MULTICULTURALISM AND DIVERSITY

School Counselors as Mediators of Culture

SHARON M. RAVITCH, PH.D.

AMERICAN
SCHOOL
COUNSELOR
ASSOCIATION

1101 King St., Suite 625, Alexandria, VA 22314
(703) 683-ASCA, (800) 306-4722, fax: (703) 683-1619
www.schoolcounselor.org

ISBN 1-929289-07-3

The American School Counselor Association (ASCA)
supports school counselors' efforts to help students focus on
academic, personal/ social and career development so they
achieve success in school and are prepared to lead fulfilling lives
as responsible members of society. ASCA, which is the school
counseling division of the American Counseling Association,
provides professional development, publications and other
resources, research and advocacy to professional school
counselors around the globe. For more information visit
www.schoolcounselor.org.

Table of Contents

PREFACE
Multicultural Counseling: "Fourth Force" but Top Priority for School Counselors

Michael J. Nakkula, Ed.D.
Harvard Graduate School of Education

As Sharon Ravitch points out in this timely volume on the diverse array of knowledge and skills required for effective school counseling, multiculturalism has been pegged the "fourth force" in counseling and psychotherapy, following psychodynamic, behavioral and humanistic approaches (Pederson, 1999). Given the issues Ravitch and her fellow contributors outline in this volume, however, it is quite clear that this fourth force needs to be a top priority in counselor training and ongoing professional development. In this era of hyper-standardization, we risk reverting to models of homogeneity rather than diversity in the ways we teach, counsel and simply understand the issues facing students and their families in our schools. School counselors are called upon to help an ever-more-diverse group of students "master" a progressively more standardized curriculum. The ability to match such extraordinary diversity with such hyper-standardization requires a level of multicultural skill development not previously experienced within our profession.

We even hear and witness the move toward standardization in seemingly progressive educational reform initiatives. "No Excuses" schools, for example, have cropped up as a particular approach to closing the "achievement gap" by promoting academic excellence for low-income students of color (Meyerson, 2000). Although the "no excuses" descriptor is intended to apply to the schools' stance that there are no excuses for under-educating students, the reality is that students either meet the no-excuse high standards of the school or are transferred out to a less-competitive setting. Although such efforts work for some students, resulting in exceptional achievement levels, they pay no regard to the structural issues that make high achievement so intensely difficult for some students and as a result tend to have extremely high attrition rates. Although such schools may serve a racially diverse student body, they implicitly state that diversity in the capacity to meet high standards is unacceptable. When high achievement in the present becomes the only standard by which students are assessed, the humanity within our educational processes is deeply compromised.

The counseling profession is built on a diversity platform; we are trained as counselors to understand the array of human experience that our clients bring. But historically we have been trained to appreciate intrapsychic diversity primarily, differences in family influence secondarily, with culture providing the context within which to understand individual and interpersonal variation. As Ravitch and the contributors to this volume make strikingly clear, it is time for our understanding of multiculturalism to move beyond the contextualizing of cultural differences; it is time to view multiculturalism as the core and to work within it, rather than viewing it as the outer shell that supports the core or core self, if you will. The "self" of our students is a multicultural self; it is not an autonomous self that is simply situated within cultural contexts.

What does it mean to counsel with culture as the core rather than culture as a context? The contributions to this volume provide many insightful responses to this question. Chapter Two, for example, focuses on culture, identity and social location and the interrelationships among these constructs. Working with culture at the core means beginning our counseling work with efforts to understand the multiply intersecting contributions of culture to our students' identities within and beyond school. It means working from an understanding of the role of school and formal education within the students' larger life experiences. Too frequently educators in general and school counselors, in particular, become overly school-centric in our approaches to our students. Certainly school is the primary context within which we are working and within which we hope to promote growth, but becoming overly school-centric can result in losing the students in our very efforts to help them succeed. To help them succeed in school, in many cases, we must reverse the typical orientation: we must learn to view schooling as a single context within the larger meaning structure and identity of the student rather than viewing the students' "culture" as a context informing school success. This reversal may seem arbitrary, but I would argue that it holds enormous ramifications. It can align us with the realities of our students rather than forcing them to fit within yet one more set of standards: the school-based standards guiding our efforts to understand and support our students.

In Chapter Three, Ravitch presents and organizes an impressive body of work on professional development for school counselors. In my own work as an educator of counselors, teachers and school-based prevention specialists, and as a collaborator helping to provide school counseling and prevention services, I have been struck repeatedly by the dearth of meaningful multicultural professional development opportunities for counselors and educators of all sorts, particularly as our emphasis has become progressively more standards-oriented. As Ravitch notes, this is especially problematic given the human tendency to become routinized in our ways of seeing and doing things. It is all too easy to begin seeing "common patterns" in student behavior, and to attribute those patterns to "common origins," whether they be racially based achievement motivation attitudes, ethnically based ways of asserting oneself, class-based career aspirations, or gender-based learning and subject-matter preferences. In other words, with the accumulation of experience we can become overly confident in our interpretations of student experience and behavior and inadvertently generate stereotypical ways of understanding it. Without models for professional development that encourage critical self-reflection, we run the risk of remaining trapped in our personal and professional biases. The contributions in Chapter Three help us avoid that trap.

The emphasis on systems work in Chapter Four orients us toward a different aspect of diversity: the diversity of human systems within which our students and our schools operate. It is interesting that as our schools have become more networked through computer access, they have remained too isolated in many cases on other systemic levels. For example, the disconnection between the structure and functioning of large urban high schools relative to the expectations for college success has been well-documented (see Kirst & Venezia, 2004), creating a particular challenge for counselors working within such school settings. The gap is made even greater when the disparity between educational systems is compounded by the fact that many urban students will be first-generation college students. In such cases, the family system is not prepared to help bridge the cultural differences between high school and college. Counselors are left to fill this void, often with too little training and even less time to allocate to the task. The approaches presented in Chapter Four begin to address such systems challenges and open our thinking to building upon these critical foundations.

The strategies and actions presented in Chapter Five provide either a valuable starting point or directions for expanding one's multicultural counseling repertoire, depending on one's current level of experience. Although multicultural counseling must ultimately become a way of being a school counselor, specific contributions to developing that way of being are necessary. Ravitch provides us with essential material for building strategic approaches that can become integrated into our existing knowledge and skill base. Importantly, the strategies and actions presented in Chapter Five are linked to the themes from prior chapters. Systemic approaches are critical, for example, to the broader conception of multicultural skill development. Multicultural counselors are, according to Ravitch, systemic bridge builders, consultants who help school personnel better understand and engage with families and who can help students and families better understand the expectations of college. Moving from the systems to the self, multicultural approaches center on critical self-reflection, with the goal being to better understand oneself culturally and otherwise in order to better understand and support our students. Ravitch returns to this crucial theme time and again throughout the book.

For those familiar with Ravitch's prior work, it is not surprising that this volume closes with an emphasis on practitioner inquiry. She argues strongly that counselors, like other educators, benefit enormously by making their work the focus of formal scrutiny. The critique of Ravitch's argument might be the usual refrain that "there is not time for anything extra." But like multiculturalism itself, practitioner inquiry should be viewed as central, not optional, from Ravitch's perspective. Taking on particular topics for inquiry, such as documenting personal responses and reactions to student concerns, can open up new ways of understanding, particularly if such inquiry is shared with fellow educators via peer study groups. Such processes expand critical reflection and dialogue within the larger school culture and signal a commitment to genuine multicultural professional development. As Ravitch and I (1998) have written elsewhere, systematic practitioner inquiry can have the impact not only of transforming one's work but can also substantially reshape larger aspects of self-understanding. Her contributions to Chapter Six of this volume underscore that point.

An organizing theme that runs throughout this book is the goal of emancipation in multicultural counseling. One might argue that such a goal exists in all forms of counseling: a goal for virtually all counseling models is to promote emancipation from the binds that inhibit growth and well being. But emancipation takes on particular meaning within the multicultural discussion; it emphasizes the promotion of freedom from the various structural forces that oppress people. The multicultural counselor is a professional bridge builder between the individual psyche and the various systems that help define and simultaneously impinge upon that psyche. When our efforts are successful we not only promote diversity within the contexts within which we operate, but as I have argued elsewhere (2006), we contribute to co-constructing a more diverse self – a self whose definition is based on meaningful connection to multiple contexts within and beyond school. Consistent with Ravitch's emphasis throughout this book, emancipation occurs precisely in this manner, through a diverse array of human connections that provide meaningful options for being in the world. This volume provides the necessary support for bringing such options one step closer to reality.

REFERENCES

Kirst, M. & Venezia, A. (2004). *From high school to college: Improving opportunities for success in postsecondary education.* San Francisco: Jossey-Bass.

Meyerson, A. (2000). *Low-income schools that work.* The Heritage Foundation: Research and Policy Analysis. (new.heritage.org/Press/Commentary/ED042700.cfm)

Nakkula, M. & Ravitch, S. (1998). *Matters of interpretation: Reciprocal transformation in therapeutic and developmental relationships with youth.* San Francisco: Jossey Bass.

Nakkula, M. & Toshalis, E. (In press). *Adolescent development for educators: Co-authoring life narratives with our students.* Cambridge, MA: Harvard Education Press.

Pedersen, P. (1999). *Multiculturalism as a Fourth Force.* New York: Taylor & Francis.

Introduction

The American School Counselor Association (ASCA) has long been committed to the advancement of multicultural thinking and culturally responsive school counseling practice. In response to the growing need to engage counselors in the process of becoming increasingly aware of, and responsive to, the needs of a diverse student body, in 1988 ASCA adopted its first position statement encouraging school counselors to take a proactive stance on becoming more multicultural and critically reflective about issues of equity and diversity in their work. Over the past decade, ASCA has continued to develop and revise its mission with respect to multicultural counseling. Its new statement, adopted in 2004, is called "The Professional School Counselor and Cultural Diversity" and reads as follows:

American School Counselor Association (ASCA) Position
Professional school counselors advocate for appropriate opportunities and services that promote maximum development for all students regardless of cultural backgrounds and strive to remove barriers impeding student success.

The Rationale
An increased awareness and understanding of cultural diversity is important for all school personnel, especially the professional school counselor. The professional school counselor promotes the understanding and appreciation of cultural diversity and provides cross/multicultural counseling to facilitate human development. Students of diverse cultural backgrounds may not always have access to appropriate opportunities or receive needed services, and the professional school counselor uses school, district, state and national data to provide leadership in advocating for systemic change.

The Professional School Counselor's Role

Professional school counselors take action to ensure students of culturally diverse backgrounds have access to services and opportunities promoting maximum academic, personal/social and career development. Professional school counselors use a variety of strategies to:

- increase awareness of culturally diverse persons and populations
- increase sensitivity of students and parents to cultural diversity
- enhance the total school and community climate for all students

Professional school counselors have the skills necessary to collaborate with students, parents and school personnel to identify attitudes and policies impeding the learning process of culturally diverse students. Professional school counselors strive to ensure all students' rights are respected, which allows students to maximize their potential in a supportive environment and encourages maximum growth and development.

Professional school counselors continue to seek professional development to better understand their students' cultural traditions and customs. The professional school counselor also collaborates with members of the community who provide services to students from a variety of backgrounds.

Summary

Professional school counselors have the responsibility of working to ensure the needs of all students are met. Having the skills necessary to collaborate with students, parents and school personnel to identify attitudes and policies impeding the learning process, professional school counselors foster increased awareness and understanding of cultural diversity in the school and community. Professional school counselors strive to ensure all students have the opportunity to maximize their potential in a supportive environment that encourages maximum academic, personal/social and career development.

In a focused effort to support the professional development of school counselors and counselor educators around issues of diversity and inequality over the years, ASCA has published hundreds of articles addressing issues of race, culture, ethnicity, religious and spiritual beliefs, social class, sexual identity and diverse learning needs as they relate to the schooling experiences of diverse students as well as the practices and professional development of school counselors. This volume contains a collection of selected articles published in *Professional School Counseling* and *ASCA School Counselor*. The goal of this book is to provide school counselors, and those responsible for their education and professional development, with a conceptually rich and practically useful, comprehensive resource for learning about and engaging in multicultural counseling, counselor education and multicultural professional development. The contributors are scholars, researchers, counselors and counselor educators who are working in the field of school counseling to find ways to more fully understand, respect and better serve diverse student and community populations.

The articles in this collection are at the cutting edge of theory, research and practice in the area of multicultural school counseling. One of the most exciting aspects of this book is that this collection includes both theoretical and empirical studies. The use of first-hand, practitioner-oriented research and practice-driven theory is crucial if school counselors, and those who educate them, are to better understand how current trends in multicultural counseling map onto local contexts and practices. Arguably, the hope for multicultural school counseling, and multicultural education more broadly, is a commitment on the part of practitioners to engage in inquiry-based practice. Because there are so many layers to multicultural counseling, the ability to ask questions that emerge from practice and to systematically gather data to respond to these questions, is a powerful tool for school counselors to gain perspective on and improve their practice. The articles in this volume help to pave the way for thinking about the kinds of questions and concerns so crucial for the development of inclusive, culturally responsive, critical, student-centered, emancipatory school counseling practice. Beyond a "how to," this book offers a critical conceptualization of multicultural school counseling, a framework for deepening thinking, for making theory-practice connections across populations and issues and for engaging in innovative and empowering research that can inform and guide everyday school counseling practices.

Each of the articles included in this book provides insight into school counselors', counselor educators', students' and families' experiences of counseling, learning and collaborating in and around educational contexts. These chapters provide a multi-vocal narrative of the processes, contents and ideals of multicultural school counseling as it is enacted in particular relational, institutional and pedagogical contexts. Together, these chapters provide a textured and vital collective voice of commitment to multicultural school counseling. This book, viewed as a dynamic dialogue between researchers, theorists and practitioners in the field of counseling, is an invitation for more critical, collaborative dialogue about what it means to counsel against the grain (Cochran-Smith, 1991).

The chapters of this book are organized around thematic clusters of articles, which represent areas of focus within the realm of multicultural school counseling. It is important to note that these clusters are not organized around specific racial, cultural or ethnic groups since that approach to multicultural education and counseling compartmentalizes students by one aspect of their identities/social locations rather than looking at students, counselors, schools and school counseling programs more holistically. Organizing these chapters thematically allows for a critical understanding of what Collins (1989) has termed "interlocking systems of oppression," which refers to the complex ways in which different aspects of identity and social location, such as race, social class and gender, overlap and converge. Each chapter, or thematic cluster, includes a range of perspectives and a diverse representation of major topics and concerns in the realm of school counseling. The organizing themes for the chapters are:

Intersections and Implications of Culture, Identity, and Social Location – This chapter addresses issues of culture, identity and social location in schools and school counseling and explores the ways in which school counselors should consider and continually re-consider the complex intersections of culture, identity and social location – their own and that of their colleagues and students – as well as the implications of these intersections for approaches to and experiences of multicultural school counseling. The articles in this chapter address issues of culture from various vantage points, providing school counselors and those responsible for their education and professional development with solid models of theory, research and practice in the realm of multicultural school counseling.

The Role of Professional Development in Multicultural Practice – This chapter explores the relationship between professional development, multicultural awareness and the enactment of culturally responsive school counseling. The chapter is structured around articles that represent and explore a range of conceptions of and approaches to multicultural professional development. Each of the articles contributes to counselors' and counselor educators' substantive knowledge about various domains of multicultural counseling practice as well as to their understanding of specific approaches to engaging in multicultural professional development. Together, these articles highlight the serious need for professional development that helps school counselors to reflect, learn, engage, critique, collaborate and advocate with respect to diverse students and their specific concerns and needs. This collection of articles also provides school counselors with ideas and templates for specific professional development initiatives and offers an ideal to which they can strive in their everyday professional lives.

Working within Systems: Taking a Proactive Role within Schools – This chapter contextualizes the complex and multifaceted roles that school counselors must assume within the influences of the systems in which they learn and practice. Each article in this chapter provides a specific vision of the multifaceted role of a multicultural school counselor as well as a roadmap, both conceptual and practical, to getting there. Moreover, these articles contribute to an understanding of the multiple contexts that shape the work of school counselors, helping to identify the difficulty in, the need for, and the promise of, school counselors taking a proactive role as innovative multicultural practitioners and agents of change. The articles in this chapter contribute significant understanding to the substantive and theoretical issues of central importance to support this kind of learning and practice. Together, they provide a vision for the kind of comprehensive role redefinition in which school counselors must engage in order to meet the demands of their profession in the 21st century.

Multicultural Counseling in Action: Strategies and Approaches – This chapter explores current strategies and approaches in the realm of multicultural school counseling practice. The articles in this chapter approach multicultural school counseling from a variety of vantage points and perspectives. Together, they present various entry points for the development of effective multicultural school counseling practices including constructive collaborations with colleagues, families, outside agencies and institutions, community members and organizations. As well, they offer specific approaches to student support, advocacy and empowerment along individual, social and institutional lines. This collection of articles helps school counselors and those responsible for their education and professional development to realize and appreciate the importance of practice-based research and research-based practice. Each article offers school counselors effective approaches to multicultural school counseling as well as an understanding of their ideological and theoretical underpinnings, thus informing school counselors' understandings of theory-practice connections and integrations.

Practitioner Inquiry as the Promise for Multicultural School Counseling Practice and Educational Transformation – This chapter argues for the importance of taking an inquiry stance on school counseling practice, which requires that school counselors develop and refine their sense of the role of systematic reflection in counseling practice and, further, that they view practice-based inquiry as an ethic of their everyday practice as well as a fundamental aspect of their vision of themselves as school counselors. This chapter explores practitioner research as a process enabling school counselors to engage in systematic inquiry that creates and extends their professional knowledge, skills and strategies. It argues that local, site-based practitioner research that focuses on issues of equity and reform is the promise for meaningful, evidence-based educational change. This chapter also discusses counselor education courses as centers of critical self-reflection, suggesting that one of the central goals of counselor education courses must be to encourage counselors to take an inquiry stance on their teaching and to teach them to engage in ongoing practitioner research as an ethic of their practice. Finally, this chapter suggests that through engagement in inquiry-based practitioner research, school counselors, and those who educate them, can facilitate educational change and, ultimately, social transformation.

Each chapter addresses issues critical to the development of multicultural counseling practice and to the ongoing understanding of the need for theory-research-practice connections that lead to the enactment of culturally responsive, equitable, student-centered counseling and counselor education practices.

CHAPTER ONE
School Counselors as Mediators of Culture

One of the greatest challenges facing school counselors today is the responsibility to take an active role in effectively meeting the needs of an increasingly multicultural student population. With the growing number of students from diverse backgrounds[i] attending schools across the United States, it is crucial that school counselors understand how to work and engage with a range of students, families, communities and school professionals in ways that are culturally aware, responsive and equitable (Coleman & Baskin, 2003; Holcomb-McCoy, 2004; Sciarra, 2001). Racially marginalized groups, including African Americans, Latinos and Native Americans, comprise nearly 33 percent of the under-18 population in the United States, and it is projected that by 2030, they will comprise 40 percent of this population (U.S. Bureau of the Census, 1996).

In terms of the student population, approximately 36 percent of American public school students are people of color (National Commission on Teaching and America's Future Report, 2003). In contrast, approximate-

---

[i] The terms "diverse students," "diverse backgrounds," and "diverse communities" are used throughout this book to refer to students of color, students from under-resourced communities, students with disabilities, immigrant students, ESL students, and students who are gay, lesbian, bisexual and transgender (GLBT). However, as Erickson (2004) argues, "everybody is multicultural" (p.33) and to assume otherwise, in and of itself, is a Eurocentric and privileged construction of identity and social location.

ly 71 percent of school counselors are white. More than half of these counselors are middle to upper-middle class, heterosexual, suburban-raised women, and approximately 86 percent of American public school teachers are white, middle to upper-middle class and monolingual (McIntyre, 1997; National Commission on Teaching and America's Future Report, 2003; U.S. Bureau of the Census, 2000). Research confirms that the percentage of white counselors and teachers will continue to increase as the student body grows more racially and culturally diverse[ii] (Howard, 1999; National Commission on Teaching and America's Future Report, 2003; Nieto, 2004).

The implications of these statistics have become the subject of much study and debate in current multicultural counseling[iii] and multicultural education discourse. Many multicultural counselors and educators discuss issues arising from the "cultural mismatch" between practitioners and students. Moreover, they examine the possible negative implications of the ways in which the demographics of the counseling and teaching populations, combined with the structure of schools, both reflect and perpetuate the pervasive racism and inequality that exist in American society (Delpit, 1995; Katz, 1985; Sleeter, 1996). Research in multicultural counseling overwhelmingly asserts that school counselors tend to embrace conservative views of schooling and counseling; lack awareness of structural and social issues affecting student mental health and student achievement; believe in deficit theories of students of color, low-income students, students with disabilities, immigrant students, ESL students and students who are gay, lesbian, bisexual and transgender (GLBT); and, further, that they feel ill-equipped to relate with, and effectively counsel, these students and their families. Additionally, research shows that the overwhelming majority of counselors, regardless of their own cultural backgrounds, are often under- or mis-educated about issues of cross-cultural counseling and assessment because of their own monocultural schooling and professional training experiences (Arrendondo, et al., 1996; Delpit, 1995; Katz, 1985; Ladson-Billings, 1995; Sleeter, 1996).

[ii] The terms "culture," "cultural groups," and "culturally diverse" are used in a broadened sense of the term culture, and should be understood to be inclusive of both larger or macrocultural groups such as race, social class, sexual orientation, cultural and/or ethnic background, as well as more individual or microcultural groups which include a variety of aspects of identity and social location (Erickson, 2004).

[iii] Arredondo, et al., (1996) define multicultural counseling in this way: "Multicultural counseling refers to preparation and practices that integrate multicultural and culture-specific awareness, knowledge and skills into counseling interactions. The term multicultural, in the context of counseling preparation and application, refers to five major cultural groups in the United States and its territories: African/Black, Asian, Caucasian/European, Hispanic/Latino and Native American or indigenous groups who have historically resided in the Continental USA and its territories. It can be stated that the U.S. is a pluralistic or multicultural society and that all individuals are ethnic, racial, and cultural beings" (p. 1).

Given these issues, it is not surprising that students of color and low-income students are disaffiliating from schools at staggering rates (Nieto, 2004; Ogbu, 1987/1992, 1995) and that these students tend to seek, utilize and benefit from counseling at significantly lower rates than their white, middle- and upper-class counterparts (Holcomb-McCoy, 2004). These kinds of issues, which reflect the current state of U.S. schools and the counseling programs within these schools, are at the center of multicultural critiques of school counseling, counselor education and of education more broadly. They are also a driving force behind initiatives aimed at changing the landscape of school counseling in American schools.

In an age of rapidly increasing diversity, standardization and national school accountability, the role of today's school counselor is becoming steadily more multifaceted, complex and challenging. School counselors are called upon daily to work with and counsel individual students; facilitate group sessions; and consult with parents/guardians, teachers, administrators, paraprofessionals and community constituencies. School counselors are often responsible for the development and facilitation of educational programming focusing on academic achievement, employment choices and college selections and transitions. Additionally, school counselors are responsible for writing reports about student welfare, requesting and advocating for school- and community-based services, as well as engaging in student assessment and individual and schoolwide intervention. In addition to these more traditional roles, the school counselor must now actively attend to the array of needs and concerns relating to diverse students' personal and academic success and well-being. The process of doing so is fraught with challenges created by the intersection of a multicultural student body and the Eurocentric schooling model in the United States. Significant challenges to effective multicultural service provision are also caused by both a dearth of resources and a lack of awareness of the need to support school counselors as they are expected to significantly complicate their roles and responsibilities as well as to broaden their knowledge base, skill sets and perspectives on issues central to counseling diverse students (Sue & Sue, 2003).

The lenses, value systems and worldviews that mediate counseling activities and interactions are the subject of current dialogue and debate in the fields of multicultural counseling and counselor education. A significant number of researchers and practitioners in the field of counseling focus on issues central to the development of knowledge, skills and awareness necessary for school counselors to engage in multicultural practice (e.g., Arredondo, et. al., 1996; Coleman & Baskin, 2003; Constantine & Yeh, 2001; Holcomb-McCoy, 2004). As Lee (2001) states, "School counselors are becoming increasingly aware that their practices are rooted firmly in the values of European-American middle class culture, whereas the cultural values of a significant portion of the students with whom they work represent worldviews whose origins are found in Africa, Asia, Mexico, Central America, the Caribbean or the Middle East" (p. 258). Clearly, school counselors need to challenge and shift the perspectives and assumptions from which they operate, which are steeped in a Eurocentric monoculturalism,[iv] if they are to ensure that students from diverse backgrounds have access to information, resources and services that promote optimal academic, career and personal-social development (Baruth & Manning, 2000). This challenging of their attitudes and practices requires that school counselors, and those responsible for their education and professional development, focus on the development of multicultural competencies.

MULTICULTURAL SCHOOL COUNSELING AND MULTICULTURAL COMPETENCIES

Multiculturalism, which is the ideologically based intellectual movement that created the foundation for multicultural education and multicultural counseling, first emerged during the era of the Civil Rights Movement, gained momentum in the late 1960s and has continued to be developed as a response to the cultural, social and political inequality of the United States (Gay, 1990; Sleeter, 1996). Multicultural education, which is the educational outgrowth of multiculturalism, is a response to the ways in which U.S. schools and social institutions reflect and perpetuate a hegemonic social order[v] (Banks, 1996; Erickson, 2004; Giroux, 1994; Goldberg, 1994; McCarthy, 1993; McLaren, 1994; Nieto, 2004). Goldberg (1994) describes multiculturalism as the emergence of "a new standard... a new set of self-understandings, presuppositions, principles and practices... a new way of thinking about the social and institutional,

---

[iv] Goldberg (1994) has termed the prevailing and established norms of the white cultural and political hegemony of the United States as based in a "monocultural ideal." His position is that monoculturalism acts to universalize the values, traditions, and language of a single culture (European white middle class) while marginalizing and pathologizing all "others." He posits that practices of monoculturalism are foundational in the establishment of the United States and that this has paved the way for the cultural hegemony that organizes American society. As many multicultural theorists and researchers argue society and social relations have been shaped to fit white ideals and interests and this has been systematized through many areas of social life from employment to education. As sites of the production and reproduction of monoculturalism, schools are central to the creation and perpetuation of hegemonic social practices (Goldberg, 1994; Levinson and Holland, 1996).
[v] Erickson (2004) defines hegemony in this way: "Cultural hegemony refers to the established view of things – a commonsense view of what is and why things happen that serves the interests of those people already privileged in a society" (p.48).

the intellectual and academic" (p.9). Building from the ideological framework developed within the broader multiculturalism movement, multicultural education localizes its tenets and goals within the educational realm, placing a primacy on the critical examination and reconstruction of pedagogical practices, educational institutions and issues of curriculum and resources. This examination is steeped in the critique of the broader social, political and economic forces that both shape and influence all areas of education. Gorski (2000) provides an overarching framework of multicultural education, describing it as:

"A progressive approach for transforming education that holistically critiques and addresses current shortcomings, failings and discriminatory practices in education. It is grounded in ideals of social justice, education equity and a dedication to facilitating educational experiences in which all students reach their full potential as learners and as socially aware and active beings, locally, nationally and globally. Multicultural education acknowledges that schools are essential to laying the foundation for the transformation of society and the elimination of oppression and injustice. The underlying goal of multicultural education is to affect social change. The pathway toward this goal incorporates... 1. the transformation of self, 2. the transformation of schools and schooling and 3. the transformation of society." (p. 2)

As these statements make clear, multiculturalism is an intellectual and political movement that refuses to accept the Eurocentric ideal of American society as natural and, further, that refuses to accept responses to it that do not transform the foundation of American society along cultural, political, social, educational and institutional lines (Giroux, 1994; McCarthy, 1993; McLaren, 1994). Multicultural education is the way that multiculturalism becomes conceptualized and operationalized within and across educational contexts and discourses.

Multicultural education has significantly grown over the past three decades in terms of its definition and the scope of its political and educational articulations (Gay, 1990; Sleeter, 1996; Nieto, 1999; 2004). Multicultural education has become a discourse that pushes the margins of education, actively works to re-vision American society and to develop pedagogical tools, methods and theories that operationalize a new social order reflecting the diversity, lifestyles, learning styles, and cultural and economic realities of all Americans. Proponents of multiculturalism and multicultural education view schools, from pre-school to graduate school, and the educational policies and discourses surrounding education and schooling, to be essential sites for social transformation (Erickson, 2004; Goldberg, 1994; Levinson and Holland, 1996; Nieto, 2004). From the perspective of multicultural theorists and educators, the modes and philosophies of schooling, which are based in myths of democracy, meritocracy and equality, are not acceptable given the reality of our nation's population, which is diverse, multiracial and multicultural. Therefore these mythical and oppressive systems of pedagogy and education must be critically analyzed, challenged and, ultimately, transformed.

In recent years, multiculturalism has been identified as the "fourth force" in counseling, following the psychodynamic, behavioral and humanistic movements of earlier decades. This "fourth force" found its roots during the Civil Rights Movement and other social and political movements of the 1960s (Locke, 1993; Pederson, 1999). Like the broader multicultural education movement, the multicultural counseling movement focuses not only on the need for cultural awareness and sensitivity but on the recognition of social and structural inequities and their impact on students and counselors, the contexts in which counseling takes place, as well as on the counseling process itself. The multicultural counseling movement has provoked a critique of existing school counseling and counselor education practices toward the ultimate goal of changing the existing school counseling paradigm from one that is steeped in, and blind to, social and structural inequality to one that works directly and self-consciously toward the empowerment of diverse students and their communities. One of the primary goals of the multicultural movement in counseling is to prepare school counselors to integrate a critical understanding of issues relating to culture, race, social class, ethnicity, sexual identity, religious beliefs and other aspects of identity and social location into mental health assessment and service delivery.

In order to integrate multicultural approaches effectively into school counseling processes, researchers, scholars and counselor educators advocate for the development of models of multicultural competence. These models create both the theoretical frameworks and practical strategies necessary for school counselors to develop specific competencies with regard to issues of diversity and equity (e.g., Arredondo, et. al., 1996; ASCA, 1999; Holcomb-McCoy, 2004). Constantine, et al. (2001) assert that multicultural counseling competence "refers to counselors' attitudes/ beliefs, knowledge and skills in counseling people from diverse cultural groups... One aspect of being multiculturally competent is having awareness and acceptance of both similarities and differences among others" (p.13). According to Sue and Sue (2003), a culturally competent counselor actively: (1) engages in and commits to the process of becoming aware of his or her own assumptions about human behavior, values, biases, preconceived notions and personal limitations; (2) works to understand the worldviews, perspectives and concerns of his or her clients; and (3) develops appropriate, relevant and culturally sensitive intervention strategies and skills that guide practice. More specifically, Holcomb-McCoy (2004) suggests nine areas of multicultural competency for school counselors. These are competence in: (1) multicultural counseling, (2) multicultural consultation, (3) understanding racism and student resistance, (4) understanding racial identity development, (5) multicultural assessment, (6) multicultural family counseling, (7) social advocacy, (8) developing school-family-community partnerships and (9) understanding interpersonal interactions.

Given these representative explanations of need and working definitions of multicultural competency, school counselor preparation programs and professional development initiatives must take into account the central importance of helping school counselors to develop the knowledge, skills and awareness necessary to become culturally competent practitioners. School counselors themselves must be invested in their own professional development, particularly as it relates to issues of critical self-reflection on the intersection of their personal ideologies and values and their professional perspectives and choices. Further, they must learn to actively critique their own limitations and the limitations of the contexts in which they work with respect to issues of diversity and inequality and how these forces affect their students, their school's environment, their own practice and the practices of professionals in their settings.

In perhaps what is the most comprehensive conceptualization of the competencies needed for counselors to operate from a multicultural paradigm of practice, Arredondo, et al. (1996) assert that multiculturally competent counselors must continually work toward developing the knowledge, skills and attitudes necessary to being effective in multicultural settings. What follows is an adaptation of their guidelines that is geared more specifically for school counselors. Based on the guidelines they developed, multiculturally competent school counselors must learn to:

- Build awareness of their cultural values and biases and how their own cultural backgrounds and experiences influence their attitudes, values and biases about counseling
- Recognize the limits of their multicultural competency and expertise
- Recognize their own sources of discomfort with differences that exists between themselves and their clients in terms of race, ethnicity, culture and other aspects of identity

- Gain specific knowledge about their own racial and cultural heritage and how it affects their definitions and biases of normality/abnormality and the process of counseling
- Gain knowledge and understanding about how oppression, racism, discrimination and stereotyping affect them and their work in terms of their own racist attitudes, beliefs and feelings
- Gain specific knowledge about communication style differences and their social impact on others
- Understand that they must engage in ongoing professional development, consultation and collaboration to improve their understandings and effectiveness in working with culturally diverse populations
- Constantly seek to understand themselves as racial and cultural beings and actively seek a nonracist identity
- Gain specific knowledge and information about the particular individual or group with whom they are working in terms of life experiences, cultural heritage and historical backgrounds
- Work to understand how race, culture, ethnicity and other aspects of identity may affect personality formation, vocational choices, manifestation of psychological disorders, help-seeking behaviors and the appropriateness of specific counseling approaches
- Understand and have knowledge about sociopolitical influences that impinge upon the lives of racial, ethnic and sexual minorities as well as their impact on self-esteem and self-concept and their relationship to life choices and trajectories
- Actively seek out cutting-edge research that informs their understanding of the mental health issues affecting marginalized groups as well as their overall approaches to the counseling endeavor
- Actively seek out involvement with minority groups outside of the counseling setting so their perspective on minorities transcends the school context or media
- Respect their clients' worldviews, belief systems and help-giving networks and understand that these affect their experiences of schooling as well as the counseling process
- Value bilingualism and do not view another language as an impediment to counseling
- Develop a clear and explicit knowledge and understanding of how the generic characteristics of counseling and therapy, which are culture-bound, class-bound and monolingual, might clash with the cultural values of various cultural groups
- Become aware of institutional barriers that can prevent minorities from seeking out and utilizing counseling and mental health services

- Gain knowledge of the potential bias in assessment instruments and use procedures and interpret findings bearing in mind the cultural and linguistic characteristics of individual students
- Gain knowledge of family values, structures and beliefs from various cultural perspectives
- Gain knowledge about the community in which a particular cultural group may reside and the resources in the community
- Serve as advocates, exercising institutional intervention when appropriate in order to mitigate against biases, prejudices and discriminatory practices in their settings
- Actively develop within themselves, their colleagues and their clients an awareness of and sensitivity to issues of oppression, racism, sexism, heterosexism, homophobia and classism

Arredondo, et al.'s conceptualization of the knowledge, skills and attitudes counselors must possess to understand and address the needs of their diverse student populations shows the foundational building block of what Ravitch (in review) refers to as counseling diversely, as distinguished from merely counseling diverse students, which requires a dynamic, working sense of need for critical self-, institutional and social assessment and critique around issues of diversity and inequality. This type of vision and process of school counseling must be bolstered by a commitment to engage in ongoing professional development, consultation and collaboration with diverse colleagues and a spectrum of outside resources. Counseling diversely requires that the counselor work within a clearly articulated paradigm of active learning, critical thinking, educational and social critique and rigorous self-reflection. Arredondo, et al.'s operationalization of multicultural counseling competencies calls into play the need for school counselors to continually contextualize and problematize their practices within broader sociopolitical forces as well as within the context of their own institutional settings. These contexts, from the perspective of the multicultural school counselor, shape every facet of the counseling process – perception, interpretation, communication, interaction, meaning- and choice-making – and, moreover, work both to create and constrain possibilities for authentic engagement and empowerment. Achieving this understanding of a dynamic, critical and social-justice approach to school counseling necessitates a redefinition and expansion of the role of the contemporary school counselor.

NEW ROLES FOR SCHOOL COUNSELORS

One major critique of multicultural efforts in schools is that they tend to be additive and superficial rather than integrated into the school's mission and overall functioning (Banks, 2003; Sleeter, 1996). Given that school counselors must learn to broaden their understanding of their responsibilities for becoming multicultural practitioners, the entire role of the school counselor must be reconceptualized so that rather than viewing engaging in culturally responsive practice as an added responsibility, school counselors view it as an integral part of their professional identity and their ethical responsibility as practitioners in a multicultural world.

Grant (1977) offers a redefinition of the role of teacher as a "mediator of culture" which he operationally defines as "a person who both transmits knowledge of the culture and interprets the knowledge being transmitted." (p.103). Grant offers this redefinition because, as he asserts, "the needs of our racially and culturally pluralistic society demand that the conceptual meaning of this role be increased" (p.103). What Grant suggests for teachers, namely, that their role be both deepened and expanded to include engagement with the cultural aspects of teaching as they become manifested at the individual, relational and institutional levels in schools, readily applies to school counselors. Clearly, the field of school counseling has arrived at an historical juncture in which the very nature of the role of the counselor is shifting, becoming reconceptualized and reconfigured so that it better matches the range of needs and issues that are becoming embedded within diverse school settings across the country. In the pages that follow, a range of newly envisioned roles of school counselors will be explored.

There is an ongoing debate in the field of school counseling about the role of the school counselor. The debate focuses on a difference of perspective on the primary role of school counselors, with some viewing the role primarily as one with a mental health focus and others viewing it primarily as one with an achievement focus. Sciarra (2001) has defined the role of the school counselor in a multicultural society as "one who can play a crucial role in promoting higher academic achievement and consequently higher quality jobs for low-income and underrepresented minority groups" (p. 701). Sciarra and others (e.g., ASCA, 1999, Coleman & Baskin, 2003; Sue & Sue, 2003) argue that school counselors must play a crucial role in promoting high academic achievement through working for students to achieve their full potential by acting as "skilled multicultural consultants" (Sciarra, 2001) with parents and school staff and, as well, that they must reach out to their students' communities to develop opportunity networks with community leaders and members. As Coleman and Baskin (2003) assert, "When one steps back from the day-to-day functions of school counselors, it becomes readily apparent that they are the ones in the school who have the primary responsibility for organizing, implementing and evaluating the development of socioemotional competence among school-age children, specifically as it applies to the acquisition of academic accomplishment and a successful transition from school to the worlds of work." (p. 104).

Proponents of multicultural school counseling place the issues, roles and responsibilities of contemporary school counselors squarely within the sociopolitical context of schooling in America, citing the fact that students from the three major underrepresented groups – African Americans, Latinos and Native Americans – lag behind their white and Asian counterparts across a range of educational measures (Coleman & Baskin, 2003; College Board, 1999; Sciarra, 2001; Sue & Sue, 2003). Thus, the roles and responsibilities of school counselors must be shaped by a solid understanding and critique of the realities of inequality in schools so school counselors can position themselves to work against the deficit-oriented grain of their schools (Cochran-Smith, 1991). To this end, Constantine and Yeh (2001) argue that one of the primary skills school counselors need to develop is how to adapt programming to meet both the universal and culturally specific needs of the students in their schools toward the end of equalizing opportunities for diverse students. Thus, one aspect of the role of the multicultural school counselor must be to work toward higher achievement for all students with a particular focus on reducing bias and inequality in their own school settings.

Many proponents of multicultural counseling view the role of the school counselor as a change agent and advocate for marginalized students (e.g., Holcomb-McCoy, 2004; Lee, 2001; Ponterotto, 1991; Sciarra, 2001). Lee (2001) conceptualizes school counselors as "agents of change, with the knowledge and skill to translate cultural awareness into constructive action" (p. 258). Lee suggests that school counselors must serve a number of functions in schools, including: (1) promoting the development of students' positive self-identities, (2) facilitating the development of positive relationships among students from diverse cultural backgrounds, (3) promoting high expectations and academic achievement for all students, (4) promoting attitudes and skills for school success and competency for all students and (5) facilitating career exploration and an informed process of choice-making for all students. Moreover, Lee argues that culturally responsive school counselors must focus their work on serving as advocates for marginalized students. Lee writes:

"The professional school counselor is faced with a unique dilemma. Charged with facilitating student adjustment to the system, the counselor is confronted with the reality that often it is the system that needs adjustment to the student. This is particularly evident when systemic insensitivity negates diverse cultural realities. The solution to this... is a redefinition of the counseling role to account for the fact that problems are not always found in students but often exist in the school as an educational system. Such a redefinition requires an awareness of the systemic barriers to quality education and the use of initiatives to effectively challenge them." (p. 260).

As advocates, school counselors should intervene on behalf of marginalized students in ways that mitigate against the structural inequalities found within their schools and against the prejudices of their colleagues. This role requires that school counselors initiate communication about students with administration and staff when problems arise and that they assume a more ongoing, proactive role of working to raise multicultural awareness among professionals within the school through implementing professional development initiatives that focus on educational equity, culturally responsive teaching and counseling and student advocacy (Lee, 2001). Proponents of multicultural counseling assert that school counselors must play a leading role in the development of multicultural awareness within their schools and that these efforts must include a continuing commitment to raising awareness about issues of diversity and inequality among administrators, teaching staff, paraprofessionals, students, families and outside service providers (Ponterotto, 1991; Sciarra, 2001).

Another primary responsibility of school counselors working toward equity and student empowerment is that they must be critical of standardized tests and assessment tools because, as research shows, these instruments are culturally biased and serve to diminish opportunities for students of color, low-income students, second-language learners and students with disabilities (Arredondo, et al., 1996; Nieto, 2004; Rogers, et al., 1999). As Coleman and Baskin (2003) argue, "One of the primary roles of the school counselor is to assess the needs of students and plan and then implement relevant interventions. One of the dangers facing counselors in a pluralistic society is an over reliance on standardized measures that do not take into account cultural variability" (p. 106). Therefore, school counselors must learn to integrate a contextual understanding into the choice of evaluation and assessment measures, test interpretation and into any interventions they develop and implement. Moreover, school counselors must actively work to raise their colleagues' awareness about the cultural bias inherent in traditional testing and evaluation measures as well as their influence on placement, service provision and assessment, both formal and informal, of student intelligence and performance. To do so, school counselors must be well-versed in the current multicultural counseling and education literature, particularly around issues of evaluation and assessment.

Clearly, there are various, and sometimes conflicting, perspectives on the nature and scope of the role of a multicultural school counselor. Even given this range of opinions about how school counselors should address issues of diversity and inequality, the idea that it is an ethical responsibility to increase their knowledge and understanding of diverse students and communities, to challenge their own values and guiding belief systems and to critically evaluate their institutions as well as testing and assessment tools has emerged as a central argument in the school counseling literature (Herring, 1997; Rogers, et al., 1999; Tyson & Pederson, 2000). For example, Ponterotto (1991) notes that professionals involved in the Association for Multicultural Counseling and Development believe "the counseling profession has a professional and ethical responsibility to study and to intervene in the area of prejudice" (p.216).

About the ethical importance of integrating sociopolitical critique and critical self-reflection into multicultural counseling practices, Nakkula and Ravitch (1998) argue that taking a reflective stance in relation to issues of culture, power and inequity in school counseling is a school counselor's ethical responsibility. They argue that while discussions of ethics in school counseling are typically relegated to such issues as confidentiality, appropriate relational boundaries for professional practice and guidelines for reporting abuse and neglect, the parameters of ethics in counseling must be expanded and reframed to include issues of culture and its impact on the counseling process and outcomes. Nakkula and Ravitch state that:

> "From a multicultural perspective, it becomes unethical for [school counselors] not to explore their own biases and prejudices and the contexts that shape (and misshape) them. The lack of such exploration impedes the serious and often uncomfortable consideration of the (mis)understandings that result from our biased interpretations. Without careful consideration of our preconceived notions about others, [counselors] work from an overly constricted worldview and, consequently, from a limited understanding of the various influences on the work we do and the relationships we form with youth. Given the vicissitudes of experience that influence interpretation, there is infinite room for both misunderstanding others and being misunderstood.
>
> Misunderstanding and miscommunication occur even within the closest relationships and between people from similar ethnic or cultural backgrounds. Given the way our society is structured, these phenomena can become more prevalent and troubling in cross-cultural, cross-generational, cross-racial and cross-class counseling work. Within these professional contexts, differences in interpretive authority, privilege and institutional power can exacerbate possibilities for acting from misunderstanding. Because [school counselors]

deal with something as serious as youths' lives, the possibilities for negative influence (even if unconscious) stemming from prejudices and misunderstandings, and from the assumptions these generate, must be rigorously and continuously reexamined" (p. xiii-xiv).

Framing the integration of a critically reflective multicultural perspective on counseling into everyday practice as an ethical stance shifts the dialogue about issues of diversity in counseling away from one that looks at students of color, GLBT students, students with learning challenges and disabilities, students from non-Western backgrounds, second language learners and students from low socioeconomic levels through a deficit lens to one that looks at human diversity as a resource for engaged, dynamic and responsive practice. Such a shift requires not only a commitment to learning but a commitment to unlearning – the unlearning of attitudes, beliefs and assumptions inculcated through monocultural, Eurocentric socialization – as well as a willingness to critically self-assess on multicultural knowledge and skills and to seek constructive feedback through collaboration (Hidalgo, 1993). Further, understanding multiculturalism as an ethic of counseling practice means moving from a paradigm in which cultural differences are viewed as the cause of conflict to one in which cultural differences are viewed as resources for conflict – and only when practitioners do not consider broader sociopolitical issues like structural discrimination, prejudice, monocultural socialization and cultural capitol and their direct and indirect impact on their counseling practices and the contexts in which these are carried out (Erickson, 2004). From this perspective, it is not just the students who are "culturally different." Everyone is "culturally different" from each other, and it is the ethical responsibility of school counselors to understand and view themselves as cultural beings with biases and prejudices that can create conflict around differences. This paradigm of multicultural school counseling works from the understanding that: (1) the development of culturally responsive practice is a lifelong process; (2) authentic growth is challenging, sometimes uncomfortable and replete with resistance to change; (3) the primary components of change in personal and professional development, such as risk-taking, self-reflection, reality-testing and ethical decision-making, are essential to this type of learning; (4) multicultural learning is transformative in nature; (5) best practices in counseling can be achieved by counselors developing their ability to integrate often-painful aspects about themselves and broader social realities into their self-concept and practice; and (6) it is only through engagement in multiculturally oriented practitioner inquiry that counselors can improve their practice in meaningful and lasting ways (Nakkula & Ravitch, 1998).

To enter into the process of being a multicultural school counselor, one must be prepared to make significant changes in his or her practice and even to experience levels of personal and professional transformation. Nieto (1999) argues that multicultural education is about transformation at the individual, collective and institutional levels. This is true of multicultural counseling as well. Such transformation requires that counselors invest in critical reflection on themselves in terms of their values and prejudices as well as on the society in which these were formed. As well, counselors need to look at how the micro – their individual lives – and the macro – larger sociopolitical forces – converge to shape and define the immediate contexts of their work: the practices, policies, attitudes and assessment tools that dominate their schools.

As many multicultural researchers and educators assert, educating professionals about discrimination in schools and society at large requires a re-socialization process that rests on exploring in great depth (and usually with much discomfort) their constructions of race, including white privilege, and of education and society more generally. Further, it is argued that such learning can only happen through rigorous processes of societally contextualized self-reflection (Hidalgo, 1993; Hooks, 1994; McIntyre, 1997). To this end, Hooks (1994) argues for striving toward multicultural awareness via engaging in "constructive confrontation" and "critical interrogation" of how political standpoints and ideologies shape identity. She asserts that these types of discussions necessitate dialogue about the non-neutrality of all forms of education. Moreover, Hooks asserts that such discussions mean that individual practitioners will need "to undergo a process of unlearning racism ... to fully appreciate the necessity for creating a democratic [learning] experience" (p.93). Teaching in a way that encourages such discourses, shifts in identity and perspective and, ideally, paradigm shifts, and which crosses over the boundaries of identity, social location and experience, takes not only vision and passion but courage and resiliency. It also requires access to research that is theoretically challenging and empirically grounded so school counselors can learn from existing strategies and models of effective multicultural practices.

CHAPTER TWO
Intersections and Implications of Culture, Identity and Social Location

Schools are, as Erickson (2004) asserts, "collection sites for cultural differences." Within the walls of every school exists a vast range of cultural differences. Although most people work from a belief that culture is simply race, ethnicity or religion, many multicultural educators argue that culture must be more broadly defined so it is inclusive of the complex ways in which aspects of culture, identity and social location converge (e.g., Collins, 1989; Erickson, 2004; Goldberg, 1994; Levinson & Holland, 1996; Nieto, 2004). This perspective on the concept of culture is essential to the development of meaningful multicultural counseling theories and practices.

Nieto (2004) defines culture in this way:

"Culture consists of the values, traditions, social and political relationships and worldview created, shared and transformed by a group of people bound together by a common history, geographic location, language, social class and/or religion. Culture includes not only tangibles such as foods, holidays, dress and artistic expression but also less tangible manifestations such as communication style, attitudes, values and family relationships. These features of culture are often more difficult to pinpoint but doing so is necessary if we want to understand how student learning may be affected" (pp. 139-140).

Erickson (2004) states, "Culture is in us and all around us, just as is the air we breathe. It is personal, familial, communal, institutional, societal and global in its scope and distribution... As we learn and use culture in daily life, it becomes habitual. Our habits become for the most part invisible to us. Thus, culture shifts in and outside our reflective awareness" (pp. 31-32). These conceptions of culture offer an inclusive working understanding of culture as dynamic, fluid and resulting from complex interactions between aspects of individual and group identity, social location and experience. Further, these concepts of culture help to guide a more inclusive understanding of how aspects of culture and identity map onto each other as well as how larger social and political forces shape aspects of what is typically viewed as an individual's culture. Arguably, understanding the nature and functions of culture is necessary before school counselors can operationalize multicultural concepts in ways that are student-centered, equitable and emancipatory.

In an effort to broaden and deepen educational practitioners' conceptions of culture, Erickson (2004) offers a conceptualization of what he refers to as "the politics of cultural difference." Erickson contends that cultural differences themselves are not problematic but, rather, that it is the ways in which they get politicized by institutions such as the media, industry and schools, as well as by common misunderstanding, that precipitates issues of inequality with respect to cultural differences. In terms of multicultural efforts in schools, Erickson argues that educators must become aware that they address issues of culture in an ongoing, daily way that cannot be artificially compartmentalized from the rest of their practices. He writes, "Culture, as it is more and less visible and invisible to its users, is profoundly involved in the processes and contexts of education. Culture shapes and is shaped by the learning and teaching that happen during the practical conduct of daily life within all the educational settings we encounter as learning environments throughout the human life span – in families, in school classrooms, in community settings and in the workplace...at every moment in the conduct of educational practice, cultural issues and choices are at stake" (pp. 32-33).

In order to complicate understandings about diversity and multicultural efforts in schools, Erickson asserts that not only is everyone cultural but everyone is multicultural, thereby removing the assumption of neutrality and normativity that most white people assume. Further, he offers a reconceptualization of cultural differences as variable within and across groups and as continually changing over time. Erickson advocates for a conceptualization and critical exploration of what he refers to as the "microcultures" or "subcultures" that exist within each and every cultural group. In this way Erickson argues against the exoticization of "cultural others" and the essentialization or reification of culture(s). These notions recommend much to current conversations in multicultural education and multicultural counseling, which often create cultural and racial binaries that further notions of "otherness" and create fertile ground for members of the dominant group (European, white, middle class) to impose their cultural values on others, distance themselves from issues of culture and multiculturalism and impose misattributions and stereotypes on students of color; students from under-resourced communities; students with disabilities; immigrant students; ESL students; and students who are gay, lesbian, bisexual, and transgender (GLBT). As Erickson states, "When we essentialize culture, assuming that all persons in a given social category are culturally similar and focusing on the unitary cultures of various others without reflecting on our own cultures and their diversity, we open a Pandora's box of opportunity for negative attribution. Sometimes social scientific notions of culture, especially of culture as a unified system and of group membership as culturally defined, have provided a justification for intergroup stereotypes" (p. 45). Erickson conceptualizes culture in a way that makes it possible for school counselors to re-think assumptions about what culture is and how it works in their practices and therefore to do justice to the texture and complexity of their students' lives and to the work of educating, counseling and consulting with colleagues, students, families and communities in ways that are truly equitable and empowering.

Nieto (2004) suggests that educational practitioners must understand that while cultural differences may become apparent in students' learning styles, communication and interaction styles, language differences and approaches to school, culture alone does not determine how students fare in school. Rather, Nieto argues, these aspects of identity may contribute to diverse students' schooling experiences depending, in part, on how they are viewed by those working within schools because of the potential for misunderstanding, prejudice and the projection of deficit-oriented expectations. Nieto states, "Young people whose languages and cultures differ from the dominant group must often struggle to sustain a clear image of themselves because differences are commonly treated as deficiencies by schools... Power is implicated in culture as well. That is, members of the dominant group in a society traditionally think of dominant cultural values as "normal" while they view the values of subordinated groups as deviant or wrong" (pp. 138-140). Nieto argues that cultural discontinuities between home and school can cause problems but that these discontinuities are not simply caused by cultural differences but rather by the sociopolitical context of schooling. As well, she asserts that while educators, including school counselors, must acknowledge differences, they must not assume there is a definite formula for engaging students even when they share culture. Further, she argues that multicultural education is not just about accepting students' differences but providing for them and that issues such as school failure and drop-out are necessarily a co-construction between students and educational practitioners.

These positions on culture and issues of culture in education and counseling are important in terms of helping school counselors to realize that the work of counseling is cultural work and, further, that they must work in conscious ways to both broaden and deepen their understanding of culture and its relationship to their practices, the practices of their colleagues, the structure of their schools and the experiences and behaviors of the students, families and communities with whom they work.

Given the many issues relating to culture and cultural differences between counselors and students and their families and communities, school counselors must be provided with structured learning opportunities in which they can develop their knowledge of and perspectives on a diverse range of people, reflect on and challenge their own biases and stereotypes and hone their skills for communicating, living and working within an increasingly multicultural United States and an ever-developing global community.

Each of the articles in this chapter addresses issues of culture and identity in schools. Together, they speak to the complex intersections of culture, identity and social location and the implications of these intersections for school counselors, counseling processes and, ultimately, the experiences of students, their families and communities. As a collection, these articles paint a portrait of a broadened sense of culture, one that includes not just race, ethnicity and religion but also social class, sexual orientation, gender, family background and other aspects of culture. These articles should be read with an understanding of the need for a consideration of both inter-group and intra-group variability caused by the complex intersections of race, social class, gender, sexuality and other aspects of culture, identity, positionality or social location.

Holcomb-McCoy's (2005) "Ethnic Identity Development in Early Adolescence: Implications and Recommendations for Middle School Counselors" suggests ethnic identity development should be viewed as an important component of middle school students' development. The author suggests that school counselors develop a solid understanding of race, ethnicity and adolescent identity development as well as of the relationship between stages of identity development and students' behaviors, self-esteem, academic achievement and relationships. She argues that school counselors must take an active role in enhancing middle school students' ethnic identity development by providing them with opportunities to clarify, explore and examine their ethnic identities.

Valadez's (1998) "Applying to College: Race, Class and Gender Differences" is an empirical study that explores the influences the individual, family and educational variables have on high school students' decisions to apply to college. In this study, social class emerged as a central issue as did issues of access to knowledge and information about college. Based on the data generated by this study, Valadez asserts that there is not equal access to information about applying to college and that this lack of information greatly affects the educational trajectory of students of color, students from under-resourced communities, and in some cases, female students. The author frames college access as an important social justice issue that must be integrated into counselors' working concepts of their roles.

Carter and El Hindi's (1999) "Counseling Muslim Children in School Settings: Qualitative Interviewing of Muslim Families" utilizes qualitative interviews to explore the cultural and religious differences between Muslim students, their peers and school personnel, including school counselors. The authors suggest that a primary role of a school counselor must be to advocate for Muslim students and families by disseminating accurate information about their religion and culture to school personnel and students to provide counter-images to those in the mass media. Carter and El Hindi suggest that school counselors must take into account cultural differences and their impact on counseling, including an expectation of family involvement in the counseling process. Further, they argue that school counselors must actively reach out to and communicate with Muslim families to learn to distinguish between culturally appropriate and inappropriate counseling practices for Muslim students.

Tlanusta Garret's (1999) "Soaring on the Wings of the Eagle: Wellness of Native American High School Students" is an empirical study assessing and comparing the wellness of Native American and non-Native American high school students. Findings of the study suggest that an individual's cultural identity is a larger factor in wellness than race or ethnicity. The findings of this study highlight the importance of understanding students' cultural identities as they understand them rather than making assumptions based simply on racial or ethnic background. The results of this study point to the importance of assessing a student's cultural identity and level of acculturation as well as utilizing developmentally appropriate interventions with adolescents to facilitate wellness through identity development.

Yeh's (2001) "An Exploratory Study of School Counselors' Experiences with and Perceptions of Asian-American Students" is an empirical study that explores the counseling needs of Asian-American students as well as school counselors' perceptions of Asian-American students and their educational and mental health concerns. The findings of the study point to the need for school counselors to cultivate a better understanding of Asian-American students generally as well as in relation to the particular challenges caused by cultural differences and differences in communication styles between home and school. Yeh asserts that there is a need for school counselors to learn about and develop alternative strategies that are more culturally appropriate for Asian-American students including the identification of specific issues, needs and perspectives on counseling.

Harris' (2002) "School Counselors' Perceptions of Biracial Children: A Pilot Study" is an empirical study that explores school counselors' perceptions of biracial children, filling in a gap in this area of school counseling research. The author discovered that school counselors' perceptions of biracial students are influenced by such variables as school level, years of experience and gender. It also found that counselors in schools that actively promote cultural diversity and awareness programs had more accurate perceptions of biracial children. Based on the findings of the study, Harris suggests school counselors must work to better understand the experiences and needs of biracial students as well as to promote understanding about this population within their school settings.

Day-Vines, et al.'s, (2003) "Counseling African-American Adolescents: The Impact of Race, Culture and Middle Class Status" fills in a significant gap in the multicultural counseling literature by exploring issues relevant to middle-class African-American adolescents and examining their unique needs and concerns, which often do not get addressed in research on counseling African-American students. Through the use of theoretical research and a case-study approach, the authors offer an in-depth discussion of the complex interaction between race, culture and social class and assert that school counselors must engage in culturally competent counseling practice, which necessitates an exploration of African-American cultural values, an examination of racial identity issues and a consideration of intra-racial stressors. The article addresses implications of these issues for the counseling of middle-class African-American adolescents and offers recommendations for individual and group counseling strategies.

Marinoble's (1998) "Homosexuality: A Blind Spot in the School Mirror" discusses issues and challenges confronting school counselors working with students who are gay and lesbian and students who begin to question their sexual orientation during their school years. The author suggests that school counselors must work with other school personnel to create a supportive learning environment for gay and lesbian students, which necessitates the development of school policies that help to foster an inclusive and equitable environment with respect to issues of sexuality and sexual identity. Further, Marinoble suggests that school counselors should act as advocates for inclusive schooling practices, which includes engaging with other educators in a critique of heterosexist curricula as well as offering support services and staff development around issues of sexuality and lifestyle choices.

Lopez's (2006) "Counseling Hispanic Students" focuses on the importance of school counselors educating themselves about the needs of Hispanic students given the specific barriers to their success, which relate to issues of social class, language, culture and immigration. Lopez provides strategies for school counselors to work toward the empowerment and support of Hispanic students, suggesting the importance of school guidance curricula for students and their parents; the use of data as a critical element in counseling Hispanic students; the importance of accessing local rates for school drop out, college, graduation and attendance; and the use of these data to develop an action plan for working with, and developing programs and interventions for, this population of students and families.

Clark, et al.'s (2006) "The Gender Achievement Gap Challenge: Male Underachievement" explores schools counselors' responsibilities to study, understand and address the growing phenomenon of boys' underachievement and its social, cultural and psychological influences. The authors suggest that school counselors must learn to assess disparities in their own schools and school districts and then to share this information with their school administration and staff to facilitate collaborative strategies for working to mitigate against this concerning trend.

Lonborg and Bowen's (2004) "Counselors, Communities and Spirituality: Ethical and Multicultural Considerations" suggests there are myriad ethical and multicultural issues embedded in the question of how school counselors should address spiritual issues when working in rural or small-town communities. Through the use of case vignettes, the article explores the particular professional challenges caused by differences in spirituality as well as by issues of establishing appropriate professional boundaries given issues of proximity and visibility within rural and small-town community contexts. The authors suggest that school counselors in these contexts must work to develop multicultural competence and boundaries with respect to these specific issues.

Williams and Butler's (2003) "Concerns of Newly Arrived Immigrant Students: Implications for School Counselors" explores the particular concerns and issues facing newly arrived immigrant students including English language acquisition, inadequate social support networks, post-traumatic stress disorder, racial labeling and categorization, differences in learning styles, new and different cultural scripts, lack of social acceptance and developmental issues. The authors discuss implications of these issues for school counselors and provide strategies for how they can address the concerns of newly arrived immigrant students at the national, state, district and school levels. At the school level the authors offer strategies including school-based initiatives, support groups, professional development, serving as a resource and peer counseling.

Holcomb-McCoy and Moore-Thomas' (2001) "Empowering African-American Adolescent Females" explores specific issues to be considered when counseling African-American adolescent females including racism, sexism, classism, body image and physical appearance, identity development, trust and religion/spirituality. The authors contextualize school counseling strategies within these population-specific aspects of identity and social location. The article contains a case example illustrating how a school counselor successfully assisted and empowered a member of this adolescent group.

Gibbons and Shoffner's (2004) "Prospective First-Generation College Students: Meeting Their Needs Through Social Cognitive Career Theory" utilizes a case study to explore the unique concerns and needs that must be addressed with prospective first-generation college students, including perceived barriers to success as well as issues of access and support. The article explores how the use of Social Cognitive Career Theory can assist with the career and academic decision-making of this population because of its focus on self-efficacy, outcome expectations, barriers and goals. The authors offer strategies for how to address issues of access to information and support for prospective first-generation college students as they learn about and apply to college.

The articles in this chapter address issues of culture from various vantage points, offering school counselors and those responsible for their education and professional development with solid models of theory, research and practice in the realm of multicultural school counseling. This collection of articles addresses the ways in which school counselors should consider and continually re-consider the complex intersections of culture, race, social class, gender, sexual orientation and other aspects of identity and social location – their own and that of their colleagues and students – as well as the implications of these intersections for approaches to, and experiences of, multicultural school counseling.

Ethnic Identity Development in Early Adolescence: Implications and Recommendations for Middle School Counselors

By Cheryl Holcomb-McCoy

This article originally appeared in *Professional School Counseling*, Vol. 9, No. 2, 2005.

The influence of ethnic identity development on adolescents' achievement, self-concept, and behaviors has been reviewed extensively in the literature. However, the role that school counselors play in enhancing middle school students' ethnic identity development has received little attention. This article reviews the definition of ethnic identity and J. S. Phinney's (1992) model of adolescent ethnic identity development. J. E. Helms' (1994) model of racial identity interaction theory is used as a basis for understanding how ethnic identity development may influence student-to-student and student-to-teacher interactions in middle schools. And finally, recommendations for middle school counselors are presented.

Early adolescence is a time when many changes occur. It is usually a time when children leave the small, comfortable havens of elementary schools and enter larger middle or junior high schools with more students and teachers (Retting & Canady, 2000). It is also a time when children begin to mature mentally and think more about their identity and where they fit in the world. Many authors have written about the importance of achieving an identity in adolescent development (e.g., Erikson, 1968; Waterman, 1985). Erikson suggested that one achieves an identity by means of a process of search and commitment. He also claimed that an individual's failure to achieve an identity can lead to confusion and despair.

Marcia (1980) later studied Erikson's concept of identity and focused specifically on adolescents' identity development. In assessing ego-identity statuses of adolescents, Marcia also employed two criteria, exploration and commitment. *Exploration* refers to a period of active questioning and engagement in choosing among meaningful alternatives. *Commitment* refers to the presence or absence of decisions in a particular ideology, role, or occupation. Marcia provided a model for categorizing adolescents in one of four ego-identity statuses: *achieved identity*, moratorium, foreclosed identity, and identity diffusion. The first status, an achieved identity, is characterized by a commitment that has followed a period of questioning and critical analyses. Having undergone a period of exploration, the individual is committed to his or her choice of ideology. *Moratorium* is characterized by a state of exploration without commitment to any ideology. The *foreclosed identity* status is described as the period in which adolescents express commitment without having experienced any period of exploration. Their commitment typically reflects parental beliefs and expectations and is not derived from self-choice and exploration. *Identity diffusion* is characterized by the absence of both exploration and commitment. For adolescents in this status, there is a lack of genuine concern about identity issues (Flum, 1994).

For minority adolescents, their ethnicity can play an important role in their identity development (Phinney, Lochner, & Murphy, 1990). According to Rotheram and Phinney (1988), ethnic and racial attitudes among children appear to crystallize by about 10 years of age, which highlights the importance of examining the role of ethnicity in the development of early adolescents. Most of the research related to ethnicity in adolescence has focused on the attitudes of ethnic minority adolescents toward racial and/or ethnic groups other than their own, particularly related to stereotyping, prejudice, and discrimination (e.g., Phinney, Madden, & Santos, 1998; Steele, 1999). Another body of literature and research has focused on the psychological relationship of ethnic and racial minority group members with their own group. Ponterotto and Pederson (1993) have contended that ethnic identity development is as fundamental to the establishment of an adult's healthy self-concept and positive intercultural attitudes as are more researched areas such as occupational identity and political identity. Given the tremendous ethnic diversity among adolescents in U.S. middle schools, it is critical for middle school counselors to address the significance of ethnicity in the development of the students they serve. As such, this article will focus on research related to ethnic identity development in early adolescence and its relationship to interactions in middle schools. Race, ethnicity, and ethnic identity will be discussed, followed by a review of research on the relationships between ethnic identity and adolescent developmental variables (i.e., academic achievement, self-esteem, student behaviors). Next, Helms' (1994) racial identity interaction theory will be used as a framework for understanding student-to-educator and student-to-student interactions in middle schools. Finally, recommendations for middle school counselors will be presented.

RACE, ETHNICITY, AND ADOLESCENT ETHNIC IDENTITY DEVELOPMENT

Although there is some overlap, race and ethnicity are different constructs, and they have produced different bodies of literature. Interpretations of race typically allude to genetic or biological characteristics that distinguish one group from another (Ponterotto & Pederson, 1993). According to McMahon and Watts (2002) and Helms (1993), *race* and/or *racial identity* focuses on the social and political impact of visible group membership on an individual's psychological functioning. *Ethnicity*, on the other hand, is often related to race, but it extends beyond visible group membership and includes sociohistorical experiences that explain why groups of individuals consider themselves to be a distinct people (Marshall, 2002). Simply put, *ethnicity* refers to a shared worldview, language, and set of behaviors that are associated with a cultural heritage. Ethnicity is assumed to be a meaningful variable to the extent that it has salience and centrality for the individuals involved. For instance, for many European/White Americans, ethnicity is not a salient or important part of their identity, whereas ethnicity is salient in cases where one's ethnic group membership is evident, as in the case of ethnic groups of color (Alba, 1990; Waters, 1990).

Ethnic identity is sometimes used to refer to ethnic group membership. It has been conceptualized as a fundamental aspect of an adolescent's identity because it includes the attitudes and feelings associated with that membership (Bernal & Knight, 1993). However, ethnic identity is not a categorical variable, something that one does or does not have. Rather, it is a complex, multidimensional construct that varies across members of a group (Cross, 1991).

Phinney (1989), extending the identity development work of Erikson (1968) and Marcia (1980), proposed a three-stage progression from an unexamined ethnic identity through a period of exploration to an achieved or committed ethnic identity.

According to Phinney's model, early adolescents who have not been exposed to ethnic identity issues are in the first stage, an unexamined or diffused ethnic identity. According to Phinney (1990), this early stage is characterized by an adolescent's lack of active exploration of ethnic issues. A disinterest in or lack of concern regarding ethnic issues manifests a diffused identity level. Phinney (1990) purported that early adolescents simply may not be interested in ethnicity and may have given it little thought. Alternatively, some adolescents may have made a commitment without exploration on the basis of inherited ethnic attitudes from parents or other influential adults. That is, their attitudes represent a foreclosed status. Bachay (1998) suggested that adolescents at the diffused and foreclosed statuses are at risk of accepting and internalizing negative and faulty stereotypes and beliefs.

An adolescent in the process of exploration without having made a commitment is in what Phinney (1989) described as moratorium. This process of exploration may require that an adolescent come to terms with cultural differences between the culture of origin and the dominant culture. Learning more about one's culture of origin is an integral part of this process and helps to clarify a personal perspective about the meaning of ethnicity. Intense emotional experiences may accompany the adolescent's deepening of ethnic awareness (Phinney).

A firm commitment following the process of exploration is indicative of achieved identity (Marcia, 1980). Phinney (1989) suggested that the process of search followed by commitment is referred to as ethnic identity achievement. This status is characterized by a sense of ethnic pride, belonging, and confidence. Phinney and Alipuria (1990) suggested that an achieved ethnic identity can serve as a buffer against the impact of prejudice and discrimination. Additionally, Phinney et al. (1990) suggested that this last stage of ethnic identity development requires individuals to come to terms with two problems for ethnic minorities: (a) cultural differences between their own group and the dominant group, and (b) the lower or disparaged status of their own group in society. Phinney (1990) purported that the meaning of ethnic identity achievement is undoubtedly different for different individuals and groups because of their distinct historical and personal experiences. Parham (1989) even suggested that the process of ethnic identity development does not end with ethnic identity achievement but may continue in cycles that involve further exploration or rethinking of the role or meaning of one's ethnicity.

THE RELATIONSHIP OF ETHNIC IDENTITY TO EARLY ADOLESCENT OUTCOMES

Ethnic Identity and Student Behaviors

Ethnic identity development has been significantly related to many adolescent behaviors. For instance, in a study with middle school Jewish students, Dubow, Pargament, Boxer, and Tarakeshwar (2000) found that students with more advanced levels of ethnic identity were more sensitive to culture-specific stressors (e.g., discrimination, racism). At the same time, Dubow et al. concluded that their participants' strong sense of ethnic identity helped them to use more effective coping strategies. In a similar study, Neville, Heppner, and Wang (1997) found that a higher endorsement of pro-Black sentiments was related to more stress and more avoidant and suppressive styles of coping among African American late adolescents. Hence, they hypothesized that late adolescents who are more aware of their ethnic identity and feel a greater sense of belonging and attachment to their ethnic group also may be more sensitive to culture-specific stressors and, therefore, exhibit more suppressive styles of coping behaviors. In a study of African American and mixed-race adolescents (ages 10–15), McMahon and Watts (2002) found that ethnic identity was significant in relation to the behavior adjustment among African American adolescents. Their results indicated that positive ethnic identity was associated with more active coping, fewer beliefs supporting aggression, and fewer aggressive behaviors.

Ethnic identity also has been significantly related to decreased adolescent drug use (Kulis, Napoli, & Marsiglia, 2002), positive educational adaptation of immigrant adolescents (Portes & Rumbaut, 1990), wellness (Rayle & Myers, 2004), and positive school adjustment (Phinney, Horenczyk, Liebkind, & Vedder, 2001). The influence of peer relationships/ behavior on ethnic identity development also has been investigated. Phinney, Romero, Nava, and Huang (2001) found that ethnic minority adolescents who interacted more with peers of the same ethnic background had more developed levels of ethnic identity. And finally, the role of ethnic identity as a protective factor among "high-risk" and "successful" White and African American adolescents was examined by Yasui, Dorham, and Dishion (2004). One hundred fifty-nine adolescents were assessed for depression, internalizing and externalizing behaviors, competence, and academic achievement. Their results indicated that advanced levels of ethnic identity development were a significant predictor of social adaptation and emotional adjustment for African American and White adolescents. Their results also indicated that when adolescents have negative attitudes or are uncommitted to their ethnicity, they also are more likely to experience negative psychological outcomes, including depression and internalizing and externalizing problems. More importantly, however, Yasui et al. found that ethnic identity was integral to the emotional and social adjustment of adolescents, particularly those of African American descent.

Ethnic Identity and Self-Esteem/Self-Concept

A positive correlation between ethnic identity and self-esteem has been reported in studies with various populations, including middle school (Carlson, Uppal, & Prosser, 2000), high school (Phinney, 1989), and college-age (Phinney & Alipuria, 1990) students. The research suggests that simply belonging to an ethnic minority group does not predict higher or lower levels of self-esteem. Instead, it is the sense of belonging that a student feels toward his or her ethnic group that better predicts self-esteem (Helms, 1993; McMahon & Watts, 2002; Phinney, 1992). Martinez and Dukes (1997) found among a multiracial sample of more than 12,000 adolescents that a stronger sense of ethnic identity is associated with higher self-esteem and self-confidence. Phinney and Kohatsu (1997) found that low self-regard and feelings of inadequacy accompany unexamined or low ethnic identity, whereas more developed levels of ethnic identity typically are associated with positive selfconcept and an absence of psychological distress.

In a more recent study, Bracey, Bamaca, and Umana-Taylor (2004) found that in a large sample of adolescents (n = 3,282), there was a significant positive correlation between ethnic identity and selfesteem for all ethnic groups. Furthermore, they found that biracial adolescents scored significantly higher than Whites on a measure of ethnic identity but scored significantly lower than African American, Asian, and Latino adolescents on the same measure. Other studies have found that social support from family and friends may be a mechanism by which ethnic identity is developed, leading to a higher level of self-esteem (Blash & Unger, 1995; Carlson et al., 2000).

Ethnic Identity and Academic Achievement

For middle school educators, understanding the process through which early adolescents come to see themselves as belonging to particular ethnic groups is important because it can have a tremendous bearing on their academic achievement (Phinney, 1989). Unfortunately, many schools in the United States are characterized by ethnic and/or racial segregation and widespread racial disparities in academic achievement (Education Trust, 2001). Despite some evidence of a strong correlation between ethnicity and academic performance, there is considerable confusion among researchers about how and why such a correlation exists (Fordham, 1996; Noguera, 2003). For instance, Fordham and Ogbu (1986) argued that Black students from all socioeconomic backgrounds develop "oppositional identities" that lead them to view schooling as a form of forced assimilation to White cultural values, and they come to equate academic success with "acting White." Such identity perceptions lead to the devaluation of academic pursuits and the adoption of self-defeating behaviors that inhibit possibilities for academic success. Chappell and Overton (2002) examined the deductive reasoning and school performance of African American adolescents and the relation of reasoning and school performance to socioeconomic status, ethnic identity, and self-esteem. They found that Ogbu's (1995) cultural-ecological theory, which predicts an inverse relationship between cognitive performance and ethnic identity strength, was not supported because better reasoning performance was associated instead with stronger ethnic identity.

Similarly, Steele's (1999) work on the effects of racial stereotypes on academic performance helps provide a compelling explanation of the identityachievement paradox. Through his research on student attitudes toward testing, Steele showed that students are highly susceptible to prevailing stereotypes related to intellectual ability. According to Steele, when "stereotype threats" are operative, they lower the confidence of vulnerable students and negatively affect their performance on standardized tests.

He also noted that the debilitating effects of stereotypes can extend beyond particular episodes of testing and can have an effect on students' overall academic performance.

Phinney (1992) proposed that an examined ethnic identity may insulate students from buying into automatic, internalized stereotypes that may undermine their academic confidence and influence them toward risky behaviors that interfere with school completion. She found that high school students reporting average grades of A or B had more developed levels of ethnic identity than those reporting C or D. In reporting this finding, Phinney did so for the entire sample, not separate ethnic groups, so it is unclear if this relationship would have held for each ethnic group.

Although not measuring ethnic identity, Sandoval, Gutkin, and Naumann (1997) investigated the relationship between racial identity attitudes and academic achievement among African American adolescents. They found that the adolescents' academic achievement (i.e., GPAs, California Achievement Test) was significantly related to their racial identity attitudes. In contrast, Guzman, Santiago- Rivera, and Haase (2005) found no significant relationship between the ethnic identity and self-reported GPAs of Mexican American adolescents. Although the research on ethnic identity development and academic achievement is mixed, the literature overwhelmingly supports enhancing early adolescents' ethnic identity development for reasons related to academic achievement (Banks, 1993; Irvine, 1991; Sleeter, 1994; Spencer & Markstrom- Adams, 1990). Clearly, this is an area that should be investigated further.

ETHNIC IDENTITY AND INTERACTIONS IN THE MIDDLE SCHOOL

According to Helms (1994), "everyone with whom a child comes in contact in the school environment (including teachers, peers, support staff) is also at some stage of identity development" (p. 30). Helms' interaction theory hypothesizes that the child's level of identity in combination with others' identities can result in qualitatively different educational experiences. In short, Helms believes that there are three potential interaction types that can occur in the school setting based on the racial/ethnic identity of the individuals involved. The first type, a *parallel relationship*, is one in which the educator and the student in the interaction are at the same stage of identity development. Helms believes that because both parties share the same racial attitudes, it is unlikely that the educator can assist the student to develop further. A regressive relationship is one in which the educator is less developmentally advanced with respect to racial/ethnic identity development than the student is. Helms purports that because the educator is less comfortable facing racial or ethnic issues than the student, the educator attempts to change the student's thinking and behavior in directions that feel uncomfortable and unfair to the student. As a result, disharmony, conflict, tension, and rebellion often characterize regressive relationships. Students involved in these types of relationships may engage in acting out and/or passiveaggressive behaviors to express their discomfort with the relationship. Educators, on the other hand, may engage in punitive activities because of their frustration with students who do not think as they do.

The last interaction type is a *progressive relationship*. This type of relationship is most beneficial because the educator's stage of identity development is more advanced than the student's and, therefore, the educator can recognize the ethnic identity issues of the student. The educator also can offer experiences and creative role modeling that will help the student consider alternate ways of being. Helms (1994) noted that because of the teacher's greater social power in the school, the student is likely to be responsive to alternative educational experiences particularly when introduced by the teacher.

Helms' (1994) racial identity interaction theory can be used as a framework for understanding student- to-educator interactions in middle schools. For example, a White seventh-grade history teacher gives her class an assignment in which the students are to write a reaction paper to the content of a lesson on the Revolutionary War. An African American female student writes in her paper that she gained little from the lesson because her descendents were slaves. This student, who typically receives superior grades, receives a low grade on her paper. The teacher comments on her paper that dwelling on slavery and "racial" issues should not have been the focus of her paper. Obviously, the student and teacher in this case are engaged in a regressive relationship. The student is attempting to explore the meaning of her ethnic group's history and the teacher is insisting such issues are not important and should not be explored. In this case, the teacher not only negatively impacts the student's ethnic identity development but also risks creating a tense, hostile, and unproductive relationship with the student. Discrediting students' ethnic exploration can negatively influence relationships between teachers and students and potentially impact relationships with students' families and communities.

For adolescents in racially integrated middle schools, racial identity and ethnic identity frequently take on new significance with respect to peer interactions, friendship groups, and dating (Clark, 1989). It is not uncommon in integrated settings for early adolescents to interact and form friendships easily across racial boundaries – if their parents or other adults allow them to do so (Killen, Lee-Kim, McGlothlin, & Stangor, 2002). However, in adolescence such racial boundaries become more problematic as adolescents become increasingly aware of the significance associated with group difference. In other words, early adolescents generally become more concerned with how their peers react to their participation in interracial relationships and, as a result, they may begin to self-segregate according to race and/or ethnicity (Schofield & Francis, 1982). Also, adolescents are more aware of the politics associated with race, and more cognizant of racial hierarchies and prejudice (Way, Cowal, & Gingold, 2001).

Helms' (1994) interaction theory can be used to explain interactions among middle school students. As an example, a Mexican eighth grader is actively exploring his ethnic identity without any sense of commitment (i.e., moratorium). He chooses to read novels by Latino authors, he listens only to Mexican music, and he chooses to speak more Spanish at home and at school. His close friendships are with Mexican boys with similar interests and he intentionally separates himself from boys (and girls) of other ethnic groups. He comments to a teacher that he "wouldn't dare date or be close friends with an African American or White girl." While this student's interactions with students at the same stage of ethnic identity development is comfortable, it is unlikely that the student can develop beyond this stage without some exposure to an individual with a more advanced ethnic identity.

Regressive relationships also can occur between students of the same ethnic group. If placed in the same small group for a classroom activity, two students of the same ethnic background with differing levels of ethnic identity (e.g., moratorium vs. foreclosed) might not "connect" and might be distant or detached from one another. There is also the possibility of tension in student-to-student relationships where differing levels of ethnic identity are present.

RECOMMENDATIONS FOR MIDDLE SCHOOL COUNSELORS

The foregoing discussion and the research related to ethnic identity development lead to recommendations for middle school counselors. Given the ASCA National Model® (American School Counselor Association, 2003) and its emphasis on recognizing and respecting students' ethnic and cultural diversity, it seems fitting that middle school counselors make enhancing students' ethnic identity development a major component of comprehensive middle school counseling programs. In order to do this, middle school counselors must first recognize that the failure of an adolescent to examine ethnic issues and his or her ethnic identity creates risks for poor psychological and educational adjustment (Phinney, 1992; Pizarro & Vera, 2001; Ponce, 2001).

In his clinical work, Zayas (2001) found that minority youth benefit from discussing their struggles with racism and ethnic identity. He found that in many of his clinical cases, adolescents' struggles with their ethnic identity were made salient when he purposefully elicited clarification of issues related to peer-group relations, family relations, and achievement. In this respect, providing middle school students the opportunity to clarify, actively explore, and examine ethnic issues and their ethnic identity would only enhance the development of middle school students. As an example, students in the search/moratorium stage of Phinney's (1992) model who are displaying a desire to explore their ethnic heritage should be given opportunities to do so in class assignments, advisory programs, and counseling groups.

Group work is one mode of counseling that has been indicated in the literature as a viable means to nurture adolescents' ethnic identity development (Baca & Koss-Chioino, 1997; Noam, 1999). Middle school counselors could develop and implement ethnic exploration groups in which students research their ethnic heritage, dialogue with others about their ethnic background, and learn new information about other cultures and ethnic groups. An activity for a small group of eighth-grade Korean American middle school students might include completing the following: "Being Korean in this community means ...," and "Being Korean in this school means ..." These types of activities can act as a catalyst for students' exploration of the meaning attached to their ethnicity and, in turn, enhance their ethnic identity development. In these groups, counselors also might help early adolescents process others' negative racial/ethnic perceptions (Holcomb-McCoy & Moore-Thomas, 2001). For example, a middle school Mexican male group member complains to the counselor that students are teasing him because of his Mexican name and heritage. The counselor might encourage the student to discuss his feelings in relationship to the encounter and his feelings related to experiencing racism. Other group members also should have the opportunity to share similar experiences or to share how they would feel in a similar situation.

These group discussions ultimately can lead to an exploration of students' feelings related to their ethnic membership. The counselor in this example also might guide the group in problem-solving activities and help students determine ways to handle this situation or similar situations in the future. Role playing could be implemented to help students determine appropriate solutions to problems related to their ethnic group membership. Middle school counselors also must be prepared to advocate for increased cultural sensitivity and competence of students and staff in their schools.

In contrast to the preceding case, middle school counselors must be prepared to work with students who lack an interest in exploring their ethnic background (i.e., diffused or foreclosed identities). White students, in particular, may show little interest in their ethnicity because they do not see themselves as having an ethnic background (Phinney, 1992). The literature in relation to White adolescent ethnic and/or racial identity development is very limited; however, the literature on White racial identity development has increased over the past decade (Davey, Eaker, Fish, & Klock, 2003; Ponterotto, Fuertes, & Chen, 2000). It has been suggested that White adolescents examine how their Whiteness, as an identity and cultural system, is embodied and institutionalized in many settings, including schools (Carter, 1997; Davidson, 1996; McIntyre, 1997).

Proweller (1999) stated, "The conflicts that White students experience when asked to talk openly about Whiteness as a location of racial identity reflect a profound resistance to examining their own positionality, lived experience, and racial histories of domination and oppression" (p. 808). Proweller further indicated that many White students do not avoid active engagement with race but selectively engage in "race talk" within the parameters of a polite and public discourse. For this reason, middle school counselors should provide "safe" environments for White students to discuss their racial identity so that they can be honest rather than merely "polite" about their beliefs and values. Safe environments include settings where students are expected to respect one another, where different opinions are valued and challenged, and where adults are open about their own identity development (Southern Poverty Law Center, 1999).

Also, middle school counselors should engage White students in self-awareness activities that focus on identifying and exploring their ethnic heritage (e.g., Polish, Italian, German). Having students research their families' migration to the United States is an assignment that can initiate ethnic identification and exploration. Some students might be reluctant to explore or express feelings about their ethnicity because of family and/or parental beliefs that ethnic exploration is not necessary or is harmful. If this is the case, counselors should educate parents about the benefits of ethnic exploration in early adolescence.

Considering the importance of ethnicity in the identity development of middle school students, school counselors should examine counseling strategies and resources they use for possible modification. For instance, implementing bibliotherapy with books that include all White characters reinforces a lack of ethnic exploration and acceptance. Middle school counseling offices should offer books, videos, and other resources with representation of people of color and various cultures to promote students' exploration and acceptance of their ethnic heritages. Also, middle school counselors should provide opportunities for positive acknowledgement of students' ethnic group membership. Classroom guidance lessons, small groups, and any other school counseling activity should include recognition of students' uniqueness in terms of their ethnicity and/or race.

One example is the family genogram (e.g., Rigazio-DiGilio, Ivey, Grady, & Kunkler-Peck, 2005), a counseling strategy that can be used in middle schools to explore students' cultural/family rituals, expectations, beliefs, and values.

Middle school counselors should use their knowledge of Phinney's (1992) model of ethnic identity development and Helms' (1994) interaction theory to analyze their school's racial climate and counseling program (e.g., group work, classroom guidance). In order to improve relationships within schools, middle school counselors might recommend or present staff professional development related to the influence of ethnic identity on student- to-student and student-to-educator interactions. If educators understand how ethnic identity affects their interactions and behaviors with students, they will be more equipped to change negative, ineffective relationships (with students and parents) into more positive, supportive relationships.

CONCLUDING THOUGHTS

Although there is compelling literature suggesting that ethnic identity development is an important component of adolescents' development, there is a need for more research that examines the ethnic identity development of early adolescents. More importantly, there is still very little known about what school counselors, educators, and parents should do to foster the healthy ethnic identity development of adolescents. Nevertheless, in light of its linkages to student achievement, self-concept, and behaviors, ethnic identity development should be realized as an important component of middle school students' development. ?

Cheryl Holcomb-McCoy is with the Department of Counseling & Personnel Services, University of Maryland at College Park. E-mail: cholcomb@umd.edu

REFERENCES

Alba, R. (1990). *Ethnic identity: The transformation of White America.* New Haven, CT: Yale University.

American School Counselor Association. (2003). *The ASCA national model: A framework for school counseling programs.* Alexandria, VA: Author.

Baca, L. M., & Koss-Chioino, J.D. (1997). Development of a culturally responsive group counseling model for Mexican American adolescents. *Journal of Multicultural Counseling and Development, 25,* 130–141.

Bachay, J. (1998). Ethnic identity development and urban Haitian adolescents. *Journal of Multicultural Counseling and Development, 26,* 96–110.

Banks, J. A. (1993). Multicultural education for young children: Racial and ethnic attitudes and their modification. In B. Spodek (Ed.), *Handbook of research on the education of young children* (pp. 236–250).New York:Macmillan.

Bernal, M. E., & Knight, G. P. (1993). *Ethnic identity: Formation and transmission among Hispanic and other minorities.* Albany, NY: State University of New York Press.

Blash, R. R., & Unger,D.G. (1995). Self-concept of African American male youth: Self-esteem and ethnic identity. *Journal of Child & Family Studies, 4,* 359–373.

Bracey, J. R., Bamaca, M.Y., & Umana-Taylor, A. J. (2004). Examining ethnic identity and self-esteem among biracial and monoracial adolescents. *Journal of Youth & Adolescence, 33,* 123–132.

Carlson, C., Uppal, S., & Prosser, E. C. (2000). Ethnic differences in processes contributing to the self-esteem of early adolescent girls. *Journal of Early Adolescence, 20,* 44–67.

Carter, R. (1997). Is white a face? Expressions of white racial identity. In M. Fine, L.Weiss, L. Powell, & L. M.Wong (Eds.), *Off-white: Readings on race, power, and society* (pp. 198–209).New York: Routledge.

Chappell, M. S., & Overton,W. F. (2002).Development of logical reasoning and the school performance of African American adolescents in relation to socioeconomic status, ethnic identity, and self-esteem. Journal of Black Psychology, 28, 295–317.

Clark, M. L. (1989). Friendships and peer relations of Black adolescents. In R. L. Jones (Ed.), *Black adolescents* (pp. 175–204). Berkeley, CA: Cobb & Henry.

Cross,W. (1991). *Shades of black: Diversity in African American identity.* Philadelphia: Temple University Press.

Davey, M., Eaker,D. G., Fish, L. S., & Klock, K. (2003). Ethnic identity in an American white minority group. *Identity, 3,* 143–158.

Davidson, A. L. (1996). *Making and molding identity in schools: Student narratives on race, gender, and academic achievement.* Albany, NY: State University of New York Press.

Dubow, E. F., Pargament, K. I., Boxer, P., & Tarakeshwar, N. (2000). Initial investigation of Jewish early adolescents' ethnic identity, stress, and coping. *Journal of Early Adolescence, 20,* 418–441.

Education Trust. (2001). *The Education Trust state and national data book.*Washington, DC: Author.

Erikson, E. (1968). Identity:Youth and crisis.New York: Norton.

Flum, H. (1994). Styles of identity formation in early and middle adolescence. *Genetic, Social, and General Psychology Monographs, 120,* 437–467.

Fordham, S. (1996). *Blacked out: Dilemmas of race, identity, and success at Capital High.* Chicago: University of Chicago Press.

Fordham, S., & Ogbu, J. (1986). Black students' school success: Coping with the burden of "acting white." *Urban Review, 18,* 176–206.

Guzman, M. R., Santiago-Rivera, A. L., & Haase, R. F. (2005). Understanding academic attitudes and achievement in Mexican-origin youth: Ethnic identity, other-group orientation, and fatalism. *Cultural Diversity and Mental Health, 11,* 3–15.

Helms, J. E. (1993). *Black and white racial identity: Theory, research, and practice.*Westport, CT: Praeger.

Helms, J. E. (1994). Racial identity in the school environment. In P. Pederson & J. C. Carey (Eds.), *Multicultural counseling in schools: A practical handbook* (pp. 19–37). Needham Heights, MA: Allyn & Bacon.

Holcomb-McCoy, C., & Moore-Thomas, C. (2001). Empowering African American adolescent females. *Professional School Counseling, 5,* 19–26.

Irvine, J. J. (1991). *Black students and school failure.* New York: Praeger.

Killen, M., Lee-Kim, J.,McGlothlin, H., & Stangor, C. (2002). How children and adolescents evaluate gender and racial exclusion. *Monographs of the Society for Research in Child Development, 67,* 1–132.

Kulis, S., Napoli, M., & Marsiglia, F. F. (2002). Ethnic pride, biculturalism, and drug use norms of urban American Indian adolescents. *Social Work Research, 26,* 101–112.

Marcia, J. (1980). Identity in adolescence. In J. Adelson (Ed.), *Handbook of adolescent psychology* (pp. 159–187).New York:Wiley.

Marshall, P. L. (2002). *Cultural diversity in our schools.* Belmont, CA:Wadsworth/Thompson Learning.

Martinez, R.O., & Dukes, R. L. (1997).The effects of ethnic identity, ethnicity, and gender on adolescent well-being. *Journal of Youth and Adolescence, 26,* 503–516.

McIntyre, A. (1997). *Making meaning of whiteness.* Albany, NY: State University of New York Press.

McMahon, S.D., & Watts, R. J. (2002). Ethnic identity in urban African American youth: Exploring links with self-worth, aggression, and other psychosocial variables. *Journal of Community Psychology, 30,* 411–431.

Neville, H. A., Heppner, P. P., & Wang, L. (1997). Relations among racial identity attitudes, perceived stressors, and coping styles in African American college students. *Journal of Counseling & Development, 75*, 303–311.

Noam, G. G. (1999).The psychology of belonging: Reformulating adolescent development. In A. H. Esman (Ed.), Adolescent psychiatry: *Development and clinical studies* (pp. 49–68). Hillsdale, NJ: The Analytic Press.

Noguera, P. A. (2003). How racial identity affects school performance. *Harvard Education Letter, 19*, 1–3.

Ogbu, J.U. (1995). Origins of human competence: A culturalecological perspective. In N. R.Goldberger & J. B.Veroff (Eds.), *Culture and psychology reader* (pp. 245–275). New York: New York University Press.

Parham,T. (1989). Cycles of psychological nigrescence. *The Counseling Psychologist, 17*, 187–226.

Phinney, J. S. (1989). Stages of ethnic identity in minority group adolescents. *Journal of Early Adolescence, 9*, 34–49.

Phinney, J. S. (1990). Ethnic identity in adolescents and adults: Review of research. *Psychological Bulletin, 108*, 499–514.

Phinney, J. S. (1992).The Multigroup Ethnic Identity Measure: A new scale for use with diverse groups. *Journal of Adolescent Research, 7*, 156–176.

Phinney, J. S., & Alipuria, L. (1990). Ethnic identity in college students from four ethnic groups. *Journal of Adolescence, 13*, 171–184.

Phinney, J. S., Horenczyk, G., Liebkind, K., & Vedder, P. (2001). Ethnic identity, immigration, and well-being: An interactional perspective. *Journal of Social Issues, 57*, 493–510.

Phinney, J. S., & Kohatsu, E. L. (1997). Ethnic and racial identity development and mental health. In J. Schulenberg, J. L. Maggs, & K. Hurrelmann (Eds.), *Health risks and developmental transitions during adolescence* (pp. 420–443).New York: Cambridge University Press.

Phinney, J. S., Lochner, B., & Murphy, R. (1990). Ethnic identity development and psychological adjustment in adolescence. In A. Stiffman & L. Davis (Eds.), *Ethnic issues in adolescent mental health* (pp. 53–72). Newbury Park, CA: Sage.

Phinney, J. S.,Madden,T., & Santos, L. J. (1998). Psychological predictors of perceived ethnic discrimination among minority and immigrant adolescents. *Journal of Applied Social Psychology, 28*, 937–953.

Phinney, J. S., Romero, I., Nava, M., & Huang,D. (2001).The role of language, parents, and peers in ethnic identity among adolescents in immigrant families. *Journal of Youth and Adolescence, 30,* 135–153.

Pizarro, M., & Vera, E.M. (2001). Chicana/o ethnic identity research: Lessons for researchers and counselors. *The Counseling Psychologist, 29,* 91–117.

Ponce,D. E. (2001).The adolescent. In W.Tseng & J. Streltzer (Eds.), *Culture and psychotherapy: A guide to clinical practice* (pp. 193–208).Washington, DC: American Psychiatric Publishing.

Ponterotto, J. G., Fuertes, J. N., & Chen, E. C. (2000).Models of multicultural counseling. In S.D. Brown & R.W. Lent (Eds.), *Handbook of counseling psychology* (3rd ed., pp. 639–669). New York:Wiley.

Ponterotto, J. G., & Pederson, P. B. (1993). *Preventive prejudice: A guide for counselors and educators.* Newbury Park, CA: Sage.

Portes, A., & Rumbaut, R.G. (1990). *Immigrant America: A portrait.* Berkeley and Los Angeles: University of California Press.

Proweller, A. (1999). *Shifting identities in private education: Reconstructing race at/in the cultural center.* Teachers College Press, 100, 776–808.

Rayle, A.D., & Myers, J. E. (2004). Counseling adolescents toward wellness: The roles of ethnic identity, acculturation, and mattering. *Professional School Counseling, 8,* 81–91.

Retting,M.D., & Canady, R. L. (2000). *Scheduling strategies for middle schools.* Larmont, NY: Eye on Education.

Rigazio-DiGilio, S. A., Ivey, A., Grady, L.T., & Kunkler-Peck, K. P. (2005). *Community genograms: Using individual, family, and cultural narratives with clients.* New York: Teachers College Press.

Rotheram, M. J., & Phinney, J. S. (1988). Introduction: Definitions and perspectives in the study of children's ethnic socialization. In J. S. Phinney & M. J. Rotheram (Eds.), *Children's ethnic socialization: Pluralism and development* (pp. 10–28). Newbury Park, CA: Sage.

Sandoval, S. R., Gutkin,T. B., & Naumann,W. C. (1997). Racial identity attitudes and school performance among African American high school students: An exploratory study. *Research in Schools, 4,* 1–8.

Schofield, J.W., & Francis,W.D. (1982). An observational study of peer interaction in racially mixed "accelerated" classrooms. *Journal of Educational Psychology, 74,* 722–732.

Sleeter, C. E. (1994). White racism. Multicultural Education, 1, 5–8.

Southern Poverty Law Center. (1999). *Responding to hate at school: A guide for teachers, counselors, and administrators.* Montgomery, AL: Author.

Spencer, M. B., & Markstrom-Adams, C. (1990). Identity processes among racial and ethnic minority children in America. *Child Development, 61,* 290–310.

Steele, C.M. (1999).Thin ice: "Stereotype threat" and black college students. *The Atlantic Monthly, 284,* 44–54.

Waterman, A. (1985). Identity in the context of adolescent psychology. In A.Waterman (Ed.), *Identity in adolescence: Process and contents* (pp. 5–24). San Francisco: Jossey Bass.

Waters, M. (1990). *Ethnic options: Choosing identities in America.* Berkeley, CA: University of California Press.

Way, N., Cowal, K., & Gingold, R. (2001). Friendship patterns among African American, Asian American, and Latino adolescents from low-income families. *Journal of Social and Personal Relationships, 18,* 29–53.

Yasui, M.,Dorham, C. L., & Dishion,T. J. (2004). Ethnic identity and psychological adjustment: A validity analysis for European American and African American adolescents. *Journal of Adolescence, 19,* 807–825.

Zayas, L. H. (2001). Incorporating struggles with racism and ethnic identity in therapy with adolescents. *Clinical Social Work, 29,* 361–373.

Applying to College: Race, Class and Gender Differences

By James R. Valadez

This article originally appeared in *Professional School Counseling*, Vol. 1, No. 5, 1998.

Currently, economic and social forces demand that students seek increasing levels of education for entry into the workforce. Industrial demands and technological advances change so rapidly that students must look forward to pursuing higher education and continually upgrading their skill levels for students has accelerated over the past two decades and has made postsecondary study indispensable for the economic well-being of society. The role of postsecondary institutions has evolved as the nation's gatekeeper for the professions and a training ground for all manner of skilled work (McPherson & Shapiro, 1995).

Because postsecondary education is important, understanding the factors that influence students' decision to apply to college is critical. In this study, the influences of individual, family, and educational variables on students' decisions to apply to college were examined.

THEORETICAL PERSPECTIVE

The relationship between educational aspiration, particularly aspirations for college, and educational attainment have been widely studied (cf., Sewell & Hauser, 1980; Sewell, Haller & Ohlendorf, 1970; Sewell, Haller & Strauss, 1957). Overall, models of educational attainment begin with variables describing social origin, educational achievement begin with variables describing social origin, educational achievement, and social indicators, including race, gender and ethnicity. The so-called Wisconsin model includes social-psychological variables, and shifts the emphasis toward the influences of significant others on students educational attainment (Sewell et al., 1970). Critics of the Wisconsin model point out that the model inadequately explains differences in achievement and subsequent educational attainment of students from different minority and social backgrounds (Hanson, 1994; Kerckhoff, 1990). This criticism has motivated researchers to examine societal structures that limit students' abilities to achieve their goals. Educational attainment from this perspective is seen as more than the product of hard work and ability. It takes into consideration social impediments such as racism, sexism and classism.

In the discussion of the interaction between the stratification system of society (structure) and individual desires and aspirations; a dominant theme is the influence of social class. Bourdieu (1977) posits that children from higher social classes have the cultural nuances of the educational system. Because the educational system values the cultural knowledge of the affluent, the upper classes may exchange their cultural capital for better treatment in educational settings. The effect of social structure shows students in more favored social locations are rewarded in a manner that marks their social positions (Kerckhoff, 1990).

The central argument of the present study is that students follow through on their plans for educational attainment based on their experiences and interactions with the social structure. Stratifications systems work in favor of certain students, particularly those who come from upper and middle class backgrounds.,

METHOD

Data Source
Participants for this study were drawn from the base year and the first and second follow-up surveys in the National Educational Longitudinal Study of 1988 (NELS:88) (1994). The NEL surveys were designed to inform educational practitioners, policy makers, and researchers about changes in the educational system over time and abou the effects of school attributes on students' experiences. The National Center for Education Statistics (NCES) initiated NELS:88 with a sample of 24,599 eighth graders in 1,052 schools. For the first follow-up in the spring of 1990, 17,424 students completed the questionnaires. NCES conducted a second follow-up in 1992 with 16,842 students completing their questionnaires. A third follow-up was conducted in 1994 with the data released in 1996.

To reduce the effects of students moving from school to school during their high school years, students who remained in the same school from the 10th to the 12th grades were selected for this study. Since this study focused on students who were planning to go to college, the sample was limited further. Only those students who expressed aspirations for completing a 4-year college degree were selected. Using these filters, a final sample of 10,080 students was identified.

Independent Variables
The variables in the model used to explain differences in applying to college included parental, peer, individual, and educational variables as well as background (race, class, and gender) variables that were of special significance for this study. Research on the processes by which educational

attainment was reached consistently states that these sets of variables – parental, peer, individual and educational – are important (Alexander & Eckland, 1974; Coleman, Hoffer & Kilgore, 1982; Hanson, 1994). These variables also represent the resources or cultural capital that research on educational stratification finds to be critical for educational success (Bourdieu, 1977; Bourdieu & Passeron, 1977; Hanson, 1994, Kerckhoff, 1990; Lareau, 1987).

The individual level variables chosen for the study included background (stratification) variables that describe the student's race, gender, and socioeconomic status (SES), and *attitudinal* variables that provide a measure of the student's outlook on life. The SES variable is a composite variable created by NCES (see Appendix) that includes information on the students' family incomes, parent' educational levels, and parental occupations.

Variables that measure the student's *locus of control* and self-concept were selected. The locus of control variable is an NCES-created composite variable that consists of six items selected from the base-year student survey. The items probed students about whether they have control over their lives; if they feel something gets in the way every time they get ahead; if their plans hardly work out; if they can make plans work and if chance and luck are important in their lives. The locus of control composite variable purportedly estimates the amount of control students exert over their own lives. A high score on this measure signifies and internal locus of control meaning that students control their own destinies, while a low score shows an external locus of control that means external factors (luck) are responsible for the student's condition. The self-concept variable is also an NCES-composite consisting of seven items. The item describe whether students feel good about themselves; whether they feel they can do things as well as others; how satisfied they are with themselves; their feelings of usefulness; if they feel they are any good; and how proud they are of themselves.

To understand the communication between parents and students, *family* variables were selected that characterize the types of conversations parent have with students about their futures. The variables estimate time parents talk to children about college and time parents talk to students about getting jobs after high school. The *peer* variables give related information. These variables describe how important it is for the students' friends to get a job after high school or to go to college after school.

Two levels of educational variables were selected. On one level were those variables that describe the students' *academic* experiences. The NCES composite score on the standardized tests in English and mathematics (administered in the students' senior years) was selected as a proxy for students' academic abilities. *Academic experience* variables include information on the on the students' grades in English and math courses. In addition, variables measuring the number of Carnegie units in math and English courses earned by the students were included. Finally, a dichotomous variable that showed whether or not a student had taken the Preliminary Scholastic Assessment Test (PSAT) was created.

The second level of educational variable described the students' school experiences. A composite variable that measures the amount of academic encouragement schools gave their students were used. This variable includes items that suggest that students place high priority on learning; teachers encourage academic achievement, and all students are expected to do homework. To provide information about the racial composition of the schools, a dummy variable that showed whether or not students attended schools with high proportions of minority students (more than two-thirds African-American and Latino) was created.

Variables that estimate the degree to which schools help students with their college intentions were also used. These variables disclose how much time school personnel help students to fill out their financial aid and college applications.

Dependent Variable

The outcome variable was designed to measure students' intentions to attend college. The *applied to college* variable shows whether the students had applied to at least one college. The variable was coded as 1 if the student had applied to at least one college, and zero (0) if the student had not applied to any. It is important to note that, for this measure, all of the students had shown that they had aspirations for at least a 4-year college degree.

Procedures

The goal of this study was to describe the variation in students' intentions for a college education by race, gender and class. The analytic strategy for this study encompassed two phases. First, descriptive information concerning students' intentions to apply or not apply to college was provided. The second phase involved testing multivariate models that included race, class, gender, as well as parental, peer, attitudinal, and educational variables. Because of the dichotomous dependent variable and its skewed distribution, logistic regression models were used to estimate the multivariate equations for explaining the variation among groups (race, class, gender) and their intentions to go to college.

The logistic regression analyses took two steps. First, a series of mulivariate, recursive models were tested to examine the effects of both distal (stratification variables) and proximal (attitudinal, academic, school, parental, and peer experiences) factors on applying to college. Second, the final multivariate model from the second phase was estimated separately for males, females, Whites, Non-Whites, and high and low socioeconomic (SES) students to examine how the effects of the independent variables varied from group to group.

RESULTS

Descriptive Analyses

Table 1 (see the Appendix for NCES variable names and for descriptions of the variables) shows the means and standard deviations, as well as the results of T-tests between groups. Results displayed show that males reported a higher socio-economic status than females and that males and females are nearly evenly distributed among the racial groups.

Results of the attitudinal measures are mixed. Females report a higher locus of control (more control over their lives) than males. Males, on the other hand, report higher scores on the self-concept measure (feel good about themselves).

The academic measures in Table 1 show that females score higher on the standardized English and mathematics tests (ability) and have higher grades in English and math courses than males. Males earn slightly more Carnegie units in math, and females earn significantly more Carnegie units in English. A higher percentage of females (56%) than males (47%) take the PSAT. On the school experience measures, males report more academic encouragement from their schools than females. The other school experience measures are not statistically significant. Both males and females report nearly the same amount of help in filling out financial aid forms and college applications. The high minority school measure indicates whether students attend schools with more than two-thirds minority students. For males who attend high minority schools, the mean percentage of minority students in these schools is 85%. For females, the percentage is 84%.

Family and peer measures show that females talk to their parents more frequently than males about getting jobs after high school and going to college after high school. Females are more likely to have peers who think it is important to go to college after high school. Males and females report no difference in the importance their peers place on getting jobs after high school.

Table 1 also shows the means, standard deviations, and differences in the means by racial and ethnic group. White students report higher social class standing than Non-White students. In the educational measures,

TABLE 1 MEANS (AND STANDARD DEVIATIONS), T-TESTS, CHI-SQUARE TESTS OF ASSOCIATION FOR VARIABLES IN APPLIED TO COLLEGE MODEL BY GENDER, RACE AND SES WITH ASPIRATIONS FOR COLLEGE, NELS: 88

Variables	Total Mean (S.D.)	Male Mean (S.D.)	Female Mean (S.D.)	White Mean (S.D.)	Non-White Mean (S.D.)	High SES Mean (S.D.)	Low SES Mean (S.D.)
Background Variables							
Gender (female=1, male=0)	.51 (.49)			.51 (.39)	.52 (.39)	.50 (.50)**	.50 (.50)**
SES	2.93 (1.07)	2.96 (1.06)**	2.90 (1.07)**	3.13 (.96)**	2.20 (1.11)**	3.61 (.48)**	1.59 (.49)**
White	.72 (.41)	.49 (.50)	.51 (.50)	—	—	73.77 (.48)&	26.23 (.48)
Non-White	.21 (.41)	.48 (.50)	.52 (.50)	—	—	39.23 (.48)&	60.77 (.48)&
Attitudinal Variables							
Locus of Control	.15 (.62)	.10 (.63)**	.20 (.60)**	.18 (.60)	.09 (.67)**	.19 (.61)**	.07 (.65)**
Self Concept	.08 (.79)	.17 (.78)**	-.01 (.79)**	.05 (.79)**	.22 (.78)**	.09 (.79)**	.06 (.81)**
Academic Variables							
Ability	54.61 (9.26)	54.40 (9.60)*	54.80 (8.89)*	56.09 (8.48)**	48.20 (9.28)**	56.9 (8.35)**	50.13 (9.32)**
Preliminary Scholastic Assessment Test (PSAT)	52.22 (.49)	.47 (.49)**	.56 (.49)**	.54 (.49)**	.40 (.49)**	.59 (.49)**	.38 (.48)**
Math Grades	6.71 (7.85)	6.31 (8.96)**	7.11 (6.57)**	7.07 (7.19)**	4.92 (10.24)**	7.27 (6.68)**	5.63 (9.65)**
English Grades	8.05 (2.36)	7.51 (2.39)**	8.58 (2.22)**	8.31 (2.28)**	6.75 (2.29)**	8.41 (2.22)**	7.24 (2.43)**
Math-Carnegie Units	3.45 (.61)	3.48 (.87)	3.43 (.92)*	3.48 (.87)*	3.23 (.95)**	3.58 (.83)**	3.19 (.96)**
English-Carnegie Units	4.10 (.77)	4.07 (.78)**	4.15 (.75)**	4.10 (.72)	4.09 (.95)	4.14 (.71)**	4.04 (.87)**

TABLE 1, CONT.

Variables	Total Mean (S.D.)	Male Mean (S.D.)	Female Mean (S.D.)	White Mean (S.D.)	Non-White Mean (S.D.)	High SES Mean (S.D.)	Low SES Mean (S.D.)
School Experience							
High Minority School	.84 (.35)	.85 (.35)	.84 (.36)	.81 (.38)**	.95 (.81)**	.83 (.37)**	.85 (.35)**
Academic Encouragement	7.64 (1.19)	7.68 (1.17)**	7.60 (1.17)**	7.70 (1.17)**	7.37 (1.20)**	7.68 (1.17)**	7.60 (1.17)**
Help-financial aid forms	3.64 (.61)	3.63 (.62)	3.65 (.59)	3.60 (.63)**	3.78 (.64)**	3.61 (.63)**	3.70 (.54)**
Help-college applications	3.85 (.41)	3.85 (.40)	3.85 (.42)	3.83 (.44)**	3.91 (.31)**	3.86 (.40)*	3.84 (.43)*
Family and Peer Influence							
Parents talk about jobs	1.92 (.70)	1.87 (.68)**	1.98 (.72)**	1.93 (.69)**	1.98 (.69)**	1.90 (.71)**	1.96 (.70)**
Parents talk about college	2.45 (.62)	2.36 (.65)**	2.54 (.62)**	2.48 (.61)**	2.36 (.61)**	2.53 (.58)**	2.27 (.68)**
Peer plans-job	1.97 (.71)	1.98 (.70)	1.98 (.71)	1.94 (.70)**	2.15 (.70)**	1.90 (.70)**	2.13 (.69)**
Peer plans-college	2.61 (.59)	2.55 (.62)**	2.68 (.56)**	2.62 (.59)**	2.58 (.61)**	2.65 (.57)**	2.54 (.62)**
Outcome Variable							
Applied to college	.77 (.41)	.73 (.43)**	.81 (.39)**	.80 (.39)**	.65 (.47)**	.84 (.36)**	.65 (.47)**

N=10,080
&Chi Square Test of Association
*p>.05
**p<.01

White students score higher on standardized English and mathematics tests, have higher grades in English and mathematics, and accumulate more Carnegie units in math courses. The Analysis shows, however, that White students do not earn significantly more Carnegie units in English courses than Non-White students.

White students score higher in the locus of control measure, and Non-White students score higher in the self-concept measure. The school experience measures show that White students receive more academic encouragement, and Non-White students are more likely to report getting help from the school in filling out their college applications. Non-White students attend schools with higher proportions of minorities than White students and report that they are more likely to get help from the school in filling out college financial aid forms.

Family and peer influences show that White students talk to their parents more about going to college and Non-White students talk to their parents more about getting jobs after high school. Non-White students are more likely than white students to have peers who believe that getting a job after high school is important. A substantial difference exists between the two groups in the applied-to college outcome variable. Eighty percent of White students report that they applied to college compared with 65% of the Non-White students.

The differences in the low and high SES groups followed predictable patterns. The results of a Chi-Square analysis show that a disproportionate number of Non-white students occupy the lower SES strata. Upper SES students perform better on cognigtive tests, have higher grades, and earn more Carnegie units in math and English than lower SES students. Higher SES students report a higher locus of control. No significant difference was found between SES groups in the self-concept measure.

The information gives one insight into the amount of resources that different groups of students have – resources shown to be important for educational attitudes and achievement. The background (stratification) variables do not necessarity explain these patterns. The findings, however, provide evidence that if groups show fewer resources needed to shape their decisions to apply to college, they are less likely to follow through on their aspirations.

In what follows, the multivariate phase of the study is described. Results of the logistic regression model run on the full sample of students and then run separately for gender, race, and social class (SES) are reported.

Gender Effects

Table 2 shows that in the logistic equation run for the full sample, gender has a significant effect in the reduced model, but its effect is suppressed in

TABLE 2: PREDICTED ODDS RATIOS FOR APPLIED TO COLLEGE MODEL FOR HIGH SCHOOL SENIORS WITH ASPIRATIONS FOR COLLEGE; NELS: 1988

Variables	Total Reduced	Total Full	Male Reduced	Male Full	Female Reduced	Female Full	Whites Reduced	Whites Full	Non-Whites Reduced	Non-Whites Full	High SES Reduced	High SES Full	Low SES Reduced	Low SES Full
Background Variables														
SES	2.222**	1.151**	1.621**	1.275**	1.657**	1.023	2.594**	1.393**	1.622**	.847	2.878**	1.435**	1.684**	.826
Gender (F=1, M=0)	1.878**	1.146	—	—	—	—	1.928**	1.079	1.872**	1.392*	2.003	1.187	1.741**	1.102
Race (W=1, NM=0)	1.153**	1.146	1.172	1.108	1.076	1.136	—	—	—	—	1.423**	1.765**	1.050	.864
Attitudinal Variables														
Locus of Control		.978		.981		.956		1.135		.958		.878		1.133
Self Concept		1.044		.979		1.023		.970		1.071		1.083		1.003
Academic Variables														
Ability		1.026**		1.022**		1.031**		1.024**		1.006		1.024**		1.031**
Preliminary Scholastic Assessment Test (PSAT)		2.211**		2.525**		1.917		1.992		3.758**		1.962**		2.625**
Math Grades		.996		.994		.995		.984		1.011		.998		.994
English Grades		1.226**		1.260**		1.212**		1.232**		1.295**		1.254**		1.189**
Math-Carnegie Units		1.214**		1.219**		2.360**		1.219**		1.183		1.220**		1.202**
English-Carnegie Units		.936		.949		.922		.949**		1.213		.877**		1.041

TABLE 2, CONT.

Variables	Total		Male		Female		Whites		Non-Whites		High SES		Low SES	
	Reduced	Full	Reduced	Full	Reduced	Full	Reduced	Full	Reduced	Full	Reduced	Full	Reduced	Full
School Experience														
Academic Encouragement		1.021		1.008		.956		1.008		1.071		1.039		.990
High Minority School		.705**		.578**		1.101		.578**		1.033		.707**		.691**
Help-financial aid forms		.710**		.734**		.833		.734**		.520**		.720**		.731**
Help-college applications		1.532**		1.540**		1.245		1.540**		1.401		1.631**		1.353**
Family and Peer Influence														
Parents talk about jobs		.708**		.603**		.706**		.603**		1.062		.689**		.735**
Parents talk about college		2.841**		3.473**		3.033**		3.473**		1.601**		3.098**		2.530**
Peer plans-job		.710**		.665**		.783**		.665**		.920		.687**		.754**
Peer plans-college		1.339		1.366**		1.431**		1.366**		1.181		1.235**		1.454**

N=10,080
*p<.05
**p<.01

the full model. This indicates that the effects of gender may be explained by other variables in the model. This issue was examined further by running separate logistic regression models for males and females. The findings show that different processes are at work for males and females in making decisions about going to college. For males there are direct effects of SES and school experiences are suppressed in the full model for females.

What these findings suggest is that differences in resources between males and females, along with differences in processes, help to explain why females apply to college at much higher rates than males. Females have more resources, particularly in the educational and the parental and peer-influence variables, and are more effective than males in converting these resources into the cultural capital needed by groups to persist in education. It is also important to note the strong influence of SES that contributes to increasing the odds of males to apply to college, while for females, the influence is largely indirect and presumably explained by other variables in the full model.

Race Effects

An examination of the logistic regression equations regarding the racial and ethnic groups shows some surprising results. In Table 2 a comparison of the reduced and full models for the full sample of students show that while the effects of race are suppressed in the full model, its presence in the reduced model indicates that its effects are mediated by other variables in the model. While the effect of race cannot be identified as a significant predictor in the full applied to college model, it points to the complexity of the issue in understanding the processes at work in shaping students' decisions concerning college. Understanding the issue requires a deeper look into how different racial and ethnic groups use the resources embedded within families, schools, and communities.

The differences in the predictors among racial and ethnic groups support the idea that groups differ in their ability to convert available resources for shaping decisions about going to college. The groups seem to behave similarly in some processes involved in shaping decisions, but in other areas they differ markedly. White and Non-White students both convert educational resources into positive decisions about going to college. But as Table 1 indicates, White students have more of these resources available. Table 1 also shows that schools appear to give significantly more assistance to Non-White students than White students in filling out college applications and financial aid forms. Curiously, the results listed in Table 2 show that getting help from the school to apply to college increases the odds for applying to college for White students, but is non-significant for Non-White students. This suggests that White students are more effective in converting this resource into decisions to apply to college. For both White and Non-White students, Table 2 also shows that getting help in filling out financial aid forms for college decreases the odds for applying to college.

As far as parental and peer influences are concerned, talking to parents about college increases the odds of applying to college for White students by 350%, compared to 60% for Non-White students. Having peers who plan to go to college increases the odds of applying to college by 36%, but is nonsignificant for Non-White students. For White students, both talking to parents about jobs and having peers who plan to get jobs after high school decreases the odds for applying to college (Table 2). In contrast, for Non-White students, talking to parents about jobs or having peers planning to get jobs after high school is not a significant predictor.

Finally, it should be said that SES complicates this issue. The logistic regression equations show that SES has an indirect effect for both Whites and Non-Whites, and a direct effect for White students. This suggests an apparent advantage for students in higher socioeconomic classes that gives them an edge in converting available resources for making decisions about going to college. In the next section, this complex issue is examined.

The Effects of SES

The key to understanding the difference that propels the higher SES group of students toward college and depresses the aspirations of the lower SES group of students is the fact that SES directly affects students applying to college, irrespective of other resources. A deeper understanding, however, requires an examination of the unequal distribution of resources between the two groups. Table 1 outlines the differences in resources, particularly those that are influential in guiding students toward college. The differences in grades, courses taken, test scores, parental conversations about college, and school assistance in filling out college applications are significant.

To understand the different processes of the higher and lower SES groups, separate logistic regression equations were run for both groups. Some striking differences emerged. For the higher SES groups, the effect of SES was significant in the reduced and full models. The effect of race, however, is also a significant predictor in the reduced and full models for the upper SES group. This suggests that higher SES students convert these resources effectively into decisions to apply for college. These findings contrast with those of lower SES students. Gender and SES are significant in the reduced model, but the effects are suppressed in the full model. The other variables in the model behave similarly for both SES groups. The significant predictor variables point to the importance of ability, having taken the PSAT, grades in English courses, and accumulating math Carnegie units in shaping decisions about applying to college.

Other significant variables that increase the odds of applying to college for high and low SES groups are getting help from the schools to fill out college applications, talking to parents about college, and having peers who plan to go to college. Variables that lower the odds for applying to college for both groups are attending a school with a high percentage of minority students, getting help completing college financial aid forms, talking to parents about jobs after high school, and having peers who plan to work after high school.

SES and race have significant direct effects for higher SES students but not for lower SES students. This indicates that, for high SES students, the variables identified in the model do not fully explain the processes involved in applying to college. The findings also show that the different processes involved in the decision to apply to college, and vast differences in resources between higher and lower SES groups, give the advantage to higher SES groups in following through on decisions to apply to college.

DISCUSSION

Bourdieu and Passeron (1977), Clark (1960), and others suggest that aspirations for higher education need to be encouraged, but society has the tendency to cool out the ambitions of certain students by imposing certain criteria, including the influence of race, class and gender. In this study, all of the students expressed a desire to attend college, yet not all students followed through on their intentions. Of the variables considered of most interest in this study (race, class, and gender), it was social class that had a significantly large effect in the predicted direction. In other words, higher SES groups were more likely than lower SES groups to apply.

The finding on social class was consistent with Bourdieu's notion that lower SES groups are likely to be selected out of the educational process leading toward higher education and subsequently higher status occupations. Other variables that contribute to the explanation for why students do not follow through on their plans to apply to college include such school-level and family-level variables as the number and type of math courses taken and discussions with parents about college. These variables indicate that certain students have access to knowledge that helps them with their decision to apply to college. Students who talk to parents or significant others about college may receive information on college preparatory activities such as appropriate courses to take, preparation for college entrance exams, and discussions a bout college plans. Those variables that seem to have a negative effect include peer pressure to find work after high school.

An unexpected finding is the lack of consistency concerning measures of academic effort, specifically math grades. When background and high school experiences are controlled, getting good grades in math seems less important than the types of math courses students take. Although high grades in English courses may be related to increasing the odds of applying to college, the results show that taking more math courses, possibly higher level math courses, is a powerful predictor of whether a student applies to college or not.

While social class has significant direct effects, the effect of gender and race are largely mediated by other variables in the model. This finding agrees with other research on minority students' educational achievement that indicates most all the observed differences in educational achievement of African Americans and Latinos can be accounted for by differences in family backgrounds (Rumberger, 1983, 1995, Belez, 1989). Closer examination of the individual groups in the present study, however, shows the varied effects of the stratification variables. For instance, there is a direct effect of SES for males but not females. Direct effects of SES for higher SES students, but not lower social class students. Direct effects of SES for White students, but not Non-White students. These seemingly mixed findings model the different processes used by the various social groups in making decisions about college. Unfortunately, what persists in this discussion of group differences in applying to college is that status maintenance systems apply. Simply put, higher SES students are more likely to take advantage of the resources needed to shape decisions about college than lower SES students. The issue of race, however, cannot be discounted. Both race and the influence of social class combine toward preserving a system in which White middle and upper class children successfully use their cultural capital to move toward higher education and eventually positions at the top of the economic ladder.

Implications for Educational Policy

This study has important implications for educators, school counselors, and administrators. The results indicate that certain students do not have access to knowledge that helps them with their decisions to apply to college. Having aspirations to college is simply not enough. Counselors, teachers, and parents need to have appropriate information concerning curricula, college entrance exams, and activities that promote and encourage students' plans for college attendance. All of us involved in education need to be aware that all students do not necessarily have equal access to information that may be critical in guiding their decisions about applying to college.

Efforts made by school counselors, such as informational programs or interventions, may be crucial for encouraging students, particularly low-income students to apply to college. Activities that provide direct help and information, such as helping students with their college applications or arranging frequent informational meetings about college, may be effective means for encouraging students' aspirations for college. Programs for parents should emphasize helping them advise their children about course-taking patterns and educating families about college life and college requirements.

In the spirit of social justice, it is important that educators reach out to schools, particularly schools with high proportions of low-income students, to give them information about college opportunities. This is an important challenge for educators as we attempt to overcome the inequities of the social structure in order to give all students the opportunity for access to higher education.

REFERENCES

Alexander, K.L., & Eckland, B.K. (1974). Sex differences in the educational attainment process. *American Sociological Review, 39*, 668-682.

Bourdieu, P. (1977). Cultural reproduction and social reproduction. In J. Karabel & A. Halsey (Eds.) *Power and ideology in education* (pp. 487-510). Oxford: Oxford University Press.

Bourdieu, P. & Passeron, J.C. (1977). *Reproduction in education, society, and culture.* London: Sage.

Clark, B. (1960). *The open-door college.* New York: McGraw-Hill.

Coleman, J. Hoffer, T, & Kilgore, S. (1982). *High school achievement, public and private schools compared.* New York: Basic Books.

Hanson, S. (1994). Lost talent: Unrealized educational aspirations and expectations among U.S. youths. *Sociology of Education, 67*, 159-183.

Kerckhoff, A. (1990). *Diverging pathways: Social structure and career deflections.* Cambridge, MA: Cambridge University Press.

Lareau, A. (1987). Social class differences in family-school relationships. *Sociology of Education, 60*, 73-85.

McPherson, M.L., & Shapiro, M.O. (1995). Skills, innovations and values: Future needs for postsecondary education. *Change, 27* (4), 26-32.

National Educational Longitudinal Study of 1988. (1994). *Base year, first follow-up, second follow-up electronic codebook/cd-rom.* Washington, DC: National Center for Education Statistics.

Rumberger, R.W. (1983). Dropping out of high school: the influence of race, sex and family background. *American Educational Research Journal, 20*, 199-220.

Rumberger, R.W. (1995). Dropping out of middle school: A multilevel analysis of students and schools. *American Educational Research Journal, 32* (3), 583-625.

Sewell, W.H., Haller, A.O., & Ohlendorf, G.W. (1970). The educational and early occupational attainment process: Replications and revisions. *American Sociological Review, 35*, 1014 – 1027.

Sewell, W.H., Haller, A.O., & Strauss, M.A. (1957). Social status and educational and occupational aspiration. *American Sociological review, 22*, 67-73.

Sewell, W.H. & Hauser, R.M. (1980). The Wisconsin longitudinal study of social and psychological factors in aspirations and achievement. *Research in Sociology of Education and Socialization, 1*, 59-99.

Velez, W. (1989). High school attrition among Hispanic and Non-Hispanic white youths. *Sociology of Education, 62*(2), 199-133.

APPENDIX

Descriptions of Variables, National Educational Longitudinal Study of 1988

Variable	Type[2]	Description (NCES variable names)
Background Variables		
Gender	D	(F2SEX; Male = 0, Female = 1)
SES	FC	(F2SES1Q)
White	D	(F2RACE1 = 4)
Nonwhite	D	(F2RACE1 = 2, 3)
Attitudinal Variables		
Locus of control	FC	(F2Locus 2)
Self-Concept	FC	(F2CNCPT)
Academic Variables		
Ability	C	(F22XCOMP)
Preliminary Scholastic Assessment Test (PSAT)	D	Student took PSAT = 1, Student did not = 0 (F2S44A)
Math grades	C	(F2RHMAG2)
English grades	C	(F2RHENG2)
Carnegie units – Math	C	(F2MAT_C)
Carnegie units – English	C	(F2ENG_C)

School Experiences

High minority school Black (F2C22C)	C	Percent Latino (F2C22B) Percent
Academic encouragement	C	Researcher-created factor-based scale (F256B, F256D, F256K)
Help – financial aid Applications	C	School report, 1=never, 2=seldom, 3=sometimes, 4=often (F2C12C)
Help – college	C	School report, 1=never, 2=seldom, 3=sometimes, applications 4=often (F2C12D)

Parental and Peer Influences

Parents talk about job	C	Student reports, 1=never, 2=seldom, 3=sometimes, 4=often (F299G)
Parents talk about college	C	Student reports, 1=never, 2=seldom, 3=sometimes, 4=often (F299F)
Peer plans – job	C	Student reports, 1=not too important, 2=some importance, 3=very important (F2S68K)
Peer plans – college	C	Student reports, 1=not too important, 2=some importance, 3=very important (F268H)

Outcome Variable

Applied to college	D	Student applied to one or more colleges =1, none=0 (F2S60A)

Variable type is: dummy (D), continuous (C) or factor composite (FC).

James R. Valadez, Ph.D., is an associate professor, Educational Leadership and Policy Studies, University of Washington, Seattle. This research was supported by a grant from the American Educational Research Association Grants Program.

Counseling Muslim Children in School Settings

By Richard B. Carter, Ph.D. and Amelia E. El Hindi, Ph.D.

This article originally appeared in *Professional School Counseling*, Vol. 2, No. 3, 1999.

Although many religious groups in the United States are experiencing a decline in membership, Islam is the nation's fastest growing religion (Cooper, 1993). Recent estimates show that Islam claims approximately 6 million U.S. adherents (Bedell, 1993). Due to immigration and conversion, Muslims (adherents to Islam) are becoming more and more numerous in all facets of American life. American Muslims represent many cultures and include immigrants from Pakistan, Iran, India, Southeast Asia, Indonesia, the Middle East, and Afghanistan as well as African Americans who have adopted the faith as part of the Nation of Islam movement.

Negative stereotyping of Muslims as fanatical extremists may possibly have caused school personnel to view Muslim students and their families in a different light than other students. Confronted with this stereotyping coupled with the outright racist response from other cultures, Muslims have found it difficult to merge into mainstream U.S. society and maintain their identity as Muslims (Jackson, 1995). At the least, counselors and other educators who do not take the time to become aware of the Muslim students' cultural needs may unwittingly find themselves working contrary to the students' religious and cultural values.

Religiously and culturally, Muslims espouse values different from those of mainstream U.S. society (Banawi, 1993). Because of the rising numbers of Muslims who are becoming integrated into society (Kelly, Aridi, & Bakhtiar, 1996), it is essential that sensitivity to this population be demonstrated by U.S. school personnel. Kelly et al. (1996) noted that Muslims place high value on benevolence and conformity while generally disdaining such Western values as power, hedonism, and excessive stimulation. Since school counselors often find their role includes assisting students in adjusting to the school environment (Myrick, 1997), they can play a major role in helping Muslim students adjust.

Counselors often find themselves lacking knowledge of Arab and other Muslim populations. Little has been written either in multicultural texts (c.f. Sue & Sue, 1993) or in the research literature on counseling Muslim students in public schools (Banawi, 1993) or for that matter on counseling Muslims in general (Haddad & Lummis, 1987; Jafari, 1993; Kelly, et al, 1996). Jackson (1995) has only recently offered information for school counselors regarding the culture and values of Arabs, which though a representative group of Muslims, is still a minority of Muslims worldwide. Therefore the purpose of the present article is to describe some basic issues regarding the education and counseling of Muslims and to offer some general suggestions to help school counselors work effectively with Muslim students.

ORGANIZING THEMES

The authors interviewed several Muslim families with children ranging in age from 3 to adulthood. While such a small sample cannot be deemed representative of U.S. Muslims as a group, from the dialogues several themes emerged that illustrate issues expressed by other writers. Each of these areas has implications for school counseling. These themes can be divided into the following areas:

- Home/school relations
- Family issues
- Peer relations and dating
- Self-identity
- Dietary issues
- Cultural events
- Curricular problems

These psycho-social issues are a result of interaction of religion, family, Muslim culture, and mainstream U.S. culture. (Jackson, 1995).

Home/school relations
Muslim families place a high value on education and hold educators in high esteem (Jackson, 1995). Because of this, Muslim parents hesitate to disturb the operation of the school by requesting conferences or confronting educators regarding cultural issues. The parents want educators to approach them and begin dialogues about the children and their educational needs. It seems they fear being misunderstood, both culturally and as a result of low self-efficacy stemming from their limited English skills. They are most pleased with those educators who proactively express a desire to learn more about Muslim values. This issue is underscored by Jackson (1995), who added that fear of being misunderstood by school officials is a major issue for Muslim families.

Family
Family is important to Muslims, both immediate and extended family. Family often includes a network of relatives extending back to the coun-

try of origin. (Jackson, 1995). Elders in the "old country" are often consulted before any major decisions are made. A strong sense of loyalty exists to this kinship network. Jackson (1995) describes a strict line of order and authority – the father being responsible for external family affairs; the mother maintaining responsibility for internal family affairs. Family life resembles the traditional American nuclear family. The bond between parents and children is very apparent. Respect for parents is paramount for children. One child, when chastised for singing Chanukah and Christmas songs, seemed more concerned about disappointing her family than breaking religious teaching. Family members are quick to support each other in times of crisis or conflict. Siblings come to each other's aid in times of conflict. Parents regularly come to the school for clarification of children's problems. Indeed, they expect to be called if there is a problem.

Peer relations

The Muslim children often experience a certain amount of prejudice from some of their non-Muslim peers (Chan,1991). This prejudice usually takes the form of stereotypical images of Muslims. Problems tend to cluster around certain political crises – the Gulf War or the World Trade Center and Oklahoma City bombings. Chan's report also related incidents of mosque desecration, name calling, and assaults during crises that the media blamed on Arabs. One high school student, a Palestinian by birth, reported being called "Iraqi" during the Gulf War. A parent mentioned being called Iranian, during the time when the U.S. diplomats were being held hostage in Iran.

Muslim children who have generally positive experiences in school enjoy school, while those whose experiences are less than positive tend not to enjoy school. Most are generally popular students with many friends. Their friends do not always understand their faith, however, most respect it. Peers perceived by the Muslim students as closed-minded are usually dismissed as potential friends. Siblings come to each other's support when one has problems with peers. The only instances of fighting by the Muslim boys interviewed by the authors were to defend their faith and the honor of sisters or younger siblings.

Muslim children also report difficulty with peers when the outward signs of their religion are displayed, such as the wearing of the hijab (head covering for females) and fasting during the holy month of Ramadan. This is reflected in statements from the children such as they had to "make a fight" to defend their faith, or "I don't like nobody to bully me about my religion," or "We're not terrorists."

The Muslim children generally view such remarks as a lack of knowledge on the part of the other students. According to the families interviewed by the authors, incidents of so-called Islamic terrorism are considered criminal by most Muslims. One adult compared such incidents to incidents of gang violence in America. They asserted that this perception is true, regardless of the target of the terrorism, even in the Middle East. Muslims stress that Islam is a religion of peace. Chan (1991) adds that racist behaviors of others often lead to feelings of shame and humiliation.

Dating

Dating was an issue with both students and parents. The Koran, the sacred book of revelations made to Muhammad by Allah, forbids unmarried individuals to be alone together. Boys report little difficulty with this, probably because society generally gives the boy the responsibility for initiating a dating relationship and they can simply avoid asking girls out. Girls, however, have to deal with such issues regularly and have to be ready with a response when asked out by a boy who does not understand the prohibition. This issue was noted by Kelly et al. (1996), who point out that in some Muslim households, dating can become a major point of controversy.

Self-identity

The Muslim children themselves are ready to identify themselves as Muslim, and many report a strong sense of pride in being Muslim. They welcome honest inquiries about their faith and enjoy sharing certain customs, such as holidays and Ramadan with their friends. High school students also report a sense of pride in their ability to speak Arabic as well as English. Being bilingual seems to give them a certain status with their peers. Some, however, report teasing about their Arabic names. Counselors must be sensitive to such identity issues (Jafari, 1993; Kemp, 1996).

Jackson (1995) describes some issues regarding students' identity as Muslims. Immigrants tend to be concerned with maintaining their traditional culture, while those children born in this country tend to loose their traditions and become Americanized. This often creates a rift between parent and child. One of the developmental tasks of Arab-American youths, Muslim or not, is to recognize this dichotomy and work to successfully merge both cultures.

Dietary issues

Dietary needs for Muslims go beyond physical nutrition to include the spiritual part of a person. Muslims on the whole eat a diet rich in vegetables and vegetable protein. They are prohibited from eating pork and any meat not killed in a ritualistic manner and cooked with special utensils

(Hampton, 1992). Such meat is referred to as halal or allowed. One mother indicated that her children had been forced to eat only bread and desert one day when the school served a meal that was primarily pork and vegetables cooked with pork seasoning. She blamed a menu change that did not allow her to plan ahead and send an appropriate lunch with her child. At the least, she felt the school could have contacted her so she could have brought her child some lunch. Hampton added that schools with a high proportion of Muslim students might offer alternative or halal menus. While this may not be possible in most schools, certainly some allowance could be made for students who cannot eat the standard menu.

Cultural events

Non-Muslim holidays can be difficult. One child interviewed by the authors had experienced some difficulty on the previous Valentine's Day because it had fallen during Ramadan and she was fasting during the daylight hours. She had to sit in the school office during a Valentine's breakfast her class was having, but when she returned, the class was still eating. That made her uncomfortable about her lack of participation in the festivities and standing out from the other children. Parents fear problems can result from their children being perceived as different. Children expressed some discomfort with school observances of Christmas and Chanukah. One noted that her mother had spoken to the school after hearing her and her friends singing "holy, holy, holy." It turned out that the words were part of a Chanukah song. The mother discussed this incident with the school and explained this was a violation of their faith. This issue was worked out satisfactorily with the child being given the responsibility for excusing herself from the class. Most Muslim children seem comfortable with such an arrangement, but some believe that it causes embarrassment about leaving their friends and missing fun classroom activities. Parents also noted that even in cases where there were no Jewish children in a class, Chanukah was still observed (their description). Chan's (1991) report recommends recognition of Muslim as well as Christian and Jewish holidays.

Curricular problems

Muslim children note discrepancies between the picture of Islam portrayed by teachers and in textbooks and their own personal experience and religious teaching. This theme is echoed by parents who express delight with educators who respect their way and want to learn more about it in order to help the children. Parents also express concern that many educators allow a distorted image of Islam and Muslims to be conveyed by textbooks.

Another problem expressed by Muslim parents is the issue of equal coverage in the curriculum (Siraj-Blatchford, 1993). A Muslim parent reported that her child's spelling book had included a unit on Chanukah. She questioned the fact that there wasn't anything comparable on Islam. Muslim parents tend to support the inclusion of curricular materials on various cultures and religions, but they have strong feelings that any such materials should devote equal coverage to all cultures and religions, including Islam. They further feel that such information should present an accurate picture of the culture under consideration. Many Muslim parents are willing to come to school and volunteer to share aspects of their culture.

Courses such as art, drama, music, and physical education (PE) can be of concern to Muslim parents. Siraj-Blatchford (1993) suggests that during Ramadan, the month of fasting, schools waive the requirement for the uniform short outfits for PE, that they not demand showers for Muslim students in light of their religious requirements for washing several times a day, and provide alternative activities for Muslim students who may lack energy because of fasting. Schools should be open to examining their policies in light of religious dictates.

IMPLICATIONS FOR SCHOOL COUNSELING

The Role of the School Counselor

Problematic peer interactions and lack of understanding of Islam by adults in school highlight a need for someone in the school to take the lead in the dissemination of accurate images of Muslims to teachers and to students (Kelly et al., 1996). Like most students in U.S. schools, Muslims hold a variety of perceptions regarding school counseling. Most who see their school counselors see them for academic support, credit checks, or college scholarships in the high school or study issues in the elementary and middle school. Other problems reported by the students interviewed by the authors for which they had sought the services of the school counselor included name calling by peers and derogatory comments about their ethnicity during a crisis such as the Gulf War, the World Trade Center bombing, or the Oklahoma City tragedy (also noted by Chan, 1991).

The parents seemed hesitant about their children discussing family issues with a school counselor. Family issues are to be handled within the family, according to Muslim traditions and the Koran (Jackson, 1995). Counseling regarding family issues is seen as an intrusion into the privacy of the family. Parents are concerned that counselors could attempt to circumvent family involvement in their children's issues. At the very least, parents expect to be involved in the personal counseling of their children. Counselors should appreciate the value of family involvement in the overall counseling relationship. Jackson adds that in career and educational planning, it is important to consult the family, especially the father.

Parents also express concern that, especially in cross-gender situations, counselors do not work with Muslim children behind a closed door. Prohibitions in the Koran are cited here also. They suggest that if privacy becomes an issue, the counselor can talk to students where they will not be overheard, but the two of them can be seen. This is in line with Jafari (1993) and Kelly et al. (1996), who note that Muslims, while supportive of counseling per se, are reluctant to go to a counselor whom they feel does not understand their values.

Counselors should consider the level of acculturation when designing counseling interventions (Jackson, 1995). Indicators of acculturation include: (a) the ability of the child to speak and understand English, versus their ability to speak and understand Arabic, (b) whether or not the child is foreign born, (c) how accepting versus how rejecting they are of Muslim values, (d) if their family name has been Americanized, and (e) the amount of social contact the family has with other Muslims. Such issues affect the student's actually seeking out counseling, and how accepting of counseling services he or she will be.

Counseling Interventions
In general, it would seem that counselors can become involved in meeting the needs of Muslim children in several ways. First, they can reach out to Muslim families in order to learn about their needs. (Kelly et al., 1996) They can share that new knowledge through faculty in-services and consultations with individual teachers. Counselors can involve Muslim parents and perhaps even the children themselves in this dissemination. They should also become aware of the limitations placed on participation of Muslims in certain aspects of the school curriculum by Islamic traditions and help those limitations to be seen in a positive light by staff and students alike. Abdudabbeh (1991) suggests that cognitive approaches to counseling children of Arab descent may be useful because of reluctance to express feelings towards outsiders. He adds that many Arabs consider it impolite to use the word "I" in a counseling interview, suggesting that counselors use phrases such as "In my professional judgment" instead of "I think."

Through various interventions, counselors create positive experiences, which lead to an improved self-concept and educational experience for Muslim children (Jafari, 1993). Interventions that help all children increase positive peer involvement could be designed. Through classroom guidance and faculty in-service, counselors can help create a more accurate picture of Muslims and Islam.

Adaptation of traditional counseling practice needs to occur in order to more effectively meet the needs of Muslim students (Kemp, 1996). It must be remembered that Muslims draw their identities from their religion (Jafari, 1993). School counselors finding themselves in a counseling relationship with Muslim students may need to redefine traditional conceptions of counseling by re-thinking the notion of privacy and confidentiality. Since family concerns take precedence over individual concerns, the involvement of the family is vital to the counseling relationship. The family is the Muslim child's strongest support system. When working with Muslim children, especially in cross-gender situations, it is important that the Muslim child not be placed in a situation that is contrary to their culture and religion. Touching such as hugging and handshaking is not appropriate. This would include being alone with the counselor in an isolated room.

Finally, individual counseling would seem to be more acceptable to Muslims than group counseling. It could be considered a violation of family privacy to place Muslim children in counseling groups where family issues would be explored (Jafari, 1993; Kelly et al., 1996). Muslims past the age of puberty should not be expected to participate in co-educational counseling groups. When group techniques are used with Muslim students, greater structure is required. If family issues are to be discussed, the school counselor might consider family counseling if individual counseling is not an option. If family counseling is recommended, it is equally important to involve the father as cultural leader of the family if at all possible. Counselors should be open to discuss their own ignorance of the Muslim culture with the families should problems arise. By this, they display a sensitivity to religious dictates when involving Muslim children in counseling.

Consultative Interventions

A close working relationship between the school and the family would seem to be the catalyst for the successful integration of Muslim students into the school (Kemp, 1996). Consultation with Muslim families should be a two-way interaction. Approaching Muslim families from the stance of the expert who knows what is the best way to educate ALL children can place an impediment in the relationship. Rather it would seem to be better to approach consultation from the standpoint of being mutual learners, that is from the standpoint that as counselors, we do not have all the answers. If an issue comes up where cultural impediments hinder the education of the child, it is best to open the issue for discussion immediately, rather than brush it aside.

In course selection, school counselors should consult with parents before placing students in art, music, or physical education classes to ascertain if there are any cultural limitations about which the family may be concerned (Siraj-Blatchford, 1993). If a child is excused from a school activity, such as a Christmas program, counselors can provide meaningful experiences for Muslim students with the emphasis on learning (Javed, 1994), instead of that child having to sit in the principal's office waiting for the program to end.

Program Development and Leadership

In the area of program development and leadership, counselors have a vital role in helping all students and teachers to better understand the impact of religion and culture on all aspects of the Muslim's life (Chan, 1991). Counselors can help change negative stereotypes of Muslims. Like all other immigrants, they come to the U.S. seeking opportunity. There is no hidden agenda to convert or conquer the rest of us. They are eager, however, to share their beliefs and help others to understand that Muslims desire to be productive citizens.

School counselors can serve as advocates for Muslim families with various aspects of the school system (Jackson, 1995). They can serve as an information clearinghouse on Islam and Muslim customs for teachers and administrators. For example, counselors can disseminate information to the staff about Muslim diet and the fasting requirements of Ramadan. This may forego any nutritional concerns for the children and help school personnel to understand that the children are not starving, that they have eaten before daylight and will eat again after sunset. Such information helps to clarify any apparent conflict between child welfare laws and religious faith before conflicts arise. Counselors can organize planning meetings and workshops involving the school staff, parents, and leaders from the Muslim community to develop interventions that will meet the academic and social needs of Muslims students (Jackson, 1995). They can provide teachers with curricular materials on courageous Muslim leaders and the culture (Javed, 1994). Finally, counselors can attend to the fair treatment of Islam and Muslim culture in the academic curriculum.

This article was designed to help school counselors to understand Islam in general and to distinguish between culturally appropriate and inappropriate counseling practices. In conclusion, as the numbers of Muslims in the schools grow, it is important that public schools adapt to the needs of this rather large minority. Since by the year 2000 it is expected that more than 5 percent of public school students will be Muslims, educators are challenged to seek to understand this growing minority population and proactively try to meet their needs and promote the cultural understanding necessary for citizenship in a global society.

Richard B. Carter, Ph.D., is an assistant professor of Counselor Education, College of Social and Behavioral Sciences, Northeastern State University, Tahlequah, OK. Amelia E. El Hindi, Ph.D., is an assistant professor of Curriculum and Instruction, College of Education, Texas Tech University, Lubbock. This research was supported in part by a grant from Texas Tech University. Correspondence regarding this article should be addressed to Dr. Carter, Department of Psychology and Counseling, Northeastern State University, Tahlequah, OK 74464; email carterdr@cherokee.nsuok.edu.

REFERENCES

Abdudabbeh, N. (1991). Cultural differences should be considered in treating Arab-Americans. Interview conducted by Rojean Wagner. *Psychiatric Times: Medicine and Behavior, 8*(4), 15–17.

Banawi, R. (1993). Islamic values relevant to group work with practical applications for the group leader. *Journal for Specialists in Group Work, 18*, 151–160.

Bedell, K. (1993). *Yearbook of American and Canadian churches.* Nashville: Abington Press.

Chan, C. (1991). *Violence and intimidation toward Arabs and Muslims: A report on a public hearing.* Los Angeles: County Commission on Human Relations. (ERIC Document Reproduction Service Report No. 337 522)

Cooper, M. H. (1993, April 30). Muslims in America. *CQ Researcher,* 368–383.

Haddad, Y. Y., & Lummis, A. T. (1987). *Islamic values in the United States.* New York: Oxford.

Hampton, H. (1992). One of the small details that got overlooked: School meals as a response to cultural diversity. *Research Papers in Education, 7*, 173–194.

Jackson, M. L. (1995). Counseling youth of Arab ancestry. In C. C. Lee (Ed.), *Counseling for diversity: A guide for school counselors and related professionals* (pp. 41–60). Boston: Allyn & Bacon.

Jafari, M. F. (1993). Counseling values and objectives: A comparison of Western and Islamic perspectives. *The American Journal of Islamic Social Studies, 10*, 326–339.

Javed, N. (1994). Gender identity and Muslim women: Tool of oppression turned into tool of empowerment. *Convergence, 27*(2/3) 58–67.

Kelly, E. W., Jr., Aridi, A., & Bakhtiar, L. (1996). Muslims in the United States: An exploratory study of universal and mental health values. *Counseling & Values, 40*, 206–218.

Kemp, C. (1996). Islamic cultures: Health care beliefs and practices. *American Journal of Health Behavior, 20*(3) 83–89.

Myrick, R. D. (1997). *Developmental guidance and counseling: A practical approach*. Minneapolis, MN: Educational Media.

Siraj-Blatchford, I. (1993). Ethnicity and conflict in physical education: A critique of Carrol and Hollingshead's case study. *British Educational Research Journal, 19*(1) 77–82.

Sue, D. W., & Sue, D. (1993). *Counseling the culturally different: Theory and practice*. (2nd ed.). New York: Wiley.

Soaring on the Wings of the Eagle: Wellness of Native American High School Students

By Michael Tlanusta Garrett, Ph.D., NCLSC

This article originally appeared in *Professional School Counseling*, Vol. 3, No. 1, 1999.

There are many definitions of the term, Native American. The U.S. Bureau of Indian Affairs (1988) legally defines Native American as a person who is an enrolled or registered member of a tribe or whose blood quantum is one-fourth or more, genealogically derived from Native American ancestry. The U.S. Bureau of the Census (1991) relies on self-identification to determine who is Native American. Oswalt (1988) points out, however, that "if a person is considered an Indian by other individuals in the community, he or she is legally an Indian... [in other words], if an individual is on the roll of a federally recognized Indian group, then he or she is an Indian; the degree of Indian blood is of no real consequence, although usually he or she has at least some Indian blood" (p. 5). The term Native American as used here, refers to any individual who self-identifies as Native American and maintains cultural identification as a Native American through membership in a Native American tribe recognized by the state or federal government or through other tribal affiliation and community recognition.

Currently, an estimated 2.3 million Native Americans live in the united States and the population is steadily growing (USBC, 1991). Native American people exhibit varying levels of acculturation, and they not only come from different tribal groups with different customs, traditions, and beliefs, but also they live in a variety of settings including rural, urban, or reservation (Garrett & Garrett, 1994). Native Americans represent a wide-ranging diversity illustrated by 252 different languages and 558 different tribal nations (Russell, 1988; Thomason, 1991). At the same time, a prevailing sense of Indianness based on a common worldview and common history seems to bind Native Americans together as a people of many peoples (Herring, 1990; Thomason, 1991). Although acculturation is a major factor in the Native American worldview, there tends to be a high degree of psychological homogeneity and a certain degree of shared cultural standards and meanings, based on common core values that exist for traditional Native Americans across tribal groups (DuBray, 1985; Heinrich, Corbine & Thomas, 1990; Honigmann, 1961; Oswalt, 1988; Peregoy, 1993; Sue & Sue, 1990).

Nationwide, the Native American population consists of a large proportion of young people with an average age of 17.3 years and an average life expectancy of 47.5 years, compared to 29.5 years and an average life expectancy of approximately 75 years for the rest of the U.S. population (Office of Minority Health [OMH], 1990). From an educational standpoint, the relative youth of this population would seem to imply enormous social and economic potential. Several studies have demonstrated that tests and teacher reports show that Native American children function at the average to superior range up to the fourth grade (Cummins, 1992; Deyhle, 1991; Hornett, 1990; McLaughlin, 1994; Tierney, 1992). However, although many Native American children enter school with an eagerness and willingness to learn, beyond about the fourth grade, their academic performance rapidly declines (Cummins, 1992; Sanders, 1987; Swisher, Hoisch, & Pavel, 1991), resulting in a 40% to 60% school dropout rate, the highest in the nation (National Center for Education Statistics [NCES], 1991). Several reasons for this trend have been suggested, including changes in the quality of family life, institutional racism and discriminatory practices, the cultural irrelevance of educational curriculum, and the social and economic pressures related to competition for success (OMH, 1990; Tierney, 1992).

The current social and educational status of native Americans may serve as an indicator of the social costs of dropping out of school. Statistics show that Native Americans have the highest suicide rate (15%), a median income that is only 50% of that for whites, an alcoholism rate that is double the national average, and have some of the highest rates of poverty (24%) and unemployment (40% to 80%) in the nation (Hodgkinson, 1990; NCES, 1991; OMH, 1990; USBC, 1991).

Several studies have been conducted using ethnographically-based questionnaires and interviews to identify sources of Native American school dropout rates. Colodarci (1983) found that Native American high school students indicated the following as reasons for dropping out of school:

- Student-teacher relationships (teachers do not care about me – 37%; teachers do not provide enough assistance – 39% disagreements with teacher – 33%)
- Content of schooling (school is not important to what I want to do in life – 44%; school is not important to me as a Native American – 24%)
- Lack of parental support (problems at home – 44%; lack of parental encouragement – 39%)

In a similar study, Deyhle (1992) found that Navajo and Ute students left school due to: student-teacher relationships, content of schooling, parental support, the need to work, distance from school, reading problems, and feelings of being unwanted. Likewise, Brandt (1992) found that Navajo students' reasons for leaving school included; boredom with school, problems with other students, retention in grade due to absenteeism, pregnancy/marriage, problems with teachers, legal problems, substance/alcohol abuse, family demands, disciplinary problems, academic failure, being older than the other students, poor transportation, language problems, medical reasons, and work.

Many Native American children tend to show in their self-concepts less emphasis on formal education and possessions and more emphasis on family ties, traditional customs and beliefs, and intrinsic worth (Rotenberg & Cranwell, 1989; Simmons & Barrineau, 1994). At the same time, studies have known that Native American children tend to view themselves more negatively than their White American counterparts (Cummins, 1992; Mitchum, 1989).

With such a strong cultural emphasis on one's relationship with others and the greater surroundings, Native American children are susceptible to encountering a variety of difficulties in a school setting that emphasizes individual uniqueness, competition, and achievement over the contrasting values of group harmony, cooperation, and sharing (Garcia & Ahler, 1992; Romero, 1994). In fact, programs designed to increase self-esteem and improved self-concept through techniques such as praising oneself, teachers giving praise, increasing student popularity with popular peers, and self-pride programs have been less successful with Native American students than other students due to violations of basic Native American cultural values concerning what is important and the appropriate way of going about it (Kleinfeld & Nelson, 1991; McCarty, Wallace, Lynch & Benally, 1991; Mitchum, 1989). Native American youth face many cultural conflicts in the school setting, even with something, for example, as well-intended as self-esteem improvement programs. Differences in cultural values and expectations have become the object of inquiry into the declining academic performance and personal difficulties faced by many Native American students.

Native American children raised with traditional Native American values, beliefs, and customs often enter the public school environment with a set of cultural assumptions and expectations concerning the purpose of learning and what is considered appropriate behavior that is different than mainstream American values (Garrett, 1995, 1996; Little Soldier, 1985; Sanders, 1987). Hulburt, Koreker, and Gade (1991) noted a higher incidence of feelings of rejection, depression, and anxiety reported by

Native American students in comparison to other students. Around fifth and sixth grade, many Native American students, along with corresponding personalandsocial difficulties ahs been attributed, in part, to the difficulty that many Native American students have in reconciling existing cultural differences (Garcia & Ahler, 1992; Kleinfeld & Nelson, 1991; Little Soldier, 1985; Sanders, 1987; Tierney, 1992). According to Sue and Sue (1990), the split between Native American tradition and mainstream expectations provides added stress to the already difficult challenge of identity formation.

Theorists have discussed the significance of adolescence and early childhood as a time of rapid changes occurring in physical, cognitive, and social growth (Erikson, 1963, 1968; Muuss, 1988; Smith, 1991; Sprinthall, 1988). Erikson's (1968) theory of identity development emphasizes the need for individuals to complete certain developmental tasks during specific developmental stages in order to maintain a healthy personality and successfully progress through subsequent developmental stages. Adolescence (12 to 19 years of age) has been characterized by Erikson (1968) as the stage of identity versus identity confusion in which the individual's developmental task is to establish a meaningful sense of personal identity. Identity achievement implies that the individual must assess his or her personal strengths and weaknesses to determine the best way of establishing a sense of congruence with his or her self-concept (Cohn & Osborne, 1992; Muuss, 1988). This involves answering such questions as: Where did I come from? Who am I? What do I want to become?" The inability to sufficiently answer such questions, according to Erikson (1968), results in identity confusion, which is accompanied by feelings of alienation, isolation, and uncertainty.

The involvement of cultural values as a mediating factor in the process of identity development is of critical importance for Native American youth (Deyhle, 1992; Hornett, 1990; Sanders, 1987). Brendtro, Brokenleg , and Van Bockern (1990), have suggested that, in order to establish a healthy cultural identity, natie American youth must find ways of satisfying the need for purpose through a sense of belonging, mastery, independence, and generosity. The process of acculturation experienced by many Native American students from early adolescence to early adulthood influences not only their definition of themselves as individuals, but also their social, emotional, intellectual, and spiritual well-being (Cummins, 1992; Little Soldier, 1985; Mitchum, 1989; Tierney, 1992). This presents an additional challenge for Native American youth in achieving a meaningful sense of personal/cultural identity through bicultural competence, defined as the ability of an individual to effectively utilize "dual modes of social behavior that are appropriately employed in different situations"

LaFromboise & Rowe, 1983, p. 592). Therefore, the role of cultural values during this developmental period is of essential importance in determining the student's ability to cope with internal and external stressors.

Myers, Witmer, and Sweeney (1995) have defined wellness as "a way of life which is oriented toward optimal health and well-being in which body, mind and spirit are integrated in a purposeful manner by the individual with a goal of living life more fully within all spheres of functioning: social, personal, environmental" (p. 1). A great deal of research supports the benefits of wellness (Witmer & Sweeney, 1992). Unhealthy lifestyles have been related to numerous physical and mental disorders; deviant behaviors; diminished self-esteem; increased heart disease, strokes, and cancer; and excessive anxiety (Omizo, Omizo, & D'Andrea, 1992; roman, 1992). The United States Public Health Service (cited in Witmer & Sweeney, 1992, p. 140) reported in 1979 that as many as 53% of the deaths in the United States each year are caused by lifestyle and self-destructive and negligent behavior. Moreover, the federal government spends more than 75% of its health care dollars on chronic diseases such as heart disease, strokes, and cancer, while less than 1% is spent to prevent these same diseases (Witmer & Sweeney, 1992).

As a concept advocating the integration of mind, body and spirit in a purposeful manner, wellness is just as important for children and adolescents as it is for adults (Omizo et al., 1992). In a survey examining the stress experienced by over 90,000 school-age youth (Minnesota Department of Education, 1989), 16% to 18% of 6th graders, 24% to 22% of 9th graders, and 35% to 48% of 12th graders reported that they experience stress either "quite a bit" or "almost more than I could take." In a society in which children are exposed to an overwhelming number of social and environmental stressors on a daily basis (Romano, 1992), the need for a strong sense of personal identity and meaningful purpose through a balance of belonging, mastery, independence, and generosity is critical for today's youth (Brendtro et al, 1990).

In Native American terms, wellness involves walking the path of good Medicine (living a good way of life) in harmony and balance (through the harmonious interactin of mind, body, spirit, and natural environment) with all our relations (with all living creatures that surround us) (Garrett & Garrett, 1994, 1996). In Cherokee tradition, for instance, wellness of the mind, body, spirit, and natural environment is an expression of the proper balance in the relationship of all things (Garrett & Garrett), 1994; Locust, 1988). If one disturbs or disrupts the natural balance of relationship, illness may be the result, whether it be expressed in the mind, body, spirit or natural environment (Garrett & Garrett, 1996; Locust, 1988).

In many Native American languages (e.g. Cherokee) there is no word for religion, because spiritual practices are an integral part of every aspect of daily life, which is necessary for the harmony and balance or wellness of individual, family, clan and community (Garrett, 1998; Locust, 1988). Healing and worship are considered as one and the same. For Native people, the concept of health and wellness is not only a physical state, but a spiritual one as well. Therefore, an understanding of a Native American student's cultural values, level of acculturation, and source(s) of stress provides a better understanding of that student's developmental issues in a culturally specific framework, including the interaction of personal, social, and environmental components.

Omizo et al. (1992) described the need to promote the wellness of students in order to assist "their academic, social, emotional, and physical development...[through] services designed to improve value clarification and self-understanding, stress management, physical fitness, and self-care." (p. 194). The goal of being able to assess and understand more fully Native American cultural values is to promote the wellness of Native American students. This might be accomplished, for example, through interventions designed to enhance identity development and bicultural competence in Native American students (LaFromboise & Rowe, 1983), utilizing techniques such as values clarification, self-awareness exercises, stress management, and communication skills enhancement. By understanding the counseling needs of Native American students, school counselors may be able to develop more effective counseling interventions for helping Native American students deal with personal, social, and environmental difficulties resulting from cultural discontinuity and the process of acculturation (LaFromboise, Trimble, & Mohatt, 1990). The purpose of the present study was to assess and compare the wellness Native American 9th, 10th, 11th, and 12th grade students with Non-Native American 9th, 10th, 11th, and 12th grade students.

METHOD

Participants consisted of Native American and non-Native American 9th, 10th, 11th, and 12th grade students from two rural counties of North Carolina. These geographic locations offered, among the native American participants, a range along the acculturation continuum from very traditional to assimilated (Neely, 1991). The choice of 9th, 10th, 11th, and 12th grade was made to include students both younger and older than the mandatory school attendance age of 16 (NCES, 1991) while also being able to examine an age range designated by Erikson (1968) as a period of identity development during adolescence and early childhood in which an individual's personal values are established.

The resulting total sample of 155 participants consisted of 16 class-rooms of Native American and non-Native American 9th, 10th, 11th, and 12th grade students. There were 132 White American students and 20 Native American students in the sample, and 3 cases with incomplete demographic data. The following tribes were represented by the Native American students in the sample: Cherokee nation, Eastern Band of Cherokee, Lumi, Mewoke, Seminole, and (Lakota) Sioux.

INSTRUMENTATION

Integrating research and theoretical concepts from a variety of disciplines including anthropology, education, medicine, psychology, religion, and sociology, Witmer and Sweeney (1992) proposed a holistic model of wellness that considers the healthy functioning of the individual in the context of a family, religion, education, business/industry, media, government, and community. According to this model of wellness, there are five major life-tasks.
- Spirituality
- Self-regulation (sense of worth, sense of control, realistic beliefs, emotional responsiveness and management, intellectual stimulation, problem-solving and creativity, sense of humor, nutrition, exercise, self-care, stress-management, gender identity, and cultural identity)
- Work, recreation, and leisure
- Love
- Friendship

Based on this model, the Wellness Evaluation of Lifestyle (WEL) was created to assess an individual on each of the five life tasks (17 total subscales).

The WEL can be administered individually or in groups and requires approximately 15 to 20 minutes to complete. A special version of the WEL, the WEL-G, which has a 7th grade reading level, was used in the present study (Myers et al., 1995). The WEL-G differs from the original instrument by substituting a "school work" on items which originally included the term "work." For the 98 total items, participants rate each statement according to a five-point Likert scale ranging form strongly agree to strongly disagree. Each response is converted to a numerical score, and the sores are summed for each subscale. Subscale scores are then converted to a percentage of the total possible points.

Based on the results obtained from groups of graduate and undergraduate male and female students (n=99), aged 18 to 32 years, Myers et al. (1995) reported 2-week test-retest coefficients ranging from .68 to .94. Alpha coefficients for the 18 scales on a group of 723 adult male san females, aged 18 to 92 years, ranged from .58 to .89 for the scales. Consistent with reliability coefficients reported in previous studies, alpha coefficients obtained for the WEL-G in the present study, based on a sample size of 130, ranged from a low of 0.60 to 0.81 with a mean of 0.64.

Concurrent validity, based on results obtained from a group of male and female graduate students, aged 22 to 49 years, has been demonstrated through correlation coefficients with the Testwell, ranging from .35 to .77 on the scales (Myers et al., 1995).

PROCEDURE

Data collection. A written set of instructions for the administration of the instruments was given to the coordinating school counselors. The coordinating school counselors and teachers of participating classrooms supervised the completion of the Wellness Evaluation of Lifestyle by each of the students. A Demographic Information form was completed by all students indicating the name of their school, date of administration, their initials and date of birth (for coding purposes) age, gender, grade level, primary ethnic designation, and tribal affiliation.

Data collection took place during a 5-week period on various occasions with intact 9th, 10th, 11th, and 12th grade classrooms. Students completed, in one class period, the questionnaire packet consisting of the Demographic Information form, and Wellness Evaluation of Lifestyle. Results for each student on the questionnaires were coded using the student's initials and date of birth.

Data analysis. The dependent variables were participant scores on the Wellness Evaluation of Lifestyle. The independent variables were cultural/ethnic background (Native American and non-Native American) and grade level (9th, 10th, 11th, 12th). A Multiple Analyses of Variance (MANOVA) was performed on the dependent variables to compare wellness by grade level for ethnicity and gender. Univariate Analyses of Variance (ANOVA) were further used to examine group differences on individual scales. An alpha confidence level of .05 was used.

RESULTS

Means and standard deviations for participants' scores on the 17 scales of wellness by ethnicity and grade level are presented (see Table). The MANOVA did not indicate any significant overall difference between students on wellness by ethnicity.

A MANOVA indicated that there was a significant difference in the 17 scales of wellness between students in different grade levels. Multivariate $F(3, 122) = 1.62$, $p < .01$. Univariate ANOVAs indicated that students in different grade levels differed significantly on Spirituality F (3, 122) = 3.28, p - .023, Sense of Worth, F (3, 122) = 3.95, p = .010, Realistic Beliefs, F (3, 122) = 3.90, p = .011, Emotional Responsiveness, F (3, 122) – 3.46, p = .019, Sense of Humor, F (3, 122) = 3.18, p = .027, Gender Identity, F (3, 122) = 3.86, p = ..011, Cultural Identity, F (3, 122) = 3.25, p = .024, Friendship, F (3, 122) = 4.55, p = .005, and Perceived Wellness, F (3, 122) = 3.65, p = .015. Overall, 10th graders scored higher on Emotional Responsiveness, 11th graders scored higher on Spirituality, Sense of worth, Realistic Beliefs, Gender Identity, Cultural Identity, Friendship, and Perceived Wellness, and 12th graders scored higher on Sense of Humor.

DISCUSSION

This study involved several limitations that either existed or were imposed for reasons of practicality, therefore affecting the generalizability of the results. The geographic region being considered in the study was limited to a rural setting in one general location of the country. Other geographic settings, suggested by the literature as being indicative of varying levels of acculturation, include urban and reservation areas (Garrett & Garrett, 1994).

The participation of students in the study depended entirely upon permission from the schools as well as the students themselves, which presented a potential limitation that was dealt with by eliciting participation and full cooperation from the superintendents, principals, school counselors, teachers, and students. The fact that all information obtained through the questionnaires was self-report presented another possible limitation of the study. Several authors have provided evidence, however, that self-report measures may provide dependable estimates of personality-related variables (Hattie, 1992; Howard, 1990; Howard, Maxwell, Weiner, Boynton & Rooney, 1980).

The resulting sample consisted of 155 participants, with 135 non-Native Americans, and 20 Native Americans. The number of Native American students in the sample was obviously small, therefore, generalization of results must take into consideration the limited number of Native American participants and limited number of tribes represented in the study. Furthermore, the results of the study may have been affected by the unequal sample size as well as the possibility of mono-measure bias. Overall, the results of this study should be considered in light of these factors which limit the extent to which the results can be generalized.

The findings of this study support Erikson's (1968) theory of identity development, designating this period as the stage of "identity versus identity confusion" in which the individual's primary developmental task is to

MEANS AND STANDARD DEVIATION OF PARTICIPANTS' SCORES ON THE WELLNESS EVALUATION OF LIFESTYLE BY ETHNICITY AND GRADE LEVEL

	Non-Native American (n=114)				Native American (n=16)			
Scale	9	10	11	12	9	10	11	12
Spirituality								
M	3.54	3.82	3.97	3.98	3.93	2.56	3.95	3.33
SD	0.75	0.53	0.68	0.47	0.64	0.00	0.54	0.00
Sense of Worth								
M	3.66	3.49	4.13	3.94	3.83	4.75	4.09	3.75
SD	0.70	0.90	0.65	0.70	0.38	0.00	0.68	0.00
Control								
M	3.66	3.59	3.88	3.59	3.50	3.50	3.89	3.75
SD	0.67	0.75	0.60	0.81	0.00	0.00	0.61	0.00
Realistic Beliefs								
M	3.37	3.32	3.62	3.33	3.60	3.80	3.86	3.60
SD	0.56	0.73	0.67	0.64	0.20	0.00	0.56	0.00
Emotional Responsiveness								
M	3.55	3.66	3.75	3.81	3.83	4.00	3.89	3.75
SD	0.67	0.58	0.63	0.63	0.64	0.00	0.53	0.00
Intellectual Stimulation								
M	3.55	3.66	3.75	3.81	3.83	4.00	3.89	3.75
SD	0.78	0.66	0.75	0.46	0.52	0.00	0.56	0.00
Sense of Humor								
M	3.56	3.86	4.03	4.09	4.27	5.00	4.00	4.00
SD	0.80	0.54	0.54	0.55	0.64	0.00	0.64	0.00
Nutrition								
M	3.41	3.22	3.49	3.16	3.00	2.50	3.57	2.50
SD	0.83	1.10	0.83	0.81	0.66	0.00	0.69	0.00
Exercise								
M	3.83	3.74	4.04	3.88	3.42	3.75	4.11	3.50
SD	0.67	0.91	0.91	0.72	0.14	0.00	0.82	0.00
Self-Care								
M	3.58	3.43	3.83	3.76	4.27	4.80	3.95	4.40
SD	0.78	0.97	0.82	0.68	0.50	0.00	0.81	0.00

MEANS AND STANDARD DEVIATION OF PARTICIPANTS' SCORES ON THE WELLNESS EVALUATION OF LIFESTYLE BY ETHNICITY AND GRADE LEVEL, CONT.

Scale	Non-Native American (n=114)				Native American (n=16)			
	9	10	11	12	9	10	11	12
Stress Management								
M	3.32	3.63	3.61	3.43	3.67	4.17	3.85	2.50
SD	0.66	0.72	0.66	0.62	0.29	0.00	0.72	0.00
Gender Identity								
M	3.71	3.90	4.24	4.09	4.50	4.50	4.30	3.25
SD	0.71	0.73	0.67	0.56	0.50	0.00	0.55	0.00
Cultural Identity								
M	3.64	3.70	3.96	3.74	4.40	4.20	4.16	3.80
SD	0.64	0.73	0.65	0.71	0.72	0.00	0.43	0.00
Work, Recreation, & Leisure								
M	3.33	3.29	3.55	3.45	3.80	3.90	3.60	3.00
SD	0.76	0.85	0.71	0.38	0.46	0.00	0.53	0.00
Friendship								
M	3.67	3.87	4.06	3.97	3.80	4.30	4.03	3.30
SD	0.68	0.68	0.57	0.39	0.10	0.00	0.48	0.00
Love								
M	3.73	3.78	3.88	3.86	3.42	3.91	4.01	3.64
SD	0.64	0.54	0.68	0.49	0.11	0.00	0.67	0.00
Perceived Wellness								
M	3.83	3.78	4.30	3.88	3.67	5.00	4.24	3.00
SD	0.61	0.96	0.64	0.60	0.33	0.00	0.52	0.00
Total	**32**	**24**	**38**	**20**	**3**	**1**	**11**	**1**

establish a meaningful sense of personal identity through changing perceptions of the self based on self-assessment of strengths and weaknesses,
likes and dislikes. This is also a period of development (ages 12 to 19)
which highlights the importance of peer group relationships, self-definition through love relationships, preoccupation with physical appearance,
the development of a vocational identity, and the formation of personal
ideologies (Muuss, 1988; Sprinthall, 1988). This could account for differences in wellness scores between students in different grade levels, with

the students in the upper grade levels scoring higher on a number of wellness scales. This also implies that the lower grades of high school (i.e., 9th and 10th grade) may be a critical time for intervention in order to promote the development of young people faced with the difficult task of identity development.

The results of the present study have a number of implications for school counselor practice and training. No significant overall difference was found in wellness between Native American and non-Native American students. This finding supports the notion that an individual's cultural identity is a more important factor in that person's wellness than his or her race/ethnicity. For counselors, this finding highlights the importance of understanding the client's cultural identity as he or she understands it, rather than making assumptions based on racial or ethnic background.

Although the results of this study show no significant differences in wellness based on ethnicity, there were significant differences between grade levels on wellness. This finding suggests the importance of promoting the identity development of both Native American and non-Native American students by incorporating developmentally appropriate interventions. These interventions can take into account the importance of self-definition by focusing on peer group relationships, love relationships, physical appearance, vocational aspirations, and personal ideologies. The higher wellness scores by students in higher grade levels also emphasize the need to intervene early.

The literature indicates that people who demonstrate higher levels of spirituality, sense of worth, sense of control, realistic beliefs, emotional responsiveness, intellectual stimulation, sense of humor, nutrition, exercise, self-care, stress management, gender identity, cultural identity, satisfaction with work, recreation, and leisure, connection through friendship, and connection through love are the people who tend to demonstrate higher levels of wellness (Myers, et al., 1995). One of the primary goals of school counselors is to facilitate the optimum human development and functioning of the client in the educational, career, social, and personal realms (Baker, 1996; Myers, 1991; Myrick, 1996; Paisley & Hubbard, 1994). The results of this study point to the importance of assessing the client's cultural identity and level of acculturation and utilizing developmentally appropriate interventions with adolescents in order to facilitate wellness through identity development. Understanding the client's cultural frame of reference is essential in utilizing appropriate counseling interventions and modes of communication to promote the wellness of both Native American and non-Native American youth during this critical period of development.

Michael Tlanusta Garrett, Ph.D., NCLSC, is an assistant professor of Counseling in the Department of Human Services at Western Carolina University at Cullowehee, NC and a member of the Eastern Band of Cherokee. The author wishes to express the deepest appreciation to Dr. Jane E. Myers, Dr. John Hattie, Dr. Willie Baber, Dr. James Fuller and Dr. Tom Sweeney for their assistance in the completion of this project.

REFERENCES

Baker, S.B. (1996). *School counseling for the twenty-first century* (2nd ed.). Englewood Cliffs, NJ: Merrill.

Brandt, E.A. (1992). The Navajo area student dropout study: Findings and implications. *Journal of American Indian Education, 31*, 48-63.

Brendtro, L.K., Brokenleg, M., & Van Bockern, S. (1990). *Reclaiming youth at risk: Our hope for the future.* Bloomington, IN: National Education Service.

Cohn, B. & Osborne, W.L. (1992). *Group counseling: A practical self-concept approach for the helping professional.* Chappaqua, NY: L.S. Communications.

Colodarci, T. (1983). High school dropout among Native Americans. *Journal of American Indian Education, 23*, 15-22.

Cummins, J. (1992). The empowerment of Indian students. In J. Reyhner (Ed.), *Teaching American American Indian students* (pp. 3-120). Norman, OK: University of Oklahoma Press.

Deyhle, D. (1991). Empowerment and cultural conflict: Navajo parents and the schooling of their children. *Journal of Qualitative Studies in Education, 4*, 277-297.

Deyhle, D. (1992). Constructing failure and maintaining cultural identity: Navajo and Ute school leavers. *Journal of American Indian Education, 31*, 24-47.

DuBray, W.H. (1985). American Indian values: Critical factor in case-work. Social Casework: *The Journal of Contemporary Social Work, 66*, 30-37.

Erikson, E.H. (1963). *Childhood and society* (2nd ed.) New York: Norton.

Erikson, E.H. (1968). Identity: Youth and crisis. New York: Norton.

Garcia, R.L. & Ahler, J.G. (1992). Indian education: Assumptions, ideologies, strategies. In J. Reyhner (Ed.) *Teaching American Indian students* (pp. 13-32). Norman, OK: University of Oklahoma Press.

Garrett, J.T. & Garrett, M.T. (1994). The path of good medicine: Understanding and counseling Native Americans. *Journal of Multicultural Counseling and Development, 22*, 134-144.

Garrett, J.T. & Garrett, M.T. (1996). *Medicine of the Cherokee: The way of right relationship*. Santa Fe, NM: Bear.

Garrett, M.T. (1995). Between two worlds: Cultural discontinuity in the dropout of Native American youth. *The School Counselor, 42*, 186-195.

Garrett, M.T. (1998). *Walking on the wind: Cherokee teachings for harmony and balance*. Santa Fe, NM: Bear.

Hattie, J. (1992). *Self-concept*. Hillsdale, NJ: Lawrence Erlbaum.

Heinrich, R.K., Corbine, J.L. & Thomas, K.R. (1990). Counseling Native Americans. *Journal of Counseling and Development, 69*, 128-133.

Herring, R.D. (1990). Understanding Native American values: Process and content concerns for counselors. *Counseling and values, 34*, 134-137.

Hodgkinson, H.L. (1990). *The demographics of American Indians: One percent of the people; Fifty percent of the diversity*. Washington, DC: Institute for Educational Leadership.

Honigman, J. (1961). North America. In F. Hsu (Ed.), *Psychological anthropology; An assessment of culture and personality* (pp. 145-227). Homewood, IL: Dorsey Press.

Hornett, D. (1990). On the construct validity of self-reports: what do the data say? *American Psychologist, 45*, 292-294.

Howard, G.S., Maxwell, S.E., Weiner, R. L., Boynton, K. S., & Rooney, W. M. (1980). Is a behavioral measure the best estimate of behavioral parameters? Perhaps not. *Applied Psychological Measurement, 4*, 293-311.

Hulburt, G. Kroeker, R. & Gade, E. (1991). Study orientation, persistence, and retention of Native students: Implications for confluent education, *Journal of American Indian Education, 30*, 16-23.

Kleinfeld, J. & Nelson, P. (1991). Adapting instruction to Native American learning styles: an iconoclastic view. *Journal of Cross-Cultural Psychology, 22*, 273-282.

LaFromboise, T.D. & Row, W. (1983). Skills training for bicultural competence: Rationale and application. *Journal of Counseling Psychology, 30*, 589-595.

LaFromboise, T.D.,Trimble, J.E. & Mohatt, G.V. (1990). Counseling intervention and American Indian tradition: An integrative approach. *The Counseling Psychologist, 18*, 628-654.

Little Soldier, L. (1985). To soar with the eagles: Enculturation and acculturation of Indian children. *Childhood Education, 61*, 185-191.

Locust, C. (1998). Wounding th spirit: Discrimination and traditional American Indian belief systems. *Harvard Educational Review, 58*, 315-330.

McCarty, T., Wallace, S., Lynch, R., & Benally, A. (1991). Classroom inquiry and Navajo learning styles: A call for reassessment. *Anthropology and Education Quarterly, 22*, 42-59.

McLaughlin, D. (1994). Critical literacy for Navajo and other American Indian learners. *Journal of American Indian Education, 33*, 47-59.

Minnesota Department of Education. (1989)). Minnesota Student Survey report, St. Paul, MN: Author.

Mitchum, N.T. (1989). Increasing self-esteem in Native American children. *Elementary School Guidance and Counseling, 23*, 266-271.

Muuss, R.E. (1988). *Theories of adolescence* (5th ed.). New York: McGraw-Hill.

Myers, J.E. (1991). Wellness as the paradigm for counseling and development: The possible future. *Counselor Education and Supervision, 62*, 3-10.

Myrick, R.D. (1996). *Developmental guidance and counseling: A practical approach* (3rd ed.) Minneapolis, MN: Educational Media.

National Center for Education Statistics. (1991). *Dropout rates in the United States: 1990.* Washington, DC: U.S. Department of Education, Office of Educational Research and Improvement.

Neely, S. (1991). *Snowbird Cherokees: People of persistence.* Athens, GA: University of Georgia Press.

Office of Minority Health. (1990). *Closing the gap.* Washington, DC: U.S. Department of Health and Human Services.

Omizo, M.M., Omizo, S.A., & D'Andrea, M.J. (1992). Promoting wellness among elementary school children. *Journal of Counseling and Development, 71*, 194-202.

Oswalt, W.H. (1988). *This land was theirs: A study of North American Indians* (4th ed.). Mountain View, CA: Mayfield.

Paisley, P.O. & Hubbard, G.T. (1994). *Developmental school counseling programs: From theory to practice.* Alexandria, VA: American Counseling Association.

Peregoy, J.J. (1993). Transcultural counseling with American Indians and Alaska Natives: Contemporary issues for consideration. In J. McFadden (Ed.), *Transcultural counseling: Bi-lateral and international perspective* (pp. 163-191). Alexandria, VA: American Counseling Association.

Romano, J.L. (1992). Psychoeducational interventions for stress management and well-being. *Journal of Counseling and Development, 71*, 199-202.

Romero, M.E. (1994). Identifying giftedness among Keresan Pueblo Indians: The Keres study. *Journal of American Indian Education, 34*, 35-53.

Rotenberg, K.J. & Cranwell, F.R. (1989). Self-concept in American Indian and white children. *Journal of Cross-Cultural Psychology, 20*, 39-53.

Russell, G. (1998). *American Indian facts of life: A profile of today's tribes and nations*. Phoenix, AZ: Author.

Sanders, D. (1987). Cultural conflicts: An important factor in the academic failures of American Indian students. *Journal of Multicultural Counseling and Development, 15*, 81-90.

Simmons, G., and Barrineau, P. (1994). Learning style nad the Native American. *Journal of Psychological type, 29*, 3-10.

Smith,E. (1991). Ethnic identity development: Toward the development of a theory within the context of majority/minority status. *Journal of Counseling and Development, 70*, 181-188.

Sprinthall, N. (1988). *Adolescent psychology: A developmental view*. New York: McGraw-Hill.

Sue, D.W. & Sue, D. (1990). *Counseling the culturally different: theory and practice* (2nd Ed.). New York: Wiley.

Swisher, K. Hoisch, M. & Pavel, d.M. (1991). *American Indian/Alaskan Native dropout study, 1991*. Washington, DC: National Education Association.

Thomason, T.C. (1991). Counseling Native Americans: An introduction for non-Native American counselors. *Journal of Counseling and Development, 69*, 321-327.

Tierney, W. (1992). *Official encouragement, unofficial discouragement: Minorities in academe – the Native American experience*. Norwood, NJ: Ablex.

United States Bureau of Indian Affairs. (1988). *American Indians today*. Washington, D.C. : Author.

United States Bureau of the Census. (1991). *1990 Census counts of American Indians, Eskimos, or Aleuts and American Indian and Alaska native areas*. Washington, DC: Author.

Witmer, J.M. & Sweeney, T.J. (1992). A holistic model for wellness and prevention over the life span. *Journal of Counseling and Development, 71*, 140-148.

An Exploratory Study of School Counselors' Experiences with and Perceptions of Asian-American Students

By Christine J. Yeh, Ph.D.

This article originally appeared in *Professional School Counseling*, Vol. 4, No. 5, 2001.

Of the 720,000 new immigrants who came to the United States in 1995, 268,000 originated from Asia and the Pacific Islands. From 1980 to 1990, the Asian-American population doubled, and it will double again between 1990 and 2020. In addition, the number of school-age Asian-Americans increased from 212,900 in 1980 to almost 1.3 million in 1990 (Lee, 1998). To date, "Asian-American" as a racial category represents 29 distinct ethnic groups (Atkinson, Morten, & Sue, 1993). Moreover, there is considerable social and economic variation between recent Asian immigrants in comparison to Asian-American communities that have been in the United States for generations (Lee, 1998). These demographic shifts have contributed to a significant influx of Asian-American students in many of the nation's public school systems, particularly on the East and West Coasts (Lee, 1998).

The American School Counselor Association (ASCA) position statement on Cross-Cultural and Multicultural Counseling (ASCA, 1999), included the statement that "School counselors take action to ensure students of culturally diverse backgrounds have access to appropriate services and opportunities promoting the individual's maximum development." Hence, this research seeks to help school counselors understand the counseling needs of Asian-American students.

Asian-American students are an important group to investigate for a number of reasons. In particular, although Asian-American students are characterized as the "Model Minority" (Lee, 1997, p. 442), they do have serious psychological, social, and developmental concerns that are often ignored by professionals (Morrissey, 1997; Uba, 1994). The Model Minority myth contributes to the perception that Asian-Americans perform well academically and emotionally and that they do not need help from a counselor. In contrast, numerous Asian-American students are vulnerable to many of the problems associated with adjusting to a new culture (Sodowsky & Lai, 1997).

Asian-American students may experience culture shock from trying to negotiate competing cultural value systems (Henderson, Millhouse, &

Ling, 1994). Cultural differences may also contribute to depression (Flaskerud & Nguyen, 1988; Nicassio, Solomon, Guest, & McMullough, 1986), social isolation (Lin, 1986), anxiety (Kinzie, 1989; Lin, 1986), low self-concept (Timberlake & Cook, 1984), relationship problems (Sodowsky & Lai, 1997), and academic and career concerns (Sodowsky & Lai, 1997). However, since many Asian-Americans mask their psychological problems with physical manifestations or somatization (Moore & Boehnlein, 1991; Nicassio, 1985), many problems may be unnoticed by school counselors.

In addition, research has consistently shown that Asian-Americans severely underutilize mental health and counseling services (Atkinson, Lowe, & Matthews, 1995; Leong & Tracey, 1986; Sue, Fujino, Hu, Takeuchi, & Zane, 1991). Although underuse could indicate a lack of need for these services among Asian-Americans, studies have demonstrated prevalence of psychological problems among Asian-American samples (e.g., Abe & Zane, 1990; Buchwald, Mansen, Dingas, Keane, & Kinzie, 1993; Loo, Tong, & True, 1989; Mollica, Wyshak, & Lavelle, 1987). In fact, research indicates that Asian-Americans are at increased risk for cultural adjustment problems in comparison to other ethnic minority populations (Leong, 1986).

Several factors have been identified as possible reasons for the underutilization of mental health services by Asian-Americans including: (a) lack of familiarity with, or misconceptions about, counseling; (b) cultural stigma and shame over mental health problems; (c) availability of alternative resources to traditional counseling; and (d) linguistic barriers (Uba, 1994). Moreover, a dearth of culturally sensitive personnel has been observed as a factor in underutilization (Atkinson & Matsushita, 1991; Atkinson, Poston, Furlong, & Mercado, 1989; Uba, 1994). Hence, teachers and other school personnel may be unaware of how to recognize Asian-American mental health problems to facilitate appropriate referrals. These factors do not point to a lack of need for mental health care among Asian-American students; rather, they highlight the unique barriers to the use of mental health services among this population. It remains to be established how Asian-American students cope with such difficulties.

An extensive literature search yielded no articles concerning school counselors' experiences with, or perceptions of, Asian-American students. In addition, there were no studies regarding school counseling techniques and strategies for working with students with Asian-American cultural backgrounds. Due to the paucity of research in this important area, this study sought to explore school counselors' perceptions of counseling Asian-American students. In addition, I was interested in examining how school counseling techniques vary with Asian-American versus White-

American students. Although this is not a study comparing school counselors' experiences with White-Americans and Asian-Americans, understanding differences in specific counseling strategies across the racial groups will help to identify current counseling techniques that are culturally based and unique to Asian-Americans. In particular, the following research questions were addressed:

1. How are Asian-American students referred to school counselors?
2. What are school counselors' perceptions of Asian-American students' presenting counseling concerns?
3. What are the most common techniques school counselors use when counseling Asian-American students? How do these differ from common techniques school counselors use when counseling White-American students?
4. What challenges do school counselors encounter when counseling Asian-American students?
5. What are school counselors' perceptions of Asian-American students' coping strategies used when dealing with problems?
6. What adjectives do school counselors use to describe Asian-American students?

METHOD

Participants

The convenience sample consisted of 154 school counselors from 113 schools on the East Coast. There were 114 females (74%) and 40 males (26%) in the sample. The mean age was 40.1 (SD = 11.4) years and the ages ranged from 21 to 65 years old. The racial backgrounds of the counselors were as follows: 67.5% (n = 104) were White-American, 14.3% were Asian-American (n = 22), 7.1% were Hispanic (n = 11), 6.5% were African American (n = 10), 1.3% were American Indian (n = 2), and 1.9% (n = 3) of the counselors were mixed race. On average, Asian-American students comprised 18.5% of the participants' school and 14.5% of their caseloads. In contrast, the average percents of White students in the school counselors' schools and caseloads were 40% and 33.5%, respectively.

In terms of counseling experience, the mean number of years of participants' counseling experience was 10.5 (SD = 8.6) years. Participants also reported previous multicultural counselor training. Counselors in the sample had earned a mean of 7.4 credit hours in multicultural counseling and had attended an average of 4.4 workshops focusing on multicultural issues. School counselors in the sample reported the grade level at which they worked as follows: 60.4% (*n* = 93) were from high school, 29.2% (*n* = 45) were from junior high, 9.7% (*n* = 15) were from elementary school, and one person did not report grade level.

The percent and frequency of school counselors working with students from specific Asian-American ethnic groups were as follows (they could select more than one ethnic group): (a) 79.2% (n = 122) counseled Chinese students, (b) 61% (n = 94) counseled Korean, (c) 37% (n = 57) counseled Japanese, (d) 25.3% (n = 39) counseled Vietnamese, (e) 24.7% (n = 38) counseled Filipino, (f) 23.4% (n = 36) counseled Indian, (g) 11.7% (n = 18) counseled Pakistan. In addition, less than 10% of the participants were working with the following Asian-American ethnic groups: Thai, Cambodian, Taiwanese, Laotian, Malaysian, and "mixed" Asian-American students.

Instruments
Demographic Information Sheet. On the demographic information sheet, participants provided their gender, age, race, years of counseling experience, multicultural training, and grade level at which they worked. In addition, participants estimated the racial compositions of their schools and their individual caseloads.

Perceptions of Asian-American Students Questionnaire (PASQ). Since there has been no previous research in this area of inquiry, a questionnaire assessing the perceptions and experiences of school counselors' work with Asian-American students was developed. The PASQ is a 24-item questionnaire consisting of two sections. The first section included questions about Asian-American ethnic groups at the counselors' school and Asian-American ethnic groups that the participant had previously counseled. This section also included questions about how Asian-American students are typically referred to counseling at the participant's school.

The second section consists of six open-ended questions covering the following topics: primary or most frequent presenting concerns of Asian-American students, most common techniques used when counseling Asian-American students, most common techniques used when counseling White-American students, and top challenges encountered when counseling Asian-American students. In addition, participants were asked about the most frequent coping strategies that Asian-American students used when dealing with problems and adjectives school counselors used to describe Asian-American students at the their school setting. For each question, participants could list up to five responses.

The initial items for the PASQ were developed based on numerous conversations with a group of eight school counselors. Moreover, the author is also experienced in the area of Asian-American counseling and mental health. The PASQ was then reviewed by four experts in the areas of multicultural counseling and Asian-American counseling, and revisions were made based on their feedback. Next, the questionnaire was reviewed by 10 school counselors, and the feedback and editing process was repeated before the questionnaire was distributed.

Separate sets of coding categories were generated for the following areas of the PASQ: Asian-American students' presenting concerns, Asian-American/ White-American counseling techniques, challenges encountered when counseling Asian-American students, Asian-American students' coping strategies, and adjectives used to describe Asian-American students.

Procedure

Questionnaires were disseminated to school counselors by a research assistant at the "Guidance Exposition," a conference sponsored by the New York Counseling Association, and at several local meetings of school counselors in New York City. Three master's- and two doctoral-level research assistants (two White-American and three Asian-American) distributed questionnaires from a table in the conference exhibition hall. Participants who approached the table were asked if they would be interested in participating in the study. Research assistants then explained the purpose of the study and responded to any questions. Two master's-level and one doctoral-level research assistant also attended the local meetings of school counselors in the New York City Metropolitan area. At these meetings, research assistants made an announcement describing the study and inquired if anyone was interested in participating. Counselors attending the meeting could then decide to participate. If they approached the research assistants, they were offered a description of the study and could ask questions about the research. The questions took about 20 minutes to complete and were completed at the time of distribution. In total, 193 surveys were distributed and 154 (81%) of the surveys distributed were returned.

Due to the exploratory nature of the PASQ, the questionnaire produced a wealth of qualitative data. For each of the open-ended questions of the PASQ, the raw data were read several times by a team of three research assistants and coded for main themes and patterns (Miles & Huberman, 1994). An interrater reliability of .89 was assessed for three raters using Cohen's Kappa.

RESULTS

How are Asian-American students referred to school counselors?

School counselors in the sample reported the people who had referred

Asian-American clients to them. Teachers had made the most referrals (57.1%, n = 88) of Asian-American students. Next, 47.4% (n = 73) were self-referred, 27.2% (n = 42) were referred by a parent, 21.4% (n = 33) were referred by another school counselor, 15.6% (n = 24) were referred by the principal, and 12.3% (n = 19) were referred by a friend of the students. Less than 10% of the referrals were made by nurses, coaches, students' siblings, and other sources.

What are school counselors' perceptions of Asian-American students' presenting counseling concerns?

In total, there were 10 categories that participants used to describe Asian-American students' presenting concerns. The most common concerns were as follows: (a) 90.9% (n = 140) listed academic pressure/expectations, (b) 51.3% (n = 79) mentioned family concerns, (c) 42.2% (n = 65) listed social concerns, and (d) 40.2% (n = 62) cultural customs/barriers. Less common concerns of Asian-American clients were (e) mental health concerns (23.4%, n = 36), (f) language/communication problems (18.2%, n = 28), (g) school functioning/logistics issues (18.2%, n = 28), (h) problems with isolation (11.7%, n =18), (i) a lack of knowledge about mental health services (5.8%, n = 9), and (j) financial difficulty (5.2%, n = 8).

What are the most common techniques/strategies school counselors use when counseling Asian-American students? How do these differ from common techniques/strategies school counselors use when counseling White-American students?

Participants reported counseling techniques and strategies used with Asian-American versus White-American students in their caseloads. Nine different techniques and strategies were determined in response to this particular inquiry (see Table). The counseling techniques and strategies utilized for Asian-Americans versus White-American students were compared using chi-square analyses. Chi-square analyses indicated significant differences between counseling techniques and strategies used for Asian-American students versus White-American students.

Specifically, school counselors in the sample were more likely to report using group counseling, x2(4, N = 154) = 99.51, p < .0001; family counseling, x2 (4, N = 154) = 128.57, p < .0001; and creative arts activities, x2(4, N = 154) = 101.17, p < .0001, when working with Asian-American versus White-American clients. In addition, school counselors reported utilizing counseling techniques and strategies that demonstrated an awareness of cultural issues more when working with Asian-American clients, x2 (4, N = 154) = 96.2, p < .0001.

NUMBER AND PERCENT OF SCHOOL COUNSELORS USING SPECIFIC COUNSELING TECHNIQUES/STRATEGIES WITH ASIAN-AMERICAN VERSUS WHITE-AMERICAN STUDENTS (N = 154)

Counseling Technique	Asian-American students		White-American students	
	n	%	n	%
Rogerian therapy techniques	94	61	90	58.4
Directive counseling	49	31.8	51	33.1
Family contact	52	33.7	43	27.9
Awareness of cultural issues	29	18.8	17	11.0
Group counseling	27	17.5	20	12.9
Creative arts activities	23	14.9	10	6.5
Information	22	14.7	23	14.9
Referral	10	6.5	9	5.8
Non-verbal behaviors	6	3.9	5	3.2

What challenges do school counselors encounter when counseling Asian-American students?

School counselors' most frequent challenges when working with Asian-American were as follows: (a) 38.9% (n = 60) reported a lack of family involvement in counseling, (b) 37.6% (n = 58) reported student stigmatization of counseling, (c) 35.1% (n = 54) mentioned overcoming cultural barriers, (d) 33.1% (n = 51) reported students' lack of self-disclosure, (e) 26.6% (n = 41) mentioned overcoming language barriers, and (f) 11.0% (n = 17) reported a student lack of direct communication in counseling. Less than 10% of the school counselors reported the following challenges with counseling Asian-American students: dealing with student perfectionism, helping students address social concerns/pressures, understanding student mental health concerns, and helping students manage school logistics.

What are school counselors' perceptions of Asian-American students' coping strategies used when dealing with problems?

Nine coding categories were established based on the counselors' perceptions of Asian-American coping strategies. Participants in the study responded that Asian-American students cope using the following strategies: (a) 67.5% (n = 104) internalize/avoid the problem, (b) 49.3% (n = 76) seek social support, (c) 25.9% (n = 40) act out, (d) 20.1% (n = 31) see a school counselor, (e) 18.8% (*n* = 29) focus on academics, (f) 14.2% (*n* = 22) involve parents, and (g) 11.6% (*n* = 18) engage in impulsive/injurious behavior. Less than 10% of the participants reported that Asian-American students' coping strategies included mental health concerns developing into a health problem, engaging in creative arts, and seeking religious resources.

What adjectives do school counselors use to describe Asian-American students?

Finally, the PASQ inquired about adjectives counselors used to describe Asian-American students. Results indicated that the following adjectives were used most frequently to characterize Asian-American students: (a) 76.6% (*n* = 118), *hardworking/academic*; (b) 46.8% (*n* = 72), *quiet/guarded*; (c) 31.2% (*n* = 48), *family/other-oriented*; (d) 27.9% (*n* = 43), *compliant/obedient*; (e) 25.9% (*n* = 40), *intelligent*; (f) 13.6% (*n* = 21), *responsible*; and 13.6% (*n* = 21), *sociable*. Less than 10% of the participants reported the following adjectives: *depressed, angry, independent, involved, and culturally cliquish.*

DISCUSSION

The purpose of this investigation was to explore school counselors' perceptions of Asian-American students and their mental health concerns. Moreover, this study sought to understand commonly used counseling techniques and strategies for Asian-American and White-American students as well as school counselors' challenges working with Asian-American students. Since this is the first study to explore these important areas, a questionnaire was developed to answer the research questions.

The results suggest that Asian-American students tend to seek help for concerns relating to academics, family issues, social concerns, and cultural conflicts. These presenting concerns are reflective of Asian-American cultural values emphasizing academic achievement (Chia, 1989; Lin & Fu, 1990), family cohesion (Morris, 1990; Tsui & Schultz, 1988), and collectivism (Markus & Kitayama, 1991). Specifically, the interdependent nature of Asian-American identity mandates a self that values interpersonal harmony and strong family ties. Such goals are achieved when Asian-American children maintain "face" and positive relations in the family. Asian-American students may "lose face" and disrupt interpersonal harmony at home when they fail to thrive academically (Hess, Chang, & McDevitt, 1987). Hence, Asian-American students are socialized to achieve and focus academically as well as interact socially. When these important agendas are interrupted, mental health concerns may arise.

School counselors in the sample tended to address Asian-American students' presenting concerns by utilizing Rogerian therapy techniques, directive counseling, group counseling; involving social and family networks; having an awareness of pertinent cultural issues; and engaging the clients in creative arts activities. Although there is a wealth of literature describing the unique culturally specific needs of Asian-Americans in a counseling context (e.g., Chin, 1998; Tang, 1997; Tsui, 1997; Ying, 1997), school counselors reported using similar counseling techniques when working with White-American clients. However, the results suggest that school counselors are significantly more likely to use counseling techniques involving social and family networks, being aware of cultural issues, and engaging in creative arts activities when working with Asian-American as compared to White-American clients.

Due to the strong importance Asian-American students place on social and family relations, it seems essential that counselors' techniques with Asian-American students would tend to involve interpersonal networks (Mau & Jepsen, 1988; Yeh & Wang, 2000). In fact, utilizing significant relationships should be a central focus of helping Asian-American clients. Moreover, since Asian-American values de-emphasizing self-disclosure and emotional expression are contrary to the traditional counseling process (Sue & Sue, 1993), it seems critical that counselors be more aware of cultural issues that impact the therapeutic alliance and process.

The findings also suggest that school counselors used more creative arts techniques when working with Asian-American versus White-American clients. Due to the strong focus on aesthetics and arts as well as the de-emphasis on direct verbal communication (Sue & Sue, 1993; Yeh, 1996) in many Asian-American cultures, counselors should consider nonverbal means of emotional expression that may seem less threatening to Asian-American students. Such interventions may include journal writing, drawing, poetry therapy, and music therapy (Alexander & Sussman, 1995; Hendersen & Gladding, 1998). However, there are also many individual differences when it comes to preferences for creative interventions and personality factors should also be considered when considering the use of creative arts techniques.

The results suggest that school counselors have challenges with counseling Asian-American students such as overcoming student stigmatization of counseling, dealing with a lack of parental involvement in counseling, overcoming cultural barriers in counseling, and dealing with students' lack of self-disclosure about emotional concerns. These challenges to counseling Asian-Americans are integrally related to Asian-American cultural contradictions with current models of counseling. In particular, many Asian-Americans stigmatize the counseling process because of their discomfort with self-disclosure (Lee, 1996) and because of a fear of losing face (Uba, 1994). Similarly, Asian-American parents may be reluctant to connect with a counselor or encourage counseling since having a child in counseling may be shameful and embarrassing in Asian-American circles (Kim, 1996). Research has shown that Asian-American clients often present to counseling with academic, or nonemotional, concerns in order to save face (Tracey, Leong, & Glidden, 1986).

Participants in this study reported Asian-American coping strategies that involved seeking social support, internalizing/avoiding problems, and acting out more frequently than seeing a counselor. These coping strategies may be related to strong cultural stigmas that contribute to Asian-American underutilization of mental health services (Atkinson & Gim, 1989). Since Asian culture emphasizes restraining emotional expression (Cheung, 1985), Asian-American students may be inclined to find more culturally consonant methods for dealing with problems. Asian-American student preferences for seeking help from social ties is consistent with previous research indicating that Asian-Americans tend to seek relational or familial rather than professional sources of help (Atkinson, Whiteley, & Gim, 1990; Root, 1985; Suan & Tyler, 1990; Yeh & Wang, 2000). Such tendencies for social as opposed to professional intervention may be reflective of an Asian-American cultural emphasis on collectivism and interpersonal ties (Yeh & Wang, 2000).

Finally, this research assessed adjectives school counselors' used to describe Asian-American students. The most frequently used adjectives included hardworking/academic, quiet/guarded, compliant/obedient, and intelligent. In many ways, these descriptions reflect many common stereotypes of Asian-American students as Model Minorities. In particular, since many Asian-American students are seen as compliant and quiet, it may be difficult for school counselors and teachers to identify their mental health problems. Such positive characterizations of Asian-Americans, coupled with an Asian-American cultural reluctance to seek help, may contribute to a general lack of sensitivity to, and identification of, Asian-American mental health concerns.

LIMITATIONS

There are several limitations of the current research investigation that should be mentioned. First of all, the convenience sample only included school counselors who attended particular meetings and were predominantly from the East Coast, so generalizability of the results is limited. Since there were no research questionnaires in the area investigated, an exploratory instrument was developed for the specific purposes of this study. In addition, the study was limited in that school counselors were asked primarily about their experiences with and perceptions of Asian-American students. Future research could explore more in-depth accounts of school counselors' experiences with a range of culturally diverse students and offer comparisons with White students. Methodologies employed could include interviews, narrative accounts, ethnographic approaches, and scale development.

IMPLICATIONS

Research has failed to keep up with dramatic increases in the Asian-American student school population and the vast ethnic and socioeconomic heterogeneity within this racial group. As a result, I believe that school counselor training programs may be unequipped to prepare counselors to work with vulnerable populations within the Asian-American community. The current study offers information that may be useful to school counselors in their future work with Asian-American students.

Specifically, from these research findings, school counselors can learn to recognize common presenting concerns of Asian-American students. Learning to identify Asian-American students' psychological concerns is especially important since many Asian-American students keep their emotional difficulties to themselves and are often reluctant to seek help from a counselor. In addition, school counselors can become familiar with culturally based coping methods among Asian-American students and help teach them new and more adaptive ways of addressing mental health problems.

Understanding school counselors' techniques with Asian-American as compared to White-American students will help to identify and highlight alternative counseling methods that may increase mental health utilization by Asian-American students. Specifically, while current methods of school counseling heavily rely on individual counseling, alternative techniques may integrate Asian-American coping styles that emphasize family and social group ties (i.e., peer groups, parent/student workshops, community outreach). Education and prevention programs can also be informed by research that clarifies the relationship between acculturation, self-concept, and mental health utilization attitudes, behaviors, and patterns among Asian-American students. Such strategies may in fact decrease Asian-American stigmatization of counseling and may, in turn, increase counseling utilization rates.

An additional contribution of this research is the identification of top challenges that school counselors experience with Asian-American students. For example, school counselors reported that Asian-American students had a lack of family involvement in counseling, tended to stigmatize counseling, and were uncomfortable with self-disclosure and direct communication in counseling. It is important for future school counselors to be aware of such challenges so they do not misinterpret these behaviors as a lack of interest in, or need for, counseling.

School counselors are part of a larger institutional setting where students can seek and receive help for mental health concerns. Sometimes, school counselors are the only option for students in need of intervention due to economic, social, and linguistic factors. However, Asian-American students may not be initially comfortable with asking for help for their concerns. Thus, school counselors offer a unique avenue to help Asian-American students become educated about, and comfortable with, coping strategies and resources.

By assessing school counselors' experiences with Asian-American youth, inaccurate stereotypes may be challenged and areas for improvement identified. Determining school counselors' current understanding of Asian-American students' psychological functioning will help highlight gaps in the training of counselors and teachers. In this present increasingly diverse society, knowledge and research concerning differing cultural mental health practices is critical. Researchers, school counselors, and counselor educators must be equipped to recognize, evaluate, and address student development in the broadest sense.

Christine J. Yeh, Ph.D., is an assistant professor, Department of Counseling and Clinical Psychology, Teachers College, Columbia University, NY. Email cy101@columbia.edu.

REFERENCES

Abe, J. S., & Zane, N. W. S. (1990). Psychological maladjustment among Asian and White American college students: Controlling for confounds. *Journal of Counseling Psychology, 37,* 437–444.

Alexander, C. M., & Sussman, L. (1995). Creative approaches to multicultural counseling. In J. G. Ponterotto, J. M. Casas, L. A. Susuki, & C. M. Alexander (Eds.), *Handbook of multicultural counseling* (pp. 441–455). Thousand Oaks, CA: Sage.

American School Counselor Association. (1999). *The professional school counselor and cross/multicultural counseling.* Alexandria, VA: Author. Retrieved August 23, 2000 from the World Wide Web: http://www.schoolcounselor.org/position_statements_(pdf).html

Atkinson, D. R., & Gim, R. (1989). Asian-American cultural identity and attitudes toward mental health services. *Journal of Counseling Psychology, 36,* 209–212.

Atkinson, D. R., Lowe, S., & Matthews, L. (1995). Asian-American acculturation, gender, and willingness to seek counseling. *Journal of Multicultural Counseling and Development, 23,* 130–138.

Atkinson, D. R., & Matsushita, Y. (1991). Japanese-American acculturation, counseling style, counselor ethnicity, and perceived counselor credibility. *Journal of Counseling Psychology, 38,* 473–478.

Atkinson, D. R., Morten, G., & Sue, D. W. (1993). *Counseling American minorities: A cross-cultural perspective* (4th ed.). Dubuque, IA: William C. Brown.

Atkinson, D. R., Poston, W. C., Furlong, M., & Mercado, P. (1989). Ethnic group preference for help providers. *Journal of College Student Development, 31,* 155–161.

Atkinson, D. R., Whiteley, S., & Gim, R. H. (1990). Asian-American acculturation and preferences for help providers. *Journal of College Student Development, 25,* 448–452.

Buchwald, P., Mansen, S., Dingas, E. K., Keane, E., & Kinzie, J. D. (1993). Prevalence of depression among established Vietnamese refugees in United States: Detection in primary case settings. *Journal of General Internal Medicine, 8,* 76–81.

Cheung, F. M. (1985). An overview of psychopathology in Hong Kong with special reference to somatic presentation. In W-S. Tseng & D. Wu (Eds.), *Chinese culture and mental health* (pp. 287–304). New York: Academic Press.

Chia, R. (1989). Pilot study: Family values of American versus Chinese-American parents. *Journal of the Asian American Psychological Association, 13,* 8–11.

Chin, J. L. (1998). Mental health services and treatment. In L. C. Lee & N. W. S. Zane (Eds.), *Handbook of Asian American psychology* (pp. 485–504). San Francisco: Sage.

Flaskerud, J., & Nguyen, T. A. (1988). Mental health needs of Vietnamese refugees. *Hospital and Community Psychiatry, 39,* 435–437.

Henderson, D. A., & Gladding, S. T. (1998). The creative arts in counseling: A multicultural perspective. *The Arts in Psychotherapy, 25,* 183–187.

Henderson, G., Millhouse, V., & Ling, C. (1994). Crossing the gap: An analysis of Chinese students' culture shock in an American university. *College Student Journal, 27,* 380–389.

Hess, R. D., Chang, C-M., & McDevitt, T. M. (1987). Cultural variations in family beliefs about children's performances in mathematics: Comparisons among People's Republic of China, Chinese-American, and Caucasian-American families. *Journal of Educational Psychology, 79,* 179–188.

Kim, B-L. C. (1996). Korean families. In M. McGoldrick, J. Giordano, & J. K. Pearce (Eds.), *Ethnicity and family therapy* (pp. 281–294). New York: Guilford.

Kinzie, D. J. (1989). Therapeutic approaches to traumatized Cambodian refugees. *Journal of Traumatic Stress, 2,* 75–91.

Lee, E. (1997). *Working with Asian Americans: A guide for clinicians.* New York: Guilford.

Lee, C. L. (1998). An overview. In L. C. Lee & N. W. S. Zane (Eds.), *Handbook of Asian American psychology* (pp. 485-504). San Francisco: Sage.

Leong, F. T. L. (1986). Counseling and psychotherapy with Asian-Americans: Review of the literature. *Journal of Counseling Psychology, 33,* 196–206.

Leong, F. T. L., & Tracey, T. J. (1986). Help seeking and problem perception among Asian Americans. *Journal of Counseling Psychology, 33,* 331–336.

Lin, K-M. (1986). Psychopathology and social disruption in refugees. In C. Williams & J. Westermeyer (Eds.), *Refugee mental health in resettlement countries* (pp. 61–73). Washington, DC: Hemisphere.

Lin, C-Y., & Fu, V. (1990). A comparison of child-rearing practices among Chinese, immigrant Chinese, and Caucasian-American parents. *Child Development, 61,* 429–433.

Loo, C., Tong, B., & True, R. (1989). A bitter bean: Mental health status and attitudes in Chinatown. *Journal of Community Psychology, 17,* 283–296.

Markus, H., & Kitayama, S. (1991). Culture and self: Implications for cognition, emotion, and motivation. *Psychological Review, 98,* 224–253.

Mau, W., & Jepsen, D. A. (1988). Attitudes toward counselors and counseling processes: A comparison of Chinese and American graduate students. *Journal of Counseling and Development, 67,* 189–192.

Miles, M. B., & Huberman, A. M. (1994). An expanded sourcebook: Qualitative data analysis. Thousand Oaks, CA: Sage.

Mollica, R. F., Wyshak, G., & Lavelle, J. (1987). The psychosocial impact of war trauma and torture on Southeast Asian refugees. *American Journal of Psychiatry, 144,* 1507–1572.

Moore, L., & Boehnlein, J. (1991). Treating psychiatric disorders among Mien refugees from highland Laos. *Social Science and Medicine, 32,* 1029–1036.

Morris, T. (1990). Culturally sensitive family assessment. *Family Process, 29,* 105–116.

Morrissey, M. (1997, October). The invisible minority: Counseling Asian Americans. *Counseling Today,* pp. 21–22.

Nicassio, P. (1985). The psychosocial correlates of alienation: Study of a sample of Indochinese refugees. *Journal of Cross-Cultural Psychology, 14,* 337–351.

Nicassio, P., Solomon, G. S., Guest, S., & McCullough, J. E. (1986). Emigration stress and language proficiency as correlates of depression in a sample of Southeast Asian refugees. *International Journal of Social Psychiatry, 32,* 22–28.

Root, M. P. P. (1985). Guidelines for facilitation therapy with Asian American clients. *Psychotherapy, 22,* 349–356.

Sodowsky, G. R., & Lai, E. W. M. (1997). Asian immigrant variables and structural models of cross-cultural distress. In A. Booth (Ed.), *International migration and family change: The experience of U. S. immigrants* (pp. 211–234). Mahwah, NJ: Lawrence Erlbaum.

Suan, L. V., & Tyler, J. D. (1990). Mental health values and preferences for mental health resources of Japanese-American and Caucasian-American students. *Professional Psychology: Research and Practice, 21,* 291–296.

Sue, D., & Sue, D. W. (1993). Ethnic identity: Cultural factors in the psychological development of Asians in America. In D. R. Atkinson, G. Morten, & D. W. Sue (Eds.), *Counseling American minorities: A cross-cultural perspective* (5th ed.; pp. 199–210). Madison, WI: Brown & Benchmark.

Sue, S., Fujino, D., Hu, L., Takeuchi, D., & Zane, N. (1991). Community mental health services for ethnic minority groups: A test of the cultural responsiveness hypothesis. *Journal of Consulting and Clinical Psychology, 59,* 533–540.

Tang, N. M. (1997). Psychoanalytic psychotherapy with Chinese Americans. In E. Lee (Ed.), *Working with Asian Americans: A guide for clinicians* (pp. 323–341). New York: Guilford Press.

Timberlake, E., & Cook, K. (1984). Social work and the Vietnamese refugee. *Social Work, 29,* 108–113.

Tracey, T. J., Leong, F. T. L., & Glidden, C. (1986). Help-seeking and problem perception among Asian Americans. *Journal of Counseling Psychology, 33,* 331–336.

Tsui, P. (1997). The dynamics of cultural and power relations in group therapy. In E. Lee (Ed.), *Working with Asian Americans: A guide for clinicians* (pp. 354–363). New York: Guilford.

Tsui, P., & Schultz, G., (1988). Ethnic factors in group process: Cultural dynamics in multi-ethnic therapy groups. *American Journal of Orthopsychiatry, 58*, 136–142.

Uba, L. (1994). *Asian Americans: Personality patterns, identity, and mental health.* New York: Guilford.

Yeh, C. J. (1996). A cultural perspective on interdependence in self and morality: A Japan-U.S. comparison. *Dissertation Abstracts International, 57*(2), 162B.

Yeh, C. J., & Wang, Y-W. (2000). Asian American coping attitudes, sources, and practices: Implications for indigenous counseling strategies. *Journal of College Student Development, 41*, 94–103.

Ying, Y. W. (1997). Psychotherapy for East Asian Americans with major depression. In E. Lee (Ed.), *Working with Asian Americans: A guide for clinicians* (pp. 252–264). New York: Guilfojrd.

School Counselors' Perceptions of Biracial Children: A Pilot Study

By Henry L. Harris, Ph.D., LPC

This article originally appeared in *Professional School Counseling*, Vol. 6, No. 2, 2002.

Biracial children represent a growing segment of America's increasingly diverse population. According to Kalish (1995), data from the National Center for Health Statistics (NCHS) showed between 1978 and 1992, the number of biracial children born in the United States increased more than 50%, "rising from about 63,700 to almost 133,200" (p. 1). During the same period, biracial births grew from 2.1% to 3.9% of all births (Kalish). Jamison (1999) suggested the number of biracial individuals at between 2 million and 5 million, and noted this is a significant underestimation. Past societal guidelines and restrictions have contributed to this underestimation because, in many situations, biracial children were simply identified with the parent of color. According to the 2000 Census report, the most recent numbers indicate that people of two or more races made up 2.4 % (6,826,228) of the national population, and 42% (2,856,886) of them were under the age of 18 (U.S. Bureau of Census, 2001). In this article, a biracial individual is defined as someone having biological parents from two different racial or ethnic groups (Winn & Priest, 1993).

   The research on the unique issues biracial children encounter has produced mixed results. Some studies found biracial children were more likely to experience higher degrees of problems associated with racial identity development, social marginality, isolation, sexuality conflicts, career dreams, and academic and behavioral concerns (Brandell, 1988; Gibbs, 1987; Gibbs & Moskowitz-Sweet, 1991; Herring, 1992; Teicher, 1968; Winn & Priest, 1993). However, other investigations yielded more positive results discovering biracial individuals overall were assertive, independent, and emotionally secure and creative individuals with a positive selfconcept (Kerwin, Ponterotto, Jackson, & Harris, 1993; Poussaint, 1984; Tizard & Phoenix, 1995). Historically, biracial individuals have been analyzed and judged from biological and sociocultural perspectives (Nakashima, 1992). Originally, the biological perspective characterized individuals from interracial unions as mentally, physically, and morally weak beings and because of their perceived genetic inferiority, they faced insurmountable social, emotional, and psychological problems (Krause, 1941; Provine, 1973). The sociocultural perspective supported the belief that biracial people were social and cultural misfits, incapable of fitting in or gaining acceptance in any racial group, destined to lead a life of loneliness and confusion. The ultimate goal behind both perspectives was racial division, which socially and legally discouraged Caucasians from marrying and/or having children with people of color (Nakashima). For example, in 1945, more than half of the states had active laws banning interracial marriages. Twenty-one years later, 19 of those states still had such laws on the books. It was not until 1967 that the U.S. Supreme Court ruled, in Loving v. Virginia, that states could not legally prohibit interracial marriages (Parker, 1999). Needless to say, the different forms of past social and legal discrimination against interracial marriages have also influenced children of such marriages in a negative manner (Wardle, 1991).

According to Kerwin and Ponterotto (1995), biracial individuals have been negatively affected by stereotyping. Stereotypes are rigid preconceptions held about all people who are members of a particular group (Sue & Sue, 1999). Stereotyping commonly leads to assigning to a single individual, characteristics associated with a group of people or extending to a group, the characteristics attached to a single individual on the basis of limited personal contact. It is important to note that not all stereotypes are unfavorable and not all stereotypes are completely inaccurate (Axelson, 1993). However, they are based upon a lack of knowledge and all incoming information is distorted to match a person's preconceived notions (Sue & Sue). There are a number of stereotypes associated with biracial individuals. One stereotype labels them as socially maladjusted outcasts, lacking culture, who will more than likely encounter identity problems stemming from their racial heritage. Suggesting that biracial children will automatically have identity problems typically refers to the perspective that these individuals do not fit neatly into socially defined categories and consequently have trouble determining their status, role, and position in society (Brown, 1990). Furthermore, this perspective assumes they will be "rejected at face value by all ethnic groups and considered marginal but not actual members of these groups" (Kerwin & Ponterotto, p. 203).

Another stereotype asserts the belief that biracial children should identify with the parent of color because society will ultimately view them from this perspective (Kerwin & Ponterotto, 1995). This point of view runs the risk of causing serious psychological harm especially if the child disregards and does not incorporate the cultural heritage of one parent into his or her identity development. The inability of the biracial child to culturally identify with both parents may cause the individual to experience feelings of disloyalty and enormous guilt over their rejection of one parent (Sebring, 1985). This theme was validated by Winn and Priest

(1993), who noted that the majority of the biracial individuals felt pressured to assume a mono-cultural identity, while at the same time experienced guilt feelings of betrayal and deception toward the parent with whom they did not identify. Finally, another stereotype involves the belief that biracial children do not like to discuss issues concerning their racial heritage. Discussing such issues may prove to be difficult for some; however, when questions are considered genuine and nonjudgmental, biracial individuals do not mind such inquiries (Kerwin et al. 1993).

Regardless of race or ethnicity, when biracial children are raised in a nurturing environment with psychologically and emotionally involved parents, "they can be expected to acquire stability and cohesiveness of the self, and those attributes (e.g., selfconfidence, capacity for empathy, self-approval, selfresiliency) intimately associated with healthy selfstructure," (Brandell, 1988, p. 180). However, Brandell further contended that biracial children operating between two cultures may have additional issues to contend with solely because of their unique racial status. Biracial children must routinely cope with glares, strange looks, and comments from people who in addition to rejecting their family structure (Steele, 1995), picture the family environment as pathological and unstable (Shackford, 1984). Even today it remains safe to assume that some social workers, psychologists, and school counselors often see problems associated with biracial individuals as a direct result of their cultural heritage.

SCHOOL COUNSELORS' PERCEPTIONS OF BIRACIAL INDIVIDUALS

In recent years, some writers in the counseling profession have specifically called upon school counselors to better address the counseling needs of biracial children in the school setting (Herring, 1992; Nishimura, 1995; Wardle, 1991, 1992). Responding to this call, Nishimura and Bol (1997) collected data from 120 school counselors investigating their perceptions of the counseling needs of biracial children. They discovered school counselors did not perceive biracial children experiencing any more or fewer problems than other children. An overwhelming majority (90%) of them indicated they were able to meet the counseling needs of biracial students without changing their current counseling program.

While Nishimura and Bol (1997) investigated school counselors' perceptions of the counseling needs of biracial children, no studies reported to date have specifically examined school counselors' personal perceptions of biracial children. Personal perceptions that school counselors hold of biracial individuals will inevitably influence their views on the severity and types of problems biracial individuals encounter. Therefore, the goal of this study was to examine school counselors' personal perceptions of biracial individuals. The following research questions were addressed:

- What personal perceptions do school counselors have concerning biracial individuals?
- What personal counseling experience do school counselors have with biracial individuals?
- Is there a relationship between school level, years of counseling experience, and school counselors' perceptions of individuals?
- Is there a relationship between gender and school counselors' perceptions of biracial individuals?
- Is there a relationship between the existence of promoted cultural diversity programs in schools and school counselors' perceptions of biracial individuals?

METHOD

Participants

Initially, 900 school counselors from 16 public school districts, ranging in size from less than 1,000 students to more than 75,000 students, were invited to participate in the study. The participants were located in nine states from the Southeastern region of the United States. Overall, 328 school counselors comprising 201 Caucasians, 122 African Americans, 3 Asian Americans, and 2 American Indians completed surveys, resulting in a 37% response rate. There were a total of 176 school counselors employed in elementary settings, followed by 89 at the middle school level, and 63 in the high schools. Eighty-seven percent (n = 285) of the sample consisted of women and 13% (n = 43) were men. The years of school counseling experience varied with 32% (n = 104) having 1 to 5 years of experience, 24% (n = 77) with 6 to 10 years of counseling experience, 21% (n = 71) with 11 to 15 years of experience, and 23% (n = 76) with 16 or more years of experience.

Cultural diversity and awareness programs were reported being promoted in 74% (n = 241) of the schools. Twenty-one percent (n = 69) of the respondents suggested such programs were not promoted, and the remaining 5% (n = 18) reported such programs were somewhat promoted. Academically, 70% (n = 230) of the school counselors had taken a multicultural counseling course and 30% (n = 98) reported no such coursework. Biracial children were also represented in 93% (n = 304) of the schools.

Participants were asked to estimate the percentage of students based upon race within their respective school. For the purpose of this study, an arbitrary decision was made by the researcher to categorize schools as

TABLE 1. COUNSELORS' PERCEPTIONS OF BIRACIAL CHILDREN DISTRIBUTED IN PERCENTAGES AND FREQUENCIES

Perception	Yes		No		Unsure	
	%	N	%	N	%	N
I believe society openly accepts biracial children	17%	54	66%	219	17%	55
It is best psychologically for biracial children to livein neighborhoods reflecting the minority parent.	10%	32	38%	125	52%	171
Biracial children have a more difficult time adjusting to society than other children.	43%	142	36%	116	21%	70

Note. n = 328

diverse if 30% or more of the student body consisted of individuals from two or more racial groups. Schools were categorized as nondiverse when one specific racial group of students comprised 71% or more of the student body. Thirty-seven percent (n = 122) of the school counselors reported a diverse student body, 40% (n = 131) reported a student body consisting primarily of African-American students, 23% (n = 73) indicated a student body consisting of mainly Caucasian students, and .6% (n = 2) indicated a student population made up of primarily Hispanics.

Instrument

Participants were asked to complete to a 25-item survey covering a broad range of issues regarding biracial children. The survey was created by the researcher and based upon a review of literature exploring a variety of personal and social issues confronting biracial individuals (Brandell, 1988; Brown, 1990; Buttery, 1987; Foeman & Nance, 1999; Gibbs & Moskowitz-Sweet, 1991; Hatcher, 1987; Kerwin & Ponterotto, 1995; McRoy & Freeman, 1986; Nakashima, 1992; Nishimura, 1995; Wardle, 1991, 1992; Winn & Priest, 1993). Colleagues familiar with the topic served as reviewers and provided valuable feedback, especially in the wording of the survey items. Originally, the first version of the survey contained 30 items. However, after consulting with colleagues, 5 items were eliminated because they were considered vague and confusing.

Demographic information was requested on eight survey items inquiring about the participants' race, gender, years of experience as a school counselor, racial composition of the student body in their school, whether or not biracial individuals were represented in their school, counseling experience with biracial individuals, school grade level, and if they had taken a formal multicultural counseling course. Three survey items briefly explored their personal counseling experience with biracial children. Thirteen items addressed the school counselors' individual perceptions of biracial children focusing predominantly on academic, behavioral, and identity related matters (see Appendix and Table 1). The final question was open-ended, inviting additional written comments addressing other concerns school counselors held of biracial individuals. Overall, 18 of the 25 items asked participants to respond by checking "yes," "no," or "unsure." One survey item that inquired about whether or not cultural diversity and awareness programs were promoted in the schools, asked counselors to respond by checking "yes," "no," or "somewhat" (see Table 3).

Procedure
The school counselors who participated in this pilot study were selected primarily because of their location in the Southeastern region of the United States. The address of each school was obtained by contacting the central office or by searching each district's Web site. Individual packets were mailed to each school addressed to the attention of the school counselor. A decision was made by the researcher to mail the elementary schools only one packet because they typically had only one counselor on staff. The middle and high schools were mailed two individual packets because in most schools, but not all, they had two or more counselors on staff. The packet included a cover letter, the survey, and a business reply self-addressed return envelope. The cover letter informed participants about the purpose of the survey and assured them their responses would remain confidential. The cover letter also provided participants with the phone number and e-mail address of the researcher to answer any potential questions or concerns. Due to limited funding and resources, follow-up reminders were not sent out to individual school counselors.

Research Design
Survey research is one form of quantitative descriptive research and, according to Babbie (1979), the objectives are to describe, explain, or explore phenomena. This research project, exploratory in design, is most often used

when little is known about a phenomenon and the researcher desires to learn more about it (Heppner, Kivlighan, & Wampold, 1999). In this case, the phenomenon was school counselors' perceptions of biracial children. Descriptive statistics were computed for all items on the survey. Chi square analysis was employed to investigate possible associations between school counselors' perceptions and school level, years of counseling experience, gender, and the existence of cultural diversity programs in schools.

RESULTS

What Personal Perceptions Do School Counselors Have Concerning Biracial Individuals?

Sixty-seven percent of the school counselors did not believe society openly accepted biracial children, and 43% indicated they would have a difficult time adjusting to society (see Table 1). When biracial children's social skills and attitudes toward adults were compared with other children, 63% ($n = 214$) of the school counselors sensed there was no such difference, 26% ($n = 78$) indicated there was a difference, and 11% ($n = 36$) were uncertain. Ninetythree percent of the participants supported the belief that biracial children should culturally identify with both parents. However, when addressing the opinion that it was in the best interest socially and psychologically for biracial children to live in a neighborhood reflecting the minority, only 38% of the school counselors disagreed, while over half (52%) answered unsure (see Table 1).

What Personal Counseling Experience Do School Counselors Have With Biracial Individuals?

The results showed that 82% ($n = 262$) of the school counselors reported having some personal counseling experience with biracial individuals. In addition, 82% ($n = 270$) of the respondents indicated they would feel comfortable providing counseling services to biracial students. Forty-four percent ($n = 143$) of the school counselors expressed the opinion they did not need additional preparation or information to more effectively provide counseling services to biracial students. However, 45% ($n = 146$) held contrary positions, suggesting a desire for additional information and preparation.

Is There A Relationship Between School Level, Years of Counseling Experience, and School Counselors' Perceptions of Biracial Individuals?

Chi square analysis revealed that the elementary grade level was found to be directly related to the perception that biracial children tend to have

TABLE 2. FREQUENCIES AND PERCENTAGES
FOR SIGNIFICANT CHI SQUARE RESULTS

School Level	Yes	No	Unsure	Total
Biracial children in schools tend to have more behavioral problems.				
Elementary	19 (11%)	131 (74%)	26 (15%)	176
Middle	5 (6%)	60 (67%)	24 (27%)	89
High	2 (3%)	55 (87%)	6 (11%)	63
Totals	26	246	56	328
Minorities are more accepting of biracial children than non-minorities.				
Elementary	59 (34%)	73 (42%)	44 (25%)	176
Middle	37 (42%)	23 (26%)	29 (33%)	89
High	30 (47%)	16 (25%)	17 (27%)	63
Totals	126	112	90	328

Experience	Yes	No	Unsure	Total
Presenting problems of biracial more likely result of identity conflicts.				
1-5 years	38 (37%)	27 (26%)	39 (38%)	104
6-10 years	20 (26%)	37 (48%)	20 (26%)	77
11-15 years	15 (29%)	29 (41%)	27 (38%)	71
16 or more	25 (33%)	30 (40%)	21 (27%)	76
Totals	98	123	107	328
I automatically categorize biracial child with the minority parent.				
1-5 years	35 (34%)	61 (58%)	8 (8%)	104
6-10 years	21 (27%)	54 (70%)	2 (3%)	77
11-15 years	18 (25%)	51 (71%)	2 (3%)	71
16 or more	11 (15%)	57 (75%)	8 (10%)	76
Totals	98	123	107	328

Gender	Yes	No	Unsure	Total
Biracial children in schools tend to have more academic problems.				
Male	6 (14%)	24 (55%)	13 (30%)	43
Female	13 (05%)	206 (72%)	66 (23%)	285
Totals	26	246	56	328
Minorities are more accepting of biracial children than non-minorities.				
Male	24 (56%)	8 (18%)	11 (26%)	43
Female	102 (36%)	104 (37%)	79 (27%)	285
Totals	126	112	90	328

more behavioral problems when compared to other children, X^2 (4, N = 328) = 13.92, p = .008. Secondary school counselors perceived minorities were more accepting of biracial children than nonminorities, X^2 (4, N = 328) = 9.94, p = .041 (see Table 2). School counselors having 1 to 5 years of counseling experience were associated with the notion that presenting problems from biracial children were more than likely the result of identity conflicts, X2 (6, N = 328) = 13.27, p = .039. In addition, the perception of automatically categorizing biracial children specifically with the minority parent was significantly related to school counselors with 1 to 5 years of counseling experience, X2 (6, N = 328) = 14.07, p = .029 (see Table 2).

Is There a Relationship Between Gender and School Counselors' Perceptions of Biracial Individuals?

Male school counselors perceived biracial children experiencing more academic problems when compared to other children, X^2 (2, N = 328) = 7.91, p = .019. Furthermore they were more likely than female school counselors to perceive that minorities were more accepting of biracial children than nonminorities, X^2 (2, N = 328) = 7.46, p = .024 (see Table 2).

Is There a Relationship Between the Existence of Promoted Cultural Diversity Programs in Schools and School Counselors' Perceptions of Biracial Individuals?

The impact of the existence of actively promoted cultural diversity and awareness programs in schools was significantly related to a number of perceptions. For example, the majority of school counselors who were uncertain whether or not biracial children exhibited more behavioral problems were in schools that somewhat promoted cultural diversity and awareness programs, X^2 (4, N = 328) = 15.04, p = .004 (see Table 3). School counselors who agreed with the concept that biracial children should identify most with the minority parent were in schools that did not actively promote cultural diversity and awareness programs, X^2 (4, N = 328) = 13.08, p = .011. Another statistically significant relationship showed that school counselors who agreed with the perspective that presenting problems biracial children encounter were more than likely the result of identity confusion also worked in schools that did not actively promote cultural diversity and awareness programs, X^2 (4, v = 328) = 14.64, p = .005 (see Table 3).

The majority of school counselors who instinctively categorized biracial children with the minority parent were employed in school environments that did not actively promote cultural diversity and awareness programs, X^2 (4, N = 328) = 19.97, p = .001. The opinion that biracial children would

TABLE 3. FREQUENCIES AND PERCENTAGES FOR SIGNIFICANT CHI SQUARE RESULTS

Promoting Cultural Programs	Yes	No	Unsure	Total
Biracial children in schools tend to have more behavioral problems.				
Yes	19 (8%)	183 (76%)	39 (16%)	241
No	6 (9%)	055 (80%)	08 (11%)	69
Somewhat	1 (5%)	8 (44%)	9 (50%)	18
Totals	26	246	56	328
Biracial children should culturally identify most with minority parent.				
Yes	13 (6%)	155 (64%)	73 (30%)	241
No	9 (13%)	39 (57%)	21 (30%)	69
Somewhat	0 (0%)	7 (39%)	11 (61%)	18
Totals	22	201	105	328
Presenting problems of biracial more likely the result of identity conflicts.				
Yes	69 (28%)	98 (41%)	74 (31%)	241
No	23 (33%)	25 (36%)	21 (30%)	69
Somewhat	6 (33%)	0 (0%)	12 (67%)	18
Totals	98	123	107	328
Automatically categorize biracial child with the minority parent.				
Yes	48 (20%)	176 (73%)	17 (7%)	241
No	32 (46%)	35 (51%)	2 (3%)	69
Somewhat	5 (28%)	12 (66%)	1 (6%)	18
Totals	85	223	20	328
Biracial children will have fewer problems living in a racially diverse community.				
Yes	166 (69%)	9 (4%)	66 (27%)	241
No	38 (55%)	9 (13%)	22 (32%)	69
Somewhat	11 (61%)	1 (6%)	6 (33%)	18
Totals	215	19	94	328
Minorities are more accepting of biracial children than non-minorities				
Yes	84 (35%)	86 (35%)	71 (30%)	241
No	37 (53%)	22 (32%)	10 (15%)	69
Somewhat	5 (28%)	4 (22%)	9 (50%)	18
Totals	126	112	90	328

not experience as many problems relating to racial identity providing they live in a racially diverse neighborhood was associated with participants that actively promoted cultural diversity and awareness programs, X^2 (4, N = 328) = 10.16, p = .038. Finally, school counselors who perceived minorities more accepting of biracial children than nonminorities worked in school environments that did not actively promote cultural diversity and awareness programs, X^2 (4, N = 328) = 14.41, p = .006 (see Table 3).

DISCUSSION

This pilot study exploring school counselors' perceptions of biracial children generated some intriguing results. Similar to Nishimura and Bol's (1997) findings, biracial individuals were represented in nearly all of the schools, which demonstrates to some degree they are a more recognized population. Even though biracial individuals are more recognized today, this does not amount to societal acceptance. School counselors validated this perspective as they strongly supported the position that biracial children were not genuinely accepted by society. Schools in many aspects are a microcosm of society, and if biracial children are not genuinely accepted by society, then how genuinely are they accepted in the schools? School counselors' perceptions, to some degree, suggest that biracial children, because of the manner in which society perceives their family environment, may still face additional stressors that other children do not necessarily encounter.

Elementary school counselors who perceived biracial children having more behavioral problems than middle or high school counselors may be linked to the cognitive/emotional stage of development these children are experiencing. Elementary children in general are not as guarded in expressing their true feelings, yet as they grow older and mature, certain emotions once openly expressed may be internalized and seen as immature. Elementary school counselors may also see more behavioral problems because they are likely to spend more time providing counseling-related services to children at this age than do middle or high school counselors. The Tennyson, Miller, Skovholt, and Williams (1989) study supported this view because they found in their survey that secondary school counselors reported that, as a group, they were involved in scheduling more often than in any other activity, including providing counseling-related services to students. Elementary school counselors, according to Morse and Russel (1988), preferred to conduct more group work with students focusing on enhancing their self-concept, developing problem-solving skills, and learning appropriate social skills. Finally, it must be taken into consideration that biracial students may choose not to see counselors as often in middle or high schools because of the stigma associated with seeing a school counselor.

Male school counselors as compared to female school counselors perceived biracial children experiencing more academic problems, and one has to question the impact of gender role socialization upon this perspective. When females reach adulthood, they often become more caring, supportive, and empathetic, while males become more independent, self-reliant, and unexpressive. Males in general, are also more likely to show anger toward strangers, especially other males, when they feel they have been challenged (Santrock, 1997).

Another important finding of this study indicated that school counselors who worked in school environments that actively promoted cultural diversity and awareness programs held more accurate perceptions of biracial children. For example, they did not believe that biracial children should identify most with the minority parent nor did they perceive minorities more accepting of biracial children than nonminorities. School counselors should not automatically assume that minorities are always more accepting of biracial children than nonminorities. This sometimes is a controversial issue for both the minority and majority communities (Buttery, 1987).

Identity development has been one of the primary topics of concern for researchers focusing on biracial children (Brandell, 1988; Gibbs, 1987; Herring, 1992; McRoy & Freeman, 1986; Poston, 1990; Sebring, 1985; Teicher, 1968). School counselors who perceived identity confusion as the major cause of emotional problems for biracial children were in schools that did not actively promote cultural diversity programs, and they also were the least experienced counselors. Herring cautioned school counselors not to automatically assume the presenting problems of biracial children are always the direct result of identity conflicts. Even when a biracial child enters counseling, school counselors should not necessarily assume the presenting problems biracial children are experiencing are direct results of identity conflicts. McRoy and Freeman contended that it is highly possible that racial identity concerns will not be among the presenting problems for biracial children who are referred to counseling. Instead, referrals are made for other matters such as poor academic achievement, social isolation, off-task behavior, and negative attitudes toward adults. When such problems occur, it is, however, therapeutically appropriate for school counselors to explore and investigate if there is "a direct link between being biracial and the presenting problems" (Winn & Priest, 1993, p. 30).

Some writers believe that it is best socially and psychologically for interracial families to live in racially diverse neighborhoods as it may help facilitate positive development of racial identity in biracial children by exposing them to different cultures (Buttery, 1987; McRoy & Freeman, 1986). Counselors employed in school settings that actively promoted cultural diversity and awareness programs also supported this view.

School counselors who reported they were more likely to automatically identify biracial children with the minority parent had less than 5 years of counseling experience and were in schools that did not promote cultural diversity and awareness programs. School counselors should thoroughly explore reasons that lead to such characterizations. One way this task can be accomplished is by conducting a personal analysis using the following questions as a guide: How do I honestly feel about interracial marriages and partnerships? Do I judge them differently when compared to non-interracial marriages and partnerships? What preconceived notions do I have regarding biracial individuals? What type of experiences have I had with biracial individuals? What type of experiences have I had with parents of biracial children? How do those experiences impact my perceptions? What factors cause me to identify biracial children with the minority parent? Is it the way the child appears physically? Is it the manner that he or she speaks or the neighborhood in which the child lives? What personal feelings do I have regarding biracial children? Do I label all biracial children with the minority parent or only biracial children from certain types of interracial unions? How does my school environment contribute to my perceptions? If I hold negative or inaccurate perceptions of biracial individuals and or multiracial families, what can I personally do to do overcome them? Exploring questions of this nature may be difficult for some; however, the intent is to help school counselors become more aware of their personal biases.

Implications for School Counselors

Based upon the results of this pilot study, school counselors who were employed in schools that actively promoted cultural diversity and awareness programs held more accurate perceptions of biracial individuals. Therefore, all school counselors should genuinely strive to promote cultural diversity and awareness programs in their respective school, thus creating a multicultural school environment. Establishing this type of environment provides fellow counselors, school administrators, teachers, students, other staff members, and possibly the community with unique opportunities to increase their awareness, knowledge, and understanding of individuals from culturally different backgrounds. This is a significant factor relating to perceptions of biracial individuals, because even though societal attitudes towards them have evolved over the years, some of the stereotypic perceptions remain in place today. School counselors must also continuously examine, explore, and become aware of their own personal values toward biracial individuals (McRoy & Freeman, 1986) and, furthermore, recognize how their values may influence their perceptions. Wardle (1992) believed that professionals working with biracial individuals and their families must strive to overcome personal prejudices, gain accurate information to defeat stereotypic views, and then help create an environment that is supportive for biracial individuals.

In order to promote a better understanding of biracial individuals, school counselors must continue to develop and improve their knowledge base about the identity development of biracial individuals. One of the earlier models of identity development such as the one developed by Stonequist (1937) conceptualized individuals who had more than one racial group heritage as marginal members to these particular groups. They were often negatively perceived as people who were "more likely to be restless and race conscious, aggressive and radical, ambitious and creative" (Stonequist, p. 25). However, more recent models of identity development such as those proposed by Kerwin and Ponterotto (1995), Kich (1992), and Poston (1990) provide more accurate perspective of identity development for biracial individuals. School counselors should recognize that identity development for biracial individuals is a developmental process and may sometimes be demonstrated in manners which appear negative (Hatcher, 1987). Finally, school counselors must take into consideration that biracial children are individuals, with emotional needs and desires in many ways similar to other children.

CONCLUSION

This exploratory study investigated school counselors' perceptions of biracial children and the results indicated school level, years of counseling experience, and gender influenced certain perceptions. School counselors' perceptions were also affected by the presence of actively promoted cultural diversity and awareness programs. When cultural diversity and awareness programs are actively promoted in schools, they create an environment in which a variety of cultures are celebrated and genuinely valued. Furthermore, racial issues are openly discussed (Wardle, 1992). This is a significant issue for school counselors to be aware of because biracial children are one of the fastest growing segments in U.S. society today, and this investigation demonstrated that some of the traditional beliefs concerning biracial individuals remain intact.

This exploratory project is not without limitations. First, the results can only be generalized to school counselors working in the nine states located in the Southeastern region of the United States. The generalizations should also be cautiously interpreted because there is no assurance that all participants honestly responded to each item on the survey. In addition, the sample of respondents, especially males, should be increased and expanded to include a national pool of school counselors where regional and other cultural elements could be taken into consideration.

In conclusion, it is important to emphasize that this study attempted to contribute to an area of research concerning biracial individuals that has been literally ignored over the years. Hopefully, the information gained will help all school counselors develop a more accurate perception of biracial individuals and foster ways to improve the cultural climate in their respective schools.

Henry L. Harris, Ph.D., LPC, is an assistant professor, Counseling, Development and Higher Education, University of North Texas, Denton. E-mail: hharris@coefs.coe.unt.edu

REFERENCES

Axelson, J. (1999). *Counseling and development in a multicultural society* (3rd ed.). Pacific Grove, CA: Brooks/Cole.

Babbie, E. R. (1979). *The practice of social research* (2nd ed.). Belmont, CA:Wadsworth.

Brandell, J. R. (1988).Treatment of the biracial child:Theoretical and clinical issues. *Journal of Multicultural Counseling and Development, 16*, 176–187.

Brown, P. M. (1990). Biracial identity and social marginality. *Child and Adolescent Social Work, 7*, 319–337.

Buttery, T. J. (1987). Biracial children: Racial identification, selfesteem and school adjustment. *Delta Phi Record, 22*, 50–53.

Foeman, K. A.,& Nance,T. (1999). From miscegenation to multiculturalisn perceptions of interracial relationship development. *Journal of Black Studies, 29*, 540–557.

Gibbs, J.T. (1987). Identity and marginality: Issues in the treatment of biracial adolescents. *American Journal of Orthopsychiatry, 57*, 265–278.

Gibbs, J.T.,& Moskowitz-Sweet, G. (1991). Clinical and cultural issues in the treatment of biracial and bicultural adolescents. *The Journal of Contemporary Human Services, 12*, 579–592.

Hatcher, C. L. (1987). *It's only half of me:The interracial child: The need for balance.* Unpublished manuscript,Denver, CO. (ERIC Document Reproduction Service No.ED 336970).

Heppner, P. P., Kivlighan,D. M., & Wampold, B. E. (1999). *Research design in counseling* (2nd ed.). Belmont, CA:Wadsworth.

Herring, R.D. (1992) Biracial children:An increasing concern for elementary and middle school counselors. *Elementary School Guidance and Counseling, 27,* 123–130.

Jamison, R. L. (1999,May 24). Mavin: A new voice for the young and mixed and proud. *Seattle Post Intelligencer,* p. B15.

Kalish, S. (1995). Multiracial births increase as U.S. ponders racial definitions. *Population Today: News,Numbers, and Analysis, 23,* 1–2.

Kerwin, K., & Ponterotto, J. G. (1995). Biracial identity development. In J. G. Ponterotto, J.M. Casas, L. A. Suzuki, & C.M. Alexander (Eds.), *Handbook of multicultural counseling* (pp. 199–217).Thousands Oaks, CA: Sage.

Kerwin, K., Ponterotto, J. G., Jackson, B. L.,& Harris, A. (1993). Racial identity in biracial children:A qualitative investigation. *Journal of Counseling Psychology, 40,* 221–231.

Kich, G. K. (1992).The developmental process of asserting a biracial, bicultural identity. In M. P. P. Root (Ed.), *Racially mixed people in America* (pp. 304–320).Newbury Park, CA: Sage.

Krause,W.W. (1941). Race crossing in Hawaii. *Journal of Heredity, 32,* 371–378.

McRoy, R. G., & Freeman, E. (1986). Racial identity issues among mixed raced children. *Social Work in Education, 8,* 164–174.

Morse, C. L., & Russel,T. (1988). How elementary school counselors see their role. *Elementary School Guidance and Counseling, 23,* 54–62.

Nakashima, C. L. (1992).An invisible monster: The creation and denial of racially mixed people in America. In M. P. P. Root (Ed.), *Racially mixed people in America* (pp. 162–180). Newbury Park, CA: Sage.

Nishimura, N. (1995). Addressing the needs of biracial children: An issue for school counselors in a multicultural school environment. *The School Counselor, 43,* 52–57.

Nishimura, N., & Bol, L. (1997). School counselors' perceptions of the counseling needs of biracial children in an urban educational setting. *Research in the Schools, 4,* 17–23.

Parker, S. (1999,March 23). Erasing a remnant of Jim Crow South from law books. *The Christian Science Monitor, 3,* p. 3.

Poston,W. S. C. (1990).The biracial identity development model:A needed addition. *Journal of Counseling and Development, 69,* 152–155.

Poussaint, A. F. (1984). Study of interracial children presents positive picture. *Interracial Books for Children Bulletin, 15,* 9–10.

Provine,W. B. (1973).Geneticists and the biology of race crossing. *Science, 182,* 790–796.

Santrock, J.W. (1997). *Life-span development* (6th ed.). Dubuque, IA: Brown & Benchmark.

Sebring, D. L. (1985). Considerations in counseling interracial children. *Journal of Non-White Concerns, 13*, 3–9.

Shackford, K. (1984). Interracial children: Growing up healthy in an unhealthy society. *Interracial Books for Children Bulletin, 15*, 4–6.

Steele, M. (1995).Mixed-race families still find a mixed reception. *Teaching Tolerance, 49*, 44–49.

Stonequist, E.V. (1937). *The marginal man: A study in personality and culture and conflict.* New York: Russell & Russell.

Sue, D.W., & Sue,D. (1999). *Counseling the culturally different: Theory and practice* (3rd ed.).New York: John Wiley.

Teicher, J.D. (1968).Some observations on identity problems in children of Negro-White marriage. *Journal of Nervous and Mental Disease, 146*, 249–256.

Tennyson,W.W.,Miller, G.D., Skovholt,T.G.,& Williams, R.G. (1989). Secondary school counselors: What do they do? What is important? *The School Counselor, 36*, 253–259.

Tizard, B., & Phoenix, A. (1995).The identity of mixed parentage adolescent. *Journal of Child Psychology and Psychiatry, 36*, 1399–1410.

U.S. Bureau of Census. (2001). Mapping census 2000:The geography of U.S. diversity.Washington, DC: U.S.Government Printing Office.

Wardle, F. (1991). Interracial children and their families: How school social workers should respond. *Social Work in Education, 13*, 215–223.

Wardle, F. (1992). Supporting biracial children in the school setting. *Education and Treatment of Children, 15*, 163–172.

Winn, N. N.,& Priest, R. (1993). Counseling biracial children: A forgotten component of multicultural counseling. *Family Therapy, 20*, 29–35.

APPENDIX

Personal Perceptions of Biracial Individuals Questionnaire

1. I believe biracial children in school settings tend to have more academic problems than other children.
Yes_____ No_____ Unsure_____

2. Individuals from different racial/ethnic backgrounds should avoid having children because of social pressure the children may encounter.
Yes_____ No_____ Unsure_____

3. I believe biracial children in school settings tend to have more behavioral problems than other children.
Yes_____ No_____ Unsure_____

4. I believe biracial children have social skills and attitudes toward adults no different than other children.
   Yes_____ No_____ Unsure_____
5. I feel that biracial children should culturally identify most with the minority parent.
   Yes_____ No_____ Unsure_____
6. I feel presenting problems from biracial children are more than likely the result of identity conflicts.
   Yes_____ No_____ Unsure_____
7. I believe biracial children should culturally identify with both parents.
   Yes_____ No_____ Unsure_____
8. When I see a biracial child, I automatically categorize him/her with the minority parent.
   Yes_____ No_____ Unsure_____
9. Biracial children will have fewer problems relating to racial identity if they live in a diverse community.
   Yes____ No_____ Unsure_____
10. I believe minorities are generally more accepting of biracial children than are non-minorities.
    Yes____ No_____ Unsure_____

Counseling African American Adolescents: The Impact of Race, Culture, and Middle Class Status

By Norma L. Day-Vines, Ph.D., James M. Patton, Ed.D., and Joy L. Baytops

This article originally appeared in *Professional School Counseling*, Vol. 7, No. 1, 2003.

A substantial body of literature addresses the concerns of African American youngsters who experience social distress, academic difficulties, poverty, despair, and violence. This article focuses on issues of particular relevance to school counselors working with middle-class, African American youngsters whose lives may have little relationship to the above-mentioned stressors. The article begins with an overview of African American socioeconomic status, continues with a discussion of the complex interaction between race and class, addresses culturally competent counseling practice, explores African American cultural values, examines racial identity issues, considers intra-racial stressors, and addresses implications for counseling of middle-class African American adolescents. The authors present a case study to examine each of these issues.

A large corpus of literature documenting the social and educational experiences of African American adolescents usually focuses on economic despair, poverty, poor health, crime, violence, and inadequate education. Such portrayals often lead to inaccurate generalizations that fail to address the interaction of race and middle-class status for African American youngsters (Ford, 1997). Although middle-class status insulates African American youngsters from certain exigencies associated with Black life, these adolescents often confront challenging social circumstances that, without appropriate support and intervention, could potentially jeopardize their healthy social and emotional adjustment.

In this article, the authors explore the complex interaction among race, culture, and social class, its impact on middle-class African American adolescents, and culturally responsive counseling. Although many issues addressed in this article reflect issues all African American adolescents confront, the nuances of race, culture, and class often operate differentially for middle-class African Americans. Simply put, middle-class status can serve as a protective mechanism against poverty, dilapidated housing, inferior education, and malnutrition, yet it does not shield young people from the manacles of racism and discrimination (hooks, 2000). So while some

African American youngsters may have advantages based on their social class, they may still endure forms of racial oppression as well as inter- and intraracial strife.

The article opens with definitions of culturally responsive counseling and middle-class status, continues with a discussion of African American cultural values, explores identity issues and intra-racial stressors, and provides culturally responsive recommendations for working effectively with middle-class African American adolescents. We present a case study to examine each of these issues. The terms African American and Black are used interchangeably.

DEFINING CULTURALLY RESPONSIVE COUNSELING

Culture is often viewed as incompatible from one cultural context to the next. That is, patterns of thought, behavior, and functioning may be deemed normative and acceptable in one cultural milieu yet construed as deficient or deviant in another cultural milieu. Culturally responsive counseling practice requires an ethic of caring and understanding in an effort to build bridges between children whose cultures and backgrounds do not necessarily mirror the cultural dictates of mainstream American society. Elsewhere Lee (2001) and Gay (2000) have articulated characteristics indicative of culturally responsive counseling practice. We proffer that culturally responsive counseling practice refers to the inclusion of diverse perspectives into the counseling process in a manner that validates and affirms children from marginalized groups and recognizes the contextual dimensions of race, culture, class, gender, religion, sexual orientation, and geography. In this article, we concentrate on the complex and dynamic interaction of race, culture, and class and discuss implications for delivering culturally responsive counseling services.

African American Socioeconomic Status

The contemporary Black middle class emerged with the advent of the Civil Rights movement (Walker & Wilson, 2002). As sweeping social and political changes placed fewer restrictions on social mobility, educational access, and residential patterns of African Americans, this expanded opportunity structure permitted more people of African descent to improve their socioeconomic status and enter the ranks of the middle class.

Middle-class status has been variously defined. For instance, Conley (1999) defined middle-class status as two times the poverty rate. According to the U.S. Census Bureau (2000), the average poverty threshold for a family of three was $13,738 and $17,603 for a family of four. By these rather inclusive guidelines, a sizable proportion of African

Americans are in the middle class. In fact, Sue and Sue (2003) noted that more than one third of the African American population can be classified as middle class.

Ford (1997) described the Black middle class as a diverse population encompassing individuals who vary in class standing from lower middle and upper middle to the elite social strata. That is, middle-class African Americans range in scope from the working poor to the affluent. Although much variability exists in employment, lifestyle, and material possessions – depending upon the rung of the social ladder one occupies – on the whole, each group (i.e., lower middle, upper middle, elite) shares core values related to a strong work ethic, achievement orientation, racial pride, and adherence to mainstream American social norms (Sue & Sue, 2003). The unifying element among members of the Black middle class appears to be a common value orientation and motivation toward social mobility.

In the main, middle class African Americans remain woefully underrepresented in the professional literature. Although erroneous, prevailing assumptions regard the Black population as a monolithic entity that is largely poor and undereducated. Such stereotypes obscure the vast heterogeneity that characterizes this population and minimizes the specific and unique concerns that confront middle class African American adolescents. Culturally responsive school counselors should recognize that social class standing can shield youngsters from concerns about economic well-being, but at the same time exacerbate feelings of guilt related to middle class status, feelings of isolation and alienation from other African Americans, and experiences with racism. Recognition of the complex issues related to race, culture, and class will better position counselors to deliver more effective counseling services. Next, we present a case study to facilitate discussion of the impact of race, culture, and class on the counseling process.

CASE STUDY

Tiffany is a 10th grade African American female student who performs well academically. She is enrolled in three advanced placement (AP) courses, and she is a member of the orchestra and the gymnastics team. Both her parents are attorneys, and she lives comfortably in an upper middle-class neighborhood. Although there are several other African American youngsters in her community, most of them are either older, younger, or attend private school.

Tiffany scheduled an appointment with her counselor to request removal from two AP courses, citing preparation for the statewide gymnastics competition as the reason. This request puzzled the counselor because Tiffany makes the honor roll consistently. Confused, the counselor, who happened to be Caucasian, probed for a more in-depth explanation from Tiffany. Although Tiffany insisted that her reason related to shifting priorities in athletics and an after-school job, the counselor speculated that more might be going on. She finally asked Tiffany to what extent her request might result from her being one of very few African Americans in her class. At that point, Tiffany felt the counselor truly understood the challenges academically successful African American children such as herself must endure. Tiffany wept as she explained to the counselor that her African American peers teased her for working hard to obtain good grades, speaking standard English, participating on the gymnastics team, and living in an affluent community. In essence, she was accused of "acting White." She confided to her counselor that the stress was overwhelming. Additionally, her White peers limited their contact with her only to expressing interest in her friendship when they could receive answers for homework assignments and speaking to her outside of class as long as no other Whites were present. They also jokingly queried about whether her parents sold drugs to afford their lifestyle, and her teacher intimated that her term paper was so well written that it may have been plagiarized.

The counselor appropriately validated Tiffany's concerns and shared that over the years she had worked with other African American females who had expressed similar concerns. She recognized that in many ways Tiffany was isolated from both her Black and White peers and was truly an outsider within two disparate peer groups. The counselor had Tiffany prioritize her concerns and establish related goals. Tiffany decided that she wanted to find an African American peer group who shared her interests, have teachers respect the quality of effort she invested in her work, and experience less antipathy from her White peers.

Between sessions, the counselor consulted with two people of color, the only African American counselor in her department and a local minister of a predominantly African American congregation who served on the guidance department's Advisory Board. The African American counselor was instrumental in helping the White counselor recognize issues such as the competing demands that African American youngsters negotiate and the simultaneous pressure that students often experience from their same race peers. She recommended to the White counselor that Tiffany consider joining civic organizations whose purpose is to provide service and, at the same time, assist cultivating positive identity formation in African American youngsters. The minister recommended that the counselor inquire about Tiffany's church affiliation and have her consider joining a church youth group, which would bring her into closer contact with other conscientious African American youngsters.

At the next scheduled appointment, Tiffany discussed with the counselor strategies for meeting other African Americans with whom she appeared to have more in common. Tiffany also expressed an interest in joining the African American history club. The counselor recommended that Tiffany participate in a small group entitled, "Sisters on the Move," a support group for academically successful African American adolescents. When the counselor registered Tiffany for classes for the following year, she made certain to enroll her in AP classes where she would not be in the minority and receive some support from other students of color.

Concerned that the racial climate may be somewhat unhealthy for students of color, the Caucasian counselor approached the school improvement team and the principal about in-service workshops to address cultural competency issues in the classroom. The counselor recognized that some issues would require policy and institutional changes to more positively influence the social and educational experiences of minority children.

During their remaining sessions, the counselor helped Tiffany realize she did not have to sacrifice academic performance for peer acceptance. For the duration of the year, Tiffany seemed to be in much better spirits.

INTERSECTION OF RACE AND CLASS
AMONG MIDDLE-CLASS ADOLESCENTS

Race and Class

The interlocking paradigms of race and class have been inadequately addressed in the literature, and the few researchers who have examined these topics have typically treated these paradigms as mutually exclusive entities wherein race functions independently of class. Hooks (2000) cited a number of causal factors for the separate treatment of race and class. First, class, unlike race which is an immutable aspect of one's identity, can be camouflaged with conspicuous consumption. In other words, people can deflect attention from their impoverished social circumstances by possessing the accoutrements of money such as clothing and cars. Second, racism in this society is so virulent that it frequently deflects attention from class. Historically, African Americans have banded together to combat racial oppression as opposed to class oppression. Moreover, racial solidarity could be achieved because all African Americans experienced bias on the basis of skin color; whereas, class distinctions created a caste system that did not engender similar forms of economic solidarity. Third,

because this society maintains a hedonistic obsession with material accumulation and negative attributions are often made about the poor being
responsible for their plight, few people openly acknowledge personal dep-
rivation and want. Society has made the poor internalize a sense of shame
about their class status; consequently, people seldom volunteer information about their social position unless it is patently obvious.

A culturally responsive counselor would recognize the complex intersection of race and class embedded within Tiffany's presenting problem.
Although Tiffany did not worry about food, shelter, or safety, she did experience ostracism from some of her peers. For instance, her African American
peers isolated Tiffany because of their perceptions of her social class standing and concerns that she was "acting White," given her decision to excel
academically. Her White peers could only accept stereotyped constructions
of African Americans as criminals involved in the drug trade. The varying
forms of ridicule she experienced from both her African American and
Caucasian peers left her feeling dejected and alienated.

Privilege and Middle-Class Status
McIntosh (1989) provided groundbreaking analyses of White and male
privilege as a sociopolitical force that confers a set of benefits to one
group while concurrently denying those same benefits to a marginalized
group with less status, power, and prestige. Her discussion of White privilege focused exclusively on the benefits that race grants European
Americans. Perhaps a more useful discussion of privilege would examine
this system of advantages in a domain-specific context. Privilege can occur
along different binary dimensions that include class distinctions between
the haves and have-nots; differences in sexual orientation primarily
between heterosexuals and homosexuals; contrasts between males and
females; distinctions between physical attractiveness and unattractiveness;
differentials between the young and old; and differences in language such
as standard and nonstandard English. In each case, society accords status
and privilege to individuals who possess more preferred attributes such as
higher social class standing, heterosexual orientation, maleness, attractiveness, youth, and the ability to speak standard English.

As defined herein, a middle-class African American who lacks privilege
on the basis of race may well experience privilege on the basis of socioeconomic status. Although middle-class status creates for Tiffany greater
economic advantages, a wider assortment of personal choices, and a
shield from poverty, her middle-class status does not provide complete
protection from the often inevitable experiences with racism in a racially
ambivalent society (Tatum, 1997; Wiley, 1992).

Hooks (2000) noted that class frequently serves as a mediating variable

against racism. For instance, Tiffany believes that the accusation of pla-
giarism was a form of discrimination. Although social class standing may
not protect her from racist assaults, class may mitigate against some consequences of racism. Thus, Tiffany has a degree of potential protection
because of class that may not be available to other students of the same
race. In comparison to a parent from the lower socioeconomic class,
should Tiffany's parents construe the teacher's accusation as a racist incident and opt to respond to allegations of racism, they are more apt to
know how to maneuver within the educational system. Tiffany's parents
would likely know how to schedule a teacher conference, enlist an administrator if necessary, articulate their concerns to school personnel, and
exude confidence and self-efficacy in the process. Class privilege may also
mean that Tiffany's parents would likely have reliable transportation and
the ability to take time from work without having to decide between loss
of pay or inquiring about a child's school-related concerns (Patton &
Day-Vines, 2003). Provided the allegations were true and in the event the
situation was not resolved at the building level, a middle-class parent
would likely have the resources to pursue other channels to seek redress,
including accessing community leaders, school board members, and the
media. Yet while many middle-class African American parents may have
access to formal and informal resources within organizations and agencies, the depth and breadth of this access still does not approximate the
resources available to their European American counterparts of equal
class standing.

While class does not thwart egregious violations of an African
American child's personhood, it can certainly interrupt the vicious cycle of
racism, particularly when parents have the resources in money, time,
knowledge of the educational system, and status in the community.
Outcomes for middle-class parents may be markedly different than those
for African Americans who lack class privilege. Although one's race may
contribute to oppression on the basis of skin color, class status may
assuage at least partially the detrimental results of racist discrimination.

AFRICAN AMERICAN CULTURAL VALUES

Many of the cultural values prevalent in African American communities
originated in West Africa (Holloway, 1990). As is the case with many
nonwestern peoples, some dominant American cultural values and African
American values are often at odds. For instance, an American cultural orientation or worldview promotes individualism, competition, material
accumulation, nuclear families, religion as distinct from other parts of culture, and mastery over nature (Sue & Sue, 2003). In marked contrast,

many African Americans, particularly those with traditional worldviews, embrace values such as the significance of the collective over the individual, kinship and affiliation, extended families, spirituality, connectedness, harmony with nature, and holistic thinking (Asante & Gudykunst, 1989; Nobles, 1991). Middle-class African Americans are often likely to adopt value orientations that encompass elements from both African American and mainstream American cultural perspectives (Sue & Sue). Tiffany experienced a collision of these competing worldviews. More specifically, she did not feel a sense of belonging in either peer group and consequently felt vulnerable to feelings of confusion, uncertainty, and distress.

Code Switching

Social class variables often influence the extent to which African Americans express certain culturally derived behaviors such as code switching, a practice in which individuals alter their behavioral patterns to conform to the current environment (Celious & Oyserman, 2001). For example, an adolescent may speak and behave in the Black English vernacular when interacting with African American peers, yet modify speech and behavioral patterns to coincide with the norms and expectations valued in more integrated settings.

For some youngsters, code switching can create a certain amount of psychological distress, particularly as they negotiate various cultural settings simultaneously (i.e., home, school, church, neighborhood) that may require markedly different communication styles and responses. In such instances, students must determine which setting requires which communication style (i.e., standard vs. nonstandard English), the consequences of each communication style, and when and whether one mode of communication should take precedence over another mode. For instance, communicating in nonstandard forms of English may curry favor with peers but engender disapproval from teachers as well as negative attributions about a youngster's cognitive abilities. When communicating with peers and teachers separately, the decisions about communication patterns may be somewhat obvious. What happens, however, when a student is immersed in two environments at once, say the classroom where a teacher and peers are present? Which communication pattern will prevail and how will teachers or peers react to a youngster's communication style? These issues may pose a confusing and stressful dilemma for students in general, and for middle-class African American youngsters in particular.

Middle-class African Americans may be less likely to live in more homogeneous, segregated communities and more likely to commute regularly between several disparate cultures (i.e., home, school, community, church, peer group) that require different nuances in communication, as in Tiffany's case. Additionally, communication style is a critical factor in a youngster's development and potential for success. Any dilemma posed by this navigation can be mitigated by the use of culturally responsive counseling practices. For these youngsters to make 'situationally intelligent' decisions it would be important for counselors to first recognize code switching as an important cultural marker and to normalize the student's need to navigate multiple and simultaneous norms and values (Perry & Fraser, 1993). Lack of awareness about these and other issues may leave counselors ill-equipped to work effectively with African American adolescents.

The Extended Family and The Church

Relative to cultural values, two institutions have weighed prominently in African American life – the extended family and the church. The extended family provides considerable social and emotional support for its members and consists of nonfictive, biological relatives such as grandparents, aunts, uncles, and cousins as well as fictive family members composed of close friends and associates (Billingsley & Caldwell, 1991). Traditionally, extended family members have participated actively in the growth and development of African American children. As African Americans prosper and employment opportunities move them away from extended family networks, close family ties require more effort to maintain (Tatum, 1999). Given Tiffany's residence in a predominantly White community it is possible that she experiences a sense of geographical dislocation from other African Americans.

The church has also served a significant role in the socialization of African American youngsters. In particular, the church has provided educational support, religious guidance, mentoring, pastoral counseling, financial assistance, and political activism as mechanisms for enhancing social and cultural outcomes (Richardson & June, 1997).

Culturally responsive school counselors can use what they know about the cultural attributes of African American youngsters to foster the familiar cultural contexts to which youngsters are accustomed and subsequently improve counseling outcomes. To know someone is to know her or his culture. Far too often the culture of the home and the culture of the school remain unsynchronized for minority children (Patton & Day-Vines, 2003). Culturally responsive counselors accommodate the emerging demands of children from culturally distinct groups. As such they recognize students' culturally derived behaviors, and interpret those behaviors appropriately and without construing such behavior as peculiar or inferring pathology in a student. Moreover, culturally responsive counselors demonstrate comfort exploring and processing the specific and unique manner in which culture may impact a student's values, viewpoints, and interpretation of stimuli. Unequipped with the requisite knowledge of culture, counselors may inadvertently avoid, ignore, overlook, or minimize the contextual dimensions of race, culture, and class.

Even as the shared cultural values of African Americans are examined, one should remember that a marked degree of heterogeneity or intra-group difference exists within any group and that social class may influence the manifestation of these cultural attributes (Pedersen, 1994; Sue & Sue, 2003). Conceptualizing information in terms of broad or modal characteristics of groups precludes one from viewing all groups as monolithic entities.

IDENTITY AS AN IMPORTANT CORRELATE
IN THE COUNSELING PROCESS

Psychologists and other social scientists underscore the importance of identity and belonging as a means of achieving psychological anchorage and acceptance. White and Parham (1990) defined identity as "the adoption of certain personal attitudes, feelings, characteristics, and behaviors and the identification with a larger group of people who share those characteristics" (p. 42). Bulhan (1979) defined identity as a core human need that reflects the manner in which an individual defines self in relationship to other group members. Lack of a sense of connectedness or identity leads to nihilism, or what West (1993) defined as a "profound sense of psychological depression, personal worthlessness, and social despair" (p. 13). Analogously, Erikson (1955) contended that failure to sort out identity issues leads to a bifurcated sense of self. Some researchers have documented the protective function of positive ethnic and racial identities (Goodstein & Ponterotto, 1997; Poindexter-Cameron & Robinson, 1997; Smith, Walker, Fields, Brookins, & Seay, 1999).

Given the importance of identity to healthy development, school counselors should seriously consider addressing identity issues in the context of counseling. Racial identity development theory permits counselors to understand the unfolding transformations that occur in individuals as they transition from stages wherein ethnic and racial group membership have limited salience to students, through to positions and statuses wherein ethnic and racial group membership become prominent and well-integrated features of students' lives. Elsewhere Vandiver (2001) has discussed, in more depth, racial identity development theory and implications for counseling.

Triple Quandary

Boykin and Toms (1985) proposed that African Americans, in general, and children, in particular, have the difficult task of integrating three distinct identities. Referred to as the "triple quandary," these identities are at once complex, competing, and contradictory. Boykin and Toms argued convincingly that this quandary reflects three interlocking arenas of experience or consciousness that include (a) mainstream American, (b) minority, and (c) African American identities.

First, African American children receive socialization experiences into mainstream American culture by virtue of their existence within the dominant culture. These socialization experiences might include a predilection for television, computers, and peer involvement as well as the adoption of certain American cultural values such as individualism, competition, and the accumulation of material goods. These preferences often derive more from one's upbringing in American culture than they do from membership in a particular racial group.

Second, for African American children, socialization occurs based on their minority status as members of a race who suffer victimization and oppression. For instance, many African Americans learn early on that their minority group status predisposes them to discriminatory treatment and constant reminders about their subordinate position in a society that devalues blackness. Often, these lessons begin during childhood. Residence in more integrated communities may increase the likelihood that middle-class African Americans endure certain indignities because of skin color. For example, when White peers are invited to attend a social event or gathering, an African American child might be excluded from participating primarily on the basis of skin color (Tatum, 1997). Within the case study, Tiffany's Caucasian peers questioned the legitimacy of her residence in an affluent community and her parents' occupations, and instead endorsed stereotypical constructions of financial well-being among African Americans. This particular kind of racial discrimination may be less of an issue for children from the lower socioeconomic levels who may reside in largely segregated communities.

At school, African American children may not be encouraged to take rigorous classes and may instead be urged to pursue vocational versus college preparatory programs of study. Similarly, African Americans remain over-represented in special education programs and underrepresented in gifted education programs, often being recommended for lower-level courses (Patton, 1998). Such experiences erode the emotional well-being of African American children, and parents frequently find themselves trying to overcompensate for the psychic wounds inflicted upon their children's personhood.

Third, socialization experiences prompt African American children to become conscious of their status as African Americans with a rich heritage linked to the West African cultural experience. Some African

American children may be exposed to African American history in their homes, churches, and social organizations. Other youngsters may even participate in Kwanzaa, an African American cultural celebration, learn facets of African and African American history that have been excluded from school curricula, or surround themselves with images and themes that validate and affirm the African American experience. In either case, possession of ethnic artifacts and literature as well as exposure to cultural events and information tends to be a prerogative of the middle class. As an example, poor families may have less disposable income after paying for food, shelter, child care, and transportation.

Boykin and Toms (1985) argued that a healthy identity rests upon successful, simultaneous negotiations of each of these three identity domains. Given that many middle-class African American adolescents often find themselves in integrated educational and residential settings (Graham, 1999; Tatum, 1999), it seems plausible that many of these youngsters would have multi-dimensional identity structures that accommodate the separate contexts in which they have been socialized. For Tiffany and many other middle-class African American adolescents, socialization within an American and an African American identity can pose dilemmas because the two identity structures often function as antithetical forces. Negotiating two or more opposing cultural forces can create tension, inner turmoil, and psychological distress for some African American adolescents. Tiffany struggles to gain acceptance by both her African American and Caucasian peers. Culturally responsive school counselors who recognize these potential dilemmas are in a better position to provide supportive and encouraging counseling interventions for African American adolescents. Recognition of the identity issues students confront permits counselors to recognize healthy and unhealthy identity functioning, provide more accurate case conceptualizations of students' concerns, facilitate students' self-understanding, and promote self-acceptance. Fordham's (1988) discussion of fictive kinship networks provides an appropriate illustration of the personal conflict that can result when youngsters experience difficulty reconciling multiple aspects of their identity.

INTRA-RACIAL ISSUES
Fictive Kinship Networks
In her study of high-achieving African American high-school students, Fordham (1988) concluded that successful students are plagued with the burden of choosing between either social acceptance by peer group members or academic success. More precisely, Fordham contended that the peer group, which she termed "fictive kinship networks," discourages stu-

dents from pursuing scholastic achievement. In effect, fictive kinship networks espouse a set of values that operate as the direct antithesis of mainstream American cultural values, which concomitantly endorse individualism, achievement, and success. The particular value orientation sanctioned by fictive kinship networks demonstrates racial solidarity among group members and operates as an oppositional response to mainstream American cultural values.

Torn between two competing value systems, fictive kinship networks on the one hand and mainstream American cultural values on the other, achievement-oriented African American students such as Tiffany, who elect mainstream American cultural values, often endure ridicule and ostracism from members of the fictive kinship network. For instance, students who choose to excel academically may be accused of "talking White" or more precisely speaking standard English versus vernacular English such as Ebonics. Other students may encounter criticism for participating in activities sparsely populated with African Americans such as lacrosse, the debate team, or swim teams. Even establishing friendships outside African American peer groups or listening to music regarded as having a White orientation may subject a youngster to relentless censure.

For many African American adolescents, an orientation toward dominant cultural values exacts a hefty price at the expense of healthy identity functioning and psychological well-being (Fordham, 1988). Under these circumstances, high achieving students must make a mutually exclusive choice between loyalty to fictive kinship networks and adherence to dominant cultural values. As such, Fordham noted that given limited alternatives, students who opt for academic achievement frequently adopt a "raceless persona" in which they, in many respects, ignore and minimize any vestiges of an African American racial identity to obtain the accouterments of success. Relatedly, Tiffany and other middle-class youngsters often find themselves belonging to several different communities at once – the neighborhood community, the school community, the African American peer group, and the church group – yet never realizing a sense of belonging in any setting. Although discussed in a separate context, Lorde (1984) referred to this phenomenon as the "outsider within," meaning that membership in a particular group does not guarantee belonging and connection to others. As a member of the gymnastics team, the orchestra, and one of few African Americans in her class, Tiffany feels a sense of personal isolation from her White peers with whom she only seems to share academic and athletic interests. Tiffany's distress seems to result from the fact that, unlike her White peers, shared interests and sustained contact with other youngsters does not seem to engender more close friendships for her. Among her African American peers, Tiffany seems only to share a commonality in racial group membership.

Successful counseling interventions with middleclass African American clients must explore these critical social issues and offer, by way of remedy, the proposition that students can occupy space within fictive kinship networks and the American cultural mainstream simultaneously. Although the values of each group appear diametrically opposed, they do not have to be mutually exclusive. Students need not adopt a raceless persona. Indeed, it is possible both to have a strong African American identity and to maintain an orientation toward success. In support of this contention, the professional literature propounds a theoretical and empirical relationship between racial identity and psychological well-being. In a similar study of gifted African American high school students, Townsend and Patton (1995) provide elaborate responses from students regarding their experiences navigating between three separate and distinct experiences: (a) mainstream American culture; (b) African American culture, and (c) gifted culture. The authors documented the importance of maintaining an awareness of conflicts experienced by students and implementing culturally mediated social development enhancement strategies. Townsend and Patton endorse a culturally affirming framework that integrates African and African American cultural norms and orientations historically associating effort with success and positive outcomes. These authors contend that progressing one's knowledge and functioning has been a valued tradition of people of African descent from classical to contemporary times. They argue, in fact, that excelling academically is consonant with being African American and thus expressive of the values of hard work, upward mobility, and success as has been attained by those of middle-class status. In contrast to Fordham (1988), Townsend and Patton maintain that many African American students are just as likely to express achievement as a condition of being African American, taking the position that to do otherwise would be to deny their 'Blackness." Under these conditions, many African American students choose not to deny their racial identity. Although Tiffany has encountered considerable difficulty, she has adopted an orientation in which she is working to occupy both a success orientation and membership with African American peers without compromising either position. Culturally responsive counseling interventions would help Tiffany recognize that her feelings of distress and her difficulty reconciling two competing worldviews is normal for students who navigate two dissimilar cultural settings.

Politics of Hair and Skin Color

The politics of hair and skin color has been a contentious intra-racial issue within the African American community, irrespective of social class

(Robinson & Howard-Hamilton, 2000). This phenomena stems back to slavery and the practice of miscegenation, when slave masters accorded preferential treatment and status to their bi-racial offspring who usually had lighter skin and straighter hair textures (Okazawa-Rey, Robinson, & Ward, 1987). Following the demise of slavery, many African Americans continued to assign greater value to individuals who approximated a White European aesthetic. Even today, many African American youngsters endure teasing and ridicule because of their appearance, especially individuals who lie at either extreme along the skin color and hair texture continuum. These experiences can erode one's feelings of self-worth and sense of personal adequacy (Holcomb-McCoy & Moore-Thomas, 2001). In the context of counseling, some African American adolescents may need reassurance about their appearance, strategies for coping with their perceptions of physical attractiveness, skills to resist internalizing negative messages imposed by society, and opportunities to openly process their experiences and reactions about issues of hair and skin color. Reinforcing notions of self-acceptance represents an appropriate counseling strategy. Although Tiffany did not cite the politics of hair and skin color as a presenting concern, a culturally responsive counselor should demonstrate an openness towards addressing such sensitive issues when they arise in a manner that validates and affirms the child. It is critically important that counselors not avoid these topics because of their personal discomfort or because they do not recognize these issues as artifacts of culture.

Geographic Dislocation

The civil rights movement of the 1960s resulted in unprecedented growth of the Black middle class. Upward social mobility and fewer housing restrictions contributed to large numbers of African Americans flocking from urban settings to suburban White communities. Although important outcomes of this movement included better schools and improved housing conditions, these new residential patterns dislocated many African Americans from predominantly Black social outlets and extended family networks (Tatum, 1999). For adolescents, manifestations of this phenomenon often meant being the only African American in a class or activity, lacking a Black peer group, and being isolated from the African American community that had served as an important socializing agent for many of their parents. School counselors should recognize that isolation from the African American community could prompt adolescents to adopt a raceless persona described by Fordham (1988). Maintaining such attitudes leaves youngsters ill-prepared for the often inevitable experiences they encounter when confronted with racism and discrimination and is particularly salient for African American youngsters once they reach puberty and their peer relationships change with the onset of the dating process (Tatum).

School counselors can help foster well-being by permitting youngsters to verbalize and sort through these issues in an accepting environment. During the counseling process, Tiffany's counselor can explore the extent to which her geographic dislocation impacts her relationship with both her African American and Caucasian peers as well as identify strategies that will help reduce her current stress level and enhance her ability to maneuver successfully between both peer groups. An appropriate counseling goal is to help Tiffany become bi-cultural or multicultural, such that she functions equally well in African American, mainstream American, or other cultural settings. Culturally responsive counselors recognize the central properties of mainstream American and African American culture, promote bi-cultural functioning by affirming and validating both cultural orientations, normalizing the demands and expectations of each cultural group, and helping students maneuver fluidly between both cultures.

COUNSELING RECOMMENDATIONS

In this section we enumerate a number of strategies that counselors can implement when counseling middle-class African American adolescents. These strategies integrate what is known about the cultural values, social institutions, peer expectations, and racial identity functioning of African American adolescents into the school counselor's repertoire. Such strategies can help decrease African American adolescents' dissatisfaction with the counseling process and reduce premature termination rates, while simultaneously accommodating the students' backgrounds during the counseling process. School counselors can capitalize on the significance that African Americans place on social relationships by fostering relationships that parallel the familiar cultural experiences of many African American youngsters. Cultivation of favorable counseling climates serves as a prerequisite for establishing trusting relationships that cannot be understated (Ford, 1997). Failure to do so can have adverse consequences on the therapeutic alliance and contribute to dissatisfaction and early termination.

Individual Counseling

Initially, counselors may confront concerns of African American adolescents during individual counseling. In most instances, students will not seek counseling because of their race or social class; however, issues of race and class may be embedded in their presenting problems. Counselors should be cognizant of these hidden issues and approach counseling with an aura of acceptance and openness in an effort to understand the complex interaction between race, culture, and class. Further, a student's perception that a counselor does not comprehend contextual variables related to race and class may lead to superficial self-disclosures, unhelpful counseling interventions, dissatisfaction with counseling services, and premature termination. Counselors must exude comfort in addressing the sociopolitical issues of race and class.

Tiffany's counselor recognized the complexities of race and class and created a safe environment in which she could talk openly. The counselor demonstrated an interest in Tiffany and probed Tiffany for a more complete understanding of Tiffany's concerns. Had the counselor made a literal interpretation of Tiffany's request to change classes the counselor would have missed important contextual dimensions of Tiffany's presenting problem. Instead, the counselor broached the subject of race and class by asking Tiffany how the dearth of African Americans in accelerated classes influenced her decision to pursue less rigorous coursework. This accurate conceptualization of Tiffany's dilemma made Tiffany feel understood and helped her self-disclose. Such a question serves a diagnostic purpose. If the student does not perceive that race or class may be germane to the counseling concern, the student is likely to say so. If the student recognizes the impact of race and class on that concern, the student may feel comfortable exploring those issues in more depth and be willing to articulate concerns that might otherwise be withheld for fear the counselor lacks insight regarding the Black experience.

Culturally responsive school counselors should be comfortable enough to allow a student to explore feelings, concerns, and perceptions without becoming defensive or de-legitimizing the student's problems, especially when the student addresses the issue of racism. Appropriate strategies for processing concerns about racism may be to allow the student to sort through the concerns in a nonjudgmental fashion. The counselor should exercise caution and not permit the student to wallow in self-pity or maladaptive criticisms of school personnel. Instead, the counselor may help the student devise strategies for coping with and confronting racism appropriately.

Given the embeddedness of racism and discrimination in our society, counselors may need to perform alternative roles as advocates and change agents in which counselors work within the system to institute changes in school policy or climate (Sue & Sue, 2003). This strategy may require counselors to conduct in-service training on topics such as diversity, advocate on behalf of students, and model appropriate behavior in efforts to improve the social and educational experiences of African American adolescents. Counselors must also recognize that although interracial tensions consume a considerable amount of psychic energy of African American adolescents, so too do intra-racial issues such as fictive kinship networks and the politics of hair and skin color.

Group Counseling

Group counseling permits adolescents to process their individual and collective experience, learn coping strategies, and feel less isolated. Incidentally, this particular counseling modality incorporates communal dynamics that are valued among many African Americans (Ford, 1997). Of course, such a group would likely not convene around issues pertaining to middle-class status, especially since, as hooks (2000) notes, people are quite reticent about issues of social class. Although social class may not be the presenting problem, issues of class and race may be embedded in students' concerns. For instance, group members might express concerns about the pressure to conform to the demands of fictive kinship networks described by Fordham (1988), process the challenges associated with being one of few minorities in a class, or sort out identity issues. Tiffany's counselor recommended her for participation in a support group which would help Tiffany process some of her conflicts with other African American students who had similar concerns.

Cultural Informants

At times, school counselors may need to acquire additional information about working effectively with middle-class African American adolescents by consulting with cultural informants. Cultural informants are people who provide insight about an indigenous group who may be unfamiliar to outsiders (Patton & Day-Vines, 2003). Usually, cultural informants are bicultural, meaning they can maneuver fluently both in mainstream American culture and in their own indigenous culture, while respecting the central properties of both cultures. Often their ability to commute between two disparate cultures permits them to understand the expectations of both their own and the culture of the "other." These individuals serve as guides and have an abundance of resources upon which school counselors can capitalize. African Americans employed in the school, members of African American social and civic organizations, and personal contacts can all serve as suitable cultural informants. Tiffany's counselor consulted with an African American school counselor in her department as well as a local minister who served on the department's advisory board. Her interactions with these individuals broadened her depth of understanding of middle class African American adolescents and helped her identify culturally responsive counseling interventions for Tiffany.

REFERRALS TO AFRICAN AMERICAN ORGANIZATIONS

African American civic, social, and religious organizations in particular have functioned as enduring parts of the African American community's vitality (Day-Vines, 2000). Most notably these organizations have supplemented the social and cultural experiences of many African American children, which have been particularly important for African Americans who live in predominantly White communities. Parents may express some comfort with the academic preparation their children receive in school yet harbor concerns about their children's social experiences and limited exposure to other African Americans. To create a balance between the academic experiences at school and social experiences in the community, many parents have relied on civic and social organizations to reinforce Black culture, instill confidence, and provide positive peer groups and adult role models for their children (Graham, 1999). This struggle for balance has been especially necessary for families living in suburban communities that are sparsely populated with African Americans. These civic and social organizations often have youth components aimed at promoting healthy identity functioning, civic responsibility, leadership training, and racial uplift. An abbreviated list of national organizations with local chapters includes the National Association for the Advancement of Colored People (NAACP) and the National Urban League; fraternities such as Alpha Phi Alpha, Omega Psi Phi, Kappa Alpha Psi, and Phi Beta Sigma; and sororities such as Alpha Kappa Alpha, Delta Sigma Theta, and Sigma Gamma Rho. Counselors working with students who have limited contact with the African American community may suggest participation in these organizations and may maintain a list of local referrals they can disseminate to children and their families. Many of the social and cultural needs children have lie outside the realm of the school counselor's expertise, so counselors need to draw on resources indigenous to the Black community to complement the educational and social experiences of African American adolescents. Optimally, a counselor would maintain contacts within the Black community. Incidentally, the African American counselor who served as a cultural informant recommended that Tiffany consider membership in a civic organization.

Within the African American community, the church is considered one of the most viable institutions. Historically, the church has provided religious, spiritual, social, educational, mental health, political, and economic sustenance to its members through numerous programming and outreach ministries (Nettles, 1991). For many African Americans, seeking help external to the family is patently discouraged, yet counselees who are reluctant to work with a counselor may consider sharing their concerns with a clergy member. Richardson and June (1997) recommended that counselors form alliances with Black churches particularly because churches instill in African Americans a positive Black identity. In the case study, the minister recommended that the counselor inquire about Tiffany's church affiliation.

SUMMARY

This article addresses the interaction between race, culture, and social class and underscores that middle-class African American adolescents may have concerns that bear little relationship to poverty and its attendant pressures. Cultural conditioning may prompt some counselors to assume that all African American adolescents, irrespective of social class differences, may experience an identical set of life stressors. This belief could not be farther from the truth. Social class issues frequently affect the social experiences that people confront. A counselor working with middle-class African American adolescents needs to be attuned to the specific and unique issues that middle-class youngsters experience and avoid looking at African Americans as monolithic entities. The manifestation of culturally responsive counseling involves a deliberate effort to bridge the cultural divide through the demonstration of understanding, respect, and competence in dealing with cultural differences.

Given broad variability in income distribution among members of the Black middle class, middleclass status may better reflect a mentality, mode of thought, or value orientation geared toward social mobility and respectability (Ford, 1997). African Americans have distinctive cultural patterns and behaviors that may be mediated by factors of social class, and counselors need to recognize these issues in the context of counseling. Identity is a critical component of psychological functioning, and failure to negotiate identity issues can create personal distress for some youngsters.

An important part of the counseling process may involve referrals to other individuals and institutions that have demonstrated respect and authority in the African American community. These individuals and agencies serve as positive role models to African American youngsters by maintaining and promoting a positive African American experience. Culturally responsive counselors recognize the student first as an individual and then in a cultural context in an effort to avoid some of the stereotyping that can have negative consequences during the counseling process. School counselors can attain some familiarity with and understanding of social issues such as fictive kinship networks, the politics of hair and skin color, and the impact geographic dislocation can have on youngsters.

Maintaining current referral lists, contacts within the Black community, and access to cultural informants are all skills on which school counselors can rely to improve their responsiveness to and multicultural competence with African American adolescents. A counselor who has some familiarity with the specific and unique issues that concern middle-class African American youngsters is better poised to listen empathically, recognize the relationships between race and social class, and less likely to discount or unintentionally avoid prominent features of adolescents' lives.

Norma L. Day-Vines, Ph.D., is an assistant professor. James M.Patton, Ed.D., is a professor. Both are with the School of Education, The College of William and Mary, Williamsburg, VA. Joy L. Baytops is a specialist, Teacher Quality Enhancement, Virginia Department of Education, Richmond.

REFERENCES

Asante, M. K.,& Gudykunst, W. (Eds.). (1989). *Handbook of international and intercultural communication*. Newbury Park, CA: Sage.

Billingsley, A., & Caldwell, C. H. (1991).The church, the family, and the school in the African American community. *Journal of Negro Education, 60,* 427–440.

Boykin, A., & Toms, F. (1985). Black child socialization: A conceptual framework. In H.McAdoo & J.McAdoo (Eds.), *Black children: Social, educational, and parental environments* (pp. 33–51). Beverly Hills, CA: Sage.

Bulhan, H. (1979). Black psyches in captivity and crises. *Race and Class, 22,* 243–251.

Celious, A., & Oyserman, D. (2001). Race from the inside: An emerging heterogeneous race model. *Journal of Social Issues, 57,* 149–165.

Conley, D. (1999). *Being Black, living in the red: Race,wealth and social policy in America*. Berkeley: University of California Press.

Day-Vines, N. (2000). Ethics, power, and privilege: Salient issues in the development of multicultural competencies for teachers serving African American children with disabilities. *Teacher Education and Special Education, 23*(1), 3–18.

Erikson, E. (1955). *Identity: Youth and crisis*. New York: Norton.

Ford, D. (1997). Counseling middle-class African Americans. In C. Lee (Ed.), *Multicultural issues in counseling: New approaches to diversity* (2nd ed., pp. 81–107). Alexandria, VA: American Counseling Association.

Fordham, S. (1988). Racelessness as a factor in Black students' school success: Pragmatic strategy or pyrrhic victory. *Harvard Educational Review, 58*, 54–84.

Gay, G. (2000). *Culturally responsive teaching: Theory, research, and practice.* New York: Teachers College Press.

Goodstein, L., & Ponterotto, J. (1997). Racial and ethnic identity: Their relationship and contribution to self-esteem. *Journal of Black Psychology, 23*, 275–292.

Graham, L. (1999). *Our kind of people: Inside America's black upper class.* New York: Harper Collins.

Holcomb-McCoy, C., & Moore-Thomas, C. (2001). Empowering African American adolescent females. *Professional School Counseling, 5*, 19–25.

Holloway, J. (1990). The origins of African American culture. In J. Holloway (Ed.), *Africanisms in American culture* (pp. 1–18). Bloomington, IN: Indiana University Press.

Hooks, B. (2000). *Where we stand: Class matters.* New York: Routledge.

Lee, C. (2001). Culturally responsive school counselors and programs: Addressing the needs of all students. *Professional School Counseling, 4*, 257–261.

Lorde, A. (1984). *Sister outsider: Essays and speeches.* New York: Book of the Month Club.

McIntosh, P. (1989, July/August).White privilege: Unpacking the invisible knapsack. *Peace and Freedom*, pp. 10–12.

Nettles, S. (1991). Community contributions to school outcomes of African-American students. *Education and Urban Society, 24*, 132–147.

Nobles, W. (1991). African philosophy: Foundations for Black psychology. In R. Jones (Ed.), *Black Psychology* (3rd ed., pp. 47–53). Berkeley, CA: Cobb & Henry.

Okazawa-Rey, M., Robinson,T., & Ward, J. (1987). Black women and the politics of skin color and hair. *Women and Therapy, 6*, 89–102.

Patton, J. M. (1998).The disproportionate representation of African Americans in special education: Looking behind the curtain for understanding and solutions. *The Journal of Special Education, 32*(1), 25–31.

Patton, J.,& Day-Vines, N. (2003). *Strategies to guide the training of special and general education teachers.* Williamsburg, VA: The College of William and Mary, School of Education.

Pedersen, P. (1994). *A handbook for developing multicultural awareness* (2nd ed.). Alexandria,VA: American Counseling Association.

Perry, T., & Fraser, J. (Eds.). (1993). *Freedom's plow: Teaching in the multicultural classroom.* NY: Routledge.

Poindexter-Cameron, J., & Robinson, T. (1997). Relationships among racial identity attitudes,womanist identity attitudes, and self-esteem in African American college women. *Journal of College Student Development, 38,* 288–296.

Richardson, L., & June, L. (1997). Utilizing and maximizing the resources of the African American church: Strategies and tools for counseling professionals. In C. Lee (Ed.), *Multicultural issues in counseling: New approaches to diversity* (2nd ed., pp. 155–170). Alexandria,VA: American Counseling Association.

Robinson, T., & Howard-Hamilton, M. (2000). *The convergence of race, ethnicity,and gender: Multiple identities in counseling.* Upper Saddle River, NJ:Merrill.

Smith, E., Walker, K., Fields, L., Brookins, C., & Seay, R. (1999). Ethnic identity and its relationship to self-esteem, perceived efficacy and prosocial attitudes in early adolescence. *Journal of Adolescence, 22,* 867–880.

Sue, D., & Sue, D. (2003). *Counseling the culturally different: Theory and practice* (4th ed.). New York: John Wiley.

Tatum, B. (1997). *"Why are all the Black kids sitting together in the cafeteria?"and other conversations about race.* New York: Basic Books.

Tatum, B. (1999). *Assimilation blues: Black families in white communities: Who succeeds and why?* New York: Basic Books.

Townsend, B. L., Patton, J. M. (1995). *Three "warring souls" of African American high school students.* (ERIC Document Reproduction Service No. ED400250).

U. S. Census Bureau. (2000). *Poverty in the United States: 2000.* Washington, DC: U.S.Government Printing Office.

Vandiver, B. (2001). Psychological nigrescence revisited: Introduction and overview. *Journal of Multicultural Counseling and Development, 29,* 165–173

Walker, L., & Wilson, B. (2002). *Black Eden: The Idlewild community.* East Lansing,MI:Michigan State University.

West, C. (1993). *Race matters.* Boston: Beacon Press.

White, J. L., & Parham,T. A. (1990). *The psychology of Blacks: An African American perspective* (2nd ed.). Englewood Cliffs, NJ: Prentice Hall.

Wiley, R. (1992). *Why Black people tend to shout: Cold facts and wry views from a Black man's World.* New York: Penguin.

Homosexuality: A Blind Spot in the School Mirror

By Rita M. Marinoble

This article originally appeared in *Professional School Counseling*, Vol. 1, No.3, 1998.

A favorite self-esteem activity among elementary school children involves listening to a story about a "very special person" who can be seen by opening a colorful box. One-by-one the children lft the lid, peer inside, and see their own reflection in a mirror glued to the bottom of the empty box. Most children giggle with glee, pride, or self-consciousness. It is fun, and it encourages children to feel good about the person they see in the mirror.

For some children though, the mirror begins to develop a blind spot – a part of themselves that they cannot see or, at best, cannot bring into focus. As these children progress through children and adolescence, their schools, families and communities, often collaborate to reinforce the blind spot. The results of this collaboration may range from mild to tragic.

The blind spot is homosexuality – a sexual orientation that appears to be natural for approximately 10% of the population. It is safe to say that the same percentage can be applied to school children; that is, approximately 10% will eventually come to identify themselves as gay or lesbian (Schneider, 1988). When driving an automobile, a blind spot can be very dangerous. When looking at oneself, a blind spot can have serious consequences. This article focuses on the issues and challenges that confront school counselors in working with students who begin to exhibit a homosexual orientation during their school years.

DIFFICULTIES EXPERIENCED

While not all sexual minority youth experience difficulties in growing up, a number of issues frequently confront students who begin to perceive themselves as gay or lesbian. These include identity conflict, feelings of isolation and stigmatization, peer relationship problems, and family disruptions (Friends of Project 10, 1989). Each of these difficulties will be discussed in terms of how it may manifest itself, and possibly be aggravated, in the school setting.

Identity Conflict

Growing up is, for all children, a process of discovering who they are in relationship to self and others. In a predominantly heterosexual society tha tconstatnly and pervasively reinforces heterosexual behavior, it is inevitable that some type of identity conflict will occur for most persons who have a homosexual orientation. It is not always easy to see manifestations of identity conflict in gay and lesbian students, but many homosexual adults who reflect on their childhoods can recall going through such a conflict. Whether manifested or not, there is a sense of being somehow different than the world expects them to be, and this is a source of considerable identity conflict for most homosexual students (Gonsiorek, 1988).

Traditional schooling contributes heavily to the identity conflicts experienced by gay and lesbian youth. Books, films, classroom discussions, guest speakers, and field trips almost always reinforce heterosexual norms and values. Lesbian and gay adults – teachers or other school staff members – most often are closeted, thus depriving gay and lesbian youth of positive role models. Occasional training may be given to counselors regarding gay and lesbian students, but the overall school climate rarely supports positive identity development among these young people.

Feelings of Isolation and Stigmatization

Perhaps the most extreme and most tragic example of the isolation and stigmatization felt by gay and lesbian youth was provided in 1989 when a federal task force conducted a study on youth suicide. Results indicated that suicide is the number one cause of death among lesbian and gay teenagers, and that suicide attempts occur two or three times more often among homosexual teens than among heterosexual teens (U.S. Department of Health and Human Services, 1989). Although much social progress has been made in de-stigmatizing homosexuality, it continues to be feared and misunderstood by many people. While suicide is certainly the extreme case, there is no doubt that feelings of isolation and stigmatization occur for many students who discover their homosexual orientation.

Gay and lesbian students frequently may shy away from social activities that involve the presumption of heterosexuality. They may find themselves victims of name-calling by other students who suspect their homosexual orientation. In some cases, the isolation results in run-away behaviors or academic problems that seem to have no logical explanation. Many lesbian and gay students exhibit depression and anxiety that seems inconsistent with the visible aspects of their lives.

The school environment often intensifies the isolation and stigmatization felt by gay and lesbian students (Rofes, 1989). Counselors and teachers fail to reprimand students who make derogatory remarks or joke about homosexuality. As social rituals begin, students are presumed to be interested in dating a person of the opposite sex. Students who are brave enough to express concern about their sexual orientation often encounter homophobic teachers, counselors, or administrators who fail to adequately address the issue or make an appropriate referral. Academic difficulties are assumed to have academic explanations, or, if they have emotional explanations, they do no tinclude the possibility of a sexual orientation issue.

Peer Relationship Problems

Gay and lesbian students frequently exhibit difficulties in their interactions with peers. Sometimes these students keep a safe distance from other students by excelling academically but declining to participate in extracurricular or social activities. Homosexual adolescents often have trouble establishing close friendships, either for fear of being discovered to have homosexual feelings, or from an inability to identify with the majority of students who are developing the more typical heterosexual interests. Self-consciousness, awkwardness, and worries about acceptance often plague homosexual students, diminishing their opportunities to interact in a normal and relaxed fashion with their peers, both in and out of the classroom.

Ideally, schools should be places for children to learn how to interact with others. When peer difficulties present themselves, school personnel usually seek to help children resolve them. Unfortunately, when an important dimension of the problem is obscured from view, as is often the case with homosexual students, the solutions are tenuous at best. Once again, schools can aggravate the problem by failing to include sexual orientation as a possible factor in peer relationship difficulties.

Family Disruptions

Family attitudes toward homosexuality are varied. Some homosexual students find considerable acceptance from their families. Frequently, however, the suspicion or confirmation that a child in the family has a homosexual orientation is met with negative responses ranging from mild panic to total rejection. As with other familial conflicts, students bring these experiences to their learning environment at school. Unexplained anger, hostility, depression, or inability to concentrate are among the possible manifestations of family disruption experienced by the homosexual student. In some cases a parent may consult the school about a child's problems, neglecting to mention the sexual orientation issue. As the web of silence expands, the student may be driven deeper into feelings of inadequacy and rejection.

Although schools continue to recognize the need for partnership with families in helping children succeed, most educators are reluctant to bring up the sexual orientation issue with parents or guardians. It is a sensitive area, and the path of least resistance is often most appealing. By ignoring this possibility, however, the family and school may be collaborating to diminish the homosexual student's opportunities for a successful life experience.

CREATING A SUPPORTIVE LEARNING ENVIRONMENT

Regardless of when students become aware of their homosexuality, the learning environment is a significant factor in how these students ultimately will deal with their sexual orientation (Friends, 1989). At all grade levels, counselors can play an important role in promoting a helpful school environment for gay/lesbian students. School policies, curriculum, support services, and staff development are the primary areas to be addressed. Awareness and action in each of these areas is essential in meeting the learning needs of homosexual students.

School Policies

If the learning climate is to be inclusive and equitable, school policies must be sensitive to the issue of homosexuality. While administrators have primary responsibility in this area, counselors can exert their influence in an advisory capacity to principals and policy-making committees. Some suggested strategies include:

- Lobby for the inclusion of sexual orientation in the language of nondiscrimination clauses of teacher contracts and in written school policy regarding treatment of students and parents.
- Establish and enforce a school policy that forbids slurs and jokes regarding homosexuality.
- Mandate human relations sessions for staff and students that include sexual diversity issues.
- Allow books that portray homosexuality in a positive manner to be included in school libraries.
- Permit gay/lesbian topics to be mentioned in school newspapers and other school publications.

Curriculum

In meeting the learning needs of homosexual students, school texts and other aspects of school curriculum are vital areas for attention. On a daily basis, children formulate images of themselves and their lives based on what they see, hear, and experience in their curriculum. Even before discovering their homosexuality; students must form positive images if they are to eventually deal with this difference in themselves in a positive manner. Some suggested strategies include:

- Urge curriculum committees to adopt texts that accurately portray gay/lesbian history and their culture.
- Present the topic of homosexuality in realistic – not homophobic – terms. This requires reducing reducing homophobia among school staff, which will be addressed later in the staff development section.
- Encourage teachers to select classroom reading materials that portray gays and lesbians in an accurate and positive light, including information on families where the parent is gay and lesbian.
- Use lesbian or gay guest speakers. These could be parents or other community members who might have something to share about accepting differences among people.
- Assist teachers in developing lesson plans for discussing gay/lesbian issues in the context of contemporary community or world events.
- Use nongender-specific language in discussing relationships of a serious nature (e.g., "partner" or "significant other").
- Use film and video to positively reflect lesbian and gay lives, and acknowledge the sexual orientation of persons who have made historical contributions (e.g. James Baldwin, Gertrude Stein, Walt Whitman, and many others).

Support Services

Counselors usually fall within this category in terms of school organization. Also included are nurses, psychologists, and other support personnel. It is in this area that the informed school counselor can probably exert the most direct influence. Since 1988, the National Education Association's annual meeting has included among its resolutions an affirmation of the need for attention to gay/lesbian issues in the schools. Resolution C-26, entitled "Student Sexual Orientation," states

All persons, regardless of sexual orientation, should be afforded equal opportunity within the public education system. The Association further believes that every school district should provide counseling by trained personnel for students who are struggling with their sexual orientation. (The 1992-93 Resolutions of the National Education Association, 1992, p. 27.)

Most districts around the country have done little to implement this important resolution. Some suggested strategies include:

- Place gay/lesbian-sensitive literature in the offices of counselors and nurses. Include pamphlets about support groups for gay/lesbian teens and genera information about homosexuality. This literature can be displayed appropriately among the many other items regarding student well-being that are typically found in these offices.

- Conduct parent information meetings that address the topic of homosexuality in a realistic, accurate, and sensitive manner.
- Select a staff member at every school site who can function as a resource person for gay/lesbian students or issues.
- Become familiar with community agencies and programs that serve gay/lesbian youth and make referrals when appropriate. Visit these programs before making referrals.

Staff Development

Most educational organizations recognize the need for staff development in order to create and maintain the best possible learning experience for students. Typical staff development offerings cover a broad range of topics, but in many cases give little or no attention to the area of homosexuality. Educators in all settings and at all levels need accurate information about homosexuality and about gay/lesbian students if they are to teach and serve these young people appropriately. Often the school counselor can serve as the impetus behind improving staff development in this area.

To better prepare for this role, school counselors should consider incorporating the gay/lesbian topic into their own professional development plans. Attendance at conference workshops, exchanging information with colleagues, and regular reading of new books and articles are examples of helpful professional development activities. These activities not only improve the counselor's effectiveness with gay and lesbian students, but also enhance the counselor's readiness to plan and implement staff development programs. Some suggested staff development strategies include:

- Conduct in-service training that is designed to inform all staff members about homosexuality, to reduce/eliminate homophobia, and to provide ideas for working with gay/lesbian students. Some offerings could be broad in scope, with others designed for specific areas of expertise such as teachers, counselors and nurses.
- Provide extensive training for selected staff members who will then train others to become resource persons for each school site.
- Support lesbian or gay staff members who wish to serve as role models for students. Use these individuals in assemblies, parent meetings, staff training, and elsewhere in order to affirm them as both knowledgeable resources and appropriate role models. School counselors who themselves are openly lesbian or gay are in a unique and important position to guide their colleagues in this process.

- Urge principals to release teachers and support staff members to visit community agencies that serve gay/lesbian youth so that they are better informed about issues and available services.

Implementation of some of the suggestions in these four areas can go a long way toward making schooling a more positive and supportive experience for students who ave a homosexual orientation. There are many additional benefits as well. All students gain from a learning environment that acknowledges and affirms diversity in every aspect of life. Students who may have a parent who is gay or lesbian – and there are far more of these students than meet the eye – receive important support for their own unique family dynamics. Lesbian and gay staff members may be helped to achieve fuller integration of their own lives, many of which have remained fragmented, partly as a result of early schooling that in no way affirmed their sexual orientation.

CONCLUSION

The analogy of a blind spot in the mirror expresses the frequent invisibility of homosexuality as a concern in the lives of many young people. It is hoped the information contained here can somehow contribute to elimination of this dangerous blind spot for educators and others who help children to succeed in school and in life. Since awareness of a homosexual orientation sometimes occurs quite early in life, it is vital that school counselors at all levels be active and informed in addressing this topic.

There are countless testimonials from gay and lesbian adults for the need to attend to these issues. One such testimonial was shared by a lesbian educator at a teacher's form on gay/lesbian concerns in the schools. She concluded as follows:

My journey would have been much less painful if, in those earlier years, I had received some sense that my feelings were not horrible and deviant, some hint that there were others like me, or some examples of healthy adults with a homosexual orientation. Perhaps a teacher or counselor could have provided that assistance, but they did not, and so for a longtime I struggled alone. I encourage all adults who work with children to be mindful that homosexuality is reality of the world, and that young people struggling with issues of sexual orientation need understanding, support and love. (Marinoble,1992, p. 6.)

As with so many challenges in education, only a concerted effort by all will yield the desired outcome – a full measure of recognition, celebration, and support of students with a homosexual orientation.

REFERENCES

Friends of Project 10. (1989). *Project 10 handbook: Addressing gay and lesbian issues in our schools.* Los Angeles: Author.

Gonsiorek, J.C. (1988). Mental health issues of gay and lesbian adolescents. *Journal of Adolescent Health Care, 9,* 114 – 122.

Marinoble, R. (1992, May). *Reflections of a school counselor.* Paper presented at the Gay/Lesbian Educational issues forum, San Diego Teachers' Association, San Diego, CA.

Rofes, E. (1989). Opening up the classroom closet: Responding to the educational needs of gay and lesbian youth. *Harvard Educational Review, 59,* 444-453.

Schneider, M. (1988). *Often invisible: Counseling gay and lesbian youth.* Toronto: Central Toronto Youth Services.

The 1992-93 Resolutions of the National Education Association. (1992, September). *National Education Association Today,* p. 27.

U.S. Department of Health and Human Service. (1989). *Report of the secretary's task force on youth suicide.* Washington, DC: U.S. Government Printing Office.

SUGGESTED ADDITIONAL READING

Clark, D. (1987). *The new loving someone gay.* Berkeley, CA: Celestial Arts.

Fairchild, B. & Hayward, N. (1981). *Now that you know.* New York: Harcourt, Brace, Jovanovich.

Harbeck, K.M. (ed.). (1992). *Coming out of the classroom closet: Gay and lesbian students, teachers and curricula.* Binghamton, NY: Haworth Press.

Heron, A. (Ed.) (1983). *One teenager in ten: Writings by gay and lesbian youth.* Boston: Alyson Publications.

Rench, J.E. (1990). *Understanding sexual identity: A book for gay and lesbian teens and their friends.* Minneapolis, MN: Lerner Publications.

Scanzoni, L. & Mollenkott, V. (1978). *Is the homosexual my neighbor?* San Francisco: Harper & Row.

BOOKS AND OTHER RESOURCES

The following books are especially designed for use with children. They either deal primarily with gay or lesbian characters, or have a gay or lesbian character somehow incorporated into the story. These books may not be available in most libraries, but can be ordered from any large bookstore. With that in mind, the ISBN numbers are listed instead of the publishers.

For secondary school students

Fricke, A. & Fricke, W. *Sudden strangers*. (ISBN 0-312-05869-1). (A nonfiction book that deals with a father/son relationship and the son's homosexuality.)

Garden, N. *Annie on my mind*. (ISBN 374-40413-5/0325).

Garden, N. *Lark in the morning*. (ISBN 0-374-343338-1).

Koertge, R. *The Arizona kid*. (ISBN 0-380-70776-4).

For elementary school students

Heron, A. *How would you feel if your dad was gay?* (ISBN 1-55583-188-5).

Newman, L. *Gloria goes to gay pride* (ISBN 1-55583-185-0).

Newman, L. *Heather has two mommies*. (ISBN 1-55583-180-X).

These three books are part of the Alyson Wonderland series published by Alyson Publications. This publisher has an ongoing commitment to supporting children's literature that conveys positive images of gays and lesbians. Other titles are expected in the future. For more information, contact: Alyson Publications, P.O. Box 4371, Los Angeles, CA 90078 (or call: (800) 526-9766).

Other Resources

Bay Area Network of Gay and Lesbian Educators (1040 Park Avenue, San Jose, CA 95126)

Gay and Lesbian Youth Advocacy Council, 55 Mason Street, San Francisco, CA 94102.

National Federation of Parents and Friends of Lesbians and Gays, 8020 Eastern Avenue NW, Washington, DC 20012.

National Gay Youth Network, P.O. Box 846, San Francisco, CA 94101.

Project 10, c/o Dr Virginia Uribe, Fairfax High School, 7850 Melrose Avenue, Los Angeles, CA 90046.

Counseling Hispanic Students

When it comes to counseling Hispanic students, although they may have different barriers to success than other students, they require the same type of comprehensive school counseling program as every other student.

By Hilda Lopez

This article originally appeared in *ASCA School Counselor*, Vol. 43, No.3, 2006.

Two years ago, I presented a session on the topic "Counseling the Hispanic Student" at a state conference. Granted, I work in Texas, where there is a high concentration of Hispanic students, but the fact that every seat was full is testament to the degree of interest in the topic. When you look at the numbers, it's no wonder school counselors across the country are searching for information on counseling Hispanics, the fastest-growing population in the United States. In some states, such as Texas and other parts of the Southwest, they are already the "minority majority."

Nationally the Hispanic population grew 58 percent over 10 years, from 22.4 million in 1990 to 35.3 million in 2000, compared to an increase in the total population of 13.2 percent over the same time frame. The Census Bureau estimates that by the year 2020, one in five Americans will be Hispanic. The medium age of Hispanics in the United States is 24, and one-third of all Hispanics are under 18. This means that one-third of the fastest growing population are in our schools today.

When I talk about this issue with others the first question they often ask is, "What do you prefer to be called anyway? Hispanic? Latina? Mexican-American? American of Mexican descent? Chicana?" What exactly is in a name anyway? The U.S. Census Bureau classifies Hispanics as Spanish-speaking people of any race. When completing the 2000 census, people could identify themselves as Mexican, Puerto Rican, Cuban or "other Spanish/Hispanic/Latino," and more than 35 million people identified themselves as Hispanic or Latino.

A MELTING POT

So, how do you counsel Hispanic/Latino students when the very term embodies many races, nationalities, languages and cultures across various socio-economic levels? Complicate that further with the fact that some students may be undocumented immigrants, first-generation Americans or, like my husband's ancestors, their families have lived in the same area for several generations. In fact, my husband's maternal grandmother's family was in this area before Texas became an official state.

When preparing for my presentation on counseling Hispanic students, I took a good look at our own districtwide comprehensive school counseling program. My district, in El Paso, Texas, is 90.9 percent Hispanic, 6.8 percent white and 1.6 percent African American. Some 73 percent of our students are classified as economically disadvantaged, and 30 percent are considered English language learners. The question asked myself was, "Given our demographics, what are we doing different than any other school counseling program in the country?"

After much reflection, I decided the answer was, not much.

A CLOSER LOOK

Foundation: The school counselors in our district share the beliefs and philosophy that every student can achieve. Although students come to us with different barriers to learning, the barriers are never an excuse for not excelling in school. Nationally, Hispanic students lag behind students from other ethnic groups in educational attainment. Figures from March 2004 show that 18.4 percent of whites complete four or more years of college, 7.9 percent of African Americans but only 7.6 percent of Hispanics. The differences at the high school completion level are even more drastic. Ninety percent of whites complete high school, 80.6 percent of African Americans but only 58.4 percent of Hispanics.

In our district, 89 percent of the students graduate under the college preparation track, and about 60 percent enroll in a two- or four-year college. As a district we are constantly looking for and analyzing our data to help us plan. We are looking for data that will tell us how many students finish college; how long it takes them to finish; why, if almost 90 percent are prepared to attend college, only 60 percent actually enroll, etc.

We encourage students who come to our schools with a language other than English to continue developing that language in addition English. My parents used to tell me, "*El que sabe dos idiomas cuenta por dos.*" ("Those who can speak two languages count as two.") When students attend our schools, they must learn English, but programs are additive, not subtractive when it comes to the language. The learning standards set by the state and No Child Left Behind are the same standards a child in El Paso, Dallas, or Houston must master. Counselors are part of the team that looks at barriers to learning and are part of the solution as to how to remove them so students can succeed.

Delivery system: The school guidance curriculum is even more critical for Hispanic students given the number of students who are considered economically disadvantaged. The College Board's 2001 report, "Swimming Against the Tide: The Poor in American Higher Education" notes that the primary source of post-secondary information for students of low socioeconomic status is the school counselor. The report goes on to say that by the ninth grade and sometimes as early as the seventh grade students have formed occupational and educational expectations strongly related to socio-economic status. When school counselors practice "threshold counseling," i.e. we counsel only those students who walk across our threshold, we are limiting information to the masses. Students who typically seek out the counselor's help are usually top students who would make it with or without our guidance. The students who need us the most are the ones who never come and are sitting in the classrooms waiting for us.

And it's not just the students who need our help. School counselors also need to consider the needs of Hispanic parents. My mother didn't speak English when I was growing up, and both my parents had limited schooling. My parents are intelligent, but with their limited formal education, they have no knowledge on how to navigate the school system. There are many students just like me – first-generation college students who would greatly benefit from guidance lessons on a variety of topics, and their parents would benefit from your lessons as well. Don't limit your guidance lessons to students; we hold many parent meetings beginning in elementary school. As we survey our parents, the topics reflect the community of the school. What is consistent is the information we provide parents on college preparation, financial aid and college opportunities. These aren't handouts given to just the students; we encourage parents to partner in this journey of knowledge so they can support their children. Given our high number of Spanish-speaking parents, we hold many of our meetings in English and Spanish.

From the career inventory to the development of a five-year plan (four years of high school and one year of post-secondary), students are encouraged to take the most rigorous courses. School board policy has already mandated four years of math to include algebra I, algebra II, geometry and a senior-level math course, and counselors encourage a fourth year of science as well. We also encourage students to enroll in pre-advanced-placement, advanced placement and dual-credit classes. Through an agreement with the local community college, students do not pay to take the college placement class and can take dual-credit classes free of charge. Counselors look at data to see if students are taking AP, SAT and ACT exams. Last year, school counselors across the district examined data and discovered a discrepancy between the number of students who said they wanted to go to college, were prepared to go to college and then took the college entrance exams. We then made it a districtwide counseling goal to increase the number of PSAT and SAT/ACT test takers.

Management system: The use of data is one of the most critical elements in counseling students, and Hispanic students are no different. School counselors should examine their graduation rate, dropout rate, college-going rate, attendance rate and more. Are you students mastering learning standards? If not, why? And what are you going to do about it? That's were action plans come in. Develop your plan to address these student needs.

Accountability system: In our district, we annually present results reports to the superintendent, all district counselors and administrators. Sometimes the goals set are not met, but the learning and insight gained is powerful.

If you were looking for a recipe on how to counsel the Hispanic student, there is none. Have high expectations for all students, and have the system in place to figure out how to make success for all a reality. We owe it Hispanic students, to African American students, to white students, to Asian students, to every student.

Hilda Lopez is a school counselor with Socorro Independent School District in El Paso, Texas, and a judge for the Recognized ASCA Model Program (RAMP). She can be reached at hlopez06@sisd.net.

The Gender Achievement Gap Challenge

Diversity isn't just about race and socioeconomic status. Gender also plays a role, particular when it comes to achievement in schools.

By Mary Ann Clark, Ph.D., Erin Oakley, Ed.S., and Heather Adams

This article originally appeared in *ASCA School Counselor*, Vol. 43, No. 3, 2006.

"Mom, why do you think I should put all these projects and tests on a calendar? All I have to do is look at my assignment book the night before something is due, and I can work on it then. It's too confusing to think about all of these assignments at the same time." A 12-year-old middle school boy rolls his eyes, and his mother throws up her hands in despair.

This is a familiar scenario to many of us, both as educators and parents. The majority of students referred to school counselors for academic and disciplinary concerns are boys. How many times have we been asked to address study skills and organizational issues with boys, either individually or in a small-group format? Or to participate on the child study team working with special education referrals with a large number of boys on the agenda? Or to be on a committee to discuss the possibility of retention for an "immature" boy?

Although many of us may believe boys eventually "land on their feet" and end up being productive members of society, as educators we are challenged with a growing issue of male underachievement. This issue, if gone unchecked, can result in boys who don't seem to have as many options for their futures or limit their own choices because of their discouragement or disinterest in school.

With the exception of an occasional newspaper article, there is little in the national educational literature about the topic of male academic underachievement, one that has been virtually ignored with regard to the widely publicized "achievement gap." The gap we all read about refers to the difference in high-stakes achievement test scores between white students and students of color. Gender is rarely mentioned.

EXAMINING DATA

The gender gap in public education has become both a national and international issue over the past decade. In the United States, boys are achieving at lower levels than girls as shown by test scores, grades and drop out rates. They have a higher incidence of ADHD, discipline referrals, and special education referrals and placements. Reports show that boys represent more than two-thirds of high school students with disabilities including physical, learning and emotional. Women have surpassed men not only in high school graduation rates but in university enrollment and degree completion. In this country, girls capture more academic honors, outscore boys in reading and writing and score about as well on math at the three grade levels (fourth, eighth and 12th) tested by the National Assessment for Educational Progress exam. On local levels, many of us have noticed that the majority of honor graduates of area high schools are girls.

Internationally, fourth-grade girls significantly outperformed boys in every G8 country that participated in the 2001 Progress in International Literacy Study. Fifteen-year-old girls outperformed boys among the 28 Organization for Economic Cooperation and Development countries participating in the 2000 Program for International Student Assessment.

In addition to achievement data, there are attitudinal and motivational data that indicate boys as a group do not seem to think school is as important in their lives as do girls. In a recent national survey of 12th-graders over the course of a decade, male students consistently reported, at a much higher rate than female students, that they fooled around in class, failed to complete assignments and seldom tried to do their best work. This study also reported that girls found coursework more meaningful and interesting than the boys did and more often saw the importance of their schoolwork later in their lives. Data from a national educational database showed that 10th-grade girls sought out college information in greater percentages than boys from nine out of 10 sources. The only resource boys used more frequently than girls was talking to coaches.

Such data paint a picture of girls who, as a group, take more initiative with regard to future planning. They set goals, seek out resources and follow through on necessary deadlines and dates.

WHAT ARE THE DIFFERENCES?

Girls are utilizing school success skills more readily than boys. They tend to be more compliant and exhibit organizational skills such as planning and studying ahead. Teachers are still predominantly women, and tend to be role models for the girls. And girls tend to be more mature, physically and emotionally, than boys until about age 16 when boys start catching up. So during these important years while students are establishing their academic records, which affect their futures, girls have a considerable advantage.

Clearly, a variety of anthropological, psychological, biological and sociological issues overlap in a complex way. Brain research shows differences

in the male and female brain that can affect learning styles and preferences for communication. Societal norms about appropriate male and
female roles, particularly for adolescents, may be contributing to this gap.

There appears to be a common perception supported by some research
that it is not as "cool" or acceptable for boys to be seen as serious students as it is for girls. As a veteran elementary teacher recently shared
with us, "It's a challenge just keeping primary-grade boys in their seats.
And by the time they get to fifth grade they don't think it's cool to be a
good student." Such an attitude can become even more pronounced in
middle school and beyond as many boys begin to measure their self-worth
with regard to sports and other traditionally masculine outlets, rather
than grades and academic achievements.

As counselors, we are aware that in general, boys and girls show differences with regard to the expression of their social and emotional selves.
Outlets for boy's emotions may be more limited than for girls, whether it
is the use of a feeling-word vocabulary or the overt display of their emotions. For example, displaying anger and sarcasm seems to be more
acceptable for males than showing sadness and despair. Not having
appropriate outlets for emotions can result in acting out, in the school or
community, with negative consequences for academic achievement.

Although there is an increasing amount of brain research that has
implications for the male mind, little research in the professional educational literature exist concerning male students' specific needs or effective
interventions for working with them. However, there are several popular
authors who have written books addressing the social, emotional, cognitive and physical needs of boys, with recommendations for the adults in
their lives.

SCHOOL COUNSELORS' ROLES

As school counselors and counselor educators, we are pivotal people who
can contribute to consultation efforts with parents and teachers as well as
engage in local research with what works best with boys.

As a profession, we have utilized individual, small-group and large-
group work in direct interventions with students. In our evolving roles as
educational leaders and advocates, our indirect contributions as consultants, collaborators and coordinators are becoming increasingly significant.
In the examination of gender disparities, we need to focus our efforts on
working with parents, teachers, administrators and other adults who are
key figures in students' lives. We can be an important part of a support
team that contributes to research and best practices that have a positive
impact on boys.

Although the task of helping to reduce the gender achievement gap (or any achievement gap for that matter) can be daunting, there are a number of ways we as school counselors and counselor educators can make contributions. Instead of feeling we must be engaged in all possible interventions, it is more practical to think about the optimal way or ways in which each of us can lead or assist as part of a team effort.

Following are suggestions that dovetail with the philosophies of the ASCA National Model®, the National Center for School Counseling Outcome Research and the College Board's National Office for School Counselor Advocacy. All of these models emphasize the importance of systemic interventions to include family-school collaboration and the use of data and outcomes to demonstrate school counseling program rationale and effectiveness. Most of these recommendations apply to helping all students, while addressing the special needs of boys.

Meet with your district-level school counseling colleagues, supervisors and administrators to discuss any local evidence of existing gender disparities. School and district group data should be available to examine gender differences on test scores, discipline referrals, dropout rates, special education referrals and placements and student retention rates. Are there any glaring discrepancies that need to be addressed? If so, which themes seem to be of major concern? Your group may want to choose one particular issue to target for intervention. Decide what data you will need to measure outcomes of your intervention. Microsoft Excel can be used to track such data points as absences, grades, referrals and test scores to examine school or district trends.

Read literature on boys' special needs to include brain research, optimal learning environments and communication styles. Consider facilitating a reading group in which your faculty reads a book such as Michael Gurian's "The Minds of Boys." Create an open faculty forum for discussion about best practices to include trying out new teaching strategies. Encourage teachers to become engaged in "teacher inquiry," which involves them in their own classroom research, the results of which they can share with the whole faculty. If the district can arrange for re-certification credits, that could serve as an incentive for schoolwide efforts.

Think about and share with your faculty the communication strategies you have found to be the most useful and age-appropriate in counseling boys. For example, the use of various media such as books, puppets, games, music, art, creative dramatics, technology, play counseling and physical movement can help engage boys in communicating about issues of concern. Bombarding them with a series of questions does not help them to open up. Teachers, parents and administrators can also use these strategies in communicating with their children/students.

Sponsor workshops for parents in which some of the above issues are described, offering positive and practical ways for them to become involved. As school counselors we have knowledge of community resources and people that could lead or contribute to these sessions. Examples of topics could include finding developmentally appropriate books that appeal to their sons, using technology for finding career and educational planning information and helping boys organize their school work and schedules. Invite interested parents to participate in career days and job shadowing experiences and to be mentors for individual or small groups of boys.

Partner with a local university. Partnerships between schools and universities are an excellent way to engage in best practices and research opportunities. We all learn from one another. Having the support of each other adds credibility and feasibility to our work. With the increased emphasis on accountability at the local, state and national levels, collaboration can be an important and mutually beneficial way to improve educational outcomes. Collecting and sharing results of collaborative interventions with stakeholders is an essential part of this process.

Involve your local business partners and civic organizations. Many are happy to make contributions to the school but are not sure specifically what to do. Not only can businesses make financial donations but they can also offer their time to help with mentoring, tutoring and career education initiatives. They may also sponsor community projects in which students can become involved. Our experience has been that involving businesses is a win-win situation and that students and adults benefit from the interaction with one another.

Use technology as a motivational tool. Many boys enjoy using computers and may appreciate e-mail as a means of communication with school-sponsored mentors and business partners. They may also enjoy contributing to an in-school morning TV broadcast, helping to get out the news on important events and deadlines. Use peers or older students to demonstrate important educational and career planning Web sites.

Tie in your school counseling strategies and interventions with the academic curriculum, so you're a partner with teachers for educational success. For example, large-group lessons can tie in with the reading curriculum for the grading period. If "community" is an elementary reading series theme, that would be an optimal time to plan career education, work experience and community-service activities. Conduct some of your lessons in the school media center, where the media specialist can help recommend specific follow-up materials that may be age- and gender-appropriate, and help tie the lesson to the curriculum.

Engage middle and high school students, both boys and girls, in talking about school-success factors. Such discussions can take place in either small- or large-group formats. Provide statements for focus group discussions or encourage students to contribute their ideas to what seems to be important for boys to be successful and what contributes to the success of girls. There will be overlap, but some true differences may emerge, and such data can provide the impetus for change possibilities at the classroom and school level. Students will appreciate being a part of the solution. Talking about success rather than failure puts a positive spin on the topic. Resources and barriers can be an important part of such discussions.

Share your results with your faculty, your district and in publications. Writing for the local paper is an excellent way to publicize your interventions and to solicit community interest and support. Join forces with other schools in your district or state to share and publicize your work.

Believe in the importance of your efforts. School counselors can and do make a difference.

As educators, we need to continue to explore which teaching, communication and counseling techniques may work best with boys. We need to instill hope and offer encouragement as boys mature into men. Having faith that the future holds a potentially positive outlook is so important with regard to motivation and perseverance. Often, gang members and youth who are in trouble with the law have held little hope for their futures.

Educational achievement of our young people affects all of us, our future generations and family structures. There are major societal implications here. A basic question we need to explore is, "Do we push boys to take on attributes that are not particularly natural for them but that contribute to educational success, or do we meet them on their territory by providing more physical space and accommodating their learning and communication styles, as well as their reading interests?"

This is a question that affects all underachievers, whether the variable is gender, race or socioeconomic status.

Mary Ann Clark, Ph.D., is an associate professor in the Department of Counselor Education at the University of Florida. She is currently involved in an internationalizing the curriculum research project examining male underachievement supported by the Center for International Studies at the University of Florida. She can be reached at maclark@coe.ufl.edu. Erin Oakley, Ed.S., and Heather Adams are doctoral students in the same department.

FOR MORE INFORMATION

"The Minds of Boys: Saving Our Sons from Falling Behind in School and Life," by Michael Gurian. Jossey-Bass, 2005.

"Boys and Girls Learn Differently! A Guide for Teachers and Parents," by Michael Gurian. Jossey-Bass, 2001.

"The Wonder of Boys: What Parents, Mentors and Educators Can Do to Shape Boys into Exceptional Men," by Michael Gurian. Tarcher/Putnam, 1997.

"Handbook of Counseling Boys and Adolescent Males: A Practitioner's Guide," by Arthur Horne and Mark Kiselica. Sage Publications Inc., 1999.

"Boys Will be Boys: Not," by Mark Kuranz. *ASCA School Counselor,* May/June 2003.

"Raising Cain: Protecting the Emotional Life of the Boy in Your Life," by Dan Kindlon and Michael Thompson. Ballantine Publishing Group, 2000.

Counselors,Communities and Spirituality: Ethical and Multicultural Considerations

By Susan D. Lonborg, Ph.D. and Neal Bowen, Ph.D.

This article originally appeared in *Professional School Counseling*, Vol. 7, No. 5, 2004.

The ethical implications of spiritual diversity for school counseling in rural and small world communities are explored in this article. Multicultural competencies are proposed as a framework for conceptualizing and responding to these professional challenges. Specific recommendations for school counselors and counselor educators are provided.

Much attention has been focused on the important role school counselors play in the establishment and maintenance of a positive school environment (e.g., Lapan, 2001). By design, members of the counseling profession assist students and clients in the important process of identity development, of which spiritual identity is one important aspect (e.g., King, 2003; Maples, 2001; Poll & Smith, 2003; Richards & Bergin, 1997). Conseuently, we propose that school counselors must be able to work with their colleagues to create a school climate in which people of differing spiritual traditions feel welcome.

Counselors as individuals may be on their own spiritual journeys; however, as school professionals, their challenge is to find ways to live out their own spiritual traditions and beliefs while carrying out their important responsibilities to a school community that likely enjoys tremendous spiritual and religious diversity. In our thinking about school counseling and spiritual diversity, we find ourselves drawn to an exploration of the counseling profession's ethical standards and multicultural competencies for guidance, particularly as we consider the challenges associated with working as highly visible counselors in either rural communities or urban "small world" communities. When using the term *small world communities*, we are referring to relatively small, selfidentified groups (e.g., ethnic or religious communities) that often exist "within the supposed anonymity" (Schank, 1998) of highly populated urban or suburban settings. Counselors who belong to these small world communities are often highly visible and may experience professional challenges (e.g., dual relationships) not unlike their counterparts in rural settings.

It is interesting to note that there is a well-developed and growing body of literature addressing ethical and multicultural issues in school counseling (e.g., Herring, 1997; Tyson & Pedersen, 2000), yet there is relatively little discussion of the challenges associated with rural school counseling practice. In fact, comparatively few articles address ethical issues in rural practice, regardless of professional specialty, and most rely on clinical experience rather than empirical data. However, several general themes have emerged from what literature exists in this area (e.g., Barnett & Yutrzenka, 2002; Schank, 1998; Schank & Skovholt, 1997). The themes particularly germane to school counseling practice include: (a) professional challenges associated with the high visibility of the practitioner's personal life; (b) the potential for unavoidable nonsexual dual relationships with clients or patients; (c) confidentialityrelated concerns; (d) questions concerning boundaries of competence; (e) community values and expectations; and (f) practitioners' personal needs and self care.

We suggest that the unique professional challenges encountered by rural school counselors are especially salient when issues of spiritual and religious diversity emerge. How school counselors might best address, or even encourage, the spiritual well-being of students is clearly controversial, particularly given the legal issues associated with the separation of church and state (e.g., Fischer & Sorenson, 1991; Staver, 1998). We believe this becomes even more problematic in rural and small world communities, where the counselor's own spiritual orientation may be known to students, parents, and staff. This visibility may both invite and prevent conversations about spiritual diversity in the school setting. Although not focused specifically on rural issues or the school counseling profession, Richards and Bergin (1997) provided a very thoughtful discussion of ethical issues related to counseling and spirituality.

The purpose of this article is to assist counselors and counselor educators in thinking about the variety of issues encountered by school counseling professionals as they express their spiritual identities in the communities in which they live. In addition, we hope to illuminate the discussion of spirituality through the framework of multicultural counseling competencies. Finally, we provide some practical suggestions for school counselors working in rural and small world communities as well as for counselor educators preparing the next generation of school counselors. In doing so, we rely on a very broad and inclusive definition of spirituality. (See Sink & Richmond in this issue.)

We believe it to be good practice to indicate the authors' motivation for exploring these themes, as this transparency may help readers evaluate our observations and suggestions more effectively. As counselor educators and parents of school-age children from different spiritual traditions living in a rural community, we have heard about or observed a number of conversations about spirituality in our local schools. These incidents have both fostered exclusion of children from non-dominant spiritual traditions and provided opportunities for greater understanding. Such experiences were, in part, the impetus for us to consider more carefully the ethical and multicultural issues described in this article.

SPIRITUALITY AS AN ETHICAL ISSUE IN RURAL AND SMALL WORLD COMMUNITIES

One of the most frequently discussed ethical issues in counseling concerns the problem of multiple relationships. More specifically, counselors are cautioned to maintain clear boundaries between their personal and professional lives when working with clients and to avoid multiple relationships (American School Counselor Association [ASCA], 1998; Herlihy & Corey, 1997). Clearly, this recommendation poses particular problems for those counselors working in rural or small world communities, wherein the counselor may enjoy much less personal privacy than those working in urban and suburban communities (Jennings, 1992; Schank, 1998; Schank & Skovholt, 1997). One area of the counselor's life that may be particularly open to inspection is his or her participation, or lack thereof, in religious or spiritual activities in the local community. Consequently, community members form impressions about the counselor's value system based on these observations. This may be particularly problematic when the counselor's behaviors or values are perceived as incongruent with dominant community norms. Counselors may also find themselves in overlapping social relationships (e.g., club member, parishioner, patient) with students and their caregivers. Rural counselors should expect that they cannot completely avoid dual relationships; however, there are many ways in which such relationships might be anticipated and managed.

Inadvertent threats to students' confidentiality should be expected in rural and small communities. For example, a counselor who also sees students at a religious ceremony or activity may be tempted to use that encounter to follow-up on conversations begun at school, unaware that family and friends may not know about a particular problem or concern. Similarly, parents who become acquainted with the counselor through social and spiritual gatherings may use the familiarity of this relationship to inquire about their child's well-being. When these professional and personal roles overlap, the burden is on counselors to keep confidential the content of conversations with students except where otherwise permitted by ethics or law (Glosoff & Pate, 2002).

Rural practitioners often experience pressures related to the boundaries of their professional competence (Roberts, Battaglia, & Epstein, 1999; Schank, 1998). In some rural communities, the school counselor may be

TABLE 1. MULTICULTURAL COMPETENCIES

	Awareness of Self	Awareness of Client	Appropriate Strategies
Attitudes and Beliefs	■ Assumptions, biases and values ■ Religious and cultural traditions ■ Limits of expertise	■ Understand the worldview of clients ■ Accept this as legitimate perspective ■ Awareness of stereotypes held	■ Respect religious beliefs and values ■ Value culture specific help-giving networks
Knowledge	■ Understanding of the impact of discrimination and oppression, particularly of dominant discourse ■ Ways the counselor has benefited from their tradition and orientation	■ Possess specific knowledge of groups worked with ■ Understand impact of culture on identity development ■ Appreciate impact of sociopolitical influence on clients	■ Awareness of institutional barriers to effective help-seeking ■ Know family structures and community characteristics ■ Understand relevant practices that may adversely impact clients
Skills	■ Seek out training, consultation and education for working with diverse others ■ Constantly seek to understand self as cultural being	■ Actively seek experiences that broaden understanding and appreciation of others ■ Be familiar with literature on impact of culture on mental health of group	■ Ability to implement approaches appropriate to diverse clients ■ Ability to intervene institutionally for clients ■ Willingness to consult appropriate religious leaders

Note. This table is based on Sue et al. (1998), simplified for format.

the only counseling professional in the area, and as such, might be called upon to consult more broadly about mental health and psychosocial issues. Thrust into this expert role and lacking sufficient referral resources, school counselors may fail to question their professional and multicultural competence.

SPIRITUALITY AS A MULTICULTURAL ISSUE

Within the abundant literature on the implementation of multicultural counseling (e.g., Atkinson, 2004; Helms & Cook, 1999; Smith, 2004; Sue & Sue, 1999), multicultural competencies are generally organized around three dimensions (self, client, and strategies) and three areas of practice (attitudes, knowledge, and skills). The competencies are presented schematically here (see Table 1), since a lengthy discussion of them is beyond the bounds of the present article. It is important to note that the items given in the cells of the table are simply examples, rather than a comprehensive listing.

Although some authors have included spiritual diversity as an application of multicultural competencies (e.g., Richards, Keller, & Smith, 2004; Sue et al., 1998), the particular challenges of working on questions of meaning across disparate spiritualities has yet to be fully explored within the framework of the specific competencies. Yet, use of the competencies in work across spiritual differences could ensure the provision of ethical counseling services.

Much of the literature on working with diversity has identified the concept of worldview as a central component (e.g., Ibrahim, 1985; Smith, Richards, MacGranley, & Obiakor, 2004). Generally, a worldview is seen as an individual's explanation for how and why reality behaves as it does. Certain components of human experience are understood to contribute in powerful ways to the construction of a worldview, including spiritual traditions in shared cultural and unique family environments (e.g., Thompson, 2004).

We have chosen to indicate one proposal for developing competence in working with diversity that places worldview at the center of the model. Jane Treviño (1996) suggested that worldview is a useful construct for understanding therapeutic change. Effective counseling is possible, she posited, when counselor and client are able to achieve congruence at the general level of worldview, with discrepancy at the specific level. The general worldview refers to global explanations, such as "humans are basically good," while the specific level refers to individual elaborations of the global level, such as "therefore, I can change the school environment by just being reasonable." Discrepancy at the specific level can provide traction for positive psychological change, while respecting and leaving intact the general level explanations.

It should be noted that achieving congruence at the general level is possible through either matching (provision of services to members of one's own group), or through the use of an 'ethnographic' approach, in which the counselor attempts to understand the client's worldview from the client's perspective. Given the under representation of many groups, and the organization of school counseling services, particularly in rural and small world environments, the 'ethnographic' approach may be the best option available.

When considering the belief that spirituality reflects a revelation of truth, it is not surprising that the ability to provide congruence across faith traditions, particularly in terms of "valuing other's perspectives as valid," is challenging for counselors. However, multiculturalism in no sense requires a repudiation of one's own culture. On the contrary, a full understanding and appreciation of one's own worldview is obligatory (e.g., Helms & Cook, 1999; Smith et al., 2004; Sue & Sue, 1999).

This, then, is one area where the value of Treviño's (1996) model becomes clear. If the task of the counselor is to provide congruence, rather than matching, there is no requirement to either deny or hide one's own spirituality. Counselors, however, must make clear that their spiritual commitment does not interfere with their ability to hold the client's independence as a guiding ethical principal. Further, counselors must be able to accurately anticipate the impact on potential clients of a specific display of affiliation or belief. Thus, an implication of multicultural competence may be a choice to moderate such displays when it is clear that they may limit equal access to the school counselor's professional services.

In order to provide services to all members of the community, the school counselor needs to have both underlying knowledge of the spiritual values of those in the school community and an understanding of how to access appropriate, specific resources (such as spiritual leaders from other faiths) in order to develop effective environments for working with those from other faith traditions.

CASE VIGNETTES AND ANALYSIS

We have constructed two fictitious case vignettes to illustrate the ethical considerations we have raised, and how multicultural competencies may provide guidance in responding to them, especially in the context of rural and small world school counseling practice.

TABLE 2. APPLICATION OF THE ASCA ETHICAL STANDARDS TO THE CASE VIGNETTES.

ASCA Ethical Standard		Christine	Nathaniel
Preamble	Each person has the right to respect and dignity as a human being and to counseling services without prejudice as to person, character, belief, or practice regardless of age, color, disability, ethnic group, gender, race, religion, sexual orientation, marital status, or socioeconomic status.	✓	✓
A-1a	*Responsibilities to Students* The professional school counselor (PSC) has a primary obligation to the counselee who is to be treated with respect as a unique individual.	✓	✓
A-1c	The PSC refrains from consciously encouraging the counselee's acceptance of values, lifestyles, plans, decisions, and beliefs that represent the counselor's personal orientation.	✓	✓
A-4	*Dual Relationships* The PSC avoids dual relationships which might impair her or his objectivity and increase the risk of harm to the client…If a dual relationship is unavoidable, the counselor is responsible for taking action to eliminate or reduce the potential for harm.	✓ (direct)	✓ (indirect)
B-1c	*Parent Rights and Responsibilities* The PSC is sensitive to cultural and social diversity among families and recognizes that all parents, custodial and noncustodial, are vested with certain rights and responsibilities for the welfare of their children by virtue of their role and according to law.	✓	✓

ASCA Ethical Standard		Christine	Nathaniel
C-1b	*Professional Relationships* The PSC treats colleagues with professional respect, courtesy, and fairness.	✓	✓ (indirect)
C-1c	The PSC is aware of and optimally utilizes related professions and organizations to whom the counselee may be referred.	✓	✓
D-1b	*Responsibilities to the School* The PSC informs appropriate officials of conditions that may be potentially disruptive or damaging to the school's mission, personnel, and property while honoring the confidentiality between counselee and counselor.	✓	✓
D-1e	The PSC assists in developing: (1) curricular and environmental conditions appropriate for the school and community	✓	✓
D-2	The PSC collaborates with agencies, organizations, and individuals in the school and the community in the best interests of counselees and without regard to personal reward and remuneration.	✓	✓
E-1b	*Responsibilities to Self: Professional Competence* The PSC monitors personal functioning and effectiveness and does not participate in any activity which may lead to inadequate professional services or harm to a client.	✓	✓
E-2	*Responsibilities to Self: Multicultural Skills* The PSC understands the diverse cultural backgrounds of the counselees with whom he/she works. This includes, but is not limited to, learning how the school counselors own cultural/ethnic/ racial identity impacts her or his values and beliefs about the counseling process.	✓	✓

Note. The ✓ suggests the ASCA standard should be considered for this vignette.

Vignette 1: Christine

Christine is an experienced school counselor in a well-to-do private academy located in a large Southwestern city. Although non-sectarian, the academy has a large concentration of Anglican teachers, parents, and students. Christine is also Anglican, and participates in a prayer breakfast with many others in the school cafeteria once a week. She wears a discreet gold cross on a necklace every day. One day Bahira calls Christine about Abdullah, her 14-year-old son. Christine had earlier recruited Bahira to sit on a parent advisory council for the school that Christine convenes monthly. Bahira reports that Abdullah has become unusually withdrawn at home, reluctant to talk with either of his parents and somewhat surly. She further notes that when she approached him, he said he was 'fed up' with a "Christian student" who, in the course of an argument, addressed him with a racial epithet. Christine reflects that Abdullah has been an outstanding student who seemed to get along well with his peers, and begins to plan how she might invite him to talk, only to be surprised when Bahira asks for a referral to "someone who would be able to work with him," since she expects that Christine will be unable to work with him because he is Moslem. This vignette raises a number of important ethical questions relevant to Christine's role as school counselor. First, her spiritual views are likely communicated to students, parents, and staff through her jewelry and participation in prayer breakfasts held on the school grounds. Although expression of her freedom of religion may be normative for staff in the private academy, the school serves students from other faith traditions (e.g., Moslem). As a school counselor, Christine has a responsibility to proactively communicate to students and families her respect for diverse spiritual and religious traditions, especially given her ethical obligation to provide services without discrimination.

The importance of being well-informed about spiritual perspectives within the community is key here. Christine holds central responsibility for fostering a school climate of respect for diversity, and it is difficult to imagine how she might accomplish this without actively seeking out information about the actual values and attitudes held by members of the school community (Carey & Boscardin, 2003). It is clear that developing an environment in which diversity is valued requires a broad distribution of multicultural competencies, implying that Christine should work to provide opportunities for students, staff, and parents to develop their own competence in living in a multicultural environment.

As Bahira clearly understands, within the school community the counselor plays an important role in identifying and developing psychosocial referral resources. Therefore, the question of how well Christine has become acquainted with referral resources in the local community arises.

Has she established any contacts with Moslem professionals or imams in this city? Should Bahira insist on it, would she be able to facilitate an appropriate referral? In this context, it is helpful to think of an appropriate role for counselors, that of facilitator of indigenous support systems (Atkinson, 2004).

Vignette 2: Nathaniel

Nathaniel is a newly certified school counselor who is midway through his first year as the only counselor in the local high school of 350 students. As the new counselor in town, Nathaniel is frequently asked to give talks to local community organizations. Sometimes the speaking requests are for counselingrelated topics; at other times, Nathaniel is encouraged to talk about whatever is of interest to him. Since moving to this small, rural community, Nathaniel has found himself frustrated by the seeming "lack of religious diversity" and decides that his next talk will be entitled, "Alternatives to Organized Religion: Best Practices for Identifying the Spiritual in Everyday Living." After giving what he thought was a successful and intellectually stimulating presentation to a local civics group, Nathaniel is surprised to find himself the target of letters – both supportive and critical – to the newspaper editor. After receiving a number of calls from concerned parents, Nathaniel's principal has also asked to meet with him to learn more about what has provoked such a controversy.

First, from a legal standpoint we must recognize Nathaniel's rights to freedom of religion and speech. However, as we consider the case of Nathaniel and the ASCA (1998) ethical standards, more questions than answers come to mind. First, as a newly certified school counselor, was Nathaniel adequately prepared for the unique experience of working in a rural community? Second, what was Nathaniel's motivation for giving this particular talk? Is Nathaniel feeling isolated in the community and hoping to identify community members with whom to establish personal relationships? Third, when preparing his speech to the local group, did Nathaniel consider the potential impact of his visibility and alternative views on the perceptions of local community members, and in turn, his ability to function effectively as a counselor to all students in his school? Fourth, did Nathaniel consult with any of his school colleagues or members of the local community in an effort to gauge, in advance, how his views might be received? Fifth, the title of Nathaniel's speech raises questions about his personal attitudes toward organized religion. Does Nathaniel have particular negative beliefs about organized religion; were those beliefs communicated to his audience in a way that might have been construed as disrespectful? How then, might these attitudes also be communicated to members of the school community as he interacts with them on a daily basis?

Sixth, what challenges might Nathaniel face now given the highly charged public debate his talk has generated? How will he be perceived by students and parents? How will he go about restoring effective working relationships with those whom may be offended by his spiritual views? Finally, what, if anything, will Nathaniel learn from this highly visible experience about: (a) his role as school counselor in a rural community, including his impact on school climate; (b) his own spiritual identity development; (c) his professional competence; (d) the quality of his personal life (i.e., self-care) within this particular rural community; and (e) his need for ongoing professional training and consultation? Table 2 provides a summary of ASCA ethical considerations for both the "Christine" and "Nathaniel" vignettes.

SUMMARY AND RECOMMENDATIONS

In this article we suggest that there are a myriad of ethical and multicultural issues embedded in the question of how counselors address spiritual issues when working in rural or small world communities. Although we recognize the many positive aspects of living and working in such communities, there are also some particular professional challenges. Perhaps most notable is the counselor's struggle to balance his or her personal and professional lives in light of one's greater visibility in these settings and to develop multicultural competence.

In closing, we offer school counselors and counselor educators a number of specific recommendations. First, school counselors in rural or other small communities should anticipate the ethical challenges associated with their highly visible lives. Second, counselors should identify and be prepared to use an ethical decision-making model (e.g., Forester-Miller & Davis, 1996) when confronted with questions about multiple relationships, confidentiality, or boundaries of competence. Third, counselors must become familiar with community norms and values so that they may thoughtfully consider the impact of their personal and professional behavior on the school community as well as the lives of their current and future clients. Fourth, ethical school counseling requires an understanding of one's own worldview, including spirituality, as well as an awareness of the diverse worldviews existing within one's rural or small community. Fifth, in light of their important role in promoting school climate, school counselors should advocate for multicultural competence in all members of the school community (Carey & Boscardin, 2003). Finally, we recommend that counselor educators prepare students more explicitly for practice in small world communities and extend discussions of multicultural competence to include spirituality. More specific recommendations are

TABLE 3. RECOMMENDATIONS FOR SCHOOL COUNSELORS WORKING WITH RELIGIOUS AND SPIRITUAL ISSUES

Ethical/ Multicultural Issue	Recommendation
Respect	School counselors should: • respect students' rights to hold spiritual and religious beliefs different from their own[a]; • not proselytize or attempt to convert students to their own religious perspective or denomination[a]; • demonstrate respect for students' spiritual leaders and avoid making demeaning or critical remarks about them[a]; • in public school settings, use great caution in pursuing spiritual goals in counseling; doing so only when students have explicitly expressed a desire to do so and when appropriate written consent has been obtained[a]; • avoid direct spiritual interventions (e.g., praying with clients, quoting Scriptures) with students, given issues concerning the separation of church and state.
Informed Consent	Where appropriate and when written informed consent is obtained, school counselors may find it helpful to consult and collaborate with the counselee's spiritual leaders.
Multiple Relationships	School counselors should: • where possible, avoid counselor-religious leader and counselor-religious associate dual relationships[a]; • consult frequently with professional colleagues when dual relationships exist.
Confidentiality	When school counselors encounter students and families in community settings (e.g., houses of worship) beyond the school, particular care should be taken to avoid inadvertent breaches of confidentiality.

Ethical/ Multicultural Issue	Recommendation
Professional Competence	In order to be proactive, school counselors new to the rural community practice setting should inform themselves through independent reading, consultation, and training about the unique challenges often encountered by rural practitioners.
Multicultural Competence	School counselors should: ▪ when working in rural settings, become informed about the variety of worldviews both within the school setting and the larger community. ▪ consult with colleagues or spiritual leaders when working with clients from religious or spiritual traditions about which the counselor is not well informed.
Self-awareness	School counselors should: • recognize the values embedded within their own spiritual traditions and beliefs and be thoughtful about ways to manage these values when counseling diverse groups of students and families; • be proactive in addressing potential conflicts between their spiritual values or activities and their professional role; • recognize the impact of their role in creating and managing a healthy school climate that contributes to student learning, growth, and development.
Training and Supervision	School counselor educators should: ▪ provide opportunities for candidates to become informed about ethical issues in rural school counseling practice; ▪ ensure that issues of spiritual and religious diversity are addressed as part of candidates' training in multicultural counseling.

[a] Adapted from Richards & Bergin (1997)

provided in Table 3. Clearly, the process of living one's own spiritual values and traditions while responding ethically to students with diverse spiritualities is a complex one; thus, we hope that these recommendations will provide a useful springboard for further discussion among professional school counselors and counselor educators.

Susan D. Lonborg, Ph.D., is director of the School Counseling Program and Neal Bowen, Ph.D., is an assistant professor of Psychology. Both are with Central Washington University, Ellensburg. E-mail: lonborg@cwu.edu

REFERENCES

American School Counselor Association. (1998). *Ethical standards for school counselors.* Alexandria,VA: Author.

Atkinson,D. R. (2004). *Counseling American minorities* (6th ed.). New York:McGraw-Hill.

Barnett, J. E., & Yutrzenka, B. A. (2002). Nonsexual dual relationships in professional practice, with special applications to rural and military communities. In A. A. Lazarus & O. Zur (Eds.), *Dual relationships and psychotherapy* (pp. 273–286).New York: Springer.

Carey, J. C., & Boscardin, M. L. (2003). Improving the multicultural effectiveness of your school in the context of state standards, accountability measures, and high-stakes assessment. In P. B. Pedersen & J. C. Carey (Eds.), *Multicultural counseling in schools: A practical handbook* (2nd ed., pp. 270–289). Boston: Allyn & Bacon.

Fischer, L., & Sorenson, G. P. (1991). *School law for counselors, psychologists, and social workers* (2nd ed.). New York: Longman.

Forester-Miller, H., & Davis,T. (1996). *A practitioner's guide to ethical decision-making.* Alexandria,VA: American Counseling Association.

Glosoff, H. L., & Pate, R.H. (2002). Privacy and confidentiality in school counseling. *Professional School Counseling, 6,* 20–27.

Helms, J. E., & Cook,D. A. (1999). *Using race and culture in counseling and psychotherapy: Theory and practice.* Needham Heights, MA: Allyn & Bacon.

Herlihy, B., & Corey, G. (1997). *Boundary issues in counseling: Multiple roles and responsibilities.* Alexandria,VA: American Counseling Association.

Herring, R.D. (1997). *Multicultural counseling in schools: A synergistic approach.* Alexandria,VA: American Counseling Association.

Ibrahim, F. A. (1985). Effective cross-cultural counseling and psychotherapy: A framework. *The Counseling Psychologist, 13*, 625–638.

Jennings, F. L. (1992). Ethics of rural practice. *Psychotherapy in Private Practice, 10*, 85–104.

King, P. E. (2003). Religion and identity: The role of ideological, social, and spiritual contexts. *Applied Developmental Science, 7*, 197–204.

Lapan, R.T. (2001). Results-based comprehensive guidance and counseling programs: A framework for planning and evaluation. *Professional School Counseling, 4*, 289–299.

Maples,M. F. (2001). Spirituality: Its place in counseling children. In D.S. Sandhu (Ed.), *Elementary school counseling in the new millennium* (pp. 223–237). Alexandria,VA: American Counseling Association.

Poll, J. B., & Smith,T. B. (2003).The spiritual self: Toward a conceptualization of spiritual identity development. *Journal of Psychology and Theology, 31*, 129–142.

Richards, P. S., & Bergin, A. E. (1997). *A spiritual strategy for counseling and psychotherapy.* Washington, DC: American Psychological Association.

Richards, P. S., Keller, R. R., & Smith,T. B. (2004). Religious and spiritual diversity in counseling and psychotherapy. In T. B. Smith (Ed.), *Practicing multiculturalism: Affirming diversity in counseling and psychotherapy* (pp. 276–293). Boston: Pearson Education.

Roberts, L.W., Battaglia, J., & Epstein, R. S. (1999). Frontier ethics: Mental health care needs and ethical dilemmas in rural communities. *Psychiatric Services, 50*, 497–503.

Schank, J. A. (1998). Ethical issues in rural counseling practice. *Canadian Journal of Counselling, 32*, 270–283.

Schank, J. A., & Skovholt,T. M. (1997). Dual relationship dilemmas of rural and small community psychologists. *Professional Psychology: Research and Practice, 28*, 44–49.

Smith,T. B. (Ed.). (2004). *Practicing multiculturalism: Affirming diversity in counseling and psychotherapy.* Boston: Pearson Education.

Smith,T. B., Richards, P. S.,MacGranley, H., & Obiakor, F. (2004). Practicing multiculturalism: An introduction. In T. B. Smith (Ed.), *Practicing multiculturalism: Affirming diversity in counseling and psychotherapy* (pp. 3–16). Boston: Pearson Education.

Staver,M.D. (1998). *Faith and freedom: A complete handbook for defending your religious rights* (2nd ed.). Orlando, FL: Liberty Counsel.

Sue, D.W., Carter, R.T., Casas, J.M., Fouad, N. A., Ivey, A. E., Jensen, M., LaFramboise, T., Manese, J. E., Ponterotto, J. G., & Vazquez-Nutall, E. (1998). *Multicultural counseling competencies: Individual and organizational development.* Thousand Oaks, CA: Sage.

Sue, D.W., & Sue, D. (1999). *Counseling the culturally different: Theory and practice*. New York: John Wiley.

Thompson, C. E. (2004). Awareness and identity: Foundational principals of multicultural practice. In T. B. Smith (Ed.), *Practicing multiculturalism: Affirming diversity in counseling and psychotherapy* (pp. 35–56). Boston: Pearson Education.

Treviño, J.G. (1996).Worldview and change in cross-cultural counseling. *The Counseling Psychologist, 24*, 198–215.

Tyson, L. E., & Pedersen, P. B. (Eds.). (2000). *Critical incidents in school counseling* (2nd ed.). Alexandria,VA: American Counseling Association.

Concerns of Newly Arrived Immigrant Students: Implications for School Counselors

By Franklyn C. Williams and S. Kent Butler, Ph.D.

This article originally appeared in *Professional School Counseling*, Vol. 7, No. 1, 2003.

The concerns of newly arrived immigrant students include the need for English language acquisition, the lack of social support networks and of social acceptance, racial labeling and categorization, acquiring new learning styles, post-traumatic stress syndrome, different cultural scripts, and the typical development issues that all students face. Also addressed are the typical responses of some educators to newly arrived immigrant students with these issues. The author also discusses implications for school counselors and how school counselors can address the concerns of newly arrived immigrant students at the national, state, and district or local levels.

As immigrant populations expand in major urban areas throughout the United States, public school systems will be serving growing numbers of immigrant students. School systems in California, New York, Texas, Florida, Illinois, New Jersey, Massachusetts, New Mexico, and Pennsylvania will be most affected (Kellogg, 1988, p. 204).

Kellogg (1988) issued this statement almost 15 years ago. It is just as true today as it was back then. For example, the most recent census data indicate that three of the above-mentioned states – California, Florida, and Texas – along with Georgia and Arizona – had the greatest population gain of any others in the years from 1990 to 2000 (Perry & Mackun, 2000). Further, cities such as New York, Los Angeles, Chicago, Washington, San Francisco, Philadelphia, Boston, Detroit, and Dallas all posted significant gains in population (Perry & Mackun). The majority of the 30 million immigrants (11% of the total population and 43% of all foreign-born residents) that came to the United States since 1990 settled in these cities or in others in the aforementioned states.

It follows that, as a state's total immigrant population grows, so does the share of immigrant students in its school systems. In fact, the percentage of children of immigrants (children with at least one foreign-born parent) in school systems across the country rose from 6.3% in 1970 to nearly 20% in 1997 (Ruiz de Velasco & Fix, 2000). As is the case with officials who are responsible for other social services, the challenge is for leaders of affected school districts to ensure provision of the necessary academic and support services to an ever-increasing immigrant student population.

With specific regard to school counseling and guidance, districts and schools are challenged to ensure that counselors and counseling programs reflect a concern for the special needs of newly arrived immigrant students. McDonnell and Hill (1993) reminded school counseling practitioners that these students cannot be ignored because their numbers will continue to increase. In addition, these students will comprise a key segment of the future labor force in this country (McDonnell & Hill).

This article highlights the issues that concern newly arrived immigrant students from the guidance and counseling perspective, how school systems have responded to these issues, and the implications for school counselors concerning what can be done to better serve newly arrived immigrant students. For the purposes of this writing, newly arrived immigrant students are those who have arrived in this country within the 12 months prior to first enrollment in a U.S. public school.

ISSUES THAT CONCERN NEWLY ARRIVED IMMIGRANT STUDENTS

All newly arrived immigrant students do not face the same issues. Some concerns may be related to their specific countries of origin. For example, Haitian immigrant students might be confronted with racism for the first time while immigrant students from Kosovo might be concerned with the effects of war. Additionally, the circumstances under which some immigrants come to America can vary depending upon their particular financial or social status prior to moving here. Students who are immigrants from very privileged families have very different concerns and needs than those who come from poor families – even if their countries of origin are the same.

Nevertheless, according to the literature, there is a set of issues that many immigrant students, in general, face. Most notably, these issues include English language acquisition (Rong & Preissle, 1998), posttraumatic stress disorder (Jay, 2000), racial labeling and categorization (Perkins, 2000), different learning styles (Jay), inadequate social support networks (Cardenas & Taylor, 1993; James, 1997), lack of social acceptance (James), and cultural scripts that are new and unfamiliar to American school personnel (First, 1988; Perkins). In addition, newly arrived immigrant students are also concerned with the same developmental issues that all other students must face (Jay).

English Language Acquisition

Developing verbal and written competence in the English language is an important concern for newly arrived immigrant students (Jay, 2000; Rong & Preissle, 1998). At the very least, they require this competence in order to know and understand what is going on in their classrooms. Optimally, though, this competence will allow them to excel academically and also demonstrate their ability to perform just as well as they did in schools in their home countries and in their native languages. The rate at which newly arrived immigrant students acquire English language skills depends on a variety of factors such as age, length of time in this country, socioeconomic status, parental education, and residence location (Rong & Preissle).

Post-traumatic Stress Disorder
Many newly arrived immigrant students arrive here from countries (e.g., Vietnam, Cambodia, Laos, El Salvador, Guatemala, Nicaragua, and Haiti) that have been affected by war and other types of conflict (First, 1988). As a result, some of these students may have been firsthand witnesses of such occurrences as death, homelessness, and poverty. They may also know what it means to be forcibly and unwillingly separated from parents, friends, and other relatives (Jay, 2000). Further, some of these students may have been refugees. This is certainly the case for Sudanese students in the Omaha (Nebraska) public school system. As a result of these kinds of experiences, such students may exhibit the various symptoms of post-traumatic stress disorder. These symptoms include – among others – flashbacks, avoidance of relationships and other social situations, irritability, insomnia, memory loss, and panic attacks (American Psychiatric Association, 1994).

Inadequate Social Support Networks
Because some newly arrived immigrant students may have left parents, friends, and other relatives behind in their home countries when moving to this country, they may no longer have an adequate social support network in place. Further, some of these students may be living in homes with relatives or friends that they barely even know. Inadequate social support networks result in isolation, fear, and grief (Cardenas & Taylor, 1993). Depression, confusion, hopelessness, frustration, and lowered self-esteem are also effects of an inadequate social support system (James, 1997).

Racial Labeling and Categorization
School records in the United States typically include information about a student's race. In their school records, students are often identified as White, Black, or Hispanic. This type of labeling might be new to many newly arrived immigrant students. Many of them are moving from countries where ethnic categories are more important than racial categories or where categorization is not even an issue at all. For example, in some

Muslim countries, it is more important to be identified by sect – Sikh or Sunni – than it is to be identified by skin color. Newly arrived immigrant students must now learn how to become accustomed to racial labeling and categorization (Perkins, 2000). This may also mean assuming a new identity and sense of self according to race (Rong & Preissle, 1998). Related to this is the major challenge of figuring out how to be assimilated into American culture and society while simultaneously figuring out how to remain a part of one's original culture and heritage (Rong & Preissle).

Different Learning Styles

Learning and teaching takes on different forms in different countries. For example, in Haiti, students are taught by the rote method where they are expected to write down the teacher's words verbatim (Jay, 2000). This is in contrast to the teaching style of most American schools where taking notes in class may involve summarizing or simply writing down the basic gist of a teacher's thoughts. Newly arrived immigrant students must learn to adjust to this style of teaching and learning (Jay). They must also become accustomed to new types of tests such as the multiple-choice test. This type of test is not common in parts of the world outside of the United States.

Included in this issue of different teaching and learning styles is the need to help newly arrived immigrant students understand how American schools operate (Olsen & Jaramillo, 2000). Moving from one class to another, being taught by several different persons each day, timing (i.e., length) of classes and the school day, and the earning of academic credit may be new and foreign to the newly arrived immigrant student. Newly arrived immigrant students may need advice and assistance in coping with and adjusting to these modes of operation within American schools.

New and Different Cultural Scripts

First (1988) reminded us that some newly arrived immigrant students are entering "U. S. classrooms with cultural scripts modeled on the material and social environments of their homelands" (p. 206). Cultural scripts include the behaviors, ideas, thoughts, and roles that are peculiar to a particular culture. For example, in many countries, older children may leave school at a certain age in order to help raise younger siblings and to help contribute to the household income by working full-time. The cultural scripts of many newly arrived immigrant students are likely very different from those found here in the United States. For example, in the home countries of some newly arrived immigrant students, gender roles might be reversed; their societies might be more matriarchal than patriarchal in nature. These cultural scripts might also include values such as family interdependence, filial piety, respect for authority, and stoicism that run counter to dominant values in America (Perkins, 2000).

The challenge for newly arrived immigrant students is to manage discrepancies or differences between their own cultural values and those of the dominant school culture (James, 1997). They also may need advice and assistance in managing these same discrepancies between their cultural values and those of the society outside of the school environment.

Lack of Social Acceptance

Newly arrived immigrant students may be faced with the challenge of not being accepted by their peers and teachers when they first enter the American school system (James, 1997). This lack of acceptance might occur because of misunderstandings based on differences in language, dress, and patterns of speech. It might also occur because of unwillingness by peers and teachers to accept, understand, and learn about things that make newly arrived immigrant students unique. Often, lack of acceptance by peers and teachers can result in a diminished sense of self and of belonging (James).

Developmental Issues

Jay (2000) reminded us that newly arrived immigrant students face the same developmental issues that all students face. All students – newly arrived immigrant or not – must confront the challenges of transitioning between childhood and adulthood. For example, in adolescence, Eriksonian psychosocial theory asserts that this involves establishing a new identity by considering questions such as "who am I?" and "what is my reason for being?" It also involves exploring life goals and aspirations. These are all, essentially, developmental and existential issues. Because of their training in child development, school counselors are well positioned to assist newly arrived immigrant students in confronting these issues.

RESPONSES TO NEWLY ARRIVED IMMIGRANT STUDENTS

Some school districts simply overlook or ignore the needs of newly arrived immigrant students. However, for those that do attend to these needs, two responses have been identified: (a) schools created solely for these students (commonly known as newcomer schools) and (b) individual school-based initiatives such as transition programs or support groups that are contained within the larger school context (Feinberg, 2000). Neither of the latter two responses is counseling specific. Nevertheless, they still warrant an examination in this discussion.

Newcomer Schools

As of 1996–1997, there were seven newcomer high schools across the country. One such school is Liberty High School in New York City. Another is Newcomer High School in San Francisco, which was actually the first newcomer school when it opened in 1979 (Perkins, 2000). As noted previously, newcomer schools are those that only serve newly arrived immigrant students. In other words, these schools are strictly devoted to addressing the special needs of these students. This is done within the context of a complete educational program or stateapproved curriculum. These schools are fully staffed by administration, teachers, counselors, and support personnel just as any other school. Students are expected to remain at such schools anywhere from one year to – in the case of high schools – the full 4 years. The length of attendance depends on the school and upon predetermined time limits on attendance.

With regard to counseling and guidance, these schools may or may not offer specific mental health or other social services. As a matter of fact, most of them focus more so on language issues than any other issues. Even when mental health and other social services are offered, they may not necessarily be guidance and counseling specific.

School-based Initiatives

School-based initiatives designed to help newly arrived immigrant students include a variety of services that addresses their special needs. These initiatives vary from school to school and from district to district. According to data from the Center for Applied Linguistics (2000), there were more than 110 programs in 26 states that catered to the special needs of newly arrived immigrant students. Most of these programs are designed as separate programs within regular middle or high schools (Short, 2000). Many of them are full school-day programs, some are half day, and others are after school programs. For the most part, the instructional components of many of these programs focus on developing both language and academic skills so that students might eventually transfer to the regular ESL or bilingual programs within their schools or districts of origin (Short). Further, to assist newly arrived immigrant students with becoming more familiar with life in American public schools and American society, many of these school-based programs offer courses in cultural orientation.

Support groups are also an important component of some school-based initiatives. One example of a successful support group is the bicultural group offered at one Los Angeles public high school (Cardenas & Taylor, 1993). Newly arrived immigrant students in this group meet regularly during a set time in the school day. They discuss issues that are important to them such as difficulties with language, lack of adequate social support, and academic performance in a new environment and atmosphere of learning. Participants in this specific group claimed that is has been invaluable in providing them with the motivation and support that they need to be successful in their new school environments in this country (Cardenas & Taylor). One young man even shared how the support group was a key factor in convincing him to remain in school until graduation. For sure, there are other programs around the country that embody the same mission and produce the same results as this above-mentioned group.

It is important to note two things here. For one, it must be reiterated that each program in each school or district operates differently according to the needs of the local population of newly arrived immigrant students. No two programs are exactly alike. Second, it is notable that the literature has been silent on how school counselors in particular deal with the issues – separate and aside from initiatives developed and implemented by school administrators – that newly arrived immigrant students bring along when they enroll in American public schools. Greater emphasis has been placed on academic and language proficiency while lesser emphasis has been placed on the mental health and social concerns of these students.

IMPLICATIONS FOR COUNSELORS

The issues of newly arrived immigrant students infer several implications for the school counseling profession on the national level, the state level, and on the district/local school level.

National Level

It would be important for the national professional organization of school counselors, the American School Counselor Association (ASCA), to more explicitly state its intention with regards to serving newly arrived immigrant students. This needs to be done as a matter of urgency given the special needs of these students and their sheer numbers in some school districts. ASCA can lead the way in addressing the concerns of newly arrived immigrant students in academic circles by going beyond general statements in its strategic plan and in its code of ethics. A specific position statement concerning the issues of newly arrived immigrant students can demonstrate a proactive stance by ASCA.

ASCA has already developed other position statements on a number of school counseling-related issues such as cross-multicultural counseling, special needs students, and students-at-risk. However, none of these statements refers specifically to the concerns of immigrant students. A position statement dealing with the issues of newly arrived immigrant students would go beyond the current ASCA statement on cross/multicultural counseling by mentioning a commitment to ensuring that they have equal access to services and opportunities that allow for their adequate adjustment and settlement into schools in this country. Of course, such a statement – like all other ASCA position statements found on its Web site at www.schoolcounselor.org – would also include a rationale, a description of the school counselor's role, and a basic summary.

From the standpoint of training, the Council for the Accreditation of Counseling and Related Education Programs (CACREP) can influence counselor education programs to prepare school counselors to be more adept at serving newly arrived immigrant students. Counselor education programs, especially those in or near major metropolitan areas such as New York, Los Angeles, Chicago, and Philadelphia can be encouraged to offer more than one single course in multiculturalism and diversity (First, 1988). Course offerings might be expanded to include more intense study of demography, cultural nuances, and the history of the countries that newly arrived immigrant students are coming from (First). For example, in a cultural history class, the focus might be on the legacy of the peoples of Latin America, Asia, and the Caribbean since it is a wellknown fact that the greater majority of immigrants to the United States are arriving from those regions. Of course too, in such a class, the relationship between history and counseling would have to be emphasized.

The main point is that adjusting counselor education programs to more adequately prepare school counselors to work with newly arrived immigrant students is of utmost importance with regards to effectiveness in the work of these counselors. CACREP, as the accrediting body for counselor education programs, can be influential in bringing about this adjustment.

State Level

At the state level, guidance and counseling efforts to assist newly arrived immigrant students can be orchestrated by state education officials. Specific laws and mandates can be drafted and implemented by such officials in order to ensure that all students within a particular state have equal access to available transition programs. Such laws and mandates would also ensure that all such programs within that state are of the same quality, content, and methodology with regards to guidance and counseling components.

In Florida, for example, one such state law or mandate could require that all schools provide cultural orientation classes for newly arrived immigrant students within a certain number of days after enrollment, for a specified period of time, and if the population of such students exceeds a certain number or percentage of the total school population. Other than

Florida, new laws and mandates might be especially urgent in states such as California and Texas where the percentages of newly arrived immigrant students continue to steadily increase.

All in all, specific laws and mandates would ensure consistency between programs in the same state. Further, they would help lessen the instances of piece-meal, individually school-based approaches.

District/Local Level

District officials with responsibility for guidance and school counseling can develop and conduct regular in-service professional development programs for the counselors in their schools (James, 1997). Appropriate in-service professional development might focus on such things as how to more accurately assess and diagnose the needs of each individual newly arrived immigrant student in culturally sensitive ways. In-service professional development might also take the form of workshops to teach about cultural adjustment. In a district such as Orange County (Florida), for example, these workshops might also focus learning about the culture and history of the countries such as Puerto Rico, Jamaica, and Haiti where immigrants in that district mainly originate. Regular in-service professional development would allow school counselors to remain current in their knowledge and level of proficiency as far as newly arrived immigrant students are concerned.

Another example of how districts can implement a system-wide approach is by setting up centralized intake centers – coordinated and run by school counselors – for newly arrived immigrant students. At these centers, school counselors could have information about area schools readily available and onhand when immigrant students and their parents first come in to register for enrollment (First, 1988). Some of these are already in operation in several schools and districts (Feinberg, 2000). School counselors are usually the first major contact person that newly arrived immigrant students encounter. Hence, counselors are well positioned to inform students of available services that can assist them in transitioning into American public high schools. Counselors are also well positioned to foster the belief that it is important to do well in school as a prerequisite for academic success (Feinberg, 2000). Within the local school, counselors can also help immigrant students better cope with their academic, developmental, social, and other needs and issues such as English language acquisition, posttraumatic stress syndrome, and racial labeling.

While school counselors are also in a good position to ensure individualized attention for and service to newly arrived immigrant students in all these different areas, it has been well established that group work is quite effective and successful in school settings. Thus, school counselors would do well to consider group work with newly arrived immigrant students. On a group level, school counselors can lead the way in academic circles by offering and conducting transition and support groups such as the bicultural group offered at the Los Angeles high school (Cardenas & Taylor, 1993). A useful transition group, for instance, could focus on study skills and test-taking skills as a way of addressing the different learning styles of newly arrived immigrant students. Transition and support groups would be offered with the goal of assisting newly arrived immigrant students in becoming more adept at survival in their new scholastic environments. Peer counselors could be used in transition and support groups. Peer counselors would work collaboratively with school counselors to assist in the facilitation of the overall adjustment of newly arrived immigrant students as well as their involvement and participation in transition and support groups.

The approaches that can be taken to assist newly arrived immigrant students require creativity and innovation on the part of individual school counselors. The important thing is to account for the needs of the targeted population of such students in one's local school or district. Of course, this can be achieved by way of a needs assessment followed by adjusting one's guidance and counseling curriculum or model according to the needs identified.

CONCLUSION

This article about the needs of newly arrived immigrant students brings several things to light. Firstly, many existing programs are still in their infancy but are very promising in terms of their effectiveness. This is especially true of the work of school counselors considering the fact that their roles in current programs have been limited. Opportunity for greater input and service definitely exists. Secondly, existing programs must constantly evolve to meet and accommodate students' needs. The ethnic and cultural composition of the immigrant student population has continually changed and continues to do so. Depending on the region of the United States, even the specific countries of origin as well as the numbers can change over time. For example, in Miami-Dade County, Florida, newly arrived immigrant students typically came from Cuba. Nowadays, there are increasing numbers coming from a variety of Central and South American countries. Hence, as the composition and numbers of newly arrived immigrant students change, so must programs that serve these students. If not, these programs run the risk of becoming obsolete and ineffective for the populations that they serve.

It may well be that many of the aforementioned suggested implications for school counselors infer a major paradigm shift in the way that school guidance and counseling is practiced. School counselors would need to be encouraged to continue to go the extra mile for their students – in this case, those who are newly arrived in this country. No matter what interventions are implemented or what programs are proposed, however, counselors must remember that foremost of all are the needs of their students. As discussed above, newly arrived immigrant students have special needs. These needs deserve attention just as do the needs of any other students. Once school counselors recognize and attend to these needs, newly arrived immigrant students will be better helped within American public schools.

Franklyn C. Williams is a doctoral candidate in the Counselor Education program, Department of Child, Family, and Community Sciences. E-mail: frwillia@mail.ucf.edu. S. Kent Butler, Ph.D., is an assistant professor, Division of Counseling and Family Therapy. Both are with the University of Central Florida, Orlando.

REFERENCES

American Psychiatric Association. (1994). *Diagnostic and statistical manual of mental disorders* (4th ed.). Washington, DC: Author.

Cardenas, J., & Taylor, L. (1993). Transition support for immigrant students. *Journal of Multicultural Counseling and Development, 21*(4), 203–210.

Center of Applied Linguistics. (2000). *Newcomers: Language and academics programs for recent immigrants.* Washington, DC: National Center for Research on Education, Diversity, and Excellence.

Feinberg, R. C. (2000). Newcomer schools: Salvation or segregated oblivion for immigrant students. *Theory Into Practice, 39*, 220–227.

First, J.M. (1988). Immigrant students in U.S. public schools: Challenges with solutions. *Phi Delta Kappan, 70*, 205–210.

Immigrant teens: Overlooked and underserved. (2001, March/April) *Leadership, 30*(4), p. 6.

James, D. C. S. (1997). Psychosocial risks of immigrant students. *The Education Digest, 63*, 51–53.

Jay, J. (2000). Issues in counseling immigrant college students. Community College of *Journal of Research and Practice, 24*, 577–586.

Kellogg, J. B. (1988). Forces of change. *Phi Delta Kappan, 70*, 199–204.

McDonnell, L. M., & Hill, P.T. (1993). Immigrant education: The incredible shrinking priority. *Education Digest, 59*, 35–39.

Olsen, L., & Jaramillo, A. (2000).When time is on our side: Redesigning schools to meet the needs of immigrant students. In P. Gándara (Ed.), *The dimensions of time and the challenge of school reform* (pp. 225–250). Albany, NY: State University of New York.

Perkins, L.M. (2000). The new immigrants and education: Challenges and issues. *Educational Horizons, 78*(2), 67–71.

Perry, M. J., & Mackun, P. J. (2000). *Population change and distribution.* Washington, DC: U.S. Census Bureau.

Rong, X. L., & Preissle, J. (1998). *Educating immigrant students: What we need to know to meet the challenges.* Thousand Oaks, CA: Corwin.

Ruiz de Velasco, J., & Fix, M. (2000).*Overlooked and underserved: Immigrant children in U. S. secondary schools.* Washington, DC: Urban Institute.

Short,D. J. (2000). *Secondary newcomer programs: Helping recent immigrants prepare for school success.* Washington, DC: Center for Applied Linguistics.

Empowering African-American Adolescent Females

By Cheryl C. Holcomb-McCoy, Ph.D. and Cheryl Moore-Thomas, Ph.D.

This article originally appeared in *Professional School Counseling*, Vol. 5, No. 1, 2001.

In the past two decades, there has been a small but growing body of literature pertaining to the issues and counseling needs of African-American adolescent females (e.g., Boyd-Franklin, 1991; Harris, 1992; Muller, 2000). This increase of literature is due, in part, to the growing numbers of African-American females experiencing depression (White, 1990), eating disorders (Lester & Petrie, 1998), and suicide (Gibbs, 1988). Furthermore, African-American adolescent females are contending with typical developmental tasks in the context of a society that has historically devalued and portrayed African-American women either as poor, welfare-dependent, working-class women, or as mothers of illegitimate, impoverished, and delinquent children (Coultas, 1989; hooks, 1981). These negative societal images and stereotypes have adversely affected the self-esteem and, consequently, the academic and emotional development of young African-American females (Neal & Wilson, 1989). For this reason, African-American adolescent females are prime candidates for counseling in schools.

The purpose of this article is three-fold: (a) to review issues that can be considered when counseling African-American adolescent females; (b) to discuss counseling implications based on those issues; and (c) through the use of a case example, to illustrate a school counselor successfully assisting and empowering a member of this adolescent group.

COUNSELING ISSUES

This section discusses relevant issues to consider when counseling African-American adolescent females. These issues were selected based on our experiences as African-American females and on the literature pertaining to the mental health of African-American women. By no means are these the only issues that African-American adolescent females experience or present in counseling. However, school counselors might consider these highlighted general issues when conceptualizing cases involving these adolescents.

The phrase *African-American adolescent females* is used in this article to describe adolescent females who identify themselves as Black or African American. Since these adolescents are not a homogeneous group, the reader is advised to use the information presented in this article as one of many resources to understand the complexities of growth and development an African-American female experiences.

Racism, Sexism, and Classism

According to Almquist (1995), African-American women have the distinction of being the only group that was enslaved and brought to the United States to "work, produce, and to reproduce" (p. 577). Numerous social scientists and researchers have written about the continued dual oppression that Black women face because of racism and sexism (e.g., Beale, 1970; Giddings, 1984; Greene, 1992; Harley & Terborg-Penn, 1997; Murray, 1970; Reid, 1988). Others (e.g., Blumberg, 1991; hooks, 1993) have addressed the triple oppression based on race, gender, and class with which African-American women contend because of the disproportionate number of them who are economically disadvantaged.

The effects of dual and triple oppression are significant when conceptualizing the problems and concerns of African-American adolescent females. For instance, a school counselor might ask a 15-year-old African-American female with a 3.75 grade point average why she has not applied to college. The student might respond by stating, "Why should I? My family can't afford to pay for it, and they won't accept me anyway because I'm Black!" This student's response reflects feelings of hopelessness as a result of her family's financial as well as racial background. Or, another example might be a 12-year-old African-American female student who expresses discontent in school because she believes that she is not capable. When asked why she feels this way, she responds, "I'm not a Black boy, so I can't be a "star athlete" and I'm not White, so I can't be a "star student!" These perceptions linked to gender, race, and socioeconomic status can ultimately lead to feelings of powerlessness among African-American female adolescents (Fordham, 1993).

Body Image and Physical Attractiveness

The American ideals of beauty (e.g., blond hair, blue eyes, thin) as defined by White American males have been noted in the literature as having a damaging effect on Black women's sense of self (e.g., Okazawa-Rey, Robinson, & Ward, 1987; Perkins, 1996; Reid, 1988; Smith, Gurlew, & Lundgren, 1991). Hooks (1993), in the following passage, captured images of "black femaleness":

...the dearth of affirming images of black femaleness in art, magazines, movies, and television reflects not only the racist white world's way of seeing us, but the way we see ourselves. It is no mystery to most black women that we have internalized racist/sexist notions of beauty that lead many of us to think we are ugly. (p. 84)

Examples of African-American women's struggles with physical attractiveness are found in African-American literature. For instance, Sinclair's 1994 African-American novel, *Coffee Will Make You Blacker*, is replete with examples of how African-American women despair over their skin color, hair texture, and body features. The main character, Stevie, reflected on her mother's hopes for her:

Mama says she wishes I'd gotten more of Daddy's lighter color and especially his curly hair. She says she prayed that if I were a girl, I'd have good hair that didn't need to be straightened. Mama says one reason she married Daddy was cause she was looking out for her children. She says it was almost unheard of for a colored man to marry a woman who was darker than him. Mama was lucky she's glad I don't have a wide nose and big lips. (p. 8)

Unfortunately, a woman's physical attractiveness can be a significant factor in her life. Female physical attractiveness has been linked to such factors as mate selection (Hollender & Schafer, 1981), preferential treatment (Lynn & Simons, 2000), and job selection (Watkins & Johnston, 2000). For African-American females, physical attractiveness has been a source of great stress and many have been deeply scarred by negative reactions to African physical features (Fordham, 1993). Even more damaging is the degrading manner in which African-American females are treated by other African Americans who have internalized society's messages about African-American physical features and female attractiveness (Gainor, 1992; Powell, 1982). An African-American father who openly wishes his young daughter had lighter skin or an African-American teacher who favors lighter-skinned African-American adolescent females with naturally "straight" hair are instances in which negative perceptions of physical features can have a long-lasting affect on the self-concept of young African-American females.

Ethnic Identity Development

Identity formation, as seen by Erikson (1968), is the primary developmental task of the adolescent years. Although all adolescents struggle with identity issues, not all adolescents think about themselves in racial or ethnic terms. Phinney (1990) proposed a model of ethnic identity based on Marcia's (1966) four identity statuses, which are determined by the presence or absence of exploration and commitment. Phinney's model characterizes the variation in the ethnic identity search process as follows: (a) diffuse, a state in which there has been little exploration or active consideration of ethnicity, and no psychological commitment to any ethnic group; (b) foreclosed, a state in which a commitment has been made to a particular ethnic group's beliefs, values, and/or customs, without actively searching or exploring one's ethnic heritage or ethnicity; (c) moratorium, a state of active exploration of one's ethnicity in which no commitment has yet been made; and (d) achieved, a state of strong personal commitment to a particular ethnic identity following a period of high exploration or crisis.

Phinney (1990), like Marcia (1966), proposed that an individual needs a period of ethnic exploration in order to secure an achieved ethnic identity. Tatum (1997) suggested that it is this need for ethnic exploration that causes African-American students, particularly African-American female adolescents, to frequently socialize with each other in school. In an exploratory study of the experience of identity in late-adolescent African-American females, Shorter-Gooden and Washington (1996) found that ethnic identity was the most salient aspect of this population's self-definition. Other research has indicated that there is a relationship between ethnic identity and African-American females' self-esteem (Phinney, Cantu, & Kurtz, 1997), ethnic socialization (Marshall, 1995), and selection of friends (Hamm, 2000).

Development of Trust

The willingness of a client to trust a counselor has long been considered an important aspect of the counseling relationship (Rogers, 1942). A number of investigators have even indicated that mistrust plays a significant role in the counseling process involving Black clients and White counselors (Terrell & Terrell, 1984; Thompson, Neville, Weathers, Poston, & Atkinson, 1990; Watkins & Terrell, 1988). African-American clients' mistrust of White counselors has been linked to the prejudicial and discriminatory practices of White Americans towards African Americans (Grier & Cobbs, 1968; Thompson, Worthington, & Atkinson, 1994). The term *cultural paranoia* has been used to describe this type of African-American mistrust (e.g., Ridley, 1984).

When counseling African-American adolescent females, school counselors should consider mistrust as a possible barrier to counseling. Terrell and Terrell (1981) purported that many Black students distrust White school personnel because of past prejudicial contact with White teachers and White individuals outside of the school. For instance, an African-American student, regardless of how he or she performs academically, may perceive a White teacher to be biased against him or her based on his or her race. This perception may also extend to White counselors. Therefore, school counselors, particularly White counselors, need to be cognizant of mistrust as a possible variable in the counseling process and, as a result, place emphasis on developing trust and rapport with African-American adolescent females.

Religion and Spirituality

Religion and spirituality have historically played important roles in the lives of many African Americans, particularly African-American females (Chatters, Taylor, & Lincoln, 1999; Constantine, Lewis, Conner, & Sanchez, 2000; Nobles, 1991). For many African Americans, religion and spirituality are embedded deeply in their day-to-day activities and rituals (Constantine et al., 2000). For instance, studies (e.g., Taylor, Chatters, Jayakody, & Levin, 1996) over the past 10 years have reported that a majority of African Americans are affiliated with a religious denomination and, more specifically, African Americans have reported higher levels of attendance at religious services than Whites have. Interestingly, Broman (1996) found that African-American women are more likely than others to use prayer in response to interpersonal, physical, and emotional problems.

Considering the general importance of religious and spiritual beliefs in the lives of many African-American families, African-American adolescent females' behavior may be affected and shaped by these beliefs. For instance, an African-American female student may talk of prayer as a means of coping with her concerns, or she may be more focused on activities related to her church rather than those related to school.

IMPLICATIONS FOR SCHOOL COUNSELING

As the previous counseling issues illustrate, African-American adolescent females may present a challenge for many school counselors. We believe that school counselors can play a pivotal role in empowering African-American adolescent females' sense of self. This section addresses several implications for school counselors when working with these adolescents.

Since many African-American adolescent females may have experienced rejection, disapproval, and/or prejudice in and outside the school setting, they may approach counseling with a great deal of anxiety, distrust, and apprehension. School counselors can minimize these emotions by demystifying the counseling process and focusing on developing a trusting relationship with these young females. By briefly and simply describing the counseling process before initiating it, the school counselor provides the young African-American female student the opportunity to ask questions about "what counselors do" and to identify the limitations of counseling. Counselors might also meet with these students in informal settings (e.g., cafeteria, school courtyard, playground, hall), which are less intimidating and are perceived as "neutral" territory. Gibbs (1990) even suggested that initially African-American youths are more concerned about the counselor's interpersonal skills than the counselor's counseling skills. Gibbs, therefore, recommended that it is imperative for counselors to develop rapport with African-American adolescents so that trust is gained for future counseling.

One area in which school counselors can empower African-American female adolescents is assisting the adolescents to develop an attitude that reinforces their willingness to take responsibility for changes that need to be made in their life or schooling. According to Edwards and Polite (1992), this attitude positions African Americans to have a sense of control over their environment, which is often perceived as racist and hostile. This attitude also enhances the potential of African-American female adolescents' to achieve in the context of a society that has historically devalued their reference groups (e.g., women, African Americans). Young African-American females who take personal responsibility rarely talk of luck or chance but have the attitude that expresses, "If I want it, I have to go for it, work for it."

In order to instill this attitude of taking personal responsibility for one's success, school counselors can assist African-American female adolescents in developing procedural or goal sequences that lead to planned action. Although school counselors and other school professionals assist all students in developing goals, African-American adolescent females seem to benefit from this intervention because of the seemingly overwhelming barriers they face due to their race and gender. To begin this process, school counselors might ask young African-American females, "What do you want to be doing in 5 years? 10 years? 25 years? How do you plan to achieve your goal in 10 years?" By developing goals, organizing a plan to achieve the goal, implementing the plan, and then evaluating the outcome of the plan, an African-American female adolescent has a useful approach to achieving success in not only her schoolwork but also her personal life.

School counselors can also empower African-American female adolescents by helping them manage the impact of others' negative perceptions. While many African-American adolescent females may not dwell on their racial, gender, or economic status, coping with others' faulty perceptions based on stereotypes is an ongoing and difficult task that will likely impact the adolescents' lives (Boyd-Franklin & Franklin, 2000). The goal then is for these youths to avoid letting others' negative perceptions block their achievements. This, according to Edwards and Polite (1992), is a difficult but necessary task that requires African Americans to possess a "heightened sense of consciousness, a finely tuned sense of control, an ability to assess a situation, make critical judgments, and take appropriate action" (p. 249).

Assisting African-American female adolescents in managing the impact of others' negative faulty perceptions can be done by using case scenarios depicting problems involving racism, sexism, and/or classism as catalysts for discussions. During these discussions, it is important for school counselors to take a "nonexpert" role so that the adolescents feel comfortable expressing their feelings. Counselors can ask questions that provide the adolescents with an opportunity to not only articulate their feelings about racism but also brainstorm new ways of challenging and managing racist encounters. Examples of questions might include "What do you feel as you read/listen to this scenario?" "What is your first reaction to the scenario?" "What might happen next after your reaction?" and "How might others deal with this situation?"

As stated previously, living in a society that devalues one's race and gender can be a devastating and challenging experience that impacts one's self-esteem and self-concept. For this reason, instilling self-acceptance is a critical aspect of empowering African-American adolescent females. School counselors can assist this population to in developing self-acceptance by reminding the youths of their inner as well as outer beauty and the significant aspects of their African-American heritage. School counselors might invite African-American women from the community or community organizations (e.g., churches) to serve as mentors or "buddies" for African-American adolescent females struggling with self-acceptance.

School counselors might also encourage these students to research their ethnic heritage by reading selected literature, attending cultural exhibits, and interacting with "experts" on African-American history/culture. Developing groups for African-American females has been supported in the literature as one way in which to encourage ethnic identity exploration (Gainor, 1992; Muller, 2000).

And, lastly, incorporating spirituality and religion into the counseling process can be an important consideration when counseling African-American female adolescents. Recognizing the importance of religion and spirituality in the lives of these adolescents enables school counselors to more fully appreciate indigenous support resources (e.g., deacons, ministers, pastors) in the adolescents' communities. School counselors may invite the support individuals to be part of open counseling groups, or the counselors may develop professional alliances with these persons to consult on specific cases, within the mandates of confidentiality. Counselors who recognize and encourage the disclosure of religious and spiritual beliefs in counseling may provide their African-American female clients with an important source of empowerment.

CASE EXAMPLE

Determining the appropriate counseling intervention for an African-American female adolescent requires the school counselor to consider many of the issues previously discussed. The following case example is presented to illustrate an effective and empowering counseling intervention used with a 13-year-old African-American female student.

Angela is a student at Western Middle School (fictional name), which is located in a predominately White suburb of a large city. Two years earlier, Angela's family had moved to the suburbs from a predominately Black community in Chicago. The relocation was quite difficult for Angela. She missed her friends and was unaccustomed to being a numerical "minority" among fellow students.

After a few months at Western, Angela's grades (which had been all A's and B's) declined, and she complained of having difficulty developing friendships. In addition to her academic and friendship concerns, Angela accused her teachers of being racist and discriminatory. She also reported that many students called her "racial names" and that she felt like an "outsider." Before long, Angela became involved in several confrontations with students and teachers. Teachers, consequently, perceived Angela to be a "problem student."

Initially, the school counselor requested that Angela meet with her for a short "get-to-know-you" conference. During the conference, the school counselor spent a significant amount of time listening and empathizing with Angela's concerns. Because it was apparent from Angela's body language (e.g., crossed arms, lack of eye contact, frowning, sitting in a chair far away from the counselor) that she was not comfortable, the counselor focused primarily on Angela's interests and hobbies.

Over the next month, Angela met with the school counselor informally. She shared her perceptions that many of Western's teachers and students were prejudiced and racist. Although the counselor was unsure of the accuracy of Angela's accusations, the counselor validated and listened to her concerns. In order to better understand the racial incidents, the counselor asked Angela to describe and then role play the incidents. When processing the role plays, the counselor did not take on an "expert" role. Instead, she allowed Angela to discuss her thoughts, feelings, and perceptions. Following these conversations with Angela, the school counselor met with the principal to discuss her concerns about the possible racial insensitivity among faculty and students. Based on informal meetings with ethnic minority students and parents regarding the school's climate, the principal initiated a series of professional development workshops on cultural sensitivity for the school's faculty.

As Angela's trust in the counselor grew, Angela agreed to set goals and discuss strategies for getting better grades and feeling more comfortable at school. The school counselor asked Angela to develop at least one goal related to academics and one related to making friends or feeling more comfortable at school. Angela's first goal was to increase her semester grades by one letter grade. Her second goal was to attend a school-sponsored dance. As Angela and the counselor discussed her goals, it became apparent that Angela linked her inability to feel more comfortable at school to her race/ethnicity. She disclosed that she felt alienated from the other girls because of her physical features (e.g., dark skin, full lips, and short curly hair). The counselor engaged Angela in activities that required her to assess society's unfair definitions of beauty. They reviewed magazines for hidden messages about beauty and how different cultures define beauty. The school counselor also made sure to highlight Angela's positive personality and academic characteristics so that physical attributes were not the sole focus of defining beauty. It is important to note that the counselor had read literature pertaining to the social and emotional development of African-American females to further her understanding of Angela's experiences (see Appendix for listing of books about African-American women).

After several meetings with the school counselor, Angela opened up about her anxieties about being Black at Western and her fears of not being accepted. The counselor used empathy, encouragement, reflection of feelings, and clarifying to empower Angela to be more self-accepting. By the end of the year, Angela had two best friends and her grades increased dramatically. Although she was still a bit uncomfortable with many of her teachers, she reported that school was "O.K!"

CONCLUSIONS

As the case example illustrates, school counselors who understand the distinct issues and challenges associated with being African American and female in America constitute a potent force for making educational and social empowerment for African-American adolescent females a reality. In his work on African-American young males, Lee (1992) suggested that counselors should have "a solid Black cultural knowledge base to address the educational challenges facing Black males" (p. 16). We believe the same is true for African-American female adolescents. In order for school counselors to serve these female adolescents effectively, the counselors must be attuned to the social realities of the youths' environments as well as to the stereotypes and faulty perceptions about African-American women held by many (Greene, 1994).

Adhering to the recommendations outlined in this article will likely empower African-American female adolescents; however, school counselors must not stop with these recommendations. The process of becoming more sensitive to the needs and issues of these youths is ongoing. We believe that concerned school counselors should also participate in professional development activities that promote cultural responsiveness with African-American female adolescents. Examples of such activities that provide opportunities to enhance school counselors' work with this population include, but are not limited to, the following:

1. Examine one's own attitudes, stereotypes, and biases regarding African Americans and, in particular, African-American females.
2. Read relevant literature pertaining to African-American culture, particularly that of African-American females (see the Appendix).
3. Develop a professional support network with African-American female counseling professionals.
4. Participate in professional development activities (e.g., workshops, conference sessions) that specifically address issues related to African American females, particularly young African-American females.

School counselors must be aware that young African-American females are faced with the difficult task of resisting negative stereotypes about African-American women. Therefore, school counselors who understand this task, along with the challenges that confront African-American women because of their race, gender, and, oftentimes, socioeconomic background, are better equipped to empower and assist young African-American females in acquiring optimum development.

Cheryl C. Holcomb-McCoy, Ph.D., is an assistant professor, Department of Counseling and Personnel Services, University of Maryland at College Park. Cheryl Moore-Thomas, Ph.D., is an assistant professor, Department of Education, Loyola College in Maryland, Baltimore.

REFERENCES

Almquist, E. M. (1995). The experiences of minority women in the U.S.: Intersections of race, gender, and class. In J. Freeman (Ed.), *Women: A feminist perspective* (pp. 573–606). Mountain View, CA: Mayfield.

Beale, F. (1970). Double jeopardy: To be Black and female. In T. Cade (Ed.), *The Black woman* (pp. 90–100). New York: New American Library.

Blumberg, R. (1991). Afterword: Racial ethnic women's labor: Factoring in gender stratification. In R. Blumberg (Ed.), *Gender, family, and economy: The tri-overlap* (pp. 201–208). Newbury Park, CA: Sage.

Boyd-Franklin, N. (1991). Recurrent themes in the treatment of African American women in group psychotherapy. *Women and Therapy, 11*, 25–40.

Boyd-Franklin, N., & Franklin, A. J. (2000). *Boys into men: Raising our African American teenage sons.* New York: Dutton.

Broman, C. L. (1996). Coping with personal problems. In H. W. Neighbors & J. S. Jackson (Eds.), *Mental health in Black America* (pp. 117–129). Thousand Oaks, CA: Sage.

Chatters, L. M., Taylor, R. J., & Lincoln, K. D. (1999). African American religious participation: A multi-sample comparison. *Journal for the Scientific Study of Religion, 38*, 132–146.

Constantine, M. G., Lewis, E. L., Conner, E. L., & Sanchez, D. (2000). Addressing spiritual and religious issues in counseling African Americans: Implications for counselor training and practice. *Counseling and Values, 45*, 28–39.

Coultas, V. (1989). Black adolescent females and self-esteem. *Gender and Education, 1*, 283–294.

Edwards, A., & Polite, C. K. (1992). *Children of the dream: The psychology of black success.* New York: Doubleday.

Erikson, E. (1968). *Identity: Youth and crisis.* New York: Norton.

Fordham, S. (1993). Those loud black adolescent females: Black women, silence, and gender passing in the academy. *Anthropology and Education Quarterly, 24*, 3–32.

Gainor, K. (1992). Internalized oppression as a barrier to effective group work with Black women. *Journal for Specialists in Group Work, 17*, 2–6.

Gibbs, J. T. (1988). Conceptual, methodological, and sociocultural issues in Black youth suicide: Implications for assessment and early intervention. *Suicide and Life-Threatening Behavior, 18*, 73–89.

Gibbs, J. T. (1990). Mental health issues of Black adolescents: Implications for policy and practice. In A. R. Stiffman & L. E. Davis (Eds.), *Ethnic issues in adolescent mental health* (pp. 21–52). Newbury Park, CA: Sage.

Giddings, P. (1984). *When and where I enter: The impact of black women on race and sex in America.* New York: Bantam Books.

Greene, B. (1992). African American women: The burden of racism and sexism. *American Family Therapy Association Newsletter, 48,* 20–23.

Greene, B. (1994). African American women: Derivations of racism and sexism in psychotherapy. In E. Toback & B. Russ (Eds.), *Sexism and racism: Challenges to genetic explanations of diversity.* New York: Feminist Press.

Grier, W. H., & Cobbs, P. M. (1968). *Black rage.* New York: Basic Books.

Hamm, J. V. (2000). Do birds of a feather flock together? The variable bases for African American, Asian American, and European American adolescents' selection of friends. *Developmental Psychology, 36,* 209–219.

Harley, S., & Terborg-Penn, R. (1997). *The Afro-American woman: Struggles and images.* Baltimore: Black Classic Press.

Harris, D. (1992). A cultural model for assessing the growth and development of the African American female. *Journal of Multicultural Counseling and Development, 20,* 158–163.

Hollender, J., & Schafer, L. (1981). Male acceptance of female career roles. *Sex Roles: A Journal of Research, 7,* 1199–1204.

hooks, b. (1981). *Ain't I a woman: Black women and feminism.* Boston: South End Press.

hooks, b. (1993). *Sisters of the yam.* Boston: South End Press.

Lee, C. C. (1992). *Empowering young Black males.* Ann Arbor, MI: ERIC/CASS.

Lester, R., & Petrie, T. A. (1998). Physical, psychological, and societal correlates of bulimic symptomatology among African American college women. *Journal of Counseling Psychology, 45,* 315–321.

Lynn, M., & Simons, T. (2000). Predictors of male and female servers' average tip earnings. *Journal of Applied Social Psychology, 30,* 241–252.

Marcia, J. (1966). Development and validation of ego identity status. *Journal of Personality and Social Psychology, 3,* 551–558.

Marshall, S. (1995). Ethnic socialization of African American children: Implications for parenting, identity development, and academic achievement. *Journal of Youth and Adolescence, 24,* 377–396.

Muller, L. E. (2000). A 12-session, European-American-led counseling group for African American females. *Professional School Counseling, 3,* 264–269.

Murray, P. (1970). The liberation of Black women. In M. L. Thompson (Ed.), *Voices of new feminism* (pp. 87–102). Boston: Beacon Press.

Neal, A., & Wilson, M. (1989). The role of skin color and features in the Black community: Implications for Black women and therapy. *Clinical Psychology Review, 9,* 323–333.

Nobles, W. W. (1991). African philosophy: Foundations of Black psychology. In R. L. Jones (Ed.), *Black psychology* (pp. 47–63). Berkeley, CA: Cobb & Henry.

Okazawa-Rey, M., Robinson, T., & Ward, J. (1987). Black women and the politics of skin color and hair. *Women and Therapy, 6,* 89–91.

Perkins, K. R. (1996). The influence of television images on Black females' self-perceptions of physical attractiveness. *Journal of Black Psychology, 22,* 453–469.

Phinney, J. (1990). Ethnic identity in adolescents and adults: A review of research. *Psychological Bulletin, 108,* 499–514.

Phinney, J., Cantu, C. L., & Kurtz, D. A. (1997). Ethnic and American identity as predictors of self-esteem among African American, Latino, and White adolescents. *Journal of Youth and Adolescence, 26,* 165–185.

Powell, G. J. (1982). The impact of television on the self-concept development of minority group children. In G. L. Berry & C. Mitchell-Kerman (Eds.), *Television and the socialization of the minority child* (pp. 105–131). New York: Academic Press.

Reid, P. T. (1988). Racism and sexism: Comparisons and conflicts. In P. A. Katz & D. Taylor (Eds.), *Eliminating racism: Profiles in controversy* (pp. 203–221). New York: Plenum.

Ridley, C. R. (1984). Clinical treatment of the nondisclosing Black client: A therapeutic paradox. *American Psychologist, 39,* 1234–1244.

Rogers, C. R. (1942). *Counseling and psychotherapy.* Boston: Houghton Mifflin.

Shorter-Gooden, K., & Washington, N. C. (1996). Young, Black, and female: The challenge of weaving an identity. *Journal of Adolescence, 19,* 465–475.

Sinclair, A. (1994). *Coffee will make you blacker.* New York: Hyperion.

Smith, L., Gurlew, A., & Lundgren, D. (1991). Black consciousness, self-esteem, and satisfaction with physical appearance among African American female college students. *Journal of Black Studies, 22,* 269–273.

Tatum, B. D. (1997). *Why are all the Black kids sitting together in the cafeteria? And other conversations about race.* New York: Basic Books.

Taylor, R. J., Chatters, L. M., Jayakody, R., & Levin, J. S. (1996). Black and White differences in religious participation: A multisample comparison. *Journal for the Scientific Study of Religion, 35,* 403–410.

Terrell, F., & Terrell, S. L. (1981). An inventory to measure cultural mistrust among Blacks. *Western Journal of Black Studies, 5,* 180–184.

Terrell, F., & Terrell, S. (1984). Race of counselor, client sex, cultural mistrust level, and premature termination from counseling among Black clients. *Journal of Counseling Psychology, 31,* 371–375.

Thompson, C. E., Neville, H., Weathers, P. L., Poston, W. C., & Atkinson, D. R. (1990). Cultural mistrust and racism reaction among African American students. *Journal of College Student Development, 31,* 162–168.

Thompson, C. E., Worthington, R., & Atkinson, D. R. (1994). Counselor content orientation, counselor race, and Black women's cultural mistrust and self-disclosure. *Journal of Counseling Psychology, 41,* 155–161.

Watkins, L. M., & Johnston, L. (2000). Screening job applicants: The impact of physical attractiveness and application quality. *International Journal of Selection and Assessment, 8,* 76–84.

Watkins, C. E., & Terrell, F. (1988). Mistrust level and its effect on counseling expectations in Black client-White counselor relationships: An analogue study. *Journal of Counseling Psychology, 35,* 194–197.

White, E. (1990). *The Black woman's health book: Speaking for ourselves.* Seattle, WA: Seal Press.

APPENDIX

Selected Literature Related to African-American Females

Angelou, M. (1970). *I know why the caged bird sings.* New York: Bantam.

Angelou, M. (1974). *Gather together in my name.* New York: Random House.

Angelou, M. (1977). *Singing and swinging and getting merry like Christmas.* New York: Bantam Books.

Angelou, M. (1981). *The heart of a woman.* New York: Random House.

Angelou, M. (1986). *All God's children need traveling shoes.* New York: Random House.

Bambara, T. C. (1970). *The black woman.* New York: Random House.

Benjamin, L. (1991). *The black elite: Facing the color line in the twilight of the twentieth century.* Chicago: Nelson-Hall.

Boyd-Franklin, N. (1989). *Black families in therapy: A multisystems approach.* New York: Guilford.

Cole, J. B. (1993). *Conversations: Straight talk with America's sister president.* New York: Doubleday.

Davis, A. (1983). *Women, race, and class.* New York: Vintage Books.

Gibbs, J. T., & Huang, L. N. (1989). *Children of color: Psychological interventions with minority youth.* San Francisco: Jossey-Bass.

hooks, b. (1992). *Black looks: Race and representation.* Boston: South End Press.

Hurston, Z. N. (1991). *Their eyes were watching God.* Chicago: University of Illinois Press.

Lorde, A. (1984). *Sister outsider.* Freedom, CA: Crossing Press.

Morrison, T. (1972). *The bluest eye.* New York: Washington Square Press.

Naylor, G. (1983). *The women of Brewster place.* New York: Penguin.

Rudwick, B. M. (1971). *Black matriarchy: Myth or reality?* Belmont, CA: Wadsworth.

Russell, K., Wilson, M., & Hall, R. (1992). *The color complex: The politics of skin color among African Americans.* New York: Harcourt Brace Jovanovic

Prospective First-Generation College Students: Meeting Their Needs Through Social Cognitive Career Theory

By Melinda M. Gibbons and Marie F. Shoffner, Ph.D.

This article originally appeared in *Professional School Counseling*, Vol. 8, No. 1, 2004.

First-generation students, or students whose parents did not attend college, represent 27% of all graduating high school students. They have unique needs that separate them from other students and that must be addressed in counseling. This article examines how school and career counselors can help these students through the use of Social Cognitive Career Theory. This theory and its focus on self-efficacy, outcome expectations, barriers, and goals can help with career and academic decision-making. A case example working with a high school junior is provided as an example of how this theory can assist this population. Implications for future research and counseling strategies are suggested as well.

One of the many duties that high school counselors perform is assisting with the career development of their students. School counselors generally agree that all students need to understand the relationship between interests, abilities, and the world of work, and how to identify and act on information pertaining to furthering their education (Barker & Satcher, 2000). In addition, the American School Counseling Association recently released its new model for school counseling programs (ASCA, 2003) based on the National Standards (ASCA, 1997). Within this National Model, it is suggested that school counselors should promote programs designed to enhance the academic, career, and personal/ social domains of students. The model promotes three standards specifically related to career and includes student competencies such as developing career awareness, identifying career goals, and gaining understanding of information and how to apply this to reach career goals. The authors of the model also suggest that its structure benefits all students by helping to promote a challenging course of study and increases access to educational opportunities for everyone (ASCA, 2003). Clearly, one of the roles of the school counselor is to be involved with the career development of all students in their schools.

In spite of this, some populations remain underserved in this regard, either because of oversight or a lack of knowledge. One of these groups is prospective first-generation college students. According to information gathered from the National Education Longitudinal Study of 1988 (Horn & Nunez, 2000), approximately 27% of high school graduates in 1992 were first-generation students, or students whose parents did not attend college. Of these students, half were from low-income families and, compared to students with college-graduate parents, were more likely to be Hispanic or African- American. This growing population of students has unique needs that must be addressed by school counselors so that all students may have the same opportunities for appropriate and challenging higher education. The 1994 U.S. Census Bureau (as cited in Indiana Career and Postsecondary Advancement Center, 2000) found a direct correlation between higher education and higher salaries, with 4- year college graduates earning an average of $17,000 more per year than someone with only a high school diploma. To date, however, almost no one has focused on how to assist prospective firstgeneration college students before their arrival to college. Only one article could be located (Fallon, 1997) that focused specifically on primary prevention strategies in working with this population while they are in high school. No theoretical model, however, was applied, and little attention was given to assistance in overcoming barriers to attending college.

The purpose of this article is to examine how school counselors can assist prospective first-generation college students prior to college entrance. This article focuses on how the needs of these students may be met through the application of Social Cognitive Career Theory (Lent, Brown, & Hackett, 1994). The use of the term *college* refers to any formal education beyond high school leading to a degree. This can, and often does, include community college. The first section of this article centers on the unique needs of these students, followed by an explanation of the theory. A case example relevant to working with first-generation students is given to assist in practical application of the theory. Implications for future research are provided as well.

FIRST-GENERATION COLLEGE STUDENTS

Empirical research on first generation college students has helped to identify several unique characteristics of this population. Inman and Mayes (1999) examined differences of first-generation community college students and found that they were more likely to be female, older, come from lower-income families, and to have more financial dependents than other students. Horn and Nunez (2000) also found that first-generation college students tended to be from low-income families and were more likely to be Hispanic or African-American. Students in this population have a strong desire to attend college (Solorzano, 1992; Valadez, 1998), perceive themselves as being as capable as other college students (McGregor, Mayleben, Buzzanga, Davis, & Becker, 1991), and recognize the importance of course options at the college level (Inman & Mayes). Other strengths of these students included a stronger desire to accomplish degree goals than other students (Inman & Mayes) and a commitment to college equal to that of other college students (York- Anderson & Bowman, 1991). There are five specific areas in which first-generation college students seem to have different demographics than other college students. Differences are evident in the lack of parental experience with the college application process, how these students prepare for college both personally and academically, why they choose to attend college, and in their personal experiences and overall personality traits.

1. **Prospective first-generation college students face the daunting task of applying to college without the assistance of parental experience.** Due to a lack of knowledge, parents may be unable to help with many of the logistical requirements related to career and college planning. Horn and Nunez (2000) found that firstgeneration students were less likely to choose high school programs of study with their parents, while York-Anderson and Bowman (1991) found that these same types of students perceived less support from their families for attending college. This possible lack of involvement by parents only strengthens the need for school and career counselors to be proactive in their assistance with prospective first-generation students. However, while students from low-income families viewed school counselors as a source of college information, these students viewed the information provided as not useful for them (Chapman, O'Brien, & DeMasi, 1987).

2. **Preparation for college life while still in high school seems to make a difference for these students.** First-generation students are more likely to leave college or higher education altogether than were other students, although usually for reasons other than academic failure (Brooks-Terry, 1988). This attrition may be due, in part, to inappropriate college choice or familyrelated constraints. Research has indicated that these students perceived adapting to the stresses of the college environment as more difficult than other students (McGregor et al., 1991). Overall, students from lower SES groups lack access to information to help them with decisions related to college planning (Valadez, 1998). However, low-income students who participated in community service and had successful leadership experience in high school were more likely to show academic progress at the college level (Strage, 1999; Ting, 1998).

3. **First-generation students seem to differ in academic preparation.** Horn and Nunez (2000) found that only 14% of prospective first-generation students took algebra in the eighth grade, compared to over one third of students with college graduate parents. This led to fewer first-generation students completing advanced level math courses, which prohibited them from pursuing college degrees. Riehl (1994) also found differences in academic preparation for first-generation students. His comparison of these students to other college students identified differences in SAT scores, high school grade point average, and overall first-year college performance, with firstgeneration college students scoring lower in each area. Academically, first-generation college students may be less prepared for college than other college-bound youth, leading to another possible barrier to completing college and obtaining a job that will support them financially.

4. **First-generation college students perceive the college experience differently than other college-bound youth.** Higher education is often seen solely as a means to a good job for first-generation students (Brooks-Terry, 1988). This perception, combined with a strong desire to go to school close to home (Inman & Mayes, 1999), could be another reason that so many first-generation students leave college before completing their degrees. Again, lack of information about the many factors regarding college choice may lead these students to select a college that does not meet their needs.

5. **Personality and basic living differences exist for first-generation students as well.** Researchers examining personality differences identified differences in self-esteem, social acceptance, humor, and creativity, with first-generation college students scoring lower in each of these areas when compared to other college students (McGregor et al., 1991). However, global selfworth, job and scholastic competence, and social relationships did not differ for these populations. Clearly, first-generation students have differences in family support and differences in personal qualities when compared to other college students. Other characteristics that differentiate first-generation college students include a higher likelihood to live at home and work part-time (Brooks-Terry, 1988), and a tendency to have more financial dependents, lower family incomes, and work more hours per week (Inman & Mayes, 1999). First-generation students may be less likely to be involved in campus activities due to their work requirements and commute from home, leading to more difficulties in connecting with college life.

Clearly, school counselors need to build upon the strengths of this population and work with these students who want to continue their education while meeting their specific needs. Counselors cannot assume that all college-bound youth are the same, and the evidence is clear that this portion of the population needs specific skills, information, and direction that other college-bound students may already possess. One approach that school counselors can use in assisting this growing population is Social Cognitive Career Theory (Lent et al., 1994).

SOCIAL COGNITIVE CAREER THEORY

Theoretical Overview

Social Cognitive Career Theory (SCCT) was developed as a way to explain career development through focusing on socio-cognitive constructs (Lent, Brown, & Hackett, 1996). Grounded in Bandura's (1986) social cognitive theory, SCCT examines how career and academic interests mature, how career choices are developed, and how these choices are turned into action. This is accomplished through a focus on three primary tenets: self-efficacy, outcome expectations, and goals (Lent et al., 1994).

Self-efficacy refers to the beliefs people have about their ability to successfully complete the steps required for a given task. These beliefs are not fixed, but are rather constantly changing based on interactions with other people, the environment, and one's own behaviors. Individuals develop their sense of self-efficacy from personal performance, learning by example, social interactions, and how they feel in a situation (Lent et al., 1996). For example, Lisa is a 15-year old sophomore who wants to attend college but says she will never go because she lacks the resources and knowledge needed to complete a degree program. Specifically, she says her math grades are terrible and that she feels just plain stupid in class because her math teacher has told her she will never make it in Algebra II next year. Lisa has the belief that she is unable to complete the steps needed to be successful in college based on interactions with others and her performance in math class.

Outcome expectations are beliefs related to the consequences of performing a specific behavior. In contrast to self-efficacy, which refers to a person's belief about the ability to accomplish a particular goal, outcome expectations focus on the consequences someone believes will occur if a particular behavior is performed. Extrinsic reinforcement, selfdirected consequences, and basic task understanding all can be tied to outcome expectations. Typically, outcome expectations are formed through past learning experiences, either direct or vicarious, and the perceived results of these experiences. These expectations are often influenced by self-efficacy, especially when outcomes are based on the quality of a person's performance (Lent et. al., 1994, 1996). Juan, a 17-year old senior, enjoys his course in TV broadcasting, but says he will not pursue a job in journalism because he believes that he will be discriminated against because there is a lack of Latinos in that field. In this example, Juan has perceived a lack of Latinos in journalism, and this has created a negative outcome expectation for this career field.

Finally, goals are seen as playing a primary role in behavior. People are seen as determiners of their own behavior, with environment and genetics playing a secondary role. A goal is defined as the decision to begin a particular activity or future plan. Behavior is organized and sustained based on these previously set goals. SCCT views goals, outcome expectations, and self-efficacy as having a constant, complex, and ever-changing relationship that affects career and academic development and choice (Lent et al., 1994, 1996).

SCCT focuses on the psychological and social effects of race and gender, rather than the physical aspects. The relevance of these factors to career is related to the environmental and personal reactions that gender or race may create. Of particular importance is how gender or race affects the self-efficacy or outcome expectations related to specific vocational interests. Race and gender may limit or expand exposure to various careers, or may influence how a person views the possibility of achievement related to a particular interest. Biases and role socialization are also relevant to this issue (Lent & Brown, 1996).

For example, students of minority ethnicity may lack appropriate role models for various careers. This may create a sense for them that people from their ethnic background do not enter these careers. This could cause students to foreclose on these careers. For example, Xavier, a 16-year old African-American in a low-income urban school, may not be exposed to people of his ethnicity who have college degrees. He may begin to believe that he does not have the ability to get a 4-year degree (self-efficacy). Or consider Jason, an Asian-American who has an interest in art and sculpture. He has been debating going into engineering or graphic design, and has decided on engineering because he believes that Asians have more success in that field (outcome expectation). Both of these students had self-efficacy and outcome expectation beliefs that were directly influenced by their race. In addition, Xavier was also influenced by socioeconomic status. These contextual factors can directly influence students' beliefs about their potential success in career and college.

Perceived Barriers to Success

In SCCT, career interests are regulated by self-efficacy and outcome expectations, meaning people form lasting interests in activities when they experience personal competency and positive outcomes. On the other hand, a belief of low competency or in negative outcomes will lead people to avoid certain activities. Goals are formed based on experiences and their perceived outcomes in different activities. These goals may lead to practice efforts, which may in turn change or reinforce previous self-efficacy and outcome beliefs. SCCT interprets this as a process in constant flux through adolescence. After this time, vocational interests typically stabilize and do not change unless new exposures occur. Perceived barriers such those related to gender, ethnicity, age, socioeconomic status, or family constraints may create negative outcome expectations, even when people have had prior success in the given area.

For example, Charlotte, a 16-year old sophomore with an 8-month old son, believes that her family constraints prohibit her ability to pursue her associate's degree in nursing. She feels that college is too expensive and that she must work during the day once she graduates from high school to support her child. She has resigned herself to the idea that she can only work as a certified nursing assistant, a certification she can complete while still in high school. Students such as Charlotte may develop narrowed career interests and perceived barriers due to lack of exposure to efficacy-building activities, because of inaccurate self-efficacy or outcome expectation beliefs. SCCT also examines the effects of aptitudes and values as mediators in the development of vocational interests (Lent & Brown, 1996).

Interests will turn into occupational choices when an individual perceives few or no barriers to success in that occupation. If barriers to success are perceived as too difficult to overcome, a person will eliminate that occupational choice, even if success in the occupationally related tasks had been achieved. Perceived barriers play a mitigating role in SCCT, where they can shape each experience and directly influence interests and choices (Albert & Luzzo, 1999). In their work with at-risk populations, Chartrand and Rose (1996) recommended addressing environmental and socioeconomic barriers to career success, and applied the constructs of SCCT because of its recognition of these areas.

The career choice process emphasizes the connection between interests, goals, and actions and the successes and failures that create self-efficacy and outcome expectations. SCCT highlights the variables that may influence this choice, in spite of or in conjunction with interests. People may prematurely eliminate occupations because of inaccurate self-efficacy or outcome expectations. These foreclosed occupational options may be reintroduced and reexamined so that self-efficacy or outcome expectations may be judged for accuracy. Additionally, discrepancies between scores on different assessments such as a high aptitude in a particular area coupled with a low interest may be examined with potential for faulty self-efficacy in mind. Analyzing perceived career barriers might also be pertinent when working with career choice. Counselors can help clients identify and prepare for these potential barriers through a listing of any perceived barriers to goal achievement related to a specific career. Finally, SCCT recommends modifying self-efficacy beliefs through introduction of new experiences upon which new self-efficacy and outcome expectations can be built (Brown & Lent, 1996).

To illustrate these concepts, a case example is presented. Although the student in this example is an African-American, many of the issues discussed pertain to prospective first-generation college students in general. In the case of Marcus, the school counselor applies specific interventions targeting the perceptions identified in SCCT as well as incorporating other career- and college-related techniques.

THE CASE OF MARCUS

Marcus is a 16-year old African-American who is trying to decide his future plans. As a junior in high school, he knows that decisions need to be made soon regarding what he will do after graduation. He lives with his mother, a high-school graduate working as an administrative assistant, his grandmother, and his two younger siblings, ages 11 and 13. His father, a high-school dropout, does not live with the family and has had a series of jobs, primarily in the restaurant and hospitality field. Marcus is a 'B' student, takes honors-level science courses, and is involved in school athletics. His mother supports the idea of Marcus continuing his education but wants him to stay close to home so he can continue to work part-time and be available to help care for his brothers.

Marcus has had positive interactions with his school counselor during course registration, so he initiated the first meeting to talk about his future plans. The counselor began by asking him about the interest inventory he had recently completed during a classroom guidance activity so that she could develop a sense of his interests and goals. Marcus reported high scores in Investigative and Realistic (Holland Codes) related occupations, but was uninterested in any of the careers that required an advanced degree. The careers listed as highly matching his interests included engineer, chemist, computer systems analyst, physician, and science teacher. When asked to talk further about this, Marcus said that careers in the science and computer fields were for "white people, geeky white people." He stated that he was considering careers in the automotive industry and that he enjoyed repairing his car and the family car. Marcus also mentioned that his interests moderately matched those for auto mechanics on the interest inventory. When the counselor remarked on his good grades in science and math, Marcus observed that he simply had lenient teachers and that the material was easy. He also indicated that although he did well in those subjects, he would never consider jobs related to them because they would require 4 years of college, and no one in his family had gone to college. This session gave the counselor insight into Marcus's outcome expectations and barriers related to various careers as well as information about self-efficacy beliefs regarding his potential for succeeding in college.

During the second and third sessions, Marcus completed a modified card sort activity, where he sorted various occupations into categories of 'might choose,' 'would not choose,' and 'in question.' Marcus and the counselor then discussed the discarded activities and examined Marcus's reasoning for discarding these activities. The counselor noted that many of the discarded occupations were related to science and math, and Marcus provided reasons such as "there are no black people in this field" and "I could never do something this hard." Brown and Lent (1996) recommended this type of exercise in order to help clients determine if the discarded occupations were due to faulty self-efficacy or outcome expectation beliefs.

The counselor then challenged Marcus to think of other reasons that he did well in math and science classes. Marcus recognized his ability to understand the meaning of scientific theories and saw that he was able to complete complex computations without a calculator. When the counselor asked how others responded to his ability to do well in these subjects, Marcus indicated that his teachers were always pleased with his work, but that his friends often made fun of him for doing well in classes that were just for nerds. This information suggested to the counselor that Marcus might need new experiences so he could create more positive outcome expectations.

The counselor also further explored Marcus's feelings about college. Marcus stated that he wanted to go to college but that doing so would be a financial burden on his family. In addition, if he continued his education, his mother only wanted him to consider a school within a 30-mile radius. As a homework assignment, the counselor asked Marcus to attend the career fair at the high school and talk to at least five people in different careers.

Marcus began the fourth session by sharing what he had learned at the career fair. He explained that he spent a long time talking with an African American engineer who had grown up in the same neighborhood as Marcus. He indicated that the engineer had gone to a college nearby and that he knew of various scholarship opportunities for students who had good grades. He offered Marcus the opportunity to shadow him on the job to see what engineering was all about. Marcus also noted that engineering used math and science skills and could be related to the automotive industry. The counselor observed that Marcus had now begun to create new self-efficacy beliefs and outcome expectations related to science and math careers. The counselor, recognizing some potential barriers facing first-generation students, discussed with Marcus other possible financial aid opportunities and encouraged him to accept the offer of a shadowing experience. Marcus stated that he would call the engineer that evening. The counselor also recommended that Marcus discuss the opportunities of financial aid and nearby colleges with his mother.

The last session with Marcus focused on ways that he could learn more about college life. Marcus had made an appointment to shadow the engineer during winter break, and he reported that his mother had expressed interest in the information about financial aid and generally supported his efforts to continue his education. The counselor provided Marcus with brochures about two different pre-college programs offered in his state. One program was science based while the other had a more general knowledge focus; both offered scholarship opportunities and possible stipends for interested students. In addition, Marcus was encouraged to use the library's computer to visit various college websites and to explore additional careers. These activities were designed to help Marcus obtain a more accurate view of college life with the hope that some potential barriers could be eliminated. The session ended with the counselor inviting Marcus to return whenever he had questions about the college application process.

IMPLICATIONS

Much like the counselor who has helped Marcus to reconsider some of his perceptions of college and of career, school counselors working with students who will be first-generation college students provide activities and interventions to increase these students' options and to increase their success upon entry into college. Specifically, counselors can explore how individuals may perceive each of the major constructs identified in SCCT. Self-efficacy, outcome expectations, perceived barriers, and perceived supports are clearly tied to the interests, goals, and choices of individuals at various points in their educational and career development (Lent, Brown, & Hackett, 1994, 2000). Each of these constructs are addressed in turn, by addressing questions that the counselor should consider while working with a potential first-generation college student.

Self-Efficacy

What does this student believe he or she is capable of doing? In which fields? For what reasons? The initial use of interest inventories and modified card sorts (Brown & Lent, 1996) can be helpful here. Exploring faulty self-efficacy beliefs is especially important. If students say that they are not capable of succeeding in college or getting into college, it is critical that the school counselor challenge this assumption. As follow-up and to increase the acceptance of a new set of self-efficacy beliefs, the counselor can design interventions that will lead to student success and increased self-efficacy. For example, discussions between the counselor and student can focus on exploring the student's true capabilities and reasons for selecting or eliminating particular career fields. The counselor also can help the student explore the reasons behind low self-efficacy related to specific career opportunities. In addition, it is vital to discuss with students their beliefs about their ability to pay for, be successful in, and complete college to determine if these factors have inhibited self-efficacy.

Outcome Expectations

What does this student believe will be the results of entering college? Of entering particular fields? What has led him or her to hold those beliefs? The modified card sort can be useful here as well. Some outcome expectations are based on faulty thinking but others are very real aspects of institutional prejudice in the world of work. It is important to challenge faulty expectations and help students to increase their sense of 'coping self-efficacy' (Lent et al., 1994) in dealing with accurate assessments of what these students might face as they enter college and/or the world of work. The counselor's identification of potential new experiences where self-efficacy and outcome expectations can be challenged and modified is critical. The counselor can help the student find activities that might alter outcome expectations to reflect more positive and realistic views of his or her abilities and beliefs about college and the world of work. Some examples of these such as summer enrichment programs held on college campuses and job shadowing were included in the above case example.

Perceived Barriers and Supports

What barriers does this student perceive that will stand in the way of achievement of the goal of entering college and/or entering into a particular occupation or type of occupation? What supports is he or she able to identify to counterbalance these barriers? Are the perceived barriers based on faulty perceptions? If they are, it is again critical for the counselor to challenge these perceptions and to provide the student with opportunities to create new perceptions around the barriers they might face and the supports available to help them as they proceed. It also is important to prepare these students for college by helping them to understand that some of their experiences and preparation may be different from others in college but that they can nonetheless succeed. One way to do this is to provide them with role models and to establish networks of first-generation college graduates who have been successful in their college career and in their chosen occupations.

CONCLUSION

Since these students tend to differ from students who are not first-generation college students (citations), it is important to provide them with the information and support that will help to counteract inaccurate beliefs and that will serve to provide them with the knowledge that they may not be able to get from their parents or guardians. In addition, counselors can provide programs for both parents and students that can help to fill the gap in knowledge by assisting them in the search process, the decision-making process, college applications, financial aid, and preparing for college life. Small group guidance and counseling can be an effective and efficient way of providing services to a group of first generation students, who can then continue to provide support to each other throughout the process and after they have entered college. Continued contact with identified role models and those who are part of an established network can also be encouraged.

There is a need for future research related to both SCCT and working with prospective first-generation students. First, empirically based articles need to focus on the effectiveness of SCCT versus alternative approaches with this population. Second, additional investigation of applying SCCT to various diverse populations is recommended. Third, research is needed to determine if additional needs are not being met for this population. More investigations focusing on first-generation students prior to their arrival to college is sorely needed. By meeting the needs of first-generation students, counselors can increase all students' potential for success in the academic and career arenas. Failing to address these specific issues serves to alienate this portion of the diverse population that counselors work with each day.

Melinda M. Gibbons is a doctoral student and Marie F. Shoffner, Ph.D., is an associate professor. Both are with the Department of Counseling and Education, The University of North Carolina at Greensboro. E-mail: mmgibbon@uncg.edu.

REFERENCES

Albert, K. A., & Luzzo,D. A. (1999).The role of perceived barriers in career development: A social cognitive perspective. *Journal of Counseling and Development, 77*, 431–436.

American School Counseling Association. (1997). *ASCA national standards*. Retrieved November 1, 2002, from http://www.schoolcounselor.org/content. cfm?L1=1&L2=9.

American School Counseling Association. (2003). *The ASCA national model: A framework for school counseling programs, executive summary*. Retrieved February 5, 2004, from http://www.schoolcounselor.org/ library/ ExecSumm.pdf.

Bandura, A. (1986). *Social foundations of thought and action: a social cognitive theory*. Englewood Cliffs, NC: Prentice- Hall.

Barker, J., & Satcher, J. (2000). School counselors' perceptions of required workplace skills and career development competencies. *Professional School Counseling, 4*, 134–139.

Brooks-Terry, M. (1988). Tracing the disadvantages of first-generation college students: An application of Sussman's option sequence model. In S. Steinmetz (Ed.), *Family and support systems across the life span* (pp. 121–134).New York: Plenum.

Brown, S.D., & Lent, R.W. (1996). A social cognitive framework for career choice counseling. *Career Development Quarterly, 44*, 354–366.

Chapman, D.W., O'Brien, C. J., & DeMasi, M. E. (1987).The effectiveness of the public school counselor in college advising. *The Journal of College Admissions, 115*(Spring), 11–18.

Chartrand, J.M., & Rose,M. L. (1996). Career interventions for at-risk populations: Incorporating social cognitive influences. *Career Development Quarterly, 44*, 341–353.

Fallon, M.V. (1997).The school counselor's role in first generation students' college plans. *School Counselor, 44*, 384–393.

Horn, L., & Nunez, A. (2000).Mapping the road to college: Firstgeneration students'math track, planning strategies, and context of support. *Education Statistics Quarterly, 2*, 81–86.

Indiana Career and Postsecondary Advancement Center. (2000). *Connections: Future planner for 9th graders*. Bloomington, IN: Author.

Inman,W. E., & Mayes, L. (1999).The importance of being first: Unique characteristics of first generation community college students. *Community College Review, 26*(4), 3–22.

Lent, R.W., & Brown, S.D. (1996). Social cognitive approach to career development: An overview. *Career Development Quarterly, 12*, 401–417.

Lent, R.W., Brown, S.D., & Hackett, G. (1994).Toward a unifying social cognitive theory of career and academic interest, choice, and performance. *Journal of Vocational Behavior, 45*, 79–122.

Lent, R.W., Brown, S.D., & Hackett, G. (1996). Career development from a social cognitive perspective. In D. Brown, L. Brooks, & Associates (Eds.), *Career choice and development* (3rd ed., pp. 373–421). San Francisco: Jossey-Bass.

Lent, R.W., Brown, S.D., & Hackett, G. (2000). Contextual supports and barriers to career choice: A social cognitive analysis. *Journal of Counseling Psychology, 47,* 36–49.

McGregor, L. N.,Mayleben, M. A., Buzzanga, M. A.,Davis, S. F., & Becker, A.H. (1991). Selected personality characteristics of first-generation college students. *College Student Journal, 25,* 231–234.

Riehl, R. J. (1994).The academic preparation, aspirations, and first-year performance of first-generation students. *College and University, 70,* 14–19.

Solorzano, D.G. (1992). An exploratory analysis of the effects of race, class, and gender on student and parent mobility aspirations. *Journal of Negro Education, 61,* 30–43.

Strage, A. A. (1999). Social and academic integration and college success: Similarities and differences as a function of ethnicity and family background. *College Student Journal, 33,* 198–205.

Ting, S. R. (1998). Predicting first-year grades and academic progress of college students of first-generation and lowincome families. *Journal of College Admission, 158,* 14–23.

Valadez, J. R. (1998). Applying to college: Race, class, and gender differences. *Professional School Counseling, 1*(5), 14–20.

York-Anderson,D. C., & Bowman, S. L. (1991). Assessing the college knowledge of first-generation and second-generation college students. *Journal of College Student Development, 32,* 116–122.

CHAPTER THREE
The Role of Professional Development in Multicultural Practice

As the understanding that the needs of students from diverse backgrounds are not being met continues to grow, it becomes clear that school counselors must work to expand their skills sets with respect to working with diverse students and communities, deepen their knowledge base about various cultural groups, cultivate strategies to engage effectively with individuals within these groups and broaden their understandings of their own values and belief systems and how these map onto their professional practices. Beattie (1997) challenges practitioners to view the development of professional knowledge as a central precept of practice and as the basis upon which they continually improve their practice and guide their decision-making processes. For school counselors to develop their professional knowledge, it becomes necessary for them to understand how theory and practice converge in their work. Gaining this understanding requires that they seek out and engage in an array of opportunities to critically analyze their practice (Beattie, 1997).

The main goal of multicultural professional development is to deepen and expand both pre-service and experienced counselors' understandings of American society, the U.S. educational system and, ultimately, the practices of education and counseling through engagement in a critical analysis of the relationship between society, ideology and practice. For school counselors to engage in practice that works against deficit models and that is culturally aware and responsive (and therefore effective), they must make paradigm shifts that complicate and influence their views of themselves, society, their counseling practices and the schools and systems in which they work. As much of the current research on multicultural counseling indicates, teaching counselors to shift away from mainstream perspectives, which are based on Eurocentric views of society, culture, schooling and learning, is a necessary goal in helping them to become multiculturally competent (Arredondo, et al., 1996; Holcomb-McCoy, 2004; Nieto, 2004; Pederson, 1999). Creating such a significant shift requires counselors to engage in processes through which they learn to acknowledge, deconstruct and critically reconstruct their knowledge base and make shifts in their belief systems. Making shifts in one's beliefs about self, society and diverse cultural groups requires counselors to gain skills and tools to critically analyze the structure of schooling and counseling, as well as education and society more broadly. It also necessitates that counselors learn to critically reflect on themselves as people who live, and practitioners who work, within a society fraught with inequality and structural discrimination.

Generally, school counselors cannot rely on their schools, districts or supervisors to provide meaningful multicultural professional development opportunities; they must take this on as a goal for their own professional growth. Therefore, it becomes critical for school counselors to learn the value and importance of advocating for their schools to provide resources to support their professional development and for them to seek out opportunities for meaningful learning, including constructive collaborations, on their own. Specifically, school counselors need to seek out opportunities to engage in professional development around issues of culture, race, social class, ethnicity, sexual identity, religious beliefs and other aspects of identity and social location, particularly as these relate to schooling, learning and counseling.

The reason school counselors, and other practitioners in schools, must seek out reformative professional development opportunities is primarily because their professional socialization has happened within the context of pervasive racism and discrimination and an uncritical acceptance of the Eurocentric basis of educational and psychological policy and practice. As a result, stereotypes and biases about an array of marginalized groups, which lead to deficit theories and biased evaluation and interventions, tend to have shaped the formation of counselors' beliefs about counseling, students, their families and communities (Arredondo, et al., 1996; Nieto, 2004). These beliefs and assumptions must be countered at both the individual (belief) and systemic (macro social and political) levels for school counselors to engage in equitable and empowering practice. Some of this professional development must focus on content-based discussions about specific cultures, racial, ethnic and religious groups, and some of this must focus more broadly on raising counselors' awareness about what constitutes multicultural competence and culturally responsive counseling practice. This requires counselors to engage in a multifaceted process through which they deconstruct and re-define their sense of identity, beliefs and professional practice as well as their views about people of color; students from under-resourced communities; gay, lesbian, bisexual and transgender (GLBT) students; students with disabilities; and ESL students (Coleman, et al., 2003; Rogers, et al., 1999; Sue & Sue, 2003).

Hidalgo (1993) argues that practitioners must develop a multicultural approach by analyzing and learning about their own cultural belief systems and how these affect their beliefs about, and conceptions of, practice. She asserts that practitioners need to engage in "multicultural introspection," which means, in part, that they must: (1) explore their own cultural heritage and how this affects their perceptions of others; (2) clarify their values and belief systems and then explore how these affect their behaviors toward and attitudes about students of color, students with disabilities, immigrant students, ESL students and GLBT students; and (3) explore their socioeconomic backgrounds and how this informs their views of children from different social classes. Hidalgo suggests that a rigorous process of exploring their "personal social constructions," which are embedded in larger social realities, will serve to reveal practitioners' implicit social and cultural assumptions so they can examine how their professional practices are affected by these constructions. Hidalgo believes this multifaceted process of critical introspection can clarify how culture functions in schools and how professionals' values and beliefs are manifested in educational settings and professional relationships. She argues that professional training programs and professional development initiatives must create environments that foster this sort of professional development so practitioners in schools can develop not only their own multicultural competency but their students' and colleagues' multicultural awareness as well (p. 105).

Achieving this sort of school counseling practice requires engagement in ongoing, focused professional development, which requires a counselor's commitment to continuous learning as well as the development of a clear vision of the kind of practice in which he or she wishes to engage. It also requires that the concept of professional development, as well as the learning initiatives themselves, are created in ways that allow them to be meaningful, powerful and practically useful. Professional development must be conceptualized as an ongoing, centralized professional process that begins during a school counselor's formal training and continues throughout his or her career. Further, school counselors must view their own professional development as interdependent with that of their colleagues, and they must position themselves as catalysts for collaboration across their schools and the various constituencies within them. Moreover, school counselors must have access to, and more importantly, aggressively seek out, cutting-edge theory and research that helps them to reflect on, critically examine and reconfigure their counseling practices.

This chapter is structured around articles that represent and explore a range of conceptions of and approaches to multicultural professional development. Each of the articles contributes to school counselors' substantive knowledge about various domains of multicultural counseling practice as well as to their understanding of specific approaches to engaging in multicultural professional development. Several articles in this cluster address the development of multicultural competence across the career trajectory. These articles both identify areas of need and offer a host of ideas and strategies for engaging in ongoing professional development that supports the creation of the knowledge, skills and awareness necessary to becoming a multiculturally competent counselor. Other articles focus on population- and issue-specific concerns for multicultural professional development, exploring how the particular experiences and concerns of racial and cultural groups can interface with meaningful professional development.

Holcomb-McCoy's (2004) "Assessing the Multicultural Competence of School Counselors: A Checklist" highlights major areas of professional development that serve to build multicultural competence. This article offers a checklist for the development of multicultural competencies for both pre-service and mid-service school counselors. Holcomb-McCoy suggests nine specific areas of competency for school counselors, which include competency in: (1) multicultural counseling, (2) multicultural consultation, (3) understanding racism and student resistance, (4) understanding racial identity development, (5) multicultural assessment, (6) multicultural family counseling, (7) social advocacy, (8) developing school-family-community partnerships and (9) understanding interpersonal interactions. The article explores how these areas of multicultural competency can be developed and refined through engaging in professional development that supports a commitment to dynamic, responsive and emergent professional practice.

Holcomb-McCoy's (2005) "Investigating School Counselors' Perceived Multicultural Competence" is an empirical study that examines the impact of multicultural courses on school counselors' perceived multicultural competence. Based on the findings of the study, the author argues for the importance of multicultural counseling coursework during training, stating that supervisors of counseling and guidance should work diligently to provide school counselors with ongoing educational and professional support in relevant multicultural topics.

Constantine's (2001) "Theoretical Orientation, Empathy and Multicultural Counseling Competence in School Counselor Trainees" discusses the development of theoretical orientation and empathy in school counseling trainees. The author argues for meaningful learning opportunities for counselors during their training as well as over the course of their careers. Constantine offers strategies for becoming more familiar with, and therefore less judgmental of, students' backgrounds, asserting that "…in order to increase their levels of empathy with regard to culturally diverse students, school counselors may wish to consider participating in events that reflect the values, beliefs and practices of these students' cultural groups… In addition, becoming an active member of culturally diverse professional and personal organizations may provide school counselors with opportunities to interact with and better understand the experiences of individuals representing various backgrounds." (p. 347). Constantine asserts that these kinds of professional development activities are a valuable means of enhancing professional competence with respect to issues of culture and its impact on students' experiences in school and in life more generally.

Tollerud's (2003) "Examining your Own Gender Bias" helps create an understanding of the influence of gender bias in schools as well as the importance of counselor awareness about issues of gender inequity. The author suggests that school counselors must work to more fully understand the need for them to critically self-reflect on and challenge their own gender biases as well as those of their colleagues.

Schwallie-Giddis, et al.'s (2004) "Counseling the Linguistically and Culturally Diverse Student: Meeting School Counselors' Professional Development Needs" is an empirical study that investigates the challenges and professional development needs of school counselors who work with linguistically diverse students and families. The authors focus on a specific professional development initiative geared toward improving school counselors' multicultural awareness, knowledge and skills. Schwallie-Giddis, et al. discuss the importance of conducting needs assessments to determine the types of multicultural professional development most useful for counselors in their school or district. The findings of this study highlight the importance of providing ongoing, in-depth professional development for school counselors on multicultural counseling issues.

Clemente and Collison's (2000) "The Relationships Among Counselors, ESL Teachers and Students" is an empirical study that explores the nature of the relationships between counselors, ESL teachers and students. Data from this study suggest that there is a significant need for school counselors, at both the training and practice stages of their careers, to engage in professional development that educates them about the particular needs and learning issues of ESL students. Among other strategies to understand and support this group of students, the authors suggest the development of a teamwork approach between ESL teachers and counselors.

Green, et al.'s (2005) "Urban School Counseling: Implications for Practice and Training" utilizes case scenarios of two school counselors in urban schools to illustrate their specific, contextualized needs in terms of professional development. The authors argue for an ecological model of school counseling that places the students, school counselors, the school and the work of counseling within its social, familial and political contexts. The authors also suggest that school counselors gain the skills and attitudes necessary to engage in ongoing critical self- and social-reflection.

Fontaine's (1998) "Evidencing a Need: School Counselors' Experiences with Gay and Lesbian Students" is an empirical study that shows school counselors' lack of professional training in and knowledge about issues of sexual orientation and sexual identity. The authors explore the need for the creation of professional development opportunities in which school counselors can gain the knowledge and skills necessary to engage with gay and lesbian students, their families and their own colleagues in ways that empower and support this often-silenced, marginalized and misunderstood group.

Each of these articles offers insight into specific areas of need in the realm of multicultural professional development for school counselors. Together, these articles highlight the serious need for professional development that helps school counselors reflect, learn, engage, critique, collaborate and advocate with respect to diverse students and their specific concerns and needs. This collection of articles also provides school counselors with templates for specific professional development initiatives and offers an ideal to which they can strive in their everyday professional lives.

Assessing the Multicultural Competence of School Counselors: A Checklist

By Cheryl Holcomb-McCoy, Ph.D.

This article originally appeared in *Professional School Counseling*, Vol. 7, No. 3, 2004.

With the increasing number of children from diverse backgrounds entering the U. S. school systems, it is imperative that school counselors gain a working knowledge of how to best serve these children. This article provides a checklist of 51 competencies that the author believes are necessary for working with culturally diverse students. The competencies offered were gathered through a theme analysis of the literature pertaining to multicultural school counseling. Nine areas of competence are suggested: multicultural counseling, multicultural consultation, understanding racism and student resistance, multicultural assessment, understanding racial identity development, multicultural family counseling, social advocacy, developing school-family-community partnerships, and understanding cross-cultural interpersonal interactions. Implications for school counselors and school counselor educators are provided.

One of the major challenges facing the field of school counseling today is the preparation of school counselors who are able to address the needs of an increasingly diverse student population (Coleman, 1995; Hobson & Kanitz, 1996; House & Martin, 1998; Lee, 1995; Lewis & Hayes, 1991). Future projections indicate that by 2020 a majority of school-age children attending public schools will be children-of-color or children from diverse cultural, ethnic, and/or linguistic backgrounds (Hodjkinson, 1985; Sue, 1992). In fact, the current racial/ethnic distribution among students in public schools in the United States is about 1.2% Native American, 4% Asian Pacific American, 15.6% Hispanic/Latino, 17.2% African American, and 62.1% European/White American (National Center for Education Statistics, 2001). These figures, however, are expected to change in the next decade due to the increased numbers of students-of-color entering public schools.

In response to an urgent need to address the cultural diversity of students, the American School Counselor Association (ASCA) adopted a position statement encouraging school counselors to take action to ensure that students of culturally diverse backgrounds have access to appropriate services and opportunities which promote the maximum development of the individual (ASCA, 1999). Furthermore, school counseling professionals (e.g., Lewis & Hayes, 1991) have suggested that cultural knowledge, sensitivity, and awareness be integrated into existing school counseling training programs. For instance, the Council for the Accreditation of Counseling and Related Educational Programs (CACREP) specifies that school counseling students have curricular experiences which explore the implications of sociocultural, demographic, and lifestyle diversity relevant to school counseling (CACREP, 1994). However, despite ASCA's position statement on multiculturalism and the inclusion of multicultural content in the CACREP standards, the emphasis in the literature placed on the competencies necessary for school counselors to effectively serve diverse populations has been limited.

Hence, the primary purpose of this article is to recommend areas of multicultural competence that the author believes are essential for the practice of school counseling. Here, a Multicultural Competence Checklist is provided to guide professional school counselors' multicultural development and training. The Checklist includes 51 items organized along nine categories: multicultural counseling, multicultural consultation, understanding racism and student resistance, multicultural assessment, understanding racial identity development, multicultural family counseling, social advocacy, developing school-family-community partnerships, and understanding cross-cultural interpersonal interactions. The categories and items were extracted through a theme analysis of the literature pertaining to multicultural issues and school counseling (e.g., Herring, 1997; Kiselica, Changizi, Cureton, & Gridley, 1995; Lee, 2001). See appendix for the items on the Checklist.

AREAS OF MULTICULTURAL COMPETENCE FOR SCHOOL COUNSELORS

Each of the nine competency categories is presented below along with a rationale for item inclusion. The reader is advised to read the description of the competency area and then review or respond to the items on the checklist.

Competence in Multicultural Counseling

Checklist items one through eight address competence in multicultural counseling. The literature documents that ethnic minorities underutilize counseling services in part because their help-seeking behaviors and treatment expectations differ from those of the dominant culture (Giordano & Giordano, 1977; Tseng & McDermott, 1981). Although the help-seeking behaviors of ethnic minorities differ from the majority population, the majority of ethnic minority students still receive mental health services from school counselors who have been trained to expect traditional help-seeking behaviors (Canino & Spurlock, 2000). According to D'Andrea and Daniels (1995) one of the most serious problems in school counseling rests in the fact that "most counseling theories and interventions, which are commonly used in school settings, have not been tested among students from diverse student populations" (p.143). For this reason, it is imperative that school counselors become familiar with counseling interventions and approaches that are appropriate for culturally diverse youngsters (e.g., Franklin, 1982).

Competence in Multicultural Consultation
Checklist items 9 through 13 address multicultural consultation. Despite the attention focused on multicultural counseling, less emphasis has been placed on the significance of culture and ethnicity in the consultation process. Consulting is a significant responsibility for school counselors (Gerler, 1992; Kurpius & Fuqua, 1993; Strein & French, 1984) and some literature (e.g., Brown, 1983) has suggested that school counselors should act in the consultant role more often than the counselor-role. Given the amount of time school counselors spend consulting with parents, teachers, students, and administrators of diverse backgrounds, school counselors should understand the impact of culture on the consultation process. Many of the traditional models of consultation (e.g., organizational, behavioral, mental health) fail to address how cultural factors impact the consultation process. Studying and applying multicultural strategies to consultation (e.g., Gibbs, 1980) should be a requirement of school counselor training.

It should be noted that language, value differences, and prejudice may all lead to less than accurate information being obtained during the consultation process (Ramirez, Lepage, Kratochwill, & Duffy, 1998). Even more problematic is when consultees hold stereotypical beliefs and biases that affect the consultation process and outcomes. Prejudicial attitudes that affect the consultation process may rise from differences in cultural background and may be manifested in outright rejection and/or the provision of inadequate interventions (Holcomb-McCoy, 2001). School consultants should be able to detect a consultees' negative racial and/or cultural attitudes and then act to modify these inhibiting attitudes.

Competence in Understanding Racism and Student Resistance
Checklist items 14–22 are concerned with school counselors' ability to recognize and address racism in schools. In addition, these items address a school counselor's ability to handle student resistance. According to Thompson and Carter (1997), race is an elusive, perplexing, and enduring

aspect of life in the United States. Herr (1999), more specifically, argues that unresolved race issues are not only prevalent in society but also in school systems. Although racism can manifest in various forms ranging from stereotyping to committing acts of violence against persons of color, school counselors must address the range of racist attitudes held by colleagues, parents, students, and themselves. According to Gay (1999), issues related to race and racism are the causes of discrepancies in student achievement among students of color and their white peers.

Regardless of the age or backgrounds of students, it is likely that school counselors will encounter some students who offer resistance to cross-cultural interactions. An even harsher reality is that some students will exhibit racist behaviors toward their peers. The manifestation of student resistance and racism can span from mild discomfort to irrational aversion toward interactions with those who differ racially or ethnically from self (Marshall, 2002). Moreover, resistance and racism have been attributed to factors ranging from negative experiences with diverse peers to uncritical allegiance to extremist ideologies. Unbeknownst to many school personnel, however, resistance and racism are also nurtured by institutional norms and tacit cultural messages students receive from schools, families, places of worship, and the larger society. By understanding the complex nature of resistance-oriented interpersonal interactions among students from different racial/ethnic backgrounds, school counselors should be able to dispel some prominent misconceptions about racism.

Competence in Understanding Racial Identity Development

Checklist items 23–25 address the school counselor's knowledge and use of racial identity development theories. The study of racial identity development has tremendous significance for school counselors who seek to comprehend some of the more prominent complexities related to counseling in culturally diverse school settings (Gay, 1999). According to Phinney (1993), a "healthy" racial identity is reflected in an adolescent's positive selfconcept, self-accepting behaviors, low susceptibility to peer pressure, and resistance to delinquent behaviors. Phinney, Lochner, & Murphy (1990) also purport that adolescents-of-color must explore their ethnic minority status in the United States in order to develop a positive personal identity or sense of self. Therefore, a significant challenge is for school counselors to acquire an understanding of racial/ethnic identity development and then apply that knowledge to students' issues and concerns.

Competence in Multicultural Assessment

Items 26–31 address school counselors' knowledge and skills regarding multicultural assessment and the assessment process. Given the prevalence of standardized achievement and aptitude tests in schools, it is imperative that school counselors are aware of appropriate and fair testing practices as well as be able to identify appropriate assessment instruments for culturally different students (Amour-Thomas, 1992; Howell & Rueda, 1996). Examples of instruments that have been revised to minimize bias include: The Weschler Intelligence Scale for Children-Third Edition, Woodcock-Johnson Psycho-Educational Battery-Revised (has Spanish version), the Standard Progressive Matrices, the Coloured Progressive Matrices, and the Test of Nonverbal Intelligence Third Edition (TONI-3; Paniagua, 1994).

Competence in Multicultural Family Counseling

Checklist items 32–35 assess whether school counselors are knowledgeable of the impact of culture/ethnicity on the family counseling process and family rituals. In addition, item 35 specifically addresses school counselors' knowledge of diverse parenting and discipline methods. Clearly, with such an increasingly diverse student population, family behavior and development is also varied. Therefore, it is imperative that school counselors have a comprehensive understanding of a family's development, and counseling interventions with families must take into account its cultural kinship networks, socialization experiences, typical interactive patterns, and culturally linked attitudinal and behavioral arrangements (Giordano & Carini-Giordano, 1995; Sue, 1994). School counselors must be aware of norms that stem from the majority culture in assessing attitudes, beliefs, and behaviors of students' parents and families.

Competence in Social Advocacy

Items 36–43 on the checklist are concerned with whether or not school counselors are advocates for social change. A relatively new theme in multicultural literature is social action or social advocacy (Kiselica, & Robinson, 2001). Because schools have become a place where social problems can be addressed and challenged, school counselors are in a pivotal position to assist those who are victims of societal ills and those who are potential victims. Lee (1998) states that a counselor who is an agent of change "possesses the awareness, knowledge, and skill to intervene not only at an individual level but also at a system-wide level … a social change agent challenges cultural, social, historical, or economic barriers that stifle optimal mental health and human development" (p. 9). By assuming this recommended "activist" stance, school counselors adopt a sense of social responsibility. Menacker (1974) pointed out that a nontraditional, more activist role for school counselors prevents counselors from becoming a part of stifling school bureaucracies, which prevent poor and disadvantaged students from achieving academic success.

Competence in Developing School-Family-Community Partnerships

Checklist items 44–46 assess whether or not school counselors are involved in developing school-familycommunity partnerships. School counselors can play a major role in the empowerment of ethnic minority families and communities by taking a leadership role in developing school-family-community partnerships (Keys & Bemak, 1997). With the critical problems that many families face, particularly those from oppressed backgrounds, it is imperative that school counselors are skilled in developing schoolfamily- community mental health teams and case management teams (Keys & Bemak, 1998). These teams, which involve the active participation of school personnel and community members, promote collaboration between communities and schools.

In addition, school counselors should be able to direct their students' families to community resources that will assist not only their children but also their families. After-school tutorial programs, day care centers, free medical assistance centers, churches, and social service agencies are examples of the types of community supports that can be used to supplement the needed services that schools are unable to provide. Community services or supports can also become extended family support networks for families that often feel isolated and alienated from the total community.

Competence in Understanding Interpersonal Interactions

Items 47–51 on the Checklist address school counselors' ability to interact and communicate with culturally diverse students. Interaction patterns that influence students' perceptions of inclusion, affirmation, and respect in the school environment are often initiated by adults in the school and directed toward individual students. These interactions can include verbalizations such as posing questions, giving directives, and commenting on behavior or appearance. For counselors and teachers, the actual words used to communicate to individual students as well as the voice tone and volume are indicators to students about the overall atmosphere of the school environment. In addition to verbal communication, nonverbal communication including facial expressions, hand signals, gestures, body movements, paraverbal vocalizations, proxemics, and even physical appearance play a part in counselor-to-student interpersonal interaction.

The nature of counselor-to-student interaction can promote a positive climate for counseling wherein students feel affirmed and respected. But it can also create a climate in which students feel alienated, disaffirmed, and devalued. Irvine (1990) found that teacher interactions with White students tended to be both task- and person-oriented, whereas those with African American students were more often restricted to task issues. Other studies (Anyon, 1981; Weis, 1990) have found that teachers initiate more frequent and more varied interactions with students from middle and upper class backgrounds than they do with those from the poor and working classes. Research (e.g., Brantlinger, 1994) also indicates that middle and upper class students typically are received positively in schools and expect to be liked by their teachers. Although there has been no research indicating the interactions between school counselors and students, much can be applied from the research on teachers to counselors. First, school counselors should be conscious of their interactions with students based on race, gender, or parental economic status. Secondly, school counselors should monitor their interaction patterns in order to foster more inclusive and affirming counselor-to-student interpersonal interactions. This can be accomplished through anonymous feedback from students and through intermittent videotape or audiotape recordings of counseling sessions and classroom guidance lessons. In analyzing recordings, school counselors should be mindful of the manner in which they speak, the nature and consistency of their counseling strategies, and the emotional tone of their interactions. Feedback on such recordings from colleagues from different ethnic/racial backgrounds can be extremely helpful.

IMPLICATIONS FOR SCHOOL COUNSELORS AND SCHOOL COUNSELOR EDUCATION

The key to becoming more effective when counseling with culturally and ethnically diverse students is to continuously assess one's multicultural competence. This process can become a reality with the use of the checklist offered in this article. School counselors are encouraged to use the checklist as a guide for professional development activities. Also, school counselors can enhance their multicultural counseling competence by soliciting feedback on their practice and understanding of multicultural issues from others who are culturally different.

From a pre-service training perspective, it is imperative that school counselor educators take some necessary steps. First, it is important for school counseling faculty to infuse the competencies described above into their existing school counselor education curricula. The checklist can be used as a vehicle for trainees to continuously assess their strengths and needs during their pre-service training. Secondly, it is imperative that school counselor trainees be required to complete their practica and internship experiences in schools that are multiethnic, multicultural, and/or multilinguistic so that they can acquire multicultural counseling competence through exposure and experience. And thirdly, the curriculum of school counselor education should take on a more interdisciplinary approach, utilizing the contributions from related fields such as social work, anthropology, and cultural studies (e.g., Native American studies, African American studies, women's studies). Focusing on areas such as bilingual, urban, and multicultural education are possible requisites in developing multicultural counseling competence.

To accomplish an innovative multicultural school counselor education program, there should also be an adequate representation of ethnically diverse faculty and students (Atkinson, Morten, & Sue, 1993). Working with an ethnically diverse student and faculty body adds enrichment to the program since one can then be exposed to various perspectives. In addition, a consultant or full-time faculty member with multicultural school counseling expertise should be available to consult with faculty members in redesigning their courses to reflect a diverse cultural content. Faculty should also build relationships with other departments within the university to identify existing multicultural courses and experts in cultural studies.

CONCLUSION

With the increasingly diverse student population of today's schools, there is a critical need for school counselors who are able to effectively guide and counsel students of ethnically diverse backgrounds. As school counselors work with larger numbers of ethnic minority students, they may need to alter their perceptions, learn to effectively counsel and consult with diverse populations, become knowledgeable of other cultures and the manifestations of racism, and assume the role of social change agent. School counselor educators must also show a high level of commitment to produce competent school counselors capable of working with students from various cultural and ethnic backgrounds. Engagement in this process of assessing multicultural competence provides school counselors and school counselor educators with an unparalleled opportunity for personal as well as professional growth.

Cheryl Holcomb-McCoy,Ph.D., is an assistant professor, Department of Counseling and Personnel Services, College of Education, University of Maryland, College Park. E-mail: ch193@umail.umd.edu

REFERENCES

American School Counselor Association. (1999). *The professional school counselor and cross/multicultural counseling.* [Position statement]. Alexandria,VA: Author.

Amour-Thomas, E. (1992). Intellectual assessment of children from culturally diverse backgrounds, *School Psychology Review, 21,* 552–565.

Anyon, J. (1981). Social class and school knowledge. *Curriculum Inquiry, 11,* 3–42.

Atkinson, D. R., Morten, G., & Sue, D.W. (1993). *Counseling American minorities:A cross-cultural perspective* (4th ed.). Madison, WI: Brown & Benchmark.

Brantlinger, E. A. (1994).The social class embeddedness of middle school students' thinking about teachers. *Theory Into Practice, 33,* 191–198.

Brown, J. A. (1983). Consulting. In J. A. Brown & R. H. Pate (Eds.), *Being a counselor: Directions and challenges* (pp. 124–146). Monterey, CA: Brooks/Cole.

Canino, I. A., & Spurlock, J. (2000). *Culturally diverse children and adolescents: Assessment, diagnosis, and treatment.* New York: Guilford.

Coleman, H. L. K. (1995). Cultural factors and the counseling process: Implications for school counselors. *The School Counselor, 42,* 180–185.

Council for the Accreditation of Counseling and Related Educational Programs. (1994). *Accreditation procedures manual and application.* Alexandria,VA: Author.

D'Andrea, M., & Daniels, J. (1991). Exploring the different levels of multicultural counseling training. *Journal of Counseling and Development, 70,* 143–150.

D'Andrea, M., & Daniels, J. (1995). Helping students learn to get along: Assessing the effectiveness of a multicultural developmental guidance project. *Elementary School Guidance and Counseling, 30,* 143–154.

Franklin, A. J. (1982).Therapeutic interventions with urban Black adolescents. In E. Jones & S. Korchin (Eds.), *Minority mental health* (pp. 267–295).New York: Praeger.

Gay, G. (1999). Ethnic identity development and multicultural education. In R. Hernandez,& E. R. Hollins (Eds.), *Racial and ethnic identity in school practices: Aspects of human development* (pp. 195–211). Mahwah, NJ: Lawrence Erlbaum.

Gerler, E. R., Jr. (1992). Consultation and school counseling. *Elementary School Guidance and Counseling, 26,* 162.

Gibbs, J.T. (1980).The interpersonal orientation in mental health consultation:Toward a model of ethnic variations in consultation. *Journal of Community Psychology, 8,* 195–207.

Giordano, G. P., & Giordano, J. (1977). *The ethno-cultural factor in mental health: A literature review and bibliography.* New York: Institute on Pluralism and Group Identity.

Giordano, J., & Carini-Giordano, M. A. (1995). *Ethnic dimensions in family treatment.* In R. H.Mikesell,D.D. Lusterman,& S. H.McDaniel (Eds.), *Integrating family therapy: Handbook of family psychology and systems theory.* Washington, DC: American Psychological Association.

Herr, K. (1999). Private power and privileged education: De/constructing institutional racism. *International Journal of Inclusive Education, 3,* 111-129.

Herring, R.D. (1997). *Multicultural counseling in schools: A synergetic approach.* Alexandria,VA: American Counseling Association.

Hobson, S. M., & Kanitz, H. M. (1996). Multicultural counseling: An ethical issue for school counselors. *School Counselor, 43,* 245–255.

Hodjikinson, H. (1985). *All one system: Demographics of education, kindergarten through graduate school.*Washington, DC: Institute for Educational Leadership.

Holcomb-McCoy, C. C. (2001). *Multicultural competence in school settings.* Unpublished manuscript.

House, R., & Martin, P. J. (1998). Advocating for better futures for all students: A new vision for school counselors. *Education, 119,* 284–286.

Howell, K.W., & Rueda, R. (1996). Achievement testing with culturally and linguistically diverse students. In L. A. Suzuki, P. J.Meller, & J. G. Ponterotto (Eds.), *Handbook of multicultural assessment* (pp. 253–290). San Francisco: Jossey-Bass.

Irvine, J. J. (1990). *Black students and school failure.* New York: Praeger.

Keys, S. G., & Bemak, F. (1997). School-family-community linked services: A school counseling role for changing times. *School Counselor, 44,* 255–264.

Keys, S. G., & Bemak, F. (1998).Transforming school counseling to serve the mental health needs of at-risk youth. *Journal of Counseling and Development, 76,* 381–389.

Kiselica, M. S., & Robinson, M. (2001). Bringing advocacy counseling to life: The history, issues, and human dramas of social justice work in counseling. *Journal of Counseling and Development, 79,* 387–397.

Kiselica, M. S., Changizi, J. C., Cureton,V. L.,& Gridley, B. E. (1995). Counseling children and adolescents in schools: Salient multicultural issues. In J. G. Ponterotto, J.M. Casas, L. A. Suzuki, & C. M. Alexander (Eds.), *The Handbook of multicultural counseling* (pp. 516–533).Thousand Oaks, CA: Sage.

Kurpius, D. J.,& Fuqua, D. R. (1993). Consultation I: Conceptual, structural, and operational dimensions. *Journal of Counseling and Development, 71,* 596–708.

Lee, C. C. (1995). *Counseling for diversity: A guide for school counselors and related professionals.* Alexandria, VA: American Counseling Association.

Lee, C. C. (1998). Counselors as agents of social change. In C. C. Lee & G. R. Walz (Eds.), *Social action: A mandate for counselors* (pp. 3–16). Alexandria, VA: American Counseling Association.

Lee, C. C. (2001). Culturally responsive school counselors and programs: Addressing the needs of all students. *Professional School Counseling, 4,* 257–261.

Lewis, A. C., & Hayes, S. (1991). Multiculturalism and the school counseling curriculum. *Journal of Counseling and Development, 70,* 119–125.

Marshall, P. L. (2002). *Cultural diversity in schools.* Belmont, CA: Wadsworth/Thomson Learning.

Menacker, J. (1974). *Vitalizing guidance in urban schools.* New York: Dodd, Mead, & Co.

National Center for Education Statistics. (2001, May). *Statistics in brief.* Washington, DC: U. S. Department of Education, Office of Educational Research and Improvement.

Paniagua, F. A. (1994). *Assessing and treating culturally diverse clients: A practical guide.* Thousand Oaks, CA: Sage.

Phinney, J. S. (1993). A three-stage model of ethnic identity development in adolescence. In M .E. Bernal & G. P. Knight (Eds.), *Ethnic identity: Formation and transmission among Hispanics and other minorities* (pp. 61–79). Albany: SUNY Press.

Phinney, J. S., Lochner, B.T., & Murphy, R. (1990). Ethnic identity development in adolescence. In A. R. Stiffman & L. E. Davis (Eds.), *Ethnic issues in adolescent mental health* (pp. 53–72). Newbury Park, CA: Sage.

Ramirez, S. Z., Lepage, K.M., Kratochwill, T. R., & Duffy, J. L. (1998). Multicultural issues in school-based consultation: Conceptual and research considerations. *Journal of School Psychology, 36,* 479–509.

Strein, W., & French, J. L. (1984). Teacher consultation in the affective domain: A survey of expert opinion. *School Counselor, 31,* 339–344.

Sue, D.W. (1992). The challenge to multiculturalism: The road less traveled. *American Counselor, 1,* 6–14.

Sue, D. (1994). Incorporating cultural diversity in family therapy. *The Family Psychologist, 10,* 19–21.

Thompson, C. E., & Carter, R.T. (1997). Race, socialization, and contemporary racism manifestations. In C. E.Thompson & R.T. Carter (Eds.), *Racial identity theory: Applications to individual, group,and organizational interventions* (pp. 5–12).Mahwah, NJ: Lawrence Erlbaum.

Tseng, N. S., & McDermott, J. F. (1981). *Cultural mind and therapy: An introduction to cultural psychiatry.* New York: Brunner/Mazel.

Weiss, L. (1990).*Working class without work.* New York: Routledge.

APPENDIX

School Counselor Multicultural Competence Checklist

COMPETENCE
Met   Unmet

I. Multicultural Counseling

1. I can recognize when my attitudes, beliefs, and values are interfering with providing the best services to my students.
2. I can identify the cultural bases of my communication style.
3. I can discuss how culture affects the help-seeking behaviors of students.
4. I can describe the degree to which a counseling approach is culturally inappropriate for a specific student.
5. I use culturally appropriate interventions and counseling approaches (e.g., indigenous practices) with students.
6. I can list at least three barriers that prevent ethnic minority students from using counseling services.
7. I can anticipate when my helping style is inappropriate for a culturally different student.
8. I can give examples of how sterotypical beliefs about culturally different persons impact the counseling relationship.

II. Multicultural Consultation

9. I am aware of how culture affects traditional models of consultation.
10. I can discuss at least one model of multicultural consultation.

11. I recognize when racial and cultural issues are impacting the consultation process.
12. I can identify when the race and/or culture of the client is a problem for the consultee.
13. I discuss issues related to race/ethnicity/culture during the consultation process, when applicable.

III. Understanding Racism and Student Resistance
14. I can define and discuss White privilege.
15. I can discuss how I (if European American/White) am privileged based on my race.
16. I can identify racist aspects of educational institutions.
17. I can define and discuss prejudice.
18. I recognize and challenge colleagues about discrimination and discriminatory practices in schools.
19. I can define and discuss racism and its impact on the counseling process.
20. I can help students determine whether a problem stems from racism or biases in others.
21 I understand the relationship between student resistance and racism.
22. I include topics related to race and racism in my classroom guidance units.

IV. Understanding Racial and/or Ethnic Identity Development
23. I am able to discuss at least two theories of racial and/or ethnic identity development.
24. I use racial/ethnic identity development theories to understand my students' problems and concerns.
25. I have assessed my own racial/ethnic development in order to enhance my counseling.

V. Multicultural Assessment
26. I can discuss the potential bias of two assessment instruments frequently used in the schools.
27. I can evaluate instruments that may be biased against certain groups of students.
28. I am able to use test information appropriately with culturally diverse parents.

	COMPETENCE	
	Met	**Unmet**

29. I view myself as an advocate for fair testing and the appropriate use of testing of children from diverse backgrounds.

30. I can identify whether or not the assessment process is culturally sensitive.

31. I can discuss how the identification of the assessment process might be biased against minority populations.

VI. Multicultural Family Counseling

32. I can discuss family counseling from a cultural/ethnic perspective.

33. I can discuss at least two ethnic group's traditional gender role expectations and rituals.

34. I anticipate when my helping style is inappropriate for an ethnically different parent or guardian.

35. I can discuss culturally diverse methods of parenting and discipline.

VII. Social Advocacy

36. I am knowledgeable of the psychological and societal issues that affect the development of ethnic minority students.

37. When counseling, I consider the psychological and societal issues that affect the development of ethnic minority students.

38. I work with families and community members in order to reintegrate them with the school.

39. I can define "social change agent."

40. I perceive myself as being a "social change agent."

41. I can discuss what it means to take an "activist counseling" approach.

42. I intervene with students at the individual and systemic levels.

43. I can discuss how factors such as poverty and powerlessness have influenced the current conditions of at least two ethnic groups.

COMPETENCE
Met   Unmet

VIII. Developing School-Family-Community Partnerships

44. I have developed a school-family-community partnership team or some similar type of group that consists of community members, parents, and school personnel.
45. I am aware of community resources that are available for students and their families.
46. I work with community leaders and other resources in the community to assist with student (and family) concerns.

IX. Understanding Cross-Cultural Interpersonal Interactions

47. I am able to discuss interaction patterns that might influence ethnic minority students' perceptions of inclusion in the school community.
48. I solicit feedback from students regarding my interactions with them.
49. I verbally communicate my acceptance of culturally different students.
50. I nonverbally communicate my acceptance of culturally different students.
51. I am mindful of the manner in which I speak and the emotional tone of my interactions with culturally diverse students.

Investigating School Counselors' Perceived Multicultural Competence

By Cheryl C. Holcomb-McCoy, Ph.D.

This article originally appeared in *Professional School Counseling*, Vol. 8, No. 5, 2005.

This study examined the perceived multicultural counseling competence of 209 professional school counselors by using the Multicultural Counseling Competence and Training Survey–Revised (MCCTS-R; Holcomb-McCoy & Myers, 1999). Participants reported that they are at least somewhat competent on all of the multicultural competence domains of the MCCTS-R. In addition, the findings of this study suggested that participants' perceived multicultural counseling competence on the multicultural knowledge and terminology domains differed significantly based on whether they had taken an entry-level multicultural course.

Many variables concerning the multicultural counseling competence of professional counselors have been debated and discussed throughout the recent history of the counseling profession. Discussions related to the multicultural competence of professional counselors have included the development of multicultural competencies (e.g., Arredondo et al., 1996; Sue, Arredondo, & McDavis, 1992), the content of multicultural counseling courses (e.g., D'Andrea & Daniels, 1991; Howard-Hamilton & Williams, 1993), the effect of multicultural training on trainees' multicultural competence (e.g., Allison, Crawford, Echemendia, Robinson, & Knepp, 1994; McRae & Johnson, 1991), and trainee characteristics that affect their level of multicultural counseling competence (e.g., Carter, 1990; Ottavi, Pope-Davis, & Dings, 1994).

In the general counseling literature, multicultural counseling competence has been described as having three domains: awareness, knowledge, and skills (Sue et al., 1982; 1998). The first domain, awareness, stresses a counselor's understanding of personal beliefs and attitudes and how counselors are the products of their own cultural conditioning. The second domain, knowledge, addresses the counselor's understanding of the worldviews of culturally different clients. And finally, the skill domain deals with the process of actively developing and practicing appropriate intervention strategies needed for work with culturally different clients. Coleman, Wampold, and Casali (1995) further asserted that multicultural counseling competence is one's ability to demonstrate to clients that their world, not just their psychological self, is understood. Other perspectives regarding multicultural counseling competence have included understanding the history, current needs, strengths, and resources of individuals (Pope-Davis, Reynolds, Dings, & Ottavi, 1994), and one's ability to acquire, develop, and use an accurate cultural schema (Ridley et al., 1994).

In addition to exploring the domains of multicultural counseling competence, counseling researchers also have examined variables or factors that might be related to one's acquisition of multicultural counseling competence. For instance, Ottavi et al. (1994) found that counselor trainees' White racial identity development, educational level, and clinical experiences correlated moderately with multicultural competence. Constantine (2002) found that racism attitudes and White racial identity attitudes together contributed to significant variance in self-perceived multicultural counseling competence. In particular, higher levels of racism were correlated with lower levels of self-reported multicultural counseling competence.

Gender also has been cited as a factor in an individual's level of multicultural counseling competence. For instance, Carter (1990) found that women were more comfortable with racial interactions and issues than were men. In a similar study, Pope-Davis and Ottavi (1994) reported that older students experienced greater discomfort with racial interactions and issues than did younger students. Finally, Sodowsky, Taffe, and Gutkin (1991) found that the amount of multicultural client contact was related to higher levels of self-reported multicultural competence for practicing counseling professionals. Recently, Holcomb-McCoy and Myers (1999) found that professional counselors who had taken a multicultural counseling course in their entry-level training perceived themselves to be more competent on multicultural knowledge than professional counselors who had not taken a multicultural course. Interestingly, there has been no research on the effect of counseling experience (i.e., years of counseling experience) or work setting (e.g., school vs. community agency; elementary school vs. high school) on a counselor's perceived multicultural competence. Clearly, one's experience in the counseling field or work setting could be related to one's perceived and actual multicultural counseling competence.

Considering the increasingly diverse composition of school populations, this notion of multicultural counseling competence is particularly critical to school counseling professionals. As such, increased attention has been paid to multicultural counseling in school counselor education programs (e.g., Carey, Reinat, & Fontes, 1990; Lee, 1995; Lewis & Hayes, 1991), and school counselors' multicultural counseling competence has been linked to self-construals or self-perceptions (Constantine & Yeh, 2001), student advocacy (Lee, 2001), and multicultural training (Holcomb-McCoy, 2001). The American School Counselor Association (ASCA; 1999) even has included the importance of school counselors' cultural knowledge and awareness in its position statement entitled "The Professional School Counselor and Cross/Multicultural Counseling." More specifically, the statement reads, "Professional school counselors have the responsibility ... to increase awareness and understanding of culturally diverse persons and populations and to enhance the total school and community environment and climate."

PURPOSE OF THIS STUDY

Despite the increased attention paid to the preparation of multiculturally competent school counselors, there is a paucity of information regarding the multicultural competence of existing professional school counselors. Therefore, this study's primary goal was to focus on school counselors' perceptions of their own multicultural counseling competence. It is important to note that the author believes this is a first step in the process of examining school counselors' actual multicultural competence. In addition, this study was implemented in order to examine differences in perceived multicultural counseling competence across school counselor characteristics (e.g., gender, years of experience, work setting, coursework in multicultural counseling). There is limited information on the relationship between school counselors' characteristics (e.g., years of experience, gender) and multicultural counseling competence.

More specifically, the research questions for the current study were as follows: (a) To what extent do existing professional school counselors perceive themselves to be multiculturally competent based on the factors of the Multicultural Counseling Competence and Training Survey–Revised (MCCTS-R)? And, (b) does professional school counselors' perceived multicultural counseling competence differ based on selected participant characteristics (e.g., whether they had taken a multicultural counseling course, their gender, years of experience, work setting)?

METHOD
Participants and Procedures
A systematic stratified sample of 510 professional school counselors was drawn from the membership of ASCA ($N = 11,200$). The sample was stratified by state in order to ensure representation from all geographic regions of ASCA. This was accomplished by selecting every 10th school counselor from the state list and 10 from the remaining U.S. regions (e.g.,

Puerto Rico, West Indies). The MCCTS-R was mailed to 510 prospective participants along with a cover letter explaining the purpose of the survey, the anonymous and confidential nature of the survey, and instructions for completion. A self-addressed, stamped envelope was included to encourage return of the surveys. No follow-up letters or questionnaires were mailed due to lack of funds. Of the 510 surveys mailed, usable returns were received from 209 school counselors (41% return rate).

Most of the counselors had 1–4 years (37%, $n = 78$) of counseling experience while 26% ($n = 54$) had 5–10 years, 22% ($n = 46$) had 15 years or more, and 14% ($n = 30$) had 11–14 years of counseling experience. Participants' self-reported race/ethnicity was as follows: 89% ($n = 187$) White/European descent, 3% ($n = 6$) African/Black, 1% Hispanic/Latino ($n = 3$), 2% Asian ($n = 5$), 2% Native American ($n = 4$), and 2% "other" ($n = 4$). Participants worked in elementary schools (37%, $n = 79$), middle schools (23%, $n = 49$), and high schools (31%, $n = 65$), and 7% ($n = 16$) worked in other types of school settings (e.g., elementary/middle, schools with all grades).

All regions of ASCA were represented in the sample: the Midwest, 16% ($n = 33$); North Atlantic, 23% ($n = 48$); South, 46% ($n = 96$); and West, 15% ($n = 31$). A majority of the counselors were female (83%, $n = 172$). Regarding multicultural counseling training, 52.4% ($n = 109$) of the participants had taken at least one multicultural counseling course in their entry-level training program. There are no data currently available regarding the demographics of ASCA membership (M. Hare, personal communication, May 17, 2001), so it is unclear how representative this sample is of school counselors who are members of ASCA.

Instrument

The instrument used in this study was a modified version of the Multicultural Counseling Competence and Training Survey (MCCTS; Holcomb-McCoy & Myers, 1999). The MCCTS was developed to measure the perceived multicultural competence of professional counselors based on the Association for Multicultural Counseling and Development (AMCD) Multicultural Competencies and Explanatory Statements. The AMCD Competencies were developed in accordance with Sue et al.'s (1982) classic framework of multicultural counseling competence (i.e., awareness, knowledge, skills). The MCCTS is a self-report instrument containing 32 behaviorally stated items and 29 items that require participants to provide information regarding their entry-level counseling training experiences and demographics such as gender, age, race, and year of graduation.

In 1999, Holcomb-McCoy and Myers reported that there were five factors underlying the multicultural counseling competence items of the

MCCTS: Multicultural Knowledge, Multicultural Awareness, Multicultural Terminology, Knowledge of Racial Identity Development Theories, and Multicultural Skills. In the calculation of internal consistency reliability coefficients (Cronbach's alpha) for the instrument, alphas of .92, .92, .79, .66, and .91 were derived for the Multicultural Knowledge, Multicultural Awareness, Multicultural Terminology, Racial Identity, and Multicultural Skills subscales, respectively (the somewhat lower reliability coefficient for the Racial Identity subscale may have been the result of a smaller number of items included on that subscale).

The initial MCCTS was revised for the present investigation in order to reflect the language used in the school setting. For instance, the term students was used rather than *clients*. Feedback on the content and format of the revised survey was solicited from ethnically diverse and experienced school counselors (with 11, 10, and 5 years of counseling experience). They judged the items to be consistent with school counselors' experiences and relevant to the school setting.

Demographic information such as work setting, gender, and years of experience was included in a demographic section of the survey as counselor characteristics thought to be relevant to multicultural counseling competence. The main body of the instrument consisted of 32 behaviorally based statements, assessing awareness, knowledge, and skills (e.g., "I can discuss how culture affects the help-seeking behaviors of students"). Participants were asked to assess their multicultural competence for each item by using a 4-point Likert-type scale: 4 = extremely competent, 3 = competent, 2 = somewhat competent, and 1 = not competent.

Research Design and Data Analysis

Before the primary statistical analyses were conducted, exploratory techniques were used to check the data for normal distribution, homogeneity of variance, input errors, outliers, or other unusual occurrences in the data. The factor analysis for the study was conducted in two stages: factor extraction and factor rotation. As part of the first stage to determine the number of extracted factors, eigenvalues and a scree plot based on a principal components solution were obtained. Three criteria were used to determine the number of factors to rotate: the "Kaiser Rule" (i.e., eigenvalues greater than 1), the scree test, and the interpretability of the factor solution (Green & Salkind, 2003). Although there were six components with eigenvalues greater than 1, the scree plot indicated three factors with eigenvalues in the sharp descent of the plot. Based on the plot, three factors were rotated using a maximum likelihood factor analysis with an oblimin rotation procedure (i.e., oblique rotation).

For research question 1, the competence variables were defined as the factor-based scores derived from the factor analysis of the 32-item MCCTS-R. The mean scores were computed by summing the competence item means that had the highest loadings on a factor and dividing by the number of items on the factor. An analysis of means and standard deviations of the factor scores was conducted to determine in which factors the participants perceived themselves to be most competent and least competent.

For research question 2, multivariate analyses of variance (MANOVAs) were used to examine the statistical significance of mean differences across participant characteristics for the factors of perceived multicultural counseling competence. Four participant characteristic variables were used to examine research question number 2. Information for these variables was obtained from the demographic section of the MCCTS-R. "Coursework in multicultural counseling" was defined as whether the participant had taken at least one multicultural counseling course in entry-level training, and it had categories of yes or no. "Gender" was defined as the participant's reported gender and had categories of male and female. "Work setting," which was defined as the setting in which the school counselor was employed, had the following categories: elementary, middle school/junior high, and high school. "Years of experience," which was defined as the years of school counseling-related experience, was categorized as 1–4 years, 5–10 years, 11–14 years, and more than 15 years.

RESULTS

Before the research questions were addressed, a factor analysis of the MCCTS-R items was conducted. The rotated solution, as shown in Table 1, yielded three interpretable factors with eigenvalues greater than 1 and accounted for 55.11% of the variance. Only those items with a structure coefficient of an absolute value of .35 or above on a given factor were considered to be included as an item on that factor. Of the four items on factor 1, the items with the highest structure coefficients were 10 ("I can define prejudice") and 11 ("I can define discrimination"). Items from this factor were related to definitions of terms used in the field of multicultural counseling. Therefore, factor 1 was named "Multicultural Terminology."

Eighteen of the 19 items on factor 2 had structure coefficients higher than .50. Because the items referred primarily to knowledge of cultural groups and issues, factor 2 was named "Multicultural Knowledge." Items 27 ("I can discuss how the counseling process may conflict with the cultural values of at least two ethnic groups") and 28 ("I can list at least three barriers that prevent ethnic minority students from using counseling services") had the largest structure coefficients on factor 2.

Of the nine items on factor 3, the items with the highest structure coefficients were item 3 ("I am able to discuss how my culture has influenced the way I think") and item 2 ("I am aware of how my cultural background and experience have influenced my attitudes about psychological processes"). Because the items on this factor focused on an individual's cultural and self-awareness, this factor was labeled "Multicultural Awareness." A Cronbach's alpha procedure was used to assess internal consistency reliability estimates of the three resulting factors. Coefficients ranged from .85 to .97, indicating high internal consistency of the items loading on each factor (see Table 1).

Research Question 1: Professional School Counselors' Perceived Multicultural Competence

In order to examine the school counselors' perceived multicultural counseling competence, means and standard deviations were computed for each factor (see Table 2). Overall, the participants reported to be at least "somewhat competent" (i.e., mean factor score over 2.0) on all three factors.

Research Question 2: Professional School Counselors' Perceived Multicultural Competence and Selected Participant Characteristics

A series of one-way MANOVAs indicated significant differences in perceived multicultural counseling competence based on having taken multicultural coursework in entry-level training, for Multicultural Knowledge, Wilks' = .78, $F(19, 184)$ = 2.81, p < .01, 2 = .22, and Multicultural Terminology, Wilks' = .96, $F(4, 203)$ = 2.42, p = .05, 2 = .05. The multivariate 2 based on Wilks' was moderately strong for Multicultural Knowledge, indicating that 22% of the variance in Multicultural Knowledge was associated with whether counselors had taken multicultural coursework in their graduate programs. In contrast, the 2 for Multicultural Terminology was much weaker, .05, suggesting that 5% of the variance in Multicultural Terminology was associated with counselors having taken multicultural coursework.

Follow-up univariate analyses of variance (ANOVAs) were performed to determine which items were statistically significant. Because numerous univariate analyses were involved, the Bonferroni procedure was used to reduce the chances of committing a Type I error (Green & Salkind, 2003). Thus, only ANOVAs with a probability of .001 or less were accepted as statistically significant. On the Multicultural Knowledge factor, participants who had taken a multicultural counseling course reported significantly higher scores on items 19, 27, 28, and 29. The follow-up ANOVAs on the Multicultural Terminology factor were not significant. Gender, school setting, and years of experience were not significantly related to any of the factors of multicultural counseling competence.

DISCUSSION

The main purpose of this investigation was to determine how school counselors perceive their multicultural competence. The results suggested that professional school counselors perceive themselves to be at least somewhat competent on all of the domains of the MCCTS-R (i.e., multicultural knowledge, multicultural terminology, and multicultural awareness). If these findings are true, then one can assume that school counselors perceive of themselves as culturally competent in multicultural knowledge, awareness, and terminology. Although this result is encouraging, one must be cautious about inferring that school counselors are practicing culturally appropriate strategies and interventions. The extent to which counselors' perceived multicultural competence transfers to actual practice is unknown and is therefore a logical next step for future research.

Also, one must be concerned about the fact that two domains of multicultural competence (multicultural awareness and multicultural terminology) are slightly higher than the third domain (multicultural knowledge). One might infer then that school counselors have varying degrees of competence based on specific areas or domains of multicultural competence. Whether this multidimensional notion of multicultural competence influences school counselors' service to students is not known but also should be investigated.

Perhaps the most significant result of this study is the fact that school counselors who had taken a multicultural counseling course rated their multicultural knowledge and ability to define multicultural terminology significantly higher than those who had not taken a multicultural counseling course. Although this relationship should be investigated further for validation, the influence of multicultural counseling coursework on multicultural competence is encouraging and validates the presence of multicultural courses in counselor education programs. For two decades, the inclusion of multicultural coursework has been encouraged throughout the counseling literature (Corvin & Wiggins, 1989; Ibrahim & Arredondo, 1986; Parker, Moore, & Neimeyer, 1998). However, the impact of those courses on school counselors' multicultural competence has received little to no attention.

It is important to note that multicultural coursework did not significantly effect school counselors' multicultural awareness. This is puzzling because the literature has stressed the inclusion of cultural awareness

TABLE 1. STRUCTURE COEFFICIENTS, COMMUNALITY ESTIMATES, EIGENVALUES, AND VARIANCE ACCOUNTED FOR FROM MAXIMUM LIKELIHOOD FACTOR ANALYSIS (N = 209)

Item	Structure Coefficients			Commu- nality h^2
	1	2	3	
(9) I can define racism.	.89	.53	.62	.82
(10) I can define prejudice.	.97	.45	.59	.95
(11) I can define discrimination.	.97	.43	.57	.94
(12) I can define stereotype.	.94	.43	.58	.89
(8) I can discuss models of White racial identity development.	.41	.58	.36	.36
(13) I can identify the cultural basis of my communication style.	.38	.59	.53	.44
(16) I can give examples of how stereotypical beliefs about culturally different persons impact the counseling relationship.	.48	.70	.49	.54
(17) I can articulate the possible differences of the nonverbal behavior among the five major ethnic groups (i.e., African/Black, Hispanic/Latino, Asian, Native American, European/White).	.32	.73	.34	.53
(18) I can articulate the possible differences of the verbal behavior among the five major ethnic groups.	.38	.78	.37	.61
(19) I can discuss the counseling implications for at least two modals of racial/ethnic identity development.	.29	.69	.26	.48
(20) I can discuss within-group differences among ethnic groups (i.e., African American, Latino/ Hispanic, Asian American, Native American).	.31	.64	.33	.41
(21) I can discuss how culture affects a student's vocational choices.	.34	.72	.38	.53

Item	Structure Coefficients			Commu-nality
	1	2	3	h^2
(29) I can discuss how culture affects the help-seeking behaviors of students.	.37	.80	.37	.64
(23) I can discuss how culture affects the manifestations of a psychological disorders.	.35	.75	.34	.56
(24) I can describe the degree to which a counseling approach is appropriate for a specific group of people.	.34	.80	.33	.64
(25) I can explain how factors such as poverty and powerlessness have influenced the current conditions of at least two ethnic groups.	.44	.80	.43	.65
(26) I can list at least three barriers that prevent ethnic minority minority students from using counseling services.	.26	.74	.19	.57
(27) I can discuss how the counseling process may conflict with the cultural values of at least two ethnic groups.	.31	.80	.26	.65
(28) I can list at least three barriers that prevent ethnic minority students from using counseling services.	.35	.80	.31	.65
(29) I can discuss the potential bias of two assessment instruments frequently used in the schools.	.30	.68	.23	.47
(30) I can discuss family counseling from a cultural/ethnic perspective.	.40	.79	.35	.62
(31) I can anticipate when my helping style is inappropriate for a culturally different student.	.40	.62	.38	.41
(32) I can help students determine whether a problem stems from racism or biases in others.	.45	.65	.43	.46

Item	Structure Coefficients			Commu- nality h^2
	1	2	3	
(1) I can discuss my own ethnic/ cultural heritage.	.47	.32	**.77**	.60
(2) I am aware of how my cultural background and experiences have influenced my attitudes about psychological processes.	.48	.34	**.85**	.73
(3) I am able to discuss how my culture has influenced the way I think.	.57	.38	**.91**	.83
(4) I can recognize when my attitudes, beliefs, and values are interfering with providing the best services to my students.	.44	.44	**.53**	.34
(5) I verbally communicate my acceptance of culturally different students.	.34	.32	**.36**	.17
(6) I nonverbally communicate my acceptance of culturally different students.	.32	.32	**.42**	.20
(7) I can discuss my family's perspective regarding acceptable and non-acceptable codes of conduct.	.40	.18	**.47**	.25
(14) I can identify my negative and positive emotional reactions toward persons of other racial and ethnic groups.	.53	.41	**.56**	.39
(15) I can identify my reactions that are based on stereotypical beliefs about different ethnic groups.	.47	.38	**.54**	.33
Eigenvalue	13.54	3.71	1.49	
Variance accounted for	33.67	16.43	5.02	
Coefficient alpha	.97	.95	.85	

Note. These results were obtained using a maximum likelihood factor analysis with a direct oblimin rotation (N = 209). Bolded structure coefficients indicate the highest coefficient for each item. Factor 1 = Multicultural Terminology; factor 2 = Multicultural Knowledge; factor 3 = Multicultural Awareness.

activities as part of multicultural counseling training (Corvin & Wiggins, 1989). Perhaps school counselors' cultural awareness is developed through life experiences, self-reflection, and other lived experiences rather than through the content of multicultural counseling courses. Based on these results, it seems fitting then that school counselor educators evaluate and review the content of multicultural courses to ensure the coverage not only of multicultural awareness content but of all domains of multicultural counseling competence.

Implications for Future Research

Despite this study's findings that school counselors perceive themselves as at least "somewhat competent" on the domains of multicultural competence, there is still a need for further research that indicates a relationship between perceived multicultural competence and actual practice. As stated previously, whether school counselors' perceived multicultural competence is significantly related to the services that they provide students is unknown. Future studies should focus on the link or relationship between school counselors' perceived multicultural competence and their actual practice. Also, studies that focus on the difference between students' perceptions of counselors' multicultural competence and counselors' perceived multicultural competence are critical. Pragmatically, this type of research will inform us of how students perceive counselors' multicultural competence and how their perceptions relate to student outcomes (e.g., grades, graduation, behavior reduction). Clearly, this line of research is greatly needed in light of the attention placed on minority student achievement.

In the present study, school counselors' personal characteristics (e.g., gender, years of experience) did not have an influence on their perceived multicultural competence. However, future studies might examine the following aspects of school counselors in relation to their multicultural competence: (a) cultural experiences (e.g., experience in diverse schools, living in another country); (b) diversity training beyond coursework in a graduate program; (c) ethnicity; and (d) adherence to stereotypical beliefs about groups of people. This line of research will greatly influence our understanding of why particular counselors are more culturally competent than others and what types of experiences enhance the cultural competence of counselors.

Another important area for future research is the construct of social desirability and multicultural competence. Research has indicated that many multicultural self-rating instruments are highly related to social desirability (Constantine & Ladany, 2000; Worthington, Mobley, Franks, & Tan, 2000). Given the possible presence of social desirability and the

TABLE 2. MEANS AND STANDARD DEVIATIONS FOR FACTORS OF PERCEIVED MULTICULTURAL COUNSELING COMPETENCE AS A FUNCTION OF PARTICIPANT CHARACTERISTICS

	Factors					
	Multicultural Knowledge		Multicultural Awareness		Multicultural Terminology	
Characteristics	M	SD	M	SD	M	SD
Overall	2.46	.81	3.37	.62	3.41	.62
Multicultural coursework						
Yes	2.57	77	3.27	.62	3.48	.59
No	2.30	.86	3.28	.65	3.33	.64
Gender						
Female	2.44	.81	3.28	.63	3.40	.60
Male	2.46	.92	3.34	.61	3.51	.67
Years of experience						
1–4 years	2.44	.83	3.43	.61	3.29	.68
5–10 years	2.42	.79	3.53	.64	3.45	.55
11–14 years	2.48	.78	3.63	.53	3.47	.55
15 years +	2.47	.87	3.59	.59	3.52	.61
Work setting						
High school	2.42	.76	3.54	.58	3.32	.59
Middle school	2.57	.88	3.62	.52	3.52	.63
Elementary school	2.39	.81	3.44	.65	3.42	.61

Note. N = 209.

general biases inherent in self-rated assessments, future research that utilizes other methods (e.g., observations, paired comparisons) of assessing the multicultural competence of school counselors is warranted. For instance, research that incorporates the use of taped sessions in which students rate school counselors' use of strategies with ethnically diverse students would enhance our knowledge of what students perceive as being "culturally appropriate" counseling techniques.

Future investigators also are encouraged to continue exploring the dimensionality of school counselors' multicultural counseling competence. While the majority of research on multicultural competencies has focused on Sue et al.'s (1998) tripartite model of multicultural counseling competence (i.e., awareness, knowledge, skills), most instruments have deviated to some extent from the model upon which they are based. The same is true of the MCCTS-R in the present study. Although this study provides some data about the dimensionality of school counselors' multicultural competence, supplementary evidence is needed to confirm or refute the findings. Additionally, because of the importance of multicultural issues to the school counseling field, future research is warranted to identify specific variables that may facilitate or impede the development of school counselors' multicultural counseling competence.

And finally, in relation to the multidimensional nature of school counselors' multicultural counseling competence, the assessment of school counselors' multicultural counseling competence also should be multidimensional. Future studies should include multiple measures that address other related variables to multicultural competence. For instance, the use of measures such as the Interracial Comfort Index (Claney & Parker, 1989) and the White Racial Identity Attitude Scale (Helms & Carter, 1990) would be helpful in understanding related aspects or components of multicultural competence.

Implications for Practice

This study's findings have two significant implications for practicing school counselors. First, the positive influence of the multicultural counseling course on school counselors' perceived competence of the multicultural knowledge and terminology dimensions indicates the need for school counselors to engage in professional development activities (e.g., courses, workshops) to enhance their multicultural competence. If coursework can significantly influence a counselor's competence, then counselors' participation in professional development is not in vain. Supervisors of counseling and guidance should be vigilant about providing school counselors with ongoing educational and professional support on relevant diversity or multicultural topics. For instance, providing training opportunities related to racial and ethnic identity development of adolescents would enhance school counselors' multicultural knowledge and possibly their practice. And secondly, the use of an instrument such as the MCCTS-R can be a valuable tool for school counselors unsure of their level of multicultural competence. School counselors may want to evaluate their competence in order to determine areas where training or experience is needed.

Implications for Training

As previously mentioned, this study's finding that multicultural coursework significantly influenced counselors' multicultural competence validates the existence of multicultural counseling courses in counselor education. With that said, this study's most important implication for training is that multicultural coursework should be continued. School counselor educators should, therefore, continue existing multicultural courses and continuously evaluate the content of their courses to ensure that counseling trainees are receiving training in all domains of multicultural counseling competence. Even adding additional multicultural counseling courses, such as advanced courses in multicultural counseling, should be explored by counselor education faculty as a means to further enhance the multicultural counseling competence of counselors. It is interesting to note that although school counseling programs approved by the Council on the Accreditation of Counseling and Related Educational Programs are required to address multicultural issues in their curricula, it is unknown how these programs are approaching this matter. Determining how diversity issues are infused in school counseling field experiences (e.g., internships), core school counseling courses, and other program components would be noteworthy and should be documented.

Limitations

Several important limitations need to be considered when interpreting the results of this study. Perhaps the primary limitation of this study is its self-report nature, and responses may reflect participants' desire to appear competent (i.e., social desirability) rather than report accurate levels of multicultural competence. Data from this study represent counselors' perceptions rather than their actual and demonstrated multicultural competence when working with culturally diverse students. Although self-report measures, as the one used for this study, are prominent in the literature, research involving actual practice would be a major step forward. Another serious limitation of this study is that information was not gathered on the racial or ethnic composition of the counselors' school population. It is possible that the participants' perceived multicultural counseling competence is related to their exposure or lack of exposure to culturally diverse student populations.

In addition, it could be possible that this study examined the perceived multicultural competence of school counselors who are more likely to have received training beyond multicultural courses or who are less intimidated by discussions pertaining to culture, ethnicity, and/or race. Furthermore, it is unknown whether those who join ASCA are more familiar with the latest trends in the field. Although these concerns may limit the generalizability of the results, this study serves as the beginning of an empirically supported understanding of currently practicing school counselors' multicultural competence.

CONCLUSION

Given the culturally and ethnically diverse student composition of today's public schools, the multicultural counseling competence of school counselors is a critical topic. Whether counselors are able to provide counseling services that are unbiased and culturally appropriate for students and their families can make a huge difference in student achievement, particularly minority student achievement. With the availability of an instrument to assess school counselors' multicultural counseling competence, it is hoped that school counselors will expand their assessment toolbox, thus allowing for a means to assess their own multicultural competence level.

Cheryl C. Holcomb-McCoy is an assistant professor, Department of Counseling and Personnel Services, University of Maryland at College Park. E-mail: ch193@umail.umd.edu

REFERENCES

Allison, K. W., Crawford, I., Echemendia, R., Robinson, L., & Knepp, D. (1994). Human diversity and professional competence: Training in clinical and counseling psychology revisited. *American Psychologist, 49,* 792–796.

American School Counselor Association. (1999). *Position statement: Multicultural counseling.* Retrieved July 11, 2004 from http://www.schoolcounselor.org/content.cfm?L1= 100&L2=26

Arredondo, P., Toporek, R., Brown, S., Jones, J., Locke, D. C., Sanchez, J., et al. (1996). *Operationalization of the multicultural counseling competencies.* Alexandria, VA: Association for Multicultural Counseling and Development.

Carey, J. C., Reinat, M., & Fontes, L. (1990). School counselors' perceptions of training needs in multicultural counseling. *Counselor Education and Supervision, 29,* 155–170.

Carter, R. T. (1990). The relationship between racism and racial identity among White Americans: An exploratory investigation. *Journal of Counseling and Development, 69,* 46–50.

Claney, D., & Parker, W. M. (1989). Assessing White racial consciousness and perceived comfort with Black individuals: A preliminary study. *Journal of Counseling and Development, 67,* 449–451.

Coleman, L. K., Wampold, B. E., & Casali, S. B. (1995). Ethnic minorities' ratings of ethnically similar and European American counselors: A meta-analysis. *Journal of Counseling Psychology, 42,* 55–64.

Constantine, M. G. (2002). Racism attitudes, White racial identity attitudes, and multicultural counseling competence in school counselor trainees. *Counselor Education and Supervision, 41*, 162–174.

Constantine, M. G., & Ladany, N. (2000). Self-report multicultural counseling competence scales: Their relation to social desirability attitudes and multicultural case conceptualization ability. *Journal of Counseling Psychology, 47*, 155–164.

Constantine, M. G., & Yeh, C. J. (2001). Multicultural training, self-construals, and multicultural competence of school counselors. *Professional School Counseling, 4*, 202–207.

Corvin, S. A., & Wiggins, F. (1989). An antiracism training model for White professionals. *Journal of Multicultural Counseling and Development, 17*, 105–114.

D'Andrea, M., & Daniels, J. (1991). Exploring the different levels of multicultural counseling training in counselor education. *Journal of Counseling and Development, 70*, 78–85.

Green, S. B., & Salkind, N. J. (2003). Using SPSS for Windows and Macintosh: Analyzing and understanding data. New York: Prentice Hall.

Helms, J. E., & Carter, R. T. (1990). Development of the White racial identity scale. In J. E. Helms (Ed.), *Black and White racial identity: Theory, research, and practice* (pp. 66–80). Westport, CT: Greenwood Press.

Holcomb-McCoy, C. (2001). Exploring the self-perceived multicultural counseling competence of elementary school counselors. *Professional School Counseling, 4*, 195–201.

Holcomb-McCoy, C., & Myers, J. E. (1999). Multicultural competence and counselor training: A national survey. *Journal of Counseling and Development, 77*, 294–302.

Howard-Hamilton, M., & Williams, V. A. (1993). Training and teaching cross-cultural issues: A flexible workshop model. *College Student Affairs Journal, 12*, 81–84.

Ibrahim, F. A., & Arredondo, P. M. (1986). Ethical standards for cross-cultural counseling: Counselor preparation, practice, assessment, and research. *Journal of Counseling and Development, 64*, 349–352.

Lee, C. C. (1995). *Counseling for diversity: A guide for school counselors and related professionals.* Alexandria, VA: American Counseling Association.

Lee, C. C. (2001). Culturally responsive school counselors and programs: Addressing the needs of all students. *Professional School Counseling, 4*, 257–261.

Lewis, A. C., & Hayes, S. (1991). Multiculturalism and the school counseling curriculum. *Journal of Counseling and Development, 70,* 119–125.

McRae, M. B., & Johnson, S. D. (1991). Toward training for competence in multicultural counselor education. *Journal of Counseling and Development, 70,* 131–135.

Ottavi, T. M., Pope-Davis, D. B., & Dings, G. (1994). Relationship between White racial identity attitudes and self-reported multicultural counseling competencies. *Journal of Counseling Psychology, 41,* 149–154.

Parker, W. M., Moore, M. A., & Neimeyer, G. J. (1998). Altering White racial identity and interracial comfort through multicultural training. *Journal of Counseling and Development, 76,* 302–310.

Pope-Davis D. B., & Ottavi, T. M. (1994). The relationship between racism and racial identity among White Americans: A replication and extension. *Journal of Counseling and Development, 72,* 293–297.

Pope-Davis, D. B., Reynolds, A. L., Dings, J. G., & Ottavi, T. M. (1994). Multicultural competencies of doctoral interns at university counseling centers: An exploratory investigation. *Professional Psychology: Research and Practice, 25,* 466–470.

Ridley, C. R., Mendoza, D. W., Kanitz, B. E., Angermeier, L., & Zenk, R. (1994). Cultural sensitivity in multicultural counseling: A perceptual schema model. *Journal of Counseling Psychology, 41,* 125–136.

Sodowsky, G. R., Taffe, R. C., & Gutkin, T. B. (1991, August). *Development and applications of the multicultural counseling inventory.* Paper presented at the Annual Conference of the American Psychological Association, San Francisco.

Sue, D. W., Arredondo, P., & McDavis, R. J. (1992). Multicultural counseling competencies and standards: A call to the profession. *Journal of Counseling and Development, 70,* 477–486.

Sue, D. W., Bernier, Y., Durran, A., Feinberg, L., Pederson, P. B., Smith, E. J., et al. (1982). Position paper: Cross-cultural counseling competencies. *The Counseling Psychologist, 10,* 45–52.

Sue, D. W., Carter, R., Casas, J. M., Fouad, N., Ivey, A. E., Jensen, M., et al. (1998). *Multicultural counseling competencies: Individual and organizational development.* Thousand Oaks, CA: Sage.

Worthington, R. L., Mobley, M., Franks, R. P., & Tan, J. A. (2000). Multicultural counseling competencies: Verbal content, counselor attributions, and social desirability. *Journal of Counseling Psychology, 47,* 460–468.

Theoretical Orientation, Empathy, and Multicultural Counseling Competence in School Counselor Trainees

By Madonna G. Constantine, Ph.D.

This article originally appeared in *Professional School Counseling*, Vol. 4, No. 5, 2001.

As the 21st Century unfolds, school systems in the United States are becoming increasingly composed of racial and ethnic minority children (Durodoye, 1998; Johnson, 1995). This situation mandates that school counselors possess competence in working effectively with a range of culturally diverse students (Hobson & Kanitz, 1996; Lee, 1995; Reynolds, 1999). Such competence is commonly referred to as multicultural counseling competence (Sue, Arredondo, & McDavis, 1992).

Few studies in the school counseling literature, however, have examined issues related to multicultural counseling competence. In one such investigation, Constantine (in press) found that higher levels of racism and less advanced White racial identity attitudes were each related to lower levels of self-reported multicultural counseling competence. In another study, Constantine and Gushue (2000) reported that higher tolerance towards other ethnic groups was associated with higher multicultural case conceptualization ability (i.e., the ability to conceptualize a client's presenting concerns from a multicultural perspective), and that higher racism attitudes were related to lower multicultural case conceptualization ability. Constantine and Yeh (2001) found that previous multicultural training and having an independent self-construal (i.e., a tendency to base one's self-definition on one's unique attributes and abilities and on the importance of distinguishing oneself from others) were each significantly predictive of self-perceived multicultural counseling competence in female school counselors. Constantine and Yeh's findings suggested that school counselors' self-perceptions or self-conceptualizations might have an important impact on how they think about or understand multicultural issues related to their students.

One mechanism by which school counselors conceptualize the presenting concerns of culturally diverse students is through their theoretical orientation. Specifically, school counselors' theoretical orientations affect the ways in which they make sense of various issues associated with multicultural students, including these students' academic functioning, career development, and personal and interpersonal functioning (Sue, Ivey, &

Pedersen, 1996). Theoretical approaches to counseling may create the necessary structure to help school counselors work within the counseling process (Nystul, 1999). There is a wide array of theoretical orientations to counseling that has been formulated over the course of the 20th Century, including psychodynamic, humanistic, and cognitive-behavioral approaches. However, these types of orientations have been criticized at times for being dated, being biased toward a White middle-class model of counseling, and failing to sufficiently consider contextual and cultural issues in clients' lives (Nystul, 1999). Thus, in recent years, there have been trends in the direction of modifying traditional counseling approaches to include attention to issues of diversity and, increasingly, towards integrating various counseling theories (Lazarus & Beutler, 1993).

Theoretical integration involves the blending of two or more counseling theories, and appears to have stemmed, in part, from the notion that no one theory can comprehensively address the diverse needs of clients (Norcross & Newman, 1992). Some theorists assert that using an integrative or eclectic counseling approach may help counselors to more meaningfully consider salient cultural issues in clients' lives (Sue et al., 1996). However, little empirical information is available regarding the extent to which school counselors' theoretical orientations may reflect their self-perceived ability to work with culturally diverse students. This study examined theoretical orientation as a predictor of self-reported multicultural counseling competence in school counselor trainees.

Of additional interest in this study was the extent to which school counselor trainees' ability to accurately empathize with the experiences of others would relate to their perceptions of their own multicultural counseling competence. The term *empathy* refers to the ability to communicate a sense of caring and understanding regarding another person's experiences (Egan, 1994; Nystul, 1999). Constantine (2000) suggested that counselors' ability to understand the cultural experiences of others might be a vital component of effective multicultural counseling. Regardless of their theoretical orientation, school counselors or school counselor trainees who are perceived by their students as empathic are likely to develop effective working relationships with these individuals, resulting in potentially beneficial counseling outcomes (e.g., Horvath & Symonds, 1991; Luborsky, Crits-Christoph, Mintz, & Auerback, 1988). Therefore, the extent to which school counselors or school counselor trainees are able to display empathy in cross-cultural relationships may represent aspects of their multicultural counseling competence.

Because previous literature in the area of school counselor multicultural counseling competence has reported that prior academic training in multicultural counseling was associated with higher self-perceived abilities to work with culturally diverse clients (e.g., Constantine, in press; Constantine & Yeh, 2001), it seemed important to consider the potential role of such training in this study. Hence, the variance accounted for by previous multicultural training was statistically considered prior to exploring the contributions of theoretical orientation and empathy to self-reported multicultural counseling competence.

One primary research hypothesis guided this study. It was hypothesized that, after accounting for previous multicultural training, school counselor trainees' theoretical orientation and empathy would contribute significant variance to their self-perceived multicultural counseling competence.

METHOD

Participants and Procedure

The 105 participants in the study were identified through faculty contacts in school counselor training programs located in the northeast region of the United States. At the time of the study, the participants in this convenience sample were enrolled in required master's-level courses in school counseling (e.g., School Counseling Fieldwork, Counseling School-Age Children and Adolescents), and most of these students (n = 82; 78%) were matriculating in the second year of their program of study. The majority of the students (*n* = 100; 95%) were enrolled full time in their program. The participants were asked to complete a survey packet consisting of the Interpersonal Reactivity Index (IRI; Davis, 1980), the Multicultural Counseling Inventory (MCI; Sodowsky, Taffe, Gutkin, & Wise, 1994), and a brief demographic questionnaire. Because the surveys were administered and completed during specific class times, the return rate of surveys was high (99%).

The 73 (70%) women and 32 (30%) men who participated in the study ranged in age from 21 to 48 years (*M* = 30.24, *SD* = 6.44), and their racial/ethnic breakdown was as follows: 72 (68.6%) Whites, 17 (16.2%) Blacks, 8 (7.6%) Asian Americans, and 8 (7.6%) Latino(a)s. With regard to their highest educational degree, 102 (97.1%) individuals held a bachelor's degree and 3 (2.9%) held a master's degree. Some of the participants reported having had previous counseling experience (*M* = 3.67 months, *SD* = 4.36, range = 0 to 28). By theoretical orientation, 44 (41.9%) of the participants were coded as eclectic/integrative, 34 (32.4%) as humanistic, 19 (18.1%) as psychodynamic, and 8 (7.6%) as cognitive-behavioral.

Instruments

MCI. The MCI (Sodowsky et al., 1994) is a 40-item, four-point (1 = very inaccurate to 4 = very accurate) self-report scale that assesses four components of multicultural counseling competence. These components are measured by subscales known as multicultural counseling (a) Awareness (10 items, possible range = 10 to 40); (b) Knowledge (11 items, possible range = 11 to 44); (c) Skills (11 items, possible range = 11 to 44); and (d) Relationship (8 items, possible range = 8 to 32). MCI full-scale scores range from 40 to 160. The MCI Awareness subscale assesses issues such as multicultural sensitivity, multicultural interactions and experiences, general cultural understanding, and multicul- tural advocacy. The Knowledge subscale consists of items that measure knowledge of multicultural case conceptualization and treatment strategies and knowledge of cultural information. The Skills subscale assesses multicultural and general counseling skills. Finally, the Relationship subscale comprises items measuring counselors' interpersonal processes with racial and ethnic minority clients. Higher scores on each subscale indicate higher levels of self-perceived multicultural counseling competence.

According to Sodowsky et al. (1994), evidence of content validity for the MCI was obtained through expert raters' accuracy of classifying items into their appropriate subscale categories and through expert evaluation of item clarity. Criterion-related validity was established in that individuals with multicultural training or more professional experience working with culturally diverse populations obtained higher MCI scores. Exploratory and confirmatory factor analyses and tests of factor congruence provided evidence of adequate construct validity (Sodowsky, 1996; Sodowsky et al., 1994). Based on findings from previous studies using the MCI (e.g., Pope-Davis & Dings, 1994; Sodowsky et al., 1994), a mean Cronbach's alpha of .87 has been reported for the entire scale, and mean Cronbach's alphas of .78, .77, .80, and .68 have been reported for the Awareness, Knowledge, Skills, and Relationship subscales, respectively (Sodowsky, Kuo-Jackson, Richardson, & Corey, 1998). In the current study, the following Cronbach's alphas were computed: .89 for the MCI full scale, .79 for the Awareness subscale, .81 for the Knowledge subscale, .79 for the Skills subscale, and .74 for the Relationship subscale.

IRI. The IRI (Davis, 1980) is a 28-item, five-point (0 = does not describe me well to 4 = describes me very well) self-report measure of four dimensions of empathy. Each of the four subscales consists of seven items, and the possible range for each subscale is 0 to 28. The possible range for IRI full-scale scores is 0 to 112. One of the IRI's subscales, Perspective-Taking, assesses empathy in the form of individuals' tendency to spontaneously adopt other people's points of view. The Fantasy subscale of the IRI measures respondents' tendency to transpose themselves into the feelings and behaviors of fictional characters in movies, books, and plays. The Empathic Concern subscale taps respondents' feelings of concern, warmth, and sympathy toward others. Finally, the Personal Distress sub-scale assesses "self-oriented" feelings of personal anxiety and discomfort in response to others' distress (Davis, 1980; Davis, Luce, & Kraus, 1994). Higher scores are associated with greater levels of self-perceived empathy. Sex differences are reported to exist for each subscale, with women tending to score higher than men on each subscale (Davis, 1980).

Several investigations have provided evidence of construct validity for the IRI's subscales (e.g., Bernstein & Davis, 1982; Carey, Fox, & Spraggins, 1988; Davis, 1983). The IRI subscales have been reported to have satisfactory internal reliabilities (range = .71 to .77) and test-retest reliabilities (range = .62 to .80) (Davis, 1980). In the current study, Cronbach's alphas of .70, .79, .79, and .68 were computed for the Perspective-Taking, Fantasy, Empathic Concern, and Personal Distress subscales, respectively. The Cronbach's alpha for the full scale of the IRI was .78.

Demographic questionnaire. Participants were asked to indicate their race/ethnicity, sex, age, highest degree earned, theoretical orientation to counseling, number of months of previous counseling experience, and the number of formal academic courses taken previously related to multi-cultural issues. Respondents who indicated more than one theoretical approach to counseling were coded as eclectic/integrative.

Results

Table 1 presents the means and standard deviations for the study's scales, along with the intercorrelations of these variables. Because of the high intercorrelations of the MCI subscales, only the MCI full-scale score (as opposed to the four individual subscales) was used as the index of self-reported multicultural counseling competence. For the preliminary analyses, a multivariate analysis of variance (p = .05) was computed to determine whether school counselor trainees differed significantly by sex and race/ethnicity with regard to the MCI full-scale score and the four IRI subscales. Results revealed no significant interaction [$F(10, 190) = .38$, p > .05] or main effect differences by sex [$F(5, 94) = .89$, p > .05] or race/ethnicity [$F(15, 288) = 1.02$, p > .05]. Thus, sex and race/ethnicity were not included as independent variables in the main analysis.

For the main analysis, a hierarchical multiple regression analysis was computed using the MCI full-scale score as the criterion variable. To account for the role of previous multicultural training in the regression analysis, the number of formal multicultural counseling courses taken was entered into the first step. In the second step, counselor theoretical orientation was entered, for which the four groups (i.e., eclectic/integrative, humanistic, psychodynamic, and cognitive-behavioral) were entered simul-

TABLE 1. MEANS, STANDARD DEVIATIONS, AND INTERCORRELATIONS OF THE STUDY'S SCALES

Variables	M	SD	1	2	3	4	5	6	7	8	9	10	11
1. MCI Full-Scale score	126.32	13.01	—	.78†	.80†	.81†	.62†	.04	.18	-.21*	.41†	-.17	.29†
2. MCI Awareness subscale	28.85	5.31	.78†	—	.52†	.45†	.24*	.08	.04	-.12	.36†	-.05	.20*
3. MCI Knowledge subscale	35.35	4.32			—	.57†	.30†	.13	.24*	-.13	.44†	-.12	.23*
4. MCI Skills subscale	37.90	3.01				—	.51†	-.02	.25*	-.23*	.27†	-.22*	.25*
5. MCI Relationship subscale	24.22	3.57					—	-.10	.05	-.17	.12	-.18	.35†
6. IRI Full-Scale score	75.21	10.83						—	.43†	.80†	.37†	.76†	-.07
7. IRI Perspective-Taking subscale	20.01	3.56							—	-.00	.36†	-.07	.28†
8. IRI Fantasy subscale	15.92	4.96								—	-.12	.83†	-.21*
9. IRI Empathic Concern subscale	20.78	4.08									—	-.16	.04
10. IRI Personal Distress subscale	18.50	5.04										—	-.17
11. MC Courses	1.00	.48											—

Note. MCI = Multicultural Counseling Inventory (Sodowsky et al., 1994); IRI = Interpersonal Reactivity Index (Davis, 1980); MC Courses = Number of multicultural or cross-cultural counseling courses taken.

$p < .05$. $*pr < .01$. †$p < .001$

taneously with three dummy codes. The eclectic/integrative orientation was coded as zero, serving as the constant. The four IRI subscales (i.e., Perspective-Taking, Fantasy, Empathic Concern, and Personal Distress) were entered simultaneously into the third step.

Table 2 provides a summary of the hierarchical regression analysis for variables predicting the MCI full-scale score. In the first step, higher multicultural counseling training was associated with higher self-reported multicultural counseling competence, $F(1, 103) = 5.39$, $p < .05$, $R^2 = .05$ (adjusted $R^2 = .04$). After controlling for prior multicultural training, counselor theoretical orientation made additional significant contributions to the MCI full-scale score, R^2 change = .11, $F(4, 100)$ change = 4.56, $p < .01$, $R^2 = .16$ (adjusted $R^2 = .13$). Specifically, school counselor trainees with an eclectic/integrative orientation reported significantly higher levels of multicultural counseling competence than did trainees with a psychodynamic or cognitive-behavioral theoretical orientation. After accounting for the previous variables, the IRI subscales together added significant variance to the MCI full-scale score, R^2 change = .13, $F(8, 96)$ change = 4.39, $p < .01$, $R^2 = .29$ (adjusted $R^2 = .23$), with Empathic Concern scores alone making a unique positive contribution. The full regression model, consisting of previous multicultural training, counselor theoretical orientation, and the IRI subscales, accounted for 29% of the variance in self-reported multicultural counseling competence.

Discussion

The primary purpose of this study was to examine the extent to which school counselor trainees' theoretical orientation and empathy would predict their self-reported multicultural counseling competence. As expected, higher levels of multicultural counseling training were related to higher self-perceived multicultural counseling competence. These findings echo the results of other school counselor investigations reporting significant positive relationships between these variables (e.g., Constantine, in press; Constantine & Yeh, 2001). The current study's findings underscore the importance of school counselor training programs attending to multicultural issues in the context of curriculum offerings in order to help trainees feel efficacious about working with culturally diverse students. Moreover, these findings suggest that practicing school counselors may benefit from continuing education activities that focus on increasing their competence and feelings of efficacy in working with diverse students.

After accounting for previous multicultural training, theoretical orientation contributed significant variance to school counselor trainees' self-reported multicultural counseling competence. Specifically, trainees with an eclectic/integrative orientation reported significantly higher levels of

TABLE 2. SUMMARY OF THE HIERARCHICAL MULTIPLE REGRESSION ANALYSIS FOR VARIABLES PREDICTING THE MCI FULL-SCALE SCORE

Variables	B	SE B	b	t
Step 1				
MC Courses	6.04	2.60	.22	2.32*
Step 2				
Theoretical Orientation				
Humanistic	−.13	2.77	−.00	−.05
Psychodynamic	−8.72	3.34	−.26	−2.61*
Cognitive-Behavioral	−12.65	4.66	−.26	−2.72**
Step 3				
IRI Subscales				
Perspective-Taking	.09	.35	.02	.26
Fantasy	−.50	.42	−.19	−1.18
Empathic Concern	1.11	.30	.35	3.66***
Personal Distress	.30	.40	.12	.75

Note. MCI = Multicultural Counseling Inventory (Sodowsky et al., 1994); IRI = Interpersonal Reactivity Index (Davis, 1980); MC Courses = Number of multi-cultural counseling courses taken.

$*p < .05.$ $**p < .01.$ $***p < .001$

multicultural counseling competence than did trainees with a psychodynamic or cognitive-behavioral theoretical orientation. These findings suggest that school counselor trainees' ability or willingness to use perspectives and techniques from various counseling theories may be indicative of their competence in working with culturally diverse students. A potential implication of these findings for both school counselor trainees and professional school counselors is the importance of being somewhat flexible in incorporating various counseling conceptualizations and treatment strategies with diverse student populations so as to effectively address their mental health needs. Although there may be benefits to utilizing a core or primary theory of counseling (e.g., consistency in conceptualization and counseling techniques), it is likely that no individual theory could address the mental health issues of every student (Nystul, 1999).

After accounting for prior multicultural counseling training and counselor theoretical orientation, the IRI subscale scores as a whole contributed significant variance to school counselor trainees' self-perceived multicultural counseling competence, with Empathic Concern scores alone making a unique positive contribution. Similarly, Constantine (2000), in an investigation of counselors and counselor trainees, found that Empathic Concern scores were positively correlated with self-reported multicultural counseling competence. The current study's findings suggest that school counselor trainees' feelings of concern, warmth, and sympathy may reflect, to some degree, their ability to work with culturally diverse students. A crucial implication of these findings is that school counselor training programs may wish to consider facilitating the development of multicultural counseling competence in their trainees by focusing on increasing their ability to emotionally understand diverse students' concerns. That is, interventions designed to increase school counselor trainees' levels of empathic listening and affective responding may indirectly contribute to higher levels of competence in working with culturally diverse students (Constantine, 2000). In particular, didactic and experiential exercises that encourage school counselor trainees to identify and process their own experiences of discrimination, oppression, and prejudice may aid them in better understanding and relating to such issues in the lives of racial and ethnic minority students.

The above-mentioned findings also have important implications for professional school counselors. For example, it is possible that school counselors who successfully communicate a sense of caring and understanding regarding their students' cultural experiences may be perceived by these students as multiculturally competent. Thus, in order to increase their levels of empathy with regard to culturally diverse students, school counselors may wish to consider participating in events that reflect the values, beliefs, and practices of these students' cultural groups (e.g., attending a religious service at a predominantly Black church, participating in certain American Indian ceremonies or rituals) (Constantine, 2000). In addition, becoming an active member of culturally diverse professional and personal organizations may provide school counselors with opportunities to interact with and better understand the experiences of individuals representing various backgrounds. Such activities may be valuable means to enhance their professional competence in addressing cultural issues in the lives of their students.

There are several potential limitations of this investigation. First, generalizability of the findings is cautioned because the sample consisted of school counselor trainees who were matriculating in programs in the northeast region of the United States. Future research should examine the study's variables in a more geographically diverse sample of trainees. Second, although the participants reported adhering to one or more theoretical orientations to counseling, it is important to note that acknowledging a preference for a particular orientation may not be synonymous with actually working with clients from this perspective. In addition, because the study's measures were self-report in nature, the trainees may have responded to the instruments in ways that did not accurately reflect their attitudes, beliefs, or behaviors. In a related issue, it is possible that the school counselor trainees in this sample may have over-estimated their levels of multicultural counseling competence in an attempt to appear socially acceptable to the researcher. This phenomenon has been noted as an artifact of some self-report multicultural counseling competence measures (Constantine & Ladany, 2000; Sodowsky et al., 1998).

Future investigators are encouraged to continue exploring the associations among the variables addressed in this study, particularly in professional school counselors. Specifically, the constructs of counselor theoretical orientation and empathy need to be examined more fully in order to further understand their potential roles in the development and maintenance of school counselors' relationships with diverse students. Moreover, future research is needed that explores other attitudinal and skill-based correlates (e.g., cognitive flexibility, interpersonal warmth) of both self-perceived and demonstrated multicultural counseling competence in practicing school counselors and school counselor trainees. There is also a need for research that examines the impact of specific types of multicultural training activities on the development of demonstrated multicultural competence in school counselor trainees and practicing school counselors.

Madonna G. Constantine is an associate professor, Department of Counseling and Clinical Psychology, Teachers College, Columbia University, NY. Email mc816@columbia.edu.

REFERENCES

Bernstein, W. M., & Davis, M. H. (1982). Perspective-taking, self-consciousness, and accuracy in person perception. *Basic and Applied Social Psychology, 3,* 1–19.

Carey, J. C., Fox, E. A., & Spraggins, E. F. (1988). Replication of structure findings regarding the Interpersonal Reactivity Index. *Measurement and Evaluation in Counseling and Development, 21,* 102–105.

Constantine, M. G. (in press). Racism attitudes, White racial identity attitudes, and multicultural counseling competence in school counselor trainees. *Counselor Education and Supervision.*

Constantine, M. G. (2000). Social desirability attitudes, sex, and affective and cognitive empathy as predictors of self-reported multicultural counseling competence. *The Counseling Psychologist, 28,* 857–872.

Constantine, M. G., & Gushue, G. V. (2000). *School counselors' ethnic tolerance and racism attitudes as predictors of their multicultural case conceptualization ability*. Unpublished manuscript.

Constantine, M. G., & Ladany, N. (2000). Self-report multicultural counseling competence scales: Their relation to social desirability attitudes and multicultural case conceptualization ability. *Journal of Counseling Psychology, 47,* 155–164.

Constantine, M. G., & Yeh, C. J. (2001). Multicultural training and self-construals as predictors of school counselors' multicultural counseling competence. *Professional School Counseling 4,* 202–207.

Davis, M. H. (1980). A multidimensional approach to individual differences in empathy. *JSAS Catalog of Selected Documents in Psychology, 10,* 85.

Davis, M. H. (1983). Measuring individual differences in empathy: Evidence for a multidimensional approach. *Journal of Personality and Social Psychology, 44,* 113–126.

Davis, M. H., Luce, C., & Kraus, S. J. (1994). The heritability of characteristics associated with dispositional empathy. *Journal of Personality, 62,* 369–391.

Durodoye, B. A. (1998). Fostering multicultural awareness among teachers: A tripartite model. *Professional School Counseling, 1*(5), 9–13.

Egan, G. (1994). The skilled helper: A model for systematic helping and interpersonal relating (5th ed.). Monterey, CA: Brooks/Cole.

Hobson, S. M., & Kanitz, H. M. (1996). Multicultural counseling: An ethical issue for school counselors. *The School Counselor, 43,* 245–255.

Horvath, A. O., & Symonds, B. D. (1991). Relation between working alliance and outcome in psychotherapy: A meta-analysis. *Journal of Counseling Psychology, 38,* 139–149.

Johnson, L. S. (1995). Enhancing multicultural relations: Intervention strategies for the school counselor. *The School Counselor, 43,* 103–113.

Lazarus, A. A., & Beutler, L. E. (1993). On technical eclecticism. *Journal of Counseling and Development, 71,* 381–385.

Lee, C. C. (1995). School counseling and cultural diversity: A framework for effective practice. In C. C. Lee (Ed.), *Counseling for diversity: A guide for school counselors and related professionals* (pp. 3–17). Needham Heights, MA: Allyn & Bacon.

Luborsky, L., Crits-Christoph, P., Mintz, J., & Auerback, A. (1988). *Who will benefit from psychotherapy? Predicting therapeutic outcome.* New York: Basic Books.

Norcross, J. C., & Newman, C. F. (1992). Psychotherapy integration: Setting the context. In J. C. Norcross & M. R. Goldfried (Eds.), *Handbook of psychotherapy integration* (pp. 3–45). New York: Basic Books.

Nystul, M. S. (1999). *Introduction to counseling: An art and science perspective.* Needham Heights, MA: Allyn & Bacon.

Pope-Davis, D. B., & Dings, J. G. (1994). An empirical comparison of two self-report multicultural counseling competency inventories. *Measurement and Evaluation in Counseling and Development, 27,* 93–102.

Reynolds, A. L. (1999). Working with children and adolescents in the schools: Multicultural counseling implications. In R. H. Sheets & E. R. Hollins (Eds.), *Racial and ethnic identity in school practices: Aspects of human development* (pp. 213–229). Mahwah, NJ: Lawrence Erlbaum.

Sodowsky, G. R. (1996). The Multicultural Counseling Inventory: Psychometric properties and some uses in counseling training. In G. R. Sodowsky & J. C. Impara (Eds.), *Multicultural assessment in counseling and clinical psychology* (pp. 283–324). Lincoln, NE: Buros Institute of Mental Measurements.

Sodowsky, G. R., Kuo-Jackson, P. Y., Richardson, M. F., & Corey, A. T. (1998). Correlates of self-reported multicultural competencies: Counselor multicultural social desirability, race, social inadequacy, locus of control racial ideology, and multicultural training. *Journal of Counseling Psychology, 45,* 256–264.

Sodowsky, G. R., Taffe, R. C., Gutkin, T. B., & Wise, S. L. (1994). Development of the Multicultural Counseling Inventory: A self-report measure of multicultural competencies. *Journal of Counseling Psychology, 41,* 137–148.

Sue, D. W., Arredondo, P., & McDavis, R. J. (1992). Multicultural counseling competencies and standards: A call to the profession. *Journal of Multicultural Counseling and Development, 20,* 64–68.

Sue, D. W., Ivey, A. E., & Pedersen, P. B. (1996). *A theory of multicultural counseling and therapy.* Pacific Grove, CA: Brooks/Cole.

Examining Your Own Gender Bias

Treating all students the same doesn't necessarily result in a school counseling program that isn't gender biased. Part of the school counselor's responsibility is to provide career and academic counseling in ways that help all students succeed and work to their greatest potential.

By Toni R. Tollerud, Ph.D.

This article originally appeared in *ASCA School Counselor*, Vol. 41, No. 5, 2003.

Each day, students barrage school counselors, seeking help with issues affecting their futures. This isn't a small responsibility and requires school counselors to ensure they are being as fair, open-minded and equitable as possible with each and every student who sits down to talk and consider future plans and options. Consider this example.

Marcus enters your counseling office during the spring of his eighth-grade year. He wants to talk about high school and discuss what courses he thinks he should take. You have known this young man for two years in middle school, and you believe he's going to struggle in high school, although he is seldom in trouble. He is currently passing his classes, but his grades are slightly below average. He is an average student in school but he just doesn't seem to apply himself to schoolwork. He has told you he would like to be a nurse at the local hospital.

If you're honest with yourself, you admit thinking, "Marcus want to be a nurse? Wouldn't an auto mechanic be better?" You ask yourself how you can best help him select appropriate courses, think about career options and prepare for the future.

Part of the responsibility we share as school counselors is to provide career and academic counseling in ways that help all students succeed and work to their greatest potential. But what is the best way to go about this? What skills must school counselors use to facilitate this growth and garner success? How much do we try to influence students who have expectations that are way beyond their potential or way below their gifts and talents? And how much does the gender of the student influence our choice?

To best answer these questions it's crucial for school counselors to understand their own biases and ensure the academic and the career counseling done with students at any grade reflects gender equity and promotes nontraditional awareness and selection. Counselors must maintain a constant vigil in order to enable all students to have the opportunities, information, motivation and support to truly be what they want to be in life.

Often I hear counselors say, "I am equitable because I treat everyone the same in my school; boys and girls all get the same set of information about college programs, career opportunities and academic choices." But, this attitude isn't sufficient to overcome the pitfalls of gender bias, and often it perpetuates the status quo. To move beyond treating our students equally and addressing their needs equitably, school counselors need to practice gender fairness in working with students about course selection, curriculum programs, college considerations and career options. This also includes introducing all students, especially girls, to nontraditional career options, informing them of the barriers and risks in entering these careers, providing extra support for those who do follow a more nontraditional path in school and intentionally informing all students of the importance of curriculum in reaching future goals.

PROJECTING A BIAS

For school counselors to practice gender equity, they should make every effort to provide all students the full range of opportunities and benefits to be successful in their lives. Although this sounds easy enough to do, counselors often get caught in two common practices that may end up inhibiting students from achieving this end.

First, counselors project their own bias when they assume that men and women have certain interests, talents or abilities because of their gender, and these beliefs result in their treating students differently. For example, we may encourage boys to take computer courses because we believe they achieve better in these classes and will need computer skills for future employment, while we may discourage girls because we assume they will not need such advanced skills in the types of jobs they might do. When our actions prohibit girls from taking certain classes in technology or limit boys from taking courses in the health care arena, we are exhibiting gender discrimination in our role.

A second practice inhibiting a student's potential occurs when the counselor, by informing particular students of their limitations, tarnishes a student's ambition or dream. Counselors sometimes justify their behaviors because of test scores, grades or school work ethic. Although these may be important pieces of information, it's important to note that basing a child's total future on such information is narrow, just as narrow as telling a boy like Marcus that he would be better off in auto mechanics or computers than in nursing.

In a 1999 American Association of University Women (AAUW) study of high school graduates, the impact of the school counselor in these students' lives received mixed reviews. Only 41 percent felt "somewhat satisfied" with the help they received from their counselors regarding college and career planning. Twenty percent to 33 percent thought their counselors could have provided them with more information and time. The study also reported that students felt counselors told them only what they couldn't do, rather than what their future possibilities could be and how the students could achieve their educational goals, even if not right after graduation.

Kenneth Gray, in his book "Getting Real: Helping Teens Find their Future," encourages counselors to work with students to identify a path that will allow students to achieve their dreams or desires. But, he goes on to say that counselors shouldn't stop at one choice; in the current economy, it is prudent to help students identify a plan B or even C in their future.

OVERCOMING GENDER BIAS

The school counselor's first task in overcoming gender bias is to look within. Ask yourself the following questions. As you review the questions, think about your attitudes regarding gender, and honestly critique how you address these with your students.

- Do I encourage every student to make academic, career and personal decisions based on individual interests, abilities, aptitudes and values rather than gender?
- Do I encourage every student to pursue his or her career aspirations and dreams even if they are dominated by the opposite gender?
- Do I talk about nontraditional careers with all of my students, both the boys and the girls?
- Do I use examples and resources on nontraditional careers in my school, including role models, guest speakers, mentors, bulletin board displays and reading material?
- Do I discuss job salaries with all my students, pointing out that typical male-dominated jobs mean higher salaries and typical female jobs mean lower salaries in the workplace?
- Do I talk about nontraditional options with all students, even if they already have a tentative career decision planned?
- Do I talk with students about employment rights and discrimination laws in the workplace so they will be informed when they enter the workforce?
- Do I speak to all students about the barriers preventing them from choosing nontraditional occupations?
- When students talk about taking courses that are composed mostly of the opposite gender, do I discuss the barriers that may be encountered and how these can be addressed?

■ When students take a nontraditional course in my school, do I meet with them and provide support for their courage and a forum for them to discuss the problems they face?

Addressing issues of gender bias is difficult because of our culture's socialization process, which often limits people in their career choices and their beliefs in their abilities. This socialization has an extremely strong impact on young people. Even in a society advocating that students can become what ever they aspire to be, other messages are equally powerful. Messages such as: girls don't do well in math or science, boys are better at computers, girls are detrimental in the trades, boys in nursing are sissy, and girls can't handle the stress in high-level or technological jobs. These messages are coupled with the fact that girls and boys who enter nontraditional careers are highly criticized, ridiculed or even harassed. This negativity often begins in the classes of our schools, especially in areas of technology, advanced math and science and technical education.

Because of this tremendous socialization pressure, it's clear that counselors must do more for those in the minority or nontraditional areas. Students come to us already influenced by this socialization. Therefore, if we treat everyone "equally," we fall short of addressing the true needs of students who may have the initial interest and ability to enter nontraditional fields. Girls may have already decided that succeeding in higher math classes is beyond their abilities because of negative feedback from peers, parents or even teachers. The resulting anxiety can lead girls to perform poorly. School counselors need to intervene for the sake of all our students.

The way information and technology are taught may also discourage a girl from success in certain technological fields. In the book "Tech Savvy: Educating Girls in the New Computer Age," from AAUW, the authors propose that girls must get more involved in computer literacy not just as consumers but as designers and leaders who are comfortable participating in the constant development and integration of computers into everyday living. Girls need to break the stereotype of people who work with computers. Girls can be taught to see the human and social dimensions and applications of computers, not just the technical aspects.

PROACTIVE STRATEGIES

School counselors are in a strategic position to combat these stereotypes. Once school counselors become committed to work intentionally on their gender bias and to promote fairness, there are many ways they can contribute to equity and student success. ASCA's National Model and National Standards advocate that school counseling programs be comprehensive in scope and developmental in nature in order to provide a proactive program for all students. The topic of gender equity should be woven into the career, academic and personal/social domains. Professionally produced curriculums such as "The Real Game" and "How to...Career Activities for Every Classroom" offer excellent exercises counselors can use.

In promoting gender equity in academic counseling, consider the following key elements:

- Encourage girls to enroll in math and science and to take computer science classes as early as possible so they do not fall behind the boys.
- Help all students select courses they are sincerely interested in and who have abilities and skills that can be enhanced or tested by the curriculum.
- Do not limit a student from taking courses because of gender.
- Talk to girls about not limiting their course selection in school even if they think they may not work their entire lives or they may choose to be stay-at-home moms.
- Intentionally encourage girls to enroll in advanced placement math, science and computer courses and to take the exam.
- Address the issues of test anxiety for those in advanced classes, both girls and boys.
- Help boys who are interested in the arts, health sciences or nontraditional areas to consider the coursework needed to achieve their educational and career goals.
- Provide support for students who choose nontraditional classes (i.e; girls in automotive and boys in child care).

School counselors can also work with students to begin to understand labor-market information in ways that will have positive outcomes for both girls and boys as they prepare for the workplace and select a career. Knowledge about the world of work is a powerful tool. Consider some of the following elements in counseling students optimally about their future:

- Help girls and boys prepare intelligently for work in the 21st-century workforce by using current occupational information. For example, students will need to know about the proper educational credentials to enter business or finance: they will need to be willing to work long hours, develop and use interpersonal/people skills – especially management skills, demonstrate competency on the job and be willing to take risks by being innovative and creative on projects.
- Encourage girls and boys to explore factors beyond internal interests, skills and values in selecting a workplace. They should also take into account external issues such as the availability of child care, flex time, wage structures, paid parental leaves and control over working hours.

- Encourage girls to look beyond their own occupational preferences to consider important data on hiring practices and policies used within specific companies and organizations.
- Educate all students in the labor market so they will understand the hierarchy of jobs. Help girls understand that jobs at the top pay more but generally have fewer female workers. Encourage students to consider not just economic survival or salary achievement in the job but opportunities for advancement, benefits, lifelong learning, responsibility to make the world a better place and retirement.

School counselors are important professionals in the educational world of students. What counselors say and do in the counseling office can have a lasting influence on students' self-concept, academic direction and career decisions. Let's be sure we do this in ways that best serve our students, regardless of their gender.

Toni R. Tollerud, Ph.D., LCPC, NCC, NCSC, ACS, is an associate professor in counseling, Northern Illinois University and executive director of the Illinois School Counselors' Academy. She can be reached at tollerud@niu.edu.

Counseling the Linguistically and Culturally Diverse Student: Meeting School Counselors' Professional Development Needs

By Pat Schwallie-Giddis, Ph.D., Kristina Anstrom, Ed.D., Patricio Sánchez, Victoria A. Sardi, Ph.D., and Laura Granato, Ph.D.

This article originally appeared in *Professional School Counseling*, Vol. 8, No. 1, 2004.

This study used qualitative methods to investigate the challenges and professional development needs of elementary and secondary school counselors who work with linguistically and culturally diverse students and families, and their perceptions of the impact of a 9-month professional development program focused on improving school counselors' multicultural awareness, knowledge, and skill.

In schools across the United States, linguistically and culturally diverse (LCD) students face dilemmas stemming from racial, ethnic, linguistic, and religious discrimination; language barriers; and stereotyping. Incongruities between LCD students' home cultures and values and those of the school can result in these students disengaging from school and eventually dropping out. Linguistically diverse students may also experience academic problems due to language barriers and lack of academic preparation in their native language. Though school counselors are called on to address the diverse needs of LCD students, they frequently do so without support or the requisite educational preparation. Professional development is one means of providing school counselors with the knowledge and skill necessary to counsel LCD students, parents, and other family members effectively.

An important consideration in designing effective multicultural professional development programming is counselors' perceptions of the challenges they face in their work with diverse students. Despite its importance, we know very little about counselors' perceived challenges in this area. Nor do we know the kind of professional development school counselors believe they need to help them meet the challenges they face in counseling LCD students. Finally, assessments of professional development efforts designed to address the challenges counselors face in their work with LCD students and families are critical. Studies that address these three areas will contribute to the development of a knowledge base on which inservice multicultural professional development programs for school counselors can be premised.

A primary purpose of this study is to describe the challenges and professional development needs of school counselors who work with linguistically and culturally diverse students in K–12 public schools. A second purpose is to describe the school counselors' perceptions of the impact of a 9-month multicultural professional development effort.

CULTURALLY COMPETENT COUNSELING: CHALLENGES FOR SCHOOL COUNSELORS

Research in the area of multiculturalism and school counseling has focused on counselors' perceptions of their own multicultural competence. Five underlying factors appear to be influential in school counselors' perceptions of themselves as multiculturally competent practitioners. These factors are an understanding of racial identity development, facility with multicultural terminology, multicultural awareness, multicultural knowledge, and multicultural skills (Holcomb-McCoy, 2000). Additional research indicates that school counselors feel competent in multicultural awareness and understanding of multicultural terminology, but perceive themselves as incompetent in racial identity development and multicultural knowledge (Holcomb-McCoy, 2001). Lack of knowledge of racial identity development is particularly problematic because "racial identity development has been linked to interpreting student behaviors and interactions" (Holcomb-McCoy, 2001, p. 199). Findings from these studies point to the importance of ensuring that information on racial identity development and development of multicultural knowledge are included in multicultural training.

In addition to their work with individual students and families, school counselors are frequently asked to assume responsibility for creating culturally accepting environments in their schools. Research undertaken to determine how well school counselors promoted and provided students with opportunities to develop multicultural awareness found that though most schools set aside special days to expose students to various cultures, there were not many ongoing programs to promote multicultural awareness. School counselors can be instrumental in developing and implementing ongoing school-wide programs that advocate tolerance and multicultural knowledge among faculty, students, and parents (Johnson, 1995).

A primary motivation for school counselors to seek multicultural training is the support they believe it provides in encouraging academic achievement among minority students. Counselors viewed multicultural training as important in helping them know how to prevent minority student dropout and to motivate minority students academically (Carey, Reinat, & Fontes, 1990). They also felt that multicultural training should address ways of working more effectively with families from different cultural backgrounds and improving cross-cultural communication skills and racial awareness. Counselors believed that multicultural training should also help them address their own stereotypes, cultural values, and biases (Carey et al.).

The literature on school counselors' perceptions of multicultural competence and the needs and challenges they face in their work with LCD students and families highlights general areas that multicultural professional development should address. The Multicultural Counseling Competencies (MCC), a framework developed by Sue, Arredondo, and Mc- Davis (1992) for professionals engaged in cross-cultural work, can also inform multicultural professional development efforts for school counselors. The MCC address three distinct dimensions (beliefs and attitudes, knowledge, and skills) of three domains (awareness of our own worldview, awareness of the other's worldview, and appropriate interventions). Most of the research findings in this area, including the studies cited here, used structured questionnaires that rely on a predetermined set of choices. What is lacking is an understanding of school counselors' perceptions of their work as multicultural counselors from their own perspectives and in their own words. Additionally, research is needed on school counselors' perceptions of the effectiveness of inservice multicultural professional development efforts.

METHODS

The essential questions that framed this study were:

1. How do school counselors perceive the challenges they face in counseling linguistically and culturally diverse (LCD) students and families?
2. How do school counselors define their professional development needs in the area of counseling LCD students and families?
3. How do school counselors, who work with LCD students and families, perceive the effectiveness of a 9-month, multicultural professional development program?

Researchers used a qualitative approach to explore, capture, and analyze participants' viewpoints relative to the three research questions posed above. The qualitative method used to address these three research questions and how data were analyzed are addressed below.

Sample and Participant Selection

Qualitative data were gathered through individual interviews with 13 of the 35 counselors who participated in a multicultural professional development program that consisted of seven monthly sessions during the 2001 to 2002 school year. The interviewees were selected from the pool of those program participants who had attended five or more of the seven sessions. The participants in this study were predominantly female, with the exception of one male participant. The majority (9) ranged in age between 40 and 60 years. The mean for age was 48 years. All participants had obtained at least a master's degree. Of the 13 participants, 10 were European American, two were Hispanic, and one was African American.

Participants' professional experience in school counseling was very heterogeneous. Forty percent of the participants had significant experience (10 to 20 years) working as a school counselor, while another 40 percent had less than 5 years of experience. The overall mean was 10 years of experience in school counseling.

Other than school counseling, the majority of the participants (9) had between 0 and 10 years of experience in education. The overall mean of the sample was 10 years of educational experience. Areas of expertise included teaching in K–12 education and special education.

The majority of the participants (7) had significant experience working with LCD students. This experience ranged from 15 to 20 years. Two participants had more than 25 years of experience. The mean for all participants was 15 years of experience working with LCD students. Four participants were bilingual counselors; three were fluent speakers of Spanish; and one was fluent in French. All 13 participants came from schools in a large, highly diverse, suburban school district.

Multicultural Professional Development Program

The school counselors in this study participated in seven interventions over the course of 9 months. Each of the interventions consisted of a didactic professional development session along with an interactive and processing component. The researchers facilitated five of the sessions and counselor educators, who specialize in multicultural counseling, conducted the other two sessions.

For each of these sessions, specific methods, group dialogue, and instructional materials were used in order to address and meet specific multicultural counseling competencies. Several of the 31 multicultural counseling competencies were integrated into each professional development session. These outcome-based learning objectives were used to assess the awareness, knowledge, and skills obtained by the participants. The sessions were conducted in this fashion to educate the participants to be more culturally competent and enable them to apply the knowledge and skills acquired.

The first professional development session was designed to address the first set of multicultural competencies, which addresses counselors' awareness of their own assumptions, values, and biases. The session began by viewing a student-developed videotape from The State University of New York. It depicted a family crisis caused by a situation in school dealing with a young girl, her teacher, and her counselor. The film addressed cultural biases coupled with ineffective counseling techniques, which created serious unresolved problems. After watching the film presentation the participants were ask to react to the way the situation was handled. This resulted in a very lively discussion about the insensitivities of the teacher and the counselor towards the student and her family. Other examples of this kind of bias were shared and many suggestions were made about how that situation could have been handled with a greater understanding of the student's cultural background.

The second professional development session focused on the multicultural competencies of understanding the worldview of culturally different clients. This session entailed processing case studies of LCD students in which participants were asked to apply a framework to the cases in order to examine the factors, variables, and processes school counselors need to consider when assessing, diagnosing, and treating diverse clients. The participants worked in groups of three or four people and each group was given a different case study to process. After much discussion, the individual groups made brief presentations describing the case study situation and discussing the alternative approaches to the presenting problem. At which point, all the participants were encouraged to dialogue and provide feedback and suggestions regarding each case study. The overall evaluation of the session indicated that the participants received practical ideas about how to handle each situation. Several of the participants commented that the case studies illustrated very common situations in the schools and that the discussion had been helpful. As one counselor stated, "We never have time at school to talk to our colleagues about many of these situations that come up, and so we never get feedback on whether we handled the problem appropriately or not."

The third and fourth sessions consisted of half-day workshops conducted by a counselor educator who specializes in multicultural counseling. Both professional development sessions were designed to focus upon the multicultural competencies that develop appropriate intervention strategies and techniques to work with the LCD client. Specifically, in the third session, Dr. Patricia Arredondo addressed how in light of the tragic events of September 11, 2001, multicultural competencies for counselors can provide a strong platform for comment and interventions. She encouraged participants to examine their own beliefs, values, assumptions, and practices since this tragic event. She also provided an overview of the skills that are necessary and fundamental to becoming an efficient multicultural counselor and educator of culturally and linguistically diverse students. This session was a precursor to the more indepth training that followed in the fourth session. In the fourth session, the multicultural competencies were discussed in light of their applicability for practice. The first part of this session dealt with discussing and learning about emotional reactions toward other racial, ethnic, and linguistic groups within a counseling setting. The second part of the session focused upon how ethnicity, culture, and race affect counseling and teaching and how our own worldviews impact our work with students and clients. The final part of this session provided handson practice in utilizing the multicultural competencies in counseling and teaching culturally and linguistically diverse students.

The fifth session addressed the multicultural competencies of understanding the worldview of culturally different clients. This session was comprised of a panel presentation conducted by three women. Each of these women came from different cultures and talked about their experiences with their children in the schools. After all these women had spoken, there was an open question and answer session in which the participants were able to ask additional questions of the panelists. The differences in each culture were interesting to hear about, but the issues were very similar. The lack of open communication seemed to be the biggest issue for all of them and as one panelist commented, "If the teacher or counselor had just called and told me what was happening with my child I could have explained why they might be upset." The participants' evaluation of this session indicated that hearing directly from these three parents was extremely helpful and insightful for them.

The sixth session focused upon developing appropriate intervention strategies and techniques to work with the LCD client. In this session, participants were given an opportunity to have an open dialogue regarding their frustrations and issues around multicultural issues. They discussed the challenges of dealing with multiple cultures and not having enough information about any of them. They voiced serious concerns about their own ability to be able to respond appropriately to a variety of different situations. They shared some of their personal stories in which they felt they had not done all they needed to do. The issue of time or lack of time came up again and again. There seemed to be a consensus among the participants that many of these multicultural issues required more time than they had to give. However, in the final analysis they seemed to be grateful to have such diversity in their schools and saw the value for everyone involved. The written evaluations after this session indicated that having a chance to talk about participants' frustrations and concerns was helpful and reassuring in that it confirmed that they were doing a good job in spite of the time constraints.

The seventh session focused upon the multicultural competencies pertaining to counselors' awareness of their own assumptions, values, and biases. The session provided an opportunity for each participant to share with the rest of the group their experiences in their individual schools during this professional development program. Participants shared anecdotes about experiences they had with students and families from diverse cultures in their schools and how they handled these situations differently as a result of the training. Participants also reflected on new insights they gained regarding their own beliefs and behaviors and how these may impact their work with students from other cultures.

Data Source

A standardized open-ended interview protocol was used to generate the data source. Open-ended interviews allow researchers to obtain data from the participants' perspectives and thus contribute to understanding how participants understand and make sense of their world (Fontana & Frey, 1994). The common interview protocol was used to ask the same questions in the same order for all participants, thus reducing interviewer effects and bias (McMillan & Schumacher, 1993). Development of the protocol occurred in three stages. First, each member of the research team who had also developed the professional development program wrote interview questions separately. Next all questions were pooled into one set and reviewed by the team for overlap, consistency, and relevance to the areas of inquiry. A final set of questions was decided on and reviewed again, both by the team and by the independent interviewer, a doctoral student in counseling. After final revisions, two members of the research team met with the interviewer to review the protocol and discuss interview technique.

The independent interviewer who conducted all 13 interviews was not part of the research team that provided the professional development program. Each interview lasted from 30 to 45 minutes. All interviews were audio taped, then transcribed. The interview protocol questions and accompanying probes can be divided into four areas and involved 15 distinct questions. The first set of questions asked for background information on the interview participants. These questions pertained to number of years working in counseling and education, the number of years working with linguistically and culturally diverse populations, and information on prior multicultural training received in their counselor preparation programs.

The other three areas pertained directly to the research questions. All questions consisted of a main question and a set of probes to elicit further discussion and exploration of the topic. Three questions were designed to collect data on the participants' perceptions of the challenges they faced in working with LCD students and families. One question asked participants to describe how their work involved multicultural counseling, then asked them to describe a specific multicultural counseling experience, how they felt about that experience, what went well, and what they would have wanted to happen differently. A follow-up question then asked them to describe the most challenging aspects of counseling diverse students and families. Finally, participants were asked about the influence of culture, ethnicity, and race on their comfort level in counseling LCD students and families.

Four questions elicited information on the participants' perceptions of their professional development needs relevant to counseling LCD students and families. One question asked them to discuss why they decided to participate in the multicultural professional development program. They were also asked to describe ways other than the professional development program they developed their capacity to counsel diverse students and families, and what skills and knowledge they most needed to develop in this area. They were also asked to provide recommendations for future multicultural professional development.

Two open-ended questions and one structured question (the only such question in the protocol) were used to understand how participants perceived the professional development program. One question asked about the activities/speakers that had the most impact on their developing awareness, knowledge, and/or skill in counseling LCD students and families, and the other asked about any perceived changes in their practice that resulted from any of the program's activities or speakers. The structured question asked participants to rate the professional development on a scale of one to five on the overall contribution of the program to their capacity to counsel LCD students and families.

Data Analysis

Cross-case analysis was used to determine recurring themes across the 13 individual interviews. To aid analysis, data were first chunked into those segments that pertained to the research areas of inquiry and clustered by question. Numbered codes that identified respondents were attached to the data chunks so that data could be retraced to the original respondents. Each team member independently analyzed the data by defining and tallying data according to dominant themes within and across protocol questions that pertained to the three areas of inquiry. Dominant themes were those that had numerical preference in the data.

The research team met to discuss emerging themes on several occasions and to discuss any inconsistencies in theme development. As patterns emerged, the researchers came to agreement about deleting, collapsing, and redefining thematic categories. Data were then re-ordered so that they were clustered according to theme and by dominance within the overall set of data for each research question. The data were then reviewed a final time by the research team, and subsequently used for final interpretation and discussion of results.

RESULTS

Challenges

Achieving a certain comfort level and competency in working with the families of linguistically and culturally diverse students and understanding cultural differences in students across a variety of cultures were the two areas that respondents indicated were most challenging in their counseling work in diverse elementary and secondary schools. These two areas are discussed below.

Counseling linguistically and culturally diverse parents and families. Prior to discussing the specific challenges the respondents face in their work with LCD families, it is important to understand how they define their work in this area. Most of the school counselors in this study were concerned with acculturating LCD students and families to the dominant school culture. Many described their work as helping newly arrived immigrant families "figure out the hurdles or differences they encounter here." The respondents understood that differences between the U.S. school system and the school systems of other countries created difficulties for immigrant families and that an important counseling role was to help families "interpret" the U.S. school system. Others discussed their work as "making school more welcoming for multicultural families." They developed programs to bring LCD families into the schools and means for disseminating information to these families.

Finally, most participants felt that working with LCD parents and families was more complex than working with LCD students and required specific understanding of family dynamics and family structure across different cultures. For example, one respondent indicated that most of her work involved parents and "dealing with parents is different than dealing with children. The children here … they know the rules, and they know the teacher, and they know how things work. But when parents come in they don't have to abide by certain rules."

Specific challenges the respondents encountered in their work with LCD parents and families included insecurities about the cultural appropriateness of their interactions with parents and families; helping parents understand and interface with an educational system that views school and parental responsibilities differently than the educational systems in their home countries; language barriers; and assisting families with economic challenges they encounter in a new country.

A majority of the respondents conveyed some discomfort in their work with LCD parents and families. Most of this discomfort stemmed from feeling unsure about whether certain actions, mannerisms, questioning behaviors, and interventions were culturally appropriate. One respondent described her discomfort in the following manner:

> I feel uncomfortable sometimes when I ask parents a lot of questions about things to get background, I feel like I'm prying – being aware that I am speaking to parents of a different culture. I'm not sure how I come off to them, and that's something that I am still not sure of because I know internally I have the best intentions and I want to help them and I want to help their child, but I'm concerned that sometimes in my comfortableness with that fact that I overlook the things that I can do to set them at ease that are culturally appropriate for them and for their child.

Most of the respondents believed they lacked sufficient knowledge of the cultural views and beliefs of many LCD parents and families. Recent influxes of immigrant students from various Middle Eastern and African countries have brought counselors face to face with cultures previously unknown to them. Of the respondents who gave examples of cultures, other than their own, with which they felt most or least comfortable, most mentioned feeling least comfortable counseling individuals from the Middle East. On the other hand, they felt most comfortable with individuals from Hispanic cultures. In their comments, the respondents indicated that their lack of knowledge of and personal and professional experience with individuals from Middle Eastern cultures were partly responsible for their feelings of insecurity in working with Middle Eastern parents.

Though most of the school counselors in this study felt it was their responsibility to help LCD parents and families acculturate to mainstream U.S. culture, and particularly the educational system, they experienced difficulty in helping parents understand the school's role in educating children and its expectations for parents. "Parents from other countries often believe that the school has such authority and so they come to us to redirect their children. They want us to deal with issues that we in our culture consider parenting issues, not within our job." A related challenge for the counselors in this study was addressing the dissonance that arises between parents and their children when the home culture and the dominant U.S. culture collide. One participant commented:

The kids have connected very much to the culture here and want to be able particularly in a social way to do what other students do. They want to be able to date and go to parties and things like that, and that's just not an acceptable part of the parents' culture and that becomes a real problem for the kids and for the parents. In a couple of cases the students have just reached the point where they have run away from home to avoid the conflict.

A third area of challenge for the counselors in this study was language. Many respondents expressed frustration over the language barriers they experienced in working with LCD parents and families. When working with non-English speaking parents or family members, respondents felt frustration at not being able to directly communicate in the native language. Other frustrations included not having ready access to translators or having no access to translators for less-commonly spoken languages. One counselor described variations in how translators interacted with the counselor and the client. "Some translators do very good and just do translating. Other ones take on the counselor role, and they want to be the ones to be real involved, so that becomes a problem."

At times, counselors were dependent upon the child to translate. Those who discussed this situation felt that using the child as a translator was entirely inappropriate, but when emergencies occurred, and they needed an immediate line of communication with parents or family members, they relied on the child to translate. Many counselors expressed a need to learn another language or to become more proficient in a second language; however, they also expressed concern that learning another language would not alleviate the need for translators since their school served students from many different language backgrounds.

Finally, several respondents discussed the challenge of working with families who were experiencing both acculturation difficulties along with economic challenges. Tied to the issue of working with families who have economic difficulties is the challenge of helping them feel comfortable enough to seek help from other agencies where they can get the counseling/guidance they need.

Understanding cultural differences in students across a variety of cultures. The second major area of challenge expressed by the counselors in this study was understanding and working with students from a variety of cultural backgrounds. Respondents described their work within this challenge area as "being aware of differences in multicultural children" and helping students who are "trying to live in two cultures." As with their descriptions of their work with LCD parents and families, the respondents indicated that their role was to help LCD students adjust and transition to the educational system in this country. Interestingly, only one respondent felt it was her role to help mainstream students understand and "be sensitive to LCD students." Specific challenges the respondents encountered in attempting to understand and work with students from a variety of cultural backgrounds included feelings of insecurity about working with students from varying cultural backgrounds and finding time to learn about different cultures.

Feelings of insecurity in working with LCD students surfaced on a number of occasions in the interviews. One counselor's response sums up this challenge:

> I don't understand all of the cultures as comfortably as I feel with the Hispanic groups. ... I'm not always sure I'm reaching them [students from other cultural backgrounds], and I'm not always sure I should reach out as much as I do to some groups, because I'm not really sure it's appreciated. That's what's challenging – I'm not sure. I'm not really sure.

When working with LCD students, counselors found it difficult to distinguish characteristics and behaviors that might be due to cultural differences from those that might be due to individual differences. One respondent remarked about the difficulty of "keeping it all straight, walking that fine line between this might be a cultural thing, I need to check on that and clarify versus that's a 10-year-old boy thing." For several of the respondents, part of the challenge was being able to "step outside" their own cultures. Respondents realized that a first step in understanding other cultures was awareness of their own cultural values and biases.

Finding the time to learn about other cultures was overwhelming for many of the respondents in this study. One respondent stated, "There's just so much to learn, to know, and there's not enough time to do any of it." Another respondent felt that she would be a better counselor and the students would benefit more "if we had more time to really get to know more about the culture and understand. But in the school setting it's brief. The kids come in and out and we have to help them as much as we can." In summary, the major challenges school counselors in this study faced related to assisting culturally and linguistically diverse parents and families and attempting to understand and work with students from a variety of cultural backgrounds.

School Counselors' Professional Development Needs

The respondents' expressed professional development needs corresponded to the challenges they faced in their multicultural counseling work. The two areas in which the respondents expressed the most need for professional development were working with LCD parents and families and increasing their knowledge of specific cultures.

In the area of working with LCD parents and families, participants' major concern was learning how to communicate to LCD parents the importance of their involvement in the educational system. One respondent commented, "Over the years we've been ... trying to figure out how can we get these parents to buy into the importance of being a partner in their child's education." Respondents also wanted to develop skill in determining the needs LCD parents have for their children. "It's very easy to assume that what I think their kids need is what they think their kids need." This counselor viewed professional development that enhanced her skill to balance LCD parents' needs for their children with those of the school as important.

The other area in which respondents expressed a need for professional development was increasing their knowledge of specific cultures. Several respondents said that professional development focused on providing specific information on different cultural groups would enable them to feel more comfortable interacting with students and families from these groups. Some counselors specified cultures they wanted to learn about. These included various Middle Eastern cultures, African immigrant cultures, African American culture, and North and South Asian cultures.

A number of respondents specified the kind of understanding they wanted about different cultures and the types of activities that would allow them to explore issues relevant to different cultural groups. One respondent suggested that professional development should focus on how personal experiences "fit in with the culture at large and the history." Another suggested that professional development provide not only information about different cultural groups, but also particular culture-based counseling strategies. Several respondents indicated that they would benefit from guest speakers who represent different cultures. Another indicated that not only were guest speakers important, but that "opportunities to interact with people from the cultures and have them talk more from a personal basis" were critical.

Respondents also expressed a need for professional development that allowed them to share experiences with one another. Participants in this study asked for opportunities to interact with counselors from different schools to share their experiences working with LCD students. Also important were opportunities to more formally share their collective knowledge of counseling LCD students, parents, and families by designing presentations, role plays, and forums for disseminating resources.

In sum, counselors in this study voiced a need for professional development in areas directly relevant to the primary challenges they believed they face in their work with LCD students, parents, and families. Specifically they requested guidance in "translating" the culture of the U.S. school system to LCD parents in a culturally appropriate manner. They also requested guidance in understanding and relating to specific cultures, and they had specific suggestions for the kinds of cultural information and skill they believed would be helpful. Finally, they provided insight into methods of transmitting that information and skill that would be most meaningful.

Perceptions of the Effectiveness of a Multicultural Professional Development Program

Overall the participants in this study rated the multicultural professional development program highly. On a scale of one to five, with five being high and one being low, all participants rated the program at a level four or above. In terms of the type of activity used, most participants felt the guest speakers who represented and spoke about their own cultures were the most useful component of the program. Several participants also commented positively on the use of case studies. One respondent remarked that taking a framework [supplied by a guest speaker] and applying it to cases helped her think more "intellectually rather than intuitively about situations."

Participants were also asked to discuss the impact of the multicultural professional development program on their awareness, knowledge, and skill in working with LCD students, parents, and families. Overall respondents believed the program impacted their knowledge and skill more so than their awareness. They described the training as providing a "bank of information" and as influential in "causing me to think about things differently." One respondent said she was more conscious of the "academic, social, and emotional pieces of the LCD students." She also felt that she would be more "proactive as opposed to reactive" in her work with diverse students. Others commented about their increased levels of confidence in counseling diverse students.

Several participants discussed how the program had impacted how they work with LCD students. One participant described how she modified a mediation session for students, based on what she had learned in the professional development program: "It made me decide that instead of just starting with mediation, I'm going to start with where the problems occur and have them look at cultural differences among them and then look at where their similarities are." Another participant indicated that she had used activities from materials provided to all participants at the start of the program. In sum, the study participants believed the multicultural professional development program had a greater impact on their knowledge and skill than on their awareness.

The next section of this paper examines the results of a pre- and post-survey designed to assess the impact of the program on participants' multicultural awareness, knowledge, and skill. These results are compared with the self-reports of the program's impact provided in the above section. Extent of Increases in Multicultural Awareness, Knowledge, and Skills: Survey Results A paired-samples t-test was performed to learn if the 9-month professional development program had a significant impact on the counselors' perceptions of their own multicultural competencies. Means scores from the MAKSS were analyzed for the pre-test and post-test phases. Paired samples t-text revealed that the group as a whole (n = 15) achieved statistically significant gains in knowledge, t(14) = 3.25, p < .01, and skill t(14) = 2.37, p < .05. Since we were not able to establish reliability for the awareness subsection of the survey, the nonsignificant results in this subsection, t(14) = .09, p < .924, are inconclusive. However, the fact that the paired samples t-test revealed significant gains in knowledge and skill allows us to say that professional development efforts such as the one employed for this study can have a significant impact on school counselors who are interested and actively engaged in building their multicultural competencies to a higher level.

DISCUSSION

The results of this exploratory study indicate that practicing school counselors who work in diverse school environments need professional development focused on the dynamics and structure of linguistically and culturally diverse families and the implications of these differences for counseling such families within the U.S. educational system. Inherent in this expressed need is professional development that enhances counselors' understanding of educational systems that differ from the U.S. system, the expectations these systems hold for families and students, and how these expectations differ from those of the U.S. educational system. Results also indicate that counselors need ongoing opportunities to learn about the backgrounds, cultures, and language systems of immigrant students from less familiar regions of the world (i.e., various Middle Eastern, African, and Asian countries). Respondents' perceived inadequacies in these areas might be one factor responsible for their feelings of uncertainty about their effectiveness in counseling certain LCD families and students.

The fact that the respondents in this study seemed less concerned with sensitizing "mainstream" students to the cultural and linguistic differences of LCD students than with assisting LCD students to adjust to the mainstream school environment should be of concern to both providers of professional development for school counselors and institutions of higher education that prepare school counselors. School environments that value diversity are created, in part, by helping mainstream students understand and learn from those whose cultural and linguistic knowledge differs from their own. In this era of standards and accountability, much of the educational community's attention is directed toward preparing the LCD student to meet high standards and perform well on high stakes assessments. However, research has shown that when the school environment, which includes all students' perspectives and behaviors, values diverse languages and cultures, LCD students' opportunities for academic success are improved (Collier, 1995; Cummins, 1996). The school counselor has an important role to play in creating a school environment that educates mainstream students about their LCD peers. Findings from the interviews appear to indicate that the participants in the 9-month professional development program felt that their participation improved their knowledge and skill in counseling LCD students. Respondents discussed the type of knowledge they believed they had acquired and how, as a result, they were thinking about and reacting differently to their work with LCD students.

These findings support the premise that the type of professional development provided in this project, if provided on an ongoing basis, can enhance school counselors' knowledge base and their perceptions of their skill in working with LCD students. As with all professional development efforts, it is difficult to assess the true impact of the program on participants. The extent to which participants will translate their newly acquired competencies into practice is difficult to measure. Future research efforts should examine how school counselors apply new learning gained through professional development to their work with diverse students and families. There are several limitations of this study. Generalizability of the findings is limited both by the nature of the inquiry and by the geographical restrictions of the sample. Qualitative interviewing provides rich data on participants' perceptions of a given condition; however it limits the findings to comparable contexts and comparable participants. Furthermore, because the counselors who participated in the program were volunteers and indicated interest in multicultural issues prior to the training, we cannot determine whether a program of this sort would have a similar impact on counselors not as predisposed to multicultural issues as the study participants. Second, because the participants selfselected into the professional development program, generalizability is limited to those who seek professional development in multicultural counseling. Third, the study participants worked in highly diverse schools in a large suburban school district on the U.S. east coast. Data obtained from counselors in urban schools or in schools in other parts of the country might not corroborate this study's findings. Fourth, because the study's methods involved selfreport, the participants may not have expressed their actual beliefs and opinions. The nature of the professional development program, the types of interactions among the participants in the program and between participants and providers is difficult to replicate in other settings. Other professional development programs, even if they attempted to replicate this program, would involve a different set of dynamics among participants that could result in alternate results. Finally, that while the researchers took precautions to avoid bias; it is possible that bias did exist due to the fact that the researchers participated in conducting the training.

IMPLICATIONS

This study's findings highlight the importance of providing ongoing, indepth professional development for school counselors on multicultural counseling issues. It also identifies the kind of professional development counselors similar to those in this study would find most useful. Such professional development should focus on developing counselors' knowledge and skill in working with diverse families and on providing counselors' with knowledge and skill in working with specific cultural groups. An important implication of this study is that those responsible for providing professional development for school counselors conduct needs assessments to determine the type of professional development most useful for counselors in their school or district.

The expressed needs of counselors concerning their work with LCD students and families are critical to designing useful professional development. However, professional development should also address the larger issue of the school counselor's role in creating a school environment that values diversity. Counselors should be competent not only in helping the LCD student adjust and acculturate, but also in sensitizing all students to the cultural and linguistic diversity of their peers. The Multicultural Counseling Competencies (Sue et al., 1992) are an important resource, along with an ongoing needs assessment, in developing multicultural professional development that meets the needs of school counselors and helps them achieve the larger goal of preparing all students for their roles in a diverse society.

REFERENCES

Carey, J. C., Reinat, M., & Fontes, L. (1990). School counselors' perceptions of training needs in multicultural counseling. *Counselor Education and Supervision, 29*(3), 156–169.

Collier, V. P. (1995). *Acquiring a second language for school.* Washington, DC: The National Clearinghouse for Bilingual Education.

Cummins, J. (1996). *Negotiating identities: Education for empowerment in a diverse society.* Ontario, CA: California Association for Bilingual Education.

Fontana, A., & Frey, J.H. (1994). Interviewing:The art of science. In N. K.Denzin & Y. S. Lincoln (Eds.), *Handbook of qualitative research* (pp. 361–374).Thousand Oaks, CA: Sage.

Holcomb-McCoy, C. C. (2000). Multicultural counseling competencies: An exploratory factor analysis. *Journal of Multicultural Counseling and Development, 28*(2), 83–97.

Holcomb-McCoy, C. C. (2001). Exploring the self-perceived multicultural counseling competence of elementary school counselors. *Professional School Counseling, 4,* 195–201.

Johnson, L. S. (1995). Enhancing multicultural relations: Intervention strategies for the school counselor. *School Counselor, 43,* 103–113.

McMillan, J. H., & Schumacher, S. (1993). Research in education: A conceptual introduction (3rd ed.). New York: HarperCollins College.

Sue, D., Arredondo, P.,& McDavis, R. J. (1992). Multicultural counseling competencies and standards:A call to the profession. *Journal of Counseling Development, 70,* 477–486.

The Relationships Among Counselors, ESL Teachers, and Students

By Roberto Clemente, Ph.D., and Brooke B. Collison, Ph.D.

This article originally appeared in *Professional School Counseling*, Vol. 3, No. 5, 2000.

The multicultural counseling movement gained momentum in the 1970s when some mental health professionals noticed the poor quality of services that members of minority groups received (Sue, 1977). The terms *cross-cultural* or *multicultural* have been used to refer to counseling American minorities who were seen as culturally different. The term *culturally different* has led many researchers to study how certain cultures differ from the mainstream U.S. culture and how traditional counseling theories and techniques have to be adapted and improved in order to be applicable (Das, 1995).

One of the first articles written about multiculturalism was "The Culturally Encapsulated Counselor" by Wrenn (1962). This article pointed out some of the client needs and flaws in counseling services. Since then, many articles have been published addressing the need to be "culturally appropriate, culturally relevant," and "culturally sensitive" in regard to minority groups. Many techniques have been developed to counsel certain groups (Pederson, 1999; Sue, 1989, 1990, 1991).

Due to the fact that the Hispanic/Latino population has risen sharply in recent years and is expected to keep increasing, the counseling field has placed special attention on this group (Lee, 1997). Since 1980, the Latino population has increased an estimated 69% nationwide. According to the National Council of La Raza (1990), the Mexican-American population alone increased from 2.1 million to 13.3 million in the past 30 years. To create context and perspective in regard to these statistics, the United States has the fifth largest Latino population in the world. The Latino population is considered the fastest-growing ethnic group in the nation, and it is expected to grow at a proportion three to five times faster than any other group (Casas & Vasquez, 1996; Hayes-Batista, Shink, & Chapa. 1988; U.S. Bureau of the Census, 1992). This growth can be attributed to recent immigration patterns and to the proportion of young people of childbearing age (Amaro & Russo, 1987).

Educational, political, and social issues that impact the general population have accompanied this demographic phenomenon. Particular cultural characteristics, magnified by linguistic differences, have posed a challenge to educators and school counselors. Multiple studies have pointed out the need to accommodate this particular school population if success is expected (Agular, 1972; Cuellar, Harris & Jasso, 1980; Marín & Marín, 1991; Moyerman & Foreman, 1992; Orozco, Thompson, Kapos, & Montgomery, 1993; Padilla & Salgado de Snyder, 1985). Proponents of multicultural counseling emphasize the need to modify therapeutic practices to reflect the Hispanic/Latino client's cultural characteristics as well as to "promote bilingualism rather than monolingualism" (Sue, Arredondo, & McDavis, 1992, p. 479). It has been shown that members of minority groups have shown higher levels of responsiveness when culturally sensitive strategies have been utilized in counseling sessions (O'Sullivan, Peterson, Cox, & Kirkebyu, 1989).

It is somewhat ambitious to define and describe the impact and complexities of the Hispanic/Latino culture in the United States of America in this study. Due to the diversity of the Hispanic/Latino community (especially in terms of racial composition), historically, the U.S. Census has used the term *Hispanic* to encapsulate members of Spanis-speaking groups regardless of racial or ethnic origin. In an effort to develop a unique identity detached from the Spanish colonialism, the term Latino (Latina for female) has been used to stress roots in a language (Latin roots) as opposed to roots in a country (Spain) (Auilar, 1972; Dana, 1993). A general Latino population does not exist from an ethnocultural point of view; instead, there are multiple groups that are distinguished by the modification of the Spanish language, distinctive culture, or unique location where they live (García & Zea, 1997). Even in the Latino community within the counseling field, it is not easy to find a consensus regarding definitions. This lack of consensus for defining Latinos has been analyzed in the last decade by Padilla and Salgado de Snyder (1985) and Baptiste (1987). Acknowledging the racioethnic diversity among Latinos and employing appropriate identification descriptors according to the person's country of origin have proven to be an important factor when providing services to this population (Falicov, 1998).

According to the Bureau of the Census (1993), there are 17 million Spanish-speaking Latinos in the United States, and of these, 8.3 million either do not speak English at all or do not speak it well. These data seem to be consistent with a previous study conducted by Ramírez and McAlister (1988), in which it was found that Spanish is the most salient characteristic among Latinos. It is clear that the demand for Spanish-speaking services is high, and there are not sufficient professionals with both training in their field and Spanish proficiency to satisfy the need. It is also not clear what language should be utilized if the client is bilingual. This issue of language selection and utilization to effectively deliver services goes along with the lack of cultural and linguistic instruments developed for specific Latino subgroups (Rozensky & Gómez, 1983).

The use of interpreters with minimum translation skills often leads to unwanted short cuts of verbalizations, distortions, and misunderstandings (Bamford, 1991). Further, even well-trained interpreters sometimes area unable to transmit all paralinguistic messages to the counselor. These paralinguistic messages may include emotional content, intonation, and subliminal linguistic sarcasms (Bamford, 1991).

Translators are also expected to abide by the counseling code of ethics (Erzinger, 1991). Acost and Cristo (1981) developed a program for interpreters in mental health settings and found that clients expressed greater satisfaction working with those formally trained than with those without training.

Research Purpose and Questions

This study was designed to investigate the multidimensional relationship between middle school counselors and ESL Latino students and the role ESL faculty play in this relational equation. Three research questions guided the study: (1) How do school counselors and ESL instructors describe student issues and needs for both Latino and European American students?, (2) How do students (Hispanic/Latino and European American) perceive counseling services and school counselors?, and (3) What are the predominant issues between students (Latino and European America) as perceived by them? This study was intended to serve as a foundation for future studies.

METHOD

Student Participants

Forty-eight students from four middle schools (grades 6-8) located in small-to-middle-size Oregon communities participated in this study. The socioeconomic status of the participants ranged from low to middle class. These schools were selected on the basis of their significant Hispanic/Latino population (Latino enrollment ranged from 10% to 35% or more). Participants were randomly selected from enrollment lists provided by the schools indicating student name, grade, gender, ethnicity, and whether the student was enrolled in the ESL (English as a second language) program.

Counselor and Instructor Participants

One school counselor and one ESL instructor were interviewed in each of the four schools. An additional counselor was selected for an interview in one school due to her ethnicity (Hispanic/Latina). Of the four ESL instructors, two were European Americans and two were Hispanic/Latina. One counselor was Hispanic/Latina and four were European Americans. All participants (instructors and counselors) were females with the exception of one male counselor.

School counselors and ESL instructors ranged in experience from 3 to 18 years and worked at the middle school level (6-8). The primary duties of ESL instructors were to teach basic English skills to nonnative speakers in order to facilitate their transition into the mainstream school population.

Research Design

The design of this study followed standard procedures of qualitative design suggested by Bogdan and Biklen (1992). The design indicates that in order to find comparable data across participants, a format of semi-structured interviews must be utilized. Two sets of interviews are necessary in order to exhaust emerging themes. The first interviews are audio-taped and later transcribed. A maximum of 2 weeks should elapse between the first and second interview.

Data were analyzed (by highlighting common themes on the transcription manuscript) and codified (labeled) by categories. Following qualitative guidelines documented by Bord, Gall, and Gall (1993) and Bogdan and Biklen (1992), the researchers used these codes as a catalyst to further explore inconsistencies in the previous interview or to pursue in-depth issues regarding a topic during the second interview.

Qualitative research is based on the assumption that each individual, culture, and setting is unique. This uniqueness provides context-dependent information that differs from the traditional quantitative design (Borg, Gall & Gall, 19993; Kopala & Suzuki, 1999). Thus, the issues of validity and reliability in a qualitative research design must be analyzed according to a categorical and not a normative approach. That is, validity and reliability are confined to statements about what is, not what should or ought to be. Therefore, from a post-modern point of view, validity and reliability are expected to be high because there are not abstract, theoretical, or conceptual definitions prior to the research. Moreover, there is a mere description of behavior-statements that have been directly observed and labeled after the fact.

PROCEDURE

Group Interviews

Parent-student consent forms and guideline questions for the group interviews were written in Spanish and English for the benefit of monolingual Spanish speakers. Two one-hour interviews were conducted in groups of six. Group interviews for the Hispanic/Latino students were conducted in Spanish, occasionally combined with English, utilizing code-switching techniques – interchange of language use – depending on the needs and level of language literacy/mastery of the students. One researcher used bilingual skills to facilitate all the interviews (group and individual). Therefore, interview consistency was maintained. Group interviews of Hispanic/Latino and European-American students were conducted separately. In each of the four schools a total of 20 students (10 Hispanic/Latino and 10 European American) were identified as potential participants in order to select 12 students per school for a total of 48. The 48 participants were equally distributed by gender (24 females and 24 males), grade level (6th grade-16 students, 7th grade-16 students, and 8th grade-16 students), and ethnicity (24 Hispanic/Latinos and 24 European Americans).

Individual Interviews
School counselors and ESL teachers were interviewed individually in order to encourage an open conversation that could have been limited by the presence of other professional colleagues. The interview questions for the staff (ESL instructors and school counselors) paralleled the content and format of the student questions, but with the particularity of being relevant to their professional field and contextual reality.

Interview Questions
The interview questions were generated as an extension of the research questions and revolved around the participants' perceptions toward the following themes: services, interethnic relationships, language, professional training, school and community issues, staff-student interactions, academic progress, and general concerns. The following are the questions used during the interviews:

School Counselors Interview Questions:
1. How long have you been working as a counselor? At this school?
2. Have you had previous experience in the classroom as a teacher? How long did you teach? Where?
3. From which school did you get your degree? What kind of school counseling license do you have? (e.g., standard, basic, emergency, or misassignment)
4. What are the predominant issues in the school district? At your school?
5. What measures has the school district taken regarding these issues? Your school?
6. Has the school district developed special policies and procedures to deal with these issues? Your school?

7. How many students in the last week have you seen in individual sessions? White (European American)? Latino/Hispanic? Others?
8. What have been the main reasons in general for the sessions?
9. How often do you get in contact with the ESL/Bilingual staff? What are the main reasons for approaching the ESL/Bilingual staff?
10. How would you describe language and cultural interaction among the student body?
11. How many languages do you speak? How would you consider yourself with regard to cultural issues?

Faculty Interview Questions:

1. How long have you been working as an ESL/Bilingual teacher? At this school?
2. Have you had previous experience in the classroom as a teacher? How long did you teach? Where?
3. From which school did you get your degree? In what area? (Ex. Bilingual education, ESL, etc.)
4. What are the predominant issues in the school district? At your school?
5. What measures has the school district taken regarding these issues? Your school?
6. Has the school district developed special policies and procedures to deal with these issues? Your school?
7. What is the student distribution of the ESL participants with regard to ethnic/racial origin?
8. In the last week, how many students have you seen? As a group? Individually?
9. How often do you see the school counselor? Under what circumstances?
10. How would you describe language and cultural interactions among the student body?
11. How many languages do you speak? How would you consider yourself with regard to cultural issues?

Group Questions for Students:
The same sets of questions were used for both Hispanic/Latino groups and European American groups except for question 2. In addition, Hispanic/Latino groups' interviews were conducted using code-switching language techniques.

1. What are the main issues in the school? In the surrounding community? (¿Cuáles son los asuntos principales en la escuela? ¿En la communidad circundante?)

2. How would you describe the ESL classes or English classes (for European Americans)? (¿Como describirías las clases de Inglés Como Segunod Idioma?)
3. During this year, how many of you have sent eh school counselor? Under what circumstances? (Using a hand check count approach) (¿Durante este año, cuántos de ustedes han estado en contacto con el (la) consejero (a) escoloar? Bajo qué circunstancias?)
4. Did the school counselor call you or did you stop by your own initiative? (Using a hand check count approach) (¿El (la) consejero (a) escolar te llamó o tú le visitaste por iniciativa propia?)
5. How do you perceive and describe the school counselor's functions? (¿Cómo percibes y describirías las funciones de el (la) consejero (a) escolar?)
6. What do you think about what the school counselor does in the school? (¿Qué piensas en relación a lo que el (la) consejero (a) escolar hace en la escuela?)
7. As a group, what are your major concerns/needs? And, how do you propose these needs/concerns should be addressed? (Cómo grupo, ¿cuáles son sus mayors preocupaciones/necesidades? Y, ¿cómo ustedes propondrían que estas necesidades y preocupaciones sean atendidas?)

Transcription and Analysis

The initial group interview session was audio taped and then transcribed; the second group interview session was audio taped, but not transcribed. During the first session all participants were interviewed by means of the guideline questions, then after the transcription and analysis of the interview, emerging patterns were codified into categories. The second session was used to verify these categories with the interviewees and to cover inconsistencies found during the first interview. Taping and analysis of the second interview complemented the first interview; conclusions were drawn based upon the integration of both interviews.

A reflective journal with field notes was used during the research process; the researcher started recording events, behaviors, and thought beginning with the firs telephone contact. This reflective journal was comprised of two main aspects: descriptive and reflective notes (Bogdan & Biklen, 1992).

Results

Data from 16 hours of group interviews with students and from 10 hours of interviews with counselors and ESL faculty resulted in conclusions about counseling services. The analysis sections are based on the perceptual/qualitative data according to the counselors, ESL instructors, and students (European Americans and Hispanic/Latino). The comments of all participants in the study were qualitatively analyzed to find common patterns among interviewees and unique and distinctive experiences for each. Categories were clustered into codes, subcodes, and themes depending on the degree of interdependence (Strauss & Corbin, 1990). The study results are reported in three parts as follows: (1) school counselors, (2) ESL instructors, and (3) students.

School Counselors

Overpopulated schools. Overcrowded schools are a major concern for some school counselors. As a result of school overcrowding, excessive energy and time must be invested in remedial interventions rather than innovative student programs.

Isolation of ESL students from the rest of the population. All counselors agreed that ESL Hispanic/Latinos experience a high degree of segregation from the rest of the academic population. This segregation is physical and intellectual due to different academic needs. Academic interaction between groups is limited to some elective courses. One participant stated: "I feel for them, I hardly see them during the day. They appear to be isolated physically and academically."

Minimal counselor involvement with ESL staff and students. With the exception of the Hispanic/Latino counselor, absence of communication and collaboration between school counselors and ESL staff was evident. School counselors view ESL teachers and programs as independent entities within the educational system. Issues regarding academic performance and partial preparation of schedule of classes are left to the discretion of ESL teachers. Minimal feedback is given to ESL students or teachers during registration or scheduling processes. One school counselor said: "ESL teachers do not ask me for help or advice. Usually they make their own decisions, and I have little involvement in the decision-making process.

TAG (talented and gifted) referrals by teachers to school counselors. A plan to identify potential TAG children among ESL groups by means of bilingual methods of evaluation does not appear to be implemented in any of the schools; furthermore, it does not appear to be part of the school counselor's agenda. The primary reasons for referring students to school counselors are based on the need to intervene with behavioral situations, schedule of classes, and academic deficiencies.

Most of these referrals carry a remedial approach as opposed to a proactive motivation originated by the teacher or the school counselor. None of the school counselors mentioned the possibility of having TAG students among the Limited English Proficiency (LEP) students belonging to the ESL program. Although TAP programs are seen as independent units from the school counseling program, neither one showed a record of TAP children among the ESL students.

Caste system among Hispanic/Latino students. Some school counselors voiced concerns about the existence of a caste system among Hispanic/Latino students. School counselors acknowledged the oppressive nature of this interactional dynamic and that it presents an obstacle to optimal educational achievement and rapid integration into the student mainstream population. A plan to ease those intra-group differences among the students was lacking. One participant said: "It is interesting to see how those that have been longer in the country and have good English-speaking skills ignore those who came recently and only speak Spanish. Also, skin color seems to be a factor. Dark-brown skin is associated with indigenous and Mexican descendants.

Utilization of bilingual-bicultural home school consultant as a school counselor. As an alternative measure, and in order to meet the needs of the Hispanic/Latino population one of the schools, a home school consultant has served the Hispanic/Latino students, families, ESL teachers, and school. This home consultant functioned as a social worker and guidance counselor for the Spanish-speaking population. The home consultant did not possess professional training in school counseling; she was hired for her cultural and linguistic knowledge but performed several functions that normally might be part of a counselor's job.

Need for Spanish-speaking counselors. Most counselors agreed on the linguistic disparity and difficulties in establishing a counseling relationship with monolingual Spanish speakers, emphasizing the need for bilingual counselors capable of meeting the needs of Hispanic/Latino students. Those counselors who have been in the field for less than 5 years agreed with the need to strengthen their Spanish skills to increase their effectiveness. Those counselors who have been in the field longer than 5 years agreed on the need to have bilingual school counselors, but showed a lack of personal commitment in learning or refining their second language skills. One participant stated: "I wish I could speak Spanish or at least have a fair command of the language and not to rely on interpreters." In a similar fashion, another participant verbalized: "I took basic Spanish for 2 years, but I don't feel competent enough to maintain a conversation in Spanish. However, I'm willing to brush up my skills."

Importance and characteristics of interpreters during counseling sessions. Some counselors have used the services of interpreters during counseling sessions with monolingual Spanish speakers. According to the school counselors, relatives are not the best interpreters due to confidentiality concerns, counseling relationship quality, ethical issues, and their lack of professional training in effectively translating technical and educational terms. Most school counselors said there was a lack of well-trained interpreters available to work in school settings.

ESL Instructors

Existence of a self-contained school. Some ESL programs – depending on the ESL student population size – have an independent program operating within the mainstream school activities. With the exception of Physical Education and perhaps other elective courses, ESL students take all courses with the same ESL group. Interaction with the mainstream population is minimal.

Less than 20% of the ESL Hispanic/Latino students attend college. Linguistic deficiencies of the Hispanic/Latino students may have an impact on the socioeducational future of these students. College does not seem to be a priority for most of the students participating in ESL programs, especially for those that initiated their academic education at the middle school level in the USA. Social class and the economic necessity to work at an early age appear to deter interest in a college education. Their level of frustration and anxiety seem to increase as academic demands of the high school level make it difficult to keep up with the average mainstream student. One interviewee said: "Most of these students come to our system with academic deficiencies from their countries and on top of that they have to deal with cultural and linguistic differences. It is very difficult."

ESL programs at an initial phase of development. It appears that due to inexperience with non-English speakers, these schools are still trying to find the best method to work with linguistically different populations. In Oregon this immigration phenomenon has been evident during the last 10 to 15 years; therefore, most ESL instructors are implementing teaching strategies that are unique and relevant to this context.

Low interaction with school counselors. As a strategic measure, ESL staff has learned to operate independently with regard to student services. This situation may be a result of the independent nature of ESL programs and the unfamiliarity with regard to the mechanics of the program by most school counselors. One instructor pointed out: "I only see the school counselor during staff meetings or when I get stuck with class schedules for my ESL students. Otherwise, I don't speak with her.

Students Hispanic/Latino

Examples of participants' comments made in Spanish have been translated to English for the benefit of readers.

English mastery equated with jobs but acknowledging the importance of keeping both languages, Spanish and English. Most students acknowledged the importance of mastering the English language in order to compete in the job market. However, the idea of losing the Spanish language was not embraced by them, especially by newcomers.

Trust issues and school counselors. The inability to communicate effectively through the English language with the school counselors appears to be associated with racial-cultural tensions. Another factor that seems to account for stressful relationships between ESL students (Spanish being the first language) and English monolingual counselors is the inability of students to voice their concerns in stressful situations using a second language. One interviewee indicated: "When I am upset and hurt I can not say what I want to say in English. I don't know if she understands me very well."

ESL students and the isolation experienced in school. Almost all ESL students interviewed manifested feelings of isolation, segregation, and disconnectedness with regard to the mainstream population. It appears that the nature of self-contained ESL programs in combination with cultural and linguistic factors generate physical and emotional separation from the school environment. Most students indicated interest in interacting more with non-ESL students. One student said: "At times I feel that I am not part of the school because I only hang out with ESL students. I wish I could do more things with the American students.

Assertiveness and language. Students participating in ESL programs appear to have multiple variables to work with regarding adaptation, including new culture, different teaching styles, expectations, and language. Linguistic confidence appears to be related to level of active participation and confidence in school activities.

Pressure and stereotypes. Some students face the dilemma of belonging to a group or staying out of groups and facing consequences. Being Hispanic/Latino and a gang member appear to be associated by many students in the schools; however, many Hispanic/Latino students are uncomfortable with that assumption. One participant indicated: "I am not a gangster. Some people believe that all Mexicans and Latinos belong to a gang."

Minimal contact with school counselor and bilingual issues. Similar to the ESL teacher experiences, students in the ESL program appear to have limited contact with school counselors. The need to voice concerns in their native language and lack of cultural understanding are important issues for some students.

Students European American
Association between gangs and Hispanic/Latinos/Mexicans. European American students associate Hispanics/Latinos and gang behavior in some

schools. The gangster stereotype has been attached to Hispanic/Latino persons based on past negative experiences in the community and school. One female student declared: "Sometimes I want to talk with some of the new Hispanic boys, but I am a little bit scared."

Strategies to solve tensions with Hispanic/Latino students. Some European American students avoid contact and ignore Hispanic/Latino students as a strategy to solve the strains between groups. Lacking understanding of cultural and linguistic differences leads them to adopt these behaviors. One interviewee said: "I pretty much don't say anything to them unless they talk to me first."

Inter-ethnic friendships and relationships. Interaction between European Americans and Hispanic/Latino students appears to be affected by assumptions rather than by facts based on communication of their particular needs, apprehensions, fears, and concerns. Lack of physical proximity and limited interactions in mainstream classrooms appear to affect potential relationships with ESL Latino students.

Linguistic frictions. There appears to be a degree of frustration and intolerance based on the inability to understand Spanish. The discomfort manifested by some European American students could be based on sensations of powerlessness and feelings of exclusion. It is not clear if Spanish-speaking students prefer to utilize their native language among themselves for comfort reasons or if it is used as a mechanism to exclude European American students and to keep a tighter circle. One student stated: "Sometimes I hear them speaking Spanish very loud and fast. I think they talk about us because they look at us and laugh."

Rationalization of gang behavior manifested by some Latino students. Some students conceptualize gang behavior and hostility manifested by some Hispanic/Latino students as a construct rooted in intolerance, frustration, and reverse prejudice projected against society. In addition, antisocial behavior is paralleled with poor academic performance and low productivity. Low socioeconomic status is linked with erratic conduct in schools and in the community.

School counselors are seen as mediator and agents that apply corrective interventions. All students, with the exception of one, described school counselors as individuals who take care of problems (individual and familial) – and prepare schedules and intervene with academically deficient students. The school counselor seems to be viewed as a reactive agent as opposed to a proactive agent anticipating future needs and providing strategies and information as preventive measures. One participant said: "I know that I am in trouble if the school counselor calls me to his office."

Implications and Recommendations for the Counseling Profession

There has been a tendency to overcompartmentalize professional disciplines, causing a fragmented view of issues that could be resolved utilizing a mutual-dependence approach in which every opinion is important and vital for the solution of an issue. In higher education, colleges, departments, and programs have operated semi-independently, protective of their knowledge and beliefs. These higher education dynamics are also observed in the K-12 school system. As the study reflected, ESL staff and school counselors are not engaged in conversations with the purpose of benefiting Hispanic/Latino ESL students. Some recommendations based on the study are presented.

1. A multilinguistic training approach for counselors as an alternative. A counselor preparation program could be developed with the collaborations of a liberal arts college and language department as a minor or certificate with the intention of licensure and specialization as a Spanish/English bilingual counselor. The courses would not be designed for international, native, Spanish speakers, but for nonnative speakers or native Spanish-speaking Hispanic/Latinos of the United States without formal linguistic training.

    These courses could be based on psycholinguistics and multiculturalism. All classes should be conducted in English and Spanish with an emphasis on the latter. A bilingual minor/certificate could be developed in conjunction with standard specializations such as school, community, vocational/rehabilitation, or mental health counseling. Implementation of such courses in counseling training programs would respond to the psycholinguistic needs of the Latino population. This psycholinguistic training is consistent with the importance of using a native language (Spanish) and/or a translator or interpreter when counseling or evaluating (Acosta & Cristo, 1981; Erzinger, 1991; Padilla et. Al., 1991; Samuda, 1998).

2. Devise and implement a TAG program for ESL Latinos. Limited English skills seem to be equated with limited intelligence and capacities. Although school staff and programs would deny such a harsh statement, why is it that there are so few ESL Hispanic/Latino students labeled as gifted and talented? There is a need to utilize nontraditional methods of evaluation. If counselors do not have training in these methods, consultation with culturally competent helping professionals seems appropriate for exploring alternate routes for standardized psychometric evaluations. Similarly, Samuda (1998) reported that using alternative methods to measure intelligence increases the chance to find out the potential of individuals that could have been ignored by traditional measures.

Some alternative assessment methods, such as interviews, self-reports, autobiographies, and portfolios can also be used to identify gifted and talented minority language students. ESL teachers ought to be included in the conversations with school counselors, because eventually the ESL teacher will serve as a bridge between school counselors and students.

3. Intragroup training. There is a need to provide intragroup training to Hispanics/Latinos belonging to different cultural generation in order to increase awareness and sensitivity regarding immigrants of the same ethnic group. Also, an additional purpose is to improve intercultural relationships and have a healthier school climate.

4. Promotion of bilingualism and not foreign language in schools to increase tolerance in the European American community. An implicit element that surfaced in some of the interviews was the confusion between foreign and second language. Although both terms seem to have the same meaning, the underlying message is different. The foreign language concept may be associated with the imposition of an external element not connected with daily life; therefore, something that is not relevant and practical. The potential of developing an adversarial position toward the language and anything that represents it is possible. On the other hand, the acquisition and learning of a second language is better associated with an addition, carrying a positive practical connotation.

A positive approach toward a second language acquisition is associated with a healthier interaction between Spanish-speaking people interacting in schools and communities. This concept ought to be promoted by both ESL teachers and school counselors in order to ensure a healthier environment in the school setting and superior relationships among the students. The idea is for students to understand and associate languages with cultures and how both are intertwined.

5. Development of teamwork approach between ESL staff and school counselors. In order for school counselors to improve services conferred to ESL/Hispanic/Latino students, it is recommended that they maintain conversations with ESL staff at least once a week. The purpose would be to discuss issues and concerns regarding ESL students and how these can be remedied before the end of the year. Ideally, the students should view the school counselor as an important part of the ESL staff, and not as a removed agent who deals with schedules and corrective behavior interventions. In order to portray an active image of the school counselor to ESL students, a close relationship has to start with ESL staff.

6. Interpreters. In coordination with the ESL staff, a list of potential interpreters and translators should be available to school counselors. Selecting potential interpreters should be based on language mastery, cultural knowledge, and personal traits compatible with the school counselor's style of work. A student's relatives should not be used as interpreters. Also, translators should be identified for the translation of documents that will reach the Spanish-speaking population.

    Culturally and developmentally sensitive interventions. In order to have successful interventions in a middle school, it is necessary for the school counselors to have an understanding of the influence of culture on personality in human development, and how human behavior differs when embedded in a bicultural environment (Dana, 1998; Pedersen, 1999). While a monocultural adolescent is struggling with the developmental stage of identity versus role confusions, bicultural Latinos are also struggling with ethnic and linguistic identity.

7. Consistent with the interview's outcome, the majority of ESL Latino students are in a disadvantageous position with regard to power. Therefore, counseling interventions should be geared toward student empowerment. For instance, some interventions that could serve as empowerment tools are (a) problem-solving skills to develop self-confidence and cultural pride, (b) planning skills consistent with the student's family system to establish goal setting, (c) leadership skills that go across ethnic groups, and (d) integration skills to develop self-acceptance.

LIMITATIONS OF THE STUDY

The dissension between ethnic groups in the United States is not new, and neither is the difficulty experienced by helping professionals when providing services to clients from diverse backgrounds, specifically nonnative English speakers. As with any other research study, only pieces of truth are revealed through these findings and not a universal truth that could shed light over every challenge. This study serves as a foundation for future studies. The following recommendations should be considered if a similar study is to be conducted:

1. Selection of only one school with multiple in-depth interviews with teaching and administrative staff, community (including religious organizations) leaders, school district staff, and family, as opposed to multiple schools. This type of qualitative study would be more time consuming, but would provide an in-depth perspective of multiple dimensions of the socioeducational system in one school.

2. From a developmental point of view, middle school dynamics are different and unique in comparison to elementary or high school dynamics. Acknowledging this developmental dynamic, it would be useful to conduct a similar study with a different school level in order to explore what can be attributed to age developmental circumstances or ethnolinguistic issues.

3. The qualitative study could be enriched by adding some type of paper-pencil quantitative measure. This could add a different dimension of analysis based on quantitative analysis of information.

CONCLUSIONS

Changes in demographics have been evident in the school system and have forced counselors and related professionals to embrace the multicultural and diversity paradigm as a suitable alternative to improve services rendered to multiethnic and multilingual populations. Including the linguistic variable as an important element during training and continuous education increases the likelihood of targeting more students with a higher degree of accuracy. In view of the fact that the nation is becoming more multilingual and will keep changing, counselors need to be at the forefront of these changes and start revisiting traditional training curricula.

ESL Hispanic/Latino students are the larger population among ESL students in the nation, therefore, deserving the attention not only from ESL staff but from school counselors in order to provide academic options for the future and to facilitate the adjustment process within the school system. Updating training methodology and shifting traditional curricula for school counselors to multilingual principles at the higher education levels deserves to be considered. Based on the results of this study, pilot studies in school counseling programs are encouraged in which multilinguistic approaches influence the direction of programs.

Roberto Clemente, Ph.D., is an assistant professor, School and Mental Health Counseling, University of Northern Iowa, Cedar Falls. Brooke B. Collison, Ph.D., is professor emeritus, Counselor Education, Oregon State University, Corvallis.

REFERENCES

Acosta, F. X., & Cristo, M. H. (1981). Development of a bilingual interpreter program: An alternative model for Spanish speaking services. *Professional Psychology: Research and Practice, 12,* 474-482.

Aguilar, I. (1972). *Initial contacts with Mexican American families.* Understanding and counseling ethnic minorities. Springfield, IL.: Charles C. Thomas.

Amaro, H., & Russo, N. F. (1987). Hispanic women and mental health: An overview of contemporary issues in research and practice. *Psychology of Women Quarterly, 11,* 393-407.

Bamford, K. (1991). Bilingual issues in mental health assessment and treatment. *Latino Journal of Behavioral Sciences, 13,* 377-390.

Baptiste, D. A. (1987). Family therapy with Spanish-heritage immigrant families in cultural transition. *Contemporary Family Therapy, 9,* 229-251.

Bogdan, R. C., & Biklen, S. K. (1992). *Qualitative research for education: An introduction to theory and methods.* Boston: Allyn & Bacon.

Borg, W. R., Gall, J. P., & Gall, M. D. (1993). Applying educational research: A practical guide. New York: Longman.

Casas, J. M., & Vasquez, M. J. T. (1996). Counseling the Hispanic: A guiding framework for a diverse population. In P. B. Pedersen, J. G. Draguns, W. J. Lonner, & J. E. Trimble (Eds.), *Counseling across cultures* (4th ed., pp. 146-176), Thousand Oaks, CA: Sage.

Cuellar, I., Harris, L. C., & Jasso, R. (1980). An acculturation scale for Mexican-American normal and clinical populations. *Hispanic Journal of Behavioral Sciences, 2,* 199-217.

Dana, R. H. (1993). *Multicultural assessment perspectives for professional psychology.* Boston: Allyn & Bacon.

Dana, R. H. (1998). *Understanding cultural identity in intervention and assessment.* Boston: Allyn & Bacon.

Das, A. K. (1995). Rethinking multicultural counseling: Implications for counselor education. *Journal of Counseling and Development, 74,* 45-52.

Erzinger, S. (1991). Communications between Spanish speaking patients and their doctors. Culture, *Medicine and Psychiatry, 15,* 91-100.

Falicov, C. (1998). *Latino families in therapy: A guide to multicultural practice.* New York: Guilford.

García, J., & Zea, M. (1997). *Psychological interventions and research with Latino populations.* Boston: Allyn & Bacon.

Hayes-Batista, D. E., Shink, W. O., & Chapa, J. (1998). *The burden of support: Young Latinos in an aging society.* Stanford, CA: Stanford University.

Kopala, M., & Suzuki, L. (1999). *Using qualitative methods in psychology.* Thousand Oaks, London: Sage.

Lee, C. (1997, April). Counseling Latinos. *Counseling Today,* pp.1-3.

Marín, G., & Marín, B. V. (1991). *Research with Hispanic populations.* (Applied Social Research Method Series, Vol. 23). Newbury Park, CA: Sage.

Moyerman, D., & Forman, B. (1992). Acculturation and adjustment: A meta-analytic study. *Hispanic Journal of Behavioral Sciences, 14,*(2), 163-200.

National Council of La Raza. (1990). *Hispanic education: A statistical portrait 1990.* Washington, DC: Author.

Orozco, S., Thompson, B., Kapos, J., & Montgomery, G. (1993). Measuring the acculturation of Mexican-Americans: A covariance structure analysis. *Measurement and Evaluation in Counseling and Development, 25,* 149-155.

O'Sullivan, M. J., Peterson, D., Cox, G. B., & Kirkeby, J. (1989). Ethnic populations: Community services ten years later. *American Journal of Community Psychology. 17,* 17-30.

Padilla, A. M., Lindholm, K. J., Chen, A., Duran, R., Hakuta, K., Lambert, W., & Tucker, G. R. (1991). The English-only movement: Myths, reality and implications for psychology. *American Psychologist, 46,* 120-130.

Padilla, A. M., & Salgado de Snyder, N. (1985). Counseling Hispanics: Strategies for effective intervention. In P. Pedersen (Ed.), *Handbook for cross-cultural counseling and therapy* (pp. 157-164). New York: Praeger.

Pedersen, P. (1999). *Multiculturalism as a fourth force.* PA: Brunner/Mazel.

Ramirez, A. G., & McAlister, A. L. (1988). Mass media campaign-A su salud. *Preventive Medicine, 17,* 608-621.

Rozensky, R. H., & Gómez, M. Y. (1983). Language switching in psychotherapy with bilingual: Two problems, two models, and case examples. *Psychotherapy, Theory, Research and Practice, 20,* 152-160.

Samuda, R. J. (1998). *Psychological testing of American minorities.* Thousand Oaks, CA: Sage.

Strauss, A., & Corbin, J. (1990). *Basics of qualitative research: Grounded theory procedures and techniques.* Newbury Park, CA: Sage.

Sue, D. W. (1998, December). *Cultural specific techniques in counseling: A counseling framework.* Paper presented at the Southeast Asia Symposium on Counseling and Guidance in the 21st Century, Taipei, Taiwan.

Sue, D. W. (1990). Culture specific techniques in counseling: A conceptual framework. *Professional Psychology: Research and Practice, 21,* 424-433.

Sue, D. W. (1991). A model for cultural diversity training. *Journal of Counseling & Development. 70*, 99-105.

Sue, S. (1977). Community mental health services to minority groups: Some optimism, some pessimism. *American Psychologist, 32*, 616-624.

U. S. Bureau of the Census. (1992). *1990 Census of population and housing summary: Tape file 3A.* Washington, DC: Department of Commerce, Data user Services Division.

U. S. Bureau of the Census. (1993). *Latino Americans today.* Washington, DC: U. S. Government Printing Office.

Wrenn, C. G. (1962). *The counselor in a changing world.* Washington, DC: American Personnel and Guidance Association.

Urban School Counseling: Implications for Practice and Training

By Alan G. Green, Ph.D., Jacqueline A. Conley and Kim Barnett

This article originally appeared in *Professional School Counseling*, Vol. 8, No. 3, 2005.

The authors present two school counselors' case scenarios to illustrate training and the delivery of effective school counseling services in an urban society. Urban education is viewed here as being more than the teaching of low-status people and represents the opportunity to create awareness and promote change through such awareness. Developments in the literature related to the topic of urban school counseling are discussed. This article provides a glimpse at some of ways in which the profession can respond to the changing demographics of society and the demands for increased accountability in academic achievement for all students.

The school counseling literature recently has reflected a commitment by some in the profession to better serve culturally diverse students through what has been referred to as urban school counseling programs and services (Green & Keys, 2001; Holcomb-McCoy, 1998, 2001; Lee, 2001). Expanding upon existing comprehensive developmental guidance counseling models (Gysbers & Henderson, 2000, 2001), urban school counseling focuses on students and schools that present challenges extending beyond traditional developmental perspectives (Green & Keys). Typically, the term urban is synonymous with the inner city and school counseling refers to addressing problems of violence, low achievement, and poverty. Although many challenges exist, the cultural richness of any urban environment creates opportunities for exchange through diversity that can promote healthy development for all students (Sink, 2002).

To provide effective programs, urban school counseling must be approached from a critical perspective of the urban environment as a whole. Urban school counseling is defined here as school counseling personnel and programmatic services that are specifically geared toward meeting the multiple and often complex needs of students living and attending school in culturally diverse environments. Because of the cultural richness in the urban setting, where values and perspectives are often in competition with one another, awareness of one's self and the developmental context is critical (Green & Keys, 2001).

As the profession makes strides toward better serving urban students, many suburban and even rural school systems across the country have faced a change in student and community demographics that reflects challenges previously associated with the inner city. Disruptive students and poor academic achievement are no longer bound by the geographic boundaries of the city alone. Gordon (2003) reminds us that due to modern technology, particularly in the forms of communication and travel, we are living in an urban nation-state where throughout most of this society, culturally diverse people are increasingly living in close proximity of one another. As communities and their schools evolve to reflect the cultural diversity of our larger society, so too must our profession if it is to continue the tradition as an adaptable and viable program and service provider to public schools. Thus there is a need for school counselors, regardless of setting, to become knowledgeable about the principles and practices of urban school counseling.

Exactly what are the challenges faced by educators today in our society? What does this mean to the delivery of comprehensive developmental guidance services in our schools? How best can we continue the tradition of the profession by responding to the complex developmental needs of students and those who seek to educate them in an urban society? This article will address these specific questions as a contribution to the growing literature focusing on the topic of urban school counseling. Two counselors' case scenarios, which will be described below, represent the ever-changing reality of school counseling in our urban society. They are presented here to help articulate how the training and practice of school counselors can be more responsive.

URBAN STUDENT NEEDS

Typically, the term *urban education* denotes an implicit and oftentimes explicit reference to the teaching of low-status people (Gordon, 2003; Gordon & Armour-Thomas, 1992). This perspective fails to account for the social and ecological factors that over time have created a high concentration of crime, violence, and poverty in many urban environments. A broader definition of the concept should not negate the importance of addressing the needs of poor and disenfranchised inner city groups, but rather should provide scholars and practitioners with a more useful conceptualization of the term. A more critical perspective allows us to tackle the deeper societal challenges associated with diversity and mobility that are inherent to the urban setting, and it prepares the way for more effective school counseling strategies.

Green and Keys (2001) provided the school counseling literature with guidelines for working with students in the 21st century. Using an ecological perspective (i.e., Bronfenbrenner, 1979), they suggested that, regardless of geographic location, the needs of urban students must be addressed through a perspective that accounts for the complex environments in which they live. As federal, state, and local demands for accountability increase, schools are finding it difficult to promote learning for all students. The persistent gap in learning, across contexts, suggests that low achievement and disruptive behaviors need to be viewed from a broader perspective.

According to Gordon (2003), "an urban environment is characterized by diversity, conflicting lifestyles, cultural richness, a high concentration of material resources, rapid communication and travel, and the coexistence of fluidity and rigidity in institutional and personal behavior" (p. 189). Due to the high concentration of different cultural practices competing with one another in an urban society, some groups and practices become more acceptable than others. In addition to content knowledge, urban education must teach students about the dominant and accepted practices of society. Many of today's struggling students resist learning because of internalized failure, a byproduct of the disconnect between the student's learning style and needs and the preferred learning style and needs of the broader environment (Adelman, 2002). From an ecological perspective, contextual awareness becomes an important skill for students and those who work with them. The mission of the school counselor is to implement developmental programs for all students. In the urban environment, these programs should promote an understanding of dominant cultural practices and facilitate awareness of the relationship between one's own personal background and culture and the broader context.

For a better understanding of the context of urban schools and students, Holcomb-McCoy (1998) provided six factors that influence urban school counseling: (a) diversity of students, (b) lack of resources, (c) poverty, (d) family issues, (e) violence, and (f) high dropout rates. Given the expansion of the urban environment beyond traditional city limits, counselor educators and school counseling practitioners everywhere should partake in the delivery and consumption of such training. An ecological perspective allows for a better understanding of student needs and can lead to more effective school counseling programs and interventions.

URBAN SCHOOL COUNSELOR EDUCATION MODELS

Just as urbanization is occurring across multiple school and community contexts, so too are opportunities to develop an urban perspective on school counseling. A Web-based search of the term urban school counseling produced several hits related to graduate-level training that specializes or offers course content on the topic. The findings suggest that a change in the profession is underway. Previously, counselor education programs have only incorporated issues of diversity and multiculturalism into existing graduate course work as subcategories. The development of specialized programs in urban school counseling represents the growing commitment to transforming the profession.

In line with professional standards set forth by the Council for Accreditation of Counseling and Related Educational Programs (2001), most urban school counseling education programs offer training in professional identity, social and cultural diversity, human growth and development, career development, helping relationships, group work, assessment, research, and program evaluation. Specialized programs incorporate an urban perspective for each of these courses, thereby allowing students to develop competences relevant to the urban environment. For example, coursework in professional identity must create a perspective among counseling students that reflects an understanding of the ecological and self-awareness foundations essential to any successful urban program (Day-Vines, Patton, & Baytops, 2003; Green & Keys, 2001). This perspective will be useful as urban school counselors consult with teachers, collect and analyze needs assessment data, and interact with parents.

Traditional graduate-level courses in group work address objectives that include understanding group types, leadership styles, theories, methods, dynamics, and the evaluation of groups. A course specializing in urban group counseling will cover each of these topics plus focus on specific issues related to urban school environments. For example, group leadership course work will introduce strategies for facilitating critical awareness of the factors contributing to behavior among disruptive or challenging students (Carlson, 2003).

Specialized urban school counseling programs also offer required and elective course work for working with urban families and collaborating with teachers, special educators, and administrators. Course offerings in urban ethical and legal issues, applied behavioral interventions, and applied research supplement the curriculum. Practicum and internship opportunities in urban programs are coordinated with local school systems and can be linked with other professional development partnerships from other education disciplines. Supervision from practicing school counselors who have adopted critical perspectives in urban issues benefits young students and counselor trainees alike (Clark, 2003).

A transformation in the profession is required in order to better work with the needs of urban students. Green and Keys (2001) have offered seven guiding principles for counselor education and school counseling programs. They have recommended that programs (a) promote self and contextual awareness, (b) utilize an ecological framework for problem solving, (c) utilize indirect service models, (d) use collaboration to achieve comprehensive program objectives, (e) align school counseling goals with local reform and improvement strategies, (f) use evidence-based best practices, and (g) use outcome-based evaluation strategies. For a detailed review of the six influential factors of urban school counseling and of the seven guiding principles, see Holcomb-McCoy (1998) and Green and Keys, respectively.

CASE SCENARIOS

The remainder of this article will elaborate on two counselors' case scenarios to describe the influence of urban school counselor education programs on the practice of school counselors working in an urban setting. Based on actual experiences of practicing counselors in both contexts, these cases offer guidance on future steps for the profession.

Counselor Scenario 1

Mrs. Taylor is currently in her 5th year as the only school counselor at Tagor Elementary School located in a large, urban school district on the Eastern seaboard of the United States. Tagor Elementary recently has been recognized for its much improved academic performance and school climate over the past 3 years. This progress can be attributed to the dedication and hard work of the entire school family as well as the leadership of the principal. Serving more than 600 students, this counselor works closely with her principal and relies heavily on her master's degree training in urban school counseling to meet the diverse needs of students, staff, and parents affiliated with the school.

When Mrs. Taylor first arrived at Tagor Elementary 5 years ago, she recently had completed her graduate training in urban school counseling at a local university. Prior to that, she was a third-grade teacher in the same urban school district. What had bothered Mrs. Taylor the most about her school was the negative attitudes other adults had toward students and their families. Every time she heard an adult solely blame a child for poor behavior or low academic performance, it bothered her. After attending an open house for graduate training in education at the local university, she became interested in the school because it offered special master's degree training in urban school counseling. She applied and was admitted.

Over the next 3 years, Mrs. Taylor was immersed in her counselor education program but felt particularly committed to better understanding how she could be effective working with urban students. In her courses, each of the core objectives was grounded in an ecological perspective of school counseling. Although she did not grow up in the inner city herself,

Mrs. Taylor appreciated gaining a better perspective on cultural diversity, particularly awareness about the historical and sociopolitical background of diverse groups. "My training helped me gain the knowledge, skills, and awareness I needed to better understand myself, my students, and the urban setting," she stated.

In one particular course, Multicultural Counseling with Urban Youth and Families, Mrs. Taylor gained awareness about the ecological and historical antecedents that played a major role in the issues facing her school. From this course, she learned that many of the problems her students brought to school were less intimidating once she stopped judging students and their families by her middle-class values. She realized that most parents and teachers wanted their students to learn and be successful, but that oftentimes ecological factors from the past and present made education a secondary priority at best. Mrs. Taylor also realized that growing up in a Southern rural community imbedded in her a strong commitment to getting a college education and giving back to society. She also felt that her upbringing was filled with a stronger opportunity structure than many of her students, which helped her to pursue her goals in life.

After completing a family genogram for herself and her husband in the multicultural family counseling course, Mrs. Taylor began to better appreciate the struggles her husband's family had endured migrating from the South to a Northern industrial city. She learned about how, in order to take care of seven children, her mother-in-law had to find work as a maid and a dishwasher for pennies a day after the family's father was incarcerated for a crime he did not commit. Mrs. Taylor realized that her husband's mother had made tremendous sacrifices so he and his siblings could get an education. While processing her emotions associated with the genogram exercise, Mrs. Taylor realized how proud she was of her husband for overcoming those obstacles, and also how fortunate he was for having the benefit of a strong and hardworking mother and an extended family structure to see him through. She then began to reflect on the many children she had encountered as a teacher who had to face similar challenges but did not have the right combination of personal, social, and environmental support structures available to make it through. Rather than blaming those students, she felt a need to temporarily set aside her values and recognize their struggles and validate them for their efforts however self-defeating they may be. She learned that this was the most important part of any counseling relationship.

This fresh perspective did wonders for her ability to connect with troubled students. Mrs. Taylor realized that working successfully in the urban school setting was about helping youth build awareness of themselves and their situations as a precursor to using established counseling strategies that lead to effective change. Mrs. Taylor also realized that success had to be defined by the student through awareness of self and not by a definition that was externally imposed upon the student. During the remainder of her graduate course work, Mrs. Taylor pursued a commitment to helping urban students and those who work with them through building awareness of self.

During her internship experience, Mrs. Taylor was placed in an urban elementary school and supervised by a counselor who, 5 years prior, had graduated from the same urban school counseling program. This experience taught her how to establish and maintain what was called a Comprehensive Development Urban School Counseling Program (CDUSCP), which based most of its effectiveness on a philosophy of respect and awareness. Mrs. Taylor's internship supervisor taught her how to address needs through direct and indirect services that were aligned to the school's overall mission and reform goals.

As a new counselor at Tagor, Mrs. Taylor first set out to implement her own CDUSCP by collecting needs assessment data to identify which particular students were doing well socially and academically. After studying closely what was working well, she developed a plan to coordinate the delivery of contextually appropriate developmental guidance for the more successful students. This included classroom guidance lessons and school-wide activities that stimulated their interest in the local and global world around them, connecting it to their educational and personal goals both present and future. Mrs. Taylor then identified targeted students for more intense interventions based on office referrals, suspension data, and feedback from teachers and other staff. Focusing on the school's improvement goals of attendance, standardized testing, and climate, the counselor focused on students with severe attendance and behavioral problems. After separating students with health, transportation, and other functional issues from those who were dealing with serious personal and family issues, she developed specific strategies for each.

Students with personal and family issues were targeted for individual, group, and culturally and "urban" sensitive outside resources. At every step of the way, Mrs. Taylor was concerned with providing age-appropriate, social skill utilization strategies based on awareness and affective processing. She also worked with the teachers and, when possible, the parents of the targeted students. With teachers, she consulted with them on individual problems, serving as a resource provider, listener, and model regarding effective interactions with challenging students.

In one difficult situation, a fourth-grade teacher quit unexpectedly due to a particularly disruptive class. Mrs. Taylor was able to locate two qualified potential replacements from her university graduate program who had been exposed to a similar urban perspective as her own. Once a replacement was hired, they worked collaboratively to stimulate and engage all of the students in that class as well as provide targeted interventions when necessary. Their work paid off as evidenced by a moderate improvement in all measured outcomes, which surprisingly contributed significantly to the school's overall performance.

Counselor Scenario 2

For the past 15 years, Mr. Cox has been the school counselor at suburban Skeldon Elementary School located in the Midwestern part of the United States. During this time, Mr. Cox has seen his school's demographics change drastically due to a large influx of international students from abroad and urban students from a large nearby city. Historically, Skeldon Elementary has been among the top performing schools in its district, but 6 years ago, the school's test scores dropped dramatically and suspension and attendance rates skyrocketed. Two years ago, Mr. Cox convinced his principal to support the implementation of a comprehensive school counseling program geared toward meeting the changing needs of the school's urbanized student population. The most recent school performance data reveal a turnaround at Skeldon, placing its nearly 550 students near the top of the district's performance list once again.

Mr. Cox completed his graduate training more than 16 years ago when he received a master's degree in school counseling at a local state university. Since then, he has always been engaged in professional development and continuing education through various local, state, and national professional associations. As a result, Skeldon Elementary benefited from a comprehensive developmental guidance program delivered and coordinated by Mr. Cox. Three years ago, he began focusing his continuing education and professional development around the changing demographics of Skeldon Elementary. Specifically, Mr. Cox sought to better serve his school by addressing the negative impact that disruptive students were having on achievement and climate. Most of the teachers, administrators, staff, and local parents readily attributed the school's recent problems to an influx of families, group homes, and foster kids from the nearby big city.

Many of the schools in this suburban/urban district also were facing increased problems with fighting in school, poor attendance, office referrals, and suspensions. Teacher morale was low, and the principal was struggling to respond to teachers' demands to remove disruptive students from the classroom. The principal went to Mr. Cox for help because there was also pressure from the district office and the state to respond to new federal regulations that require a reduction of school suspensions and increased academic performance. Up to that point, disruptive students typically were sent to the office for a "cooling-off period" and then sent back to class. More serious issues were reviewed by the principal, and suspension was used as a last resort after family conferences and individual and/or group counseling services were provided. Mr. Cox conducted classroom guidance lessons on bullying, anger management, and character development to no avail.

As the numbers of students being sent to the office increased, a spare classroom located next to Mr. Cox's office was designated as the in-school suspension room. Staffed by a parent volunteer at first, the suspension room became problematic because of behavioral problems. The principal was able to utilize a teacher's aid position to hire a behavior specialist to staff the room and work with the students, yet the problems continued to increase. Because many of the disruptive students were initially coming from the local city's school system, Mr. Cox became interested in research and training offerings related to urban school counseling. His interests led him to attend workshops and read professional literature about the ecology of urban schools and successful counseling practices. He also enrolled in a post-master's certificate in urban school counseling. As a result he realized that his school was in many ways dealing with the same urban issues occurring in the nearby city. Beyond the impact of the disruptive students, the counselor also realized that the school's diversity had changed in other ways. For example, there were now seven different foreign language groups of students attending Skeldon, when in years past there were only two. This increase in English as a Second Language students also was overwhelming the school's resources and impacting achievement.

Eager to address these issues, Mr. Cox sat down in the spring 3 years ago to develop a strategy to adapt his comprehensive guidance program to the urbanization occurring at Skeldon Elementary. Prior to the end of that school year, Mr. Cox conducted a needs assessment to identify and prioritize the challenges the school faced. With the approval of the principal, he gathered data about teachers' perceptions of disruptive students as well as their thoughts about other problems faced by the school. This assessment not only inquired about the amount and types of disruptions that were occurring in the classroom and cafeteria, but it also gauged teacher attitudes and beliefs about the causes of these problems.

The results of the needs assessment proved quite useful in that it shed light on some of the hostility that teachers and staff had about the changes that were occurring in their school and collective communities. Specifically, teachers and other adults, including parents who came from families who had been a part of the school and neighborhood for generations, felt hostility toward local political and economic trends that caused the city residents to move into their bedroom community. Teachers also blamed parents and other caregivers for the behavior problems students displayed at school. Some teachers felt that after meeting and attempting to work with some of the new parents, they were more discouraged. "Now I see where this student gets her temper from," a fifth-grade teacher stated.

After interpreting the data from the needs assessment, Mr. Cox felt a bit relieved to learn that out of 550 students, there were fewer than 50 students who were identified as being repeatedly or severely disruptive. He recalled how one of the local parents had made a comment during a PTA meeting that the school seemed like a wild animal park and that every child in the building was in crisis. He was glad to learn that this was not reality. The needs assessment also revealed that many of the students who were disruptive in class also were performing low academically. Contrary to the opinion of others, Mr. Cox also found that not all of the severely or continually disruptive students were new entrants from the city and that some of the traditionally local students were in need of intervention as well.

These results made sense to Mr. Cox, after having attended a summit at his state school counseling association conference the previous summer. He learned that many schools with disruptive students appear worse than they really are, and that schools that respond negatively to a few disruptive students usually can make things worse for everyone involved. He also learned from his training on urban school counseling that many of the problems associated with disruptive students could be reduced if classroom teachers and school staff adopted better ways of relating to students by developing a positive and nonthreatening approach to addressing behavior problems. It was at that point that Mr. Cox decided to take action. He used the summer months to make a comprehensive plan for the upcoming year. He presented the plan to the principal who endorsed it right away.

During the summer months, Mr. Cox coordinated the upcoming school year's professional development opportunities being offered to Skeldon's teachers. Because he worked at a professional development school he was able to collaborate with other professionals and develop workshops around best practices for teaching in an urban environment. Mr. Cox made teacher interventions a top priority of his initiative because his data revealed that broader community issues and cultural contradictions heavily impacted the school's climate. Mindful of his inability to tackle these issues alone, he created ongoing opportunities for adults to dialogue about issues during lunch in breakout groups at the professional development workshops. He felt that by incorporating best practices training with opportunities to bring an ecological perspective to the challenges facing Skeldon Elementary, teachers would be less threatened.

In the fall Mr. Cox continued to coordinate his comprehensive developmental guidance activities as he did in the past. By partnering with teachers and staff, changing the school's climate was not as overwhelming as he once thought. Over the next 2 years, students, staff, and some parents worked on implementing the best practices in their respective fields. Although many challenges still remain, the school climate does reflect a new commitment for responding to changes and needs in ways that benefit all students.

FUTURE STEPS FOR URBAN SCHOOL COUNSELING

Governmental mandates such as No Child Left Behind and the changing demographics of public schools have compelled the profession to move forward in responding to student needs. Educators and practitioners alike are seeking effective ways of being more accountable. In the case scenario of Mrs. Taylor, connecting with students in a manner that promotes self-awareness was important. By establishing a grounded perspective of herself in the urban context, she was able to deliver a program that reflects the needs of Tagor Elementary School. For Mr. Cox, rethinking the way his guidance program impacts school climate was an effective strategy for initiating change. In his case, working closely with teacher perceptions of disruptive students had a significant impact on the school climate.

In the future, counselor educators can enhance their program offerings through standards-based specialized training that responds effectively to urban students. Practicing counselors in the field can equally benefit from adopting an expanded urban perspective toward their craft. For both educators and practitioners, the first step in this process is to develop an ecological perspective that reflects the dynamics of themselves and their students and the context within which schools and counseling programs are located.

Alan G. Green, Ph.D., is an assistant professor in the Department of Counseling and Human Services at Johns Hopkins University, Baltimore. Jacqueline A. Conley is an assistant professor in the Department of Psychology at Chicago State University. Kim Barnett is a faculty associate in the Department of Counseling and Human Services at Johns Hopkins University. E-mail: agreen@jhu.edu

REFERENCES

Adelman, H. (2002). School counselors and school reform: New directions. *Professional School Counseling, 5*(4), 235–248.

Bronfenbrenner, U. (1979). *The ecology of human development.* Cambridge, MA: Harvard University Press.

Carlson, L. A. (2003). Existential theory: Helping school counselors attend to youth at risk for violence. *Professional School Counseling, 6*(5), 310–315.

Clark, M. (2003).Training school interns to teach elementary students to respect and care for others. *Journal of Humanistic Counseling, Education and Development, 42*(1), 91–106.

Council for Accreditation of Counseling and Related Educational Programs. (2001). *Accreditation procedures manual and application.* Alexandria,VA: Author.

Day-Vines, N. L., Patton, J. M., & Baytops, J. (2003). Counseling African American adolescents: The impact of race, culture, and middle class status. *Professional School Counseling, 7*(1), 40–51.

Gordon, E.W. (2003). Urban education.Teachers College Record, 105(2), 189–209.

Gordon, E., & Armour-Thomas, E. (1992). Urban education. In M. C. Alkin (Ed.), *Encyclopedia of educational research* (6th ed., pp. 1459–1470). New York: American Educational Research Association.

Green, A., & Keys, S.G. (2001). Expanding the developmental school counseling paradigm:Meeting the needs of the 21st century student. *Professional School Counseling, 5*, 84–95.

Gysbers, N. C., & Henderson, P. (2000). *Developing and managing your school guidance program* (3rd ed.). Alexandria, VA: American Counseling Association.

Gysbers, N. C., & Henderson, P. (2001). Comprehensive guidance and counseling programs: A rich history and a bright future. *Professional School Counseling, 4*, 246–256.

Holcomb-McCoy, C. C. (1998). *School counselor preparation in urban settings.* ERIC Clearinghouse on Urban Education. (ERIC Document Reproduction Service No. ED418343)

Holcomb-McCoy, C. C. (2001). Exploring the self-perceived multicultural counseling competence of elementary school counselors. *Professional School Counseling, 4*(3), 195–201.

Lee, C. C. (2001). Culturally responsive school counselors and programs: Addressing the needs of all students. *Professional School Counseling, 4*(4), 257–261.

Sink, C. (2002). Comprehensive guidance and counseling programs and the development of multicultural student citizens. *Professional School Counseling, 6*(2), 130–137.

Evidencing a Need: School Counselors' Experiences with Gay and Lesbian Students

By Janet H. Fontaine

This article originally appeared in *Professional School Counseling*, Vol. 1, No.3, 1998.

For a variety of reasons, the needs of gay and lesbian students in our nation's schools go largely unnoticed and unmet. Their identity as a minority group is ignored even though in many schools they may be the largest minority. Their status in schools, as in the broader society, can arguably be said to be the unenviable status of most hated group. As one of the few remaining minority groups available who can be victimized with few social consequences, gays and lesbians are fair game for adults, adolescents, and children alike to harass, demean, threaten and even physically assault. Laws and institutional regulations preclude homosexuals' full participation in society – for example, marriage, tax exemptions, health benefits for domestic partners, same-sex couple attendance at school proms. And more subtle forms of culturally-sanctioned discrimination are often officially condoned by governmental, religious and other social institutions.

Homosexuals are probably the most frequent victims of hate crimes, which appear to be on the rise in parts of our nation (Herek, 1989). The consequences of this intimidation by threats and acts of violence take many forms, but perhaps none more subtle than the restriction of behavior options for both heterosexual and homosexual persons alike (Herek, 1989). Antigay harassment serves to enforce rigid standards of gender-appropriate behavior. Both heterosexuals and gays avoid deviating from society's heterosexual sanctioned norms for fear of being labeled as homosexual and thus subjecting themselves to the potential for verbal and physical abuse.

Marino (1995) believes no part of the homosexual community suffers more than gay, lesbian and bisexual adolescents. Their high need for peer group approval, tenuous dependent economic and legal status, and lack of financial independence severely restrict their options for dealing with emotionally and physically threatening environments and persons. Statistics support this vulnerability. One in three adolescent suicides have been attributed to youth dealing with sexual-identity issues (Gibson, 1989). Several studies have documented higher incidences of substance abuse, utilization of psychiatric services, difficulties in school, and running away among homosexual youth (Remafedi, 1987; Remafedi, Farrow &

Deisher, 1991). More than 80% of the gay and lesbian adolescents studied by Remafedi (1987) still in school reported declining academic performance and other school-related problems.

Schools, with their documented high incidents of harassment and violence, have been shown to be among the most homophobic institutions in America (Governor's Task Force, 1988; Remafedi, 1987; Unks, 1994). A survey of junior and senior high school students in the state of New York found higher levels of hostility toward gays than toward racial or ethnic minorities (Governor's Task Force, 1988). In a recently-published teen interview on the topic of sexuality, a question was posed about how difficult it would be for students to be openly gay or bisexual in their schools (Pratt, 1995).Two poignant responses represent the blatantly anti-gay hostility permeating their institutions:

> A few years ago, two girls were walking down the hall at my school, holding hands, and they kissed briefly. This mob came and harassed them. A person who witnessed it said that if the people had had rocks in their hands they would have stoned them to death. (p. 5)

> If my friends found me hugging another dude...that ain't gonna happen. They would slap me. (p. 5)

Homophobic and intolerant educational environments can only exist with the implicit and/or explicit cooperation of school officials and personnel. Evidence suggests that teachers, counselors, and administrators exhibit distressingly high levels of homophobic attitudes and feelings (Dressler, 1985; Price & Telljohann, 1991; Rudolph, 1988; Savin-Williams , 1990; Sears, 1992). In a comparison of several studies, Sears (1992) found 8 out of 10 preservice teachers exhibited negative attitudes toward homosexuals. Two-thirds of the school counselors surveyed expressed negative attitudes; both groups, according to the instruments used, had scores in the homophobic range.

Educators and counselors may believe that they exhibit a nonjudgmental demeanor, but their biased feelings and attitudes are often communicated in subtle ways. Southern gay and lesbian students, interviewed after they graduated from high school, indicated that they lacked trust in their teachers and counselors, thought them to be unsupportive of their orientation, would not seek out school counselors to discuss their lifestyle problems, and said teachers avoided the topic of homosexuality in their classes (Sears, 1991, 1992).

This institutionalized homophobia – evidenced by many examples of benign neglect such as subject omission from curricula, nonexistent or unenforced antidiscrimination policies, and lack of visible services for gay and lesbian youth – serves to deny the very existence of homosexual students in the schools. In turn, this denial and lack of affirmation perpetuates the homosexual student's survival need to remain invisible within an educational system that fails to exhibit an interest in his or her safety and welfare.

One result of this elective invisibility is to permit school officials to deny the need for services for homosexual youth by rationalizing that a population of any consequence does not exist. The reality is, however, that various estimates of homosexuality claim 3% to 10% of the population to be gay or lesbian. Deisher (1989) estimated that approximately 3 million young people between the ages of 10 and 20 are predominantly or exclusively homosexual. Statistically then, if we consider the involvement of siblings of homosexual youth and parents who identify as gay or lesbian, as many as 9 student sin a classroom of 30 could be affected by homosexual issues (AFSC Gay/lesbian Youth Program, 1991). Given the high at-risk status of gay and lesbian students and the potential number of individuals involved, there appears to be a substantial population in need of support from our schools and, especially, our school counselors.

Little empirical evidence is available to provide information about the issues gay and lesbian students face in our nation's schools or about the services provided for them. A content review of three major journals available to school counselors (*Journal of Counseling and Development, The School Counselor*, and *Elementary School Guidance and Counseling*) for the 11-year period from August 1984 to August 1995, yielded a total of 14 articles dealing with homosexuality, excluding the Special Issue Vol. 68 of the *Journal of Counseling and Development.* Of these14, only five were found in *The School Counselor*, none were found in the *Elementary School Guidance* and *Counseling* journal. The majority of these existing articles however, were either normative essays that identified the needs of homosexual students and called for various professionals to respond to them or were discussions of ethical issues related to counselors and HIV clients. Few contained empirical evidence.

One exception is the work of Price and Telljohann (1991), who sought to identify the extent of the contact that secondary and junior high school counselors had had with homosexual adolescents. In addition, they assessed such varied issues as the type of services provided to these youth, counselors' knowledge of homosexual issues, training counselors had received, and the attitudes school counselors held toward homosexuality. Their data dispel the myth that counseling gay and lesbian students is an infrequent activity in our public schools. An overwhelming majority (71%) of their sample of high school and junior high counselors (N=289) indicated that they had counseled at least one gay or lesbian student.

Most of these students (58%) sought counseling on their own; only 18% having been referred by classroom teachers. Although they were optimistic about their findings, Price and Telljohann noted that theirs was the first study to examine school counselors' experiences and perceptions of adolescent homosexuality and cautioned about excessive generalization of their results. They also cautioned about the possibility of a sampling bias in that counselors who were more supportive of gay and lesbian issues might have been more inclined to return their surveys, despite the high response rate.

The study presented here is designed to replicate aspects of Price and Telljohann's (1991) work and to extend it in several ways. First, data were collected from K-12 counselors because it was believed that counseling needs can exist at any grade level. (For example, an elementary school student may have gay or lesbian parents or have a gay or lesbian adolescent sibling.) Evidence supports the fact that many more adolescents will question their sexual identity than will actually claim a homosexual identity; therefore, school counselors may frequently work with students who are struggling with sexual identity issues but who would not, using Price and Telljohann's criteria, be included in their results because they did not identify themselves as gay or lesbian. The current study extends existing information by including data regarding current school environments and policies toward both racial and sexual minorities. School counselors' knowledge about homosexual issues (for example, causes and frequency of homosexuality) was also surveyed. Information was also collected on issues of professional development, that is, how counselors acquired their knowledge of homosexuality and what they perceived as resources that would be helpful to them and other school personnel in expanding their knowledge.

METHOD

Participants
Some 250 surveys were distributed at the Annual Conference of the Pennsylvania School Counselors' Association (PSCA) in April 1995. A total of 101 surveys (29%) were returned for analysis from 22 men and 79 women. The mean age for the group of respondents was 42.4 years, with a range from 24-58. The vast majority (96%) were European American, 2% were African American, and 2% did not respond to the question about ethnic identity.

Two categories of school counselors, elementary and junior/senior high school, composed the responding groups. The largest proportion of counselors was junior/senior high school counselors (N=55, 56%); 43 (43%)

were elementary school counselors. Both gender and school type (elementary or junior/senior high school) distributions of respondents were determined to be representative of the overall distribution of PSCA membership statistics. The average length of time participants served as a school counselor across all work settings was 11 years. Less than one-half (40%) of respondents reported that they were members of the American School Counselor Association.

The majority of respondents (56%) were from moderately-sized schools (501-1,000 students); 22% worked in schools with 1-501 students. Larger schools (1,001-1,500) were the setting for 13% of the respondents. Only 5% were employed in schools having student populations over 1,500 students. The location of schools was predominantly rural (38%); suburban locations accounted for 37% of the settings. About 1 in 10 counselors (13%) was from inner city schools.

To summarize, the typical respondent was a 42-year-old white female from either a junior or senior high school setting with 11 years of work experience in a small-to-moderately-sized school in a rural or suburban setting.

Survey instrument

The instrument used in this study, the School Counselor Survey of Sexual Minority Youth Issues (SCSSMY), was an expansion of the survey used by Price and Telljohann (1991). It consisted of 23 items about school counselors' experiences with homosexual youth and students who were questioning their sexual identity. The 4-page SCSSMY was divided into five sections:

I.   Demographic Information, which consisted of questions about gende,r age, race, years of guidance experience, ASCA membership, employment setting, school size and school location.
II. Personal Experiences, which assessed professional encounters with gay or lesbian students and/or those questioning their sexual identity, the types of problems presented by these students, and source(s) of referrals.
III. School Environment, the level of homophobia perceived, incidents of harassment, and any existing anti-discrimination policies.
IV. Perceptions Regarding Homosexuality, which was a list of commonly-held beliefs regarding the causes of homosexuality that was similar to the items utilized by Price and Telljohann (1991).
V.   Professional Development, which assessed levels of competence, sources of knowledge, and desire for further training on counseling homosexual students.

344 • SCHOOL COUNSELING PRINCIPLES

Responses were recorded in three formats. Yes/No responses were provided for questions about direct experience. Check lists were used to identify types of student concerns, counseling actions taken, and sources of knowledge of homosexual issues. The remaining items employed a five-point Likert-type scale, which solicited degrees of agreement (Strongly Agree/More tolerant/Great Deal to Strongly Disagree/Less Tolerant/Very Little) on attitudinal and perception items.

The SCSSMY was introduced to participants through an accompanying cover letter that explained the purpose of the study, guaranteed anonymity and confidentiality, and provided directions for returning the surveys.

Procedure

The surveys and cover letters were distributed at the PSCA Conference, which was attended by approximately 675 school counselors, counselor educators, and graduate students. Counselors, either individually or in small groups, were approached by the author or one of her graduate students, provided a brief overview of study, and asked if they would be willing to complete the SCSSMY. Completed surveys were to be returned to a collection box in the main conference area. Of the 101 surveys (29%) collected, 98 were returned to the survey return box and 3 were mailed directly to the author, an alternative return format that was offered in the cover letter. As the surveys had been distributed anonymously, no method was available for followup on unreturned SCSSMYs.

This method of distribution, although not random, afforded a unique opportunity for direct dialogue with respondents that provided valuable qualitative information, which will be discussed in the last section of this article.

RESULTS

Counselors' Experiences

Both junior/senior high and elementary school counselors had substantial experience counseling students with sexual identity issues. More than half (51%) of the junior/senior high school counselors who responded reported that they had experience working with at least one student who was confused about sexual identity issues; 42% had worked directly with at least one self-identified gay or lesbian student.

As might be expected due to students' developmental levels, elementary counselors had fewer such experiences. Nonetheless, it is noteworthy that at least 21% of elementary school counselors knew of students in their schools who were either identifying as gay or lesbian and/or questioning their sexual identity.

Counselors were also asked to indicate the gender of students with whom they had contact. Overall, male students were more likely than females to seek assistance. Elementary school counselors had seen a total of nine students (five male; four female) who were questioning their sexual identity. Junior/senior high counselors saw a total of 104 such students (63 male; 41 female). Self-identified homosexual students were also more commonly male than femalel (37 gay males and 25 lesbians had been seen.)

As might be expected, at the elementary level the frequency of contact increased with increasing grade levels. The majority of contact with students was in grades five and six. Junior and senior high school counselors' patterns of contact were similar, with the frequency peaking in grades 10 and 11.

A list of mental health problems was provided and counselors were asked to indicate the types of problems presented by their gay and lesbian students. As only three elementary counselors (7%) had seen students who self-identified as gay or lesbian, the summary data below is only for junior/senior high counselors. Counselors were asked to check all problems each student presented or discussed.

The three most common problems of homosexual students – poor self-esteem (33%), depression (32%), and self-doubt (31%) – can be broadly grouped into sense-of-self issues. In many ways, these results support prior findings of the effects of marginal group status, in the social stigmatization tends to create a negative self-concept.

Specific fears composed a second cluster of presenting problems. Fear of disclosure to peers (26%) and parents (22%) as well as fear of rejection by family (24%) was the second-highest cluster of reported problems. The high need for secrecy that gay and lesbian students maintain requires a tremendous expenditure of psychic energy. Attempts to avoid exposure create social distance from peers and family, which, in turn, enhances feelings of difference and social isolation, a problem reported by 24% of the students. Robinson (1994) indicated social isolation to be the biggest factor for any minority group member struggling for acceptance within the larger group. Homosexual students appear to be no exception to this isolation, even though their minority status is based on a nonvisible characteristic.

Although a recent study of homosexual adolescents seeking services from an urban mental health service reported that more than 30% had attempted suicide (Remafedi, Farrow & Deisher, 1991), the current findings are more in line with earlier reports that 39% of lesbians and 40% of gay males had either attempted or seriously contemplated suicide (Jay and Young, 1979). The counselors reported that 22% of students had seriously thought about suicide or had attempted at least once in the past (15%). Current estimates of overall high school sudent suicide attempts range from 6 to 13% (Garland & Zigler, 1993; Schneider , Farberow & Kruks, 1989), so it appears that gay and lesbian students from the schools surveyed in this study are at a slightly or moderately higher risk than students in general.

The threat or occurrence of verbal harassment was reported more frequently by students (24%) than any fears of physical violence (11%). Counselors reported that students in their schools were more concerned with verbal and other forms of abuse than with acts of physical violence by their peers. This finding is supported by actual counselor observations of abuse incidents of gay and lesbian students (see School Environment below).

Few students who self-identified as gay or lesbian reported to their counselors a desire to change their sexual identity (6%) or experienced difficulty resolving their sexual identity with their religious beliefs (2%).

The majority of gay and lesbian students (51%) actually seen by counselors were self-referred. Fewer than 1 in 16 (5.5%) students were referred by classroom teachers or other school personnel. Counselors indicated that 1 in 8 times (13%) they themselves identified the students as in need of assistance and sought them out.

School Environment

This section of the SCSSMY was designed to assess school climate for gay and lesbian students by surveying such things as incidents of harassment and the existence of any school antidiscrimination/antiharassment policies.

Among junior/senior high school counselors, 22% reported being aware of at least one openly gay male or lesbian student in their schools. A total of 11 gay male and 16 lesbian students were known to this responding group. At the elementary level, only two gay male students were known to openly identify as homosexual.

Schools that do not actively provide for the protection of minority group members implicitly lend support to their marginal citizenship status. Toleration of incidents of harassment is one manifestation of this implicit support. Thirty-three percent of junior/senior high counselors reported observing over 43 separate incidents of harassment of students believed to be gay or lesbian. In addition, 26% of elementary school counselors reported awareness of 19 such incidents. The content of this harassment took the form of such benign activities as name calling, teasing, ridicule, and exclusion by fellow students to more severe forms such as physical intimidation, pushing, hitting and shoving. One counselor stat-

TABLE 1. MEAN RATING OF COUNSELORS' PERCEPTIONS OF GROUP ATTITUDES TOWARD HOMOSEXUALITY

Responding Group	Students	Faculty	Administrators
Elementary School	2.15	2.65	2.77
Junior/Senior High School	2.04	2.44	2.76

Note: 5-point scale with 5=unsupportive, 3=neutral, 1=intolerant

ed that a male student had quit school because of continuous homophobic comments made to him. Counselors indicated that such harassment was ongoing because of such things as appearing effeminate or having parents who were gay or lesbian.

School policies to protect racial minorities against harassment were more common than policies to protect sexual minorities. In 66% of junior/senior high schools, policies existed to protect racial minorities. Only 44% of these schools had policies to protect sexual minority students. Fifty-eight percent of elementary schools had racial discrimination policies, whereas only 35% had antiharassment policies to protect homosexual youth.

Table 1 presents results of counselors' assessments of the attitudes of their students, faculty, and administrators toward homosexuality. The average response was 2.4 across all grade levels and constituents (students, faculty and administrators). That is, no group within the school was perceived by counselors to be neutral toward the subject of homosexuality. To the contrary, counselors believed that students, faculty and administrators all hold views that range from negative to intolerant, with administrators faring best. In the counselors' assessments, administrators were rated closest to neutral (M=2.7), and students were rated as possessing the least tolerant attitudes (M=2.1).

Various articles found in the general press and in counseling literature have helped to create visibility for gay and lesbian issues in recent years. Several special issues of eminent journals have been devoted to the counseling needs of gays and lesbians (*Journal of Counseling and Development*,1989; *The Counseling Psychologist*, 1991). Given this visibility and the nonpathological perspective of the articles, it seems reasonable to expect that attitudes toward homosexuality might have become, over the past few years, more tolerant. When asked whether any shift in attitude of students, faculty and administrators had taken place in their institutions over the past 10 years, the counselors responded that there had been little change. On a five-point scale (1 = less tolerant, 3 = no change, 5 = more tolerant), average ratings across settings and constituents was 3.2, slightly above a no-change position. Although these data are distressing, a more positivistic interpretation could be that at least there has been no regression toward less tolerant views. When asked to assess any change in their own level of homophobic attitudes over the past 10 years, counselors rated their own progress more positively. That is, their overall self-rating averaged 3.9, which indicates movement in a more tolerant direction.

Literature on positive minority identity development strongly indicates the need for positive adult role models. For gay and lesbian students, having a faculty member, counselor, and/or administrator who is gay or lesbian could fill such a need. Counselors were asked if any faculty member or administrator in their school was openly gay or lesbian. Six counselors, all at the high school level, indicated there was at least one faculty member at their school who was out.

Although the sexual orientation of respondents was not solicited by the SCSSMY, two respondents indicated in the Comment section that they were homosexual. It is unclear whether these two individuals were part of the six out faculty noted above.

Knowledge of Homosexual Issues

Counselors were given a list of eight commonly held beliefs about the causes of homosexuality and asked to rate, on a 5-point scale, the degree to which they believed each contributed to the formation of a homosexual identity. Table 2 provides overall mean ratings and the percent of counselors who selected each item grouped by either (a) No Contribution = 0, (b) Low Contribution = 1 and 2, or (c) High Contribution = 4 and 5. Although counselors did not appear to support the idea that students chose a gay or lesbian lifestyle due to a lack of heterosexual options or the influence of a gay or lesbian adult, commonly held myths, they did believe that a homosexual lifestyle was chosen by the person. "Choice as a lifestyle" was seen as significantly more of a contributor than the other factors provided. One implication of this finding is that students may potentially be able to be counseled into choosing a heterosexual lifestyle also.

The majority of counselors (55%) estimated that only 1% to 5% of their student population was homosexual. This finding defies evidence that estimates approximately 10% of the population is predominantly homosexual (Kinsey, Pomeroy & Martin, 1949). Only one in five counselors believed their student population consisted of between 6% to 10% of gay/lesbian students. Eleven percent of school counselors (mainly ele-

TABLE 2. COUNSELORS' RATINGS OF FACTORS CONTRIBUTING TO A HOMOSEXUAL IDENTITY

Contributing Factors	Percentages			Mean
	None	Low	High	
Choice as a Lifestyle	6	23	44	4.02
Childhood Sexual Experience	10	28	35	3.63
Hormone Imbalances	14	25	33	3.62
Heredity	14	25	31	3.60
Parental Upbringing	11	31	33	3.60
Negative Heterosexual Experience	13	34	27	3.31
Influence of Gay/ Lesbian Adult	18	35	20	3.10
No Heterosexual Options	24	37	15	2.74

Note: % = percent of respondents who selected each item; Mean Rating = average rating on a scale of 0 = no contribution, 1 and 2 = low contribution, and 4 and 5 = high contribution.

mentary counselors) even indicated that they had not one student who was gay or lesbian in their schools.

Professional Development

This section of the SCSSMY was designed to assess several areas of the counselors' perceptions and experiences. First, counselors were asked to rate, on a 5-point scale (1 = Not at All; 5 = Very), their own level of perceived competence in counseling sexual minority youth. Fewer than one in 10 (8%) indicated a high level of competence, and close to the same number (8%) indicated little to no competence whatsoever. The vast majority of counselors rated themselves as possessing varying levels of ability to counsel gay and lesbian youth, with a mean rating of 2.9. When asked about interest in obtaining further training in the area of counseling skills to deal with issues of sexual minority youth, 89% of responding counselors indicated interest of varying levels; 11% responded they had no such interest.

The major sources of knowledge from which counselors obtained information about homosexuality were, in descending order: professional journals (66%), mass media (56%), gay/lesbian friends (50%), workshops and professional conferences (37%), and textbooks (30%). Only 2% of the respondents reported any school in-service as providing information to them on homosexuality. Written responses in this category under "other" were informative. Three counselors indicated that they had obtained information from gay family members. Two counselors said their information came from personal experience as a homosexual. One individual attributed his or her knowledge base to "the Bible."

General Comments Section
At the completion of the SCSSMY, counselors were invited to add any additional comments they desired. Nineteen (19%) chose to do so. A review of these comments found they could be classified into three general groupings: (1) those supporting sexual minority students, (2) those holding negative attitudes, and (3) a neutral group that focused mainly on comments about the survey itself.

Comments of a neutral nature (37%) either provided insufficient information to categorize the response or were of a general survey format nature. That is, some referred to the survey format itself or situations about the respondents' work settings (For example, "How will you or will you be dealing with religious issues!?"; "I work in an elementary school. If a child is teased about being gay or lesbian is the most I deal with the subject. My principal would be upset if I talked about this often. I usually tell him when the subject comes up.").

The comments that were nonsupportive of gay and lesbian students (21%) cited a variety of reasons from personal beliefs and prejudices to religious beliefs. Although several counselors indicated that because of this bias they would refer such students to someone else for counseling, one counselor stated: "Gay/lesbians turn me off based on my own beliefs/prejudices. I find this morally reprehensible, yet as a counselor I am morally bound to help such a student. If a youngster approaches me, only then will I do what I must do, to inform myself, not be judgmental, and to offer appropriate counseling." Another stated, "Because of my religious belief, I believe that the gay/lesbian lifestyle is a sin! And is in contradiction to the Bible.... Please do not take me wrong, I hate the sin, but I love the person." One can only wonder about the type of counseling a gay or lesbian student might receive from someone holding such strongly negative attitudes.

Comments reflecting more counselor support and understanding were the second largest category (26%) of responses, and they mainly expressed concern for the intolerance in their schools and school boards. Several indicated their dismay over progress toward tolerance with these comments: "I live in a very traditional, socially narrow community, which still views feminism and racial minorities suspiciously. Tolerance for homosexuality will be a long time coming." Another noted the depressing reality of the lack of progress on many fronts: "In our school, the sadness is that differences of any kind (race, sexual orientation, handicaps) are not well tolerated. I personally have been verbally attacked because I am pro-choice. Welcome to backward, rural, redneck, Born-Again Christian America!"

DISCUSSION

Gay adolescents face the same developmental challenges as their hetero-sexual counterparts, with the added burden of attempting to incorporate a stigmatized sexual identity. Recent evidence suggests that schools provide little support for this latter task. Teachers either avoid the topic of homo-sexuality in their classrooms or, when discussed, more frequently present it in a negative manner. Nor do homosexual students view school coun-selors as someone with whom to share their problems (Sears, 1992; Telljohann & Price, 1993). Since the most common problem faced by gay youth is social, emotional, and cognitive isolation (Hetrick & Martin, 1987), schools appear to be barren wastelands to a needy proportion of students.

This study examined the extent to which school counselors had worked with two types of sexual identity issues – adolescents questioning their sexual identity and those clearly identifying as gay or lesbian. At the jun-ior and senior high school level, more than 93% of responding counselors saw students with these concerns, which is contrary to what many ele-mentary counselors believe – that is, the issue of homosexuality is devel-opmentally premature for their level of students. Some caution may be warranted in generalizing these results due to the relatively low response rate (29%) and the possibility that those counselors choosing to respond may more likely have been those who had some type of experience work-ing with gay or lesbian students.

In this study, many of the types of problems presented to counselors by gay and lesbian youth were similar to those documented in previous research – self-doubt, depression, poor self-esteem, social isolation, and fear of exposure to family and friends. Thirty-seven percent of counselors reported that the gay and lesbian youths they had seen had either made suicide attempts or contemplated suicide.

It appears that if gay or lesbian students are going to be seen by a school counselor, they will take the initiative themselves. If a counselor is perceived to be receptive, that counselor will see other homosexual students. More than half of the students cited in this study were self-referrals, which indicates that students felt comfortable approaching their counselors. It is interesting that the four counselors whose general comments fell in the negative attitude category did not report seeing any student who self-identified as gay or lesbian. It may be that gay and lesbian students are able to detect those counselors who are receptive to their struggles.

Given the reported high incidence of harassment and violence against students who are perceived as homosexual in our schools and the fact that perpetrators of violent antigay acts are usually groups of juvenile or young adult males, it is crucial to the mental and physical well-being of gay and lesbian students that counselors take an active role in advocating for services and policies for this group.

A particularly confusing finding in this study is that respondents indicated professional journals as their major source of information on homosexuality in light of the fact that only a total of five articles published over the past 11 years have been in the two primary school counseling journals, that is, *The School Counselor* and the *Elementary School Guidance and Counseling* journal. One wonders which journals are actually providing this information. Special issues such as this seem an appropriate place to start providing the needed skills and education for our school counselors to work effectively with our sexual minority youth population.

REFERENCES

American Friends Service Committee,Gay/Lesbian Program. (1991). *Manual for anti-bias training.* Seattle, WA.

Deisher, R.W. (1989). Adolescent homosexuality: Preface. *Journal of Homosexuality, 17*, xiii-xv.

Dressler, J. (1985). Survey of school principals regarding alleged homosexual teachers in   the classroom: How likely (really) is discharge? *University of Dayton Law Review, 10*(3), 599-620.

Garland, A.F., & Zigler, E. (1993). Adolescent suicide presentation: Current research and social policy implications. *American Psychologist, 48*, 169-182.

Gibson, P. (1989). Gay male and lesbian youth suicide. In *Report of the Secretary's Task force on Youth Suicide,* vol. 3, 110-142. U.S. Department of Health and Human Services. Washington, DC: U.S. Government Printing Office. DHHS Publication NO. (ADM)89-1632.

Governor's Task Force on Biased-Related Violence. (1988). *Final report* 2(1), 77-89. (Available from Division of Human Rights, 55 West 125th Street, New York, NY 10027.)

Herek, G.M. (1989). Hate crimes against lesbians and gay men. *The American Psychologist, 44*(6), 948-955.

Hetrick, E.S. & Martin, A.D. (1987). Developmental issues and their resolution for gay and lesbian adolescents. *Journal of Homosexuality, 14*, 25-43.

Jay, K., & Young, A. (1979). *The gay report: Lesbians and gay men speak out about sexual experiences and lifestyles.* New York: Summit.

Kinsey, A.C., Pomeroy, W.B. & Martin, C.E. (1949). *Sexual behavior in the human male.* Philadelphia, PA: W. B. Saunders.

Marino, T.W. (1995, May). To be young and gay in America. *Counseling Today,* Vol. 37(11), 1-8.

Pratt, J. (1995, September 22-24). Teens talk about sexuality . *USA Weekend*, 4-6.

Price, J.H., & Telljohann, S.K. (1991). School counselors' perceptions of adolescent homosexuals. *Journal of School Health, 61*(10), 433-438.

Remafedi , G., Farroe, J.A., & Deisher, R.W. (1991). Risk factors for attempted suicide in gay and bisexual youth. *Pediatrics, 87*(6), 869-875.

Robinson, K.E. (1994). Addressing the needs of gay and lesbian students: The school counselor's role. *The School Counselor, 41*, 326-332.

Rudolph, J. (1988). Counselors' attitudes toward homosexuality: A selective review of the literature. *Journal of Counseling and Development, 67*, 165-168.

Savin-Williams, R.C. (1990). Gay and lesbian adolescents. *Marriage and Family Review, 12*(3/4), 197-216.

Schneider, S.G., Farberow, N.L., & Kruks, G.N. (1989). Suicidal behavior in adolescent and young adult gay men. *Suicide and Life-Threatening Behavior, 19*, 381-394.

Sears, J.T. (1991). *Growing up gay in the South: Race, gender and journeys of the spirit.* New York: The Haworth Press, Inc.

Sears, J.T. (1992). Educators, homosexuality, and homosexual students: Are personal feelings related to professional beliefs? In K.M. Harbeck (Ed.), *Coming out of the classroom closet: Gay and lesbian students, teachers, and curricula* (pp. 29-79). Binghamton, NY: Harrington Park press.

Telljohann, S.K., & Price, J.H. (1993). A quantitative examination of adolescent homosexuals' life experiences: Ramifications for secondary school personnel. *Journal of Homosexuality, 26*(1), 41-56.

Unks, G. (1994). Thinking about the homosexual adolescent. *The High School Journal, 77*(1&2), 1-6.

CHAPTER FOUR
Working within Systems: Taking a Proactive Role within Schools

As stated in Chapter One, school counselors' roles are becoming increasingly multifaceted and complex in response to the growing diversity and increased accountability and standardization in American schools. In addition to their more traditional roles and responsibilities, school counselors are now becoming more responsible for serving as "mediators of culture" (Grant, 1977) within educational systems, meaning they have within their purview the responsibility of integrating healthy, positive and socially responsible understandings of, and approaches to, diverse students and an array of cultural differences into their counseling services as well as into the daily functioning of their schools. Thus, school counselors must actively work to reconceptualize their roles and engage in a simultaneous process of critical self- and systemic-reflection toward the goal of empowering themselves and their colleagues, as well as the students, families and community members with whom they work to engage in and experience a more equitable, student-centered and empowering educational process.

School counselors' role in our multicultural nation must be significantly deepened and expanded so they contribute to the affirmation and support of diverse students and communities and, further, to the countering of prejudice and injustice found in their schools and in the educational system more broadly. I believe that although social transformation must take place via systemic reform, schools are sites of immense possibility for some of this work to happen, and school counselors must be at the center of a collaborative effort toward this vision. From this perspective, schools, and the practitioners working within them, are viewed as active agents in a process of social change and transformation (Delpit, 1995; Erickson, 2004; Goldberg, 1994; Nieto, 2004).

An explicit, well-defined approach to the role of the multicultural school counselor can help school counselors to actualize multicultural ideals because it is thoughtful in its approach to the following: (1) issues of culture and cultural differences as they relate to schooling, counseling and education more broadly; (2) terminology and concepts surrounding race, ethnicity, culture and other aspects of identity; (3) the effects of power on pedagogy, schooling and school-based counseling practices; (4) making connections between schooling and larger systems of oppression; (5) challenging Eurocentric notions of knowledge and deficit orientations toward non-Western knowledge; (6) the role of schooling in the transformation of society; (7) academic achievement and its relationship to broader societal oppression; (8) the intersection of the personal and the political as it relates to the conduct of social life and specifically as it relates to pedagogical and counseling practices; (9) the need for educators to critically examine their biases and presuppositions in relation to race, social class and gender discrimination and to critically explore their own internalized Eurocentrism; and (10) the affirmation of the voices and realities of marginalized students, families and communities in educational and counseling processes.

The articles in this chapter individually and collectively contribute to a more sophisticated perspective on the multiple and complex roles of school counselors in the 21st century. Each article provides a specific vision of the multifaceted role of a multicultural school counselor as well as a roadmap, both conceptual and practical, to getting there. Moreover, the articles in this chapter contribute to an understanding of the multiple contexts that shape the work of school counselors, helping them to realize and appreciate the difficulty in, the need for, and the promise of, taking a proactive role as innovative multicultural practitioners and agents of change.

Fusick and Charkow Bordeau's (2004) "Counseling At-risk Afro-American Youth: An Examination of Contemporary Issues and Effective School-Based Strategies" focuses on the multifaceted role school counselors must play to provide support to their African-American students. According to the authors, this reconfigured role includes: (1) building relationships with diverse students and families through proactive outreach; (2) creating a sense of membership in the school community; (3) contributing to the creation and maintenance of a bias-free, safe environment; (4) helping set high expectations for all students along with the provision of necessary tools to reach their full potential personally, socially and academically; (5) providing comprehensive career development; and (6) helping students to develop positive ethnic and racial identities.

Eschenauer and Chen-Hayes' (2005) "The Transformative Individual School Counseling Model: An Accountability Model for Urban School Counselors" explores a model of urban school counseling that bridges the gap between research and practice, reconceptualizing urban school counselors as "school counselor-researchers" who create and utilize data for accountability purposes, thereby engaging in and contributing to evidence-based best practices. This article focuses on the importance of data-driven practice and inquiry-based decision making for school counselors working in urban contexts.

Lee's (2001) "Culturally Responsive School Counselors and Programs: Addressing the Needs of All Students" discusses the role of the school counselor as an agent of change who must work toward the development and maintenance of a culturally responsive school. The author suggests that school counselors develop comprehensive guidance and counseling programs that reflect the needs and realities of diverse students. Lee views the role of a culturally responsive school counselor as a facilitator of student development and as a student advocate who serves as a liaison and bridge between students, school and families, addressing divergences and making the system more responsive to culturally diverse communities.

McCall-Perez's (2000) "The Counselor as Advocate for English Language Learners: An Action Research Approach" presents an action research design in which the school counselor enlists the participation of numerous professional and community stakeholders in a site-based inquiry focused on issues relevant to English language learners. The author offers a model for school counselors to conduct their own professional needs assessment regarding their readiness to serve immigrants and adolescent English language learners. McCall-Perez suggests school counselors must understand their central role in the success of English language learners and that they must serve as advocates for this often marginalized and struggling student population.

Milsom and Hartley's (2005) "Assisting Students with Learning Disabilities Transitioning to College: What School Counselors Should Know" suggests that school counselors should play central roles as advocates, collaborators and direct service providers for students with learning disabilities, helping to prepare them for life after high school, including college. The authors suggest that school counselors should support students in a number of ways, including: (1) cultivating a collaborative approach to transition planning with special educators, (2) proactively addressing students' needs, (3) striving to develop working relationships with college personnel and (4) assisting students with college admissions.

Benedetto and Olisky's (2001) "Biracial Youth: The Role of the School Counselor in Racial Identity Development" addresses the role of the school counselor in assisting biracial youth to develop a positive racial identity. The article highlights interventions focusing on awareness of particular issues of biracialism to facilitate a secure biracial identity, provide students and staff with exposure to race and ethnicity and help to create a multiculturally sensitive atmosphere in which biracial students experience high levels of support, validation and acceptance from the counselors, educators and peers in their schools.

McFarland and Dupuis' (2001) "The Legal Duty to Protect Gay and Lesbian Students From Violence in School" discusses the responsibility of school counselors to support and ensure safety for gay and lesbian students through creating professional development for all staff around homophobia and heterosexism as well as providing school-based counseling and support groups for gay, lesbian and heterosexual students. The authors assert that the school counselor must function as "the leader of a coordinated effort to influence other school personnel and students in the effort to make the school environment more inviting for gay and lesbian students" (p. 177). The article provides strategies for school counselors such as disseminating information across the school and in each classroom as well as attending to their own professional development to acquire the skills and knowledge necessary to support and validate gay and lesbian students.

Lee's (2005) "Urban School Counseling: Context, Characteristics and Competencies" explores how school counselors can promote academic, career and personal-social development and success within the context of under-resourced urban schools in which there is pervasive academic failure. Lee asserts that urban school counselors must confront the complex contextual factors and structural dynamics that undermine school success for urban students and posits that they must shift from an individual focus to a systemic focus. Lee suggests that urban school counselors should collaborate with other educational stakeholders to bring about systemic change and to have more extensive involvement as leaders in the school and in the community more broadly.

Tarver-Behring, et al.'s (1998) "School Counselors and Full Inclusion for Children with Special Needs" discusses the ways in which the roles of school counselors have evolved within the context of educational reform. The authors suggest that school counselors must become informed and prepared to be active participants in facilitating the full inclusion of students with disabilities into general education classrooms. They assert that the role of the school counselor must include collaboration with general and special education teachers to provide consultation to teachers and services to students that help to promote successful full inclusion. Tarver-Behring, et al. suggest that school counselors, in addition to providing direct counseling services, must work to facilitate social adjustment by assisting teachers and students in understanding and promoting peer acceptance and helping teachers to implement social skills curricula. Further they argue that the school counselor's role in promoting inclusion must incorporate consulting with families and helping teachers learn to effectively collaborate with parents.

Looking across the myriad roles and responsibilities set out for school counselors in this chapter, it becomes clear that school counselors are being challenged to broaden their roles and deepen their knowledge and skills in unprecedented ways. It also becomes clear that "A school counselor cannot do it all" (Erford, 2003). Rather, as Bryan (2005) states, "[I]t is suggested that school counselors be actively involved in activities to engage their schools' stakeholders; this identifies school counselors as team facilitators, advocates and collaborators with members of their schools, families and communities..." (p. 223). Thus, as school counselors work to develop their knowledge base, skills and levels of awareness and to redefine their roles, one role that must span across specific domains and skills is that of the facilitator of collaboration and change with respect to issues of diversity and equity. This overarching role will help school counselors to enlist the support and buy-in of their colleagues as well as family and community advocates and service providers. This kind of comprehensive collaboration is necessary because, indeed, school counselors do not typically have the time or the resources to do everything alone. The articles in this chapter contribute significant understanding to the substantive and theoretical issues of central importance to support this kind of learning and practice. Together, they provide a vision for the kind of comprehensive role redefinition in which school counselors must engage in order to meet the demands of their profession in the 21st century.

Counseling At-Risk Afro-American Youth: An Examination of Contemporary Issues and Effective School-Based Strategies

By Lisa Fusick, M.S.Ed., and Wendy Charkow Bordeau, Ph.D., LPC, NCC

This article originally appeared in *Professional School Counseling*, Vol. 8, No. 2, 2004.

Many Afro-American children are considered to be "at-risk" due to a variety of social and economical factors. This article first reviews the effects of racism on Afro-American youth and examines the results of barriers caused by negative stereotyping within counseling services, schools, and communities. Next, a historical overview of issues and approaches used in counseling Afro-American youth in schools is presented, along with a discussion of the limitations of each. Lastly, practical implications for multicultural competence and effective contemporary interventions are recommended for school counselors to assist this population, via both direct counseling and consultation with other school, family, and community members. School counselors can utilize this information to enhance at-risk Afro-American students' ethnic identity development, as well as academic, career, social, and personal growth.

Since the publication of the National Commission on Excellence in Education's 1983 study, *A Nation at Risk*, educators and counselors across the country have struggled to identify and assist "atrisk" youth populations. By definition, any young person is "at risk" for educational and social failure when his or her potential for becoming a responsible and productive adult is limited by barriers at home, at school, or in the community. Risk factors – including racism, poverty, lack of parental supervision, illegal drug use, high school incompletion, teenage pregnancy, juvenile crime, and suicide – during the past decade have adversely affected a growing number of American children (McWhirter, McWhirter, McWhirter, & McWhirter, 1998).

Although at-risk factors affect youth of diverse racial and ethnic backgrounds, we chose to focus this review of counseling issues and strategies

---

[1] For the purposes of classification, all students identifying themselves as Afro-American, African American, Afro-Caribbean, and of African descent will be described in the more inclusive term of "Afro-American," and all students identifying themselves as Caucasian, White, or of European descent will be described in the more inclusive term of "Euro-American."

on atrisk Afro-American[1] youth for several reasons. First, recent psychological research has begun to focus on the widening achievement gap between Afro-American and Euro-American students (Barton, 2003; Harpalani & Gunn, 2003). Lower IQ and standardized test scores have raised many questions regarding societal and educational expectations and the preparedness of minority status students (Carlson & Lewis, 1993). Further, Afro-American youth are less likely than Euro-American youth to graduate from high school; national statistics indicate a graduation rate of 56 percent for Afro-American youth, as compared to 78 percent for Euro-American youth (Stanard, 2003). Contemporary statistics also indicate that Afro-American youth are significantly more likely than their Euro-American counterparts to face poverty, unemployment, teen pregnancy, victimization, and incarceration (Kempf-Leonard, Pope, & Feyerherm, 1995; Substance Abuse and Mental Health Administration [SAMHSA], 1999). As disproportionate numbers of Afro-American youth face risks to their safety, physical and mental health, and future success, we believe it is important to understand specialized risk factors and counseling interventions, particularly in light of past research that suggests that counseling services often are perceived as culturally insensitive to the needs of Afro-American clients (McDavis, Parker, & Parker, 1995).

Of course, this is not to suggest that all Afro-American children are "at-risk" or that suggested counseling interventions for Afro-American youth should be uniformly applied. Lee (1991) wisely counseled against assuming a monolithic perspective in which "all black people are the same and that one methodological approach is universally applicable in any counseling intervention with them" (p. 561). The inherent danger in discussing shared cultural factors is the inadvertent creation or propagation of stereotypes about Afro-Americans without respecting uniqueness and within-group variation. Therefore, we encourage counselors to use this information to further their understanding of potential issues facing Afro-American youth, but not to impose stereotypes (Boyd-Franklin, 1989; McDavis et al., 1995). Further, we hope to encourage counselors to examine not only risk factors, but also the strengths and potential that Afro-American youth bring to counseling relationships.

AT-RISK AFRO-AMERICAN YOUTH AND MULTICULTURAL COUNSELING ISSUES

School counselors nationwide are being called upon to provide support and empowerment for at-risk Afro-American youth (Muller, 2002; Nettles & Perna, 1997; Thompson & O'Quinn, 2001). The American School Counselor Association (ASCA) recently published a comprehensive national framework for school counselors that focuses on equitable access of direct services to all students (2002). Many school counselors and counselors-in-training have undergone cultural sensitivity training in an effort to understand the specific issues faced by many Afro-American youths and to develop multiculturally competent counseling approaches (Sue, Arrendondo, & McDavis, 1992). However, multicultural counselor training programs face many challenges in actually enhancing multicultural competence; although multicultural training has been associated with counselors' self-perceived multicultural counseling competence and case-conceptualization abilities, little data currently exist to indicate whether and how this training impacts the actual work between counselors and diverse students (Constantine, 2001). The ASCA National Model (2002) challenges school counselors and administrators to be accountable for their practice and to demonstrate the effectiveness of their work in "measurable terms," such as results reports, adherence to performance standards, and program audits (p. 2). Therefore, counselor education efforts toward increased multicultural competence similarly require measurable accountability data to ensure the provision of high-quality counseling services.

Unfortunately, many traditional counseling and training programs are still ill-prepared to meet the contemporary needs of Afro-Americans in counseling, as these programs often are based on theories and clinical experiences with middle-class, Euro-American clientele (Graham, 1992; Jones, 1990; Sue & Zane, 1987). Most counseling models are built upon traditional European values such as individuality, uniqueness, and survival of the fittest, which conflicts with traditional African principles of cooperation, collective responsibility, and survival of the group (Mays, 1985; Nobles, 1976). This majority status culture bias leads to the phenomenon of labeling behaviors that differ from mainstream or Euro-American norms as "deviant" or "pathological" (Miller, 1993).

Further, traditional counseling models may lead to discomfort, misdiagnosis, and perceived counselor insensitivity among Afro-American clients (Lewis-Fernández & Kleinman, 1994). Three theories that are almost universally taught in counseling programs today are person-centered therapy, cognitive-behavioral therapy, and psychoanalysis (Corey, 1996). Though these theories entail many aspects helpful to developing strong counseling relationships, they may not always be appropriate for at-risk Afro-American clients. For example, person-centered therapy advocates a nondirective approach, which may be ineffective for Afro-American clients who may be more comfortable, especially in the critical beginning point of counseling, with structure and evidence of solutions to problems (Ziter, 1987). Youth who are facing very realistic problems that require immediate action may perceive a nondirective approach that places the direction of the counseling solely on the client as disrespectful or unhelp-ful. In addition, the psychoanalytic concept of resistance may hinder counselors working with Afro-American youth as they mistake the child's appropriate preliminary mistrust as a refusal on the client's part to truly work in therapy or as indicative of psychic conflict (Corey). Finally, cogni-tive therapies that place the locus of change or control on the child's thought processes may not pay enough attention to the influence of sys-temic qualities, such as racism and the socioeconomic residual effects of slavery, on the client's world view and life circumstances.

Additionally, much of the past literature in the mental health field has racist overtones and encourages the misdiagnosis and mistreatment of Afro-American clients (Atwell & Azibo, 1992; Bulhan, 1985; Greene, 1985; Jones, 1990; Mays, 1985). Current counseling and mental health-related systems continue to discriminate against Afro-Americans by focus-ing on pathology rather than goals, although the discrimination occurs in much more subtle forms (SAMHSA, 1999). For example, the problems of misdiagnosis and mistreatment are exacerbated by the uniform use of biased assessment instruments and diagnostic criteria designed for the majority status population in evaluation and treatment planning (Jones; Mays; Smart & Smart, 1997). Therefore, it should come as no surprise that many Afro-Americans often are reluctant to seek counseling and there is a tendency of Afro-Americans to frequently terminate counseling services after only one session (McDavis et al., 1995; Terrell & Terrell, 1984).

Counselors providing multiculturally competent counseling services to at-risk Afro-American youth must be aware of the origins of this popula-tion's initial "healthy cultural paranoia," or understandable wariness, toward counseling and should work to prevent unintentionally furthering these discriminatory practices (Ridley, 1984). Additionally, multiculturally competent counselors recognize the impact of racism on psychological health and understand that the subjugated history of Afro-Americans in the United States affects the current perceptions and barriers surrounding Afro-American identity and achievement. Accurate conceptualizations of Afro-American clients cannot occur without acknowledging the insidious nature of racism, which can force Afro-Americans to negotiate a bicultur-al identity to function in both the majority status and marginalized cul-tures (Wilson & Stith, 1997; Ziter, 1987). For example, Afro-American students experiencing academic, behavioral, and emotional difficulties in school may be struggling with institutional racism and stereotyping that have been undetected or ignored by administrators and teachers, or they may be employing coping tactics such as "stereotype threat" as survival mechanisms in a perceived hostile environment (Sue & Sue, 2003).

To facilitate therapeutic relationships, competent Euro-American counselors serving Afro-American children must first be prepared to deal with
their clients' historical hostility, feelings of mistrust, and fear resulting from
300 years of oppression (Vontress & Epp, 1997). Counselors quickly must
develop rapport and trust to alleviate any mistrust or skepticism Afro-
American children might feel. Counselors can establish trust by first clarifying the relationship between counselor and client and the nature of the referral, and by discussing confidentiality (Harris, 1995). Counselors must be
careful not to mistake the Afro-American client's possible preliminary resistance, mistrust, and hesitancy to self-disclose as a refusal on the child's part
to engage in therapy; rather, Afro-American clients are likely to work hard
and succeed with therapy when given ample opportunity for sensitive relationship development (Corey, 1996; Ridley, 1984; Sanchez- Hucles, 2000).

Several researchers have suggested that Afro-American children and
adults prefer same-race counselors (Bass & Coleman, 1997; Lee, 1991;
Muller, 2002) and might therefore fare better in counseling with Afro-
American counselors. Jones (1991) noted that Afro-American clients
referred to Afro-American counselors frequently say "they would not feel
comfortable talking with a white person about their problems; they do
not feel that a white therapist will understand them; they cannot be convinced of the white therapist's interest in them; they feel too angry with
whites to be able to focus on anything else in their presence" (p. 653).
However, as a shortage of Afro-American counselors exists in the nation's
schools and communities, all counselors must work to assist at-risk Afro-
American youth (Muller; SAMHSA, 1999). Further, current research indicates that Afro-American youth initially view the counselor's interpersonal
skills and ability to establish rapport of utmost importance, regardless of
the counselor's race (Holcomb-McCoy & Moore-Thomas, 2001; Muller).
According to Boyd-Franklin (1989), "the person-to-person connection is
the most important in work with Afro-Americans" (p. 97). Ultimately,
effective counselor-assisted ethnic identity development and the completion of related tasks in therapy are more beneficial to the client than the
racial match between counselor and client.

Counselors of all races and ethnicities have the potential to work successfully with Afro-American youth when they have engaged in active
exploration and resolution of their biases and make a commitment to furthering their own multicultural knowledge and skills. To aid clients in the
development of effective racial identity, multiculturally competent counselors must first be aware of both their own misconceptions toward people of other races and the differential counseling needs of their Afro-
American clientele (Jones, 1990; Sue, Arredondo, & McDavis, 1992).
Afro-American clients generally are very attuned to subtle racist commu-

nicative nuances and other nonverbal messages expressed by the counselor, and these subliminal "vibes" determine whether the client will be treated with respect in a safe environment (Boyd-Franklin, 1989).

Counselors must be careful to avoid communication that appears to be condescending or patronizing. Stances taken by Euro-American counselors that can be detrimental to their relationships with Afro-American clients include paternalism, in which the "omnipotent" counselor attempts to solve the problems of the disadvantaged client, often fueled by guilt over racism (Boyd-Franklin, 1989). Euro-American counselors, in an effort to avoid confrontation with Afro-American clients, also might unquestioningly comply with the rhetoric of "Afro-American power," adopt a subservient role in the relationship, speak ebonics or use "black slang" to connect with the client, or show too much admiration for the ability of Afro-Americans to "work the system" (Boyd-Franklin). All of these behaviors will likely be viewed by the Afro-American youth as patronizing, inauthentic, and contraindicative to effective counseling.

Although counselor-client race homogeneity may enhance perceptions of therapeutic relationships with Afro-American clients, Afro-American counselors also must be aware of their biases and potential toward cultural insensitivity. For example, Afro-American counselors working with Afro-American clients may exhibit patterns such as moralizing, overidentifying with the client, rescuing, premature problem solving, and advice giving. These approaches, while well-meaning, also are detrimental to the client's ability to function independently (Boyd-Franklin, 1989; Hunt, 1987).

Hardin and Wampold (2001) suggested that one method counselors can use to establish rapport with Afro-American youth is to consider their own situation-dependent coping strategies when dealing with diversity. As Afro-American youth tend to express disdain for cultural "wannabees," or people who deny their own identity when trying to fit into another group, counselors who attempt to assimilate too quickly with client culture will likely be disregarded by their clientele. When creating therapeutic alliances and conceptualizing client concerns with Afro-American clients, counselors will likely benefit from informally assessing clients' acculturation styles and coping strategies for dealing with diversity. For example, a student "who attempts to assimilate into a predominantly White school environment and is rejected will have one set of concerns and a student of color who uses a separation strategy in that context will present with a very different set of issues" (Hardin & Wampold). Ramseur (1991) asked the question, "Do blacks and whites differ in their appraisal of the severity or meaning of different stressors?" and discussed several important factors related to Afro-Americans' resiliency, including religious orientation and reliance on informal social networks (p. 372). Ramseur also addressed a key stressor that is more prevalent for Afro-Americans than Euro-Americans: racial discrimination, and the economic, social, academic, and career barriers that accompany it.

Whereas counselors will fail to gain rapport with Afro-American clients if they behave in accordance with stereotypes or biases, it does not benefit the counselor-client relationship if counselors claim to be "color blind" and counsel all clients in similar ways regardless of race. To be blind to race is to ignore the impacts of race and racism. Greene (1985) advised that "clinicians cannot accurately assess and interpret the meaning of behavior (i.e., what is healthy or maladaptive) without an awareness of the norms of a particular client's cultural environment" (p. 390). The client's ethnicity or race, and how one is treated by society based on his or her cultural background, is an integral part of identity formation; counselors should therefore convey to their clients the message that race and culture are important, are valued, and are worthy of focus in counseling (Boyd-Franklin, 1989).

Jones (1991) proposed that all Afro-Americans face distinct psychological tasks and has developed an interactive model that addresses reactions to racial oppression, that is, coping mechanisms; the influence of both the majority status and home cultures on Afro-Americans' formulation of identity and lifestyle; and individual and family experiences and strengths. Lee (1991) cited several social and economic factors affecting the mental health of Afro-Americans, including limited access and glass ceilings, double standards, exclusion and isolation, powerlessness, voicelessness and invisibility, token status, second guessing, pigeonholing, guilt by association and group stereotyping, and ethnic identity conflict issues.

Counseling supervisors should assist school counselors working with Afro-American youth to avoid perpetuating these stressors and to combat common errors made in counseling minority status clients, such as expecting cooperation from the client as proof of counselor competence, bombarding the client with too many questions early on in the process, and hiding behind the professional role of therapist – practices that hinder the development of rapport (Hunt, 1987). In addition, supervisors can help counselors reveal maladaptive patterns of relating (e.g., self-effacing, moralizing, rescuing) to Afro-American clients. Techniques beneficial for this type of supervision include (a) facilitating concrete practice, (b) viewing tapes of counseling sessions to isolate times in which cultural conflicts are present, (c) helping the supervisee identify the impact of the client's "cooperation" level on himself or herself, (d) assisting the trainee to understand the impact of counselor anxiety on the client, and (e) using role reversal exercises in which the supervisor plays the client and then processes the experience with the trainee. See Table 1 for a listing of potential counseling barriers, strategies, and limitations in addressing these barriers.

Finally, the goal of multiculturally competent counselors and supervisors should be to facilitate a process of empowerment in which the client gains a sense of personal control and self-efficacy in order to "reduce the powerlessness of Afro-American clients" (Ziter, 1987, p. 131). This emphasis on empowerment differs from the traditional therapeutic goal of adjustment, in which clients were encouraged to accept and cope with current living conditions (Thomas & Dansby, 1985). Instead, the multiculturally competent counselor acknowledges racism and its effects, and he or she works actively with the client to accomplish victories, effect change in discriminatory social structures, and combat patterns of learned helplessness (Seligman, 1975).

AT-RISK AFRO-AMERICAN YOUTH IN THE SCHOOLS

In addition to the possible counseling biases already discussed, school-based counselors need to be aware of the disturbing inequities that exist in predominantly Afro-American urban school districts, where nearly 40 percent of Afro-American students attend school in the United States (Nettles & Perna, 1997). The conditions in public schools funded under Title I of the Elementary and Secondary Education Act of 1965 are generally far inferior to those in suburban schools, including the danger of asbestos and poor quality drinking water (Kozol, 1991). Afro-American students in these districts frequently have fewer resources, such as updated textbooks and access to modern technology. Students in city schools often are forced to rely on public transportation instead of the convenience and safety of school buses. Afro-American students often are uncomfortable and may feel unsafe in their school environments and in their travels to and from school. On the surface, possible causes for perceptions of insecurity and danger include the common presence of security guards, metal detectors, weapons, and gangs in city schools. More than twice the percentage of Afro-American students as Euro-American students in grades 6 through 12 reported the presence of security guards in their schools, with more than 6 times the presence of metal detectors (Nettles & Perna).

Rather than simply adding conventional security measures at schools, we must address the root causes of fear, anxiety, and danger among at-risk student populations to genuinely change the school environment and student potential for the better. First, the underrepresentation of Afro-American teachers, counselors, and principals to serve as role models has been cited as a serious problem in contemporary schools. According to Nettles and Perna (1997), Afro-American teachers make up approximately 7% of public school teachers and just 3% of private school teachers,

TABLE 1: COUNSELING BARRIERS, RECOMMENDED STRATEGIES, AND LIMITATIONS

Counseling Barrier	Recommended Strategy	Limitations
Counselor bias	Self-exploration, supervision, cultural sensitivity training, coursework in multiculturally competent counseling; awareness of nonverbal gestures	Counselor's willingness to explore personal biases and admit prejudices
Counselor ignorance of client population and effective strategies	Self-exploration, supervision, consultation, diversity training, extensive reading, targeted workshops, seminars, coursework; awareness of overgeneralizations and stereotypes	Counselor's access to resources and commitment to change
Counselor rescuing	Self-awareness of "rescuer"tendencies; explorationof personal biases and feelings of guilt; awareness of paternal approach and/or feelings toward client	Limited research on this topic
Counselor oversympathizing	Self-awareness of counselor anxiety; role reversal exercises with supervisor, colleagues; authenticity and genuineness	Limited research on this topic

Counseling Barrier	Recommended Strategy	Limitations
Cultural conflict between client and counselor	Awareness; confrontation; exploration of racial issues and concept of identity; taping and reviewing sessions; peer mediation and conflict resolution	The presence of cultural conflict tends to be minimized or ignored in institutions; limited research on this topic
Client resistance	Counselor patience; establishment of rapport and trust; awareness of countertransference	Client tends to be blamed for lack of progress, rather than encouraged; high termination rate
Client mistrust	Counselor awareness and acknowledgment of historical hostility; rapport and trust-building; awareness of client's personal impact on counselor; directive approach	Same as above; client's efforts to seek help marginalized and/or acknowledged
Client ignorance of counseling process	Counselor explanation of counseling process, goals, and mutual expectations; informed consent; explanation of confidentiality as applied to minors	With Afro-American youth, referral to a counselor is often in conjunction with disciplinary efforts and is viewed as a punishment
Client bias	Counselor patience; mutual examination of bias and prejudices, in context of hindering counseling progress; possible referral	Client has little opportunity to vent anger and/or hostility; discouraged from expressing and exploring bias

which is disproportionate to both Afro-American representation in the U.S. population (~13%) and Afro-American representation among the nation's public school students (~17%). To alleviate this disparity, Ladson-Billings (1994) recommended recruiting teachers and counselors who have expressed "a desire and an interest to work with Afro-American students" (p. 131).

Second, educational personnel must recognize that Afro-American students appear to be as ready to learn and succeed as their Euro-American counterparts (Nettles & Perna, 1997). However, potential does not necessarily directly translate to achievement. Lee (2001) suggested that multiculturally competent and culturally competent school initiatives are based on "the premises that (1) all young people can learn and want to learn; and (2) cultural differences are real and cannot be ignored" (p. 2). In a sample of 40,000 suburban secondary students surveyed by the Minority Student Achievement Network (2001), 40% of Afro-American students reported having grade averages at or below satisfaction level, despite having positive attitudes about education (Fletcher, 2002). A recent National Assessment of Educational Progress report indicated that by the eighth grade, students who are Afro-American, Latino, and economically disadvantaged are approximately four grades behind other students in terms of school achievement. By 12th grade, the average 17-year-old Afro-American student is at the same academic level as the typical Euro-American 13-year-old (Haycock, Jerald, & Huang, 2001). Other studies show that Afro-American children from low socioeconomic status families enter school less prepared than their peers from more advantaged backgrounds (Connell & Prinz, 2002; Thompson & O'Quinn, 2001). Therefore, ameliorating schoolrelated difficulties of Afro-American youth entails close work with wider community contexts to prevent the many negative effects of poverty and socioeconomic inequalities. However, poverty and a lack of resources should not excuse schools from also working within their walls to enrich at-risk students' learning experiences.

According to Haycock, Jerald, and Huang (2001),

The American education system has been in thrall to a myth for more than 30 years. The myth says that student achievement has much more to do with a child's background than with the quality of instruction he or she receives. ... The myth is powerful. It is pervasive. And it is wrong. No one who has visited as many urban classrooms as we have would argue that poverty and racism don't make both teaching and learning more challenging. But more challenging doesn't mean impossible. All across the country, there are examples of high-poverty schools that perform at or near the top on state tests. (p. 5)

Additional explanations offered for the achievement gap between Afro-American and Euro-American students include a mismatch between Afro-American learning styles and Euro-centric curricula, a lack of cultural affirmation in the schools, a lack of home-based enrichment, overpopulated classrooms, and difficulty attracting highly qualified teachers to at-risk school districts (Barton, 2003; Bass & Coleman, 1997; Carlson & Lewis, 1993; Robelen, 2002). These conditions must be remedied for at-risk Afro-American students to achieve their potential and contribute to a safe and harmonious school environment.

White and Johnson (1991) challenged the stereotypes revolving around Afro-American achievement and motivation, noting that "the assumption is made that a standard of excellence is embedded in urban schools and that black children and youth are not motivated to compete with these standards" (p. 412). These authors discussed the possibility that Afro-American children have been socialized according to different norms, including the belief that "black children and youth are not educable," and that certain goals are not attainable for all (p. 413). A particularly relevant quote to the present argument is that "black children and youth are encouraged to stay on the same conveyor belt notwithstanding the fact that they do not inherit the same range of choices" (p. 414). Counselors serving Afro-American youth must first facilitate the process of choice, empowerment, and availability of equal opportunities for their students before focusing on inconsistencies in performance.

As Knowles and Prewitt (1969) illustrated in their landmark book *Institutional Racism in America,* "the problem is not a lack of interest in education, but a lack of power" (p. 33). Although Afro-American parents typically encourage and value education, it is not uncommon for Afro-American parents, particularly single mothers, to feel powerless and ineffectual in working with school authority. Parents' lack of self-efficacy may trace back to their own experiences with racism and disempowerment in America's schools (Kuykendall, 1991). School personnel also need to be sensitive to the fact that many Afro-American parents, in an effort to improve the quality of education for their children, often are forced to move frequently or travel extensively due to limited work opportunities. These conditions can consequently limit stability and parental accessibility, and they stem from institutional racism in the United States (Knowles & Prewitt).

Further, teacher and counselor expectations, as well as school climate, directly impact student performance and perception of self-worth. This is particularly true of urban students who attend so-called "ghetto" schools, where students and teachers often have less access to resources and opportunities, and therefore experience diminished expectations (Kozol,

1991). In addition, as a response to the oftexperienced chaos and lack of structure in at-risk schools, teachers often resort to authoritarian teaching styles that limit students' abilities to express themselves, engage in identity exploration, and perform to their potential (Haberman, 1991). More than 30 years ago, Silberman (1971) found that 80% of Afro-American children have positive self-images when they enter school, but only 5% still do by their senior year in high school. Current case studies suggest that high achievement continues to be regarded by teachers and students alike as attainable for Euro-Americans only, and Afro-American students who do succeed are perceived by their peers to be "acting white" and forsaking their "Afro-Americanness" (Bradley, 2001; Harris, 1995). According to Steinberg (1992), "Afro-American students are more likely than others to be caught in a bind between performing well in school and being popular among their peers" (p. 728). Afro-American students who are successful in school may face a lack of peer support or peer rejection, and they then must find ways to downplay their successes to become accepted (Lee, 1991; Tatum, 1997).

Research also indicates that Afro-American elementary, middle, and high school students are less likely to participate, or have the opportunity to participate, in extracurricular school and community activities than their Euro-American peers (Kozol, 1991; Kuykendall, 1991). This is particularly alarming when one considers that students who participate in academic and non-academic extracurricular activities are more likely to stay in school and experience enhanced personal and social development (MacKay & Kuh, 1994; Tinto, 1993). One explanation for this lack of involvement in school activities is that Afro-American students also reported receiving significantly less support and encouragement from educators than do their Euro-American peers (Bass & Coleman, 1997; Muller, 2002). For example, Afro-American children are more likely to be suspended from schools than Euro-American students (Robelen, 2002). Interaction among these youth, their parents, and school administrators is therefore likely to be negative and not conducive to the formation of extracurricular school-based relationships and interests.

Of course, a multitude of other factors interplay in the academic and social success of Afro-American children, including problems at home and with peers. However, this article is limited to a discussion of the factors school counselors can work to change within their means and available resources. School counselors have a duty to assist Afro-American youth in the acquisition of the necessary attitudes, skills, and knowledge required for effective learning and successful personal development despite external obstacles. If it is true that children learn what they live, then it should come as no surprise that Afro-American children are more likely to submit to a negative self-fulfilling prophecy that has been strengthened by negative stereotypes, pessimistic school personnel perceptions, low societal expectations, and minimal opportunities for achievement. The burden of providing a sanctuary as well as opportunities for success for at-risk children lies with their families, schools, and communities. School counselors, when supported, are ideally situated to provide the necessary professional intervention with at-risk students and consultation with school systems to address these underlying problems.

IMPLICATIONS FOR SCHOOL COUNSELING INTERVENTIONS

This section will first address suggested interventions for individual school counselors working with at-risk Afro-American youth. Second, recommended group and career counseling interventions will be presented. Finally, we will focus on ideas for school counselors to utilize in their consultative and preventive roles with teachers, parents, and their respective communities.

Although school counselors are theoretically in an optimal position to facilitate opportunities for at-risk Afro-American youth, they often do not make contact with at-risk students until those students are sent to counseling following punishment (Lee, 1991). The ASCA National Model (2002) states that appropriate school counselor responsibilities include counseling students with disciplinary problems, but it excludes performing disciplinary actions. To facilitate productive school counseling relationships, school counselors' policies should be to establish contact and rapport with all their assigned students before problems arise. A brief, informal group meeting with students by grade level or a personal interview with each student early in the year is necessary in promoting a positive school climate (Kuykendall, 1991). To be successful, school counselors, as well as other personnel, also must be very explicit in their expectations of their clients in terms of behavior and interaction. When working with Afro-American students, school counselors must communicate the following message clearly from the start: "I care about you and I expect from you the same as I would everyone else. I expect you to treat me fairly in return."

ASSISTING ETHNIC IDENTITY DEVELOPMENT

As the development and affirmation of ethnic identity within a group context may be an important correlate to academic achievement and social success, school counselors also are encouraged to conduct group counseling focused on ethnic identity development with at-risk Afro-American youth (Benedetto & Olisky, 2001; Bradley, 2001). According to Cross,

Parham, and Helms (1991) and Lee (1991), counselor-assisted ethnic identity development – or the acculturation into individual and group membership in regard to roles, status, language, spirituality, and socialization – is a critical task in empowering young Afro-Americans, especially as ethnic identity is heavily influenced by racism, class, and unbalanced economic conditions. Specifically, counselors can work with Afro-American youth as they explore their ethnic and racial identities. The Cross model of "nigrescence" (1991, 1995) describes ethnic identity as a stage process for Afro-Americans: pre-encounter, immersion-emersion, internalization, and internalization-commitment. During each of these stages, youth struggle with their identities as Afro- Americans by asking not only "Who am I?" but "What can I do, given my social context?" Identity formation is essential for any youth, but it often is shortchanged and marginalized for Afro-Americans (Sue & Sue, 2003).

School counselors facilitating ethnic identity groups should be aware of their own biases and limitations when it comes to ethnic identity exploration, as well as current best practices in this counseling format. Though it is beyond the scope of this article, many resources are available to use in counseling groups focused on ethnic identity development (e.g., Bradley, 2001; Cross, 1995; Cross et al., 1991; Lee, 1991; Merchant & Butler, 2002; Muller, 2002; Sue & Sue, 2003). All counselors working with clients on ethnic identity development should employ culturally specific counseling techniques to cultivate pride and potential by promoting (a) selfawareness of abilities, interests, and values; (b) an expansion of educational and occupational options; (c) educational and occupational decision making based on knowledge and experience; and (d) encouragement to anticipate future events (Lee & Simmons, 1988). Lee (1991) also discussed specific strategies aimed to assist Afro-American youth in ethnic identity development, including encouraging students to share their belief systems, personal strengths, problem-solving strategies, impact of family and friends, religious celebrations, special interests, and perception of social class.

ASSISTING INTERPERSONAL DEVELOPMENT

McWhirter et al. (1998) advocated for target approaches for at-risk youth, which are "aimed at groups of young people who share some circumstance or experience that increases the probability that they will develop problems in the future" (pp. 207–208). Target approaches can be used with Afro-American students who are feeling isolated within the community or discriminated against in school. Target approaches also can be used to create themes for peer groups to bond together, such as conflict resolution using peer mediation, supported by booster follow-up sessions when needed. For example, peer facilitators can aid in the development of resistance and refusal training to help peers resist negative social influences through role play and discussion (McWhirter et al.). Counselors also can provide assertiveness training and instruction in relaxation techniques as necessary. All of these approaches benefit Afro-American youth by facilitating optimism, resiliency, and self-control in adverse situations.

One of the personal development goals for students in school counseling set forth by the ASCA National Model (2003) is the acquisition of the knowledge, attitudes, and interpersonal skills that will help them understand and respect themselves and others, which relates strongly to the needs for cultural identity development and social skills applicable to diverse relationships among at-risk Afro-American youth. Peer mediation programs that focus on conflict resolution have proven to be effective in this arena (ASCA; McWhirter et al., 1998). Peer mediators are students who have been trained to intervene in conflicts between peers and to provide a supportive alliance for adolescents. Program trainees and qualified school counselors teach designated teachers and students appropriate helping skills to assist peers in crisis situations, in consultation with school counselors, as well as to provide them with access to community resources and hotline numbers students can turn to for advice. Together, counselors and students can work to plan for and promote peace, tolerance, and understanding of differences in the school climate.

ASSISTING CAREER DEVELOPMENT

The ASCA National Model (2003) encourages school counselors to assist their student clientele in three very important career development goals: the acquisition of skills necessary for the world of work, the ability to make informed career decisions, and the employment of successful strategies to achieve career satisfaction. The ASCA model recommends the use of goal setting, the creation of academic counseling groups, and the development of career centers to aid students in this process. Although Afro-American youth are unfortunately limited in their career paths in some instances due to discriminatory hiring practices and inadequate school and social skills training, school counselors are mandated to provide these services, regardless of the perceived obstacles. School counselors can implement career programs to accommodate the needs and interests of Afro-American students in their career exploration and development using resources cited below.

Lee and Simmons (1988) recommended the implementation of a life-planning model for Afro-American adolescents designed to teach them the necessary social and academic skills for successful living. Suggested activities include shared reactions to culturally representative films and novels; role-play skits regarding gender roles, occupational choices, and parental options; and life scenario exercises that require youth to make decisions about possible life changes. An example of such an exercise is, "What would you do if the job you really wanted did not exist when you finished your schooling?" (Lee & Simmons, p. 7). The establishment of a supportive network of community and parental role models who can assist students with school-to-work decisions is being implemented in many urban communities, such as Trenton, New Jersey, and Philadelphia, Pennsylvania, where large school districts have developed career interest-centered curricula and have partnered with local businesses to provide funding, resources, and the opportunity for internships and job training for students. Funds were previously available via the School-to-Work Opportunities Act (1994).

ASSISTING ACADEMIC DEVELOPMENT

School counselors also can assist at-risk students by consulting with other personnel to ensure that tracking practices, or placing students together in terms of academic ability, do not further discriminate and disenfranchise at-risk Afro-American youth. Tracking has long been a debate in U.S. schools, as students in upper tracks often learn skills and concepts that the lower-track students do not. Historically, Afro-American students have been disproportionately placed by school counselors into lower, remedial tracks, and they often remain "at the bottom of the ladder" permanently (Thompson & O'Quinn, 2001). Carlson and Lewis (1993) advised counselors to "monitor the use of standardized test results for purposes of classification and placement of ethnic minority students [and] to take the lead in dispelling the myth that any test score is fixed or is a stable index of what the child can achieve" (p. 246). According to the ASCA National Model (2003), school counselors' duties include interpreting cognitive, aptitude, and achievement tests with proper training. These data are to be used to monitor student progress and develop action plans to help close the achievement gap between Afro-American and Euro-American students (ASCA). Counselors also are encouraged to educate school staff on the validity and reliability of test score interpretations, and to provide alternate methods of assessing student ability. Counselors' duties also include preparing students for postgraduation and ensuring the availability of a wide range of choices and options, including college (ASCA). School counselors can help school personnel and youth understand that students who are assigned to or who elect to take only remedial coursework, which include a disproportionate number of Afro-American students, are at a disadvantage for competitive job selection, college acceptance, and other career opportunities.

TABLE 2: COUNSELING AT-RISK AFRO-AMERICANS IN A VARIETY OF SETTINGS: RECOMMENDED APPROACHES AND LIMITATIONS

Counseling Setting	Recommended Approach	Limitations
Schools	▪ Combination of peer group, individual, and family counseling ▪ Early intervention ▪ Counselor-assisted ethnic and racial identity development ▪ Peer academic support groups ▪ Career and vocational exploration and development ▪ Peer mediation and conflict resolution training ▪ Goal-setting activities and curriculum ▪ Target approaches ▪ Booster sessions ▪ Coping and adaptive skills training*	Limited access to role models, racial and gender matches, due to underrepresentation; limited access to equitable systems support; inadequate responsive services
Wraparound services	▪ Combination of peer group, individual, and family counseling ▪ Parental skills training* ▪ Community-based intervention ▪ School-based intervention	Limited or inadequate systems support; inadequate responsive services; ineffectual relationships among community resources, state agencies, and schools

* If necessary

ASSISTING SCHOOL PERSONNEL
IN PROFESSIONAL DEVELOPMENT

School counselors can furthermore encourage fellow educators to hold high expectations for all students, and to not simply accept poor performance from Afro-American students. Rousseau (1979) defined the "tyranny of indulgence" as a systematic abuse of power that occurs when a child is "unsure of what is valued and what behaviors will gain approval" (p. 28). If educators apply this theory to Afro-American students in a Euro-American culturally biased or nonaffirming school setting, school personnel will experience the same results. When expectations are low, unequal, or uncertain, delinquency and poor performance become the rule rather than the exception (Rousseau). Lee (2001) perceptively described the salient aspects of culturally responsive schools to include a centered, equitable, and fair curriculum that "accurately reflects the contributions of many cultures"; a diverse staff of committed educators; high levels of parental involvement; attention to lingual and cultural diversity; and a definition of cultural diversity that encompasses people with disabilities and people of different sexual orientations, religions, races, ages, and languages (p. 2).

The role of the school counselor becomes pivotal in assisting staff to explore what methodologies work best for Afro-American students. For example, several researchers have suggested that at-risk Afro-American students achieve more when they engage in "teaching for meaning" or a curriculum that lends itself to observable and direct application (Knapp et al., 1995). Also, some research has indicated that atrisk students tend to exhibit better performance when placed in smaller classes (e.g., a student-teacher ratio of 15 to 1) (Molnar, Smith, & Zahorik, 2000). Obviously, these potential solutions would necessitate the cooperation of school administration and funding sources in addition to counseling personnel.

The ASCA National Model (2003) recommends counselors collaborate with teachers to present "proactive, prevention-based guidance curriculum lessons" (p. 3). Counselors also are directed to assist in the identification and delivery of "the knowledge and skills all students should acquire" (ASCA, p. 1). In addition to the strategies discussed above, school counselors also can meet this goal by facilitating discussions and workshops for educators to explore their own cultural stereotypes and expectations for minority status students. Carlson and Lewis (1993) suggested that "particular attention could be given between pupils' typical styles of perceiving and processing information and the teachers' own preferred modes of instruction" (p. 246). For example, if a teacher's style includes lecture and recitation, he or she may find it beneficial to incorporate more handson activities to address the diverse learning styles of the students. Differentiated instruction is recommended, of course, for all student populations.

ASSISTING FAMILIES

Several parent training models exist to serve Afro-American families in the development of successful child-rearing techniques, such as the Effective Black Parenting Program and the Black Parenting Education Program, although counselors should exercise sensitivity and proper judgment when making these referrals (McWhirter et al., 1998). The purpose of family- and community-based interventions is to facilitate strong bonds among home, school, and community, and not further alienation and mistrust. Afro-American families who rarely have contact with their child's counselors will be naturally suspicious of a sudden home visit, and they most likely will react with hostility to any suggestions of inadequate parenting or need for support.

Prevention programs can be used to garner community support and involvement, and early intervention programs can help develop social and cognitive skills in schools (McWhirter et al., 1998). Peer tutors, for example, can organize study groups for Afro-American students struggling with language difficulties or academic adjustment. However, caution should be used when naming and developing these interventions; for example, it would be detrimental to student morale to propose a dropout prevention or teen pregnancy early intervention program targeted specifically for the Afro-American school population. Peer-led initiatives and afterschool drop-in programs would be better received than teacher-led or counselor-mandated approaches in these instances.

Fortunately, counselors are trained and skilled in facilitating dialogue, providing opportunities for growth and identity development, and fostering a positive social climate within schools. As with all populations, school counselors need to involve family and community whenever possible. School counselors are likely to have a positive impact on their atrisk Afro-American clients if they refer to and consult with other treatment providers in a "wraparound" services program. Wraparound services programs provide opportunities to develop formal and informal support networks for at-risk youth in an individualized and coordinated treatment setting. This type of service, also referred to as "systems of care," is a contemporary, popular model for mental health service delivery that draws on strengths of the family and cultural resources as well as traditional therapeutic interventions.

Overall, wraparound programs have suggested promising results in lowering risk factors and creating successful opportunities for their at-risk clients when treatment providers coordinate effectively and collaboratively (Burchard, Bruns, & Burchard, 2002). Specifically, at-risk youth who participate in wraparound programs that strongly adhere to the wraparound philosophy are more likely to avoid residential placements and delinquency, as well as have better outcomes in terms of prosocial behaviors, school completion, more concentrated career focus, higher-quality job performance, and higher grades than at-risk youth who participate in more traditional mental health service programs.

Lee (2001) suggested that when counselors bring comprehensive services to their clients' families and communities, it demonstrates that "counselors are sensitive to the fact that not all parents perceive schools as welcoming environments" (p. 5). Additionally, youth are best served when they feel free to express their concerns in a language and environment most comfortable to them; counselors should make efforts to visit the students in their homes to express their care, support, and willingness to work with the child's family. Sue and Sue (2003) also emphasized the need for multiculturally competent counselors to expand their roles to include consultation and outreach services. Counselors functioning in the "ombudsman role," for example, actively work toward social change by identifying potential barriers and protecting their clients from "bureaucratic mazes and procedures" (Sue & Sue, p. 23).

The school setting is the optimal place in which to coordinate the wraparound team service delivery, as schools already have the structure to interact with students and families and have opportunities to provide effective role models, support people, and coordinated holistic health services. We encourage school counselors to refer to the research cited above for further ideas and strategies in coordinating wraparound programs.

Resources available to school counselors also include religious and spiritual leaders (e.g., deacons, ministers, pastors) to form alliances among the home, school, and community (Holcomb-McCoy & Moore-Thomas, 2001; McWhirter et al., 1998). School counselors can invite Afro-American role models, such as community leaders and professionals, to speak to the student body on designated career days or serve as mentors. They might arrange for students to meet with representatives from historically Afro-American colleges and universities or arrange field visits to cultural exhibits. Students must feel that their culture is honored and valued in and out of school, and this accomplishment requires a coordinated community effort. See Table 2 for a comprehensive description of recommended approaches and potential limitations for serving atrisk Afro-American youth in a variety of settings.

CONCLUSION

It is imperative that school counselors and other professionals serving youth populations participate in finding positive ways to reach out to at-risk Afro-American children and fully welcome them as members of our communities. Schools need to provide a bias-free, safe haven in which all students are held to high standards and empowered with the necessary tools to reach their academic, personal, and social potential. School counselors should continue to abide by the ASCA National Model guidelines and work to assist Afro-American youth in career exploration, academic achievement, and ethnic identity formation. School counselors also are called upon to foster and strengthen peer, community, and family affiliations by establishing and maintaining highquality, multiculturally competent programs and services for at-risk Afro-American youth.

Lisa Fusick, M.S.Ed., is with the University of Pennsylvania, Philadelphia. E-mail: lfusick@hotmail.com Wendy Charkow Bordeau, Ph.D., LPC, NCC, is an assistant professor of Psychology at Georgian Court College, Lakewood, NJ. E-mail: wbordeau@optonline.net The authors wish to acknowledge contributor Andrene M. Taylor, M.A., of Howard University.

REFERENCES

American School Counselor Association. (2003). *The ASCA National Model: A framework for school counseling programs.* Alexandria,VA: Author.

Atwell, I., & Azibo, D. A.Y. (1992). Diagnosing personality disorder in Africans (Afro-Americans) using the Azibo nosology: Two case studies. In A. K. H. Burlew,W. C. Banks, H. P. McAdoo, & D. A.Y. Azibo (Eds.), *African American psychology: Theory, research, and practice* (pp. 300–320).Newbury Park, CA: Sage.

Barton, P. E. (2003). *Parsing the achievement gap: Baselines for tracking progress.* Princeton, NJ: Educational Testing Service.

Bass, C. K., & Coleman, H. L. K. (1997). Enhancing the cultural identity of early adolescent male African Americans. *Professional School Counseling, 1*(2), 48–51.

Benedetto, A. E., & Olisky, T. (2001). Biracial youth: The role of the school counselor in racial identity development. *Professional School Counseling, 5*(1), 66–69.

Boyd-Franklin, N. (1989). *Afro-American families in therapy: A multisystems approach.* New York: The Guilford Press.

Bradley, C. (2001). A counseling group for African-American adolescent males. *Professional School Counseling, 4*(5), 370–373.

Bulhan, H. A. (1985). Afro-American Americans and psychopathology: An overview of research and theory. *Psychotherapy, 22*(2), 370–377.

Burchard, J.D., Bruns, E. J., & Burchard, S. N. (2002). The wraparound approach. In B. J. Burns & K. Hoagwood (Eds.), *Community treatment for youth: Evidence-based interventions for severe emotional and behavioral disorders* (pp. 69–90).Oxford:Oxford University Press.

Carlson, J., & Lewis, J. (Eds.). (1993). *Counseling the adolescent: Individual, family, and school interventions* (2nd ed.). Denver, CO: Love Publishing Company.

Connell, C. M., & Prinz, R. J. (2002).The impact of childcare and parent-child interactions on school readiness and social skills development for low-income African American children. *Journal of School Psychology, 40*(2), 177–193.

Constantine, M.G. (2001). Multicultural training, theoretical orientation, empathy, and multicultural case conceptualization ability in counselors. *Journal of Mental Health Counseling, 23*(4), 357–373.

Corey, G. (1996). *Theory and practice of counseling and psychotherapy* (5th ed.). Pacific Grove, CA: Brooks/Cole.

Cross Jr., W. E. (1995).The psychology of nigrescence: Revising the Cross model. In J. G. Ponterotto, J. M. Casas, L. A. Suzuki, & C. M. Alexander (Eds.), *Handbook of multicultural counseling* (pp. 93–122).Thousand Oaks, CA: Sage.

Cross Jr., W. E., Parham,T. A., & Helms, J. A. (1991).The stages of Black identity development: Nigrescence models. In R. L. Jones (Ed.), *Black psychology* (3rd ed.) (pp. 319–338). Berkeley, CA: Cobb & Henry.

Fletcher, M. E. (2002, November 20). Survey discounts attitude in races' education gaps. *The Washington Post*, p. A12.

Graham, S. (1992). "Most of the subjects were white and middle class": Trends in published research on African Americans in selected APA journals, 1970-1989. *American Psychologist, 47*, 629–639.

Greene, B. A. (1985). Considerations in the treatment of Afro- American patients by White therapists. *Psychotherapy, 22*(2), 389–393.

Haberman, M. (1991).The pedagogy of poverty versus good teaching. *Phi Delta Kappan, 73*(4), 290–294. Retrieved July 3, 2002, from http://www.enc.org/topics/equity/articles/document.shtm?input= ACQ-111376-1376

Hardin, L. K., & Wampold, B. E. (2001). Adolescent strategies for coping with cultural diversity. *Journal of Counseling and Development, 79*, 356–364.

Harpalani, V., and Gunn, R. (2003). Contributions, controversies, and criticisms: In memory of John U.Ogbu. *Penn GSE Perspectives on Urban Education, 2.* Available from http://www.urbanedjournal.org./ogbu_memorial.html

Harris, S.M. (1995). Psychosocial development and Afro- American male masculinity: Implications for counseling economically disadvantaged African American male adolescents. *Journal of Counseling and Development, 73*(3), 279–287.

Haycock, K., Jerald, C., & Huang, S. (2001, Spring). *Closing the gap:Done in a decade.* Thinking K-16, 5(2), 3–21.

Holcomb-McCoy, C. C., & Moore-Thomas, C. (2001). Empowering African-American adolescent females. *Professional School Counseling, 5*(1), 19–26.

Hunt, P. (1987). Afro-American clients: Implications for supervision of trainees. *Psychotherapy, 24,* 114–119.

Jones, A. C. (1991). Psychological functioning in African Americans: A conceptual guide for use in psychotherapy. In R. L. Jones (Ed.)., *Black psychology* (3rd ed.) (pp. 577–590). Berkeley, CA: Cobb & Henry.

Jones, F. (1991).The African American psychologist as consultant and therapist. In R. L. Jones (Ed.), *Black psychology* (3rd ed.) (pp. 653–666). Berkeley, CA: Cobb & Henry.

Jones, N. S. C. (1990). Afro-American/white issues in psychotherapy. *Journal of Social Behavior and Personality, 5*(5), 305–322.

Kempf-Leonard, K., Pope, C. E., & Feyerherm,W. H. (1995). *Minorities in juvenile justice.* Thousand Oaks, CA: Sage Publications.

Knapp, M. S., Adelman, N. E.,Marder, C.,McCollum, H., Needels, M. C., Padilla, C., et al. (1995). *Teaching for meaning in high-poverty classrooms.* New York: Teachers College Press.

Knowles, L. L., & Prewitt, K. (1969). *Institutional racism in America.* Englewood Cliffs, NJ: Prentice-Hall.

Kozol, J. (1991). *Savage inequalities.* New York: Harper Perennial.

Kuykendall, C. (1991). *From rage to hope: Strategies for reclaiming Afro-American and Hispanic students.* Bloomington, IN: National Education Service.

Ladson-Billings, G. (1994). *The dreamkeepers.* San Francisco: Jossey-Bass.

Lee, C. C. (1991). Counseling African Americans: From theory to practice. In R. L. Jones (Ed.), *Black psychology* (3rd ed.) (pp. 559–576). Berkeley, CA: Cobb & Henry.

Lee, C. C. (2001). Culturally responsive school counselors and programs: Addressing the needs of all students. *Professional School Counseling, 4*(4), 257–261.

Lee, C. C., & Richardson, B. L. (Eds.). (1991). Multicultural issues in counseling: New approaches to diversity. *ACAeNews – Counseling African Americans.* Retrieved November 17, 2002, from http://www.counseling.org/enews/ volume_1/0106a.htm

Lee, C. C., & Simmons, S. (1988). A comprehensive life-planning model for black adolescents. *The School Counselor, 36*(1), 5–10.

Lewis-Fernández, R., & Kleinman, A. (1994). Culture, personality, and psychopathology. *Journal of Abnormal Psychology, 103*(1), 67–71.

MacKay, K. A., & Kuh, G.D. (1994). A comparison of student effort and educational gains of Caucasian and African- American students at predominantly white colleges and universities. *Journal of College Student Development, 35*, 217–223.

Mays, V.M. (1985).The Afro-American American and psychotherapy: The dilemma. *Psychotherapy, 22*(2), 379–388.

McDavis, R. J., Parker,W.M., & Parker,W. J. (1995). Counseling African Americans. In N.A.Vacc, S. B.DeVaney, & J. Wittmer (Eds.), *Experiencing and counseling multicultural and diverse populations* (3rd ed.) (pp. 217–248). Bristol, PA: Accelerated Development.

McWhirter, A. M., McWhirter, B.T., McWhirter, E. H., & McWhirter, J. J. (1998). *At-risk youth: A comprehensive response* (2nd ed.). Pacific Grove, CA: Brooks/Cole Publishing.

Merchant, N. M., & Butler, M. K. (2002). A psychoeducational group for ethnic minority adolescents in a predominantly White treatment setting. *Journal for Specialists in Group Work, 27*(3), 314–332.

Miller, A.T. (1993). Social science, social policy, and the heritage of African American families. In M. B. Katz (Ed.), *The "underclass" debate: Views from history* (pp. 254–292). Princeton, NJ: Princeton University Press.

Molnar, A., Smith, P., & Zahorik, J. (2000,December). *1999-2000 results of the Student Achievement Guarantee in Education (SAGE) program evaluation.* University of Wisconsin- Milwaukee, Center for Education Research, Analysis, and Innovation. Executive summary retrieved July 3, 2002, from http://www.uwm.edu/ Dept/CERAI/documents/ sage/execsum00.htm

Muller, L. E. (2002). Group counseling for African American males:When all you have are European American counselors. *Journal for Specialists in Group Work, 27*(3), 299–313.

National Commission on Excellence in Education. (1983). *A nation at risk: The imperative for educational reform.* Washington, DC: Government Printing Office.

Nettles, M.T., & Perna, L.W. (1997). *The African American education data book,Vol. II: Preschool through high school education.* Fairfax,VA: College Fund/UNCF.

Nobles, W.W. (1976). Black people in white insanity: An issue for black community mental health. *The Journal of Afro-American Issues, 4,* 21–27.

Ramseur, H. P. (1991). Psychologically healthy black adults. In R. L. Jones (Ed.), *Black psychology* (3rd ed.) (pp. 353–378). Berkeley, CA: Cobb & Henry.

Ridley, C. R. (1984). Clinical treatment of the nondisclosing Afro-American client. *American Psychologist, 38,* 1234–1244.

Robelen, E. (2002). *Taking on the achievement gap.* Retrieved August 5, 2003, from the North Central Regional Educational Laboratory website: http://www.ncrel.org/gap/takeon/toc.htm

Rousseau, J. (1979). *Emile* (A. Bloom, Trans.). New York: Basic Books. (Original work published 1762)

Sanchez-Hucles, J. C. (2000). *The first session with African Americans: A step-by-step guide.* Indianapolis, IN: Jossey- Bass.

School-to-Work Opportunities Act. (1994).Washington, DC: U.S. Department of Education, Office of School-to-Work Opportunities. Retrieved March 11, 2004, from http://www.ed.gov/legislation/FedRegister

Seligman, M. (1975). Helplessness: *On depression, development, and death.* San Francisco: Freeman.

Silberman, C. (1971). *Crisis in the classroom.* New York:Vintage Books.

Smart, D.W., & Smart, J. F. (1997). DSM-IV and culturally sensitive diagnosis: Some observations for counselors. *Journal of Counseling and Development, 75,* 392–397.

Stanard, R. P. (2003). High school graduation rates in the United States: Implications for the counseling profession. *Journal of Counseling and Development, 81*(2), 217–221.

Steinberg, L. (1992). Ethnic differences in adolescent achievement: An ecological perspective. *American Psychologist, 47,* 723–729.

Substance Abuse and Mental Health Administration. (1999). *Mental health: A report of the Surgeon General.* Retrieved August 5, 2003, from http://www.mentalhealth. samhsa. gov/cre/fact1.asp

Sue, D.W., Arredondo, P., & McDavis, R. J. (1992). Multicultural counseling competencies and standards: A call to the profession. *Journal of Multicultural Counseling and Development, 20,* 64–68.

Sue, D.W., & Sue,D. (2003). *Counseling the culturally diverse: Theory and practice* (4th ed.). New York: John Wiley & Sons.

Sue, S., & Zane,N. (1987).The role of culture and cultural techniques in psychotherapy: A critique and reformulation. *American Psychologist, 42*(1), 37–45.

Tatum, B.D. (1997). *Why are all the Afro-American kids sitting together in the cafeteria? And other conversations about race.* New York: Basic Books.

Terrell, F., & Terrell, S. (1984). Race of counselor, client sex, cultural mistrust level, and premature termination from counseling among Afro-American clients. *Journal of Counseling Psychology, 31*(3), 371–375.

Thomas, M. B., & Dansby, P. G. (1985). Afro-American clients: Family structures, therapeutic issues, and strengths. *Psychotherapy, 22,* 398–407.

Thompson, C. L., & O'Quinn, S.D. (2001). *Eliminating the Afro-American-White achievement gap: A summary of research.* Chapel Hill, NC: North Carolina Education Research Council.

Tinto, V. (1993). *Leaving college: Rethinking the causes and cures of student attrition* (2nd ed.). Chicago: University of Chicago Press.

Vontress, C. E., & Epp, L. R. (1997). Historical hostility in the African American client: Implications for counseling. *Journal of Multicultural Counseling and Development, 25,* 170–184.

White, J. L., & Johnson Jr., J. A. (1991). Awareness, pride and identity: A positive educational strategy for black youth. In R. L. Jones (Ed.), *Black psychology* (3rd ed.) (pp. 409–418). Berkeley, CA: Cobb & Henry.

Wilson, L. L., & Stith, S. M. (1997). Culturally sensitive therapy with Afro-American clients. In D. R. Atkinson & G.Morten (Eds.), *Counseling American minorities* (5th ed.) (pp. 116–126). Boston:McGraw-Hill.

Ziter, M. L. P. (1987). Culturally sensitive treatment of black alcoholic families. *Social Work, 32*(2), 130–135.

The Transformative Individual School Counseling Model: An Accountability Model for Urban School Counselors

By Robert Eschenauer, Ph.D., and Stuart F. Chen-Hayes, Ph.D.

This article originally appeared in *Professional School Counseling*, Vol. 8, No. 3, 2005.

The realities and needs of urban students, families, and educators have outgrown traditional individual counseling models. The American School Counselor Association's National Model and National Standards and the Education Trust's Transforming School Counseling Initiative encourage professional school counselors to shift roles toward implementing comprehensive developmental school counseling programs focused on systemic change to overcome institutional K-12 school barriers. This article reconceptualizes individual counseling as a collaborative act of advocacy and accountability used by professional school counselors and researchers to close achievement and opportunity gaps. The Transformative Individual School Counseling model utilizes a functional behavioral assessment approach to define problems; systemic, solution-focused, and narrative counseling approaches to address problems; and single-case study designs to document the effectiveness of interventions.

The profession of school counseling continues to evolve in its role in K-12 educational settings. The effort to redefine professional school counseling is evidenced by the American School Counselor Association's (ASCA) National Model and National Standards and the Education Trust's National Center for Transforming School Counseling initiatives. Also, these preceding initiatives were due, in part, to the increased calls for accountability in education and increased attention to the access, equity, and success for every student (ASCA, 2003; Bailey, Getch, & Chen-Hayes, 2003; Erford, House, & Martin, 2003; Green & Keys, 2001; Gysbers, 2001; Stone & Dahir, 2004). As a precursor to the changes in professional school counseling, the introduction of educational standards to improve curricula, raise achievement, and serve as a measure for the assessment of outcomes has changed the image and functioning of K-12 schools in the United States. As a result, the idea of aligning the professional identity of a school counseling program with the educational mission and philosophy of the school became critical, and educational goals became the focus of ASCA's National Model for School Counseling Programs (Dahir, 2001;

Erford et al.; Green & Keys; Paisley & McMahon, 2001; Perusse & Goodnough, 2004).

Developing school counseling program accountability models has been addressed in the literature (Borders, 2002; Green & Keys, 2001; Hughes & James, 2001; Otwell & Mullis, 1997; Stone & Dahir, 2004). Accountability in the counseling profession, however, is not new. In 1970, Arbuckle wrote a seminal article that resulted in a spate of articles promoting accountability (Baker, 2001). What is unique about the current accountability mandate is the specificity of attention to academic outcomes (Carey & Boscardin, 2003; Colbert & Colbert, 2003; Green & Keys; Johnson, 2002; Perusse & Goodnough, 2004). The focus of this article, therefore, is to reconceptualize the role of individual counseling performed by urban professional school counselors as a tool to advocate for and demonstrate accountability in closing K-12 achievement and opportunity gaps (Johnson).

THE SCOPE OF THE NEED FOR A NEW INDIVIDUAL COUNSELING MODEL IN URBAN SCHOOLS

Although individual counseling cannot meet the needs of all students in K-12 urban schools, it can remain a vital component of a school's comprehensive program (Campbell & Dahir, 1997; Gysbers & Henderson, 2000; Myrick, 2003; Newsome & Gladding, 2003; Paisley & McMahon, 2001). There are a number of concerns, however, regarding individual counseling in the schools. These concerns include the overemphasis on individual counseling in K-12 schools, the lack of research data and accountability for individual counseling outcomes in K-12 school settings (Whiston, 2003; Whiston & Sexton, 1998), and how individual school counseling is conceptualized to address achievement and opportunity gaps. Burnham and Johnson (2000) suggested that there might be an overreliance on individual counseling because it is consistent with traditional counselor education training and/or because it is a convenient and comfortable way to work with students. However, in today's climate of accountability in urban schools, neither of these reasons is an adequate justification.

Individual counseling is part of a comprehensive counseling program that needs to be aligned closely with the educational mission and philosophy of K- 12 schools – educating all students to high levels of academic, career, and personal/social success. Within this framework, a greater emphasis is placed on interventions that benefit all students, such as group counseling and developmental school counseling lessons (Perusse & Goodnough, 2004). Individual counseling should be used when group counseling or developmental school counseling lessons are not appropriate. Providing an urban student with individual counseling during the school day lessens critical instructional time. In environments where high-stakes testing influences much of what occurs, teachers and administrators are justifiably reluctant to release students for activities that have not been empirically tested for effectiveness (Baker, 2001; Green & Keys, 2001).

What is the purpose of individual school counseling and how does it differ from mental health counseling? Should individual school counseling be offered to any students routinely? What are appropriate goals for individual school counseling? What role does research play in individual school counseling interventions? What outcome measures should be utilized to evaluate individual school counseling interventions? Addressing these questions within the K-12 school's conceptual framework or mission – facilitating student learning and development – differs significantly from an agency-based mental health perspective. Mental health models conceptualize social-emotional functioning as ends in themselves. Many school counselors, school psychologists, and school social workers currently use a mental health perspective in their roles in K-12 schools. This explains in part why some K-12 students are in individual school counseling "forever" and why school counseling goals from a mental health perspective are vague and tangential to an academic success and learning focus.

A consequence of defining individual counseling within an educational framework is that one has to rethink how problems are defined and solutions or interventions formulated. Over 25 years ago, the point was made that many problems in the field of psychotherapy remained problems because they were not formulated in a way that led to a real solution (Watzlawick, 1978; Watzlawick, Weakland, & Fisch, 1974). This also may apply to counseling and explain why students remained in counseling for an undefined period of time and seemed to make no progress. A related issue is that many urban school counselors lack knowledge and the skills to implement many types of interventions. They tend to conceptualize solutions in terms of *what they know how to do instead of what is really required in the given situation.*

The ethical codes of both the American Counseling Association (1995) and ASCA (1998) address the professional responsibility of counselors to stay abreast of current research and trends in professional counseling. In addition, best practices require that school counselors not only use empirically validated interventions and models, but that they also do their own research to evaluate interventions used in their work. A problem in this regard is that school counselors traditionally have not linked research and practice and have taken a rather negative view of research (Deck & Cecil, 1990; Green & Keys, 2001; Lundervold & Belwood, 2000; Lusky & Hayes, 2001; Whiston, 2003).

This situation must be changed if today's school counselors are to respond to the accountability mandates to demonstrate through data the effectiveness of their contributions to the school's mission (Hughes & James, 2001; Lapan, 2001; Otwell & Mullis, 1997; Stone & Dahir, 2004; Whiston & Sexton, 1998). Whiston and Sexton addressed the need for counselor educators to take a more active role in producing good consumers of research because the results of research are not easily deciphered by students unfamiliar with research designs and statistical language. School counseling students need to be given the tools to understand research articles early in their training and then opportunities to practice using those tools in the majority of their coursework.

The remainder of this article will focus on the Transformative Individual School Counseling (TISC) model, which was created by the authors as a means to illustrate accountability and to justify time-limited counseling interventions used primarily to close achievement and opportunity gaps in urban schools.

THE TRANSFORMATIVE INDIVIDUAL
SCHOOL COUNSELING MODEL

The TISC model bridges the practitioner-researcher gap while responding to the need for accountability data. Rather than accepting the dichotomy of practitioner/ researcher, the TISC model defines professional school counselors as school counselor-researchers whenever they are engaged in individual counseling. Combining these perspectives places the school counselor in a unique position of using data for accountability purposes while contributing to evidenced-based best practices. Both Brady and O'Hern (2003) and Dimmitt and Carey (2003) noted that outcome studies must be repeated within specific multicultural contexts to extend evidenced- based best practices. This model presents opportunities to do this in urban settings, and it also is applicable to suburban and rural contexts. Figure 1 includes the steps in the model.

The first step in this model involves a *paradigm shift* for school counselors trained in mental health models. Individual counseling is now to be defined within an educational framework with goals that are consistent with the school's philosophy and mission statement. The next step involves *problem definition*. Problems must be defined contextually in operational terms. This is particularly important when working with urban children and adolescents (Crone & Horner, 2000). A powerful technique to assist in defining a problem is functional behavioral assessment (Scott, Nelson, & Zabala, 2003). A functional behavioral assessment is a collaborative team effort that involves collecting data from both

FIGURE 1. THE TRANSFORMATIVE INDIVIDUAL SCHOOL COUNSELING MODEL.

Step 1: *Paradigm shift* from mental health perspective to school and academic perspective

Step 2: *Problem definition* – for example, functional behavioral assessment can be used to contextualize and operationalize a problem

Step 3: *Implementation* of intervention

- Use of solution-focused, narrative, or systemic interventions with other stakeholders as resources and allies

- Short-term counseling interventions used to maximize student ability

Step 4: *Evaluation* of individual counseling data using single-case research design

indirect and direct sources in order to conceptualize the context and function of a behavior. By contextualizing behavior, one is able to gather information regarding antecedents, behaviors, and consequences that can lead to the formulation of hypotheses as to the purpose or function of the behavior for the particular individual (Crone & Horner, 2000; Gresham, Watson, & Skinner, 2001; Scott et al.; Sugai, Lewis-Palmer, & Hagan-Burke, 2000). This information then can be utilized to formulate interventions that are customized for the individual (Crone & Horner).

The third step of this model involves the *implementation* of the intervention. The intervention strategies should be implemented by either the teacher, counselor, other specialist, parent, or student. The intervention strategies utilized in the TISC model are systemic (ASCA, 2003), solution focused (Murphy, 1997), and narrative (Winslade & Monk, 1999). And finally, the last step of the model involves *evaluation* of the intervention. Lundervold and Belwood (2000) noted that in the past, "intuition, authority, and tenacity" served as the basis of clinical judgment regarding the choice of treatment and evaluation of its results (p. 93). Such an approach would not meet today's accountability standards. In 2002, Foster, Watson, Meeks, and Young (re)introduced single-case experimental designs to school counselors and stated that "school counselors can easily take advantage of the singlesubject research paradigm to conduct outcome research and answer questions regarding the effectiveness of school counselors' interventions" (p. 147). This approach would provide professional school counselors with a vehicle for documenting their efforts to achieve their intended outcomes and, better yet, fulfilling the ASCA National Standards.

CASE EXAMPLE OF TISC MODEL IN URBAN SCHOOL SETTINGS

The following example illustrates the use of the TISC model within a K-12 urban school setting. A third-grade African American boy diagnosed with attention deficit hyperactivity disorder (ADHD) was referred for counseling because of his frequent class disruptions. The academic performance of this youngster was consistently below average in both literacy and math. His disruptive behaviors were operationally defined and were described as "talking out loud," "not being prepared to work," and "not following directions." The counseling intervention plan for this youngster had the following overall goals: to function within the classroom and to improve academic performance in literacy, math, and other subjects. Counseling was done inside and outside of the classroom setting. The counseling implemented outside the classroom focused on his understandings or self-narrative about his ADHD. Like so many other youngsters with this disorder, he translated this to mean that he was a "bad boy," but many times he was not aware of what he had done to earn that title.

The counselor then set additional goals: (a) to improve the boy's understandings of ADHD as a disorder that was separate from his identity, and (b) to help him identify how this disorder specifically affected him so that compensatory strategies could be developed. In addition, he needed training in social skills (e.g., modulating the volume of his voice, learning how to appropriately ask for help, learning about personal space). Shaping procedures, a behavioral technique, were used to develop new behaviors. In the class setting, the counseling focused on his organizational and self-monitoring skills to keep him on task. He also was taught strategies to avoid responding to inappropriate provocation from others.

His third-grade teacher, an African American woman, wanted him out of her classroom and claimed that he could not function in the general education setting. She referred him for special education placement. She would not acknowledge the small positive changes in his behavior that began to occur. These small changes were documented and analyzed by the counselor (e.g., data). Both his mother and counselor opposed the teacher's referral because they were convinced that he could achieve in his general education placement. They also were aware that too many young urban people of color, particularly boys, were inappropriately placed in special education settings. If these youngsters had been given the support of appropriate counseling, they might have been successful learners in general education.

The counselor, the parent, and the student worked collaboratively to keep him in his general class setting. He was put on medication, and the teacher, parent, and counselor who worked closely with his physician monitored the effects. The results of the counseling and medication were dramatic, but the teacher and school administrator still wanted to remove him to a special education setting. Through the combined efforts of the mother and counselor's advocacy efforts, the student was not referred to a special education setting. His counseling sessions were continued before or after school, or during his lunch break.

When this boy graduated from the fifth grade, he received the highest reading score in the entire graduating class – a major data point that showed the effective use of transformative school counseling in action. As evidenced from this example, school counselors need to become reflective and investigative practitioners.

CONCLUSION

The TISC model addresses the issue of accountability and gives school counselor-researchers tools to document the effectiveness of interventions through the collection and organization of data about their individual counseling. By monitoring their individual school counseling performance, school counselor- researchers use the TISC model to improve data-based professional practice. The outcome data from such investigations benefit both individual students receiving the service and the larger school community. The authors encourage urban school counselor-researchers to collect and publish their data regarding interventions through national programs such as the ASCA journal (*Professional School Counseling*) and the University of Massachusetts' National Center for School Counseling Outcome Research publications.

Robert Eschenauer, Ph.D., is an assistant professor and Stuart F. Chen-Hayes,Ph.D., is an associate professor at Lehman College of the City University of New York, Bronx. E-mail: robert.eschenauer@ lehman.cuny.edu

REFERENCES

American Counseling Association. (1995). *Code of ethics and standards of practice*. Retrieved July 25, 2002, from http://www.counseling.org/resources/ethics.htm

American School Counselor Association. (1998). *Ethical standards for school counselors*. Retrieved July 25, 2002, from http://www.school-counselor.org/library/ethics.pdf

American School Counselor Association. (2003). *The ASCA National Model: A framework for school counseling programs.* Alexandria,VA: Author.

Arbuckle, D. S. (1970). *Counseling: Philosophy, theory, and practice.* New York: Allyn & Bacon.

Bailey, D. F., Getch,Y. Q., & Chen-Hayes, S. (2003). Professional school counselors as social and academic advocates. In B.T. Erford (Ed.), *Transforming the school counseling profession* (pp. 411–434).Upper Saddle River, NJ:Merrill Prentice-Hall.

Baker, S. B. (2001). Reflections on forty years in the school counseling profession: Is the glass half full or half empty? *Professional School Counseling, 5,* 75–83.

Borders, L.D. (2002). School counseling in the 21st century: Personal and professional reflections. *Professional School Counseling, 5,* 180–185.

Brady, S., & O'Hern, J. (2003,October). *Integrating cultural differences into graduate training on trauma.* Paper presented at the North Atlantic Regional Association for Counselor Education and Supervision Fall 2003 Conference, Canandaiqua, NY.

Burnham, J. J., & Johnson, C. M. (2000). School counselor roles: Discrepancies between actual practice and existing models. *Professional School Counseling, 4,* 41–49.

Campbell, C. A., & Dahir, C. A. (1997). *Sharing the vision: National standards for school counseling programs.* Alexandria: VA: American School Counselor Association.

Carey, J. C., & Boscardin, M. L. (2003). Improving the multicultural effectiveness of your school in the context of state standards, accountability measures, and high-stakes assessment. In P. B. Pedersen & J. C. Carey (Eds.), *Multicultural counseling in schools: A practical handbook* (pp. 270–289). Boston: Allyn & Bacon.

Colbert, R.D., & Colbert, M. M. (2003). School counselor involvement in culture-centered education reform. In P. B. Pedersen & J. C. Carey (Eds.), *Multicultural counseling in schools: A practical handbook* (pp. 3–25). Boston: Allyn & Bacon.

Crone, D. A., & Horner, R.H. (2000). Contextual, conceptual, and empirical foundations of functional behavioral assessment in schools. *Exceptionality, 8,* 161–172.

Dahir, C. A. (2001). The national standards for school counseling programs:Development and implementation. *Professional School Counseling, 4,* 320–327.

Deck, M.D., & Cecil, J. H. (1990). School counselor research as perceived by American School Counselor Association leaders: Implications for profession. *Elementary School Guidance & Counseling, 25,* 12–20.

Dimmitt, C., & Carey, J. (2003,October). *Critical school counseling research: A Delphi study.* Paper presented at the North Atlantic Regional Association for Counselor Education and Supervision Fall 2003 Conference, Canandaigua, NY.

Erford, B.T., House, R., & Martin, P. (2003).Transforming the school counseling profession. In B.T. Erford (Ed.), *Transforming the school counseling profession* (pp. 1–20). Upper Saddle River, NJ:Merrill Prentice Hall.

Foster, L.H., Watson,T. S., Meeks, C., & Young, J. S. (2002). Singlesubject research design for school counselors: Becoming an applied researcher. *Professional School Counseling, 6,* 146–154.

Green, A., & Keys, S.G. (2001). Expanding the developmental school counseling paradigm:Meeting the needs of the 21st century student. *Professional School Counseling, 5,* 84–95.

Gresham, F.M.,Watson, T. S., & Skinner, C.H. (2001). Functional behavioral assessment: Principles, procedures, and future directions. *School Psychology Review, 30,* 156–172.

Gysbers, N. C. (2001). School guidance and counseling in the 21st century: Remember the past into the future. *Professional School Counseling, 5,* 96–105.

Gysbers, N. C., & Henderson, P. (2000). *Developing and managing your school guidance programs* (3rd ed.). Alexandria, VA: American Counseling Association.

Hughes, D., & James, S.H. (2001).Using accountability data to protect a school counseling program: One counselor's experience. *Professional School Counseling, 4,* 306–310.

Johnson, R. S. (2002). *Using data to close the achievement gap: How to measure equity in our schools.* Thousand Oaks, CA: Corwin Press.

Lapan, R. (2001). Results-based comprehensive guidance and counseling programs: A framework for planning and evaluation. *Professional School Counseling, 4,* 289–299.

Lundervold, D. A., & Belwood,M. F. (2000).The best kept secret in counseling: Single-case (N=1) experimental designs [Electronic version]. *Journal of Counseling & Development, 78,* 92–102.

Lusky, M. B., & Hayes, R. L. (2001). Collaborative consultation and program evaluation [Electronic version]. *Journal of Counseling & Development, 79,* 26–38.

Murphy, J. (1997). *Solution-focused counseling in middle and high school.* Alexandria,VA: American School Counselor Association.

Myrick, R.D. (2003). Accountability: Counselors count. *Professional School Counseling, 6*, 174–179.

Newsome, D.W., & Gladding, S.T. (2003). Counseling individuals and groups in school. In B.T. Erford (Ed.), *Transforming the school counseling profession* (pp. 209–230). Upper Saddle River, NJ:Merrill Prentice Hall.

Otwell, P. S., & Mullis, F. (1997). Academic achievement and counselor accountability. *Elementary School Guidance & Counseling, 31,* 343–348.

Paisley, P.O., & McMahon, H. G. (2001). School counseling for the twenty-first century: Challenges and opportunities. *Professional School Counseling, 5*, 106–115.

Perusse, R., & Goodnough, G. E. (Eds.). (2004). *Leadership, advocacy, and direct service strategies for professional school counselors.* Pacific Grove, CA: Thomson Learning/Brooks/ Cole.

Scott, T. M., Nelson, C. M., & Zabala, J. (2003). Functional behavior assessment training in public schools: Facilitating systemic change. *Journal of Positive Behavior Interventions, 5*, 216–224.

Stone, C. B., & Dahir, C. A. (2004). *School counselor accountability: A MEASURE of Student Success.* Upper Saddle River, NJ: Pearson Merrill Prentice Hall.

Sugai, G., Lewis-Palmer,T., & Hagan-Burke, S. (2000).Overview of the functional behavioral assessment process. *Exceptionality, 8,* 149–160.

Watzlawick, P. (1978). *The language of change: Elements of therapeutic communication.* New York:W.W.Norton & Company.

Watzlawick, P.,Weakland, J., & Fisch, R. (1974). *Change: Principles of problem formulation and problem resolution.* New York: W.W. Norton & Company.

Whiston, S. C. (2003). Outcome research on school counseling services. In B.T. Erford (Ed.), *Transforming the school counseling profession* (pp. 435–448).Upper Saddle River, NJ: Merrill Prentice Hall.

Whiston, S. C., & Sexton,T. L. (1998). A review of school counseling outcome research: Implications for practice. *Journal of Counseling & Development, 76*, 412–426.

Winslade, J., & Monk, G. (1999). *Narrative counseling in schools: Powerful & brief.* Thousand Oaks, CA: Corwin Press, Inc.

Culturally Responsive School Counselors and Programs: Addressing the Needs of All Students

By Courtland C. Lee, Ph.D.

This article originally appeared in *Professional School Counseling*, Vol. 4, No. 4, 2001.

Among the issues facing contemporary school counselors, addressing the developmental needs of the growing number of students from culturally diverse backgrounds is, perhaps, the most challenging. Demographic trends indicate that the number of students in public elementary and secondary schools in the United States increased by approximately one million from 1987–1988 to 1990–1991. More than three-quarters of this growth can be attributed to an increase in the number of Hispanic and Asian students. Data further indicate that the overall proportion of minority public school students increased from 1987–1988 to 1990–1991 while the proportion of White non-Hispanic students declined (National Center for Education Statistics, 1996). In concrete terms, these demographic estimates mean that, as never before, U.S. schools are becoming a social arena where children who represent truly diverse behavioral styles, attitudinal orientations, and value systems have been brought together with one goal – to prepare them for academic, career, and social success in the 21st Century.

Cultural pluralism has become widely recognized as a major factor deserving understanding on the part of school counselors. Significantly, the American School Counselor Association (1999) established a position statement on cross/multicultural counseling that calls for the facilitation of student development through an understanding of and appreciation for multiculturalism and diversity. This statement encourages school counselors to take action to ensure that students from culturally diverse backgrounds receive services that foster their development.

However, there is a growing realization that current school counseling services often do not have broad applicability across the range of cultural backgrounds represented by students (Baruth & Manning, 2000; Herring, 1997; Lee, 1995). School counselors are becoming increasingly aware that their practices are rooted firmly in the values of European-American middle class culture, whereas the cultural values of a significant portion of the students with whom they work represent worldviews whose origins are found in Africa, Asia, Mexico, Central America, the Caribbean, or the Middle East (Herring, 1997; Lee, 1995).

Cultural diversity must be effectively addressed in the provision of comprehensive school counseling programs. Three concepts underscore the importance of promoting cultural diversity in school counseling interventions. These are access, equity, and educational justice. All students, regardless of their cultural background and heritage, deserve equal access to a quality education. Anything less than that, for any child, is a grave educational injustice. School counselors need a different perspective from which to operate if they are going to ensure that students from culturally diverse backgrounds have access to services that promote optimal academic, career, and personal-social development (Baruth & Manning, 2000).

This article provides such a perspective. The article provides direction for planning, implementing, and evaluating culturally responsive school counseling programs. The article first explores the concept of a culturally responsive school. It next considers the ways that a comprehensive guidance and counseling program can promote such a school. Within the context of a school counseling program that is both comprehensive and culturally responsive, specific counselor roles and functions considered critical for enhancing the quality of education for all children are discussed.

SALIENT ASPECTS OF CULTURALLY RESPONSIVE SCHOOLS

For the past 20 years, I have been an active consultant to schools across the country that have been grappling with the challenges and opportunities associated with a culturally diverse student body. It has become obvious to me that schools and school systems vary widely in their response to issues of cultural diversity. Those schools that have been successful in both meeting the challenges and seizing the opportunities associated with multiculturalism and diversity appear to share a number of important characteristics. From my perspective, the salient aspects that characterize a culturally responsive school are the following:

1. The school has adopted a "salad bowl" as opposed to a "melting pot" philosophy of education.
2. The school has been able to forge a sense of community out of cultural diversity.
3. The school has been able to capitalize on cultural diversity and maintain academic standards (i.e., it has the same high academic expectations for all students).
4. The school has a curriculum that is neither Eurocentric nor Afrocentric nor Asiancentric, but rather is Centered (i.e., it has a curriculum that fairly and accurately reflects the contributions of many cultures).

5. The school goes "beyond Black History Month" (i.e., it infuses multi-culturalism and diversity in a nonstereotypical manner throughout the curriculum and the school year).
6. The school provides students with forums outside of the classroom to communicate with and learn about their peers from diverse cultural backgrounds.
7. The school has mechanisms in place to deal with racial/cultural tensions.
8. The school has committed educators who engage in ongoing staff development and are not afraid to take risks or improvise when necessary.
9. The school actively attempts to recruit a diverse staff of educators.
10. The school has high levels of parental involvement and educators consider language and cultural customs in their interactions with parents.
11. The school broadly defines cultural diversity to include people with disabilities, people with diverse sexual orientations, people with diverse religious traditions, and older people.

While no one school may possess all of these characteristics, in my opinion, those schools and school systems that exhibit a significant number of these factors are ahead of the curve in dealing with the complex issues of cultural diversity.

School counselors, because of the unique role they play in promoting development and facilitating change, can play a major role in advocating for and advancing these characteristics in schools. Comprehensive school guidance and counseling programs should promote these 11 aspects. School counselors need to develop new perspectives regarding comprehensive guidance initiatives and their role in promoting culturally responsive schools. Such initiatives can be a major influence in meeting the challenges and seizing the opportunities of cultural diversity.

A concerted effort is required to develop comprehensive guidance and counseling programs that reflect the needs and realities of all students, regardless of their cultural background. Implicit in such initiatives must be the concept that counselors are agents of change, with the knowledge and skill to translate cultural awareness into constructive action. Such action necessitates extending comprehensive counseling and guidance beyond students into the home and community.

CULTURALLY RESPONSIVE COUNSELORS AS FACILITATORS OF STUDENT DEVELOPMENT

Culturally responsive comprehensive guidance initiatives in schools should be based on two important premises: (1) All young people can learn and want to learn; and (2) cultural differences are real and cannot be ignored. A fundamental aspect of any comprehensive guidance approach, therefore, is understanding the cultural realities of children and their importance to academic, career, and personal-social development.

Through individual and group counseling as well as large-group guidance interventions, culturally responsive counselors should be able to help students from a variety of cultural backgrounds develop healthy self-concepts and learn to respect cultural diversity, while setting educational, career, and personal-social goals. This will require that school counselors be effective facilitators of student development. As effective student development facilitators, five distinct functions emerge for culturally responsive school counselors.

The first of these functions entails promoting the development of positive self-identities among students. This might be accomplished by conducting self-awareness groups that emphasize self-appreciation through a validation of cultural heritage. Counselors might consider using culturally specific curriculum materials to cultivate self-pride from a number of cultural perspectives in individual and group interactions.

The second function involves facilitating the development of positive interpersonal relations among students from diverse cultural backgrounds. Growth groups might be used to accomplish this goal by having students from diverse backgrounds explore with each other the nature and importance of positive interpersonal relationships. Cultural variations on the notion of community might be incorporated into group interactions as a way to develop mutual respect and understanding among youth from diverse backgrounds (Carter & Vuong, 1997; Hayes, 1996).

Academic achievement and promoting the attitude and skills for school success are the focus of the third and fourth functions. These involve promoting the development of positive attitudes toward academic achievement among all students and facilitating the development of academic skills and competencies.

To accomplish the former, counselors should consider developing guidance activities that focus on inherent cultural potential that incorporate the educational experiences of influential people from a variety of backgrounds. To achieve the latter goal guidance activities need to be planned in areas such as academic planning, study skills and time management, test-wiseness, and remediation. Such workshops are necessary to ensure that all young people have an opportunity to develop the skills to achieve, given cultural differences in learning styles.

The final fifth function is facilitating the career exploration and choice process among young people. For young people from many cultural backgrounds, the issues of career interest and choice become complex and challenging dimensions in their development for many reasons, including racism and socioeconomic disadvantage (Herring, 1998). From the elementary through the secondary level, therefore, it is important to provide young people from culturally diverse backgrounds with relevant guidance to the work world (Murrow-Taylor, Foltz, McDonald, Ellis, & Culbertson, 1999). For example, a comprehensive guidance initiative needs to include information forums on nonstereotyped jobs and careers. Also, counselors can sponsor "Career Days" and invite career role models from a variety of cultural backgrounds to school to share with students their perceptions and experiences in the work world. For older students, internships and cooperative experiences with culturally diverse businesses and professionals could be developed.

The role of student development facilitator in a comprehensive guidance and counseling program requires that counselors go beyond traditional school counseling practice. Specific guidance provisions are necessary for heightening awareness, expanding skills and maximizing options on the part of all students regardless of their cultural background.

CULTURALLY RESPONSIVE COUNSELORS AS STUDENT ADVOCATES

Traditionally, U.S. schools have made little allowance for cultural diversity in educational practice. School success has generally been narrowly defined in terms of White middle-class norms. Within such a framework, students whose cultural realities differ from these norms are often required to make important adjustments to ensure a measure of academic or social success. These adjustments become critical considering the lack of cultural awareness or cross-cultural sensitivity on the part of many educators. Obstacles to school success for young people from culturally diverse backgrounds, then, often come to be perceived as student inadequacies rather than considered as originating with institutional insensitivity (Lee, 1995).

Given such perceptions, the responsibility for problematic school functioning comes to rest solely on the culturally different status of a student and its divergence from the educational norm. Little consideration is given to the notion that problems and challenges may in reality be reactive responses by many students to a system that tolerates little diversity (Lee, 1995).

The professional school counselor is faced with a unique dilemma. Charged with facilitating student adjustment to the system, the counselor is confronted with the reality that often it is the system that needs adjustment to the student. This is particularly evident when systemic insensitivity negates diverse cultural realities. The solution to this dilemma in comprehensive guidance and counseling initiatives is a redefinition of the counseling role to account for the fact that problems are not always found in students, but often exist in the school as an educational system. Such a redefinition requires an awareness of the systemic barriers to quality education and the use of initiatives to effectively challenge them (Lee, 1995, Lee & Walz, 1998).

The role of student advocate represents such a redefinition and should be basic to a culturally responsive comprehensive school guidance and counseling program. In this role, a culturally responsive counselor can intervene in the educational system on behalf of students in ways designed to eliminate institutional barriers and cultural insensitivities. In addition, a student advocate becomes an important bridge across crucial cultural chasms separating culturally diverse children and the school.

Two important counselor functions form the basis of the student advocate role. The first function is facilitating educator awareness of systemic factors that may impinge upon student progress. The second function is facilitating the professional development among teachers and school administrators of culturally responsive approaches to education.

To implement the first function counselors may need to conduct individual and group consultations with teachers, administrators, and other school personnel to identify potentially culturally alienating or insensitive factors in educational attitudes, behaviors, or policies. It is important that educators become aware of their own personal "cultural blindspots" and how they might affect the development of students who come from backgrounds that are very different from their own.

The second function may be implemented through professional development groups and workshops organized by the guidance staff for teachers and other educators on ways to incorporate culturally diverse experiences into a total school program. These might entail a guidance program-initiated review of curriculum and master plans to ensure that cultural diversity is reflected in all areas related to academic, career, and personal-social development.

CULTURALLY RESPONSIVE COUNSELORS AND CULTURALLY DIVERSE FAMILIES AND COMMUNITIES

Children from culturally diverse backgrounds generally bring to the school a set of behaviors and success expectations that are fostered both at home and in their communities. Most families, regardless of cultural background, place a high value on education, considering it to be the prime factor in improving socioeconomic status. The expectations, however, of many students from culturally diverse backgrounds, their families, and communities are often at odds with the realities of schools and the educational process (Lee, 1995).

Often, cultural insensitivities inherent in the educational system tend not to validate the experiences of culturally diverse home and family life. Because of this, parents from many cultural backgrounds are often excluded from serious consideration in the education of their children. It is not unusual, therefore, to find that in many instances relations between the school and many communities are severely strained (Lee, 1995).

In such instances, it is important that comprehensive guidance and counseling programs provide ways to bridge the home and family life of culturally diverse students and the school. In order for such bridges to be constructed, it is necessary that counselors form working alliances with parents and families from diverse cultural backgrounds. An important counselor function is promoting the development and incorporation of a wide variety of family and community resources into the educational process (Carter & El Hindi, 1999).

These alliances may be operationalized in a several important ways. For example, it may be important to coordinate paraprofessional development programs to involve selected people from diverse communities in guidance-service delivery. Such individuals can be important in helping to bridge language and cultural barriers to effective academic, career, and personal-social interventions with young people and their families.

Another more innovative approach to bridge building may be making allowances for cultural differences in help-seeking attitudes and behavior and "thinking outside the box" about how and where comprehensive guidance and counseling services are to be delivered. One example of this would be a reconfiguration of the school counseling day. Reconfiguring the counseling day for some members of the counseling staff from 9 a.m. to 3 p.m. to 3 p.m. to 9 p.m. would allow for the possibility of greater access to family and communities. Counselors could conduct home visits during afternoon and evening hours to work with young people and their families on guidance and counseling concerns. These hours could maximize the possibility of greater access to parents than during the working and/or school day.

Similarly, comprehensive guidance activities could be conducted during these hours in community centers of social activity such as religious institutions or other places where people gather and experience both a feeling of safety and cultural validation. Counseling initiatives in such centers could be facilitated by paraprofessionals who are familiar with a community's language and cultural customs.

Finding ways to effectively reach out to culturally diverse communities and families by actually taking comprehensive guidance services to them would be a way to demonstrate that counselors are sensitive to the fact that not all parents perceive schools as welcoming environments. Language differences and cultural customs often make schools alienating and intimidating places for many parents. A good faith effort on the part of counselors that demonstrates that they are willing to meet parents "where they are" can help to dispel the fear or alienation many parents experience in their interactions with schools, when they are continuously forced, whether for good or bad, to make the trip to the school building.

School counselors and comprehensive guidance programs must play an active role in addressing the divergence between many communities and the educational system. Counselors can serve as an important link between the home, culturally diverse communities, and the school. A culturally responsive comprehensive guidance program can function to make the system more responsive to culturally diverse communities while at the same time increasing the level of effective participation by communities in the educational process.

CONCLUSION

Appropriate educational processes require that schools move beyond the myth of a monolithic society to the reality of cultural diversity. Professional school counselors can be on the cutting edge of this movement. As the 21st Century begins, it is becoming clear that a new American culture is emerging, a universal culture where diversity and pluralism are accepted hallmarks of the society. Young people, who represent diverse worldviews characteristic of this pluralism and are the future leaders of this new national order, are now maturing and developing their abilities and interests. They will need guidance in this developmental process from counseling professionals whose expertise includes sensitivity to human diversity and the skills to help develop talents within the context of cultural realities. When all of this is taken into consideration, professional school counselors and culturally responsive comprehensive guidance and counseling programs have the potential to be on the cutting edge of promoting access, equity, and educational justice.

Courtland C. Lee, Ph.D., is a professor of Counselor Education and dean of the School of Education at Hunter College, City University of New York

REFERENCES

American School Counselor Association. (1999). *Position statement: Cross/multicultural counseling*. Alexandria, VA: Author.

Baruth, L. G., & Manning, L. M. (2000). A call for multicultural counseling in middle schools. *Clearing House, 73*, 243–246.

Carter, R. B., & Vuong, T. K. (1997). Unity through diversity: Fostering cultural awareness. *Professional School Counseling, 1*(1), 47–49.

Carter, R. B., & El Hindi, A. E. (1999). Counseling Muslim children in school settings. *Professional School Counseling, 2*, 183–188.

Hayes, S. A. (1996). Cross-cultural learning in elementary guidance activities. *Elementary School Guidance and Counseling, 30*, 264–274.

Herring, R. D. (1997). *Multicultural counseling in schools: A synergetic approach*. Alexandria, VA: American Counseling Association.

Herring, R. D. (1998). *Career counseling in schools: Multicultural and developmental perspectives*. Alexandria, VA: American Counseling Association.

Lee, C. C. (Ed.). (1995). *Counseling for diversity: A guide for school counselors and related professionals*. Boston: Allyn & Bacon.

Lee, C. C., & Walz, G. (Eds.). (1998). *Social action: A mandate for counselors*. Alexandria, VA: American Counseling Association and ERIC Counseling and Student Services Clearinghouse.

Murrow-Taylor, C., Foltz, B. M., McDonald, A. B., Ellis, M. R., & Culbertson, K. (1999). A multicultural career fair for elementary school students. *Professional School Counseling, 2*, 241–243.

National Center for Education Statistics. (1996). *Trends in school district demographics 1986-87 to 1990–91*. Washington, DC: Author.

CHAPTER FOUR

The Counselor as Advocate for English Language Learners: An Action Research Approach

By Zaida McCall-Perez, Ed.D.

This article originally appeared in *Professional School Counseling*, Vol. 4, No. 1, 2000.

The number of students who are English Language Learners (ELLs) continues to increase across the country, with the most impact in California, New York, and Texas. Between 1990 and 1995, the number of kindergarten through 12th grade ELLs nationwide increased by approximately 47% (Macias & Kelly, 1996). In California, approximately 25% of the public school population are ELLs, also referred to as limited English proficient (LEP). Furthermore, these students are not just arriving in the elementary school years. According to the California Department of Education, 17% of all California secondary school students are identified as LEPs.

The burgeoning population of ELLs has prompted recent cross-cultural authorizations for teachers in a number of states, including California. Yet, there is no equivalent certification or licensing specifically for counselors who work with ELLs. In order to secure a California cross-cultural authorization, teachers must engage in course work, training and/or examinations. The content of these courses and examinations is designed to assure that teachers have the knowledge, attitudes, and skills to effectively teach ELLs. Although school counselors are eligible to obtain California's cross-cultural teacher certification, only a few schools require it for counselors. As a result, counselors are likely to address ELL special needs through trial and error, if at all. Some secondary school counselors are disappointed to discover how much of their time must be dedicated to scheduling students in classes. Although some counselors view student advisement as a necessary but unfulfilling aspect of their position, it is of critical importance to the success of adolescent ELLs. These students are less likely than their native-born peers to have other means of gaining information essential to their schooling decisions. Often, they do not have family members or peers who understand the U.S. school system well enough to provide guidance that will support their post-high school choices about college and career. This means many ELLs are counselor-dependent for school success in, and beyond, high school.

THE ORIGINAL PROJECT

Objectives

The present counselor study was a project within a larger demonstration project conducted by California Tomorrow (CT) – a nonprofit research and technical assistance organization in northern California that was one of the four national sites funded by the Andrew W. Mellon Foundation to conduct a project to improve secondary immigrant education. CT conducted a three-and-one-half-year demonstration project with two school districts in northern California, Hayward and Salinas (Olsen, Jaramillo, McCall-Perez, White, & Minicucci, 1999). The student outcome objectives, shared by the four national sites were to:

- Increase English literacy
- Improve mastery of academic content and skills
- Advance steadily through high school to graduation, thus increasing access to postsecondary opportunities

The CT project's overall results were measured in two categories: (1) overall success of the California Tomorrow equity-centered school change model and (2) the three national student outcome objectives. The California Tomorrow "Principles of Equitable and Responsive Schools" were advocacy, research immersion, professional development, data, student voice, time, partnerships, local design, and leadership. These are discussed more fully in both an executive summary (Olsen, Jaramillo, McCall-Perez, White, & Minicucci, 2000) and the full report (Olsen et al., 1999). The counselor professional development project, which is the topic of this paper, was a focus in the third year of the larger northern California project in Hayward at Tennyson and Hayward High Schools.

Methods and Procedures Project

Each national research site determined its own methods and procedures. In the CT project, a variety of practical measures such as grades, units earned for graduation, and the rate students became proficient in English determined the extent to which the desired student outcomes were achieved. Data were compiled for each of three student cohorts over three and one-half years, making it possible to compare the project's impact over time. Each cohort consisted of identified ELLs by grade level. For purposes of the study, cohorts were further grouped by those students who were enrolled in English-as-a-second-language (ESL) classes when they were in the ninth grade and those who were not. This distinction allowed for separate examination of subgroups of ELLs who (a) were recent arrivals (meaning they were enrolled in ESL in ninth grade) and (b) who had been here longer (meaning they were already orally fluent in English in ninth grade and therefore not enrolled in ESL during ninth grade).

COUNSELOR PROFESSIONAL DEVELOPMENT STUDY

As the CT Hayward project concluded its second year, it became evident that for truly systemic, secondary school change to take place, school counselors were both essential and pivotal to the process. The original project focus was primarily on teachers and administrators. The study presented here was contained within the larger CT project and reflects an added focus on counselor professional development as a strategy for improving schooling for secondary immigrant students. An on-the-job action research model of professional development was utilized. Counselors learned and applied the CT equity-centered school change principles as a means of gaining a deeper understanding of the schooling needs of ELLs. The premise of the model was that incorporation of the school change-process principles into the habits of counselors would serve as a catalyst for the creation of new solutions, and these in turn, would lead to greater student success. As counselors deepened their understanding and perspectives about ELLs and the issues that impact them, counselors identified and influenced changes in practices regarding scheduling, course placement, and student advising.

The Hayward site of this project-within-a-project is an urban district in northern California that is heavily impacted by past and present immigration. At the high school that is the focus of this article, more than 21 languages are spoken; approximately 35% of the 1,400 enrolled students are ELLs, and more than 50 languages are spoken in the local community. High school attendees include substantial numbers of Spanish, Farsi/Dari, Punjabi, and Vietnamese speakers.

METHODS AND PROCEDURES

An action research model of professional development for counselors was based on the premise that the equity-centered school change model, rather than a program imposed by the researchers, would yield locally designed solutions to improve schooling for secondary ELLs. The design, delivery, and content of the counselor focus were the result of collaboration and consultation among counselors, outside partners, and local project staff. Recurring cycles of inquiry, data collection, reflection, and action were characteristic of action research. These cycles were sustained through: (a) collegial relationships and dialogue; (b) student data, both quantitative and qualitative; and (c) targeted information relevant to counselors.

Collegial Dialogue and Reflection

Counselors were invited to participate in several groups that met regularly to engage in collegial dialogue and collaboration. The groups included: (a) an on-site monthly meeting of ESL and "sheltered" subject area teachers across disciplines; (b) a quarterly cross-site subject area meeting of teachers who collaborated in the development of course placement guidelines for mathematics and science classes designated for ELLs; (c) quarterly community dinner forums for the purpose of linking school personnel with each other, with students, and with individuals from community-based organizations around the theme of educating ELLs; and (d) a quarterly meeting of immigrant parents, their students, and school counselors, which was supported by the project resource teacher and bilingual community liaison. In addition, two counselors served as designated liaisons among counselors, the local project staff, and outside partners. The liaison role was critical in representing the counselor perspective in planning activities and informing fellow counselors of project activities, and student data at counselor monthly meetings.

Forums were well attended by counselors. The agenda for each forum included: presentations of local student data, briefings on literature and research, student panel presentations, and structured opportunities for reflective dialogue and discussion. One forum focused on transitions to higher education. Community agencies, secondary schools, local community colleges, state colleges and universities sent representatives to participate. A chart, collaboratively developed during one of the forums, displayed each agency's services and target populations, thus enabling participants to gain a better understanding of local and regional services available for ELLs. The chart developed during the forum can be viewed both as a product of the project, and as a primary action research strategy that generated data for reflection in determining next appropriate action steps.

Data, Student Voice, and Inquiry

Counselors learned about ELLs through inquiry, review of research, examination of local student achievement and course enrollment data, and listening and reflecting on student voices (such as student panels and questionnaires). The following are examples of data collected that contributed to this process: (a) percentage of Ds and Fs earned by ELLs not served by classes of ESL; (b) percentage of Ds and Fs earned by ELLs compared to proficient English speakers; (c) units accrued by ELLs at each grade level compared to proficient English speakers; (d) language census data for numbers and percent of ELLs served by type of program; (e) number and percentage of students redesignated as Fluent English Proficient; and (f) enrollment figures and grade point averages for ELLs in science and mathematics.

Student voice-generated data for reflection and dialogue regarding student experiences, needs, desires and dreams were conveyed through transcripts of individual student interviews, results of student questionnaires, and by student panels. Results of a senior survey revealed that ELL students' career and post-high school goals were not supported by the course choices they had made. Of the students who intended to pursue a 2-year community college degree, 47% identified careers goals which require a degree from a 4-year college. And 95% of ELL seniors were enrolled in one or more college-prep courses, however 46% of those seniors earned at least one D or F in the first semester of their college-prep courses. While a large majority of the ELL respondents expected to attend 4-year colleges and universities, only a small portion of them were actually enrolled in classes that prepared them for college. Again, while the questionnaire results can be considered a product of the study, the results were used as a springboard for reflection and dialogue from which next-step decisions were made. For example, a next-step decision in this instance was to corroborate the survey data with the actual experiences of former ELL students, now in college.

Local graduates (former ELLs now enrolled in college) served on a panel and gave personal accounts of the challenges they had faced in high school and reflected on how their high schools had or had not assisted them in getting into college or determining their educational futures. The audience seemed stunned to learn that one student who had entered U.S. schools in 6th grade at the age of 12, had had no prior schooling in Vietnam. This young man acquired literacy, graduated from high school, and was a second year student in pre-Engineering at a local state college. It had been an older brother, high school dropout, rather than any school personnel, who encouraged and assisted him to get into college.

Local data on student achievement and course enrollment also served as a catalyst for further discussion and reflection. Counselors and teacher leaders were encouraged to disseminate the data to other groups in their schools, thus expanding the dialogue about ELL issues and needs. These data helped counselors further define issues and formulate perspectives regarding the schooling of ELLs. Counselors absorbed multiple perspectives about ELLs, their needs, the obstacles and barriers they encounter, and their successes and failures. Through dialogue and reflection stimulated by both quantitative and qualitative data, these perspectives influenced change in practice and ultimately helped shape the goals and expectations within the school.

Targeted Information
The outside partners (California Tomorrow) and local project staff presented information targeted to counselors about the courses in which

ELLs were enrolled, grades earned by ELLs, and the length of time it takes for them to learn English and succeed academically in high school.

Counselors participated in a required orientation to the district's secondary newcomer center, where recently arrived ELLs participated in ESL classes. The orientation was designed specifically for counselors. After a general orientation, they observed first-hand ELL students in the classrooms at different levels of ESL instruction. After classroom observations, some counselors were surprised to note that they had greatly misjudged the levels of English proficiency of their own advisees. After observing students at different levels of ESL, counselors examined samples of student work from each ESL level and compared the work to the linguistic demands of mainstream courses.

RESULTS AND DISCUSSION

Overall, ELLs at the participating high school achieved greater school success as a result of the demonstration project. Counselor participation contributed to positive student outcomes including: (a) increased intensity of English classes and accelerated credit accrual, (b) more appropriate course placement in relation to each student's stage of English acquisition and prior academic experiences, and these contributed to (c) smoother transitions through high school and more post-high school options. Specifically, more ELLs remained in school, studied more English, enrolled in more classes, and accrued more units towards graduation and college.

Increased Time and Intensity

Length of time, a critical factor for ELLs in secondary schools, is one of the most important variables in achieving proficiency in a new language, no matter what the instructional approach. Some research suggests that, even for previously schooled students, 4 to 10 years of study are required to achieve native-level English proficiency (Collier, 1989; Cummins, 1983; Thomas & Collier, 1997). The tradition of students attending high school for only 4 years presents a major, if not insurmountable, challenge for a student who first begins to learn the English language as an adolescent. An informal analysis of ELLs in this district indicated that 6 to 7 years is the average length of time to become redesignated to English proficient. Counselors reflected on the reality faced by the ELL adolescent who is in a race against time in which every minute counts. Thinking deeply about these facts served as a springboard for counselors to develop creative solutions and strategies.

Proactive use of the block schedule contributed positively to student outcomes. In a block schedule, students have the option of taking up to 8 courses per year (32 classes in 4 years), as compared to a traditional six-period day in which there is only space for six courses per year (24 over 4 years). Although native English speakers enroll in one English course per year, ELLs were advised to enroll in English classes every term. Many students exercised the option of enrolling in more than the minimum required number of English classes and benefited continuity in their formal study of English.

Optimal use of the 4 X 4 Block schedule constituted a significant change in practice. Forty-six percent (N = 98) of the ELLs enrolled in two English courses per year (the equivalent of 2 years of English credit in one academic year) compared with 33% (N = 61) at one other local high school and 32% (N = 115) at another. Sixty-seven percent (N = 287) of high school ELLs enrolled in four blocks of courses during 1997-98 compared to 54% (N = 102) at one other local high school and 55% (N = 98) at another. Although the move to a block schedule was implemented as the project began, the new uses of the block schedule for the benefit of ELLs was a local strategy resulting from the counselor participation in the project.

Unit Accrual and School Retention

At the end of three-and-one-half years, data compiled by the outside evaluator, Minicucci Associates (Olsen et al., 1999), showed that ELL students at each grade level were earning, on average, more units each year than they had previously. The block schedule, coupled with strategic counselor advising, course placement guidelines, and individual ELL student data contributed to increased ELL access to curriculum, academic rigor, and study of English. Students were also able to enroll in other additional courses required for high school graduation and college. Students who had made steady progress, but had not been able to complete high school graduation requirements within 4 years, were allowed and encouraged to return for a fifth year (additional time) to complete high school and prepare for college.

Average unit accrual at each grade level increased for all cohorts. For example, the average unit accrual of 10th grade ELLs, who were served by ESL during ninth grade, increased from 121 units to an average of 128 units, up 5.8% by the end of three-and-one-half years. The average unit accrual of the non-ESL-served 10th grade ELL increased from 104 to 116 units, up 11.5%. The average unit accrual of the ninth grade ESL-served cohort increased from 49 to 59, an increase of 20% over the three-and-one-half year project. And for the non-ESL served ninth grade cohort, the increase was from 49 to 54 units, up 10%.

The first year of the larger study uncovered a substantial finding that 23% (N = 35) of ninth grade ELL students dropped out between the beginning of ninth grade and the beginning of 10th grade. We called this the "leave rate" or the "retention rate." These terms distinguished the phenomena from "drop-outs," who by state definition are students who leave school after 10th grade. Students who "leave" after ninth grade (and prior to entering 10th grade) are typically invisible statistics. Bringing this data to the attention of counselors prompted a focus on this particular group of students. Counselor changes in practice contributed to a decrease in the percentage of ninth grade "leavers" (an improvement in the number of students who were retained to the end of 10th grade). By the end of the third year of the project, 5% (N = 8) left during the same time period.

Increased Access to Science and Mathematics

Successive cohorts of ELLs showed increases in enrollment in gatekeeper science and mathematics classes. Prior anecdotal information indicated that some ELL students failed mathematics classes because they had insufficient English to succeed at the time they were enrolled in them. Teachers were frustrated because they were not successfully reaching their students. These problems diminished as a result of changes in counselor advising and course placement practices and procedures.

Historically, a computer software program generated the assignment of students to mathematics and science classes without regard for their linguistic skills. Although counselors with personal knowledge about a particular ELL student might hand-schedule that student, no counselor with a caseload of 1,500 students could know the linguistic and academic profile of every student. Systematizing the retrieval and transmission of individual ELL student data was an essential step towards improving ELL student advising. Counselor access to individual ELL student data made it possible for counselors to consider linguistic and academic profiles of students during advisement and when making course placement decisions. Thus, ELL enrollments increased in science and mathematics.

For instance, during the first year of the study (1994–5), only 34% (N = 27) of 10th graders who had been served by ESL during ninth grade were enrolled in science courses. By the end of the third year (1996–7), 84% (N = 27) of 10th graders who had been served by ESL during ninth grade were enrolled in science courses. The number is the same because numbers of students enrolled in ninth grade ESL had decreased from 79 to 31. This represents a 50% increase in access to gatekeeper courses for the ESL-served cohort. Other gains exceeded 50%. Gains in science enrollment for the not-served-by-ESL cohort increased from 13% to 92% by project's end. Mathematics enrollment gains for ESL-served 10th graders increased from 47% to 91%. For ESL-nonserved 10th graders, the mathematics enrollment increased from 40% to 88%. Thus, better advisement, routinely available ELL student data, and teacher-developed placement guidelines contributed to greater school success as measured by increased enrollments in mathematics and science courses.

Better Informed Course Placement

Counselors who understand the relationships among subject area content, teacher instructional style, and the student's linguistic skills and academic background can be extremely helpful to ELLs through the advising process. For example, it is helpful to schedule ELLs for their more linguistically demanding courses with unfamiliar content (e.g., U.S. History) in later high school years, when they have greater proficiency in English. Such flexibility in scheduling, however, may require relaxation of lock-step course sequences common in many high schools. It also requires that counselors have accurate information regarding ELL student English proficiency levels.

In collaboration with ESL teachers, data processing staff, and key administrators, counselors took an active role in the creation of procedures for retrieving and transmitting ELL student data. Information in the profiles of each ELL student consisted of (a) number of years the student has been in an English medium environment; (b) level of student literacy in the native language; (c) number of years of prior schooling in another country; (d) amount of previous ESL study both in the U.S. and outside; and (e) level of English proficiency in English oral, reading, and writing skills.

The importance of establishing a system for storing, retrieving, and transmitting student data cannot be overstated. Tremendous collaborative efforts among counselors, teachers, administrators, and data processing staff were necessary in order to merge separate student databases for meaningful use by counselors and teachers. Subject area placement guidelines established and agreed upon by teachers, and corresponding to student English proficiency levels (codes), were also essential. Once these elements were in place, an in-service for counselors on how to use, interpret, and apply student data and placement guidelines helped counselors to refine advisement and placement decisions.

At a systemic level, counselors influenced the master schedule development for the next year by using LEP data to inform decisions regarding courses students were likely to need, rather than, and prior to, determining course offerings solely in response to current student sign-ups. In addition to projected overall enrollment, ELL projected enrollment was estimated based on the previous school year's school language census data and counts of ELLs at each English proficiency level.

Improving Transitions through High School and Beyond

Counselors can obstruct or facilitate the journey of a student through high school and beyond. Counselor awareness is a first step to responsible advising of ELLs. Large caseloads can pressure counselors to serve only those students who seek them out. In such environments, immigrant students become invisible because they are not aware of the role and power of the counselor. In an informal local school survey, many ELL students reported not even knowing their counselor or how and where to find the counselor.

Unique ELL issues such as whether a college or university accepts Advanced ESL to fulfill English entrance requirements are not decided uniformly by all institutions (Lane, Brinton, & Erickson, 1996). An ELL who does not receive early and accurate course advising may fail to meet college admission requirements when the time arrives. Most ELLs with 4-year college and university aspirations need to be explicitly advised to include both ESL and English in their high school program. ELLs and their parents also need explicit explanations regarding college preparatory courses and their relationship to college entrance. They need to be taught how to recognize the code or symbol that indicates college prep credit on report cards and transcripts. This information enables students to make better-informed course selections on their own behalf rather than leaving these important decisions to others or to chance.

Counselors can also be pro-active in explaining to ELLs that foreign language requirements for college entrance may be fulfilled in a variety of ways not available to native-English speakers. Some immigrant students, for example, can use foreign transcripts, evidence of substantial schooling in their home country, or a letter from their principal verifying language fluency in a non-English language. Counselor awareness of this kind of explicit and pro-active advice and knowledge can make a dramatic and lasting difference to an ELL.

As counselors gain a better understanding of ELLs and recognize that ELL students have just as good a chance at college entrance as native English speakers, counselors can become effective advocates for ELLs, individually and systemically. A consequence of counselor participation in this project was to make the specific needs of ELLs more central to overall school planning. ELL students were less systemically marginalized as a result of the project. As the lead counselor reflected:

The goal is 100% of kids college-ready by the end of junior year. That means they are going to be visiting at a college level, and we're saying the ELLs that come in the ninth grade will be writing college level work by the end of 10th grade. That is a real challenge, but it is a welcome challenge. (lead counselor at Tennyson High School, 1997)

LIMITATIONS OF THE STUDY

Action research is a process, as opposed to a single research methodology. The action research approach is a process of engaging in recurring cycles of inquiry, data, reflection, and action/intervention. It draws upon both qualitative and quantitative methodologies for generating data that are then used as a springboard for either further inquiry or action (interventions). The principles for equitable and responsive schools (see Appendix B) utilized in the present study also constitute a process as opposed to a predetermined set of interventions. In this project, researchers and participants collaborated in the evolution and development of counselor professional development activities. New practices and procedures (interventions) evolved through a process of widespread collaboration, rather than from the imposition of a rigidly defined sequence of activities or predefined interventions. The challenge was not to reproduce static models or to seek to meet the letter of the law, but to create schools that are continually responsive to the mixes of cultures and languages present and to improve accountability within the school for embracing immigrant populations and for producing high achievement.

As a result, one limitation of this study is the difficulty of isolating a one-to-one correspondence between interventions and outcomes. Another limitation may be that, although student cohorts were tracked for 3 and one-half years, no standardized measures of English acquisition or academic achievement were part of the research design. On the other hand, the project's outcome measures were specifically selected for their meaningfulness to high school practitioners as indicators of student success. Success was defined as students progressing steadily through high school and accessing college preparatory curriculum. Measures were also selected because they are available in all high schools, offering ease of potential replication.

ELLs face many psychosocial and psychocultural challenges, including the prejudices, discrimination, and racism of many adults and peers in U.S. schools. The study did not measure project impact on these issues directly. However, some of the psychosocial and psychocultural challenges faced by ELLs are the result of systemic barriers, which are the manifestation of institutionalized prejudice and discrimination. Insensitive or uninformed school leaders create some policies and procedures that foster these barriers. The present study focused on enhancing the knowledge and attitudes of counselors. Counselors' actions and decisions can be critical contributors to the schooling experiences, successes, and failures of ELLs in U.S. secondary schools. As school leaders, counselors can also be central in reducing or eliminating these barriers. It was a premise of this study that by addressing the knowledge, attitudes, and practices of school counselors, there would be shifts in school policies and practices related to ELLs that would recognize the dignity and worth of all students in the system, including English Language Learners.

SUMMARY AND RECOMMENDATIONS

Counselors are encouraged to conduct their own professional needs assessment regarding their own preparation to appropriately serve immigrants and adolescent ELLs. A self-assessment checklist is included in the appendix to assist counselors. Counselors can replicate many of the action research approaches described in this article. Once a knowledge base is acquired, data systems developed, habits of inquiry and structures and time for collegial collaboration established, there are ongoing benefits, which have a life of their own. Action research offers a process through which professional service and student achievement can be enriched, leading to improvements of the educational institution and better preparation of students to successfully encounter challenges in the world of tomorrow.

Professional school counselors are encouraged to value the important and central role they play in the success of ELLs. Particularly in periods of challenges to the educational rights of immigrant and language minority students, informed counselors can serve as their most effective advocates and protectors. In some contexts, it may be the counselor who is an ELL student's only advocate. The crucial gate-keeping role of counselors can either open or close the schoolhouse door in the educational journey of ELLs.

The findings from this action research project showed positive effects on student outcomes that were achieved through enhancing the professional preparation of counselors to work with ELLs. Key strategies for impacting student outcomes were (a) collegial relationships and dialogue, (b) student data, student voice and inquiry, and (c) targeted information. Student outcomes of increased English literacy, improved mastery of academic content and skills, and smoother transitions through and beyond high school were achieved.

By embracing and applying the California Tomorrow "Principles for Equitable and Responsive Schools," counselors appeared to acquire a greater knowledge base about second language learners and integrated that knowledge with personal experience and relevant research. While no one initiative or strategy can be isolated as the cause of improved school success for ELLs, what is clear is that by gaining a deeper understanding of the school success issues faced by ELLs, caring, competent, and proactive counselors generated new solutions to old problems, which led to positive student outcomes.

Zaida McCall-Perez, Ed.D., is an associate professor and director of Cross-Cultural Teacher Certification Programs, Saint Mary's College of California, Lafayette. She is a research associate with California Tomorrow, Oakland, CA.

REFERENCES

Collier, V. (1989). How long? A synthesis of research on academic achievement in a second language. *TESOL Quarterly, 23*(3), 509–531.

Cummins, J. (1983). Language proficiency and academic achievement. In J. W. Oller (Ed.), *Issues in language testing research* (pp. 108–126). Rowely, MA: Newbury House.

Lane, J., Brinton, D., & Erickson, M. (1996). ESL students entering the University of California. *The CATESOL Journal, 91*(1), p. 101.

Macias, R. F., & Kelly, C. (1996). *Summary report of the survey of the state of limited English proficient students and available educational programs and services, 1994-95.* Santa Barbara, CA: University of California Language Minority Research Institute.

Olsen, L., Jaramillo, A., McCall-Perez, Z., White, J. & Minicucci, C. (2000). *Executive summary, igniting change for immigrant students: Portraits of three high schools.* Oakland, CA: California Tomorrow.

Olsen, L., Jaramillo, A., McCall-Perez, Z., White, J., & Minicucci, C. (1999). *Igniting change for immigrant students: Portraits of three high schools.* Oakland, CA: California Tomorrow.

Thomas, W., & Collier, V. (1997). *NCBE resource collection series: School effectiveness for language minority students, Vol. 36.* Washington, DC: National Clearinghouse for Bilingual Education.

APPENDIX A:

Counselor Professional Development Needs Assessment Checklist

If you can answer, "yes" to the following questions, you have a solid understanding of the ELLs in your school/ district – and you know whom to talk to when you encounter a problem that you alone cannot solve. In items for which you do not have a response, an action research inquiry using the Principles for Equitable and Responsive Schools may be useful counselor professional development.

1. ____ I know how many levels of ESL my school offers.
2. ____ I know the difference between Basic Interpersonal Communication Skills (BICS) and Cognitive Academic Language Proficiency (CALP).
3. ____ I know whether and which sections (if any) of required academic courses have been specially designed for intermediate and advanced English Language Learners (ELLs).
4. ____ I know which teachers are certified to teach ELLs.
5. ____ I have observed selected ELLs in classes designed for them.
6. ____ I am familiar with the linguistic demographics of my school and district: the number and percent of ELLs, their countries-of-origin, home languages and reasons for coming to the U.S. (e.g., immigrant, refugee, political asylum).
7. ____ I have a personal friend or relative who learned English as a Second Language (ESL), and I have talked to that person about the experience.
8. ____ I know which classifications and computer codes are used to designate types of second language learners in my school district.
9. ____ I know the district criteria and standards for full English proficiency and how long (on average) it takes students at each grade-span (e.g., k-5, 6-8, 9-12) to meet these criteria.
10. ____ I know what student data are kept about ELLs or can be requested.
11. ____ I know how and where to access (or make requests for) individual student data and how to use that information in planning an ELLs school program class schedule.
12. ____ There is an ESL teacher of whom I can freely ask questions.
13. ____ I know whether bilingual assistance is available and how to request it.
14. ____ I know the meanings of my school's ELL codes and how to interpret them for placement purposes.
15. ____ I know how and where to update myself regarding immigrant students' legal rights in relation to college admission and financial aid.

APPENDIX B:

California Tomorrow's Principles for Equitable and Responsive Schools

Advocacy: Create mechanisms and supports for educators to speak out and act effectively on behalf of underserved students. This includes personal advocacy for individual students as well as advocacy to change the system of schooling so that new programs and support will be institutionalized.

Research Immersion: The partnership introduced research literature to the core groups and provided forums in which they could read and consider the research and engage together in collaborative inquiry and reflection.

Professional development: Significant improvements in student achievement depend upon improving the quality of teaching and the skills and understandings of teachers about effective pedagogy. Our model provided sustained, long-term, collaborative, and inquiry-focused models of professional growth.

Data: Data is essential to help educators "see" where and how gaps in achievement are occurring. Our project sought to create data systems and habits for understanding and holding schools accountable for immigrant student access and achievement. Schools need expert help in developing data systems and strong inquiry processes for analyzing data about achievement, participation, and progress through school.

Student Voice: We worked with our schools to regularly use a wide range of strategies for eliciting, supporting and using student voice in the change process, including: student panels, focus groups, interviewing, shadowing, and questionnaires. These are essential to inform school change, to motivate educators to change, and to bring language minority students, who often have not had a voice in their schools, into the dialogue about achievement and reform.

Time: The model involves working with schools to examine their uses of time and to consider restructuring how time is used in class periods, school days, and years with an eye to maximizing instruction for immigrant students. Immigrant secondary students face the triple burdens of needing to learn English rapidly, to learn all their academic subjects at grade level, and often to overcome academic gaps in the past education.

Partnerships: Schools can be more responsive and effective when they are supported by strong partnerships with those who can provide the "critical friend" lens with providers of community supports.

Local design: Reforms are more appropriate when people within a community, who know their own students and contexts, design them. We also believe that the most lasting change occurs when those changes are "owned" by the people with the responsibility to implement change. For these reasons, our model supports each school community to design its own agenda for change.

Leadership: The model works to foster leadership within the school community as it emerges from the teaching staff, from parents and from community members who care most about immigrant students (Olsen et al., 2000, p. 6).

Assisting Students with Learning Disabilities Transitioning to College: What School Counselors Should Know

By Amy Milsom, D.Ed., and Michael T. Hartley, M.A.

This article originally appeared in *Professional School Counseling*, Vol. 8, No. 5, 2005.

Students with learning disabilities can benefit from developing specific knowledge and skills that may increase their chances of successfully completing postsecondary degrees. School counselors can play important roles as advocates, collaborators, and direct service providers. This article is a review of critical student knowledge and skill areas as well as school counselor roles in the implementation of postsecondary transition planning services for students with learning disabilities.

Learning disability is an umbrella term providing a common language for a wide range of professionals, including teachers and counselors (Thomas & Woods, 2003). Neurologically based learning disabilities manifest themselves in different ways (Brinckerhoff, 1994). According to the Individuals with Disabilities Education Act (IDEA) of 1990, students with learning disabilities may have weaknesses in one or more areas including reading, writing, spelling, listening, speaking, thinking, and mathematics. All students are unique in terms of which of these characteristics they possess.

Since the passage of the Americans with Disabilities Act (ADA) of 1990, more and more colleges and universities have implemented support services for students with disabilities. The 173% increase in the number of students with learning disabilities attending postsecondary institutions from 1989 to 1998 (Henderson, 1999) is attributed in part to that legislation (Flexer, Simmons, Luft, & Baer, 2005). It has been suggested, however, that many students with learning disabilities are encouraged to pursue vocational education rather than to attend 4-year colleges (Janiga & Costenbader, 2002). Data indicate that "only 13% of students with learning disabilities (compared to 53% of students in general population) have attended a 4-year post-secondary school program within two years of leaving high school" (National Longitudinal Transition Study, 1994, as cited in National Center for Learning Disabilities, 2004, p. 1).

Although disability legislation has helped to make postsecondary education a more realistic option for students with disabilities, the National

Joint Committee on Learning Disabilities (NJCLD) suggested "… that many students with learning disabilities do not consider postsecondary education options (2- and 4-year colleges and vocational schools) because they are not encouraged, assisted, or prepared to do so" (1994, p. 1). Hitchings et al. (2001) interviewed 97 college students with learning disabilities and found 20 reported being discouraged from pursuing college by teachers and/or school counselors.

Many students with learning disabilities do pursue postsecondary education, but they often do not complete their programs of study. The U.S. Department of Education (as cited in Janiga & Costenbader, 2002) reported that since 1989, only 53% of students with disabilities either had completed their postsecondary degree or were still enrolled, as compared to 64% of students without disabilities. Dickinson and Verbeek (2002) suggested that individuals with learning disabilities might be more successful in life if they were able to complete higher levels of education. They also indicated, however, that many students with learning disabilities end up working in low-paying jobs with few benefits and little job security. Successful transition to college opens the door for future economic success, social power, and personal well-being.

SCHOOL COUNSELOR INVOLVEMENT IN TRANSITION PLANNING

School personnel are directed to help students with learning disabilities prepare for life after high school. In 1990, IDEA mandated the inclusion of transition services in students' Individualized Education Programs (IEPs) by age 16; that age was lowered to 14 with the IDEA Amendments of 1997. Special education professionals primarily coordinate IEPs; however, IDEA mandates the participation of *related services* professionals when relevant. As such, information on college transitions should be provided to students with learning disabilities by school counselors. The American School Counselor Association (ASCA) supports school counselor involvement in transition planning, as outlined in its professional position statements Educational Planning (ASCA, 2000) and *The Professional School Counselor and Students with Special Needs* (ASCA, 2004). Additionally, the 2001 Council for Accreditation of Counseling and Related Educational Programs (CACREP) standards specify that school counselors be trained to assist with educational transitions.

Despite support for school counselor involvement in transition planning (ASCA, 2000, 2004; CACREP, 2001; Hildreth, Dixon, Frerichs, & Heflin, 1994; Satcher, 1993; Satcher & Dooley-Dickey, 1991; Taves & Hutchinson, 1993), Milsom (2002) found many school counselors reported not being involved in providing transition planning services for students with disabilities. Of participants in her national study, only 68% of high school counselors reported assisting with transition plans for students with disabilities. Additionally, Hitchings et al. (2001) found only 8% of the participating college students with learning disabilities indicated having met with a school counselor during high school to discuss coursework and requirements for applying to college.

As advocates for *all* students (ASCA, 2003), school counselors can play important roles in helping students with learning disabilities transition to college. School counselors develop working relationships with college personnel and have experience assisting students with college admissions. They are often the individuals who coordinate college admissions testing and can most easily arrange for (and help students prepare for) those tests. Finally, they possess knowledge of courses required for college admission and for success in future careers. With collaboration from special educators, school counselors can help students with learning disabilities determine and explore realistic future options and ensure that they complete the steps (e.g., coursework) necessary to pursue those options.

COLLEGE TRANSITION PLANS

All students transitioning to a postsecondary institution can benefit from participating in activities that help them develop skills in academic, career, and personal/social domains (ASCA, 2003). For example, all students should be encouraged to examine and assess their strengths in areas such as studying, time management, and organization, as these skills have been associated with success in college settings (DuChossois & Michaels, 1994). Hicks-Coolick and Kurtz (1997) conducted a qualitative study with college disability services counselors regarding the characteristics of students with learning disabilities who were successful in college. Three main themes emerged in their findings: motivation, preparation (including completion of college preparatory coursework and development of effective study skills), and self-advocacy skills.

The NJCLD (1994) stated that postsecondary transitions can be greatly affected by student participation in transition planning activities. In fact, Halpern, Yovanoff, Doren, and Benz (1995) found that students with disabilities who had engaged in some formal transition planning were more likely to pursue postsecondary education than those who had not. In general, however, there is little effectiveness data on transition programs, and no research specifically focusing on the effectiveness of school counselors in providing interventions in this area.

Many transition programs are offered to incoming freshmen by various colleges and universities (see Brinckerhoff, 1994; Dalke & Schmidt, 1987;

HEATH Resource Center, 2004), but some programs have been implemented in high schools. For example, Phillips (1990) presented the results of a program implemented to 15 students with learning disabilities over a 4-year period. Students started in ninth grade by participating in their own IEP meetings, visiting colleges, and participating in seminars during which they discussed their disabilities. Over the next 3 years, students were assisted in exploring their own learning styles, determining which accommodations were effective for them, and communicating their needs to teachers. Phillips reported upon completion of the program that students were more aware of their rights, had developed greater disability self-awareness, and could identify more potential career options.

Aune (1991) described a program focusing on individualized psychoeducational training for 55 students with learning disabilities. Student needs were assessed based on a transition model, which provided guidelines for content areas (e.g., using accommodations), desirable timelines, and optional services (e.g., consultation with parents, individual counseling). Through grant funding, a transition specialist was hired to serve as a case manager, meeting bimonthly with students one-on-one and coordinating the provision of additional services. Optional group sessions were provided during the summer months, and students continued monthly communication (often by phone) with the case manager during their first year of college. Aune reported 71% of the students pursued postsecondary courses within a year of graduating from high school and the majority were more aware of their disabilities and able to self-advocate.

IDEA mandates that students be actively involved in their own transition planning, yet research indicates that many students do not actively participate in their own IEP conferences (Grigal, Test, Beattie, & Wood, 1997; Hitchings et al., 2001; Williams & O'Leary, 2001). Consistent with the ASCA National Model® (ASCA, 2003), a comprehensive approach to postsecondary transition planning is recommended, emphasizing the involvement of various professionals as well as the student and his or her parents (Phillips, 1990; Sitlington, Clark, & Kolstoe, 2000). School counselors can assist in ensuring that transition planning is approached collaboratively and with the active involvement of students and parents.

FOUR COMPONENTS FOR EFFECTIVE COLLEGE TRANSITION PLANNING

Knowledge of Disability

Campbell and Dahir (1997) identified the awareness of personal strengths and skills as important in academic and career planning for all students. Related to this concept, students with learning disabilities can benefit from developing awareness of their disability (Cowen, 1993; Durlak, Rose, & Bursuck, 1994; Goldhammer & Brinckerhoff, 1992; Merchant & Gajar, 1997; NJCLD, 1994; Taves & Hutchinson, 1993). By learning about their disabilities, including associated strengths and deficits as well as interventions or accommodations that work, students with learning disabilities can be better prepared to set realistic future goals.

School counselors may not be experts on disability, but special educators are. Collaborating with special education teachers may be the most effective method of helping students with learning disabilities to increase awareness and understanding of their own disabilities. Special educators can be encouraged to help these students examine their disabilities and their educational histories, including successes and challenges. School counselors then can follow up with individual or small-group sessions during which they help students with learning disabilities explore the relationship between their skills and abilities and potential future careers. A discussion of required coursework also would be important at this time. More specifically, by making students with learning disabilities aware of course requirements for various college majors and encouraging them to try out rigorous academic courses, school counselors can help these students assess the reality of successfully pursuing various majors.

Knowledge of Postsecondary Support Services

All students can benefit from learning about what to expect when they go to college, including topics ranging from time management and personal motivation to extracurricular activities. Students with learning disabilities need additional information not relevant to the majority of students pursuing college. Before choosing a college, students with learning disabilities should possess knowledge of admission requirements for students with disabilities (Sitlington et al., 2000) as well as the availability of and procedures for accessing support services (Cowen, 1993; Durlak et al., 1994; NJCLD, 1994; Sitlington et al.).

According to Section 504 of the Vocational Rehabilitation Act of 1973, postsecondary schools must modify program requirements that are discriminatory and allow for the use of auxiliary aids. One modification might be a course substitution, and examples of auxiliary aids might include taped texts, exam readers, and note takers. If students become aware of what accommodations will be available in advance of graduating from high school, they would have time to test the effectiveness of those accommodations in their high school classes.

In addition to providing basic information to students with learning disabilities about common types of postsecondary support services, secondary school counselors can serve as liaisons to postsecondary institutions, helping students with learning disabilities connect with personnel who can more thoroughly discuss admissions requirements and availability of disability services. School counselors also could encourage these students to visit colleges and can help by arranging student meetings with admissions and disability services during the visit.

Providing these students with a list of important questions to ask postsecondary personnel (e.g., "What documentation do I need to obtain services??" "How do I apply for services?") can provide structure for the students and ensure they obtain enough information to help them make informed decisions. The answers to many of these questions are likely to be available via college and university Web sites, and school counselors can assist students with learning disabilities in accessing and navigating through these Web sites (Milsom, Akos, & Thompson, 2004).

Knowledge of Disability Legislation

Students with learning disabilities can benefit from learning about disability legislation, specifically IDEA, ADA, and Section 504 (NJCLD, 1994; Scott, 1991; Sitlington et al., 2000). Unless formal education is provided, many students with learning disabilities go through high school without ever being informed of the legislation that guides the provision of services to which they are entitled. Milsom et al. (2004) found that of the six 11th- and 12th-grade students with learning disabilities participating in their study (a psychoeducational group designed to help them prepare for college), none was familiar with disability legislation.

While one could argue that students can successfully complete high school ignorant of the laws that help them, the same cannot be said for students in college. Because the ADA and Section 504 mandate that postsecondary institutions provide support services only for individuals who request them, provided those individuals possess the appropriate documentation, students with learning disabilities must be aware of their rights and responsibilities. The ADA and Section 504 protect students who are otherwise qualified from unfair discrimination; in relation to college, otherwise qualified refers to meeting the requisite essential requirements for admission and academic program regardless of the disability (Scott, 1994). The essential requirements depend on the core competencies of the academic program (e.g., an essential requirement for a math degree would include the ability to successfully complete coursework in math).

Through collaboration and coordination, school counselors can help students with learning disabilities to acquire information about disability legislation. In addition to providing information to these students in a small-group format (Milsom et al., 2004), school counselors can invite disability services personnel in to talk with students with learning disabilities and their parents. Content should include a discussion of changing roles and responsibilities for students and parents. A variety of resources are available to assist school counselors, teachers, parents, and students in understanding disability legislation (see Greenbaum & Markel, 2001; Turnbull & Turnbull, 2000; Webster, Clary, & Griffith, 2005), but by consulting with their district special education administrators, school counselors can promote a collaborative effort and ensure the information they have is current.

Ability to Self-Advocate

Once students with learning disabilities possess disability awareness, knowledge of disability services available in college, and an understanding of their rights and responsibilities, they must develop skills to successfully advocate on their own behalf. Consistent with the ADA, many researchers discuss the importance of students with learning disabilities developing self-advocacy skills (Durlak et al., 1994; Goldhammer & Brinckerhoff, 1992; Hicks-Coolick & Kurtz, 1997; Hildreth et al., 1994; Lock & Layton, 2001; NJCLD, 1994). Wilson (1994) found that nearly 70% of the participating students with learning disabilities relied on their parents or teachers to communicate their needs.

Essentially, self-advocacy involves a student possessing an awareness of his or her needs and the ability to effectively communicate those needs to others. Hicks-Coolick and Kurtz (1997) identified five components for self-advocacy: self-awareness, self-acceptance, knowledge of rights and resources, assertiveness skills, and problem-solving skills. Durlak et al. (1994) used a direct-instruction approach to teach self-determination skills to students with learning disabilities, providing feedback and ongoing practice. They concluded that "...repeated practice of self-determination skills relating to self-awareness, self-advocacy, and assertiveness is essential if students with learning disabilities are to achieve some degree of comfort with, and confidence in, their ability to demonstrate these skills in post-high school environments" (p. 57). Krebs (2002) agreed that future personal and professional success is facilitated by the development of self-advocacy skills.

School counselors can again collaborate with special educators to provide opportunities for students with learning disabilities to practice self-advocacy skills. Skill instruction followed by role-play and then supervised practice with special education teachers can allow for students to gradually develop skills. Students also may be encouraged to self-advocate in their regular education classes. A psychoeducational approach can be used whereby students are first taught the basics of self-advocacy. An experiential component can follow, in which students first watch school counselors and special educators model the skills, then the students role-play, and finally they practice the skills with regular education teachers. The use of peers (perhaps older students) as models also could be effective.

SPECIAL CONSIDERATIONS FOR INDIVIDUAL PLANNING

When providing individual planning to students with learning disabilities, school counselors may consider modifying sessions based on student needs, and Wren and Einhorn (2000) have provided a variety of suggestions for counselors. For example, they suggested that counselors may need to structure shorter sessions and frequent breaks, remove distracting objects, provide noiseless objects for students to hold or squeeze, or allow students to stand, pace, or sit in different chairs throughout the session; these modifications could be helpful for students with short attention spans. They also suggested reserving a few minutes at the beginning and end of sessions to review previous material, a helpful accommodation for students who learn better with repetition. Similarly, Wren and Einhorn suggested counselors not assume that students comprehend the information they provide.

Asking for clarification, simplifying vocabulary, decreasing sentence complexity and length, and slowing speech to the students' preferred pace could be helpful. Other students with learning disabilities may benefit from counselors reviewing key ideas, illustrating points with sketches, and, when necessary, asking students to bring in written or taped notes, questions, or thoughts. All students have unique needs and school counselors must do what is necessary to clearly communicate.

As recommended with other diverse populations, school counselors must attempt to learn about and understand the experiential worldviews of students with learning disabilities. They also must acknowledge the potential effects of learning disabilities on student identity and develop interventions to help individuals cope. For example, learning disabilities have been identified as negatively affecting self-esteem (Wren & Einhorn, 2000). As such, school counselors may want to implement primary prevention interventions to promote positive self-esteem in all students (possibly through classroom guidance) and follow up with secondary prevention activities (perhaps a small counseling group) for students with learning disabilities who could benefit from additional support.

In addition, individuals with learning disabilities often experience anxiety and depression related to academic failures (Orenstein, 2000). Orenstein suggested individuals might be hesitant to register for college preparatory courses based on a fear of failure or a lack of confidence. To intervene, school counselors can provide support and encouragement to students as they explore possible postsecondary options. Testimonials from alumni who are currently attending or successfully completed college may help increase student self-efficacy.

FINAL THOUGHTS

Many students with learning disabilities have the potential to be successful in college, but not without support and encouragement. Simply by proactively addressing their needs, school counselors demonstrate belief in their potential. A collaborative approach to transition planning is emphasized by the IDEA mandate that transition services be included as part of a student's IEP; decisions must be made with input from multiple perspectives. School counselors must make sure that their voices are heard on those teams, as they possess unique knowledge about career and lifespan development.

Furthermore, in order to effectively advocate for students with learning disabilities, school counselors must be directly involved. It goes without saying that school counselors should include students with learning disabilities in any career and college planning activities offered to all students. In addition, they should provide information to parents and anticipate concerns and questions regarding what it means for a student with a learning disability to attend college. Whether they provide direct services or collaborate with others to ensure that students with learning disabilities develop additional knowledge and skills for successful transitions to college, school counselors cannot deny the importance of sharing their specialized knowledge.

Amy Milsom, D.Ed., is an assistant professor and Michael T. Hartley, M.A., is a doctoral student in the College of Education, University of Iowa, Iowa City. E-mail: amy-milsom@uiowa.edu

REFERENCES

American School Counselor Association. (2000). *Position statement: Educational planning.* Retrieved November 25, 2003, from http://www.schoolcounselor.org/content. cfm?L1=1000&L2=18

American School Counselor Association. (2003). *The ASCA national model: A framework for school counseling programs.* Alexandria, VA: Author.

American School Counselor Association. (2004). *The professional school counselor and students with special needs.* Retrieved August 19, 2004, from http://www.schoolcounselor.org/content.asp?contentid=218

Americans with Disabilities Act of 1990, PL 101-336, 42 U.S.C. § 12101 *et seq.* (1990).

Aune, E. (1991). A transition model for postsecondary-bound students with learning disabilities. *Learning Disabilities Research & Practice, 6,* 177–187.

Brinckerhoff, L. C. (1994). Developing effective self-advocacy skills in college-bound students with learning disabilities. *Intervention in School and Clinic, 29,* 229–237.

Campbell, C. A., & Dahir, C. A. (1997). *Sharing the vision: The national standards for school counseling programs.* Alexandria, VA: American School Counselor Association.

Council for Accreditation of Counseling and Related Educational Programs. (2001). *CACREP accreditation manual: 2001 standards.* Alexandria, VA: Author.

Cowen, S. (1993). Transition planning for LD college-bound students. In S. A. Vogel & P. B. Adelman (Eds.), *Success for college students with learning disabilities* (pp. 39–56). New York: Springer-Verlag.

Dalke, C., & Schmidt, S. (1987). Meeting the transition needs of college-bound students with learning disabilities. *Journal of Learning Disabilities, 20,* 176–180.

Dickinson, D. L., & Verbeek, R. L. (2002). Wage differentials between college graduates with and without LD. *Journal of Learning Disabilities, 35,* 175–185.

DuChossois, G., & Michaels, C. (1994). Postsecondary education. In C. A. Michaels (Ed.), *Transition strategies for persons with learning disabilities* (pp. 79–117). San Diego, CA: Singular.

Durlak, C. M., Rose, E., & Bursuck, W. D. (1994). Preparing high school students with learning disabilities for the transition to postsecondary education: Teaching the skills of self-determination. *Journal of Learning Disabilities, 27,* 51–59.

Flexer, R. W., Simmons, T. J., Luft, P., & Baer, R. M. (2005). *Transition planning for secondary students with disabilities* (2nd ed.). Upper Saddle River, NJ: Pearson.

Goldhammer, R., & Brinckerhoff, L. C. (1992). *Self-advocacy for college students. Their World,* 94–97.

Greenbaum, J., & Markel, G. (2001). *Helping adolescents with ADHD and learning disabilities.* San Francisco: Jossey-Bass.

Grigal, M., Test, D., Beattie, J., & Wood, W. (1997). An evaluation of transition components of individualized education programs. *Exceptional Children, 63,* 357–372.

Halpern, A. S., Yovanoff, P., Doren, B., & Benz, M. R. (1995). Predicting participation in postsecondary education for school leavers with disabilities. *Exceptional Children, 62*, 151–164.

HEATH Resource Center. (2004). 2004 summer pre-college programs for students with disabilities. Retrieved May 19, 2004, from http://www.heath.gwu.edu/PDFs/ 2004SummerPreCollege.pdf

Henderson, C. (1999). *1999 college freshmen with disabilities statistical year 1998: A biennial statistical profile.* Washington, DC: American Council on Education, HEATH Resource Center.

Hicks-Coolick, A., & Kurtz, D. P. (1997). Preparing students with learning disabilities for success in postsecondary education: Needs and services. *Social Work in Education, 19*(1), 31–43.

Hildreth, B. L., Dixon, M. E., Frerichs, D. K., & Heflin, L. J. (1994). College readiness for students with learning disabilities: The role of the school counselor. *The School Counselor, 41*, 343–346.

Hitchings, W. E., Luzzo, D. A., Ristow, R., Horvath, M., Retish, P., & Tanners, A. (2001). The career development needs of college students with learning disabilities: In their own words. *Learning Disabilities Research & Practice, 16*(1), 8–17.

Individuals with Disabilities Education Act of 1990, PL 101-476, 20 U.S.C. § 1400 *et seq.* (1990).

Individuals with Disabilities Education Act Amendments of 1997, PL 105-17, 20 U.S.C. § 1400 *et seq.* (1997).

Janiga, S. J., & Costenbader, V. (2002). The transition from high school to postsecondary education for students with learning disabilities: A survey of college service coordinators. *Journal of Learning Disabilities, 35*, 462–468.

Krebs, C. S. (2002). Self-advocacy skills: A portfolio approach. *RE:view, 33*, 160–163.

Lock, R. H., & Layton, C. A. (2001). Succeeding in postsecondary education through self-advocacy. *Teaching Exceptional Children, 34*(2), 66–71.

Merchant, D. J., & Gajar, A. (1997). A review of the literature on self advocacy components in transition programs for students with learning disabilities. *Journal of Vocational Rehabilitation, 8*, 223–231.

Milsom, A. (2002). Students with disabilities: School counselor involvement and preparation. Professional School Counseling, 5, 331–338.

Milsom, A., Akos, P., & Thompson, M. (2004). A psychoeducational group approach to postsecondary transition planning for students with learning disabilities. *Journal for Specialists in Group Work, 29*, 395–411.

National Center for Learning Disabilities. (2004). *LD fast facts*. Retrieved March 28, 2005, from http://www.ncld.org/LDInfoZone/InfoZone_FactSheetUpdate04.cfm

National Joint Committee on Learning Disabilities. (1994). Secondary to postsecondary education transition planning for students with learning disabilities. *Collective perspectives on issues affecting learning disabilities: Position papers and statements*. Austin, TX: Pro-Ed.

Orenstein, M. (2000). *Smart but stuck: What every therapist needs to know about learning disabilities and imprisoned intelligence*. New York: The Haworth Press.

Phillips, P. (1990). A self-advocacy plan for high school students with learning disabilities: A comparative case study analysis of students', teachers', and parents' perceptions of program effects. *Journal of Learning Disabilities, 23*, 466–471.

Satcher, J. (1993). College-bound students with learning disabilities: Role of the school counselor. *The School Counselor, 40*, 343–347.

Satcher, J., & Dooley-Dickey, K. (1991). *College and the LD student: Where does the school counselor fit in?* Paper presented at the annual conference of the American Association on Counseling and Development, Reno, NV. (ERIC Document Reproduction Service No. ED330963)

Scott, S. (1991). A change in legal status: An overlooked dimension in the transition to higher education. *Journal of Learning Disabilities, 24*, 459–466.

Scott, S. (1994). Determining reasonable academic adjustments for college students with learning disabilities. *Journal of Learning Disabilities, 27*, 403–412.

Sitlington, P. L., Clark, G. M., & Kolstoe, O. P. (2000). *Transition education and services for adolescents with disabilities*. Needham Heights, MA: Allyn & Bacon.

Taves, R. A., & Hutchinson, N. L. (1993). The role of the high school counsellor in transition programs for youth with learning disabilities: The case of Ryan. *Guidance and Counseling, 8*(3), 49–57.

Thomas, D., & Woods, H. (2003). *Working with people with learning disabilities*. New York: Jessica Kingsley Publishers.

Turnbull, H. R., & Turnbull, A. P. (2000). *Free appropriate public education: The law and children with disabilities*. Denver, CO: Love Publishing.

Vocational Rehabilitation Act of 1973, PL 93-112, 29 U.S.C., 701 *et seq.*

Webster, D. D., Clary, G., & Griffith, P. L. (2005). Postsecondary education and career paths. In R. W. Flexer, T. J. Simmons, P. Luft, & R. M. Baer, *Transition planning for secondary students with disabilities* (pp. 388–423). Upper Saddle River, NJ: Pearson.

Williams, J. M., & O'Leary, E. (2001). What we've learned and where we go from here. *Career Development for Exceptional Individuals, 24*(1), 51–71.

Wilson, G. L. (1994). Self-advocacy skills. In C. A. Michaels (Ed.), *Transition strategies for persons with learning disabilities* (pp. 89–106). San Diego, CA: Singular.

Wren, C., & Einhorn, J. (2000). *Hanging by a twig: Understanding and counseling adults with learning disabilities and ADD*. New York: W.W. Norton & Company.

Biracial Youth: The Role of the School Counselor in Racial Identity Development

By Amy E. Benedetto and Teri Olisky, Ph.D.

This article originally appeared in *Professional School Counseling*, Vol. 5, No. 1, 2001.

Since the 1967 Supreme Court decision of Loving v. Virginia, which prohibits anti-miscegenation laws, the number of biracial births has more than tripled (Sandor & Larson, 1994). Schwartz (1998a) reported that through 1996 more than 100,000 babies were born annually to parents of interracial marriages. Literature also suggests that a disproportionate number of biracial youth require special attention in school due to difficult behaviors (Herring, 1995; McRoy & Freeman, 1986). These behaviors are affecting school performance and, as such, counselors will likely find themselves assisting a student of biracial descent. Because school counselors are in a unique position to assist biracial youth, it is important that these professionals are multiculturally sensitive and knowledgeable about working with these students.

A reasonable amount of literature on biracialism exists (e.g., Herring, 1992; Kerwin, Ponterotto, Jackson, & Harris; 1993; McRoy & Freeman, 1985; Nishimura, 1995; Poston, 1990; Schwartz, 1998a, 1998b; Wardle, 1992; Winn & Priest, 1993). Little research, however, has been completed on biracial youth or their families. Herring (1992) noted that this lack of research was partly due to the resistance of biracial individuals and their families to being studied as well as to the small population of biracial youth. Instead, issues related to biracial youth have focused largely on explaining racial identity development. This article addresses this concept and the role of the school counselor in assisting biracial youth to develop a positive racial identity. Interventions are presented with goals of promoting the development of a healthy biracial identity and alleviating at-risk behaviors.

RACIAL IDENTITY DEVELOPMENT

Racial identification is defined as "pride in one's racial and cultural identity" (Poston, 1990, p. 152), and has been considered a key factor in any individual's development. Few of the many proposed models of racial identity development have been able to adequately address the unique issues of the biracial individual (Herring, 1995; Poston, 1990). In response to the lack of a model of biracial identity development, Poston (1990) presented

The Biracial Development Model. This model suggests that biracial individuals develop through five stages: personal identity, choice of group categorization, enmeshment/denial, appreciation, and integration.

Stage one, personal identity, is characterized by one's identity being relatively inconsistent and dependent on self-esteem developed within the family. This is a critical developmental period for a child. Family members are instrumental in helping a biracial child feel a sense of belonging and acceptance. The second stage, choice of group characterization, may be a time of crisis for a child. During this stage, the child feels compelled to select an ethnic identity, and thus must choose between parents. The third stage, enmeshment/denial, is characterized by confusion and guilt as a result of choosing an identity that may not be all-inclusive of one's biracial heritage. This stage is characteristic of adolescence during which group belonging becomes a central theme for all youth (Newman & Newman, 1999; Poston, 1990). The enmeshment/denial stage is even more difficult for biracial youth because they are struggling with dual-race membership. The fourth stage, appreciation, is a period during which the individual still identifies with one ethnic group but begins to broaden his or her understanding of multiple heritages. This is a time of exploration, resulting from the desire to know one's complete racial heritage. The final stage, integration, is characterized by the individual's ability to recognize and appreciate all of the ethnicities he or she possesses. At this point, the biracial individual feels complete and sees himself or herself as a contributing member of society.

Poston (1990) speculated that with the proper support and mastery of these stages, biracial individuals can develop a healthy racial identity and achieve a sense of wholeness in their lives. However, racial identity development is a complex process for some biracial youth, especially as they enter adolescence. Biracial adolescents may encounter conflicting values as they begin to ask, "Who am I?" and "Where do I belong?" (Newman & Newman, 1999). These youth may experience guilt and confusion about developing an identity that may not embody all aspects of their heritage (Herring, 1992; McRoy & Freeman, 1985; Poston, 1990). They may also be confronted with a lack of social acceptance due to prejudicial and stereotypical attitudes (Newman & Newman, 1999; Schwartz, 1998a). As a result, some biracial youth exhibit a variety of problems that has led researchers to label them "at risk" (Kerwin et al., 1993). These at-risk behaviors include (a) poor academic achievement, (b) off-task behavior, (c) poor social skills, (d) negative attitudes toward adults, (e) chip-on-the shoulder personas, (f) social isolation, and (g) aggressive behaviors toward peers (McRoy & Freeman, 1985; Nishimura, 1995). More importantly, biracial youth may experience depression or exhibit maladaptive behaviors such as substance abuse, psychosomatic disorders, and suicidal ideation (Herring, 1995; Poston, 1990; Winn & Priest, 1993). These behaviors may place the biracial youth at risk for academic failure. The school counselor is in a position to assist the biracial student in working through these issues, and to support the student's successful involvement and achievement within the school.

INTERVENTIONS

Awareness, communication, and exposure are areas for intervention by school counselors. These areas provide a focus for intervention as part of a school counseling program and are designed to promote the development of healthy biracial identity in youth. These intervention areas were derived from multicultural literature (e.g., Herring, 1992, 1995; Nishimura, 1995; Schwartz, 1998b; Wardle, 1992, 1998; Wehrly, Kenny, & Kenny, 1999) on interventions that can be used to help biracial youth reach Poston's (1990) final stage of integration. Specific interventions are presented for the areas of awareness, communication, and exposure in hopes of providing a more specific structure for working with biracial youth.

Awareness

Awareness is the recognition of the various factors related to biracialism, including individual and societal feelings toward interracial marriages and biracial births, a familiarity with historical and modern myths and stereotypes, and an appreciation for the advantages and disadvantages of biracialism (Schwartz, 1998a; Wardle, 1992; Wehrly et al., 1999). Awareness facilitates dealing with feelings of inadequacy or alienation, which may lead to a display of at-risk behaviors. School counselors have the opportunity to address these feelings, create awareness, and help youth find solutions that offset negative attitudes and behaviors.

School counselors may employ a variety of strategies for fostering awareness of biracialism. They can implement developmental guidance lessons to increase school-wide awareness. The lessons can address the meaning and importance of diversity and can debunk existing racial myths and stereotypes. Cultural diversity days based on the lessons taught can also be implemented school-wide. Individual responsive services can address awareness at a more personal level. For example, counselors can use questioning skills to assess a biracial student's current level of racial identity awareness; they can also use family trees to help the student gain a better understanding of his or her heritage (Schwartz, 1998b; Wardle, 1992). Counselors can address racial myths and stereotypes and use bibliotherapy to ameliorate the student's feelings about these prejudicial opinions (Wardle, 1992; Wehrly et al., 1999). Role playing can also help individuals learn how to deal with prejudice (Wardle, 1992). Counselors may want to refer the student to biracial or minority status support groups (Poston, 1990). Finally, counselors can disseminate accurate information about biracialism through reference books, articles, Web sites, and psycho-educational workshops that discuss racial identity formation and general topics about biracialism (Poston, 1990; Wehrly et al., 1999).

Communication

Communication is the time spent discussing biracialism so as to facilitate a secure racial identity. School counselors are in a unique position to foster communication about racial issues through individual counseling, group counseling, and classroom guidance. This process allows biracial youth to share feelings about their biracial identity, and to receive confirmation and assurance that these feelings are normal (Herring, 1992; Winn & Priest, 1993). The counselor can gain an understanding of how a student's racial identity is viewed, supported, and cultivated in the home as well as how the student would like it to be supported in school. Additionally, counselors can ascertain how biracial youth respond to negative comments and prejudice, and then develop positive responses to these situations (Schwartz, 1998b; Wardle, 1992).

Specific strategies to foster communication with biracial youth could include the use of diaries and/or creative writing to record uncomfortable situations (Herring, 1992). School counselors can use the writings to discuss students' reactions to the situations and to offer suggestions for future action. The use of bibliotherapy can generate questions on reading assignments, which can, in turn, initiate discussions of the negative situations (Wehrly et al., 1999). Stories about historical biracial role models could be used to develop stories about a youth's future (Herring, 1992; Wardle, 1992). Additionally, counselors can develop staff training sessions and parenting workshops (Wardle, 1992). Promoting and teaching communication skills school-wide and within the family may help these individuals involved in the workshops increase their self-awareness regarding issues related to biracial youth, which may, in turn, foster a sense of belonging for the biracial youth.

Exposure

Biracial youth need exposure to all aspects of race and ethnicity in order to understand their heritage and to acquire culturally linked coping skills (Schwartz, 1998a; Wardle, 1992; Wehrly et al., 1999). Exposure enables a biracial individual to attain more realistic attitudes and perceptions about his or her racial or ethnic background, and to become aware of prejudices and injustices (McRoy & Freeman, 1985). Through exposure, youth can learn to embrace their identity and find positive ways to respond to discrimination.

School counselors are in a position to implement school-wide and district-wide interventions to increase exposure to race and ethnicity. Specific strategies might include career days at which minority role models speak to the school body; developmental guidance lessons that focus on multiculturalism are another alternative (T, 1995; Wardle, 1998). Counselors can encourage classroom or school celebrations that observe culturally different holidays, or arrange field trips to various cultural centers on those holidays or throughout the year (Schwartz, 1998b). Counselors can have multiracial books and other literature readily available, and can ensure that the school library has a variety of such literature (Wardle, 1992). In-school support groups for biracial youth and a multicultural group for the school are other intervention options. Finally, when schools are predominantly one race, counselors can try to find biracial or minority role models within the community to assist in developing a mentoring program (McRoy & Freeman, 1985). Role models foster a sense of encouragement, especially in individuals who feel their minority status is a determinant for failure.

CONCLUDING THOUGHTS

David (not his real name) was a young biracial boy who lived in a predominantly White community. He was on the playground and many of the other kids were playing "war." He wanted to play and asked if he could join the game. One of the boys refused him saying no Black soldiers were allowed. As David entered adolescence, he began to realize that he was different. Other student's continually made negative comments about his skin color. He felt increasingly alone and more aggressive, feeling the need to defend himself at all costs. At home David was even angrier, mainly with his mother because she was White and David blamed her for his being born. As David went through high school, things did not get much better. Girls at least talked to him; however, they could not bring him home to meet their mothers. On the night of the senior prom, David had to sit in the limousine while his friends went in to pick up his prom date.

David, now a young man, could possibly have benefited from the help of a school counselor who was knowledgeable in racial identity development. The school counselor is in a unique position to help alleviate some of the confusion, guilt, and anger that biracial youth such as David may experience, and to assist them in developing a positive racial identity. School counselors who implement the interventions as part of a school counseling program can create a positive and multiculturally sensitive atmosphere, thereby helping biracial students decrease their at-risk behaviors. Individual counseling, group counseling, and classroom guidance may help in dispelling ignorance and intolerance as well as in creating a sense of belonging for biracial youth. A biracial student who feels supported, validated, and accepted in school will have the benefit of enhanced self-esteem and a well-rounded sense of the world (Schwartz, 1998a).

Amy E. Benedetto is a graduate student, School Counseling Program. E-mail: Aben711@aol.com. Teri Olisky, Ph.D., is professor and chair, Department of Counseling and School Psychology. E-mail: Loughead@ scsu.ctstateu.edu. Both are with Southern Connecticut State University, New Haven.

REFERENCES

Herring, R. (1992). Biracial children: An increasing concern for elementary and middle school counselors. *Elementary School Guidance and Counseling, 27,* 123–131.

Herring, R. (1995). Developing biracial ethnic identity: A review of the increasing dilemma. *Journal of Multicultural Counseling and Development, 23,* 29–37.

Kerwin, C., Ponterotto, J., Jackson, B., & Harris, A. (1993). Racial identity in biracial children: A qualitative investigation. *Journal of Counseling Psychology, 40,* 221–231.

McRoy, R., & Freeman, E. (1985, February). *Racial identity issues of mixed-race children: Implications for school social workers.* Paper presented at the NASW School Social Work Conference, New Orleans.

Newman, B., & Newman, P. (1999). *Development through life: A psychosocial approach* (7th ed.). Belmont, CA: Wadsworth.

Nishimura, N. (1995). Addressing the needs of biracial children: An issue for counselors in a multicultural school environment. *The School Counselor, 43,* 52–57.

Poston, W. (1990). The biracial identity development model: A needed addition. *Journal of Counseling and Development, 69,* 152–155.

Sandor, G., & Larson, J. (1994). The other Americans. *American Demographics, 16,* 36–42.

Schwartz, W. (1998a). *The identity development of multiracial youth* (Contract No. RR-93-002016). Washington, DC: Office of Educational Research and Improvement. (ERIC Document Reproduction Service No. ED 425 248).

Schwartz, W. (1998b). *The schooling of multiracial students* (Contract No. RR-93-002016). Washington, DC: Office of Educational Research and Improvement. (ERIC Document Reproduction Service No. ED 425 249).

Wardle, F. (1992). Supporting the biracial children in the school setting. *Education and Treatment of Children, 15,* 163–173.

Wardle, F. (1998). Meeting the needs of multiracial and multiethnic children in early childhood settings. *Early Childhood Education Journal, 26,* 7–11.

Wehrly, B., Kenney, K., & Kenney, M. (1999). *Counseling multiracial families.* Thousand Oaks, CA: Sage.

Winn, N., & Priest, R. (1993). Counseling biracial children: A forgotten component of multicultural counseling. *Family Therapy, 20,* 29–35.

The Legal Duty to Protect Gay and Lesbian Students from Violence in School

By William P. McFarland, Ed.D. and Martin Dupuis, Ph.D., JD

This article originally appeared in *Professional School Counseling*, Vol. 4, No. 3, 2001.

Public attention has recently focused on violence in schools in the United States. Media coverage of shootings in Arkansas, Oregon, and Colorado have shocked the nation. These violent incidents in the schools have demonstrated the alarming potential for these events to occur anytime in any school. To prevent this problem, there has been a call for understanding the causes of violence among school-age children and adolescents and a demand for action. A comprehensive approach to prevention requires the schools to address physical violence, media violence, political-economic violence, cultural-racial violence, and sexual and gender violence (Daniels, Arredondo, & D'Andrea, 1999).

Within the larger issue of sexual and gender violence is the problem of harassment and abuse directed against gay and lesbian students. The purposes of this article are to describe the violence against gay and lesbian students; demonstrate the connection between homophobia, heterosexism, and violence; examine the legal responsibility of schools to protect gay youth from harassment and abuse; and, to recommend prevention strategies to provide safe schools for gay and lesbian students.

ANTI-LESBIAN AND GAY VIOLENCE

Gay and lesbian youth have been the invisible minority in our schools. Since homosexuality has historically been viewed as only an adult issue, many people in the public schools remain uninformed about the number of gay students in schools and show little interest in the concerns of these students (Treadway & Yoakam, 1992). School counselors have made general comments during training sessions that there are no gay students in their schools or have even labeled attempts to educate about gay and lesbian issues as subversive attempts by homosexuals to take over the schools. Research by Price and Telljohann (1991) described one in five school counselors as reporting that working with gay and lesbian students would not be gratifying, but 41% of the counselors in their study also reported that schools were not doing enough to help gay and lesbian students adjust to their environment.

As further evidence that these students are ignored, Reed (as cited in O'Conor, 1994) stated, "Not only does the group remain invisible, the existence of and problems associated with gay youth are largely denied by public school educators, particularly administrators" (p. 8). Woog (1995) described a statewide survey of Connecticut teachers and administrators in 1991 where respondents indicated that they recognized the plight of gay and lesbian students, admitted that little was being done for them, and expressed hope for interventions to assist these students. Teachers were more insistent on action, whereas administrators claimed that there were sufficient programs in place to address the needs of these students.

Depending on the study, it has been reported that between 2% and 10% of the U.S. population is homosexual. Ginsberg (1998) reported using the midpoint of this range, or 6%, to indicate a national gay/lesbian population of approximately 15,000,000 which also suggests a gay and lesbian student population of 2,610,515 based on the *Digest of Education Statistics* (U.S. Bureau of the Census, 1995). Ginsberg (1998) explained:

> These estimates suggest that of the adolescents who attend the country's public schools about one in 20 is likely to be gay/lesbian. Thus, each time a middle or high school teacher addresses a class, she or he is likely to be addressing one or more gay/lesbian students. (p. 2)

School can be a dangerous and often hostile environment for gay and lesbian youth. One reason gay and lesbian students live silent and secretive lives is that to be visible, or to have come out as a teenager, means to place oneself at risk of verbal and physical abuse. O'Conor (1994) wrote, "A recent U.S. Department of Justice report states that gays and lesbians are the most frequent victims of hate crimes, and school is the primary setting for this type of violence" (p. 11). It has also been noted that crimes against gay males and lesbians in schools occur with greater frequency than crimes against the general population in the school setting. Some 25% of lesbian and gay students are crime victims, while 9% of the general population of students are crime victims (Comstock, 1991). A survey of more than 4,000 students reported in the Youth Risk Behavior Study (Massachusetts Department of Education, 1995) that gay males and lesbians were five times more likely than their heterosexual peers to skip school out of fear for their safety.

Gay and lesbian students are at risk because of societal views of homosexuality, which create unsupportive and unaccepting or even hostile environments at school and at home. Many families react badly when their child comes out, and many youths are abused by their family members with some adolescents being kicked out of their homes. Remafedi (1987) reported that 26% of gay and lesbian youth are forced to leave home because of conflicts with their families about their sexual orientation.

The pervasiveness of the general homophobic atmosphere in schools is shown by research, which found that 97% of students in Massachusetts public high schools regularly report hearing homophobic remarks from their classmates, and 53% indicated that they heard homophobic comments from school staff (Massachusetts Governor's Commission on Gay and Lesbian Youth, 1993). Anderson (1997) cited a 1992 Harris Poll which showed that 86% of high school students would be very upset if classmates called them gay or lesbian.

Teachers may often punish students for uttering racists remarks, but students who make homophobic comments are seldom challenged. An Iowa study found that the average high school student hears anti-gay epithets 25 times a day and that teachers who hear these slurs fail to respond 97% of the time (Carter, 1997).

Research by Pilkington and D'Augelli (1995) revealed that gay and lesbian youth (ages 15 to 21) experience high levels of verbal and physical assault as a result of their orientation. Of the youths in their survey, 80% endured verbal insults; 44% were threatened with violence; 33% had objects thrown at them; 31% reported being chased or followed; and 17% reported being physically assaulted. In the Youth Risk Behavior Study (Massachusetts Department of Education, 1995) it was reported that 23% of gay and lesbian youth were in a fight that required medical attention compared with 3% of heterosexual students. One gay student described the abuse he endured in school:

> I don't feel safe from abuse at my high school. I am relentlessly persecuted for being gay. By the time I was in ninth grade, listening without responding to others bashing homosexuals was more painful than the harassment I deal with now. Up to now, a person has masturbated in front of me while I was in the school lavatory, I have had cigarettes thrown at me, students have driven their car within a foot of me to drive me off the road while I was walking, and people call me vulgar names almost daily. What I am describing now is not simple child's play and name calling. It is very specific harassment that threatens my safety at school. (Youth Pride, 1997, p. 4)

THE CONNECTION BETWEEN HOMOPHOBIA, HETEROSEXISM, AND VIOLENCE

Homophobia is the widely used term that means the fear and hatred of homosexuality or perceived homosexuality (Elia, 1993). Herek (1986) described homophobia in terms of the four functions that homophobic attitudes fulfill. First, negative attitudes serve an experiential-schematic function based on past unfavorable contact with homosexuals. For example, if a person thought a gay male made a pass at him, he may conclude that all gay males are highly sexualized and. based on this belief, may oppose the employment of gay teachers in schools. Herek's second function is labeled social-expressive and means an individual may express negative attitudes towards gay and lesbian people to win approval from significant others, especially peers. The third function served by homophobia is a value-expressive function. For these people, negative attitudes towards gay and lesbian people are expressions of important personal values such as certain religious ideologies. The fourth function served by homophobic attitudes is a defensive function where gay and lesbian people are seen as legitimate targets for attack so the individual avoids personal anxieties and confusion related to his or her own sexuality.

Heterosexism refers to the belief that heterosexuality is the best and only acceptable way of living (Blumenfeld & Raymond, 1989). Institutions in our society, including the schools, harbor the fear and hatred of homosexuality as well as prejudices based in heterosexism. Homophobia and heterosexism have a negative impact on all students, both gay and straight. Masters, Johnson, and Kolodny (1992) noted that most of the attacks against homosexuals are committed by male adolescents who are trying to demonstrate their hypermasculinity to their peers. Also, Herek and Berrill (1992) reported that teenagers surveyed about their biases against a variety of minorities reacted more negatively towards gay people than to other groups. It was stated in the 1988 report of the Governors Task Force on Biased Related Violence that, "gay men and lesbians are perceived as legitimate targets that can be openly attacked" (as cited in Herek & Berrill, 1992, p. 97).

Homophobia is detrimental to other people in the schools besides gay and lesbian youth. For example, heterosexual boys who do not fit the traditional male gender role (aggressive, controlling, restricted emotions) defined by heterosexism may be punished, ostracized, and abused. These boys may be called "faggots," "fairies," "sissies," "queers," or other derogatory names. Sears (1992b) and Klein (1992) noted that males seem to experience more homophobia than females. Hetrick and Martin (1987) claimed that effeminate male youth are at highest risk for violence. Girls also experience pressure to conform to heterosexist gender stereotypes, and failing to do so is likely to result in abuse. Girls who fail to demonstrate stereotypical feminine traits (complacent, emotional, deferential) may be called "dykes," "lezzies," or other derogatory names.

Others who may be strongly impacted by homophobia are gay and lesbian parents who have school children who might experience homophobic ridicule. It is estimated that the are 4 million gay and lesbian parents with 8 to 10 million school-age children (American Bar Association, 1987). If traditional gender role behavior is breached, homophobic actions are taken to punish anyone – gay or straight, male or female – in the name of enforcing the standards of heterosexuality. Thus, students become victims of violence because of the connection between homophobia and rigid gender roles defined by heterosexism.

When harassment or violence instigated by homophobic attitudes persists in schools, students learn that it is acceptable to be intolerant of diversity. Even worse, it may appear permissible to denigrate others who are different. Young people who learn to hate, and then violently act out these feelings may be lost to the criminal justice system (Hunter & Schaecher, 1995). Therefore, both the victim and the perpetrator pay a severe price for the violence that arises out of homophobia. A gay male described the effects of a homophobic school environment:

> People kept coming up to me and making fun of me, they would call me horrible names and I would cry all the time. Letters were put in my locker saying things about AIDS and how my parents shouldn't have had me and how I should just die. Kids would threaten me after school and follow me home yelling things at me. No one should have to go through what I went through in school. (Youth Pride, 1997, pp. 3-4)

LEGAL RESPONSIBILITY OF SCHOOLS

The abuse of lesbian and gay youth is a serious issue, and education officials are being forced to take a more proactive position to ensure that schools are safe for all students. The liability for administrators for not responding appropriately to claims of harassment can be very costly, as several recent court cases demonstrate.

In a 1999 landmark decision for educational policy, the U.S. Supreme Court declared that school officials who ignore student-on-student sexual harassment can be held liable for violating the federal civil rights law under Title IX of the Education Amendments of 1972 (*Davis v. Monroe County Board of Education*, 1999). The case was brought by a mother on behalf of her fifth-grade daughter, who was inappropriately touched on an ongoing basis for 5 months by a male classmate. The male student said he wanted to have sex with her, simulated a sexual act, and rubbed-up against her. Both parent and student complained to school officials, but nothing was done to correct the problem. The mother complained to the police, and the boy pleaded guilty to sexual battery.

The Court, sharply divided in the 5-4 decision, stated that federally aided schools can be held liable when the student-on-student harassment is "so severe, pervasive and objectively offensive that it denies its victims the equal access to education" (*Davis v. Monroe County Board of Education*, 1999, p. 650), and school officials are deliberately indifferent to the sexual harassment. The harassment must go beyond simple acts of teasing and name-calling. The U.S. Justice Department has concluded that the deliberately indifferent standard would make such lawsuits rare because school officials will usually respond to such behavior, at least when it involves male and female students.

How school officials react to same-gender sexual harassment will also be an important factor in determining liability, and more importantly, for providing an educational environment conducive to learning for all students. Many gay and lesbian students report that they were made to feel responsible for their harassment since they did not conceal their homosexuality. Rather than punish the perpetrators, gay and lesbian students were often transferred to other classrooms. Administrators using such remedies may now be at risk of being deliberately indifferent.

In another case, the issue of discrimination based on sexual orientation in schools has been heard by the federal courts (*Nabozny v. Podlesny*, 1996), and the settlement agreement cost school officials nearly $1 million. Jamie Nabozny suffered verbal and physical abuse at the hands of his classmates because of his sexual orientation for the 4 years from seventh to eleventh grade. The physical attacks were so severe that Nabozny has had to have two surgeries. He attempted suicide three times during these years.

Nabozny and his parents complained on numerous occasions to his school counselors and principals. Despite promises to protect Nabozny, no action was taken against the offenders, and the abuse continued year after year. One principal even said that if Nabozny was "going to be so openly gay, that [he] had to expect this kind of stuff to happen." A teacher, upset by the disruption caused by other students taunting Nabozny, called him a "fag" and expelled him from the classroom. Nabozny sued the principals and the school district arguing that he had been denied equal protection of the law under the Fourteenth Amendment of the U.S. Constitution based on his gender and sexual orientation.

Nabozny claimed that the employees of the school district treated him differently than they treated girls who had been harassed. The school had a record of punishing boys who harassed girls, and the court even suggested that the school officials' departure from their regular practice of punishing perpetrators might be evidence of the principals' discriminatory intent.

At the jury trial to determine if in fact the school officials and the district did discriminate against Nabozny, a unanimous, seven-member jury determined that he was denied equal protection from harm while at school. Hours after the verdict, the principals quickly settled the suit for over $900,000. Interestingly, the jury did not find the school district liable, perhaps because the district had a non-discrimination policy that included sexual orientation.

In a third case, administrative remedies were sought against schools that did not protect against harassment based on sexual orientation. A gay student filed a sex discrimination complaint against the Fayetteville, Arkansas public schools with the Office of Civil Rights (OCR) of the U.S. Department of Education (*Wagner v. Fayetteville Public Schools*, 1998). The gay student was harassed from the eighth to the tenth grades. Gay bashing by a gang caused a broken nose and a bruised kidney. Criminal charges against the perpetrators were filed, and these students were given probation. The harassment by other students continued, and the school failed to take any meaningful action.

In March 1997, the OCR released new Title IX guidelines (U.S. Department of Education, 1997). Title IX is a federal statute that prohibits sex discrimination, and for the first time the guidelines made explicit reference to gay and lesbian students as being protected against sexual harassment. While the guidelines do not forbid discrimination on the basis of sexual orientation, they prohibit actions that create a sexually hostile environment. Expressing a dislike for gays and lesbians alone would not be a violation of Title IX. The actions or language must specifically be of a sexual nature to fall under the title.

The Department of Education reached an agreement with the Fayetteville Public Schools requiring the school district to "recognize the various forms of sexual harassment," including that directed at gay or lesbian students. The school district must adopt policies consistent with this understanding and provide training and education on sexual harassment for the faculty, staff, and student body. Written reports monitoring the school district's progress must be submitted for one year.

As these cases demonstrate, school districts will now be held liable for not protecting gay and lesbian students from sexual harassment by their peers. According to Lambda Legal Defense and Education Fund (1998), similar law suits have been initiated in California, Illinois, New Jersey, and Washington. Furthermore, the U.S. Supreme Court in 1998 ruled that school districts can be held liable when a teacher sexually harasses a student (Gebser v. Lago Vista Independent School District, 1998). The district must know about the harassment and be deliberately indifferent to it. These are the same standards the Court used to hold school officials responsible for not preventing students from harassing each other.

School administrators must now ensure that gay and lesbian students are provided a safe educational environment. Ignoring this type of sexual harassment could be very costly. Many professional organizations such as the National Education Association; American School Health Association; National School Board Association; American Psychological Association; American Federation of Teachers; Gay, Lesbian, Straight Education Network; American Counseling Association; and the American School Counseling Association support local schools in combating intolerance and homophobia.

STRATEGIES TO PROVIDE SAFE SCHOOLS

Klinger (1995) stated, "Prevention of anti-gay lesbian violence ... primarily involves systemic changes in homophobia at a societal level" (p. 131). While this may exceed the ability of a single societal institution to accomplish, several states have suggested specific ways to address the homophobia that causes anti-gay violence in schools. The Connecticut State Board of Education 1991 publication Equity Newsletter (as cited in Anderson, 1994) identified nine suggestions for bettering the school environment for gay and lesbian students and staff. Those suggestions are:

- Use inclusive language
- Challenge anti-gay epithets
- Designate resource people in the schools for gay and lesbian students
- Make resources and materials on homosexuality visible and accessible
- Educate staff members on homophobia
- Support gay and lesbian colleagues
- Use gay and lesbian colleagues as role models
- Refer self-identified gay and lesbian students to appropriate services
- Refer parents of gay children to organizations such as Parents and Friends of Lesbians and Gays.

In Massachusetts, the Massachusetts Governor's Commission on Gay and Lesbian Youth (1993) published a report entitled *Making School Safe for Gay and Lesbian Youth: Breaking the Silence in Schools and in Families*, which recommends taking action in five areas. The first is the establishment of school policies protecting gay and lesbian students from harassment, violence, and discrimination. Procedures for investigating and punishing harassment charges should be clear to administrators and should be uniformly applied to all accusations. Marinoble (1998) instructed school counselors to advise principals and policy-making committees to include sexual orientation in school nondiscrimination clauses of teacher contracts and in written school policies regarding treatment of students and parents. Students should know that the school district will not tolerate sexual harassment and will discipline perpetrators accordingly.

Anti-harassment rules must be carefully written so that they do not forbid speech, opinions, or beliefs in and of themselves, but instead punish impermissible conduct that targets a person for assault, threat, or vandalism on the basis of the victim's actual or perceived race, religion, national origin, disability, gender, or sexual orientation. According to Honig (1999), these rules may also forbid harassing conduct, whether or not targeted to a particular person, that is so pervasive or intense as to create a hostile environment, which hinders the ability of a person to get an education. An excellent example is the Seattle, Washington Public Schools' policy statement which includes the following:

> Every participant in Seattle Public Schools has the right to an educational environment in which differences among people are accepted and valued, including sexual orientation ... Every student has the right to learning experiences infused with the value of cultural diversity ... prohibits harassment based upon national origin, race, economic status, sex, sexual orientation, pregnancy, marital status, or disability ... by employees, volunteers, parents/guardians, and students. (Reis, 1996, p. 19)

Other anti-harassment policy models are described in *Improving School Policies and State Laws* (Lambda Legal Defense and Education Fund, 1997).

The second area for prevention efforts is training for teachers, counselors, and school staff members in crisis intervention, violence prevention, and the issues and concerns of gay and lesbian students. Black and Underwood (1998) suggested that school counselors coordinate staff development strategies such as annual presentations about gay and lesbian youth for all teachers, utilize expert speakers and panels, facilitate discussions of homophobia and its effects on all students, and provide resources for staff who have a difficult time overcoming their homophobia and prejudice. An excellent example of staff training material is *Homophobia 101: Anti-Homophobia Training for School Staff and Students published by the Gay, Lesbian, Straight Education Network* (GLSEN, 1998). These materials are designed to provide basic awareness of prejudice against sexual minorities; to provide basic information about sexual orientation; to explain stresses on gay and lesbian youth and how this impairs educational performance; to explain how prejudice against sexual minorities impairs educational performance of students; and to equip teachers with some tools and skills to use to reduce prejudice against sexual minority youth and to create an inclusive classroom and school environment. The U.S. Department of Education Office for Civil Rights, with the National Association of Attorneys General 1999 Bias Crime Task Force Education Subcommittee, has released *Protecting Students from Harassment and Hate Crime: A Guide for Schools*. The guide includes sections on developing anti-harassment policies, identifying and responding to incidents of harassment, developing grievance procedures, and creating a climate that appreciates diversity.

Another resource for staff training is *The Safe Schools Anti Violence Documentation Project* (Reis, 1996), which recommends five strategies for school staff to respond to harassing situations. First, intervene immediately when you hear anti-gay remarks or observe anti-gay harassment with the same firmness you would employ for religious or racial harassment. Second, make it safe to report an incident. Identify a safe person in the school to whom a student or staff member or parent can come to report being harassed or attacked. Third, consider both educating and disciplining the offenders. Discipline should be equitable to that used with offenses involving religion or race. Fourth, consider the needs of the targeted person such as his or her safety, support, and recovery. Fifth, consider the needs of the witnesses and the rest of the school community such as the need for reassurances that those in charge will do everything possible to keep this from happening again.

Professional development for all staff is important because many well-meaning people may have a desire to offer assistance to gay and lesbian students, but due to misunderstandings, they may do more harm than good (McFarland, 1998). Sears (1992a) discovered that less than 20% of school counselors have received any training on assisting gay and lesbian students, and many school employees have negative feelings towards gay and lesbian people. Some faculty and staff may have personal or religious views against homosexuality and may not be in favor of developing materials and programs on gay and lesbian youth. Education programs can bridge this divide by stressing professional and legal responsibilities rather than trying to change personal beliefs. Programs must emphasize that personal viewpoints should not allow a classroom to be so homophobic that gay and lesbian students cannot learn. In addition, training should also note that the ethical obligations that attach to a teaching license could require educators to prevent discrimination on the basis of sexual orientation. Such a duty provides additional incentive for staff to assist gay and lesbian students. Alaska, Connecticut, Florida, and Pennsylvania have this type of statewide education code (Lambda Legal Defense and Education Fund, 1997).

The third area for prevention efforts is school-based counseling and support groups for gay and straight students. School counselors can address the needs of gay and lesbian youth through a group counseling model (Muller & Hartman, 1998). School counselors can also assist in the creation of support groups that are not counseling or therapy groups, but rather have as their focus support, education, and socialization. These support groups could be facilitated by teachers as well as counselors. Suggestions for starting a gay/straight alliance are explained in *Gay/Straight Alliances: A Student Guide* (Blumenfeld & Lindop, 1995).

The fourth area to address is making information about gay and lesbian issues available in school libraries. Library exhibits can create awareness of contributions of gay and lesbian people similar to what many schools do for Black History Month. Anderson (1994) suggested a display for Gay and Lesbian Month in June since it marks the anniversary of the Stonewall Riot in New York City in 1969, which is viewed as the symbolic beginning of the movement to obtain civil rights for gay and lesbian Americans. The National Gay and Lesbian Task Force recognizes October as Gay and Lesbian History Month. The American Library Association has a Gay and Lesbian Caucus, which can be a source of information, booklists, and support for building a library collection.

The fifth area recommended for action by the Massachusetts Governor's Commission (1993) is a curriculum that includes gay and lesbian issues. Anderson (1994, 1997) noted that including gay and lesbian topics in the curriculum does not require developing extensive curriculum guides or spending large amounts of money. Anderson (1994) stated:

> The Latin teacher could mention that Emperor Hadrian was gay. The music teacher can choose from Tchaikovsky, Benjamin Britten, Cole Porter, and so on. Coaches need to begin valuing gay and lesbian athletes. In addition to Martina Navratilova and Bruce Hayes, coaches can mention Dave Kopay and Dave Pallone. Our social studies teachers should include the gay rights movement when discussing the various civil rights movements of this century. And no English teacher passes the year without mentioning Walt Whitman, Langston Hughes, May Sarton, Adrienne Rich, Countee Cullen, Willa Cather, Amy Lowell, W.H. Auden, Thornton Wilder, or Edna St. Vincent Millay. They were all gay. (p. 153)

Age-appropriate curriculum materials should be used. For example, teaching about gay and lesbian issues in the elementary school does not mean discussing sex. Appropriate topics include treating everyone with kindness and respect, and that families come in different forms.

Elementary resources include It's Elementary: Talking About Gay Issues in School (Chasnoff & Cohen, 1997), which is a documentary film for parents, teachers, administrators, and school boards. Appropriate materials for the elementary level include Positively Different: Creating a Bias-Free Environment for Young Children (grades K through 5; Matiella, 1991), a curriculum which teaches strategies for intervening in harassment. Another curriculum, Bullyproof: A Teacher's Guide on Teasing and Bullying for Use with 4th and 5th Grade Students (Sjostron & Stein, 1996), addresses the issue of sexual orientation-related bullying without explicitly calling it that along with a number of other kinds of harassment. Publishers who produce literature for children about gender issues include Alyson Publications, Tricycle Press, and Women's Press Interlink Publishers.

For the secondary level, Lipkin (1994) has developed a curriculum on topics such as gay and lesbian literature for use in English classes, the history of gays and lesbians in the United States for use in social studies classes, and the history and nature of homosexuality for use in biology or psychology classes. Lipkin (1992) has also developed a resource titled Strategies for the Teacher Using Gay/Lesbian-Related Materials in the High School Classroom. School counselors who use curriculum materials such as part of a developmental curriculum may impact the stigma that all students attach to homosexuality, reduce homophobic attitudes, and help create safe schools for gay and lesbian students (McFarland, 1998).

IMPLICATIONS FOR SCHOOL COUNSELING

While there is still a great deal of bias against gay and lesbian people, social acceptance has increased significantly. The gay and lesbian students in schools are coming out of the closet and shedding their status as an invisible minority. As they make their presence known, these students encounter a wall of hate. Hate is based on homophobic attitudes and results in harassment and violence. The courage of these young men and women as they attempt to break through these two walls of silence and hatred is truly inspiring. They cannot, however, wage this battle alone.

Robinson (1994) related, "It is the counselor's responsibility, however, to understand the unique stressors of gay and lesbian students, help these students cope with the social and educational barriers of homophobia, and provide appropriate information regarding resources available for needed support" (p. 329). The school counselor may function most effectively as the leader of a coordinated effort to influence other school personnel and students in the effort to make the school environment more inviting for gay and lesbian students. School counselors can ensure that schools fulfill their legal responsibilities to provide a safe learning environment for gay and lesbian students by implementing many of the previously discussed strategies through the four components of a comprehensive developmental guidance program (McFarland, 1993).

First, school counselors can infuse educational information through the guidance program curriculum component addressing issues like challenging the myths surrounding homosexuality, the contributions of gay and lesbian persons throughout history, and the struggle for legal rights for gay and lesbian people. The classroom topics could also address the personal challenges for gay and lesbian students, including decision making about coming out as well as issues related to families of gay and lesbian youth such as responding to parental grief, managing relationships with siblings, and diffusing potential inflammatory family situations.

Second, school counselors can embark on a professional development program to acquire the knowledge and skills to serve gay and lesbian students through the responsive services component of the guidance program. Through counseling interventions, school counselors can assist students to challenge internalized homophobia before it results in self-destructive behaviors.

Third, as part of their guidance program's individual planning services component, school counselors can recommend to students the school curriculum where gay and lesbian issues are addressed. School counselors should keep relevant information available for career planning and choosing colleges that are affirming of gay and lesbian students (Orzek, 1992). School counselors should be familiar with community resources for gay and lesbian youth and their families.

Finally, through the system support component of a developmental program, school counselors can help develop staff in-service training programs on such issues as how to include gay and lesbian issues into the curriculum or how to supportively respond to a student who indicates a struggle with sexual orientation issues. By addressing the needs of gay and lesbian youth through all developmental guidance program components (curriculum, responsive services, individual planning, system support), school counselors may become leaders in the effort to reduce violence against gay and lesbian youth in the schools. We are suggesting that school counselors undertake responsibilities in addition to counseling for this population. We are promoting the role of social advocate on behalf of gay and lesbian students.

School counselors may be subjected to open antagonism from the school community and the community at large for taking on the role of advocate. There are several arguments that school counselors can make when defending gay and lesbian youth. School counselors can emphasize that the educational environment for all people is enhanced when ideas are discussed openly and honestly. While some people may have religious or personal objections to homosexuality, it is important to explain that living in a democratic society involves valuing a tolerance of others. Advocacy for gay and lesbian youth is linked to the core ideals of the school: equality, respect, and citizenship.

School counselors can also note that it is the professional responsibility of all educators to provide a supportive and safe learning environment. At the very least, these obligations require schools to accommodate a diverse population, including gay and lesbian students. There is an emerging body of case law which mandates protecting all students from harassment and violence.

Critics can be told that allowing homophobic conditions to persist sends the message that certain types of discrimination are acceptable. Students should learn that it is not okay to treat others badly because they are perceived to be different. Jennings (2000), Executive Director of GLSEN, explained, "We must help [people] understand bigotry and name-calling represent a greater threat to her child's welfare than an open discussion of touchy issues" (p. 2).

School personnel have been identifying at-risk populations of students and developing programs to serve the needs of these groups for decades. Working with gay and lesbian youth and their families is a continuation of these efforts to help all students maximize their educational achievement. Ignoring these students means disregarding statistics on suicide, HIV infection rates, homelessness, and violence. If these issues were connected to other populations, there would be an outcry to intervene. Commenting on the role of school counselors in addressing critical social issues, Baker (2000) wrote:

The pervasiveness of ... social problems and the call for social action require school counselors to respond with patience and care. Setting goals and working with others to achieve them is a better strategy than working independently and impulsively to resolve issues. Demanding change may be less palatable to decision makers than leading the way with information and reasoned debate. When singular efforts fail, planning and renewed efforts are needed. These social problems may not be eradicated for a generation or more. Yet, some individuals can be helped. Many counselors attempting to help many individuals can be very influential. (p. 43)

As educators assist these young people in reaching their full potential, they will be increasingly called upon to guarantee that schools will not discriminate on the basis of sexual orientation. In addition to effective counseling, the best strategies for school counselors to use for confronting hatred of gay and lesbian students in schools are informing, debating, persuading, discussing, and lobbying for change. These tactics can achieve faster and more effective results than litigation, which takes time, is costly, and involves external mandates. However, if school districts do not respond to the reasonable and respectful leadership of school counselors to convince school personnel to provide safe schools, it seems likely that the courts will impose it.

William P. McFarland, Ed.D., is a professor, Counselor Education and College Student Personnel, and Martin Dupuis, Ph.D., JD, is an assistant professor, Political Science. Both are with Western Illinois University, Macomb, IL. Correspondence should be addressed to Dr. McFarland, Counselor Education and College Student Personnel, 1 University Circle, Western Illinois University, Macomb, Illinois, 61455. E-mail: Bill_McFarland@ccmail.wiu.edu.

REFERENCES

American Bar Association. (1987). *Family Law Reporter.* Washington DC: Author.

Anderson, J. D. (1994). School climate for gay and lesbian students and staff members. *Phi Delta Kappan, 76,* 151–154.

Anderson, J. D. (1997). Supporting the invisible minority. *Educational Leadership, 54,* 65–68.

Baker, S. (2000). *School counseling for the twenty-first century.* Upper Saddle River, NJ: Macmillan.

Black, J., & Underwood, J. (1998). Young, female, and gay: Lesbian students and the environment. *Professional School Counseling, 1*(3), 15–20.

Blumenfeld, W. J., & Raymond, D. (1989). *Looking at gay and lesbian life.* Boston: Beacon.

Blumenfeld, W. J., & Lindop, L. (1995). *Gay/straight alliances: A student guide.* Malden, MA: Massachusetts Department of Education.

Carter, K. (1997, March 7). *Gay slurs abound.* Des Moines Register, p. 3.

Chasnoff, D., & Cohen, H. (1997). *It's elementary: Talking about gay issues in school.* [Film]. (Available from Women's Educational Media, 2180 Bryant St., Suite 203, San Francisco, CA 94116).

Comstock, G. D. (1991). *Violence against lesbians and gay men.* New York: Columbia University.

Daniels, J., Arredondo, P., & D'Andrea, M. (1999, June). Expanding counselors' thinking about the problem of violence. *Counseling Today, 41,* 12, 17.

Davis v. Monroe County Board of Education, 526 U.S. 629 (1999).

Elia, J. P. (1993). Homophobia in the high school: A problem in need of a resolution. *The High School Journal, 77,* 177–185.

Gay, Lesbian, Straight Education Network. (1998). Homophobia 101: *Anti-homophobia training for school staff and students.* New York: Author.

Gebser v. Lago Vista Independent School District, 524 U.S. 274 (1998).

Ginsberg, R. W. (1998). Silenced voices inside our schools. *Initiatives, 58,* 1–15.

Herek, G. M. (1986). On heterosexual masculinity: Some psychical consequences of the social construction of gender and sexuality. *American Behavioral Scientist, 29,* 563–577.

Herek, G. M., & Berrill, K. T. (Eds.). (1992). *Hate crimes: Confronting violence against lesbians and gay men.* Newbury Park, CA: Sage.

Hetrick, E., & Martin, A. D. (1987). Developmental issues and their resolution for gay and lesbian adolescents. *Journal of Homosexuality, 14,* 25–43.

Honig, D. (1999). Enforcing rules against harassment of gay students while respecting the free speech rights of students and teachers. *The Safe Schools of Washington Trainer's Manual,* 32–33. Retrieved June 14, 1999 from the World Wide Web: http://www.safeschools-waorg/ss_aclu.html

Hunter, J., & Schaecher, R. (1995). *Gay and lesbian adolescents.* In R. L. Edwards (Ed.), Encyclopedia of social work (19th ed., pp. 1055–1059). Silver Springs, MD: National Association of Social Workers.

Jennings, K. (2000). *What does homosexuality have to do with education? An answer.* Blackboard On Line: The Website of the Gay, Lesbian and Straight Education Network. Retrieved August 14, 1999 from the World Wide Web: http://www.glsen.org/pages/sections/library/schooltools/016.article

Klein, S. S. (1992). Why should we care about gender and sexuality in education? In J. T. Sears (Ed.), *Sexuality and the curriculum: The politics and practices of sexuality education* (pp. 171–179). New York: Teachers College.

Klinger, R. L. (1995). Gay violence. *Journal of Gay and Lesbian Psychotherapy, 2,* 119–134.

Lambda Legal Defense and Education Fund. (1997). *Improving school policies and state laws.* New York: Author.

Lambda Legal Defense and Education Fund. (1998). *An outline of our school work.* New York: Author.

Lipkin, A. (1992). *Strategies for the teacher using gay/lesbian-related materials in the high school classroom.* Cambridge, MA: Harvard Graduate School of Education.

Lipkin, A. (1994). The case for a gay and lesbian curriculum. *The High School Journal, 77,* 95–107.

Marinoble, R. M. (1998). Homosexuality: A blind spot in the school mirror. *Professional School Counseling, 1*(3), 4–7.

Massachusetts Governor's Commission on Gay and Lesbian Youth. (1993). *Making schools safe for gay and lesbian youth: Breaking the silence in schools and in families.* Boston: Author.

Massachusetts Department of Education. (1995). *Youth risk behavior study.* Boston: Author.

Masters, W., Johnson, V., & Kolodny, R. (1992). *Human sexuality* (4th ed.). New York: HarperCollins.

Matiella, A. C. (1991). *Positively different: Creating a bias free environment for young children.* Santa Cruz, CA: ETR Associates.

McFarland, W. P. (1993). A developmental approach to gay and lesbian youth. *Journal of Humanistic Education and Development, 32,* 17–29.

McFarland, W. P. (1998). Gay, lesbian, and bisexual student suicide. *Professional School Counseling, 1*(3), 26–29.

Muller, L. E., & Hartman, J. (1998). Group counseling for sexual minority youth. *Professional School Counseling, 1*(3), 38–41.

Nabozny v. Podlesny, 92 F.3d 446 (W.D. Wisc. 1996).

O'Conor, A. (1994). Who gets called queer in school? Lesbian, gay and bisexual teenagers, homophobia, and high school. *The High School Journal, 77,* 7–12.

Orzek, A. M. (1992). Career counseling for the gay and lesbian community. In S. Dworkin & F. Gutierrez (Eds.), *Counseling gays and lesbians: Journey to the end of the rainbow* (pp. 23–33). Alexandria, VA: American Counseling Association.

Pilkington, N. W., & D'Augelli, A. R. (1995). Victimization of lesbian, gay and bisexual youth in community settings. *Journal of Community Psychology, 23,* 34–56.

Price, J. H., & Telljohann, S. K. (1991). School counselors' perceptions of adolescent homosexuals. Journal of School Health, 61, 433–438.

Reis, B. (1996). *Safe schools anti-violence documentation project.* The Safe Schools Coalition of Washington. Retrieved June 14, 1999 from the World Wide Web: http://www.safeschools-wa.org/ssp_part3.html

Remafedi, G. J. (1987). Adolescent homosexuality: Psychosocial and medical implications. *Pediatrics, 79,* 331–337.

Robinson, K. E. (1994). Addressing the needs of gay and lesbian students: The school counselor's role. *The School Counselor, 41,* 326–332.

Sears, J. (1992a). Educators, homosexuality, and homosexual students: Are personal feelings related to professional beliefs? In K. Harbeck (Ed.), *Coming out of the classroom closet: Gay and lesbian teachers and curricula* (pp. 29–79). New York: Harrington Park.

Sears, J. (1992b). The impact of culture and ideology on construction of gender and sexual identities: Developing a critically based curriculum. In J. T. Sears (Ed.), *Sexuality and the curriculum: The politics and practices of sexuality education* (pp. 139–156). New York: Teachers College.

Sjostron, L., & Stein, N. (1996). *Bullyproof: A teacher's guide on teasing and bullying for use with fourth and fifth grade students.* Santa Cruz, CA: ETR Associates.

Treadway, L., & Yoakam, J. (1992). Creating a safer school environment for lesbian and gay students. *Journal of School Health, 62,* 352–357.

U.S. Bureau of the Census. (1995). *Digest of Educational Statistics, Statistical Abstracts of the United States* (115th ed.). Washington, DC: U.S. Department of Commerce.

U.S. Department of Education. (1997). *Sexual harassment guidance: Harassment of students by school employees, other students, or third parties,* 62 Fed.Reg. 12,034.

U.S. Department of Education Office for Civil Rights. (1999). *Protecting students from harassment and hate crime: A guide for schools.* U.S. Department of Education Office for Civil Rights. Retrieved August 15, 1999 from the World Wide Web: http://www.ed.gov/pubs/Harassment/

Wagner v. Fayetteville Public Schools. (1998). Administrative Proceeding. U.S. Department of Education.

Woog, D. (1995). *School's out: The impact of gay and lesbian issues on America's schools.* Boston: Alyson Publications.

Youth Pride, Inc. (1997). *Creating safe schools for lesbian and gay students: A resource guide for school staff.* Providence, RI: Youth Pride, Inc. Retrieved August 20, 1999 from the World Wide Web: http://members.tripod.com/~twood/guide.html

Urban School Counseling: Context, Characteristics, and Competencies

By Courtland C. Lee, Ph.D.

This article originally appeared in *Professional School Counseling*, Vol. 8, No. 3, 2005.

This article explores the nature of professional school counseling in urban settings. An overview of key characteristics of the urban environment and urban schools first provides context for the role of the professional school counselor in such a setting. Second, specific challenges facing urban school counselors are considered. Third, a set of urban school counseling competencies is discussed.

Although the goal of education in any setting is fundamentally the same, ensuring educational success for all children, this mission takes on challenging dimensions in an urban environment. Complex issues that characterize life in cities and their immediate metropolitan surroundings often confound education in urban schools.

Professional school counselors working in urban schools must promote academic, career, and personal- social development against the backdrop of environmental issues that by degree are often more challenging than they are in suburban or rural educational settings. Although attention has been focused on rural school counseling in recent years (Hines, 2002; Morrissette, 1997, 2000), school counseling practice in an urban context has tended to be overlooked. The purpose of this article is to explore the nature of professional urban school counseling. First, an overview of key characteristics of the urban environment and urban schools will provide context for the role of the professional school counselor in such a setting. Second, specific challenges facing professional urban school counselors will be considered. Finally, suggested competencies for advancing school counseling in an urban context will be discussed.

THE URBAN CONTEXT

To fully appreciate the issues confronting urban school counselors, it is important to examine the context for those issues. It is necessary, therefore, to define what is meant by urban and examine crucial characteristics of such an environment.

The U.S. Census Bureau (2002) classifies as urban all territory, population, and housing units located within an urbanized area or an urban cluster. It delineates urban area and urban cluster boundaries to encompass densely settled territory, which consists of (a) core census block groups that have a population density of at least 1,000 people per square mile, and (b) surrounding census blocks that have an overall density of at least 500 people per square mile. According to the Census Bureau, an urbanized area consists of densely settled territory that contains 50,000 or more people. An urban cluster consists of closely settled territory that has at least 2,500 people but fewer than 50,000 people. The Census Bureau introduced the urban cluster for the 2000 census to provide a more consistent and accurate measure of the population concentration in and around places.

Concomitant with the operational definition of urban, the Census Bureau also defines the general concept of metropolitan area. This is an area with a large population nucleus, together with adjacent communities that have a high degree of economic and social interaction with that nucleus. Each metropolitan area must contain either a place with a minimum population of 50,000 or a total metropolitan area of at least 100,000. A metropolitan area contains one or more central counties. It also may include one or more outlying counties that have close economic and social relationships with the central county.

Given these Census Bureau definitions, the term urban can be conceived of as referring to cities, and in most instances the municipalities or counties in close proximity to them. Conceptualizing an urban area in this manner suggests a number of important characteristics that may help to define the nature of such places. The following is a list of characteristics that help to define the urban context. This list is by no means exhaustive, but it does represent many of the aspects that have come to characterize urban settings:

- Population density
- Structural density
- High concentration of people of color
- High concentration of recent immigrants
- High rates of reported crimes
- Per capita higher rates of poverty
- Complex transportation patterns
- High concentration of airborne pollutants
- Strong cultural stimulation
- Diversity in property values
- Inequities in the educational system
- Large, complex educational systems
- Inequities in the legal system

- Lack of community connectedness
- Cultural heterogeneity
- Inequities in access to health care.

THE URBAN CONTEXT OF SCHOOLS

Urban schools in large measure reflect the characteristics of the environment in which they are located. The status of urban public education has become a topic of much concern in recent years (Gallay & Flanagan, 2000; Kolodny, 2001; National Center for Education Statistics, 2000; Olson & Jerald, 1998; Parker, Kelly, & Sanford, 1998). It is evident that public schools in urban areas face significant issues that are qualitatively different from those confronting schools in rural or suburban contexts. Olson and Jerald, in reviewing a number of indicators, have provided an important framework for examining the context and inherent challenges of urban education:

- *The achievement gap.* Urban youth are less likely to receive a postsecondary degree and are more likely to drop out of high school compared to rural and suburban youth. In addition, they are less likely to meet the minimum standards on national tests and less likely to complete high school in 4 years. Significantly, urban youth often enter college or the workforce unprepared to succeed at competent levels, which places them in a precarious situation for attaining meaningful work.
- *Concentrated poverty.* This is a major urban phenomenon. Urban students are more than twice as likely to attend high-poverty schools. Concentrated poverty heightens the probability that schoolchildren will lack access to regular medical care, live in a household headed by a single mother, become a victim of crime, have a parent who never finished high school, become pregnant, and drop out of school.
- *The teaching challenge.* Urban school districts face major challenges hiring teachers and filling teacher vacancies. Significantly, urban schools are far more likely to hire unlicensed or underqualified teachers. In many instances, urban school systems cannot meet the salaries or working conditions that are offered by suburban districts.
- *The school climate.* On average, urban students attend bigger schools than do non-urban students. The climate in urban schools is, more often than not, characterized by teacher reports that weapons and physical conflicts among students are a problem. Significant student absenteeism and tardiness often are associated with an urban school climate. Likewise, a lack of parent involvement is often a characteristic of the climate of urban schools.

- *Access to resources.* The share of public resources for funding urban schools is often a major challenge. Nationally, urban districts spend less per student than do non-urban districts. This lack of resources often is seen in aging and crumbling school facilities where students with a lack of books and supplies attempt to learn. Urban schools also are often lagging behind in access to educational technology that is so crucial to the contemporary learning process. Significantly, funding problems in urban schools often are exacerbated by financial mismanagement on the part of educational leaders.

- *Politics and governance.* Urban school districts are, in most instances, large bureaucratic institutions that are fueled by highly charged political realities. These realities include the ever-growing influence of key political stakeholders on the educational process. Mayors, city council members, school board members, union officials, and, in some cases, state officials can be counted among these major stakeholders. The political realities of urban schools are exacerbated by central administrations that are highly bureaucratic, grossly mismanaged, and increasingly inefficient when it comes to educational governance. Within the morass of politics and governance are superintendents who, on average, serve fewer than 3 years as chief executives of urban school systems.

SCHOOL COUNSELING IN THE URBAN ENVIRONMENT

Given the contextual factors that characterize urban schools and their impact on student development, it is important to consider the nature of professional school counseling in this environment. Urban school counselors must support young people as they explore options, make choices, and prepare for life after high school against a backdrop of the challenges that confront the school systems in which counselors work.

The overarching issue confronting urban school counselors is pervasive academic failure (National Center for Education Statistics, 2000; Olson & Jerald, 1998). In their attempts to address this issue, counselors often must confront complex factors that significantly undermine the ability of many young people to achieve academic success in urban schools. They also must deal with structural dynamics that greatly impinge upon their professional roles.

The implementation of counseling programs in urban schools is hampered often by chronic student absenteeism, family instability, high levels of student transience, increasing school and community violence, and high rates of teenage pregnancy. Additionally, urban school counselors are faced with major challenges associated with increasing cultural diversity in schools. Counseling interventions are greatly impacted by language issues and value differences that come with the cultural diversity that characterizes many urban schools.

Urban school counseling is further complicated by major structural challenges to programming. These include ever-increasing workloads, meager resources, minimal professional development, unionization, expanding bureaucratic interference or indifference, and high rates of administrative turnover.

As if these issues and challenges were not enough, urban school counselors also must contend with the contemporary demands placed upon schools for greater accountability. In an era of legislative initiatives such as the No Child Left Behind Act (U.S. Department of Education, 2001), urban school counselors, like their rural and suburban counterparts, find themselves under significant public pressure to ensure that all students achieve to high academic standards.

URBAN SCHOOL COUNSELING COMPETENCIES

It is evident that school counseling in urban areas brings with it significant challenges. Counselors who work in urban educational environments must be prepared to confront serious impediments to student development. Counseling in urban schools, therefore, implies a set of competencies on the part of professionals that will enable them to effectively address the personal, interpersonal, and structural challenges that tend to stifle academic success for scores of young people. These competencies are underscored by a major movement underway to transform the nature of professional school counseling.

School Counseling Reform:
The Foundation of Urban School Counselor

Competency Within the past decade, professional school counseling has undergone a transformation. School counselors have been challenged to achieve new professional goals and assume new and more proactive roles (Education Trust, 2000; Erford, House, & Martin, 2003). Professional school counselors are being called upon to be visible leaders in national educational reform movements and central to the missions of schools (House & Hayes, 2002; Martin, 2002). The work of a school counselor in this transformational effort is predicated on the principles of access, equity, and social justice. These principles reflect a commitment to ensuring that all children, regardless of race/ethnicity or socioeconomic status, have the opportunity to achieve to their fullest potential.

School counselors are now challenged to assume roles that reflect a commitment to these principles. Accordingly, they are being asked to shift from an individual focus to a systemic focus in their work. Rather than work in isolation with individual student problems, professional school counselors are being asked to team and collaborate with other educational stakeholders and work at a macro level to bring about systemic change (Bemak, 2000). In addition, they are being called upon to move beyond a primary focus on school counseling activities to more extensive involvement as leaders in both the school and the community (Erford, House, & Martin, 2003). Finally, in an era of greater educational accountability, professional school counselors are being called upon to demonstrate with data that their efforts make a difference in the lives of the students with whom they work (Dahir & Stone, 2003).

Competencies for the Transformed Urban School Counselor

Within the context of this national reform initiative, the following represents a set of important competencies for professional school counselors in urban educational environments. These competencies reflect the knowledge set, skills, and attitudes or beliefs needed to promote student academic, career, and personal-social development given the realities of contemporary urban schools.

Cultural competence. Urban school counselors must be culturally competent (Holcomb-McCoy, 2004; Lee, 2001). They should possess the awareness, knowledge, and skills to intervene in responsive and appropriate ways into the lives of the increasingly culturally diverse student population that characterizes the urban school setting.

Skills for promoting empowerment. Urban school counselors must have individual and group counseling skills that are grounded in the concept of empowerment. Empowerment is a developmental process in which people who are powerless or marginalized in some fashion become aware of how power affects their lives. They then develop the skills for gaining reasonable control over their lives that they use to help themselves and others in their community (McWhirter, 1994).

Given the personal and structural challenges that often confront young people in urban schools, counselors should be able to move beyond traditional counseling practice when promoting academic, career, and personal-social development. They should have the skills to engage in programmed intervention that facilitates a process in which young people become empowered to proactively address urban challenges that impede their overall educational success. As part of the empowerment process, counselors should be able to promote the development of positive attitudes toward academic achievement as well as foster academic competency among students.

Counseling for empowerment also should involve the ability to promote positive self-identity and cultural awareness in young people. This is necessitated by the failure identity fostered in many youth as a result of their experiences with educational processes that have been negatively impacted by the challenges facing urban schools.

An empowerment perspective on counseling also includes skill to promote individual and collective awareness among young people about how their ultimate academic, career, and personal-social success is linked to the potential betterment of their communities. As students become empowered, counselors should be able to help them to channel their interest and potential into helping empower their families and communities.

Systemic perspective. Urban school counselors must adopt a systemic perspective with respect to their helping roles and functions. Rather than focus exclusively on the etiology of problems originating with students, counselors should make the urban systems in which young people must develop and function also a center of attention for programmed intervention (Lee & Walz, 1998). Adopting a systemic perspective demands that counselors develop an understanding of important urban systems and how they interact to affect student development. These include the educational system, the family system, the political system, the criminal justice system, and the social welfare system.

Advocacy. Adopting a systemic perspective suggests advocacy. Urban school counselors must be advocates for their students. In this role, counselors intervene in social systems on behalf of students in ways designed to eliminate barriers to academic success (Bailey, Getch, & Chen-Hayes, 2003). As advocates, urban school counselors are systemic change agents, working to impact urban social systems in ways that will ultimately benefit the students with whom they work.

Collaboration. Urban school counselors must be able to collaborate with key educational stakeholders to promote student development (Bemak, 2000; Bryan & Holcomb-McCoy, 2004). They should be able to collaborate, for example, with urban families to help them become empowered as a proactive force in the educational success of children. Such collaboration should be based on important considerations about urban family life. Counselors must be sensitive to the economic and social realties of many urban families and meet them where they are with respect to such things as language proficiency and cultural customs.

In addition, urban school counselors must collaborate with community stakeholders to advance the educational interests of students. Counselors should be able to form alliances within the business, religious, and political sectors of urban communities to promote education. They should be able to broker such alliances so that they result in community resources being channeled into school programming to support both counseling and teaching initiatives. An example of this might be collaborating with community stakeholders and actively supporting their efforts to develop supplemental academic support programs in neighborhood religious institutions, community centers, and other areas of social activity.

Urban school counselors also should collaborate with educational stakeholders within the school setting. In particular, they should collaborate with teachers and administrators on ways to increase their educational effectiveness given the social and structural challenges with which educators often are confronted. School counselors should facilitate faculty development initiatives that focus on increasing awareness of the urban systemic factors that impinge upon student development or that introduce innovative methods for promoting student success in this environment.

Leadership. Urban school counselors must be leaders in their schools and within the larger community (Bemak, 2000). They should be in the forefront of developing new educational initiatives that promote student development. They also should be active participants on leadership teams within their respective schools and in the school district. Urban school counselors should be involved in the development of new educational policies and procedures from the board of education to the school building level.

Likewise, urban school counselors must be politically and socially active leaders in the community at large. They should seek leadership positions within strategic community organizations and institutions that affect the quality of life for young people and their families. They should be in a position to directly influence important community political decisions and policy initiatives that have a connection to the quality of education for students as well as the welfare of their families.

The Challenge of Urban School Counseling Competencies

While it may be argued that these competencies are important for school counselors in all settings, the pervasive failure and wasted potential of scores of young people that characterize much of the urban educational landscape underscore the importance and urgency of this skill set for counseling in urban schools. These competencies imply a rejection of many long-standing traditions characteristic of professional school counseling. They require school counselors who work in urban school settings to transcend the traditional boundaries of school counseling practice. The competencies challenge urban school counselors to "think outside the box" and take risks in their efforts to address the complex issues that confront them and the students with whom they work. In developing these competencies, counselors must be willing to commit themselves to understanding the complexities of the urban environment and how they directly affect young people.

They also must embrace the concept of empowerment and approach their individual and group interventions with students from such an affirming perspective. In addition, they must be willing to collaborate in innovative ways with all urban stakeholders and exert leadership within the school and community to promote educational success.

CONCLUSION

Counseling in urban schools is significantly different from school counseling in other settings. This article has provided direction for effective school counseling in an urban environment. It is based on the important notion that professional school counselors in this setting must possess the knowledge, skills, and attitudes to effectively address profound and often unique social and structural impediments to educational success for urban youth. The future of these young people and urban America demands no less.

Courtland C. Lee is professor and director of the School Counseling Program at the University of Maryland, College Park. E-mail: clee5@umd.edu

REFERENCES

Bailey, D. F., Getch,Y. Q., & Chen-Hayes, S. (2003). Professional school counselors as social and academic advocates. In B.T. Erford (Ed.), *Transforming the school counseling profession* (pp. 411–434). Upper Saddle River, NJ:Merrill Prentice Hall.

Bemak, F. (2000).Transforming the role of the counselor to provide leadership in educational reform through collaboration. *Professional School Counseling, 3*, 323–331.

Bryan, J., & Holcomb-McCoy, C. (2004). School counselors' perceptions of their involvement in school-family-community partnerships. *Professional School Counseling, 7*, 162–171.

Dahir, C., & Stone, C. (2003). Accountability: A M.E.A.S.U.R.E. of the impact school counselors have on student achievement. *Professional School Counseling, 6*, 214–221.

Education Trust. (2000). *National initiative for transforming school counseling summer academy for counselor educators proceedings.* Washington, DC: Author.

Erford, B.T, House, R., & Martin, P. (2003).Transforming the school counseling profession. In B.T. Erford (Ed.), *Transforming the school counseling profession* (pp. 1–20). Upper Saddle River, NJ:Merrill Prentice Hall.

Gallay, L. S., & Flanagan, C. A. (2000).The well-being of children in a changing economy: Time for a new social contract in America. In R.D.Taylor & M. C.Wang (Eds.), *Resilience across contexts: Work, family, culture, and community* (pp. 3–34). Mahwah, NJ: Erlbaum.

Hines, P. L. (2002).Transforming the rural school counselor. Theory Into Practice, 41, 192–202.

Holcomb-McCoy, C. (2004). Assessing the multicultural competence of school counselors: A checklist. *Professional School Counseling, 7,* 178–186.

House, R.M., & Hayes, R. L. (2002). School counselors: Becoming key players in school reform. *Professional School Counseling, 5,* 249–256.

Kolodny, K. A. (2001). Inequalities in the overlooked associations in urban educational collaborations. *The Urban Review, 33,* 151–178.

Lee, C. C. (2001). Culturally responsive school counselors and programs: Addressing the needs of all students. *Professional School Counseling, 4,* 257–261.

Lee, C. C., & Walz, G. (Eds.). (1998). *Social action: A mandate for counselors.* Alexandria,VA: American Counseling Association and ERIC Counseling and Student Services Clearinghouse.

Martin, P. J. (2002).Transforming school counseling: A national perspective. *Theory Into Practice, 41,* 148–154.

McWhirter, E. H. (1994). Counseling for empowerment. Alexandria,VA: American Counseling Association.

Morrissette, P. J. (1997).The rural school: A review and synthesis of the literature. *Guidance and Counseling, 13,* 19–23.

Morrissette, P. J. (2000).The experiences of the rural school counselor. *Professional School Counseling, 3,* 197–207.

National Center for Education Statistics. (2000). *The condition of education 2000* (NCES 2000-062).Washington, DC: U.S. Government Printing Office.

Olson, L., & Jerald, C.D. (1998). *Quality counts '98: The urban picture.* Retrieved June 18, 2004, from http://www.edweek.org/reports/qc98/challenges.htm

Parker, L., Kelly,M., & Sanford, J. (1998).The urban context of schools and education: Community, commitment, and change. *Educational Theory, 48,* 123–138.

U.S. Census Bureau. (2002). *Census 2000 urban and rural classification.* Retrieved June 9, 2004, from http://www.census.gov/geo/www/ua/ua_2k.html

U.S. Department of Education. (2001). *No Child Left Behind Act of 2001* (H.R.1).Washington, DC: Author.

School Counselors and Full Inclusion for Children with Special Needs

By Shari Tarver-Behring, Ph.D., Michael E. Spagna
and James Sullivan

This article originally appeared in *Professional School Counseling*,
Vol. 1, No.3, 1998.

The integration of children with disabilities in the same classroom with nondisabled youngsters has emerged as one of the most complex, important, and controversial practices in the field of education.

Originally, the Education for All Handicapped Children Act of 1975 required that schools provide a continuum of placement options. These options included general education classrooms, resource classrooms, special day classrooms, special day schools, hospitals, and the like. In addition, in individualized education programs, (IEPs) determined which placements were most appropriate given the special needs of children with disabilities (Smith, Polloway, Patton & Dowdy, 1995). Recently, the Act was reauthorized by Congress and is now known as the Individuals with Disabilities Education Act of 1990 (IDEA). The delivery of special education instruction and services for children with disabilities, as required by IDEA, has shifted to the regular classroom whenever possible. The practice of educating *all* students in the general education classroom, including students with special needs and abilities, is currently referred to as *full inclusion*.

Historically, a primary role of the school counselor has been to provide services that supplement and support students in general education. However, in addition to attending to the students' social, personal, educational, and life-career development – via direct counseling and guidance, and via indirect services such as consultation with parents, teachers, and support services – adjunct services to students with disabilities has been within the realm of the school counselor's duties (Baker, 1992). Children with disabilities who rejoin the classroom through full inclusion are eligible for school counseling services identical to those received by students who have been in general education all along. Children with disabilities may require the assistance of the counselor to an even greater degree since they show specific problems that might require both immediate as well as ongoing attention. For example, youngsters with disabilities often exhibit poor self-concept, difficulties with the expression and control of frustration and anger, inappropriate social behavior, low motivation, and high dependency on others (Lewis, Chard & Scott, 1994; McDowell, Coven & Eash, 1979).

Given the current legislative mandate for full inclusion, school counselors must become informed and be prepared to be active participants in facilitating the full inclusion of students with disabilities into the general education classroom (Tarver-Behring, Spagna, & Sullivan, 1996). Before describing specific ways that school counselors can assist students with disabilities, we will discuss the process, possible sources of resistance, and the benefits of full inclusion both for children with and without disabilities.

FULL INCLUSION

Full inclusion is defined as: "the existence of only one unified educational system from the beginning of formal education, encompassing all members equitably, without regard for variations in their status" (Giangreco, 1993, p. 17). According to IDEA, schools must attempt to teach children with disabilities in the general education classroom with supplemental supports and services before these children are considered for placement in a more restrictive environment. Previously, children who functioned at a level that was significantly different from their same-aged peers were often placed directly into special education classrooms with minimal-to-no access to general education settings.

Full inclusion does not necessarily mean that all students will be educated by using the same instructional methods or be expected to work toward or obtain the same educational goals (Stainback & Stainback, 1990). Rather, full inclusion means that all students will be provided appropriate educational programs that reflect their needs and abilities with the support necessary to promote success. These necessary supports can be in the form of specialized instruction, adapted equipment, and specialized personnel. For full inclusion to be successful, general education teachers must work collaboratively with special education staff as well as school counselors in order to provide meaningful and appropriate programs for all students (Sugai & Horner, 1994). Full inclusion should be viewed as a process, and this process needs to be individualized for each school, student and family. IDEA clearly identifies special education as a service, not a place.

Full Inclusion Is Not Mainstreaming

It is important to note that the term mainstreaming has been used interchangeably with full inclusion, while in fact full inclusion and mainstreaming are not similar. Mainstreaming and similar terms evolved from the existence of two parallel school systems – special education and general education. There is an assumption that the two systems are unequal. That is, integration involves allowing the minority – children of disabilities, who make up approximately 10% of the school-age population (U.S. Department of Education, 1993) – to join the majority of youngsters receiving instruction in general education or the mainstream. Therefore, the members of the minority group – students receiving instruction in special education settings – must understand that mainstreaming is contingent upon being able to participate in accordance with standards set by the majority system. In short, students with disabilities should be ready to compete in general education classrooms as they currently exist in order to be successful.

Alternately, full inclusion is the belief in one unified educational system, not minority and majority systems as implied under the mainstreaming model. The full-inclusion model, by comparison, promotes a unified system of formal education, which includes all members equally. Therefore, under this model, the need for integration is moot since there is no separation to begin with. Furthermore, according to the full-inclusion model, all students' needs, regardless of whether or not they have disabilities, will be met in one educational system.

Successful Models

There are currently a number of successful full-inclusion programs in the nation; students with disabilities, ranging from mild to severe, attend age-appropriate general education classrooms at neighborhood schools (Colvin, Karmeenui, & Sugai, 1994; Keenan, 1993). These students are considered full-time members of the general education classroom and are receiving the support necessary for them to succeed. Furthermore, these inclusive schools have abandoned the traditional dual system of special and general education, instead adopting and operating under one unified educational system. Within this one system, students with disabilities are challenged and provided educational opportunities equal to their needs and abilities. Students with disabilities are provided different methods of learning, different educational objectives as well as appropriate and sufficient support services within the general education classroom. General and special education staff have joined resources to provide the assistance and support necessary to help students with disabilities reach their potential (Sugai &Horner, 1994). In turn, general education teachers have experienced increased feelings of comfort and have become more confident when working with students with disabilities. The inclusive school fosters an appreciation of individual differences among all students and promotes diversity.

Some of the benefits of full inclusion have been documented by Snell and Eichner (1989). They propose that merging general and special education provides specific benefits that are available in inclusive programs that are not available in segregated settings. For example, students with disabilities are provided with more normal role models when educated in the general education classroom. Such role models, according to Snell and Eichner, eventually lead students with disabilities to exhibit more appropriate behaviors. Furthermore, students without disabilities learn to understand, tolerate, and appreciate individual differences of students with disabilities. For example, students without disabilities lean to accept rule modifications so that students with disabilities are able to be successful, challenged and included.

COLLABORATING AND CONSULTING

There are ways to facilitate collaboration and/or consultation between school counselors and general and special education teachers. School counselors play a unique role as consultants to teachers, assisting teacher to meet the immediate needs of students (Tarver-Behring, et al., 1996). In this context, the main purpose of consultation is to promote the successful implementation of full inclusion as children with disabilities enter general education classrooms. In particular, general education teachers require assistance to facilitate students' academic and social adjustment (Idol, 1988).

School counselors are not expected to be experts in curricular modifications, particularly as far as those adaptations impact the education of the fully included pupil with disabilities. Special education teachers are trained to assist general education teachers in developing these skills. (Kratochwill, Elliot & Rotto, 1990). School counselors can be informed of special education information and resources and, in return, share counseling skills with special education teachers through a collaborative team approach. This team can then work together to offer consultation to general education teachers about a wide variety of topics and skills critical for successful full inclusion.

As the movement toward full inclusion is taking place, general education teachers have been challenged to implement full inclusion while continuing to serve the nondisabled students in class. Full inclusion requires general education teachers to develop and implement educational plans that meet students' specific needs in an inclusive environment. Special education teachers have a responsibility to facilitate this process. Special education teachers can assist general education teachers to modify the curriculum to benefit children with disabilities rather than force children with disabilities to fit into the existing curricula. Often, general education teachers are not aware of the resources available to them to meet the variety of needs of their students with disabilities once they are included into the classrooms. Therefore, school counselors can facilitate linkage between general education teachers who possess the resources to make full inclusion successful. The school counselor/special education collaborative consultation team is an ideal method by which to identify support and resources to assist the general education teacher.

Once linked, special education teachers have been trained to share the following functions with general education teachers, according to Wiedemeyer and Lehman (1991):

(a) collaborative teaching; (b) monitoring of students; (c) developing units in social, problem-solving, or study skills, especially as required by students experiencing difficulty; (d) sharing of materials and expertise in programming; (e) developing materials at a lower level; (f) providing generalization opportunities and activities; and, (g) sharing special instructional techniques and strategies (pp. 7-8).

Each of these functions proves essential if full inclusion is to truly take place. For example, collaborative teaching means that special and general education teachers share in the planning and presenting of lessons and providing adaptations to this instruction to better meet the needs of all students – those with and without disabilities.

In particular, special education teachers are skilled in providing curricular adaptations for students with disabilities. These modifications and adaptations allow students with disabilities to participate as much as possible in the general education curriculum. To make these modifications/adaptations, special education teachers generally engage in a three-step process whereby teachers systematically determine the students' need for specific changes to the curriculum, implement these same changes, and evaluate the effectiveness of these adaptations in terms of students' progress and learning (Hoover, 1990). Several examples of these adaptations can be found in the work of Chalmers (1991), Cheney (1989), and Dowdy (1990). For example, students experiencing difficulty in writing might receive the following modifications: "allow children to circle or underline responses rather than writing them; let students type or tape record answers instead of giving them in writing; fasten materials to the desk to alleviate coordination problems" (Smith et al., 1995, p. 400).

In addition to the collaboration/consultation already mentioned, numerous resources are available to build general education teacher skills for serving the child with disabilities. For example, two recent resources have been developed that provide general education teachers with a good starting place for working with students with disabilities (*Teaching Children with Special Needs in Inclusive Settings* by Smith et al., 1995; and *Teaching Special Learners in the General Education Classroom*, by

McCoy, 1995). Of course, all general education teachers should consult with special education teachers in relation to the severity of the disability, mild-to-moderate or moderate-to-severe, when implementing any of the strategies and/or interventions listed in these resources.

Acknowledging Resistance

It is important for school counselors to acknowledge that general education teachers will have fears concerning full inclusion. General education teachers need reassurance that counselor/special education teacher consultation teams will collaborate with them to find resources and build instructional skills to address areas of concern. School counselors can prepare for possible sources of resistance to full inclusion. For example, school counselors can acknowledge that there is disagreement in the field of education about whether all children, especially those with extensive educational and social needs, belong in general education classrooms. Some writers believe that students with severe disabilities should not be fully included into the general education classroom (Baker & Zigmond, 1990; Bergen, 1990; Gallagher, 1994; Lewis et al., 1994; Reganick, 1993).

Reganick (1993) states that the needs of youngsters with severe disabilities can not be accommodated in the present educational system, primarily because general education teachers are insufficiently prepared to educate these students. Moreover, Reganick asserts that the behavior of certain students with disabilities, specifically those identified as having serious emotional disturbance, would be so disruptive that it might be harmful to other students. According to Gallagher (1994), general education classrooms are presently unable to provide the range of instruction and intensive services that special education classes supply. For example, certain students with disabilities need to learn basic life skills and concrete tasks, which are not part of the general education curriculum. Finally, Bergen (1990) reports that youngsters with disabilities who are fully included in general education classrooms increase their dependency on others instead of seeking independence.

Abundance of Professional Support

In response to teacher resistance, school counselors should also be familiar with an abundance of professionally published support of integration (see Cole & Meyer, 1991; Peck, Donaldson & Pezzoli,1990) and an ever growing amount of professional literature in support of full inclusion (Snell & Eichner,1989; Stainback & Stainback,1990). To answer an often-asked question, "do students with disabilities benefit from full inclusion?" Stevens and Slavin (1991) report that these students exhibit improved social interaction as well as increased academic performance when necessary supports are present in the general education classroom. However, it is important to note that the jury is still out regarding whether or not similar positive outcomes rare realized for all types of youngsters with disabilities who are fully included (Fuchs & Fuchs, 1990) . School counselors, in collaboration with special education teachers, can play a key role in assisting teachers and parents to be fully informed before decisions are made about full inclusion of children (Eichinger & Woltman, 1993).

BUILDING SOCIAL AND EMOTIONAL ADJUSTMENT

A primary purpose of full inclusion is to increase social competence of children with disabilities and to improve peer relationships (Snell, 1989). Yet, one of the most demanding aspects of full inclusion is the successful social adjustment of children with special needs into the general education environment.

Social adjustment in childhood is critical to overall adjustment later in life. Children with behavioral difficulties often continue to show social maladjustment in adulthood without treatment (Gersten, Langner, Eisenberg, Sincha-Fagan, & McCarthy, 1976; Parker & Asher, 1987). Many social challenges occur for such children entering general education classes. These children may come with fewer resources needed to succeed socially due to handicapping conditions such as learning disabilities or serious emotional disturbances (Lewis et al., 1994; McDowell et al., 197). Differences in physical appearance for some exceptional children may result in social isolation or rejection. The stigma of having been in a special education classroom in and of itself may adversely affect other children's attitudes towards children with disabilities (Baker, 1992). Less experience with general education peers due to having been in a special education program may have further limited these children in the acquisition of social skills which are age-appropriate (Snell & Eichner, 1989).

Promoting Social Adjustment

Of primary importance, counselors must assist teachers to promote acceptance of students with disabilities by their nondisabled peers in the general education classroom. School counselors can use their consultation skills to increase teachers' knowledge and skills about social and emotional adjustment for fully included children. Together, school counselors and teachers can develop a plan that teachers can use both for present social exchanges between students and for similar situations in the future.

School counselors can offer knowledge and skills in the consultation process to increase a disabled student's sense of belonging. Kramer and Wright (1994) have identified a number of suggestions for school counselors to make such as explaining how teachers can be good role models by demonstrating respect for all students. School counselors can reassure teachers of the positive benefits of asking students with disabilities to be accountable as much as possible for the same rules that apply to others and of encouraging these students to be active participants in all classroom and social activities. Counselors can also help teachers to create a sense of open communication and safety in expression for all students by establishing ground rules for classroom communication, such as one person speaks at a time, no one can make demeaning comments to others in the group, and so on. School counselors can further promote social adjustment by encouraging teachers to give positive feedback to nondisabled students engaging in social interactions with their classmates who have disabilities.

Implementing Social Skills Curricula

In addition to facilitating peer acceptance, special and general education teachers can benefit from training in specific social skills for students with disabilities (Horner, Diemer & Brazeau, 1992). Teachers have expressed a willingness to incorporate social skills into the educational curriculum if given the necessary support (Bain & Farris , 1991). School counselors can assist teachers in promoting specific skills, such as how to make friends, how to take turns, sharing, and initiating play (Cartledge & Kleefelt, 1991; Ridley & Vaughn, 1982).

Children who have emotional, behavioral, or learning problems often exhibit deficits in problem-solving skills such as the ability to identify social problem situations, generate solutions, and evaluate consequences. These skills can also be couched in a social skills program (Galvin, 1983; Shure & Spivack, 1980). School counselors can help teachers to build these skills via a social skills curriculum for the involvement and benefit of the entire class. In addition, school counselors can identify, in consultation with general education teachers, those peer mentors (often the popular and socially adept children in the class) who can be paired with disabled children to increase their social status and to provide role models for children in social exchanges (Dougherty & Taylor, 1983).

Providing Direct Counseling Services

When necessary, school counselors can offer direct services to students with disabilities who are experiencing social difficulties. School counselors can draw upon their expertise in counseling to facilitate successful social adaptation for these students. Impulse-control techniques, conflict resolution, coping strategies, and counseling specific to the child's difficulties can also be provided in individual counseling. Finally, school counselors can intervene with classmates in group counseling activities to promote altruistic behavior, tolerance, and compassion for the exceptional child. Students without disabilities can be guided toward an appreciation for individual differences, greater knowledge of and optimism for those who do have disabilities, and a broader perspective when facing one's own difficulties in life (Frith, Clark & Miller, 1983; Gottlieb, 1980; Salend, 1983).

CONSULTING WITH FAMILIES

Parents are often ambivalent about introducing their special education children into the full-inclusion process. Parents fear that despite the opportunity to experience success in a general educational setting, their children will receive fewer services, experience social rejection by classmates, and be the recipients of negative attitudes from the regular educational teachers who do not understand full inclusion or do not want to have the additional burden that comes with it. Parents also experience stress because of the extra skills they need to assist their children and are reluctant to add to their stressors by making changes and attempting to learn new skills relative to full inclusion.

School counselors are ideal for assisting these parents. Unlike other school personnel, counselors have more time available for contact with parents and have specific skills to collaborate and communicate with them. Counselors can share information about the benefits of full inclusion and respond to parents' fears about this process. School counselors can explain that general education teachers have been prepared with appropriate instructional strategies, that social and behavioral programs are in place for facilitating the children's adjustment, and that ongoing monitoring of the children's progress will occur via the school counselor/special education teacher team. Counselors can also provide emotional support and coping strategies for parents in relation to the demands from caring for exceptional children (Cochrane & Marini, 1977).

Helping Teachers Work with Parents

School counselors can facilitate the extension of knowledge and skills to parents for use at home via conjoint parent-teacher collaboration (Sheridan & Kratochwill, 1992). The following are some specific suggestions.

- Establish trusting relationships with parents.
- Obtain accurate and complete information from parents, listen carefully, and value what parents say.
- Help parents acquire more effective ways of handling behavior problems.

- Provide numerous options for parent involvement in the school setting, and keep in mind that involvement may be unfamiliar for parents.
- Provide assurance to those parents who may be fearful of the school bureaucracy.
- Let parents know that the school staff believes that the parents want the best for their children.
- Provide parents with special knowledge to meet the varied needs of children.
- Have parents collaborate in the process, to make them more likely to carry out recommendations successfully.
- Think of parents as experts who can contribute knowledge about and insight into their children, helping to enhance educational programs.
- Explain assessment procedures and encourage participation in conference decisions so that parents can help decide on the educational placement of their children.
- Encourage parents to involve themselves in classroom activities whenever appropriate.
- Provide opportunities for parents of disabled and nondisabled children to work together productively.

The success of school interventions, such as those identified through full inclusion, is greatly enhanced when teachers collaborate effectively with parents (Berry, 1987).

CONCLUSION

As more and more students with disabilities are fully included into neighborhood schools and general education classrooms, students, families, and teachers might become overwhelmed. These changes will require that the role of the school counselor evolve along with educational reform. In many ways, it is the school counselor who will play a crucial part in the smooth transition of children with disabilities into general education classrooms. In keeping with the spirit of federal legislation designed to include children with disabilities as much as possible into general education, school counselors can be instrumental in changing attitudes, meeting informational needs, enhancing social adjustment, assisting in the location of much needed outside resources, and building collaborative consultation teams, working with parents and teachers toward successful full inclusion.

Shari Tarver-Behring, Ph.D., is an assistant professor, and Michael E. Spagna is an assistant professor, both are at California State University, Northridge. James Sullivan is a teacher at El Rancho Unified, Pico Rivera, CA.

REFERENCES

Bain, A. & Farris, H. (1991). Teacher attitudes toward social skills training. *Teacher Education and Special Education, 15*, 49-56.

Baker, J.M. & Zigmond, N. (1990). Are regular education classes equipped to accommodate students with learning disabilities? *Exceptional Children, 56*, 515-526.

Baker, S.B. (1992). *School Counseling in the twenty-first century.* New York, Merrill.

Bergen, D. (1990). Facilitating friendship development in inclusion classrooms. *Childhood Education. 69*, 234-236.

Berry, J.O. (1987). A program for training teachers as counselors of parents of children with disabilities. *Journal of Counseling and Development, 65*, 508-509.

Cartledge, G. & Kleefeld, J. (1991). *Taking part: Introducing social skills to children.* Circle Pines, MN: American Guidance Services.

Chalmers, L. (1991). Classroom modifications for the mainstreamed student with mild handicaps. *Intervention in School and Clinic, 27*, 40-42.

Cheney, C.O. (1989). The systematic adaptation instructional materials and techniques for problem learners. *Academic Therapy, 25*, 25-30.

Cochrane, P.V. & Marini, B. (1997). Mainstreaming exceptional children: The counselor's role. *School Counselor, 25*, 17-21.

Cole, D.A., & Meyer, L.H. (1991). Social integration and severe disabilities: A longitudinal analysis of child outcomes. *The Journal of Special Education, 25*, 340-351.

Colvin, G., Karmeenui, E.J. & Sugai, G. (1994). Reconceptualizing behavior management and school-wide discipline in general education. *Education and Treatment of Children, 16*, 361-381.

Dougherty, A.M. & Taylor, B.L. (1983). Evaluation of peer helping programs. *Elementary School Guidance and Counseling, 18*, 130-136.

Dowdy, C. (1990). *Modifications for regular classes.* Unpublished manuscript. Alabama Program for Exceptional Children.

Education for All Handicapped Children Act of 1975. (1977). *Federal Register, 197*, 42474-42518.

Eichinger, J. & Woltman, S. (1993). Integration strategies for learners with severe multiple disorders. *Teaching Exceptional Children, 26*, 18.

Frith, G.H., Clark, R.M. & Miller, S.H. (1983). Integrated counseling services for exceptional children: A functional, noncategorical model. *School Counselor, 30*, 387-391.

Fuchs, D. & Fuchs, L.S. (1990). Framing the RE debate: Abolitionists versus conservationists. In J.W. Lloyd, A.C. Repp, & N.N. Singh (Eds.). *The regular education initiative: Alternative perspectives on concepts, issues, and models* (pp. 241-255). Sycamore, IL: Sycamore Press.

Gallagher, J.J. (1994). The pull of societal forces on special education. *The Journal of Special Education, 27*, 521-530.

Galvin, M. (1983). Making systematic problem-solving with children. *School Counselor, 31*, 130-136.

Gersten, J.C., Langner, T.S., Eisenberg, J.G., Sincha-Fagan, D. & McCarthy, E.D. (1976). Stability in change of behavioral disturbances of children and adolescents. *Journal of Abnormal Child Psychology, 4*, 111-127.

Giangreco, M.F. (1993). *Choosing options and accommodations for children: A guide to planning inclusive education.* Baltimore: Paul H. Brookes.

Gottlieb, J. (1980). Improving attitudes toward retarded children by using group discussion. *Exceptional Children, 47*, 106-111.

Hoover, J.J. (1990). Curriculum adaptations: A five-step process for classroom implementation. *Academic Therapy, 25*, 407-416.

Horner, R.H., Diemer, S.M. & Brazeau, K.C. (1992). Educational support for students with severe problem behaviors in Oregon: A descriptive analysis from the 1987-88 school year. *Journal of the Association of Persons with Severe Handicaps, 17*, 154-169.

Idol, L. (1988). A rationale and guidelines for establishing special education consultation programs. *Remedial and Special Education, 9*, 48-58.

Individuals with Disabilities Education Act (IDEA). 20 U.S.C. 1400 *et. seq.* (1990).

Keenan, S. (1993, October). *Planning for inclusion: Program elements that support teachers and students with E/BD.* Keynote Address at the Council for Children with Behavioral Disorders Working Forum, Inclusion: Ensuring Appropriate Services to Children/Youth with Emotional/Behavioral Disorders, Saint Louis, MO.

Kramer, B. & Wright, D. (1994). *Inclusive educational workshop.* California: Diagnostic Center.

Kratochwill, T., Elliot, S.N. & Rotto, T. (1990). Preparation of school psychologists to serve as consultants for teachers of emotionally disturbed children. *School Psychology Review, 20*, 530-580.

Lewis, T.J., Chard, d., & Scoot,t.M.(1994). Full inclusion and the education of children and youth with emotional and behavioral disorders. *Behavioral Disorders, 19*, 277-293.

McCoy, K.M. (1995). *Teaching special learners in the general education classroom* (2nd ed.) Denver, CO: Love.

McDowell, W.A., Coven, A. B. & Eash, V.C. (1979). The handicapped: Special needs and strategies for counseling. *Personnel and Guidance Journal, 58,* 228-232.

Parker, J.G. & Asher, S.R. (1987). Peer relations and later personal adjustment: Are low accepted children at risk? *Psychological Bulletin, 102,* 357-389.

Peck, C.A, Donaldson, J. & Pezzoli, M. (1990). Some benefits non-handicapped adolescents perceive for themselves from their social relationships with peers who have severe handicaps. *Journal of the Association for Persons with Severe Handicaps, 15,* 241-249.

Reganick, K.A. (1993). *Full inclusion: Analysis of a controversial issue.* Fort Lauderdale, FL: Nova University.

Ridley, C.A. & Vaughn, S.R. (1982). Interpersonal problem solving: An intervention program for preschool children. *Journal of Applied Developmental Psychology, 3,* 17-190.

Salend, S. (1983). Using hypothetical examples to sensitize nonhandicapped students to their handicapped peers. *School Counselor, 33,* 306-310.

Sheridan, S. & Kratochwill, T. (1992). Behavioral parent/teacher consultation: Conceptual and research implications. *Journal of School Psychology, 30,* 117.

Shure, M. B. & Spivack, G. (1980). Interpersonal problem solving as a mediator of behavioral adjustment in preschool and kindergarten children. *Journal of Applied Developmental Psychology, 1,* 29-44.

Smith, T.E.C., Polloway, E.A., Patton, J.R. & Dowdy, C.A. (1995). *Teaching children with special needs in inclusive settings.* Boston, MA: Allyn and Bacon.

Snell,M.E. & Eichner, S.J. (1989). Curriculum and methodology for individuals with severe disabilities. *Education and Training in Mental Retardation, 23,* 302-314.

Snell, M.E. & Eichner, S. J. (1989). Integration for students with profound disabilities. In F. Brown & D. H. Lehr (Eds.) *Persons with profound disabilities* (p. 109-138). Baltimore, MD: Paul H. Brooks.

Stainback, W., & Stainback, S. (1990). Support networks for inclusive schooling. Baltimore, MD: Paul H. Brooks.

Stevens, R.J. & Slavin, R.E., (1991). When cooperative learning improves the achievement of students with mild disabilities: A response to Tateyama-Sniezek. *Exceptional Children, 57,* 276-280.

Sugai, G. & Horner, R. (1994). Including students with severe behavior problems in general education setting: Assumptions, challenges, and solutions. In J. Marr, G. Sugai, & G. Tindal (Eds.), *The Oregon conference monograph 1994* (pp. 109-120). Eugene, University of Oregon.

Tarver-Behring, S. Spagna, M.E. & Sullivan, J. (1996). School counselors as change agents toward full inclusion. *Arizona Counseling Journal, 21,* 50-57.

U.S. Department of Education (1993). *Fifteenth annual report to Congress on the implementation of Public Law 94-142: The Education for All Handicapped Children Act,* Washington, DC: U.S. Government Printing Office.

Wiedemeyer, d. & Lehman, J. (1991). House plan: Approach to collaborative teaching and consultation. *Teaching Exceptional Children, 23*(3), 6-10.

CHAPTER FIVE
Multicultural Counseling in Action: Strategies and Approaches

Clearly, school counselors are being called upon to serve in a variety of capacities that strive to empower, educate and support students from diverse backgrounds (Arredondo, et al., 1996; Lee, 2001; Rogers, et al., 1999). In order for school counselors to be able to become multicultural practitioners, they need exposure and access to strategies and models of effective multicultural counseling. As Rogers, et al. (1999) assert, "An important step in the development of cross-cultural competence is to become informed regarding the existing knowledge base of ... professional best practice specific to work in diverse schools" (p. 244). Thus, school counselors must have exposure to approaches to multicultural practice that help them to broaden and continually refine their multicultural knowledge, skills and awareness and to develop effective strategies for serving the needs of their diverse constituencies. Once provided with access to an array of effective multicultural counseling strategies, it is then up to school counselors themselves to adapt these models in site- and population-specific ways.

Even given the resounding call for action in the field of multicultural school counseling, change has been incremental. One explanation for the slow pace of change in school counseling processes with respect to issues of diversity and inequality is that school counselors do not have access to models and strategies of multicultural practice that can provide them with the skills and the confidence necessary to explore and try out new ideas in their own schools. As Lee (2001) states, "School counselors need to develop new perspectives regarding comprehensive guidance initiatives and their role in promoting culturally responsive schools. Such initiatives can be a major influence in meeting the challenges and seizing the opportunities of cultural diversity" (p. 258). However, without access to practice-based strategies for how to achieve these goals, school counselors are left to their own devices, often without the support and guidance they need to engage in true multicultural practice.

Lee suggests that school counselors should serve as "student development facilitators" stating that, "The role of student development facilitator in a comprehensive guidance and counseling program requires that counselors go beyond traditional school counseling practice. Specific guidance provisions are necessary for heightening awareness, expanding skills and maximizing options on the part of all students regardless of their cultural background" (pp. 258-259). Serving in this capacity requires the development of specific multicultural competencies that guide practice. However, as Pope-Davis, et al. (2003) state, "Within multicultural competency research, the practical applications are often overlooked" (p.xv). The collection of articles in this chapter is a response to the call for practical applications of multicultural school counseling theories and models that focus on the development of multicultural competencies. Therefore, the focus of this chapter is on the application of multicultural competencies, approaches and strategies to school counseling practices with diverse students in an array of school settings. The articles in this chapter offer a range of innovative and effective strategies, models and approaches to the work of developing multicultural, school-based interventions, constructive collaborations, models of reflective practice, as well as conceptualizations of school counseling and consulting practice. Together, these articles offer insight into how theory and practice converge in the development of effective multicultural school counseling practices.

Sink's (2002) "Comprehensive Guidance and Counseling Programs and the Development of Multicultural Student-Citizens" advocates for school counselors to take seriously the charge to develop productive student-citizens through working within an expressly multicultural approach to guidance and counseling practice. The article addresses the valuable role comprehensive guidance and counseling programs can play in the development of multicultural student-citizens. Sink discusses comprehensive guidance and counseling programs as an educational link to multicultural citizenship development, which he argues is essential for helping prepare students to live in a global society. The article offers principles, sample competencies and activities that help to create a working model for comprehensive guidance and counseling programs.

Graham and Pulvino's (2000) "Multicultural Conflict Resolution: Development, Implementation and Assessment of a Program for Third-Graders" presents a multicultural conflict resolution intervention for third-graders and an evaluation of that intervention. The article highlights the formulation, implementation and assessment of one counselor's attempt to increase student skills in the area of conflict resolution through a six-week, curriculum-based, conflict resolution program for a third-grade class at a K-8 Catholic school. Graham and Pulvino explore the integration of multicultural considerations into a broader conflict resolution curriculum and present an exciting shift in how conflict resolution is taught in schools, bridging these areas of focus into a unified program.

Quinn and Stern's (2005) "Helping ADHD Students Help Themselves" focuses on the need for school counselors to raise their own awareness and that of others with respect to the needs and concerns of students with Attention Deficit Hyperactivity Disorder (ADHD). The authors urge school counselors to initiate and facilitate support groups that help to empower this student population. The article highlights an eight-week program curriculum that helps students deal with issues related to their ADHD and, ultimately, to feel more in control of their symptoms. The authors offer strategies for identifying, selecting and including students in a student-centered model of learning and support.

Bryan's (2005) "Fostering Educational Resilience and Academic Achievement in Urban Schools Through Family-Community Partnerships" discusses specific roles and strategies for urban school counselors in the development of family-community partnerships, which include that of team collaborator and advocate. The author suggests that school counselors serve as facilitators of specific types of partnership programs that promote academic achievement and resilience for students of color and low-income students because of their specific social-cultural-political needs and concerns. Bryan discusses the value and importance of developing school-family-community partnerships, exploring their relationship to the empowerment of diverse students and families and to students' educational outcomes. The author suggests that school counselors work to facilitate and assist in the coordination of school-family-community partnership programs in such a way as to not take on the sole responsibility for partnership building in schools but rather to elicit the active participation of various school- and community-based stakeholders.

Palladino Schultheiss' (2005) "University-Urban School Collaboration in School Counseling" offers insight into the process of developing and implementing a collaborative university-elementary school career intervention-based research program in an underserved urban school. Key elements of the process of collaboration are discussed, including developing a theoretical framework, identifying partnerships, integrating program development with programmatic research and obtaining funding. This initiative is placed in the context of innovative practices in collaborative research-practice efforts that serve to provide: (1) opportunities for social justice and social action efforts to emerge and transform participants both personally and professionally and (2) cutting-edge services to support underserved students and communities.

Giles' (2005) "Three Narratives of Parent-Educator Relationships: Toward Counselor Repertoires for Bridging Urban Parent-School Divide" draws on the concept of narrative to describe three basic patterns that underlie the roles and relationships between parents and educators in urban schools: (1) the deficit narrative, (2) the in loco parentis narrative and (3) the relational narrative. Through the use of these narratives, the article provides urban school counselors with a conceptual framework for discerning the nature and quality of their relationships with parents. The author identifies repertoires counselors can utilize to foster relationships between parents and educators and that enhance the academic achievement and social and emotional development of students.

Day-Vines and Day-Hairston's (2005) "Culturally Congruent Strategies for Addressing the Behavioral Needs of Urban, African-American Male Adolescents" explores the ecological and contextual contributions to the reality that urban African-American males experience disproportionately higher rates of discipline referrals, suspension and expulsion. The authors suggest that efforts to reduce discipline problems for this population must work from the awareness that there is a reciprocal relationship between cultural thought and the expression of particular behaviors. The article offers school counselors a conceptual understanding of the logic guiding some of the behaviors of urban African-American adolescents. Day-Vines and Day-Hairston provide tools and strategies that can help school counselors develop culturally congruent intervention strategies that improve school experiences and discipline outcomes for urban, African-American male students.

Bradley, et al.'s (2005) "School Counselors Collaborating with African-American Parents" provides school counselors with an understanding of the importance of collaboration with parents as a vital means of student support. The article offers specific strategies that can help school counselors to better collaborate with African-American parents. These strategies include: (1) engaging in critical self-reflection and a shifting of their attitudes and practices, (2) rethinking and reworking practices of parent communication and support, (3) establishing community relationships and (4) actively eliciting the support and collaboration of colleagues and the administration. The authors suggest that school counselors must become proactive advocates for creative change who dramatically improve the status of parent involvement in urban schools.

Bemak, et al.'s (2005) "Empowerment Groups for Academic Success: An Innovative Approach to Prevent High School Failure for At-risk, Urban African-American Girls" works from an understanding that there is a great need for innovative strategies that serve to close the achievement gap for low-income, culturally diverse students in under-resourced urban schools. The authors assert that school counselors must assume leadership roles in reducing academic disparity for at-risk, urban African-American girls. The article explores the experiences of urban, African-American, at-risk girls in urban schools, highlighting the unique challenges they face. The authors describe the need for school counselors to emphasize a group counseling approach that works from a multicultural perspective. Bemak, et al. present the Empowerment Groups for Academic Success approach, which seeks to prevent high school drop out and improve academic performance for this student population.

The articles in this chapter approach multicultural school counseling from a variety of vantage points and perspectives. Together, they highlight various entry points for the development of effective multicultural school counseling practices including constructive collaborations with colleagues, families, outside agencies and institutions, community members and organizations. As well, they offer specific approaches to student support, advocacy and empowerment along individual, social and institutional lines. The articles in this chapter individually and collectively provide school counselors with much-needed models for how multicultural school counseling practice is constructed and implemented. These articles help school counselors and those responsible for their education and professional development to realize and appreciate the importance of practice-based research and research-based initiatives. The contributors to this cluster of articles each offer school counselors not only effective approaches to multicultural school counseling but an understanding of their ideological and theoretical underpinnings, thus informing school counselors' understandings of theory-practice connections and integrations.

Comprehensive Guidance and Counseling Programs and the Development of Multicultural Student-Citizens

By Christopher Sink, Ph.D., NCC, LMHC

This article originally appeared in *Professional School Counseling*, Vol. 6, No. 2, 2002.

Aconsistent element in the social-moral montage of U.S. schooling is the attempt to cultivate "good" student-citizens (Anderson, Avery, Pederson, Smith, & Sullivan, 1997; Pangle & Pangle, 2000). For instance, notable 18th-century pundits such as John Adams, Benjamin Rush, and Noah Webster (see, e.g., Fraser, 2001, for a historical perspective) strongly promoted this goal. Even though the external impetus for citizenship education appeared to wane during the turbulent 1960s and 70s, contemporary authors and policymakers on all sides of the political spectrum remain convinced that school curriculum and pedagogy should, in part, aid students to engage in and contribute to society's democratic processes (Gutmann, 2000; National Commission on Excellence in Education, 1983). Similarly, in a recent article on the future direction of the school counseling profession, Sink (2002) recommended that counselors should be more closely involved in this agenda.

This article addresses the valuable role comprehensive guidance and counseling programs (CGCP) can play in developing multicultural student-citizens. More specifically, after contextualizing citizenship education in relationship to the advancement of the school counseling profession, I provide a rationale for including this domain within CGCPs. Second, the concept of multicultural citizenship is defined and clarified. Third, various characteristics of multicultural student-citizens are enumerated. Finally, I offer practical implementation strategies for school counselors.

HISTORICAL CONTEXT – SCHOOL COUNSELING AND CITIZENSHIP EDUCATION

Reminiscent of various disciplines over the past century, school counseling in the United States has gradually evolved in three general stages (e.g., Gysbers & Henderson, 2000, 2001; Herr, 2001; Myrick, 1997). Summarized briefly, the initial phase (1910s to 1950s) deployed a "position" approach, whereby guidance personnel (i.e., mostly vocational and classroom teachers) dispensed vocational and career information to high school students with the goal focused largely on job preparation and maintenance (Gysbers & Henderson). Interestingly, while citizenship education was not a component of the guidance curriculum and students' psychosocial and psychoeducational concerns received only minimal attention in schools, moral "fitness," patriotism, and civic duties were overtly fostered primarily by social studies teachers through school-wide and classroom rituals (Anderson et al., 1997; Risinger, 1996). Furthermore, during the two world wars and the Korean conflict, school personnel encouraged students to be good citizens, but school counselors' specific roles in the process appear to be undocumented.

During the second stage (approximately 1960s to 1980s), a "services" or pupil-personnel model was instituted (Gysbers & Henderson, 2001; Herr, 2001). Secondary-level counselors and other guidance personnel (e.g., nurses, attendance officers, teachers) provided psychoeducational support and reactive services to students at risk for school failure or those experiencing personal-social difficulties. While school counselors were also offering educational and career guidance to the college- or university-bound, social studies teachers continued to provide civics lessons in their classrooms (Riley, 1997, Risinger, 1996). As in the previous stage, since classroom guidance did not target citizenship formation, school counselors presumably had little influence on nurturing these skills in students.

By the late 1970s and early 1980s, several prominent school counseling and career education researchers (e.g., Norman Gysbers, Donald Dinkmeyer, Edwin Herr) maintained that a philosophical reorientation in the profession was badly needed. The antecedents for these clarion calls are well documented in multiple publications (e.g., Dinkmeyer & Caldwell, 1970; Gysbers & Henderson, 2000, 2001; Herr, 2001; Myrick, 1997; Paisley & Borders, 1995; VanZandt & Hayslip, 2001). As a result, the CGCP movement emerged as a viable alternative to a "services" orientation.

For those who are unacquainted with this programmatic approach, a CGCP is a competencybased programmatic approach (Johnson & Whitfield, 1991) which attempts to be multisystemic, collaborative, developmental, preventionminded, and educative (Borders & Drury, 1992; Campbell & Dahir, 1997; Clark & Stone, 2000; Gysbers & Henderson, 2000, 2001; Henderson & Gysbers, 1998; Keys & Lockhart, 1999; Myrick, 1997; Neukrug, Barr, Hoffman, & Kaplan, 1993; Olson & Perrone, 1991; Paisley, 2001; Paisley & Benshoff, 1996; Paisley & Hubbard, 1994; Paisley & Peace, 1995; Thompson, 2002). By the late 1990s, this programmatic view had become the most widely used organizational framework for the profession (Sink & MacDonald, 1998), endorsed by the American School Counselor Association (ASCA, 1997, 1999a, 1999b; Campbell & Dahir; Dahir, 2001; Dahir, Sheldon, & Valiga, 1999; Wittmer, 2000a, 2000b) and numerous state school counseling organizations. Despite the paucity of nationwide efficacy studies, empirical research conducted in Missouri (Gysbers & Henderson, 2000; Lapan, 2001; Lapan, Gysbers, & Petroski, 2001) and Washington (Sink & Robinson, 2002) has yielded promising results. Other recent studies on CGCPs revealed that the program implementation poses major challenges for K–12 counselors (Sink & Yillik-Downer, 2001) and numerous state models lack credible documentation of their theoretical underpinnings (MacDonald & Sink, 1999).

While many state and district CGCPs plainly assert or imply in their mission or purpose statements that one of their central outcomes is to facilitate the advancement of "good" or "productive" citizens (e.g., Coats, Ash, & Dorsey, 1998; Hatch, 2000), evidence indicates that citizenship education, like character formation, is a severely neglected developmental domain (MacDonald & Sink, 1999). As alluded to previously, a careful search of the education literature also revealed meager evidence that school counselors are formally assisting classroom teachers with citizenship development. Two recent dissertations attempted to incorporate some aspects of citizenship education into their school counseling-related studies with only mixed results (Cassell, 1995; Swen, 2000).

CGCPS AS AN EDUCATIONAL LINK TO MULTICULTURAL CITIZENSHIP DEVELOPMENT

The need for increased citizenship education in U.S. schools has received considerable attention over the past two decades. For instance, the Center for Civic Education (Calabasas, California; see Web site: http://www.civiced.org/) was established in 1981 with the expressed mission to promote citizenship education in the nation's K–12 schools. This organization helps educators cultivate enlightened, competent, and responsible citizens (Rosen, 2000). In an effort to do so, researchers/scholars associated with the Center produce and distribute citizenship education curricula and materials to school personnel.

Correspondingly, Robert Battistoni (1997), speaking in defense of citizenship education, challenged schools to graduate persons of character who are more responsive to the needs of the community, more able to contribute to society, and more civil in their expressed attitudes and behavior. These propositions resonate well with the earlier remarks made by Mustaine and LaFountain (1993) on the future of school counseling, where they argued for a more holistic view of the profession and education in general. Successful schools, in their perspective, should facilitate the competencies commensurate with productive student-citizens (e.g., good decision-making, conflict-resolution, and team-building skills).

The mission statements of many district- and state-level comprehensive programs also reflect this broader educative orientation. For instance, reiterating Washington State's CGCP mission statement, the overall aim of Highline School District's (1997) school counseling program is as follows:

All students will receive educationally based comprehensive counseling and guidance support to realize their potential *as responsible, productive, and healthy citizens contributing to a democratic society in a changing world* [italics added]. (p. C-1)

A similar goal was presented in Utah's Comprehensive Guidance Program (1998) purpose statement:

Provide in all districts and schools throughout Utah a comprehensive student services system, designed to offer comprehensive guidance, prevention, intervention, crisis and referral services for individual students, and families. *Such services will assist students in becoming healthy, respectful and contributing citizens* [italics added].

Like school counselors in general, CGCP leaders have not been held accountable for encouraging the attributes of citizenship and seem to do little to intentionally foster this aim (MacDonald & Sink, 1999). It is my contention, however, these comprehensive programs are one of the most important frameworks from which qualities of citizenship education can be instituted. To realize this goal, the first step is to propose a working definition of citizenship education that is well researched and flexible enough to be adapted by program leadership teams.

MULTICULTURAL CITIZENSHIP EDUCATION DEFINED AND ELUCIDATED

The perspective used here was drawn from current educational literature that reconceptualizes citizenship education from its more "traditional" (i.e., a narrow focus on the political rights and duties of a citizen) and incomplete renderings (Anderson et al., 1997; Clark, 1999) to what has been called *multicultural citizenship* (Kymlicka, 1995; also see Banks, 1997, 1998, 2001; Kaltsounis, 1997; Parker, 1996, for detailed discussions). Although the notion of "multiculturalism" as a socio-political construct is the subject of scholarly debate (e.g., Fuller, 1995; Lind, 2000), there is obvious common ground between multicultural education and citizenship education (Kaltsounis). This integrated approach is consistent with the contemporary positions espoused by Lee (1995, 2001) in his articles on diversity and school counseling, and in the American School Counselor Association's (1999a) position statement on multicultural counseling. To summarize the latter document, school counselors, operating within the context of a CGCP, should facilitate student development and enhance the total school and community environment through the understanding and appreciation of cultural diversities.

Subsequently, Banks (2001), one of the seminal writers in multicultural education, embedded this construct into citizenship education. He posited the following:

> Because of growing ethnic, cultural, racial, and religious diversity throughout the world, citizenship education needs to be changed in substantial ways to prepare students to function in the 21st century. Citizens in the new century need the knowledge, attitudes, and skills required to function in their ethnic and cultural communities and beyond their cultural borders and to participate in the construction of a national civic culture that is a moral and just community that embodies democratic ideals and values ... Students also need to acquire the knowledge and skills needed to become effective citizens in the global community. (p. 6)

This form of multicultural citizenship education is obviously many-sided (Cogan, 1999), embracing disparate levels of community (local and global) as well as individual differences, various task identities, and socio-political realities (Parker, 1996). In general, the orientation also seems to resolve the tensions in U.S. citizenship education (Cogan; Kaltsounis, 1997), for it attempts to unify various standards in civic education within the context of school reform (e.g., Citizenship Committee, 1983; Cogan, 1996, 1999; National Standards for Civics and Government, 1994; Riley, 1997).

CHARACTERISTICS OF MULTICULTURAL STUDENT-CITIZENS

Multicultural citizens are, in general, able to function well in their own culture, nation, and within the global community (Banks, 2001). Yet, specific characteristics of such a citizen vary in part across a spectrum of writers (e.g., Banks; Cogan, 1999; Dondero & McCoy, 1996; Meyer, 1996; Schaps & Lewis, 1998). Schaps and Lewis proposed, for example, three essential qualities of this broader view of a citizen. Students would develop a (a) deep regard for self and others, (b) personal commitment to core American values (e.g., justice, caring, fairness, responsibility, compassion), and (c) civil and considerate spirit when interacting with others dissimilar to oneself. Subsequently, Banks suggested that "good" multicultural student-citizens would learn to take humane and democratic social and civic actions to help change their communities and nation.

Perhaps the most useful way to recast the discussion is to work from two seminal studies (Anderson et al., 1997; Cogan, 1999). First, in an investigation that surveyed a random sample of American social studies teachers (N = 361) on their views regarding citizenship education, Anderson et al. reported several important findings. Across the four derived teacher perspectives, including the (a) cultural pluralists and (b) critical thinkers (both closely aligned with the aims of multicultural citizenship education), and (c) legalists and (d) assimilationists (two views that mirror the "traditionalist" orientation), there were several essential beliefs that could be readily integrated into a CGCP. A comprehensive approach to multicultural citizenship education should (a) promote tolerance and open-mindedness, (b) address controversial issues which encourage higher order thinking, (c) emphasize civic involvement (e.g., service learning), and (d) address the topic of social values (i.e., the fundamental values of the American society).

Subsequently, Cogan's (1999) research systematically questioned 182 experts/scholars across the citizenship education continuum to determine whether some consensus could be found among a host of possible citizen characteristics. These eight in descending order of importance were reported:

1. The ability to look at and approach problems as a member of a global society.
2. The ability to work with others in a cooperative way and to take responsibility for one's roles and duties in society.
3. The ability to understand, accept, and tolerate cultural differences.
4. The capacity to think in a critical and systemic way.
5. The willingness to resolve conflict in a nonviolent manner.
6. The willingness to change one's lifestyle and consumption habits to protect the environment.
7. The ability to be sensitive toward and to defend human rights (e.g., rights of women, ethnic minorities).
8. The willingness and ability to participate in politics at local, national, and international levels. (pp. 76–77)

The results from both investigations encompass many of the characteristics discussed in related citizenship education literature discussed earlier and are summarized as Grade 12 student competencies. (See Table) Where suitable, these outcomes could be woven into existing CGCP competencies, under perhaps the personal-social, educational, and career domains. Moreover, the competencies could be revised so that they are more developmentally appropriate for K–8 students.

SUMMARY COMPETENCIES OF A MULTICULTURAL STUDENT-CITIZEN WITHIN THE FRAMEWORK OF A COMPREHENSIVE GUIDANCE AND COUNSELING PROGRAM

By Grade 12, students will demonstrate

- An understanding and appreciation for their own culture and the cultures of others.
- Critical thinking in the exploration of sociocultural and political ideas.
- An ability to reason about issues from local, national, and global perspectives.
- An understanding of important American values (e.g., justice, tolerance, responsibility).
- An understanding of the basic rights of all human beings as embodied in the Bill of Rights.
- The ability to express appropriately an opinion on important social and political issues while listening and respecting the views of others.
- The ability to cooperate/collaborate with others in school and community settings.
- How to resolve interpersonal conflicts peacefully.

Various commonalties seem to emerge among the key features of CGCPs and multicultural citizenship education. Like comprehensive programs, multicultural citizenship stresses the need for collaboration, shared responsibility, and interdependence at various levels of society, including educational and community settings (Banks, 2001; Battistoni, 1997; Dondero & McCoy, 1996; Porter, Epp, & Bryant, 2000; Rowley, 2001; Schaps & Lewis, 1998). To create a civil society, and more narrowly, a school that is a caring community of multicultural studentcitizens (Sink, 2000; Sink & Rubel, 2001), opportunities must be provided for all educators, students, families, and influential community members to effectively work together to achieve CGCP competencies. Finally, CGCPs and multicultural citizenship education use systemic and developmental constructs to support them. Several ways school counselors can practically infuse multicultural citizenship education into their CGCPs are now presented.

RECOMMENDATIONS FOR IMPLEMENTATION

Initially, school counselors need to review existing CGCP (student) competencies to ascertain whether any of them are aligned with the characteristics of multicultural citizenship development (e.g., Anderson et al., 1997; Banks, 2001; Cogan, 1999; Remy, 1980). Very often CGCPs, perhaps unwittingly, focus on student outcomes that intersect nicely with those of multicultural citizenship education. For example, in the personal and social domain, CGCPs target effective communication and conflict resolution skills (e.g., Campbell & Dahir, 1997; Gysbers & Henderson, 2000, 2001; Myrick, 1997; Wittmer, 2000b), reflecting those proposed by major citizenship education writers (e.g., Cogan; Meyer, 1996). Similarly, in the educational domain, CGCPs attempt to foster higher order thinking and reasoned discussion, which would reflect salient elements of multicultural citizenship programs (Anderson et al.; Cogan). Nonetheless, supplementary performance-based and developmentally appropriate competencies may need to be included to explicitly address issues such as civic involvement, socio-political issues, diversity, and character development (MacDonald & Sink, 1999). Those offered here and in several of the previously mentioned articles are useful starting points.

Second, school counselors in partnership with classroom teachers should peruse the citizenship education literature examining it for practical activities and existing programs (e.g., Clark, 1999; Risinger, 1996; Rosen, 2000), which can be adapted for large group guidance curriculum. Since "hands on" experiences appear to be constructive teaching-learning strategies to promote aspects of citizenship education (Banks, 2001; Barber, Higgins, Smith, & Ballou, 2000; Meyer, 1996), counselors and teachers could collaboratively provide opportunities for active learning, including, for example, role-playing, simulations, project-based learning, and debates over controversial issues (e.g., Johnson, 1997; MacDonald, 1996; Westheimer & Kahne, 1998). School counselors can readily access a host of relevant multicultural citizenship education materials available at The Center for Civic Education. Additionally, guidance activity books that are related to the topic are widely available. For example, Peyser and McLaughlin's (1997) book, Character Education Activities for K-6 Classrooms, offers many elementary classroom activities that can be incorporated into social studies, health, and language arts lessons that target good citizenship and allied topics (e.g., responsibility, cooperation, character education). In short, to provide widespread exposure to and application of multicultural citizenship curriculum, experientially based guidance activities are recommended.

A third proposal involves the developmental feature of CGCPs. For multicultural citizenship education to be effective, The Center for Civic Education, in its report on civic education in America, recommended that this form of learning should be consciously reproduced in schools, starting with Grades K to 2 and proceeding through high school (Risinger, 1996).

More recently, Niemi and Chapman (1999) and Rosen (2000) posited that elementary through secondary schools' pedagogy could informally model and augment prescribed curriculum by other styles of participatory learning. As such, school counselors and other relevant parties, as part of the CGCP, should ensure that students have exposure to small and large group guidance lessons on aspects of good multicultural citizenship. The following are sample ideas:

1. Guide students through an engaging and respectful process that helps generate school and classroom rules as well as the school code of conduct (cf. Schimmel, 1997).
2. Foster good social skills to enhance civil classroom interaction and discussion, where a range of opinions can be safely voiced.
3. Teach students how to serve on student councils where issues of diversity and multiculturalism are openly addressed.
4. Assist pupils to locate and use relevant information (i.e., helping them to be more informed about their community and its diversity).
5. Work with students on how to make effective oral and written presentations to "authority figures" (e.g., school leaders and community leaders) from a range of backgrounds.
6. Assign older students with diverse backgrounds and positive social skills to be mentors for those younger students with limited exposure to religious, cultural, and ethnic differences.
7. Encourage dynamic representatives from diverse backgrounds to interact with pupils in a variety of forums that discuss important multicultural civic issues (e.g., discrimination, participatory democracy, underrepresented people groups in office).

As students mature, multicultural citizenship education should move from concrete outcomes and structured tasks used in elementary schools to those that might be called transitional objectives and activities in middle schools. During the high school years, the guidance competencies and activities should be transformational in nature, preparing students for realistic life roles in a multicultural society. For example, by the third or fourth grade, children should be able to talk about multicultural citizenship ideas (e.g., What does it mean to show "tolerance" or "intolerance"?) and act out consistently a simple performance (e.g., giving a complement or showing eye contact when another child is speaking). Transitional tasks are those that combine structured performances with higher levels of reasoning (e.g., role-playing a scripted dialogue with a peer from a different ethnicity). In the late teen years, students should be able to not only discuss and role-play complex situations, but also act in a civil manner in "real-world" situations. For instance, when high school seniors attend a public forum on a particular issue, they should be able to listen carefully to all sides, assert their perspective in a respectful manner, and acknowledge the validity of differing viewpoints (Schaps & Lewis, 1998; Spady, 1994).

Finally, to encourage a systemic approach to citizenship development, CGCPs ought to make stronger connections with parents and community members (Cogan, 1999). In Niemi and Chapman's (1999) summary of a 1996 National Center for Education Statistics' study of civic development (N = 4,212 American high school students and their parents), two salient findings were reported: (a) Parental involvement and modeling were important components in fostering citizenship characteristics; and (b) sustained community service projects for students appeared to be positively related to several dimensions of civic development (e.g., increased political knowledge and a higher level of confidence in the ability to speak at public meetings).

To engage parents and guardians in the process, I recommend that administrators team up with school counselors and other educators in creating a volunteer system that provides meaningful socialcivic activities (e.g., mentoring, small group instruction, one-on-one interaction, job shadowing, field trip chaperones). The Parent Teacher Association could be involved as well as other civic-minded service organizations (e.g., Rotary International). Additionally, community-school round-tables could be developed, where people of color, for instance, who are also parents or guardians, explore with students vital issues affecting school and community life.

CLOSING REFLECTIONS

In this article, I advocate for school counseling personnel to take seriously the charge to develop productive student-citizens written into or implied from most CGCP mission statements. Although there are numerous ways to inculcate various characteristics of citizenship, I suggest here, given America's highly pluralistic society, that a multicultural orientation is a feasible position to adopt. Even in areas where students have few contacts with different ethnic groups, the dimensions of multicultural citizenship outlined here can be beneficial to all pupils. Many students, for example, leave rural communities to attend college or seek employment in diverse settings. These most likely will require a broader perspective on the world and more finely honed social-civic skills.

Multicultural citizenship education can be harmonized with comprehensive guidance and counseling programs through a variety of workable steps:

- Modify current student competencies to include those multicultural outcomes presented in the Table and in other resources (e.g., Cogan, 1999; Northside Independent School District, 1994; Remy, 1980).
- Use large group guidance lessons as a conduit for active engagement with issues related to multicultural citizenship. (Collaboration with all school personnel is essential.)
- Initiate the multicultural citizenship formation process early, starting with kindergarten or first grade.
- Elicit parental and community involvement in developing a broad-based coalition of supporters of multicultural citizenship education.

Because they already face a multitude of responsibilities, resistance from school counselors is to be expected and openly processed (Sink & Yillik- Downer, 2001). Yet, if members of the profession desire to remain focused on all of comprehensive guidance and counseling program's major goals, this developmental "domain" should no longer be neglected. Noble CGCP mission statements must be translated into deliberate programming and measurable student outcomes. It is my hope that the principles, sample competencies, and activities offered in this article will assist school counselors to realize this important aim. Over the long run, students should benefit as well. They will become effective multicultural citizens, contributing more positively to their local communities and to society. ?

Christopher Sink, Ph.D.,NCC,LMHC, is a professor and chair, Department of School Counseling and Psychology, Seattle Pacific University, WA. E-mail: csink@spu.edu The author expresses his appreciation to Ms. Heather Robinson Stroh for her research assistance.

REFERENCES

American School Counselor Association. (1997). *The professional school counselor and comprehensive school counseling programs* (Position statement). Retrieved April 11, 2002, from http://www.school counselor.org/content. cfm?L1=1000&L2=9

American School Counselor Association. (1999a). *The professional school counselor and cross/multicultural counseling* (Position statement). Retrieved April 11, 2002, from http://www.schoolcounselor.org/ content.cfm?L1=1000& L2=26

American School Counselor Association. (1999b). *The role of the professional school counselor* (Position statement). Retrieved April 11, 2002, from http://www.schoolcounselor.org/content.cfm?L1=1000&L2=69

Anderson, C., Avery, P. G., Pederson, P.V., Smith, E. S., & Sullivan, J. L. (1997). Divergent perspectives on citizenship education: A Q-method study and survey of social studies teachers. *American Educational Research Journal, 34*, 333–364.

Banks, J. A. (1997). *Educating citizens in a multicultural society.* New York: Teachers College Press.

Banks, J. A. (1998).The lives and values of researchers: Implications for educating citizens in a multicultural society. *Educational Researcher, 27*, 4–17.

Banks, J. A. (2001). Citizenship education and diversity: Implications for teacher education. *Journal of Teacher Education, 52*, 5–16.

Barber, B. R., Higgins, R. R., Smith, J. K., & Ballou, J. (2000). *Measuring citizenship project high school study: Final report to the Ford Foundation.* Detroit, MI: The Ford Foundation.

Battistoni, R. M. (1997). *Service learning as civic learning: Lessons we can learn from our students.* In G. Reeher & J. Cammarano (Eds.), Education for citizenship (pp. 31–49). New York: Rowman & Littlefield.

Borders, L.D., & Drury, S. M. (1992). Comprehensive school counseling programs: A review for policymakers and practitioners. *Journal of Counseling and Development, 70*, 487–498.

Campbell, C. A., & Dahir, C. A. (1997). *Sharing the vision: The national standards for school counseling programs.* Alexandria,VA: American School Counselor Association.

Cassell, J. R. (1995). *Improving self-control in upper elementary students through a program of character, civic, and social education.* Fort Lauderdale, FL: Nova Southeastern University. (ERIC Document Reproduction Services No. ED386634)

Citizenship Committee. (1983). *Standards and position statements: Essential characteristics of a citizenship education program.* Retrieved October 5, 2000, from http://www.ncss.org/standars/positions/essential.html

Clark, M., & Stone, C. (2000). The developmental school counselor as educational leader. In J. Wittmer (Ed.), *Managing your school counseling programs: K–12 developmental strategies* (2nd ed., pp. 85–81).Minneapolis, MN: Educational Media.

Clark,T. (1999). Rethinking civic education for the 21st century. In D.D.Marsh (Ed.), *Preparing our schools for the 21st century* (pp. 65–87). Alexandria,VA: Association for Supervision and Curriculum Development.

Coats, R. Q., Ash, M., & Dorsey, C. J. H. (1998).*Washington state guidelines for comprehensive counseling and guidance programs from kindergarten through community and technical college.* Olympia,WA:Office of Superintendent of Public Instruction.

Cogan, J. J. (1996). Crisis in citizenship education in the United States. *International Journal of Social Education, 11,* 21–36.

Cogan, J. J. (1999). *Multidimensional citizenship as educational policy for the millennium: Putting research into practice.* Momentum, 30, 73–82.

Dahir, C. A. (2001).The national standards for school counseling programs:Development and implementation. *Professional School Counseling, 4,* 320–327.

Dahir, C. A., Sheldon, C. B., & Valiga, M. J. (1998). *Vision into action: Implementing the national standards for school counseling programs.* Alexandria,VA: American School Counselor Association.

Dinkmeyer,D. C., & Caldwell, E. (1970).*Developmental counseling and guidance: A comprehensive school approach.* New York:McGraw-Hill.

Dondero, M., & McCoy, E. (1996). R.I.C.E. – four values for civics education. *Momentum, 27,* 20–23.

Fraser, J.W. (2001). *The school in the United States: A documentary history.* New York:McGraw-Hill.

Fuller, K. (1995). The voices of rhetoric and politics in social epistemology: For a critical-rationalist multiculturalism. *Philosophy of the Social Sciences, 25,* 512–522

Galbraith, J. K. (1997). *The good society: The humane agenda.* New York: Houghton-Mifflin.

Gutmann, A. (2000).Why should schools care about civic education? In L. M.McDonnell, P. M.Timpane, & R. Benjamin (Eds.), *Rediscovering the democratic purpose of education* (pp. 73–90). Lawrence, KS: University of Kansas Press.

Gysbers, N. C., & Henderson, P. (2000). *Developing and managing your school guidance program* (3rd ed.). Alexandria, VA: American Counseling Association.

Gysbers,N. C., & Henderson, P. (2001). Comprehensive guidance and counseling programs: A rich history and a bright future. *Professional School Counseling, 4,* 246–256.

Hatch,T. (2000). *Comprehensive school counseling and guidance program: The implementation year.* Moreno Valley, CA: Moreno Valley Unified School District.

Henderson, P., & Gysbers,N. C. (1998). *Leading and managing your school guidance program staff: A manual for school administrators and directors of guidance.* Alexandria,VA: American Counseling Association.

Herr, E. L. (2001).The impact of national policies, economics, and school reform on comprehensive guidance programs. *Professional School Counseling, 4,* 236–245.

Highline School District Comprehensive Counseling and Guidance Program. (2000). Highline,WA: Highline School District.

Johnson,D.W. (1997). Academic controversy. *The National Teaching and Learning Forum, 5*(6), 1–4.

Johnson, S. K., & Whitfield, E. A. (Eds.). (1991). *Evaluating guidance programs: A practitioner's guide.* Iowa City, IA: The American College Testing Program and the National Consortium of State Career Guidance Supervisors.

Kaltsounis,T. (1997). Multicultural education and citizenship education at a crossroads: Searching for common ground. *Social Studies, 88,* 18–22.

Keys, S. G., & Lockhart, E. J. (1999).The school counselor's role in facilitating multisystemic change. *Professional School Counseling, 3,* 101–107.

Kymlicka,W. (1995). *Multicultural citizenship: A liberal theory of minority rights.* New York: Oxford University.

Lapan, R.T. (2001). Results-based comprehensive guidance and counseling programs: A framework for planning and evaluation. *Professional School Counseling, 4,* 289–299.

Lapan, R.T., Gysbers, N. C., & Petroski, G. F. (2001). Helping seventh graders be safe and successful: A statewide study of the impact of comprehensive guidance and counseling programs. *Journal of Counseling and Development, 79,* 320–330.

Lee, C. C. (1995). School counseling and cultural diversity: A framework for effective practice. In C. C. Lee (Ed.), *Counseling for diversity: A guide for school counselors and related professionals* (pp. 3–17). Boston: Allyn & Bacon.

Lee, C. C. (2001). Culturally responsive school counselors and programs: Addressing the needs of all students. *Professional School Counseling, 4,* 257–261.

Lind,M. (2000). Politics after ideology. New Leader, 83, 19–21.
MacDonald, G., & Sink, C. A. (1999). A qualitative developmental analysis of comprehensive guidance programmes in schools in the United States. *British Journal of Guidance and Counselling, 27,* 415–430.

MacDonald, M. (1996). Civic education of, by and for the students. *Momentum, 27,* 8–11.

Meyer, J. R. (1996). Citizenship development education: An imperative. *International Journal of Social Education, 11,* 1–20.

Mustaine, B. L., & LaFountain, R. M. (1993). Some thoughts on the future of school counseling. *Guidance and Counselling, 8,* 30–39.

Myrick, R.D. (1997). *Developmental guidance and counseling: A practical approach* (3rd ed.).Minneapolis, MN: Educational Media.

National Commission on Excellence in Education. (1983). *A nation at risk: The imperative for educational reform.* Washington, DC: U. S.Government Printing Office.

National Standards for Civics and Government. (1994). Calabasas, CA: Center for Civic Education.

Neukrug, E. S., Barr, C.G., Hoffman, L. R., & Kaplan, L. S. (1993). Developmental counseling and guidance: A model for use in your school. *The School Counselor, 40,* 356–362.

Niemi, R.G., & Chapman, C. (1999).Making students good citizens. *The Education Digest, 65,* 36–40.

Northside Independent School District. (1994). *Comprehensive guidance program framework.* San Antonio,TX: Author.

Olson, M. J., & Perrone, P. A. (1991). Changing to a developmental guidance program. *The School Counselor, 39,* 41–46.

Paisley, P.O. (2001). Maintaining and enhancing the developmental focus in school counseling programs. *Professional School Counseling, 4,* 271–278.

Paisley, P.O., & Benshoff, J.M. (1996). Applying developmental principles to practice: Training issues for the professional development of school counselors. *Elementary School Guidance and Counseling, 30,* 163–169.

Paisley, P.O., & Borders, L.D. (1995). School Counseling: An evolving specialty. *Journal of Counseling and Development, 74,* 150–153.

Paisley, P.O., & Hubbard, G.T. (1994). *Developmental school counseling programs: From theory to practice.* Alexandria, VA: American Counseling Association.

Paisley, P.O., & Peace, S.D. (1995). *Developmental principles: A framework for school counseling programs.* Elementary School Guidance and Counseling, 30, 85–93.

Pangle, L. S., & Pangle,T. L. (2000). What the American founders have to teach us about schooling for democratic citizenship. In L. M. McDonnell, P. M. Timpane, & R. Benjamin (Eds.), *Rediscovering the democratic purpose of education* (pp. 21–46). Lawrence, KS: University of Kansas.

Parker, W. C. (1996). "Advanced" ideas about democracy: Toward a pluralist conception of citizen education. *Teachers College Record, 98,* 104–125.

Peyser, S., & McLaughlin, M. (1997). *Character education activities for K–6 classrooms.* Minneapolis, MN: Educational Media.

Porter, G., Epp, L., & Bryant, S. (2000). Collaboration among school mental health professionals: A necessity, not a luxury. *Professional School Counseling, 3,* 315–322.

Remy, R. C. (1980). *Handbook of basic citizenship competencies: Guidelines for comparing materials, assessing instruction, and setting goals.* Alexandria, VA: Association for Supervision and Curriculum Development.

Riley, R. W. (1997, February). The importance of civic education: "National standards for civic education." *Teaching PreK–8, 27,* 6.

Risinger, C. F. (1996). Citizenship education in the curriculum: An ERIC/CHESS sample. *International Journal of Social Education, 11,* 120–122.

Rosen, L. (2000). Elementary school civic education gets good citizens started. *The Education Digest, 65,* 19–22.

Rowley, W. J. (2001). Expanding collaborative partnerships among school counselors and school psychologists. *Professional School Counseling, 3,* 315–322.

Schaps, E., & Lewis, C. (1998). Breeding citizenship through community in school. *The Education Digest, 64,* 23–27.

Schimmel, D. (1997). School rule-making and citizenship education. *The Education Digest, 63,* 40–44.

Selbourne, D. (1994). *The principle of duty: An essay on the foundations of civic order.* South Bend, IN: University of Notre Dame.

Sink, C. A. (2000). Modeling collaboration through caring communities of learners. *Professional School Counseling, 3*(5), ii–iii.

Sink, C. A. (2002). In search of the profession's finest hour: A critique of four views of 21st century school counseling. *Professional School Counseling, 5,* 156–163.

Sink, C. A., & MacDonald, G. (1998). The status of comprehensive guidance and counseling in the United States. *Professional School Counseling, 2,* 88–94.

Sink, C. A., & Robinson, H. L. (2002). *Can comprehensive school counseling programs make educational difference in Washington state's elementary schools?* Manuscript in preparation, Seattle Pacific University.

Sink, C. A., & Rubel, L. (2001).The school as community approach to violence prevention. In D. S. Sandhu (Ed.), *Faces of violence: Psychological correlates, concepts, and intervention strategies* (pp. 417–437). Huntington, NY: Nova Science.

Sink, C. A., & Yillik-Downer, A. (2001). School counselors' perceptions of comprehensive guidance and counseling programs: A survey of national trends. *Professional School Counseling, 4,* 278–288.

Spady, W. G. (1994,March). Choosing outcomes of significance. *Educational Leadership,* pp. 18–22.

Swen, S. F. (2000). Participation in a peer helpers program: Students' perception of school climate and personal growth. *Dissertation Abstracts International, 61,* 5A. (UMI No. 04194209)

Thompson, R. A. (2002). School counseling: Best practices for working in the schools (2nd ed.). New York: Brunner- Routledge.

Utah's Comprehensive Guidance Program. (1998). *Utah student services initiative for all K–12 students – Purpose statement.* Retrieved June 30, 2001, from http://www.usoe.k12.ut.us/yap/ssi.htm

VanZandt, Z., & Hayslip, J. B. (2001). *Developing your school counseling program: A handbook for systemic planning.* Belmont, CA:Wadsworth.

Westheimer, J., & Kahne, J. (1998). Education for action: Preparing youth for participatory democracy. In W. Ayers, J. A. Hunt, & T. Quinn (Eds.), *Teaching for social justice: A democracy and education reader* (pp. 1–20). New York: Teachers College.

Wittmer, J. (2000a).Developing school guidance and counseling: Its history and reconceptualization. In J. Wittmer (Ed.), *Managing your school counseling programs: K–12 developmental strategies* (2nd ed., pp. 2–13).Minneapolis, MN: Educational Media.

Wittmer, J. (2000b). Implementing a comprehensive developmental school counseling program. In J. Wittmer (Ed.), *Managing your school counseling programs: K–12 developmental strategies* (2nd ed., pp. 14–34).Minneapolis, MN: Educational Media.

Multicultural Conflict Resolution: Development, Implementation and Assessment of a Program for Third Graders

By Benjamin C. Graham and Charles Pulvino, Ph.D.

This article originally appeared in *Professional School Counseling*, Vol. 3, No. 3, 2000.

The inescapable conflict occurring between students in elementary schools provides counselors, teachers, and administrators a unique opportunity to teach students essential life skills for asserting themselves, de-escalating potentially violent situations, and appreciating individual and cultural differences. Each child comes to class with a worldview that is neither completely static nor uniform when compared to his or her peers. Using Deutsch's (1973) definition of interpersonal conflict as "two or more people who interact and perceive incompatible differences between, or threats to, their resources, needs, or values" (as cited in Kreidler, 1984, p. 12), we can view conflict in elementary schools as a natural component of the diverse gathering of perspectives learning and growing in the shared school environment.

The way that school counselors, teachers, and administrators address the area of conflict will greatly affect a school's educational environment, including how children learn to interact with each other. School authorities must actively work to utilize the potential inherent in conflict situations for teaching students the vital life skills for resolving conflicts. This can be accomplished through initiatives such as skills-based training programs, peer mediation, and modification of existing curriculums to reflect conflict resolution theory.

The intervention presented here outlines the formulation, implementation, and assessment of one counselor's attempt to increase student skills in the area of conflict resolution through a 6-week, curriculum-based, conflict resolution program for a third-grade class at a K-8 Catholic parochial school. The program will be presented by describing a brief history of conflict resolution programs, the initial assessment of the school's environment, the program itself, its evaluation, and directions for further exploration.

CONFLICT RESOLUTION IN SCHOOLS: A BRIEF HISTORY

The past 15 years have seen an abundance of conflict resolution (CR) curriculums developed to help teachers, counselors, and administrators address this important issue (Carruthers, Sweeney, Kmitta, & Harris, 1996; D'Andrea & Daniels, 1996; Johnson & Johnson, 1995a). Before describing the present program, the different forms of school-based CR programs that have been developed will be briefly reviewed.

CR programs directed at providing students with the knowledge and skills to effectively deal with conflict situations can be clustered into two types – curriculum-based and peer-mediation programs (Levy, 1989). Curriculum-based programs target all students in a class, grade level, or school, and usually consist of a series of lesson plans providing a theoretical background and social skills training. This is historically the most common approach to addressing CR in schools, and many such programs have been designed and implemented (Carruthers et al., 1996; Sweeney & Carruthers, 1996).

Peer mediation programs train a subset or all of a school's student body to serve as mediators when conflicts arise. These students receive specific skill training in negotiation and mediation, which are then used to assist in resolving conflicts in the classroom, oftentimes in lieu of traditional forms of discipline. The peer mediators gain valuable skills as well as provide modeling for their peers. In general, peer mediation programs require more coordination with teachers, administrators, and students than curriculum-based programs, but are nonetheless frequently utilized (Cohen, 1995; Johnson & Johnson, 1995b; Johnson, Johnson, Dudley, & Magnuson, 1995; Lee, Pulvino, & Perrone, 1998;).

Carruthers et al. (1996) have underscored the challenges to outcome evaluation of CR programs in schools. Personal competencies, available time, and analytic resources are only some of the hindrances to an ideal research methodology which teachers and counselors must face (Carruthers et al., 1996).

As conflict resolution programs have evolved, increasing emphasis has been placed on integrating CR training into the broader school experience, intertwining CR skills with the broader school curriculum, including such well-suited areas as the history of the civil rights movement and the multicultural classroom (Carruthers et al., 1996; D'Andrea & Daniels, 1996; Holmgren, 1996; Lee, 1995; Stomfay-Stitz, 1993; Sweeney & Carruthers, 1996). In addition, much emphasis has been placed on training those who work in the school setting in conflict management (Girard & Koch, 1996).

Teaching the role of culture in CR has been underscored as an especially important component for providing the vital skills needed for living in a pluralistic society (D'Andrea & Daniels, 1995; Sunoo, 1990). Rather than restricting the diversity issue to a specific class or unit, recent authors posit that broad, institution-wide structural and curricular changes should take place to make schools inclusive for children from diverse cultural backgrounds (Canino & Spurlock, 1994; Lantieri & Patti, 1996; Locke, 1989). These changes also serve to provide students: "An opportunity to learn skills that are not part of their native culture but that are necessary to achieve practical success in the United States" (Canino & Spurlock, 1994, p. 27).

DEVELOPMENT OF PRESENT PROGRAM

The program outlined here, "A World of Difference," utilizes the traditional curriculum-based CR approach by structuring 6 weeks of small-group workshops exploring ways of thinking about and dealing with conflict. It incorporates multicultural issues into the CR process to deepen students' understanding of the role of culture in interpersonal conflict and how such conflicts can be resolved in a way that respects the perspectives of all participants.

The present school, while having implemented CR programs in the past, did not at the time of the intervention apply such a program as part of its guidance counseling milieu. A survey was distributed to teachers in each of the eight grades in order to assess the need for a CR program. Of the six surveys returned, all indicated that conflict between students was a significant concern, supporting the need for the program. In addition, the third-grade teacher was consulted to discuss the intervention. This individual had some training in teaching CR. She had incorporated elements of Creative Conflict Solving for Kids (Schmidt & Friedman, 1991), a program from which portions of the present intervention were constructed, into her previous year's classroom. As the current year's class had not yet been exposed to the curriculum, the combination of teacher knowledge, school need, and administrative support provided an ideal environment for implementing the CR program.

In reviewing the conflict resolution and multicultural literature discussed above, it was determined that the present intervention would be built around five goals. Most elementary school CR programs aim to teach children to view conflict as either a neutral or positive phenomenon (as opposed to an inherently negative one), and to provide listening and assertiveness skills training for dealing with conflict. The present program was designed to incorporate these aims. In addition, the program was developed to meet the need for the teaching of conflict resolution from a multicultural perspective, including activities that address prejudice and stereotyping in schools. The specific program goals were defined as follows:

1. Students will learn to understand conflict as an occurrence inherent in human interaction, which presents an opportunity to creatively deal

CHAPTER FIVE

with the situation in a way that respects the other person as well as one's own interests.

2. Students will learn listening skills, specifically as they relate to successful CR.
3. Students will learn the five "Rules for Fighting Fair" outlined in Creative Conflict Solving for Kids (Schmidt & Friedman, 1991).
4. Students will better understand the role of culture in the CR process.
5. Students will learn the detrimental effects of labeling others.

This purpose of this paper is twofold. First, it serves to illustrate how existing conflict resolution programs (that do not address the role of culture in conflict) can be modified to incorporate a multicultural perspective. Second, it reports an evaluation of the effects of the integrated program described herein. The latter purpose consists of three key research questions. The first explores the program's effectiveness in changing students' conceptions of conflict to reflect a more positive view. It was expected that students would use more positive and fewer negative words in their description of conflict from pre- to post-testing. Second, the evaluation explored students' ability to discern positive approaches to conflict from other, more destructive conflict strategies before and after the program. It was expected that students would more accurately identify the "Rules of Fighting Fair" from Creative Conflict Solving for Kids (Schmidt & Friedman, 1991). Finally, the evaluation sought to determine students' understanding of the role of cultural influences in shaping perspective before and after the program. It was expected that students would offer more cultural, familial, and individual differences as possible factors in determining different points of view following the training.

METHOD

Participants

The intervention was implemented in a K–8 Catholic school in a mid-sized Midwestern city. The school contracts for counseling services through a local community agency, which provides one masters-level counselor for two days per week and one practicum student for one-half day per week. Approximately 151 students attend the school, representing many ethnic/racial backgrounds. The third-grade class, in which this intervention was focused, consisted of 22 students. Subject ages ranged from 7 to 9 years. The class was approximately half girls and half boys. The racial/ethnic backgrounds of this group consisted of Caucasian (68%), African American (18%), and Latino (14%).

Counselor Resources

Time resources of the practicum student initiating the CR program were somewhat limited. The 4 hours per week in which the student counselor worked was divided between individual, group work, and supervision. It was therefore decided that only one grade would be targeted for the intervention. An existing CR curriculum targeting third and fourth graders had been used at the school in previous years. The present intervention modified exercises from this curriculum to fit the needs of the students (as identified by teacher surveys) as well as the time constraints on counseling resources at the school.

Program Overview

A detailed outline of the program is presented in the Appendix. The present design is a modification of an existing CR program, Creative Conflict Solving for Kids (Schmidt & Friedman, 1991). This program, aimed at students in Grades 3–4, is built around several core elements. Brainstorming, role-playing, problem solving, empathetic listening, and nonthreatening statement of one's own concerns are central to the curriculum (Schmidt & Friedman, 1991).

The diverse backgrounds of the third graders at the school clearly warranted as well as provided a rich environment for efforts to understand the role that culture plays in classroom conflict. The call to incorporate multiculturalism in CR programming has been suggested by several authors (D'Andrea & Daniels, 1996; Pedersen, 1993; Sweeney & Carruthers, 1996). To achieve the goals of the present intervention, exercises from Creative Conflict Solving for Kids (Schmidt & Friedman, 1991) were interwoven with strategies aimed at exploring, understanding, and respecting diversity in the classroom. Multicultural exercises were drawn from various initiatives developed by past authors. They are cited as they appear in the outline found in the Appendix.

Brief Program Outline

A six-session intervention was used to achieve the program goals. The class was divided into three groups of seven to eight students. For the first two sessions, two groups were instructed for 25 minutes each week, so that each of the groups had 2 weeks of activities over the course of 3 weeks. The nature of the activity in the third session warranted the entire group for a single exercise lasting one hour. The remaining three sessions were conducted for each group each week for 25 minutes.

At the start of the first session, the counselor administered the pre-test assessment. The remainder of the first session consisted of a group-building exercise, emphasizing the importance of understanding each person's point of view in conflict situations. The second week of programming introduced students to the five "Rules for Fighting Fair" from Creative Conflict Solving for Kids (Schmidt & Friedman, 1991). Students were given a worksheet (that tapped family traditions, customs, and values) to complete with a family member. The third week's session involved the entire class dividing into small groups, each being given a box of cultural artifacts for a fictitious country. Students were asked to describe what life would be like for people in the respective countries, followed by an exploration of hypothetical conflict scenarios between countries. Strategies for resolving the conflicts, as well as reasons why the different countries thought differently, were discussed.

The fourth week's session began with a brief quiz to assess students' understanding of the past three sessions, followed by a listening-skills exercise. Students were given the opportunity to practice listening and assertiveness skills in a simulated conflict situation. The fifth session consisted of an exercise aimed at exploring the negative effects of labeling others, including issues around prejudice and stereotyping. The sixth and final session reviewed the nature of conflict, skills for listening/assertiveness and the role of culture in CR. An activity integrating the core curriculum was conducted, followed by a final quiz as part of the post-program evaluation.

Evaluation

In order to assess the effectiveness of the intervention, two methods were used. First, the assessment "quiz" utilized in the first session was administered after the sixth. The quiz consisted of three sections. In the first section, the counselor asked students to identify words or ideas they associated with the word "conflict." This technique has been used by past researchers to assess children's perceptions of the nature of conflict pre- and post- intervention (Johnson & Johnson, 1996). In the second section, the counselor read 11 items pertaining to things a peacemaker does to resolve conflicts. There were six correct and five incorrect responses. Students in each group individually indicated whether they agreed or disagreed, and the counselor recorded their responses. The final section of the quiz consisted of the counselor asking each group the question "What are some things that might make a person think differently than you do?"

The second method of evaluation consisted of an interview with the third-grade teacher. Questions asked during the interview were based on the five goals of the program and the three research questions. In addition, the interview explored future directions for the CR curriculum. It was expected that the interview responses would reflect students' increased understanding of issues outlined in the program goals.

In addition to the two evaluation methods employed at the end of the program, a mid-program evaluation took place at the beginning of the fourth week. This was done to assess students' understanding of the material presented in the first three weeks so that the counselor could reemphasize deficient areas, if necessary. Students were first assessed regarding their knowledge of the five "Rules for Fighting Fair" (Schmidt & Friedman, 1991) outlined in the second week. This was accomplished by the counselor reading off 10 note cards which listed different possible rules. Each group voted using a thumbs up/thumbs down method for agreeing whether or not each of the statements are one of the rules for fighting fair. The groups' responses to each card were recorded (with the three possibilities of yes, no, or lack of consensus).

In the second portion of the mid-program assessment, the counselor asked students the question from the pre-/post-test, "What are some of the reasons that a person might think differently than you do?" The counselor recorded students' responses. It was expected that students would offer responses identifying cultural upbringing and personal differences as factors influencing why two people might think differently.

RESULTS

Pre- / Post-Test Results

Student responses to words associated with the word conflict were compared by group across the pre- and post-testing. All three groups had listed primarily negative words in the pre-testing, with a few positive or neutral responses such as solving problems and peace. There was a major shift in words associated with 'conflict' in the post-testing. All three groups showed marked increases in positive words offered. Group 3 showed the greatest increase of positive versus negative responses, shifting from words such as sad stuff, murder, the KKK, and A-bomb in the pretest to not labeling, a chance to talk and give ideas, and not just be quiet in the post-test. Some negative connotations to 'conflict' still existed in some groups (guilty and war), but the overall responses for the two testings were dramatically different overall.

In the survey results from the second section, students were better able to identify the six correct responses out of the ten possible "things a peacemaker does to settle arguments" following the intervention. The most significant increases in accuracy occurred in responses to the items "Attacks the problem with everything they've got," "Lets the other person know when it's their fault," and "Clearly states why the other person is wrong."

There were some items which clearly did not seem to fit into the general increase in identifying correct 'yes' and 'no' items. For example, Group

2 showed a dramatic change in support of the statement "Criticizes the other person's way of thinking about things" at the end of the program compared to the beginning.

The third section of the pre- and post-test asked students the question "What are some things that might make a person think differently than you do?" Responses for this question were mixed. As previously stated, it was expected that students would be able to identify individual, family, and cultural differences as factors. Students showed a clear understanding of individual differences as an influence on both pre- and post-tests ("people are different," "we're different because we're human," "personal qualities"). Responses in the post-test did show some evidence of knowledge of familial and cultural influences ("family," "rich or poor," "different cultures"). For the most part, however, students did not offer responses that directly related to cultural and familial influences.

The interview of the third-grade teacher occurred one week after the final session of the intervention. In the interview, the teacher stated that the program had been well received by the students, and that they had looked forward each week to participating in the program. She stated that in several of the student disputes she had witnessed during the semester, there seemed to be an increase in students talking about each other's feelings, as opposed to the specific events of the conflict situation. This suggests that at least some students had integrated the "Steps to I-Care Listening" into their daily lives. The instructor expressed that she felt an emerging area to focus on would be the competitiveness which she saw on the playground and which she anticipates as increasing as the class moves on to the fourth grade next fall.

The mid-program feedback gathered from the students suggested that all three groups had a fairly accurate understanding of the "Rules for Fighting Fair" (Schmidt & Friedman, 1991). The groups were able to identify all of the five rules. Of the ten possible rules (five correct and five incorrect), all three groups selected six (identifying all five correct responses plus an additional erroneous rule). Their responses to the question "What are some of the reasons some people think differently than you do?" reflected some understanding of the role of culture as a factor in interpersonal conflict. Students offered responses such as "God made everybody different," "Parents teach us different things," and "Racism," suggesting some understanding of how individual, familial, and cultural differences relate to interpersonal conflict. The overall numbers of responses, however, were somewhat low.

DISCUSSION

The data from the first section of the evaluation suggest that the connotations that students place on their ideas of conflict were changed through their participation in the program. As noted earlier, this is an essential ingredient to broadening young people's understanding of conflict. The marked decrease in negatively loaded words and increase in the description of conflict as a process that holds positive potential (e.g., "A chance to talk and give ideas") is promising. Although more extensive studies of such programs are necessary, the outcomes of the present evaluation lend support to conflict taught from a multicultural perspective in reshaping children's conception of conflict.

The second section of the evaluation indicated that the program was effective in teaching the five "Rules for Fighting Fair" (Schmidt & Friedman, 1991). Students were better able to identify the five rules in the post-test compared to the pre-test, indicating that the program at least raised students' awareness of what skills are required for dealing effectively with interpersonal conflict. Exploration of students' skills in areas such as active listening and assertiveness was beyond the scope of this study, but represents a potential area for future research.

For a small number of items in the second section, student responses ran contrary to expected outcomes (i.e., Group 2 becoming more supportive of criticizing the other person as a CR strategy from pre- to post-test). This switch in expected outcome was perhaps due to limitations of the survey procedure, which may have created a pressure for consensus that was dominated by one particularly energetic student's view. Having students raise either a "thumbs up" or "thumbs down" for each statement may have placed pressure on students to conform to the answers of other students in the group, despite efforts by the counselor to encourage individual differences. Although conflict resolution programs inevitably involve a group process, taking a more individual approach to data collection would open new possibilities for analysis and address some of the shortcomings of the group approach.

Central to the present program was its incorporation of multicultural awareness raising into the teaching of CR. Although student responses in the third section of the evaluation indicated that their understanding of cultural influences was deepened somewhat, the evaluation did not conclusively indicate this. The question "What are some of the reasons some people think differently than you do?" represents only one facet of understanding conflict from a multicultural perspective. More practical evaluation approaches, possibly based on activities where students act out conflicts, might shed more light on program effectiveness. Future versions of

"A World of Difference" might include more extensive discussions and activities framing culture as a factor in CR, with sessions dedicated to defining culture and how it relates to one's experience.

The mid-program evaluation aided the implementation of the program by offering feedback that, while students appeared to have mastered the "Rules for Fighting Fair," their understanding of the role of cultural and familial influences on the CR process seemed somewhat limited. The counselor responded to this feedback by briefly revisiting lessons from the third week during the fifth week's sessions, clarifying how culture affects individual perspectives, which in turn might influence interpersonal conflict.

Several limitations are related to the evaluation methods applied in the pre- and post-tests. First, the procedures are qualitative in nature and cannot statistically support or challenge the program's success. Second, the evaluation was not a true experimental design, and therefore threats to internal validity clearly exist. Although this makes an in-depth evaluation of the program problematic, it nonetheless provides some indication of the potential effectiveness of multicultural CR programming. It has been noted that objective, statistical evaluation of such CR programs in schools is not always possible due to idiosyncrasies of the individual school and classroom (Carruthers et al., 1996). Moreover, the lack of a convincing body of research in the area of conflict resolution program evaluation has been noted by several authors (Carruthers et al., 1996; Johnson & Johnson, 1996).

Amidst the thorny realm of program evaluation in schools, however, some promising strategies have emerged. Such approaches include: (a) the use of several schools for control and training groups (Soutter & McKenzie, 1998), (b) surveys assessing students' real-life conflicts (Johnson, Johnson, Dudley, Ward, & Magnuson 1995), (c) video or actual observations (Johnson, Johnson, Dudley, & Acikgoz, 1994), and (d) use of school records (Johnson & Johnson, 1995b). In most cases, the convincing evaluation efforts have come from large-scale, well-resourced projects. Larger studies of multicultural conflict resolution programs are necessary to understand this important approach to peace education.

The implementation of the program described here brought to light several concerns and recommendations for elementary school counselors who facilitate conflict resolution and multicultural training programs. These implications are discussed below.

In response to the somewhat limited ability of students to identify the role of culture in the CR process, more explicit discussions and activities exploring culture in future programs might better promote a multicultural understanding of the CR process. Understanding one's cultural worldview is a complicated process, one with which adults often struggle. At minimum, discussions with young people must include a manageable definition of culture as well as specific activities aimed at relating this definition to students' personal experience.

The teacher interview component of the program evaluation was able to tap the perspective of the teacher, who is by far best fit to assess how the program has affected the students' day-to-day interactions at school. The interview content, however, offered little tangible feedback about how to improve the program as well as how specifically the program effected students' behavior. The interview could be improved in the future by discussing with the third-grade teacher at the onset of the intervention what behaviors would be assessed in the interview following the program's completion. A clear operationalization of what specific areas were to be assessed as well as a recording sheet for assessing these areas within a given time frame would better enable the teacher to give useful feedback regarding the effects of the program on students' behavior.

An obvious concern in implementing a program such as "A World of Difference" is the inconsistency of the school environment. Activities such as field trips, rehearsals, and special lesson planning all pose a threat to keeping the CR program on schedule in its limited time frame. Although this complicates the evaluation of the results, the flexibility needed to work in the school environment is an essential skill for the elementary school counselor (Prutzman, Stern, Burger, & Bodenhamer, 1988). Future evaluations of multicultural conflict resolution programs must inevitably incorporate this flexibility into their research design.

A related concern to implementing a program such as "A World of Difference" is the spontaneous conflicts arising at school. Since the program directly challenges students to consider the way they handle conflict, specific student conflicts will inevitably be brought into the sessions. A counselor needs to be prepared to address such spontaneous conflicts in a way that is consistent with the program curricula. These occurrences should be framed as unique opportunities for the counselor or teacher to illustrate the applicability of CR skills in students' day-to-day lives.

An incident occurred in the fifth week of programming that well illustrates this issue. In the gym class before the students met, a confrontation had happened between several students regarding the score of a kickball game. Since the event involved several of the program's participants, the scenario was explored in each of the three groups as it related to the "Different Strokes" exercise (Schmidt & Friedman, 1991).

Since the implementation of the program is contingent on teacher approval, it is important that the counselor have clear communication with the teacher in the hope of foreseeing any potential obstacles to implementing the program. Teachers and counselors working collaboratively not only makes the intervention run smoothly; it models (for students) adults working together from different perspectives. Also, clear teacher-counselor communication increases the effectiveness of the program by offering the two professionals a shared language and theoretical framework for teaching students about CR. Thus, the efforts of the teacher and counselor reinforce each other.

Future implementations might optimize this advantage by having a formal meeting before the beginning of the program to go over what is to be taught in the sessions, its ramifications for day-to-day classroom experience, and ways in which teachers can reinforce the counseling curriculum in the classroom. In turn, counselors must consult with teachers (as well as students) to understand the specific needs of the school, rather than applying a generic program. The use of teacher surveys and interviews at the beginning of the present program is one example of how this might be done. Although teachers and counselors have different roles and resources in the elementary school, their shared perspective in the area of CR will deepen students' experience of the program's goals.

Student interaction in an elementary school setting provides counselors, teachers, and administrators a unique opportunity for educating children about the conflict inherent in human interaction. The six-session program outlined here expands current CR initiatives by incorporating multiculturalism into the instruction of CR principles.

The program evaluation indicates that it was successful in challenging students' conceptualization of conflict, shifting their associations with the word from negative to positive. In addition, students were better able to identify the five "Rules for Fighting Fair" (Schmidt & Friedman, 1991) following the intervention. Feedback from the students' teacher indicated that they enjoyed participating in the program and were more likely to acknowledge their own feelings as well as the feelings of others in conflict situations. Although the class was somewhat able to articulate the role of cultural, familial, and individual differences in the CR process, their knowledge of cultural and familial influences appeared limited.

Ways in which the program might be improved include strengthening teacher-counselor communication in areas of pre-program coordination, sharing CR language and theoretical framework, and utilizing current class conflicts in CR sessions. The evaluation methodology could be improved in future implementations of the program by having students fill out individual worksheets to assess the "Rules for Fighting Fair" (Schmidt & Friedman, 1991) in the second section of the pre- and post-test. This change could also be applied to the mid-program evaluation. These changes might provide a more accurate assessment of students' knowledge by removing pressure for students to conform to their group's norm. Moreover, larger and more extensive projects should be undertaken to explore the effects of multicultural CR training programs. Implementing the program in several schools, video taping sessions, and having students record actual c

Benjamin C. Graham is project coordinator, Safe To Learn Demo Project, Illinois Violence Prevention Authority, Chicago. Charles Pulvino, Ph.D., is professor Emeritus, School of Education, Department of Counseling Psychology at the University of Wisconsin-Madison. Correspondence concerning this article should be addressed to Mr. Graham, 2014 S. 141st Circle, Omaha, NE 68144.

Helping ADHD Children Help Themselves

A school-counselor-led educational group for ADHD children can help students learn more about their disorder and, most importantly, ways to effectively manage it themselves.

By Patricia O. Quinn, MD and Judith Stern, M.A.

This article originally appeared in *Professional School Counseling*, Vol. 43, No. 2, 2005.

Professionals working with ADHD children are in the important position of helping those children and their parents understand what it means to have the disorder and how to effectively manage it. Discussions that are honest, informative and positive can have an enormous impact on these students, who deserve to know what their diagnosis is all about. When these discussions are done in a cognitively appropriate manner, children can gain a sense of hope and increased insight into how to help themselves. By adding a repertoire of knowledge and skills as the child grows, professionals can help ADHD children become more competent and independent. These are children with good cognitive skills and many talents. The difficulties that come with ADHD needn't stand in the way of future success. However, the input of parents and professionals is especially important so difficulties can be dealt with effectively and strengths be capitalized upon.

When children begin to experience problems that may be specific to their attention problems, they may become confused and frustrated. Once they have a better idea of what their ADHD entails, they are able to clarify the issues. They learn they are intelligent and capable but that some aspects of life may be a little harder for them. This opens up further discussions on what they can do to help themselves, become their own advocates and know when to ask for outside help.

Discussions should include the varied feelings that come with having ADHD. For older children and adolescents, understanding some of the current brain research, as well as an explanation of medication's impact, can be helpful. Children need to know they are part of the treatment team. They may be working with physicians, therapists and tutors who provide an important support network. Together with their parents and professionals, children with ADHD are an important part of all that can go well. A well-informed, confident child can make all the difference.

One way we have found for school counselors to be involved in this educational process is for them to set up and run children's support groups held in the school setting before, after or during school hours.

We've developed an eight-week curriculum, which helps children with ADHD deal with issues related to their ADHD and ultimately feel more in control of their ADHD symptoms.

STARTING A GROUP

When starting a group for ADHD students in your school, it's best to begin early in the school year. By getting a jumpstart on the group at the beginning of the school year, you can help the students master educational tools and techniques before they experience easily avoidable problems in the classroom or with homework. If there are a large number of children with ADHD in your school, you may want to consider running two groups, one in the spring and one in the fall.

Scheduling sessions: When it comes to groups such as these, eight sessions seem to work best. Depending on scheduling limitations, either run the group twice a week for four weeks or once a week for eight weeks. Since a full hour is recommended for most of the sessions, finding a suitable time during the school day may be a challenge. A program that begins immediately after school is probably best, since students are still in the building (for those who need reminders), and no class time will be lost. Lunchtime is another possibility, although we strongly recommend that groups not be held at the expense of an ADHD child's recess time. If you hold the group during the school day, vary the time from session to session in order to avoid missing the same academic period each week. And consider serving a snack at each session to help make the meeting more enjoyable.

Selecting age ranges: In the elementary grades, try to group students who are fairly close in age together (i.e. a third- to fourth-grade group or a fifth- to sixth-grade group). In the middle school setting, students should be able to work together regardless of grade placement. Keep groups between five and 12 students. The group should be open to boys and girls; if girls attend, make sure there is more than one.

Identifying participants: To identify students appropriate for the group, ask classroom teachers for recommendations. The school nurse is also another important resource as she frequently has contact with students who may benefit from such a group. In addition, place an announcement in the school's weekly parent bulletin and on the Web site so parents will have an opportunity to enroll their children. Before starting the group, send a written description to the parents of all prospective participants. In it you can describe the goals, time, leader's name and qualifications, session titles and any other information you wish to share. Require parents to sign a permission form allowing their children to enroll in this group.

CONTENT SUGGESTIONS FOR EACH SESSION

Session 1 - Introduction to the Group

- Introduce members, establish rules and present logistical information.
- Assess what group members already knows about ADHD, and fill in the gaps in their knowledge.
- Suggest group members discuss their treatment with their parents before the next session.
- Obtain parents' permission to discuss medication in the next session.

Session 2 - ADHD and the Brain

- Provide a brief lecture on the brain and its relationship to ADHD.
- Discuss different medications used to treat ADHD and how they work. Leave plenty of time to discuss side effects and the need to take medication as prescribed on a regular basis.
- Be sure to discuss the difference between taking ADHD medication and substance abuse.

Session 3 – Self-awareness/Self-esteem

- Have the group list the positives and negatives about having ADHD.
- Have each student define his or her positive qualities.
- Introduce coping strategies to address negative feelings.

Providing student folders: Give each student a special folder, and encourage them to keep all materials from the group in this folder. The folder will facilitate the return of homework that may be used in the next session and ensure that at the conclusion of the group, each student has a set of educational materials to refer to in the future as the need arises.

Patricia Quinn, M.D., is a developmental pediatrician in Washington, D.C. A graduate of the Georgetown University Medical School, she specializes in child development and psychopharmacolog and has worked for more than 30 years in the areas of ADHD and learning disabilities. She is the author of several books on ADHD and the director of the National Center for Gender Issues and ADHD. She can be reached at addvance@aol.com. Judith Stern, M.A. is an educational consultant in private practice in Rockville, Md., specializing in attention and learning problems in children. She consults with parents and provides workshops for schools and other parent and professional groups.

CONTENT SUGGESTIONS FOR EACH SESSION

Session 4 – Study Skills
- Discuss organization and time-management issues.
- Share ideas for becoming more organized.
- Work on making homework time more efficient.
- Introduce techniques to manage long-term assignments.

Session 5 – Friends
- Discuss way to make and keep friends
- Introduce the concept of problem-solving to address relationship issues

Session 6 – Family
- Explore ways a family can help provide support.
- Discuss problem-solving and conflict resolution.

Session 7 - Self-advocacy/Banishing Excuses
- Help the students appreciate their strengths.
- Identify individual weaknesses.
- Teach them how to ask for help.

Session 8 – Summary/Party
- Recognize positive aspects of ADHD.
- Provide an opportunity for participants to ask questions,
- Evaluate the group experience.
- Have a party.

FOR MORE INFORMATION

For more information and tools to use when working with children with ADHD, check out the following books by the authors, available from Advantage Books at *www.addvance.com*.

"Putting It All Together: A Curriculum for Conducting an 8-week Group for Children with AD/HD"

"Putting on the Brakes: A Young People's Guide to Understanding ADHD"

"The Putting on the Brakes Activity Book"

"The Best of Brakes Activity Book"

Fostering Educational Resilience and Achievement in Urban Schools Through School-Family-Community Partnerships

By Julia Bryan, Ph.D.

This article originally appeared in *Professional School Counseling*, Vol. 8, No. 3, 2005.

In this era of education reform, school counselors are among educators being held accountable for the academic achievement of minority and poor children. School counselors in urban schools serve a disproportionate number of minority and poor children at risk for school failure. Urban school counselors can play critical roles in engaging their school's stakeholders in implementing partnership programs that foster student achievement and resilience. This article discusses team facilitator, collaborator, and advocacy roles and strategies for urban school counselors and specific types of partnership programs they need to promote to foster academic achievement and resilience in minority and poor students.

In this current era of school reform, educators are being held accountable for the academic achievement of minority and poor students. This is of particular concern to urban educators because urban schools serve a disproportionate number of minority and poor students, who invariably are at risk for school failure (Wang, Haertel, & Walberg, 1998). Of the 7 million students served by the Great City Schools – which consists of 61 of the largest urban school districts in the country including Baltimore, Cleveland, and Philadelphia – over 75 percent of the students are minority students (Council of the Great City Schools, 2003). School counselors are being urged to take leadership roles in education reform aimed at reducing the barriers to academic achievement for such students (American School Counselor Association [ASCA], 2003; Bemak, 2000; Butler, 2003; Taylor & Adelman, 2000). Many urban minority and poor students tend to have multiple precipitating factors and stressors that put them at risk for school failure (Atkinson & Juntunen, 1994; Walsh, Howard, & Buckley, 1999). Urban school counselors have the challenge of helping students who daily face risk factors, such as poverty; homelessness; neighborhoods characterized by crime, violence, and drugs; and sociocultural factors such as discrimination and racial and language barriers (Atkinson & Juntunen; Holcomb-McCoy, 1998, Schorr, 1997).

Racial and ethnic minority students in many urban schools often feel powerless in a majority-dominated school culture where language, class, and culture differences are seen as deficits (Cummins, 1986; Noguera, 1996, 2001). These children are overrepresented in special education programs and underrepresented in gifted and talented programs (Ferguson, Kozleski, & Smith, 2001). Not only are the lives of a disproportionate number of racial and ethnic minority children characterized by oppression and a lack of privilege, but too often, they are "neglected, labeled, and left to wither in the lowest tracks in our schools" (Lewis & Arnold, 1998, p. 60). Efforts by schools to reduce the minority achievement gap often focus on blaming minority students for what are perceived as individual and cultural deficits residing in them, their families, and their communities (Herbert, 1999). Oftentimes, parents are regarded by school officials as adversaries instead of supporters of their children's education (Huang & Gibbs, 1992; Noguera, 1996, 2003). School officials blame differences in cultural values and family structure for poor academic achievement while parents in turn blame discrimination and insensitivity by school personnel (Atkinson & Juntunen, 1994).

For many educators, the minority achievement gap, especially in urban areas, has come to be accepted as normative and they perceive little hope for transformation in these schools. Little attention is paid to the manner in which school culture and organizational practices unconsciously act to maintain the racial inequities in academic achievement or to the effect of the assumptions, fears, and stereotypes of school personnel on their interactions with urban minority children and families (Noguera, 1996, 2001, 2003). The socio-cultural-political stressors and forces that minority students in urban schools face interact to present very complex, subtle, and seemingly insurmountable barriers to both student achievement and partnerships among schools, families, and community members. These forces are equally harmful for both low-achieving and highperforming minority students (Herbert, 1999). In spite of this drab picture, recent research on the successes of more than 4,500 high-performing, highminority, and high-poverty schools should elicit the hope in educators that urban schools, families, and communities can work together to foster the educational resilience and academic success of students (Education Trust, 2001).

DYNAMICS OF RESILIENCY

Resilience is the capacity of an individual to overcome difficult and challenging life circumstances and risk factors. *Educational resilience* is the ability of children to succeed academically despite risk factors that make it difficult for them to succeed (Benard, 1991; Wang, Haertel, & Walberg, 1997, 1998). Resilient children experience one or more difficult life circumstances or traumatic events but somehow find the power to overcome their adverse impact. Resilience in children can be fostered and promoted by establishing protective factors in their environments (Benard, 1991, 1995; Wang et al., 1997). Protective factors reduce the negative effects of adversity and stressful life events. The main protective factors that families, schools, and communities can foster to increase resiliency in children are caring and supportive adult relationships, opportunities for meaningful student participation in their schools and communities, and high parent and teacher expectations regarding student performance and future success (Benard, 1995, 1997; Wang et al., 1997, 1998). A study (Herbert, 1999) of 18 culturally diverse, high-achieving students in an urban high school revealed that a number of factors enhanced these students' ability to be resilient amid poverty, family crises, and adverse environments. Among these were supportive adults at home, at school, and in the community; extracurricular afterschool, Saturday, and summer enrichment programs; challenging educational experiences; a network of achieving peers; and a strong belief in and sense of self.

Overwhelmingly, school-family-community partnerships are promoted as potential sources of the protective factors that foster educational resilience in children (Benard, 1995; Christenson & Sheridan, 2001; Epstein, 1995; Wang et al., 1997, 1998). School-family-community partnerships are collaborative initiatives or relationships among school personnel, parents, family members, community members, and representatives of community-based organizations such as businesses, churches, libraries, and social service agencies. All partners involved work together to coordinate and implement programs and activities aimed at the increased academic, emotional, and social success of students served by the school (Davies, 1996; Epstein, 1995). Despite the fact that school-family-community partnerships are not a panacea for solving students' and schools' problems, they foster the protective factors that help overcome some of the barriers and risks that many urban students face.

School-family-community partnerships establish supportive relationships, such as parent-teacher support, and involve family, school, and community members in implementing programs that promote academic success for students. When schools, families, and communities foster protective factors, they are putting risk-reducing mechanisms in place that mediate risks in four ways: (a) Children are less impacted by the effects of risks with which they have come in direct contact; (b) the danger of exposure to the risk is reduced or the risk itself is modified; (c) children's self-efficacy and self-esteem are enhanced; and (d) children are provided with opportunities for meaningful involvement in their environments (Benard, 1991, 1995).

THE RATIONALE FOR SCHOOL-FAMILYCOMMUNITY PARTNERSHIPS

The No Child Left Behind (NCLB) Act (U.S. Department of Education, 2001) has mandated the development of school-family-community partnerships in Title I schools. Under NCLB, Title I schools are required to work jointly with family and community members to develop a school-familycommunity involvement policy. Ferguson (2003) noted that the provision concerning school-familycommunity partnerships is being overlooked; yet, such partnerships hold the key to meeting the overarching goal of NCLB, that of reducing the achievement gap between White and poor and minority students in public schools. Education reform initiatives over the past three decades, such as Goals 2000, have focused on parent involvement or school-family- community partnerships (Simon & Epstein, 2001). Inherent to NCLB and previous reform initiatives is the belief that parents, families, and community members are critical contributors to improving academic achievement.

Schools alone lack the necessary resources to address the large number of obstacles to learning that many minority and poor students in urban schools confront on a daily basis. Schorr (1997) argued, "Schools can become islands of hope in otherwise devastated neighborhoods. When schools and communities work together to give poor children the supports typically enjoyed by children in middle-class neighborhoods, they help children avoid a culture of failure" (p. 289). Family and community members can contribute extensively to the work of the school, to the planning and implementation of curricular and extracurricular activities that enhance learning, and to the infusion of the culture of students and families within the school (Brewster & Railsback, 2003; Ferguson et al., 2001; Henderson & Mapp, 2002).

Partnerships and Educational Outcomes

Research has indicated that school-family-community partnerships improve school programs and school climate, increase parents' skills and leadership, connect families with others in the school and the community, and improve children's chances of success in school and life (Epstein, 1995; Henderson & Mapp, 2002). In a longitudinal study of 293 third and fifth graders in 14 classrooms in Baltimore City schools, teachers' efforts to involve parents were found to have significant positive effects on student reading achievement from fall to spring, even after controlling for teacher quality, students' initial achievement, parents' education, parents' improved understanding of the school program, and the quality of students' homework (Epstein & Dauber, 1991). Notably, Comer's School Development Program, which was implemented first in troubled, lowincome, urban areas in New Haven, CT's schools and subsequently in many similar urban schools nationally, has had over 40 years of success in helping minority and poor students to reach and exceed national achievement norms (Comer, Haynes, Joyner, & Ben-Avie, 1996). Relatedly, Henderson and Mapp have synthesized 51 studies that highlight the positive influences of family and community involvement in schools on student academic achievement. When family members are involved in their children's education, children are more likely to earn higher grades, enroll in rigorous classes, go on to college, and have better academic-achievement- related behaviors, such as good social skills and regular attendance at school.

Recent studies have sought to dispel the myth that students in high-poverty, high-minority schools cannot perform well academically (Charles A. Dana Center, 1999; Education Trust, 2001). The Education Trust has identified 4,577 high-performing schools that serve high-minority or high-poverty students, or both. Among the critical components that these high-performing, high-poverty/highminority schools have in common are high expectations and standards for all students, access for all students to rigorous curricula, extra support for students who need it, and strong partnerships with families and community members. However, one must take note of the research that indicates that the effect of parent involvement on minority student achievement may be mediated by school-level variables that tend to affect minority and poor students more than White students (Desimone, 1996). School-level variables, such as organizational practices, school culture, and discrimination, may negate the positive effects of parent involvement on student achievement.

Partnerships and Empowerment

Parents and family members often emerge empowered by the process of participation in partnerships with schools (Davies, 1995, 1996; Winters, 1993). They gain skills, knowledge, and confidence that help them in rearing their children, in improving their economic condition, and in being good citizens (Davies, 1996). After years of working with initiatives to involve parents in schools in New Haven, CT, Milwaukee, WI, and other urban public school systems, Winters observed that low-income, single mothers seem to emerge from these programs with strengthened self-competence, new skills, and a determination to alter the direction of their lives. She reported that these parents entered these programs feeling powerlessness (believing that one's behavior cannot affect outcomes or result in what one desires), a sense of anomie or meaninglessness, social isolation, and self-estrangement. As a result of their participation in school-family partnership programs, parents reaped a number of benefits including an increased sense of well-being and personal competence.

Similarly, Cochran and Dean (1991), in a study of 160 urban families over a 3-year period, concluded that efforts to involve parents, neighborhood members, teachers, and school administrators in programs that focus on parent empowerment will have positive impacts on family-school relationships and on children's school performance. Like Winters (1993), Cochran and Dean found that parents emerged from their empowerment-focused schoolfamily- community partnership program having better self-perceptions, gaining stronger social networks, and being more willing to initiate changes in their neighborhoods.

Partnerships and Social Capital

School-family-community partnerships build social capital or networks of trust that families draw from to help their children succeed (Epstein & Sanders, 2000). More formally, social capital is further defined as "resources stored in human relationships whether casual or close ... the stuff we draw on all the time, through our connections to a system of human relationships, to accomplish things that matter to us and to solve everyday problems" (de Souza Briggs, 1997, p. 112). Partnerships among schools, families, and communities create avenues by which relationships or networks of trust can be formed among administrators, teachers, family, and community members. These relationships provide a source of connections, information, and understandings that parents can draw on to help their children succeed. Such partnerships facilitate the exchange of knowledge across cultures and lead to a bridging of the gap between home and school cultures, values, and expectations (Huang & Gibbs, 1992; Schorr, 1997).

Positive relationships between schools and families in many urban schools are infrequent because parents often do not trust the schools and school professionals in turn do not trust minority and lowincome families and communities (Cummins, 1986; Goddard, Tschannen-Moran, & Hoy, 2001). Noguera (1996, 2001, 2003) highlighted the negative attitudes that principals and teachers in urban schools frequently have toward low-income and minority students and families. Some of the barriers to trust are parents' past negative experiences with schools, poor school-home communication, parents' experiences of discrimination, and incongruent teacher and parent expectations (Brewster & Railsback, 2003). School administration, teachers, and counselors may be rigid and defensive in reinforcing rules with these families whom they perceive as "problems." Such interactions result in the accruing of negative social capital to these families who feel alienated and marginalized from schools (Epstein & Sanders, 2000; Noguera, 2003).

It has been demonstrated that among children whose backgrounds and parental expectations are inconsistent with school expectations and values, strong family-school relationships make a positive difference to student achievement (Comer et al., 1996). The creation of positive relationships and transformative partnerships among schools, families, and communities presupposes a paradigm shift. There must be a shift from seeing parents as peripheral to education, and as deficient, to seeing them as valuable resources and assets to the school and as having a shared responsibility and equal capacity to contribute to the education of their children.

THE SCHOOL COUNSELOR'S ROLES IN PARTNERSHIP BUILDING IN URBAN SCHOOLS

School-family-community partnership involvement is considered a central aspect of the school counselor's role (ASCA, 2003; Bemak, 2000; Bryan & Holcomb-McCoy, 2004, 2005; Taylor & Adelman, 2000; Walsh et al., 1999). School counselors are in an ideal position to promote and provide leadership for partnerships among school, families, and communities (Colbert, 1996). Recent studies have indicated that school counselors agree that their roles in school-family-community partnerships are important (Bryan & Holcomb-McCoy, 2004, 2005). In one study, school counselors reported that they were more involved in some partnership roles (those of advocate, team leader, and consultant) than in others (facilitator, school-home liaison, coordinator, and trainer). They also perceived some types of partnerships (e.g., mentoring and parent education programs) as more important than others (Bryan & Holcomb-McCoy, 2004).

In another study of school counselors drawn from ASCA, counselors reported being at least moderately involved in 18 school-family-community partnership role behaviors prescribed for them in the professional school counseling literature (Bryan & Holcomb-McCoy, 2005). For example, they reported being frequently involved in locating services and resources for students and their families in the community, collaborating with community agency professionals, and working with a team of school staff, family, and/or community members and professionals. Furthermore, the same study indicated that school counselors' involvement in school-familycommunity partnerships was influenced by their role perceptions, their confidence in the ability to build partnerships, and their attitudes about partnerships over and above school norms of collaboration (Bryan & Holcomb-McCoy, 2005).

Urban school counselors are in a key position to assist schools in their education reform mandates to reduce the achievement gap among low-income and minority children (Butler, 2003; Holcomb-McCoy, 1998, 2001). ASCA's (2003) National Model specifically outlined a leadership role for school counselors in school-family-community partnerships: "The school counselor provides proactive leadership, which engages all stake-holders in the delivery of activities and services to help students achieve success in school" (p. 17). Because urban school counselors work on a daily basis with a large proportion of students who feel alienated from school and are at risk for academic failure and dropping out, they have a responsibility to facilitate these students' academic achievement (Butler, 2003). It is imperative that school counselors understand how to devise programs and interventions to assist failing students in overcoming systemic barriers that impede their academic progress. Furthermore, school counselors must be willing to become involved in various partnership roles in order to connect schools, families, and communities in addressing barriers to learning and promoting student resilience and achievement (Bemak, 2000; Taylor & Adelman, 2000).

Partnership Roles for School Counselors

The school counselor cannot do it all (Erford, 2003). Rather, it is suggested that school counselors be actively involved in activities to engage their schools' stakeholders; this identifies school counselors as team facilitators, advocates, and collaborators with members of their schools, families, and communities (Bemak, 2000; Colbert, 1996; Taylor & Adelman, 2000). These roles allow the school counselor to facilitate and assist in coordinating such partnership programs without taking on the sole responsibility for partnership building in schools.

Team facilitator. Enhancing student achievement in urban schools will not be accomplished in a piecemeal fashion or by engaging parents in a few token activities (Charles A. Dana Center, 1999; Christenson & Sheridan, 2001; Ferguson et al., 2001). Schools that embrace families and community members as valued partners have comprehensive programs of partnerships that move beyond traditional partnership roles for parents, such as involvement in the parent-teacher association, to engage family and community members in working as a team at multiple levels in the school (Christenson & Sheridan). Partnership teams – referred to as family-school teams (Christenson & Sheridan), school mental health teams (Keys & Lockhart, 1999), and action teams for partnerships (Epstein, 1995) – are suggested as the best way to facilitate the designing, planning, and evaluation of partnership programs. These teams typically are composed of school personnel (e.g., administrator, teachers, school counselor, librarian, school psychologist), parents, and community members.

Teaming is the process of working with a group of individuals to accomplish common goals and objectives. Team facilitators assist teams in running smoothly and moving forward in their efforts to accomplish a task. Facilitators must have effective communication, problem-solving, and conflict resolution skills, as well as an understanding of team dynamics. Given their training in group work and more specifically in working with teams, school counselors can play a critical role as facilitators of partnership teams. It is imperative that school counselors use their team facilitation skills to help administrators and teachers work collaboratively with stakeholders who are representative of the children that most need help, that is, minority and low-income students (Ferguson et al., 2001). Oftentimes, minority parents may not voice their ideas because of their fear of the team's reaction to them. School counselors can use group process skills to ensure that minority and low-income parents' voices are heard in the collaboration and decision-making process (Brewster & Railsback, 2003; Cicero & Barton, 2003; Henderson & Mapp, 2002). In addition, school counselors can help create an environment in which team members appreciate the expertise and diverse perspectives that poor and minority parents bring to the problem-solving process.

Advocate. Lee (1998) defined advocacy as "the process or act of arguing or pleading for a cause or proposal" (p. 8). An advocate pleads or argues the cause of another. School counselors are advocates who work with school personnel, family, and community members to remove systemic barriers to student success, especially for students who have been disenfranchised due to racism and discrimination (House & Martin, 1998). School-family-community partnerships are an effective means of combating systemic barriers in urban schools (Noguera, 1996; Schorr, 1997). Success in establishing support for such partnerships will be predicated on school counselors' willingness to advocate for such partnerships. This commitment to advocacy is likely to be fueled by school counselors' understanding of the benefits that such partnerships have for minority and lowincome children. Convincing educators that urban families and communities can provide valuable resources to the school is one of the first challenges that school counselors will face given the stereotypes and fears that school personnel may have about these families and communities. In order to get principal and teacher "buy-in," school counselors will need to collect and use data and stories about successful partnerships and their impact on student achievement to elicit school-wide support for building partnerships.

Urban school counselors can increase administrator and staff awareness of the benefits of school-family- community partnerships for student achievement through staff development trainings. Staff development workshops are also forums in which counselors can help teachers examine their beliefs and stereotypes about culturally diverse students and urban communities and awaken awareness of the negative effects of viewing students from a deficit perspective. Combined workshops for school staff, family, and community members can create opportunities for all stakeholders to examine their views about how they can work together to build partnerships to foster academic achievement and the protective factors that build educational resilience in children.

Collaborator. As urban school counselors work with school personnel, family, and community members to build partnerships, they will have to use their knowledge and expertise to lay the groundwork for successful collaboration. Collaboration is a process for reaching goals that cannot be reached alone but are reached through shared vision, responsibility, and resources; parity; joint work; mutual expertise; and shared outcomes in accomplishing the goals. Successful collaboration among members of urban schools, families, and communities will take place when they see each other as equals, share common goals, and contribute equally to developing and implementing partnership plans (Keys, Bemak, Carpenter, & King-Sears, 1998; Noguera, 1996, 2003). School counselors can play a critical role in fostering collaboration by modeling open dialogue. Open dialogue, a critical component of successful collaboration, involves partners listening to each other respectfully, valuing each other's opinions, and respecting the views of diverse partners with different experiences. Such dialogue provides a starting point for partnerships through which cultural understandings and trust can be built and schoolfamily- community differences can be bridged.

As urban school counselors collaborate with school personnel, families, and communities, a necessary first step is that they become familiar with the community that the school is located in, with the understanding that community may go beyond the neighborhood surrounding the school (Dorfman, 1998). Community asset mapping is a useful tool that urban school counselors can utilize to learn who are the "point" people or people of influence in the local community, which persons and organizations have the respect of the people (e.g., pastors, priests, 4-H club), and who are the active advocates and "voices" of the community. School counselors can use community asset mapping to learn where resources are located (e.g., the social service agencies, mentoring program, libraries) and where the community meeting places are.

Getting to know the community is a first step in marshaling valuable community resources. Parents and family members from the local community are valuable resources in helping urban school counselors learn about the community. School counselors should enlist the support of "point" parents and community members so that they can build a bridge to other parents and community members who do not usually venture into the schools. If school counselors are going to be successful in their attempts to collaborate with family and community members, they will need to examine their own attitudes and stereotypes about poor and minority persons and be willing to accept cultural norms that are different from their own. To do so, they will need to be culturally competent.

Partnership Programs for Enhancing Academic Achievement

It is not enough to just build partnerships. Urban school counselors must facilitate the establishment of partnerships that foster academic achievement and resilience in poor and minority children. Such partnerships provide students with caring and supportive relationships, offer them opportunities for meaningful involvement in their school and community environments, offer after-school enrichment activities, incorporate high expectations regarding student performance and success, and enhance students' sense of self-efficacy and self-esteem (Benard, 1995; Herbert, 1999; Wang et al., 1997, 1998). Two types of partnership programs are successful in facilitating educational resilience and academic achievement: (a) family-centered partnerships such as family centers, parent education programs, and family outreach (Comer et al., 1996; Epstein, 1995; Ritchie & Partin, 1994); and (b) extracurricular enrichment partnership programs such as tutoring, mentoring, and after-school enrichment programs (Christiansen, 1997; Herbert; Walsh et al., 1999).

Family-centered partnerships. Through family outreach programs, family centers, and parent education programs, many urban schools have been effective in involving parents and guardians in their children's education (Johnson, 2001; Simon & Epstein, 2001). Through family-centered programs, school counselors can help family members become more involved in working to keep their children engaged in school. Supportive family members can help coordinate parent education and family centers, because parents reach parents more effectively (Atkinson & Juntunen, 1994). Some schools may pay for a parent liaison or coordinator out of their budget, while in others, parents may volunteer. In urban areas, where there are a large proportion of racially and ethnically diverse families, including immigrant families, it is imperative that parent education and family outreach programs identify the needs of family members and students and tailor partnership programs to meet their needs (Cicero & Barton, 2003). The school counselor should conduct needs assessment and focus groups to determine parents' and students' needs prior to designing parent workshops.

Parent education is already a role that school counselors embrace, often implementing parent workshops to educate parents about ways in which to help their children succeed in school (Ritchie & Partin, 1994). Parent workshops can help many families, such as immigrant and minority families, understand the school's policies and rules and how to advocate for their children in the school. In order to reach "hard-to-reach" parents, urban school counselors may have to take parent workshops to community meeting places such as churches and community centers. They also can network with the largest employers of their students' families to organize "Parent Days" or parent meetings at the work site. Home visits are powerful ways of connecting with families who may find it difficult to come to the school. Parents respond positively to visits from parent or teacher liaisons of the same culture (Hiatt- Michael, 2001). Wherever possible, school counselors should ask a parent liaison or volunteer of the same ethnicity to accompany them on a home visit. This will help to reduce cultural barriers because the parent may better understand the accepted cultural traditions and practices of the family.

Finding ways to reduce parents' feelings of alienation in the school necessitates that the school counselor advocate for a space for all parents in the school. School counselors are often advocates for the establishment of family and parent resource centers (Cicero & Barton, 2003). Family centers provide a welcoming space in the school, create a feeling of belongingness among parents, and provide a place where parents can come to meet with other parents, find parent resources, and have parent group meetings (Cicero & Barton). In schools where family centers have been implemented, parents reported feeling like insiders rather than outsiders (Johnson, 2001). As school counselors collaborate with school staff to incorporate the various cultures of students represented in the school into the family center (e.g., through books and posters), and throughout the school, urban family members will feel more accepted in the school culture.

Extracurricular enrichment partnership programs. Research has highlighted the positive influences of mentors and tutors in children's lives (Benard, 1992; Dubois, Holloway, Valentine, & Harris, 2002). After-school enrichment and tutoring programs are reported to be successful in fostering academic achievement and resilience in children (Hock, Pulvers, Deshler, & Schumaker, 2001). Similarly, tutoring programs are effective when tutors receive some training (Hock et al.). As school counselors advocate for the establishment of mentoring and tutoring programs and encourage parents to involve their children in these programs, they will need to ensure that coordinators of such programs are implementing best practices such as providing training for tutors and mentors.

In urban schools, school counselors must be aware of the community organizations that can serve as resources and provide academic support services for students and their parents (Atkinson & Juntunen, 1994). This will enable them to identify and partner with reputable mentoring, tutoring, faith-based, and other community programs to provide academic enrichment experiences for students. It is imperative in working with urban minority families that school counselors recognize the focal role of the church within the African-American, African, Caribbean, and Hispanic communities (Day-Vines, Patton, & Baytops, 2003). Churches often are a valuable source of mentors and tutors for students and a great medium through which to get information to families. Furthermore, urban school counselors should see colleges and universities as valuable resources for providing mentors and tutors for academic enrichment activities. Many colleges and universities, corporations, and career professionals have partnered with schools to provide pre-college academic preparation and orientation programs to reduce student attrition in middle and high schools, enhance student achievement, and prepare students for college (Fenske, Geranios, Keller, & Moore, 1997).

Also, urban school counselors can liaise with businesses and professional corporations to facilitate the implementation of Cadet programs and career clubs in the schools in order to arouse children's interest in various careers, enhance their knowledge about career options, build their career self-efficacy, and provide accurate career information to dispel myths about careers.

CONCLUSION

Partnerships among the school, home, and community increase students' chances of success by removing some of the stressors and systemic barriers to academic and personal success, especially for poor and minority students (Taylor & Adelman, 2000; Walsh et al., 1999). In preparing school counselors to work in urban settings, counselor educators must seek to address their special training needs within the existing Council for the Accreditation of Counseling and Related Educational Programs (2001) school counseling curriculum. School counselors who work with urban families and communities must have knowledge and skills in collaboration, advocacy, and leadership (Bemak, 2000; Taylor & Adelman, 2000); collaborative consultation (Keys et al., 1998); and multicultural competency (Holcomb-McCoy, 1998, 2001).

In addition, counselor educators will need to infuse knowledge about school culture, community asset mapping, and urban education issues in the school counseling curriculum (Bryan & Holcomb- McCoy, 2005). Some of these knowledge and skill areas would be better explored in greater depth in a course focusing on school-family-community partnerships, collaboration, consultation, and school restructuring. Additionally, school counseling trainees should be placed in internships where site supervisors are engaged in school-family-community partnerships so as to provide them with practical understandings of urban issues and how to build strong partnerships among urban schools, families, and communities.

Julia Bryan, Ph.D., is an assistant professor in School Psychology and Counselor Education, School of Education, College of William and Mary, Williamsburg, VA. E-mail: jabrya@wm.edu

REFERENCES

American School Counselor Association. (2003). *The ASCA National Model: A framework for school counseling programs.* Alexandria,VA: Author.

Atkinson, D. A., & Juntunen, C. L. (1994). School counselors and school psychologists as school-home-community liaisons in ethnically diverse schools. In P. Pedersen & J. C. Carey (Eds.), *Multicultural counseling in schools: A practical handbook* (pp. 103–119). Needham Heights, MA: Allyn & Bacon.

Bemak, F. (2000).Transforming the role of the counselor to provide leadership in educational reform through collaboration. *Professional School Counseling, 3,* 323–331.

Benard, B. (1991). *Fostering resiliency in kids: Protective factors in the family, school, and community.* Portland, OR: Northwest Regional Educational Laboratory. (ERIC Document Reproduction Service No. ED335781)

Benard, B. (1992). *Mentoring programs for urban youth: Handle with care.* Portland, OR: Northwest Regional Educational Laboratory.

Benard, B. (1995). *Fostering resilience in children.* Urbana, IL: ERIC Clearinghouse on Elementary and Early Childhood Education. (ERIC Document Reproduction Service No. ED386327)

Benard, B. (1997). *Turning it around for all youth: From risk to resilience* (ERIC/CUE Digest,No. 126). New York: ERIC Clearinghouse on Urban Education. (ERIC Document Reproduction Service No. ED412309)

Brewster, C., & Railsback, J. (2003). *Building trust with schools and diverse families: A foundation for lasting partnerships.* Portland, OR: Northwest Regional Educational Laboratory. Retrieved January 30, 2004, from http://www.nwrel.org/request

Bryan, J. A., & Holcomb-McCoy, C. H. (2004). School counselors' perceptions of their involvement in school-family-community partnerships. *Professional School Counseling, 7,* 162–171.

Bryan, J. A., & Holcomb-McCoy, C. H. (2005). *Factors related to school counselor involvement in school-family-community partnerships.* Manuscript submitted for publication.

Butler, S. K. (2003). Helping urban African American high school students excel academically: The roles of school counselors. *High School Journal, 87,* 51–57.

Charles A. Dana Center. (1999). *Hope for urban education: A study of nine high-performing, high poverty urban elementary schools.* Washington, DC: U.S.Department of Education, Planning and Evaluation Services.

Christenson, S. L., & Sheridan, S. M. (2001). *Schools and families: Creating essential connections for learning.* New York: The Guilford Press.

Christiansen, J. (1997). Helping teachers meet the needs of students at risk for school failure. *Elementary School Guidance and Counseling, 31,* 204–210.

Cicero, G., & Barton, P. (2003). Parental involvement, outreach, and the emerging role of the professional school counselor. In B.T. Erford (Ed.), *Transforming the school counseling profession* (pp. 191–207).Upper Saddle River, NJ: Merrill Prentice Hall.

Cochran, M., & Dean, C. (1991). Home-school relations and the empowerment process. *The Elementary School Journal, 91*(3), 261–269.

Colbert, R.D. (1996).The counselor's role in advancing school and family partnerships. *The School Counselor, 44,* 100–104.

Comer, J. P., Haynes,N.M., Joyner, E.T., & Ben-Avie,M. (Eds.). (1996). *Rallying the whole village: The Comer process for reforming education.* New York: Teachers College Press.

Council for the Accreditation of Counseling and Related Educational Programs. (2001). *Accreditation procedures and manual.* Alexandria,VA: Author.

Council of the Great City Schools. (2003). *2002-2003 Annual report.* Washington, DC: Author.

Cummins, J. (1986). Empowering minority students: A framework for intervention. *Harvard Educational Review, 56,* 18–36.

Davies, D. (1995). Commentary: Collaboration and family empowerment as strategies to achieve comprehensive services. In L. Rigsby, M. Reynolds, & M.Wang (Eds.), *School community connections: Exploring issues for research and practice* (pp. 267–280). San Francisco: Jossey-Bass.

Davies, D. (1996). Partnerships for student success. New Schools, *New Communities, 12,* 14–21.

Day-Vines, N., Patton, J., & Baytops, J. (2003). African American adolescents: The impact of race and middle class status on the counseling process. *Professional School Counseling, 7,* 40–51.

Desimone, L. (1996). Linking parent involvement with student achievement:Do race and income matter? *Journal of Educational Research, 93,* 11–30.

de Souza Briggs, X. (1997). *Social capital and the cities: Advice to change agents.* National Civic Review, 86(2), 111–117.

Dorfman, D. (1998). *Mapping community assets workbook. Strengthening community education: The basis for sustainable renewal.* Portland, OR: Northwest Regional Educational Laboratory, Rural Education Program. Retrieved January 10, 2003, from http://www.nwrel.org/ruraled/publications/com_mapping.pdf

Dubois, D. L., Holloway, B. E., Valentine, J. C., & Harris, C. (2002). *Effectiveness of mentoring programs for the youth: A meta-analytic review* [Special issue]. American Journal of Community Psychology, 30, 157–197.

Education Trust. (2001). *Dispelling the myth revisited: Preliminary findings from a nationwide analysis of highflying schools.* Retrieved January 10, 2004, from http://www2.edtrust.org/EdTrust/ product+catalog/special+reports.htm#preliminary

Epstein, J. L. (1995). School/family/community partnerships: Caring for the children we share. *Phi Delta Kappan, 76*(9), 701–712.

Epstein, J. L., & Dauber, S. L. (1991). School programs and teacher practices of parent involvement in inner-city elementary and middle schools. *The Elementary School Journal, 91,* 289–305.

Epstein, J. L., & Sanders, M.G. (2000). Connecting home, school and community: New directions for social research. In M. Hallinan (Ed.), *Handbook of sociology of education* (pp. 285–306). New York: Plenum.

Erford, B.T. (Ed.). (2003). *Transforming the school counseling profession.* Upper Saddle River, NJ: Merrill Prentice Hall.

Fenske, R. H., Geranios, C. A., Keller, J. E., & Moore, D. E. (1997). *Early intervention programs: Opening the door to higher education* (ASHE-ERIC Higher Education Report, 25, No. 6). Retrieved May 14, 2002, from the OCLC FirstSearch database.

Ferguson, D. L., Kozleski, E. B., & Smith, A. (2001). *On ... transformed, inclusive schools: A framework to guide fundamental change in urban schools.* Denver, CO: National Institute for Urban School Improvement.

Ferguson, S. (2003). Whatever happened to partnerships? *Gaining Ground, 5,* 1–2. Retrieved January 30, 2003, from http://www.ccsso.org/content/PDFs/GGSummer03.pdf

Goddard, R.D., Tschannen-Moran, M., & Hoy, W. K. (2001). A multilevel examination of the distribution and effects of teacher trust in students and parents in urban elementary schools. *Elementary School Journal, 102,* 3–17.

Henderson, A.T., & Mapp, K. L. (Eds.). (2002). *A new wave of evidence: The impact of school, family, and community connections on student achievement* [Electronic version]. Austin,TX: National Center for Family and Community Connections with Schools, Southwest Educational Development Laboratory.

Herbert, T. P. (1999). Culturally diverse high-achieving students in an urban school. *Urban Education, 34,* 428–457.

Hiatt-Michael, D. B. (Ed.). (2001). *Promising practices for family involvement in schools: A volume in family school community partnership.* Greenwich, CT: Information Age Publishing.

Hock, M. F., Pulvers, K. A., Deshler, D.D., & Schumaker, J. B. (2001). The effects of an after-school tutoring program on the academic performance of at-risk students and students with LD. *Remedial and Special Education, 22,* 172–186.

Holcomb-McCoy, C. (1998). *School counselor preparation in urban settings.* Greensboro, NC: ERIC/CASS. (ERIC Document Reproduction Service No. ED418343)

Holcomb-McCoy, C. (2001). *Examining urban school counseling professionals' perceptions of school restructuring activities.* Greensboro, NC: ERIC/CASS. (ERIC Document Reproduction Service No. ED452451)

House, R.M., & Martin, P. J. (1998). Advocating for better futures for all students: A new vision for school counselors. *Education, 119*(2), 284–291.

Huang, L. N., & Gibbs, J.T. (1992). Partners or adversaries? Home-school collaboration across culture, race, and ethnicity. In S. L. Christenson & J. C. Conoley (Eds.), *Homeschool collaboration: Enhancing children's academic and social competence* (pp. 19–52). Colesville,MD: National Association of School Psychologists.

Johnson, V. R. (2001). Family centers in schools: Expanding possibilities for partnership. In D. B. Hiatt-Michael (Ed.), *Promising practices for family involvement in schools: A volume in family school community partnership* (pp. 85–107).Greenwich, CT: Information Age Publishing.

Keys, S., Bemak, F., Carpenter, S. L., & King-Sears, M. E. (1998). Collaborative consultant: A new role for counselors serving at-risk youths. *Journal of Counseling and Development, 76,* 123–134.

Keys, S. G., & Lockhart, E. J. (1999).The school counselor's role in facilitating multisystemic change. *Professional School Counseling, 3,* 101–107.

Lee, C. (1998). Counselors as agents of social change. In C. Lee & G. R.Waltz (Eds.), *Social action: A mandate for counselors* (pp. 3–16). Alexandria,VA: American Counseling Association.

Lewis, J. A., & Arnold,M. S. (1998). From multiculturalism to social action. In C. Lee & G. R.Waltz (Eds.), *Social action: A mandate for counselors* (pp. 263–278). Alexandria,VA: American Counseling Association.

Noguera, P. A. (1996). Confronting the urban in urban school reform. *The Urban Review, 28,* 1–19.

Noguera, P. A. (2001). Racial politics and the elusive quest for excellence and equity in education. *Education and Urban Society, 34,* 18–41.

Noguera, P. A. (2003). City schools and the American dream: Reclaiming the promise of public education. New York: Teachers College Press.

Ritchie, M.H., & Partin, R. L. (1994). Parent education and consultation activities of school counselors. *The School Counselor, 41,* 165–170.

Schorr, L. (1997). *Common purpose: Strengthening families and neighborhoods to rebuild America.* New York:Doubleday.

Simon, B. S., & Epstein, J. L. (2001). School, family, and community partnerships: Linking theory to practice. In D. B. Hiatt-Michael (Ed.), *Promising practices for family involvement in schools: A volume in family school community partnership* (pp. 1–24). Greenwich, CT: Information Age Publishing.

Taylor, L., & Adelman, H. S. (2000). Connecting schools, families, and communities. *Professional School Counseling, 3,* 298–307.

U.S. Department of Education. (2001). *No Child Left Behind Act of 2001* (H.R.1). Washington, DC: Author.

Walsh, M. E., Howard, K. A., & Buckley, M. A. (1999). School counselors in school-community partnerships: Opportunities and challenges. *Professional School Counseling, 2,* 349–356.

Wang, M. C., Haertel, G.D., & Walberg, H. J. (1997). Fostering educational resilience in inner-city schools. *Children and Youth, 7,* 119–140.

Wang, M. C., Haertel, G.D., & Walberg, H. J. (1998). *Educational resilience* (Laboratory for Student Success Publication Series No. 11). Philadelphia: Temple University Center for Research in Human Development and Education.

Winters, W. G. (1993). *African American mothers: The power of participation.* New York: Lexington Books.

University-Urban School Collaboration in School Counseling

By Donna E. Palladino Schultheiss

This article originally appeared in *Professional School Counseling*, Vol. 4, No. 4, 2005.

Models of effective collaboration are needed to best serve the needs of students in 21st-century schools. The Career and Education Connection program, an elementary career intervention developed for an economically challenged urban school district, is described. The article discusses theoretical frameworks and lessons learned through professional and personal experiences with (a) initiating a collaborative research-practice initiative; (b) making connections and enhancing collaborative relationships among university faculty, graduate students, and school professionals; and (c) facilitating graduate student professional development and training.

Schools in the 21st century are facing a multitude of complex and multifactored problems (Paisley & McMahon, 2001), including poverty, violence, and poor academic achievement. The intensity of students' needs has led some to question whether school counseling programs are actually comprehensively meeting the needs of all students (Green & Keys, 2001; Whiston, 2002). Ecological (e.g., Bronfenbrenner, 1979) and developmental contextual models (e.g., Lerner, 1995) have been introduced into the school counseling literature as paradigms for understanding and responding to the needs of today's youth (Whiston). These models emphasize the interaction of personal characteristics and the context in which the person lives as central to intervening in developmental contexts such as schools.

Although such paradigms provide a powerful means of conceptualizing and intervening in the lives of children, school counselors are faced with a daunting task if left to their own devices. Thus, multiple challenges point to the need for multidisciplinary collaborative efforts (Bemak, 2000; Green & Keys, 2001). Despite repeated calls for social action and collaboration (e.g., Bemak, 1998; Keys & Bemak, 1997; Paisley & McMahon, 2001), the extant literature indicates that school counselors do not participate in the extensive collaborative program development that is needed for comprehensive developmental school counseling programs in the 21st century (Green & Keys). Moreover, demands for evidence-based practices make clear the need for programmatic research to substantiate the effectiveness of school counseling programs (Green & Keys; Whiston, 2002; Whiston & Sexton, 1998).

Given the complex challenges facing 21st-century schools, school counselors can no longer function in isolation from their communities (Hobbs & Collison, 1995). Recent literature has emphasized the importance of collaborative partnerships between school counselors and various stakeholders as a necessary component of effective school counseling programs (e.g., Bemak, 2000; Fall & Van-Zandt, 1997; Green & Keys, 2001; Hayes, Paisley, Phelps, Pearson, & Salter, 1997; Keys, Bemak, Carpenter, & King-Sears, 1998; Paisley & McMahon, 2001; Walsh, Howard, & Buckley, 1999). Although collaborative alliances are critically important, there are no standard frameworks in school counseling to guide the design and implementation of the alliance-building processes. Models of effective collaborative practice are needed to contribute to our knowledge base and sustain school counseling's professional contribution to prevention and social justice. Interprofessional collaborative efforts have great potential to improve urban schools and communities. Professional disciplines can inform one another if researchers grounded in different schools of thought suspend their initial skepticism and become more familiar with one another's work (Ferguson, 1999).

Despite best intentions, proactive efforts often are met with challenges in terms of initiating and maintaining productive interprofessional relationships that foster collaboration and personal involvement. This article provides the theoretical backdrop for reflecting on lessons learned from developing and implementing a collaborative university-elementary school career intervention-based research program, Career and Education Connection (CEC). This program, developed for an economically challenged urban school district, introduces young students to the world of work and helps them to understand the connection between what they are learning in school and what is expected in the work world. Given the effectiveness of career interventions and their apparent value in contributing to academic achievement (e.g., Evans & Burck, 1992; Peterson, Long, & Billups, 1999), this career intervention program was initiated. A brief description of the CEC program precedes a theoretical discussion of the lessons learned through professional experiences with (a) initiating a collaborative university-school venture; (b) making connections and enhancing collaborative relationships among university faculty, graduate students, and school professionals; and (c) facilitating graduate student professional development and training.

CAREER AND EDUCATION CONNECTION

The CEC program was developed to improve elementary students' career awareness and self-awareness, educational and occupational exploration, and career planning. This project represents an intervention- based research collaborative program that responds to the need for empirically based elementary school-to-work educational initiatives. This is noteworthy because most interventions designed to keep students involved and interested in the educational process – and to help them see the connection between what they are learning in school and what will be expected of them in the outside world – are often left to secondary educators. As a result, even the most effective interventions at the secondary level may be received by a smaller or less-thanengaged audience. Thus, early intervention is essential. In response to this need, a university-school intervention-based research collaborative venture was initiated. This paradigm of integrated intervention and evaluation serves as a means of combining social action, community collaboration, and accountability. The CEC program reflects the integration of a social advocacy perspective and prevention efforts – both essential in keeping our youth in school and engaged in the educational process.

The CEC program sets out among its primary objectives to (a) enhance the academic, personal/ social, and career development of elementary school youth; (b) initiate an intervention-based research initiative that directly benefits the unmet educational needs of elementary students; and (c) establish and nurture collaborative relationships with university-school partners by providing an opportunity for university faculty, graduate students, and school district professionals to integrate an innovative model of intervention and research. Given that few elementary schools consistently provide comprehensive developmental career guidance programs as outlined by organizations such as the American School Counselor Association (ASCA, 2003; Campbell & Dahir, 1997), the National Occupational Information Coordinating Committee (NOICC, 1989), the National Career Development Association (Kobylarz & Hayslip, 1996), and state education departments, this intervention-based research initiative responds to a critical need in elementary education.

The CEC program consists of a 10-week, classroom- based school-to-work intervention for fourthand fifth-grade students, conducted in weekly 30- minute structured group experiences. The intervention uses active and interactive approaches to student learning. Weekly group meetings include instruction, discussion, art and literacy projects, peer interaction, and experiential activities. They are cofacilitated by counseling graduate students and classroom teachers from the target schools. The content of the weekly sessions corresponds to the NOICC (1989) career development competencies in three major areas: self-knowledge, educational and occupational exploration, and career planning. The CEC curriculum corresponding to the self-knowledge competency includes three sessions related to learning style, family heritage, and good work habits. Educational and occupational exploration includes three sessions on how school learning relates to work and jobs, occupational information, and exploration. The final competency in career planning is represented in four sessions with activities associated with information gathering, choices and consequences, setting goals, planning, and barriers. A literacy- rich approach that includes reading and writing activities, and an interactive career-related computer program, supplements weekly group meetings. Weekly written homework is based on instructional content.

INITIATING A COLLABORATIVE RESEARCH-PRACTICE INITIATIVE

Collaboration has been described as a style of interaction in which participants actively involve each other in carrying out their functions (Friend & Cook, 1996). Thus, some degree of interdependency exists in interpersonal interactions and the accomplishment of tasks. Friend and Cook identified six distinguishing features of a collaborative style of interaction. These include acknowledgement that (a) collaboration is voluntary and members participate without coercion; (b) collaboration requires that all participants are valued equally, and each has an equal voice in decision making; (c) collaboration is based on mutual goals, otherwise commitment to the problem-solving process wanes and collaboration diminishes; (d) collaboration depends on shared responsibility for participation and decision making, creating an interdependency among participants and encouraging active involvement; (e) resources are shared between participants without efforts to control how these resources are used; and (f) collaborative partners share accountability for outcomes. Initiating a collaborative research-practice program requires time, persistence, ingenuity, and perhaps a little luck. Based on recent experience initiating an elementary career intervention-based research program, three prominent tasks are described.

1. Identifying partnerships. Relationships between universities and schools take time to cultivate, therefore it is helpful to build on existing working alliances, if at all possible. Building on established university-school relationships may facilitate the initiation of new programmatic goals. In successful existing partnerships, trusting relationships likely have been established between the university and school, and both may have experience obtaining required administrative approval or support for collaborative projects. Familiarity with this process greatly facilitates the initiation of new proposals. Existing relationships between universities and schools, such as those evident in school counseling practicum or internship training sites, are potential partnerships to consider given established training and supervisory relationships. This is not meant to imply that new alliances are not worth pursuing. In fact, developing new partnerships can be an exciting and mutually beneficial experience for all involved.

The partnership that formed the CEC program was cultivated through an existing network between a university and urban public schools. A universitybased Center for Urban School Collaboration previously had been established between the university and five urban public schools districts. Its mission was to bring together higher education and secondary and elementary schools to work on a focused agenda of community action to raise academic achievement. Networking within the center between faculty and urban school administrative leaders resulted in the formation of a partnership to address the career education needs of an urban elementary school and eventual development of the CEC program.

Forging alliances might be facilitated by engaging in conversations with university or school personnel about what each can offer, and how such collaborative efforts might be beneficial to the partner. The following relevant questions may be considered: What are the needs of the school? How can university faculty help? What can the faculty member and this program do for the school and the children? Why is this important? What will it cost the university and school in time and resources? For the CEC program, these conversations were initiated and facilitated by the infrastructure of the Center for Urban School Collaboration that provided a meeting place for university faculty and school leaders.

2. Integrating program development with programmatic research. Program development is best accomplished in conjunction with all collaborative partners. Ongoing consultation with school personnel during program development and final approval by all involved are imperative for success. Teachers, in particular, must have some ownership and "veto power" on programmatic activities. It is helpful to have a theoretical framework on which the project is based, together with specific developmental goals and objectives, to make these programmatic decisions (cf., Schultheiss, in press). Literature suggests that counselor educators are less effective in changing counseling practice in schools because they lack a grasp of the complexities associated with school environments. Likewise, school counselors have been challenged for rarely conducting systematic evaluation of counseling practices or integrating research findings into their practice (Hayes et al., 1997). Thus, collaborative interprofessional alliances that draw on multiple skill sets can facilitate the integration of program development with programmatic research.

Truly collaborative interprofessional initiatives present challenges and opportunities in program development. As trust develops and mutual problem solving emerges, this process proceeds most effectively. Moreover, intervention-based research can actually provide a rather creative solution to the multiple demands placed on faculty for research, training, and service activities. Integrating systematic evaluation into school-based programs allows the faculty member to both contribute a valuable service to community schools and conduct meaningful empirical research. In addition, involving graduate students in these endeavors provides a valuable training tool and serves as a model of social action.

For the CEC program, university faculty were relied on to seamlessly integrate the research component into the curriculum and instruction of students. Thus, data collection efforts needed to be tightly aligned with the curriculum and not require excessive time. The lack of an established psychometrically sound assessment tool to measure career progress in children provided an additional challenge for collecting outcome data on program effectiveness. This obstacle led to the development of the Childhood Career Development Scale, a theoretically derived instrument to assess childhood career development (Schultheiss & Stead, 2004).

3. Obtaining funding. Seeking funding can be a difficult and time-consuming endeavor. School personnel frequently lack the necessary training and skills to successfully prepare a competitive grant proposal. Universities could serve as a resource for support and training in the grant seeking process. Moreover, counselor education faculty with grant writing skills might be valuable collaborative partners in these endeavors. Another challenge in uncovering funding sources can be learning about various foundations, their goals, and purposes. Consultation with university development or grants offices can be very beneficial in this regard as well. In addition, meeting personally with foundation leaders can be an enlightening experience to assist in clarifying the mission and goals of the funding organization and the specific types of proposals it is interested in funding. For junior faculty focused on building a publication record and developing new courses, grant writing presents an added challenge as it is a time-consuming endeavor. One option for faculty is to turn the grant application into a relevant professional presentation or publication. Theoretically driven projects lend themselves well to these types of manuscripts.

Additional lessons learned in seeking funding include knowing the importance of professional and university relationships with funding sources, using language consistent with the mission and focus of each source, pursuing multiple sources, being persistent, and being creative in one's definition of support. Goods and services, and other in-kind contributions, can be just as useful as direct financial assistance. In fact, some grants require a matching contribution equal to all or a portion of the total support requested. Even if matching grants are not required, funding sources look favorably on projects that have already gained the support and approval of others. Therefore, seeking out collaborative funding partners can be an effective funding strategy. Collaborative partners to consider are publishers or vendors of needed materials. Publishers often are willing to provide an in-kind contribution or a discount in exchange for the visibility and empirical support their product will likely receive.

MAKING CONNECTIONS AND COLLABORATIVE RELATIONSHIPS

Nurturing new and established relationships with institutions, administrators, faculty, teachers, students, and graduates in training is essential for a program's success. However, this is not always a smooth process. School professionals have limited time away from students, and they typically receive little to no incentives to participate in these endeavors. Thus, the internal motivation and willingness to engage in the project will vary from those who enthusiastically embrace innovation to those who experience it as added work with little reward.

Contextual issues related to the school and community environment also can be very influential in developing working relationships. For example, the level of morale in the building, the teachers' relationships with the building administrator, the economic situation of the school and community, and other unique situations can and will emerge to influence one's ability to make meaningful personal and professional connections. The collaborative relationship between university faculty and school professionals becomes an essential vehicle or tool in the promotion of social justice efforts. Interventionbased research brings faculty out of their offices and into areas of their communities where they may not otherwise venture. As researchers, many faculty cross boundaries of race and privilege as they step into worlds where they hope they can make a difference. The relationship becomes a kind of psychological meeting place where university faculty, school professionals, and students come together. Thus, a sense of mutuality and collaboration is essential.

Multidimensional aspects of trust regarding motives, competence, dependability, and collegiality are essential for successful collaborative ventures (Ferguson, 1999; Stead & Harrington, 2000). Trust, a feeling or expectation of relative certainty regarding another's behavior, is thought to exist as social capital in the networks from which collaborative alliances arise (Ferguson). As such, trust is considered to be a factor at every stage of alliance development (Ferguson). For the CEC program, the alliance building process between the university and school personnel evolved over a period of time prior to the initiation of the program. Initial interactions concerned the school's need for counseling and consultation services from university counselor education faculty. In successive interactions, trust developed through a mutual understanding and acceptance of each collaborator's needs, motives, skills, and available resources. As a result, a mutually beneficial partnership was formed to respond to the unmet academic, personal/social, and career needs of students; the professional development and training needs of counseling graduate students; and the field's need for programmatic research to - substantiate the effectiveness of school counseling programs.

This alliance building process might best be understood by considering the four trust questions introduced by Ferguson and Stoutland (1999):

1. Can I trust that my allies have motives compatible with mine, so that the alliance is likely to serve, not undermine, the interests that I represent?
2. Can I trust that my allies are competent (or can become competent) to do their part in the alliance?
3. Can I trust that my allies have sufficient will and resources to be dependable?
4. Can I trust that my allies will be respectfully collegial?

The less confident that collaborative partners are that the answers to these four trust questions are yes, the less likely they will be to commit time and resources to the alliance. Thus, if there is too much doubt of others' motives, competence, dependability, or collegiality, the alliance may either never be successfully initiated or be destined to fail. Indeed, resistance to interdisciplinary collaboration has been a prominent topic in the literature (e.g., Bemak, 2000; Fine, 1990; Keys et al., 1998). Research has identified personal resistances in which members feel too threatened to incorporate new ideas or other individuals or groups into the decision-making process, or they have concerns that others either will not be cooperative or will devalue differences of opinion (Bemak; Fine).

Using Erikson's (1964) theory of psychosocial development and Tuckman and Jensen's (1977) model of group process, Ferguson (1999) outlined five tasks of alliance development to provide a knowledge base for alliance leadership. These tasks and associated tensions are thought to emerge in a developmental sequence. Success in earlier stages is thought to be important for continued success throughout the remaining stages; thus, difficulties successfully accomplishing the tasks of one stage could potentially affect later success. The tasks of alliance development, proposed by Ferguson and described next, include (a) Trust and Interest vs. Mistrust and Disinterest, (b) Compromise vs. Conflict or Exit, (c) Commitment vs.

Ambivalence, (d) Industriousness vs. Discouragement, and (e) Transition vs. Stagnation.

In the first stage, Trust and Interest vs. Mistrust and Disinterest, trust and interest are crucial to successful attempts to mobilize and unite others in a collaborative venture. Collaborative members often come from existing networks; thus people already know each other and may or may not have some shared understanding of the issues to be addressed. During the developmental stages of the CEC collaborative program, questions emerged about who would benefit from the program and how. Could a program of intervention-based research serve the needs of both the school and the university without compromising the needs of one for those of the other? The tensions at this stage also can include those involving race, class, and disparities in power.

In the second stage, Compromise vs. Conflict or Exit, the prominent task is to reach agreement on how the collaborative will operate and what its goals will be. Tensions can emerge over power, interpretation, turf, and priorities. For the CEC program, concerns were expressed by the school that the program would interfere with academic time and student preparation for high-stakes testing. Compromises had to be reached about the timing and scheduling of the program to occur after scheduled state academic proficiency testing was completed. If conflict predominates over compromise, members may drop out of the alliance and the collaboration may fail. Thus, trust is important in this stage for resolving conflicts and compromising so that the alliance can continue to progress effectively.

In the Commitment vs. Ambivalence stage, the task is to resolve problems that interfere with participants' role commitments. Tensions that could arise during this stage concern conflicting obligations from outside the alliance or from members' abilities to perform agreed-upon tasks. Ambivalence could surface if members become less confident that they possess the necessary knowledge or resources to follow through on their commitments. Conflicting obligations, competing values, or social class identity can cause guilt, which in turn creates ambivalence that can lead to decreased involvement or disengagement from the process. In the CEC program, training needs of counseling graduate students became apparent. Relevant skills in lesson planning, classroom guidance, and classroom management were lacking, and additional training and support were required. Through the coordinated efforts of university faculty and classroom teachers, necessary skill-based training, supervision, and support were provided.

The task of the Industriousness vs. Discouragement stage is to remain industrious in the face of adversity. Although one may expect that the alliance will progress effectively if it has met with success in the previously encountered tasks, it is inevitable that potentially discouraging setbacks can occur. Collaborative relationships built on trust and a history of effective problem solving are typically better prepared to emerge successfully through these challenges. For the CEC program, scheduling was sometimes a challenge with various school field trips and events requiring flexibility in delivering the structured group experiences.

The final stage, Transition vs. Stagnation, involves terminating projects and transferring resources to alternative uses, including future projects taken on by the same collaborative group. After the first year of the CEC program, the need for the development of a student assessment measure became evident, and plans for continued collaboration to make this possible were initiated. The school also became an internship site for the university's school counseling program. The failure to make transitions such as these can result in stagnation in an established collaborative alliance. Given that a prominent objective of the collaborative alliance building process is to initiate and build long-term relationships, this could present an obstacle in the process.

FACILITATING GRADUATE STUDENT PROFESSIONAL DEVELOPMENT AND TRAINING

Literature suggests that school counselors not engaging in collaboration (Paisley & McMahon, 2001) lack the necessary training, experience, and support. To counter this, faculty need to effectively integrate innovative models of teaching, service, and research into the training of new school counselors and the professional development of established professionals (Hayes et al., 1997). It is essential for counseling graduate students to embrace the needs for collaboration, acquire the necessary skills to form effective collaborative alliances, and participate in successful models of collaborative work (Bemak, 2000). Counselor educators have been called to action to nurture students to be leaders in spearheading interdisciplinary collaboration (Bemak). University-school collaborations can provide an innovative solution to meeting the unmet educational needs of underserved students and the training needs of graduate counseling students. Practical experiences with collaborative programs in the schools provide counselors-in-training with valuable skills not easily learned in the classroom. These learning experiences contribute to positive self-efficacy and outcome expectations (Bandura, 1977), which in turn increase the probability that these students, when later independent professionals, will have the necessary skills and confidence to engage in successful collaborative ventures.

An illustrative example is provided from the CEC program. A wealth of opportunities existed in this project for graduate student professional development and training. Some of these opportunities were anticipated, some were not. Anticipated was counselor growth in areas of program development, implementation, evaluation, consultation, and the development and maintenance of a social action agenda. However, despite experience with youth and schools, what was not anticipated were the challenges and training needs associated with classroom management, classroom guidance, lesson planning, and other issues associated with working with large groups of students with varied educational, developmental, social, and emotional needs. In fact, the development of appropriate program modifications to accommodate the unique needs of special needs students is a task yet to be accomplished. Most counselor education programs more than adequately prepare school counseling graduate students to perform individual and group counseling and to experience and process empathy and attunement to others. However, classroom guidance challenges all of these skills. It was learned firsthand how empathy conflicts with classroom management, and how education and counseling meet and how they differ.

The graduate students clearly communicated many of these issues. For example, one graduate student spoke of feeling pulled in many different directions and expressed the impossibility of being empathically attuned to 26 or more children at a time. Another used a metaphor to describe her feelings regarding the incompatibility of counselor training and school-based practice: "I feel like I was taught all the rules to play one game, and was then asked to play another." Needless to say, much was learned about the new training needs for students engaged in interdisciplinary collaboration. Collaboration between counselor education faculty and the schools provides an essential social action training model that can more effectively prepare the 21stcentury school counselor for the challenges that lie ahead.

Another lesson learned was how reality meets theory and one's best efforts to facilitate career development. This was illustrated by children's homework assignments. The importance of attending to the context, and the embedded and overlapping nature of career and noncareer domains of life, became clearly evident. For example, when children were asked to describe how they make important decisions, discussions of health and safety emerged, including choices related to drug use and violent behaviors. Other factors also emerged related to problematic family relationships and difficult community environments (e.g., violence, poverty, declining work opportunities), socioeconomic realities, and financial constraints. Through the words of students, the interpersonal and economic contextual realities of their everyday life were revealed. As such, ecological and developmental contextual models provide an excellent framework to conceptualize and develop effective collaborative programs.

SUMMARY

As counselor educators and school counselors explore new vistas in collaborative research-practice initiatives, opportunities for innovative social justice efforts continue to emerge and transform participants both personally and professionally. Efforts to focus attention on new models of social action and collaboration with underserved communities are rich with opportunities to make an immediate impact in the lives of many school-aged children. New paradigms of integrated theory, research, and practice encourage novel research and practicebased ventures consistent with a social advocacy perspective. Collaborative interdisciplinary interventions not only provide opportunities to be proactive in the lives of children, they also provide a valuable resource to teachers and schools and enhance the professional development of counseling graduate students by demonstrating the importance of collaboration and social action in graduate training. The theoretical frameworks provided here are offered to stimulate interest and activity in the building of collaborative alliances to respond to the complex issues facing school counseling in the 21st century.

Donna E. Palladino Schultheiss is an associate professor in the Department of Counseling, Administration, Supervision, and Adult Learning, Cleveland State University, OH. E-mail: d.schultheiss @csuohio.edu. The author would like to thank Thomas V. Palma and Graham B. Stead for their thoughtful comments on a previous version of this article, and Katie Robinson (director, Center for Urban School Collaboration, Cleveland State University) and Maureen Berg (principal, Louisa May Alcott Elementary School) for their vision and leadership. She also thanks Alberta J. Manzi and Ameerah Draper for their participation in the collaborative career program described in this article.

REFERENCES

American School Counselor Association. (2003). *The ASCA national model: A framework for school counseling programs.* Alexandria, VA: Author.

Bandura, A. (1977). Self-efficacy: Toward a unifying theory of behavioral change. *Psychological Review, 84,* 191–215.

Bemak, F. (1998). Interdisciplinary collaboration for social change: Redefining the counseling profession. In C. C. Lee & G. R. Walz (Eds.), *Social action: A mandate for counselors* (pp. 279–292). Alexandria, VA: American Counseling Association.

Bemak, F. (2000).Transforming the role of the counselor to provide leadership in educational reform through collaboration. *Professional School Counseling, 3*, 323–331.

Bronfenbrenner, U. (1979). *The ecology of human development.* Cambridge, MA: Harvard University Press.

Campbell, C. A., & Dahir, C. A. (1997). *The national standards for school counseling programs.* Alexandria,VA: American School Counselor Association.

Erikson, E. (1964). *Childhood and society.* New York:W.W. Norton & Co.

Evans, J.H., & Burck, H.D. (1992).The effects of career education interventions on academic achievement: A metaanalysis. *Journal of Counseling and Development, 71*, 63–68.

Fall, M., & VanZandt, C. E. Z. (1997). Partners in research: School counselors and counselor educators working together. *Professional School Counseling, 1*, 2–3.

Ferguson, R. F. (1999). Conclusion: Social science research, urban problems, and community development alliances. In R. F. Ferguson & W.T. Dickens (Eds.), *Urban problems and community development* (pp. 569–610). Washington, DC: Brookings Institution Press.

Ferguson, R. F., & Stoutland, S. E. (1999). Reconceiving the community development field. In R. F. Ferguson & W.T. Dickens (Eds.), *Urban problems and community development* (pp. 33–76).Washington, DC: Brookings Institution Press.

Fine, M. J. (1990). Facilitating home-school relationships: A family- oriented approach to collaborative consultation. *Journal of Educational and Psychological Consultation, 1*, 169–187.

Friend, M., & Cook, L. (1996). *Interactions: Collaboration skills for school professionals* (2nd ed.). White Plains, NY: Longman.

Green, A., & Keys, S.G. (2001). Expanding the developmental school counseling paradigm:Meeting the needs of the 21st century students. *Professional School Counseling, 5*, 84–95.

Hayes, R. L., Paisley, P.O., Phelps, R. E., Pearson, G., & Salter, R. (1997). Integrating theory and practice: Counselor educator– school counselor collaborative. *Professional School Counseling, 1*, 9–12.

Hobbs, B. B., & Collison, B. B. (1995). School community agency collaboration: Implications for the school counselor. *School Counselor, 43*, 58–65.

Keys, S. G., & Bemak, F. (1997). School-family-community linked services: A school counseling role for changing times. *The School Counselor, 44*, 255–263.

Keys, S. G., Bemak, F., Carpenter, S. L., & King-Sears, M. E. (1998). Collaborative consultant: A new role for counselors serving at-risk youths. *Journal of Counseling & Development, 76*, 123–133.

Kobylarz, L., & Hayslip, J. (1996). *National career development guidelines: K-adult handbook.* Des Moines, WA: NOICC Training Support Center.

Lerner, R.M. (1995). *America's youth in crisis: Challenges and opportunities for programs and policies.* Thousand Oaks, CA: Sage.

National Occupational Information Coordinating Committee. (1989). *National career development guidelines: Local handbook for elementary schools.* Washington, DC: Author.

Paisley, P.O., & McMahon, H. G. (2001). School counseling for the 21st century: Challenges and opportunities. *Professional School Counseling, 5*, 106–115.

Peterson, G.W., Long, K. L., & Billups, A. (1999). The effect of three career interventions on educational choices of eighth grade students. *Professional School Counseling, 3*, 34–42.

Schultheiss, D. E. P. (in press). Elementary career intervention programs: Social action initiatives. *Journal of Career Development.*

Schultheiss, D., & Stead, G. B. (2004). Childhood Career Development Scale: Scale construction and psychometric properties. *Journal of Career Assessment, 12*, 113–134.

Stead, G. B., & Harrington, T. F. (2000). A process perspective of international research collaboration. *The Career Development Quarterly, 48*, 323–331.

Tuckman, B.W., & Jensen, M. A. (1977). Stages of small-group development revisited. *Group & Organization Studies, 2*, 419–427.

Walsh, M. E., Howard, K. A., & Buckley, M. A. (1999). School counselors in school-community partnerships: Opportunities and challenges. *Professional School Counseling, 2*, 349–356.

Whiston, S. C. (2002). Response to the past, present, and future of school counseling: Raising some issues. *Professional School Counseling, 5*, 148–155.

Whiston, S. C., & Sexton, T. L. (1998). A review of school counseling outcome research: Implications for practice. *Journal of Counseling and Development, 76*, 412–426.

Three Narratives of Parent-Educator Relationships: Toward Counselor Repertoires for Bridging the Urban Parent-School Divide

By Hollyce C. Giles

This article originally appeared in *Professional School Counseling*, Vol. 8, No. 3, 2005.

Drawing on the concept of a narrative, this article describes three basic patterns underlying the roles and relationships between parents and educators in urban schools: the deficit, in loco parentis, and relational narratives. The author offers evidence for the narratives from the research literature and from her interviews and participant observation as a counselor, consultant, and researcher in urban school reform initiatives. The article concludes by identifying repertoires that counselors can use to foster relationships between parents and educators that enhance the academic achievement and social and emotional development of students.

In an op-ed piece written in *The New York Times*, Anika Rahman, a New York lawyer of Bangladeshi origin, described her thoughts in the wake of anti-Arab sentiment in the days after the attacks on the World Trade Center,

> I am so used to thinking about myself as a New Yorker that it took me a few days to begin to see myself as a stranger might: a Muslim woman, an outsider, perhaps an enemy of the city. Before last week, I had thought of myself as a lawyer, a feminist, a sister, a friend, a woman on the street. Now I begin to see myself as a brown woman who bears a vague resemblance to the images of terrorists we see on television and in the newspapers. ... I feel myself losing the power to define myself. ... (Rahman, 2001, p. A27)

Here, in a time of crisis and intense anxiety in New York City, Ms. Rahman wrote of the power of other's expectations over her own thinking, especially about herself. The pervasive stereotypic images of Arabs in the media challenged her own sense of her identity and, ultimately, her very power to define herself. Images from the media, as well as social cues that she received during everyday interactions, framed expectations about her identity, her actions, and her thoughts.

In this article, I want to suggest that in the social arena of relations in urban school reform initiatives in economically poor and working-class communities, a process similar to what Rahman experienced occurs between professional educators and parents. Whereas Rahman's sense of identity was reframed by the events following 9/11, so too, I suggest, are parents' identities reframed when they enter the educational arena to try to help to improve their children's schools. That is, a similar process occurs for parents in which social cues bear down upon, and potentially reframe, parents' sense of who they are and what their role ought to be as parents. In many cases, they receive the message that they may be called upon to help their children, but only in a limited, predefined capacity. This capacity is not defined by the parents themselves, but rather is defined for them by educators. These expectations for urban, inner-city parents about their behavior and where they fit into the school picture are transmitted via social narratives and roles. The cues for these roles may be subtle or direct, but their cumulative effect conveys powerful expectations to parents that potentially undercut their very notions about who they are, their capacity for imagining better schools for their children, and, hence, their ability to effectively transform those schools.

The purpose of this article is to offer school counselors and other educators a conceptual framework for discerning the nature and quality of their relationships with parents in urban schools. To describe basic patterns of roles and relationships between educators and parents, the thrust of the article will be to outline three "narratives" of parent-educator relationships: the *deficit narrative*, the *in loco parentis narrative*, and the *relational narrative*. The first two narratives offer more limiting and passive roles for parents, whereas the third narrative, the relational narrative, contains more active, dynamic roles for them. Evidence for all three narratives comes from both the research literature and my participant observation as a counselor, consultant, and researcher in several urban school reform initiatives.[1] After discussing the three parent-educator narratives, the article will identify repertoires, or sets of practices, that counselors can develop to change the narrative of relationships between parents and educators in their school, to a narrative that better supports the academic achievement and personal development of all of their students.

I also use the narratives as a lens through which to examine recent recommendations for school counselor approaches to use to develop relationships between parents and schools (Bemak & Cornely, 2002), and the parents' role in the conceptual framework of the Transforming School Counseling Initiative (Education Trust, 2003). My aim is that by drawing upon these narratives, counselors can determine the extent to which they and other educators may be participating in narratives of relationships

---

[1] The names of individuals and locations in my consulting and research are pseudonyms to preserve the anonymity of participants.

with parents that limit and hence undermine theirs and the parents' contribution to the education of the children or youth in their school.

THREE NARRATIVES OF PARENTEDUCATOR RELATIONSHIPS: THEORETICAL FRAMEWORK

A substantial body of research documents the contribution of strong, trusting relationships between professional educators and parents to the success of initiatives to improve urban schools and increase student achievement (Bryk & Schneider, 2002; Henderson & Mapp, 2002; Hoover-Dempsey & Sandler, 1997). Studies also show that differences in race and social class between parents and educators, and the differential power of their institutional roles, pose significant barriers to developing such relationships (Abrams & Gibbs, 2002; Giles, 2002; Gold, Rhodes, Brown, Lytle, & Waff, 2001; Horvat, Weininger, & Lareau, 2002; Lawson, 2003; Smrekar & Cohen-Vogel, 2001). A recent group of studies, however, has found that although race, class, and power differences between parents and educators clearly have a strong impact on relationships, the local culture created by educators and parents in a school can minimize the potentially negative impact of these differences. By working to transform the traditional, bureaucratic culture typically found in urban schools into a more relational culture, educators and parents in several reform initiatives, often in collaboration with community organizing groups, have developed close and fruitful relationships with each other, across differences of race and social class (Gold, Simon, & Brown, 2002; Lewis & Forman, 2002; Shirley, 1997).

To identify and explore these different cultures and patterns of relationships between parents and educators, the work of scholars recently has converged upon the concept of roles. In describing a social process similar to that reflected in Rahman's (2001) experience after 9/11, researchers note that parents' perception of the appropriate role for them in a particular school appears to be a function of the way the school treats them. Roles, defined as the expectations that groups have for the behavior of particular members (Hoover-Dempsey & Sandler, 1997), are informal and often implicit, evolve over time in the context of an organization, and influence individuals' ideas about how they should act and the nature of their relationships with people in other roles (Smrekar & Cohen-Vogel, 2001). In their observations of the daily life of urban schools, scholars have identified a variety of roles, or sets of expectations, that have emerged for parents – for example, *client, consumer, collaborator* (Gold et al., 2001; Lewis & Forman, 2002), *comrades in struggle* (Lewis & Forman), *welfare parent, parent-in-recovery, bureaucrat, citizen* (Giles, 2001), *monitor, helper, advocate, decision-maker* (Abrams & Gibbs,

2002), *supporter, and fund-raiser* (Smrekar & Cohen-Vogel). Each is shaped through a gradual social process in one's everyday interactions with educators in schools.

In this article, I will expand upon the concept of roles and invoke the concept of *narrative* to describe different logics of relationships between parents and educators in urban schools. A narrative has the advantage of pointing to distinctive ways of "ordering experience," or "of constructing reality" (Bruner, 1986, p. 11), which underlie particular parent- school relationships, as opposed to simply identifying clusters of roles. In Kathleen Casey's (1995) review of narrative research in education, she identified one strand of narratives as falling within what Gramsci (1980) called the "collective subjective," in which "a distinctive definition of the self and its relationship to others is generated" (Casey, p. 222). In this article, excerpts from individual narratives by parents and educators, along with data from observations of schools, will be offered as evidence for three larger "meta-narratives," or collective subjectives, describing patterns of relationships between parents and educators in schools.

As such, the larger narrative here is considered to be a basic story or plot that captures the essential logic underlying actors' ways of acting and interacting in a system or organization. Although the culture of a school typically is characterized by one dominant narrative between parents and educators, pockets of "counternarratives" or alternative narratives may be reflected in the language and behavior of some teachers and parents at the school. In the following sections, the three narratives – deficit, in loco parentis, and relational – will be described, with examples of each from the research literature and from my own work as a counselor, consultant, and researcher in urban schools involved in reform initiatives.

THE DEFICIT NARRATIVE

In this narrative, educators consider working-class and low-income parents to be deprived, deviant, or "at-risk" and have low expectations for their involvement in their children's education (Laosa, 1983; Lawson, 2003; Swadener, 1995). School professionals hold low expectations for educational achievement or personal growth and development for students and for their parents. Educators view the perceived pathologies and problems of families as undermining their ability as educators to successfully teach their children.

Historical evidence of a deficit narrative goes back to the origins of the role of the school counselor. William Cutler (2000) wrote, "Between 1905 and 1930, visiting teachers, vocational counselors, and school nurses joined the professional team. It was up to them to save the American family, by dispelling maternal ignorance about the nature of childhood and the principles of homemaking" (p. 9). Cutler added that many of those teachers and mental health professionals "disdained the people they professed to be helping, failing to distinguish between the real and imagined deficiencies of African-American, immigrant, and working-class parents and children" (p. 10).

Abundant evidence can be found for a deficit narrative in contemporary educational contexts. Describing their conversations with the principal and other school staff as they prepared to set up interviews with parents in an elementary school in northern California, Smrekar and Cohen-Vogel (2001) wrote,

> These officials suggested that most of the parents in the school were lazy, irresponsible, and apathetic when it came to school involvement and that these attitudes were inextricably linked to the low performance of their children. ... School officials warned that it was unsafe and unwise to enter the school neighborhood and conduct interviews at parents' homes. Teachers warned that we would be lucky to get one third of the initially contacted parents to participate. (p. 85)

The authors went on to note that, contrary to the expectations of the school staff, all but one of the 15 parents they contacted were willing to participate in their interviews, and that parents "welcomed [them] warmly and politely into all the homes" and most "responded that, if asked, they would find ways to increase their involvement at home and at school" (Smrekar & Cohen-Vogel, p. 85).

One example of the deficit narrative that surfaces over and over again in educators' descriptions of their efforts to engage parents can be found in variations of the "we even offered them food and they didn't come" script. In Lawson's (2003) ethnographic study of teachers' and parents' perceptions of parent involvement, he described a representative example of this script in one of his interviews with a teacher. The teacher said,

> Unfortunately, we're frustrated because we're not seeing parents making that commitment. And, I think it's gotten to the point where the staff feels that we're bribing the parents to come in. "We're serving dinner." "If we serve food, they'll come." "If we give out prizes, then they'll come." (Lawson, p. 110)

Lawson observed that teachers view these "bribery tactics as a signal of parental deficits" (p. 110). Referring to such "bribery tactics," another teacher in the same study concluded, "It's the only way that we can get them in here to show them what's good for them" (p. 120). Lawson's analysis of these and other teacher narratives in his study led him to conclude that in that school, teachers' theory of action (a concept similar to that of "narrative" as defined in this article) for parental change was "based on defining and then reluctantly meeting the needs of parents" (p. 121).

Another example of a deficit-based role became evident during a training activity for a community initiative to reform several urban schools in lowincome neighborhoods. A Latino father, José, told me of his experience when he approached the principal of his daughter's school. In an angry, indignant tone, José told me,

> I went to the principal to tell her that a group of us parents wanted to talk with her about some ideas about how to make the school better. She told me, "Look, I'll give you letters for welfare." I couldn't believe it! I told her that I had a job, I wasn't there for a handout.

The principal projected an image of these parents, who perceived themselves as potential allies in improving the school, as dependent, needy, and trying to "work the system" to meet their welfare requirements. I labeled this role the *welfare parent*. Other roles identified in the research literature that may be located within the deficit narrative are those of *parent-in-recovery* (Giles, 2001) and *client* (Gold et al., 2001; Lewis & Forman, 2002).

In schools with families from mixed social classes, middle-class parents often contribute to strengthening the deficit narrative, reinforcing perceptions of working-class and poor parents as deficient. Abrams and Gibbs (2002) gave an example of this dynamic in the narrative they shared from a white, middleclass parent who was talking about parents' roles in the parent-teacher association (PTA) at school,

> If none of the White parents showed up, there just wouldn't be any fundraising, there would be no activities, there would be nothing. You can call it cultural, but I think for the most part White parents are fairly middle- to uppermiddle- class. They're used to being disciplined, being on time, sticking to the subject, and getting tasks done. I don't think that this is shared across cultures. (p. 398)

This parent relied on a description of parents from other social classes as being deficient in the skills needed to run a productive meeting to explain the dominance of White, middle-class parents in the PTA. As such, the deficit-based language and behaviors of middle-class educators and middle-class parents toward working-class and poor parents of children in a school can entrench the deficit narrative ever more firmly in the school's culture. While in this example the dominant parents are White, the dynamic also occurs with parents from a variety of social identity groups (e.g., different races, ages, and immigration statuses) identifying some "other" group of parents as deficient by comparison to themselves (R. Domanico, personal communication, February 2004).

THE *IN LOCO PARENTIS* NARRATIVE

The literal translation of the Latin phrase *in loco parentis* is "in the place of a parent," and it came into use in the United States in the late 1800s in court cases debating educators' right to discipline students in the place, or absence, of their parents. In American courts, the concept of educators assuming parents' rights and responsibilities toward their children has expanded to include questions of search and seizure and reasonable rules the school can set for students, such as whether they can eat lunch off-campus or their appropriate hair length (Zirkel & Reichner, 1986). In a related but broader sense, and in the meaning drawn upon in this article, *in loco parentis* refers to educators' beliefs and practices that assume that it is their responsibility to provide an academic, and often social and emotional, education in the place of students' parents, that is, with very limited or no participation by parents. This narrative shares the assumption of the deficit narrative that working-class and poor parents generally are not capable of contributing in significant positive ways to their children's education and development. However, the in loco parentis narrative differs from the deficit narrative in that it assumes that educators will be able to compensate for parents' deficits themselves, to help students achieve to high levels. Lewis and Forman (2002) captured the essence of this narrative in their observation, "Many urban schools have taken the posture of educating students in spite of their families, rather than in concert with them" (p. 82). Another way of characterizing the in loco parentis narrative is that educators have high expectations for students, but limited or low expectations for their parents.

Approaches to working with parents generated from this narrative tend to assume that educators are "the providers of knowledge and opportunity, and parents [are] the 'receivers,'" and parents tend to feel "even in the context of parent-attracting policies and gimmicks, that their input and participation is not valued" (Smrekar & Cohen-Vogel, 2001, p. 97). Though parents may be called upon to play various roles that involve them in their children's education, such as those of supporter, fund-raiser, and helper, their help is sought for the priorities and issues identified and shaped by educators. Parents also may be called to play the role of consumer in this narrative, with schools working to keep them "happy and at a distance" (Lewis & Forman, 2002, p. 82).

Evidence of this narrative can be found in several recent reform initiatives, which exhort counselors and other educators to raise their expectations for the potential of their working-class and low-income students, and to work to narrow the achievement gap among students of different classes and races, yet they do not articulate a significant role for parents in accomplishing these objectives. For example, in the description of the "scope of work" for counselors in the Transforming School Counseling Initiative, parents are not mentioned in the "Leadership," "Advocacy," or "Teaming and Collaboration" areas of work but are identified as recipients of resources under the "Counseling and Coordination" area (Education Trust, 2003). Though the role of parents may be evolving given the newness of the initiative, it would appear from the written materials that the narrative of relationships between parents and educators currently guiding the initiative is in loco parentis.

Another example of in loco parentis can be found in the training for educators offered by several school districts around the country based on a book intended to help middle-class educators effectively teach economically poor children. Payne (1998) wrote that given that poverty is directly related to existing social relationships, those who want to escape it must sacrifice poverty-culture relationships, at least for awhile. This recommendation might be understood to mean that in order to develop middle-class values, and ways of thinking and acting, students must distance themselves from their families and communities. This kind of thinking about relationships between educators and parents suggests an in loco parentis narrative. The danger of such thinking lies in the damage that it risks inflicting on students' relationships with their families and communities, as well as in further alienating parents from the process of educating their children.

An entirely different kind of dynamic occurs in contexts where educators and parents trust and respect each other and have similar values and similar cultures. In this kind of context, the teacher acting in the place of the parent is likely to contribute positively to students' development and academic achievement. Immigrant parents from Mexico, Central America, and the Caribbean islands often tell of a more fluid relationship between home and school in which they expect the teacher to act in their place. A Mexican mother interviewed in Smrekar and Cohen-Vogel's (2001) study observed,

I believe that school is better in Mexico. ... In Mexico if the kids don't do their homework, the teachers can punish them, so the kids won't be disrespectful. ... There the teachers are like parents and they can discipline the kids, because it's for their own good. The teacher is like the second parent. School is where their behavior is formed apart from the home. (pp. 89–90)

African-Americans who attended segregated schools in the South before *Brown v. Board of Education* described a similar dynamic (hooks, 1994). Unfortunately, educators in most urban schools do not have this kind of relationship of trust and respect with the parents in their community, and an in loco parentis narrative risks further alienating and distancing parents from the school and from their children.

THE RELATIONAL NARRATIVE

In the third narrative, the relational narrative, educators work with parents, rather than for them. The Iron Rule, a principle espoused by a community organizing group involved in urban school reform, exemplifies this narrative: *Never do for another person what he can do for himself* (Cortes, 1996). Educators expect parents to bring knowledge and strengths to improving the school, and parents expect educators to do the same. They hold each other mutually responsible for their parts in educating students. They build strong, trusting relationships, often across differences of race and class, and together identify and address issues that interfere with the education of students in their school.

In Lewis and Forman's (2002) study, they described an elementary school, Metro, in which a relational narrative appeared to guide interactions between middle-class educators and low-income parents. A description of the parent conferences at the school gives a sense of the expectations for relationships between parents and educators:

Parent conferences were not viewed as a time for teachers to report to parents about a child's academic progress, but as a way for the important adults in a child's life to share not only academic information, but also social and emotional information. Expert status was understood not as the sole purview of school staff but as something shared with and encouraged in parents. (Lewis & Forman, pp. 77–78)

The authors went on to note:

Parents were rarely called upon to be fundraisers, bakers, or room moms. Instead, they were involved as members of a community, as educational collaborators with important information about their children, and as comrades in struggles related to keeping the school functioning. (p. 78)

Parents' role as "comrades in struggles" with educators, taking action together to address the many issues that typically face urban schools in lowincome neighborhoods, is a central component of the relational narrative. Lewis and Forman (2002) concluded that Metro was able to develop these kinds of relationships because of the culture established by the school's principal and teachers, characterized by "no closed doors" of classrooms or offices to other educators or to parents, an openness of conflict, a valuing of the ideas and abilities of people in every role in the school, and frequent spaces for conversations among and between educators and parents, for example a weekly parent breakfast to solicit community input on different issues. Another important finding of this study, noted by other studies as well, is that educators are more likely to develop open, collaborative relationships with parents if they themselves feel respected and powerful in their school context (Bryk & Schneider, 2002).

A narrative that envisions middle-class educators and working-class and low-income parents as partners in struggles to improve schools represents a major shift in the roles and relationships typical in urban schools (Lopez, 2003). A key moment or "tipping point" of change in one school's narrative of parent-educator relationships illustrates one way that such change may come about. The story emerged in my interviews with the principal and assistant principal of an elementary school in a working-class, low-income community in a city in the Southwest about their efforts to improve the quality of education in the school (Giles, 2001). They told the story of how a group of parents in their school, with the coaching of the education coordinator of a local community organizing group, had persuaded the school district to get rid of an infestation of rats in the school in a period of 2 weeks, something that the administrators had tried to do without success for several years. The assistant principal described sharing the news of the parents' victory with teachers,

The teachers weren't involved [in the effort to get rid of the rats], and the teachers wondered, "What's going on? Why are all these parents here so early? Are we in trouble? What did we do? Oh my gosh, it's a riot." And the next day at the faculty meeting, we told them and we shared the story with them, and they were clapping and they got all excited. It was an example of these parents advocating for their kids, maybe not in the traditional educational way that we expect, but they are. (Giles, p. 142)

The administrators were intentional about communicating to the teachers that the parents could be powerful allies. As the assistant principal explained,

> These are the examples that we bring to the teachers. Making sure that the teachers know that these things are happening because they need to understand that these parents have a lot of power. And that we need to be working with them and inviting them in, in order that they can help us because there are things that we cannot do. (Giles, p. 142)

In this example of cultural change, the administrators presented images to teachers of parents as people who can be trusted and who have power that they can use to improve the school. The administrators had begun to create a culture that was open enough that they would let the parents know that there were rats in the school in the first place. In marked contrast, the norm in many struggling urban schools is to withhold negative information about the school from parents (Mediratta, Fruchter, & Lewis, 2002).

Here, it is important to emphasize that any narrative of relationships between parents and educators emerges out of the particular power dynamics of a school. Given that the usual power arrangements in urban public schools exclude parents from knowledge about the school's functioning, and from agenda- setting and important decision-making, a first step in creating more collaborative relationships between educators and parents often has involved community groups joining with parents and community residents, and in some cases educators, to pressure schools to be more responsive to parents' concerns and priorities (Lopez, 2003). It is in this context of power relations that school counselors make decisions about the norms of relationships among educators, parents, and community members that they will work to create.

TOWARD COUNSELOR REPERTOIRES FOR BUILDING RELATIONSHIPS BETWEEN EDUCATORS AND PARENTS

As tools for counselors and other educators to use to change the narratives of relationships in schools, this section describes repertoires, or sets of practices, they can draw upon to build more fruitful relationships among the adults in the school community. As noted earlier, the three narratives outlined in this article are intended as a lens through which counselors can look to discern the nature and quality of the relationships between parents and educators at their schools. However, before looking outward, at the school, it is critical for a counselor to begin by looking inward to consider which narrative is most prominent in his or her thinking about relationships with parents. Once counselors have some clarity about their own internal narratives, they can listen to the language and observe the relationships of educators and parents in their everyday interactions at the school to discern which narrative seems to be predominant.

Counselors can consider the following questions: What language do the principal and teachers use when they talk about parents? Does their language reflect high or low expectations? What kinds of implicit and explicit cues do educators give to parents about their "proper" role in the school? Do they expect parents to be passive recipients of knowledge from them, as the experts? Or, do they expect parents to help to define the school's priorities and issues it needs to address to improve? What kinds of relationships do teachers have with each other? Are their classrooms open to each other? Are their classrooms open to parents? Are there times and places for conversations among teachers about their hopes and concerns for the school?

Once counselors have a sense for the narrative of relationships that is most evident at their school, and for the narrative driving their own relations with parents, they can decide whether and how they want to try to work toward changing the dominant narrative to a narrative that is more conducive to improving students' education. Changing a narrative takes time, persistence, and the collaboration of many people inside and outside of the school. However, counselors, by virtue of their role as liaison among parents, the community, and the school, and their training in listening skills and group and organizational dynamics, are in an excellent position to offer leadership in initiating such systemic change and to play the role of "midwife" to deepen and sustain it.

One of the most basic and important steps to take toward creating a relational narrative is to develop space where parents and educators can share their hopes and concerns with each other about the school and identify issues that they would like to take action on together. These can be individual conversations that the counselor has with parents, or small groups of parents or educators, facilitated by the counselor or others identified as educational leaders in the school. In facilitating such conversations, it is important for the counselor to shed the role of expert, and simply be a good listener, as well as to share his or her own hopes and concerns for the school. Through these conversations, the counselor and others working with him or her can discover leaders among parents and other educators who can join as "comrades in struggles" to improve the school.

The counselor also can develop a collaborative relationship with a community organization that has strong ties to parents and others in the neighborhood, which will help him or her to reach out and initiate conversations and relationships with parents, and to build their capacity to take action to improve their children's education. Given counselors' large caseloads and multiple responsibilities, a community organization with knowledge of how to engage parents and train them in leadership skills can be a crucial partner. Counselors can learn whether there is such a group in their community by contacting the Cross Cities Campaign for Urban School Reform at http://www.crosscity.org or the Institute for Education and Social Policy at http://www.nyu.edu/iesp.

To develop a deeper understanding of how other schools have developed a more relational culture between educators and parents of different social classes, counselors can read stories of reform initiatives in other urban schools. Good sources include books and reports by Gold et al. (2002), Hirota and Jacobs (2003), Mediratta et al. (2002), and Shirley (1997). In the school counseling literature, Bemak and Cornely (2002) recently proposed a model for ways that counselors can develop links between families and schools. Several of the authors' proposals reflect a relational narrative, particularly the recommendations for building bridges between schools and families "so that education becomes a two-way street" (p. 325), "creating environments that welcome families," and "encouraging family advocacy programs" (p. 327). However, some of the language in their recommendations, including using the term "marginalized families" to describe families whom they perceive to be "difficult to reach," suggests a lingering deficit narrative in their thinking. Though the authors noted that they did not intend to use the term pejoratively, the term highlights the deficits of some families, as compared to other families whom they labeled as "integrated families," those who "feel comfortable at schools, and regularly participate in PTA and booster club activities" (Bemak & Cornely, p. 323). Affixing such labels to differentiate groups of parents, even if it they are only used "in-house," masks the strengths and potential contributions of some families and risks marginalizing them further.

It is important to note that working toward a more relational narrative in a school involves altering the dynamics of power among the adults in the school community and, therefore, is likely to encounter some resistance (Gold et al., 2001). As such, it will be important for the counselor to develop relationships with powerful allies inside and outside the school. The most important ally inside the school is likely to be the principal, as the person with the most formal power, though having the support of other educators and parents who are formal and informal leaders in the school is also essential. Outside the school, a community group with experience in school reform can be a critical ally in creating strategies for overcoming educators' resistance to more collaborative relationships (Gold et al.). The likelihood that some parents will not have the time or the desire to collaborate with other parents and educators to improve their children's education should not deter a relational approach with other parents; a school with even 10% of its parents engaged as leaders is of great value in enhancing the quality of education.

It will be important for the counselor to locate and coordinate training for educators and parents to take on their new roles in a relational narrative. As observed by Gold et al. (2001) regarding the Children Achieving reform initiative in Philadelphia, part of the reason the reform did not succeed as fully as was hoped is that the district did not offer the professional development that "school principals and teachers needed to work collaboratively with parents and community members, including how to work through the inevitable tensions and conflict of changing roles and expectations" (p. 47).

CONCLUSION

The three narratives of parent-educator relationships described in this article – deficit, in loco parentis, and relational – offer a framework that can be used to observe and reflect upon the nature and quality of relationships between parents and educators in urban schools. Two of the narratives, deficit and in loco parentis, place parents in more limited and passive roles, whereas the relational narrative offers opportunities for both parents and educators to take on more active roles in which they can bring their knowledge and strengths to improving students' academic achievement and social and emotional development. Finally, the article identifies repertoires, or sets of practices, that counselors can use to "midwife" relationships among the adults in the school community that are more likely to bear fruit in students' intellectual and social lives. The repertoires needed for counselors and other educators to develop a relational narrative in their school require significant energy and commitment. However, it is helpful to keep in mind that change occurs gradually, and that the process of developing closer relationships among and between parents and educators who have been isolated and distant from each other can be a deeply gratifying, poignant experience that ultimately will benefit the children and youth in their care.

Hollyce C. Giles is an associate professor in the Graduate Program in School Counseling at Brooklyn College City University of New York. E-mail: sgiles@mindspring.com

REFERENCES

Abrams, L. S., & Gibbs, J.T. (2002). Disrupting the logic of homeschool relations: Parent involvement strategies and practices of inclusion and exclusion. *Urban Education, 37*(3), 384–407.

Bemak, F., & Cornely, L. (2002).The SAFI model as a critical link between marginalized families and schools: A literature review and strategies for school counselors. *Journal of Counseling and Development, 80*(3), 322–331.

Bruner, J. (1986). Actual minds, possible worlds. Cambridge, MA: Harvard University Press.

Bryk, A. S., & Schneider, B. (2002). *Trust in schools: A core resource for improvement.* New York: Russell Sage Foundation.

Casey, K. (1995). The new narrative research in education. In M. Apple (Ed.), Review of research in education, 21 (pp. 211–253). Washington, DC: American Educational Research Association.

Cortes, E. (1996). Organizing communities and constituencies for change. In S. L. Kagan & N. E. Cohen (Eds.), *Reinventing early care and education: A vision for a quality system* (pp. 247–266). San Francisco: Jossey-Bass.

Cutler, W. (2000). *Parents and schools: The 150-year struggle for control in American education.* Chicago: The University of Chicago Press.

Education Trust. (2003). *Scope of work: Transforming School Counseling Initiative.* Retrieved January 5, 2004, from http://www2.edtrust.org/edtrust/Transforming+ School+Counseling/

Giles, H. C. (1998). *ERIC Digest: Parent engagement as a school reform strategy.* New York: ERIC Clearinghouse on Urban Education.

Giles, H. C. (2001). A word in hand: The scripted labeling of parents by schools. In G. M. Hudak & P. Kihn (Eds.), *Labeling: Politics & pedagogy* (pp. 130–159). London: RoutledgeFalmer.

Giles, H. C. (2002).Transforming the deficit narrative: Race, class, and social capital in parent-school relations. In C. Korn & A. Bursztyn (Eds.), *Rethinking multicultural education* (pp. 127–146).Westport, CT: Bergin & Garvey.

Gold, E., Rhodes, A., Brown, S., Lytle, S., & Waff,D. (2001). *Clients, consumers, or collaborators? Parents and their roles in school reform during Children Achieving, 1995-2000.* Philadelphia: Consortium for Policy Research in Education.

Gold, E., Simon, E., & Brown, C. (2002). *Strong neighborhoods, strong schools: The indicators project on education organizing.* Chicago: Cross City Campaign for Urban School Reform & Research for Action.

Gramsci, A. (1980). *Selections from the prison notebooks of Antonio Gramsci.* New York: International Publishers.

Henderson, A.T., & Mapp, K. L. (2002). *A new wave of evidence: The impact of school, family, and community connections on student achievement.* Austin, TX: Southwest Educational Development Laboratory.

Hirota, J. M., & Jacobs, L. E. (2003). *Vital voices: Building constituencies for public school reform.* New York: Academy for Educational Development and Chapin Hall Center for Children.

Hooks, B. (1994). *Teaching to transgress: Education as the practice of freedom.* London: Routledge.

Hoover-Dempsey, K.V., & Sandler, H.M. (1997). Why do parents become involved in their children's education? *Review of Educational Research, 67*(1), 3–42.

Horvat, E.M., Weininger, E. B., & Lareau, A. L. (2002). From social ties to social capital: Class differences in the relations between schools and parent networks. *American Educational Research Journal, 40*(2), 319–351.

Laosa, L. M. (1983). Parent education, cultural pluralism, and public policy: The uncertain connection. In R. Haskins & D. Adams (Eds.), *Parent education and public policy* (pp. 331–345). Norwood, NJ: Ablex.

Lawson, M. A. (2003). School-family relations in context: Parent and teacher perceptions of parent involvement. *Urban Education, 38*(1), 77–133.

Lewis, A. E., & Forman, T. A. (2002). Contestation or collaboration? A comparative study of home-school relations. *Anthropology & Education Quarterly, 33*(1), 60–89.

Lopez, M. E. (2003). *Transforming schools through community organizing: A research review.* Cambridge, MA: Harvard Family Research Project. Retrieved May 9, 2004, from http://www.gse.harvard.edu/hfrp/projects/fine/ resources/research/lopez.html

Mediratta, K., Fruchter, N., & Lewis, A. C. (2002). *Organizing for school reform: How communities are finding their voices and reclaiming their public schools.* New York: New York University, Institute for Education and Social Policy.

Payne, R. (1998). *Framework for understanding poverty.* Highlands, TX: Aha! Press.

Rahman, A. (2001, September 19). Fear in the open city. *The New York Times*, p. A27.

Shirley, D. (1997). *Community organizing for urban school reform.* Austin, TX: University of Texas Press.

Smrekar, C., & Cohen-Vogel, L. (2001).The voices of parents: Rethinking the intersection of family and school. *Peabody Journal of Education,* 76(2), 75–100.

Swadener, B. B. (1995). *Children and families "at promise": Deconstructing the discourse of risk.* Albany, NY: State University of New York Press.

Zirkel, P., & Reichner, H. F. (1986). Is the in loco parentis doctrine dead? *Journal of Law and Education, 15*(3), 271–283.

Culturally Congruent Strategies for Addressing the Behavioral Needs of Urban, African American Male Adolescents

By Norma L. Day-Vines and Beth O. Day-Hairston

This article originally appeared in *Professional School Counseling*, Vol. 8, No. 3, 2005.

Urban, African American male adolescents experience disproportionately higher rates of discipline referrals, suspension, and expulsion, which have been attributed to numerous ecological factors, including cultural conflicts and misunderstandings between the student's culture of origin and school. Efforts to reduce discipline problems must recognize that a reciprocal relationship exists between cultural thought and the expression of certain behaviors. This article helps school counselors understand the logic that guides certain behaviors of urban African American adolescents in order that they may develop culturally congruent intervention strategies that improve discipline outcomes.

Nationwide, African American youngsters account for 16.9% of the student population yet they constitute 33.4% of all suspensions (Education Trust, 1998). Several experts acknowledge that these figures arise at least in part from racial and gender discrepancies in the dispensation of disciplinary measures that result in more severe consequences for African American males, the proliferation of zero tolerance policies in urban schools that do not abound in suburban communities, interpersonal and cultural misunderstanding, vague and ambiguous policies that can give way to bias, the attitudes of school personnel, and parenting styles that do not foster in children a sense of accountability (Bireda, 2002; Tucker, 1999). Cartledge and Middleton (1996) argued that the dynamic interaction between race and poverty doubly jeopardizes urban African American adolescents who misbehave and leads teachers to make more negative attributions about infractions committed by African Americans than their other race and gendered peers.

Ecological factors can exacerbate disciplinary actions taken against African American male adolescents in particular. For instance, factors that strain a youngster's ability to conform to school demands and profit from the educational enterprise include the high density of students in urban schools, students whose culture of origin remains unsynchronized with the demands and expectations prescribed within mainstream educational settings, dilapidated facilities, inadequately prepared teachers, inconsistent school rules and regulations, heightened levels of crime and violence, large unemployment rates, substandard housing, poor health care, persistent poverty, family challenges, substance abuse, and large immigrant populations (Holcomb-McCoy, 1998; Patton & Day-Vines, 2004). All too often, chronic discipline problems lead to academic underachievement and subsequent school dropout.

ADDRESSING DISCIPLINE ISSUES RELATED TO URBAN AFRICAN AMERICAN ADOLESCENTS

Much has been written about the academic underachievement of far too many African American adolescents (Ogbu, 2003; Tucker, 1999). According to the Education Trust (2003a, 2003b), 61% of African American students performed below basic levels on an eighth-grade measure of math attainment, in comparison to 21% of Caucasian students. Similarly, 7% of African American students earned proficient and advanced scores on this same instrument, compared with 36% of Caucasian students. Sadly, by the end of high school, African American students have math and reading skills that are comparable to White eighth graders (Education Trust, 2003b). Poverty contributes significantly to academic underachievement as well.

According to the National Center for Education Statistics (NCES, 2003), 24% of children residing in large metropolitan areas live in poverty and significant proportions of African American youngsters are more heavily concentrated in the highest poverty schools. Regrettably, an inverse relationship exists between the percentage of students eligible for free lunch and student performance. As an example, 56% of poor students in comparison to 25% of middle and affluent youngsters performed below basic levels on an eighth-grade math achievement measure (Education Trust, 2003a). Classes with high-poverty and high-minority enrollments are taught by a disproportionate number of underqualified teachers, which adversely affects learning outcomes. Finally, teachers in these districts spend less time developing reasoning skills and are more apt to rely on worksheets as the primary pedagogical approach. Students who have internalized a pervasive sense of helplessness and hopelessness and who also see no connection between their education and economic mobility remain disengaged in school and mark time until they are eligible to drop out (Tucker, 1999).

According to the NCES (2003), African Americans constitute 14.7% of all dropouts. These figures represent cause for alarm because a significant inverse relationship exists between the amount of education an individual earns and incarceration. The Justice Policy Institute (JPI, 2003) has indicated that 52% of African American males who departed prematurely from school had prison records by their 30s. Current projections indicate that 32% of African American males are likely to serve prison terms. Sadly, once incarcerated, a declining number of inmates avail themselves of educational programs (JPI). Unless African American male adolescents are taught and counseled in some radically different ways, an inordinate number of these young men will remain trapped in a social and economic caste system that severely limits their job prospects, curtails economic prosperity, and impedes overall quality of life (Patton & Day-Vines, 2004).

If education functions as the great equalizer, then educational prospects for African American adolescents must improve. Given the recent demands for systemic, outcome-oriented approaches to the delivery of school counseling programs, it is expected that school counselors will play a pivotal role in eliminating barriers that distance poor and minority children from their more economically privileged and educationally prepared peers (Butler, 2003).

This article opens with a discussion of culture and its impact on the academic performance and behavioral outcomes of urban, African American male adolescents, continues with a profile of African American male adolescents, and closes with a set of culturally congruent strategies for addressing discipline with African American males in the school setting.

Culture

Culture refers to the sum total ways of living developed by a group of human beings to satisfy biological and psychological needs. Ordinarily, culture includes patterns of thought, behavior, language, customs, institutions, and material objects (Leighton, 1982). Culture also has been defined as the integrated pattern of human behaviors that includes thoughts, communication, action, customs, beliefs, values, and instructions of a racial, ethnic, religious, or social group (Leighton). Different cultural groups have identified different solutions to cultural problems. At times, cultural differences contribute to cultural conflict, particularly when the dominant cultural group imposes a universal imperative that presumes its way of thinking, behaving, and responding to the world is superior (Patton & Day-Vines, 2004).

A mainstream American cultural orientation endorses competition, individualism, a nuclear family constellation, religion as separate from other aspects of life, and mastery over nature, whereas an African American cultural orientation promotes a collective orientation, an extended family network, religion as integral to other aspects of life, and harmony with nature. These cultural attributes reflect modal characteristics that apply to many, though certainly not all, African American adolescents. In fact, manifestations of these cultural traits may be mediated by social class, education, ethnic identification, and affiliation (Gay, 2000).

All too often, the culture of the home and the culture of the school remain at odds leading to cultural discontinuities between African American students and the schools they attend (Patton & Day- Vines, 2004). In fact, this rift between the school and the community has been attributed in large measure to academic failure, high rates of suspension and expulsion, and the overrepresentation of African American males in particular in special education programs and their underrepresentation in gifted education programs (Bireda, 2002; Lee, 1996; Patton, 1998). Moreover, as we discuss later in this article, cultural orientation contributes to the behavioral styles of many urban, African American male adolescents. Counselors who understand the central properties of urban African American culture are better positioned to develop effective interventions that improve discipline outcomes.

In order for school counselors to help change inappropriate school behavior, they must understand the logic governing certain decisions of urban, African American male adolescents. Without this critical piece of information, many well-intentioned interventions will not succeed (Noguera, 2002). With this fact in mind, the next section of this article addresses race-specific information that considers the African American male subculture and ethnic variations in communication patterns. School counselors equipped with this information will have added insight regarding the social and cultural experiences of urban African American adolescents and can use this information to design culturally congruent strategies for promoting prosocial behavior.

African American Male Subculture

The urban, African American male subculture often endorses values that reflect the direct antithesis of healthy psychosocial functioning, such as academic underachievement, aggression, substance abuse, sexual promiscuity, and illegal activity (Corbin & Pruitt, 1999; Lee, 1996; Poussaint & Alexander, 2000). These behaviors represent a reactionary stance toward a society that devalues African American manhood.

Historically, the church and the family have served as strong socializing agents within the African American community, which have deterred youngsters from certain maladaptive behaviors. Regrettably, (a) the declining significance of the family and church, (b) premature parenting by individuals whose own psychosocial needs remain unmet, (c) ineffectual adult male role models resulting from the historical emasculation of many African American males, (d) the impersonal nature of urban environments, (e) economic distress, (f) decreasing access to legitimate opportunities, and (g) dwindling school and community resources jeopardize the psychological well-being of many adolescents, leaving an alarming number of young men to construct their own misguided definitions of African American manhood (Day-Vines & Day-Hairston, 2004; Lee, 1996; Majors & Billson, 1992).

The African American male subculture makes unreasonable and coercive demands that its members exhibit a tough persona and deny personal vulnerability. Any expression of human frailty or a desire to achieve academically and engage in prosocial behaviors may engender ridicule, ostracism, and humiliation from the peer group. In the absence of a psychologically safe environment that permits the expression of personal angst and vulnerability, many adolescents outwardly exude a false bravado yet inwardly harbor feelings of self-doubt, insecurity, fear, and internal strife that lead to self-defeating and self-destructive behaviors. Tragically, several realities within the African American community may mitigate against seeking counseling services as a mechanism of social support (Day-Vines & Day-Hairston, 2004; Poussaint & Alexander, 2000).

First, African American cultural norms discourage intimate self-disclosures with strangers (Tucker, 1999). A common refrain in many African American households is as such: "What goes on in this house stays in this house" – and, by extension, the peer group. This reticence around disturbing personal experiences may preclude urban, African American male adolescents from obtaining needed relief from personal problems. Second, the family and church may no longer function as viable support mechanisms for a host of urban, African American male adolescents as described above (Poussaint & Alexander, 2000). Third, socialization within the African American male subculture endorses physical and sexual prowess, aggression, suppression of feelings, and ritualized forms of speech, gait, and demeanor, such that deviations from this identity structure are regarded as effeminate behavior (Lee, 1996; Majors & Billson, 1992). Fourth, physical and psychological strength have been extolled as virtues within the African American community to such an extent that when individuals actually encounter personal vulnerability they may equate inner turmoil and psychological distress as indicators of personal weakness (Poussaint & Alexander).

In the absence of appropriate outlets for the expression of personal angst, many adolescents may express suffering by engaging in delinquency, acting-out behaviors, hostility, and physical aggression, all of which can lead to suspension and expulsion in schools. Finally, historical experiences with racism and discrimination may contribute to a cultural mistrust of authority figures such as school personnel (Cartledge & Middleton, 1996).

School counselors can best assist urban, African American male adolescents by providing this information to those who make disciplinary decisions regarding these youngsters, by making appropriate referrals (i.e., counseling versus special education placement), and by equipping these young men with strategies to modify behavior problems. As a caveat, the manifestation of certain inappropriate behaviors should not exempt students from assuming responsibility for their actions, but should help school counselors identify an appropriate array of nonpunitive interventions that will result in antirecidivism. Just as school personnel can misconstrue student cries for help as defiance and insubordination, so too can they misinterpret African American communication styles. The next section of this article addresses ethnic variations in communication patterns.

Communication Styles

Cultural misunderstanding and misattributions between urban African American males and school personnel contribute to the preponderance of discipline referrals, suspensions, and expulsions (Bireda, 2002; Tucker, 1999). African Americans with high levels of ethnic affiliation exhibit a distinctive set of communication styles that does not conform readily to the norms and expectations required in mainstream educational settings. Many urban African American students may communicate with one another and with school personnel in a manner characterized as loud, intense, and confrontational even without having accompanying feelings of anger (Bireda; Cartledge & Middleton, 1996). Onlookers may regard this conduct as volatile and assume that a fight is impending. Contrariwise, many Caucasians rely on more dispassionate, impersonal, and emotionally restrained communication styles. Nothing is inherently wrong with either form of communication, but when interpreted outside a particular cultural context, certain interpersonal styles may be regarded as rude and inappropriate and lead to an increase in disciplinary referrals for urban African American males.

Similarly, when African American youngsters perceive a particular injustice, they may feel entitled to an explanation from authority figures without right of refusal. In comparison, European culture permits the right of refusal to a communication (Cartledge & Middleton, 1996). School counselors can best assist students by helping them recognize the dimensions of each cultural orientation and by giving urban adolescents strategies to behave in accordance with established school norms while respecting the student's culture of origin.

During general discourse, many African Americans engage in very spontaneous and interactive communication styles that do not require turn taking or permission from others to speak (Gay, 2000). This African American cultural feature can cause problems within the classroom setting for African American youngsters, particularly because European cultural dictates mandate sequential versus simultaneous patterns of interaction. Outside an African American cultural context, this stylistic orientation may be regarded as impulsive and can create considerable consternation for individuals unfamiliar with the African American cultural experience. Analogously, repeated reprimands for expressing culturally derived communication styles may irritate African American youngsters, diminish their sense of self-worth, lead to escalating discipline problems, and impede academic progress. Elsewhere, other scholars have presented a more elaborated discussion of ethnic variations in communication styles as well as strategies (Bireda, 2002; Cartledge & Middleton, 1996; Tucker, 1999).

Those unfamiliar with ethnic variations in communication patterns may not recognize them as artifacts of culture. As counselors hone their race-specific understanding of urban African American males, they will recognize ethnic variations in communication patterns as artifacts of culture. Cultural congruence results when school counselors can provide students with a repertoire of strategies for responding appropriately to the behavioral demands and expectations of schools. Counselors can enlist their leadership and advocacy skills by helping school personnel understand the central properties of culturally distinct communication patterns in ways that do not penalize urban, African American male adolescents. Consultation and in-service training may represent the most efficient means for the dissemination of this information. In the final section of this article, we enumerate several culturally congruent strategies for addressing the discipline and behavioral needs of urban African American male adolescents.

IMPLICATIONS FOR PROFESSIONAL SCHOOL COUNSELORS
Individual and Small-Group Counseling
Individual counseling and small-group counseling represent effective media for promoting healthy prosocial behaviors among urban, African American male adolescents. Such counseling approaches facilitate socioemotional well-being, self-management, empowerment, and academic achievement for youngsters at risk of engaging in maladaptive behaviors (Bradley, 2001; Holcomb-McCoy & Moore- Thomas, 2001; Lee, 1996; Tucker, 1999). Given earlier discussions regarding cultural taboos associated with counseling, the school counselor may need to dispel myths about the counseling process by helping youngsters understand the impor-

tance, benefits, and dimensions of counseling (i.e., informed consent). Further, given adolescent concerns about cultural mistrust, school counselors will have to establish relationships that exude warmth, nurturing, trust, and personal respect (Day-Vines, 2000). Even youngsters who exhibit a tough veneer silently crave positive adult attention despite the fact that they have been socialized to act otherwise.

Individual and group counseling may help some youngsters explore their personal feelings related to an internalized sense of disequilibrium within the safety of the counseling relationship. Counselors who understand the cultural dynamics and challenges that urban African American males routinely encounter may be better equipped to help these youngsters. Group counseling permits urban, African American male adolescents to process their individual and collective experience, learn new coping strategies, and benefit from the safety of the group environment. Elsewhere, Lee (1996) has developed useful protocols for facilitating the group process. Most notably, he recommended the involvement of African American adult males as role models.

Mentoring Programs

Mentoring programs represent a form of early intervention that pairs students with respected role models in the community. The nurturing relationship between the student and the mentor can be structured using activities that include individual discussions, tutoring, leisure activities, and cultural awareness sessions, all of which promote personal development and resilience (Lee, 1996). Counselors can work collaboratively with members of the African American community such as the church and social and civic organizations to coordinate these programs (Day-Vines, 2000; Day-Vines, Patton, & Baytops, 2003).

Overcoming the Counselor's Own Inhibitions

Frequently, when the first author conducts cultural competency training programs, Caucasian participants question how they can work effectively with students whose social and cultural experiences differ so markedly from their own. It may be less obligatory that counselors share cultural connections and more important that school counselors demonstrate comfort and willingness to facilitate discussions that address the urban, African American male experience. Moreover, creating a safe space within which African American males can talk openly, honestly, and confidentially about their concerns is paramount. Counselors can be most effective by inviting students to discuss their experiences using some of the following questions to guide their counseling efforts: What is your personal experience as a member of this school or community? What particular challenges do you face that make it difficult to behave appropriately? How have you managed to function despite the large number of challenges you face? What can school personnel do to help improve situations for you and other students in this school?

This series of questions relies more on an understanding of how to facilitate the counseling process rather then on the shared experience of the counselor and client. Moreover, counselors who may have difficulty relating to the students' lived experience may more readily understand the affective component of a student's concern (Ingram, n.d.). As an example, a counselor may not relate directly to the relentless teasing, taunting, and peer pressure that African American male adolescents encounter encouraging them to have contempt for prosocial behavior and academic achievement, but that counselor may readily understand feelings associated with fear, intimidation, confusion, uncertainty, and victimization. It is through this invitation to share their concerns in a nonthreatening environment that counselors will come to understand the experience of their clients more precisely and develop warm, trusting relationships with these youngsters. Bibliotherapy operates as another medium for facilitating self-understanding and personal empowerment.

Bibliotherapy

Bibliotherapy functions as a therapeutic counseling technique that can have a transformative impact on the student (Vernon, 2004). During bibliotherapy, student counselees read about literary characters who undergo experiences similar to their own. It is through this shared experience that students identify and connect with the character's situation and come to the realization that others experience similar concerns. For urban African American adolescents who might have been socialized into a culture of inferiority, encouraging them to read about people who have overcome adversity may serve as a significant source of empowerment. As an example, the critically acclaimed book The Pact (Davis, Jenkins, & Hunt, 2002) is a biography of three high school friends from Newark, NJ, who succeed despite the exigencies associated with urban living. Following a brush with the law and after attending a college recruitment seminar for minority students interested in pre-med, the young men pledge to become medical doctors. The book chronicles their path to the medical profession.

Ingram (n.d.) recommended that counselors integrate sociocultural poetry into the counseling process. Sociocultural poetry operates as a literary medium that explores unique social and cultural factors that impinge on individuals from oppressed groups in an effort to promote self-reflection and problem resolution. Counselors may refer to the work of Harlem Renaissance poet Langston Hughes.

Arguably, rap music represents a form of spoken word poetry to which many youngsters respond favorably (Corbin & Pruitt, 1999). In fact, some preliminary evidence suggests that rap music can improve counseling outcomes for at-risk and delinquent youth (Tyson, 2002). Given the prominence of hip-hop culture in urban settings, rap music may represent a suitable medium for connecting with young people and helping them sort through a number of existential issues. Of course, counselors would need to preview material for appropriate lyric and content.

Social Skill Instruction

Tucker (1999) recommended providing students with self-empowerment strategies as a means of modifying behavior problems, especially because in urban environments, self-management may function as the only viable resource upon which African American adolescents can rely. She further asserted that as school counselors work to eliminate certain behaviors, they must provide students with replacement behaviors through direct social skill instruction. Appropriate intervention goals involve teaching students to (a) develop long- and short-term goals for achieving success, (b) identify strategies for appropriate management of feelings and behavior, (c) consider consequences associated with personal choices, and (d) praise themselves for engaging in appropriate problem-solving strategies (Tucker). Direct social skill instruction helps children learn to cope in situations where they have not had exposure to appropriate behaviors. Bireda (2002) recommended teaching students to strategize for challenging situations by playing the "What would you do if?" game. This exercise engages students in behavioral rehearsals such that they practice responding appropriately to negative stimuli in preparation for real-life situations.

Code Switching

Code switching refers to the ability to move fluidly between cultural contexts such as the culture of origin and the school culture (Celious & Oyserman, 2001). Because the culture of the home and the culture of the school remain diametrically opposed, students may not realize that different sets of expectations govern behavior when students move between cultural contexts. That is, behavior considered appropriate in one cultural context may not be acceptable in other settings. School counselors can best assist students by helping them to recognize the central properties of each culture and by teaching appropriate strategies for functioning in accordance with the cultural norms of each particular group, without devaluing the merits of either culture.

As an example, Malik was a tall, imposing 17-yearold student. He was engaged in an animated discussion with a classmate and started using inappropriate language during a classroom guidance lesson. The counselor pulled Malik aside and explained that sometimes she too cursed; however, when at work, she minimized this type of language. In this instance, the counselor's self-disclosure served as a powerful medium to help teach Malik that different social settings require different types of behavior, to indicate that she was not immune from such language, and to preserve his dignity and self-worth.

Democratic Values

Campbell (2004) suggested that an effective measure to decrease inappropriate behavior in the schools is to promote democratic values by (a) teaching civic responsibility; (b) using service learning to encourage students to work with student government and social service agencies on issues that affect the community; (c) helping students understand and demonstrate fairness, justice, and mutual respect; and (d) teaching students to work collaboratively to reach goals.

INTERPERSONAL APPROACHES WITH URBAN, AFRICAN AMERICAN MALE ADOLESCENTS

SSS Method

Social relationships are highly prized among African American adolescents, and the failure to connect personally with them may erode the counseling relationship (Day-Vines, 2000). Many urban, African American male adolescents are particularly sensitive to criticism and may respond defensively when confronted about their behavior, particularly if they do not share a trusting relationship with authority figures or they feel authority figures have disrespected them. Bireda (2002) recommended the "SSS" method when working with urban African American adolescents; this method refers to a sequence of providing feedback that requires the counselor to *stroke, sting,* and *stroke.* That is, as counselors reprimand students, they must first make a positive statement that affirms the integrity of the child, then sting or issue the reprimand, and close by offering another positive statement.

In a continuance of the described example with Malik, the same incident occurred several weeks later. Instead of the counselor overreacting by embarrassing him in front of his classmates, she called Malik aside and used the SSS method to discuss her concerns about his behavior. She said, "Malik, you are such a tall, handsome, intelligent, and articulate young man with a promising future. When others hear you use that language I'm afraid they might not see your charm, good looks, and intelligence. Could you please help me by watching your language in class? I'm sure I'll be

able to count on you because you emerge as a leader among your peers."
Beaming with pride, Malik returned to class without further incident. This
scenario depicts the importance of validating and affirming youngsters to
gain their respect and cooperation.

School-Family-Community Partnerships

Several counselor educators have advocated schoolfamily- community
partnerships that rely on an integrated system of service delivery that
accounts for interactions within and between systems such as the school,
family, community, civic organizations, and social service agencies (Bryan
& Holcomb-McCoy, 2004; Bryan & Mitchell, 2004). Such an approach
enlists representatives from each system to identify problems, devise
strategies, and implement programs that can improve educational outcomes for children. Each respective team member possesses a specific and
unique area of expertise and makes important contributions toward eliminating problematic issues such as discipline within schools and communities.

Team members might comprise administrators, school counselors,
social workers, psychologists, mental health workers, juvenile justice officials, parents, students, and civic and religious leaders. The coordinated
efforts of a collective body of concerned individuals in both school and
community settings will help reduce problematic behaviors. Tasks of these
partnerships may include parent education workshops, home visits,
forums that solicit community input, and the planning and implementation of empowerment programs such as those described by Lee (1996).
Taken together, these efforts can promote mutual and reciprocal relationships among the school, family, and community and ward off troubling
discipline problems. Research has demonstrated that African American
students' achievement is higher when their parents and families are
involved actively in their education (Ford, Harris, Tyson, & Trotman,
2002). School counselors must provide parents with social capital or the
ability to access resources, information, and services that reinforce and
enhance their children's educational experience (Suarez-Orozco & Suarez-
Orozco, 2002).

CONCLUSIONS

Many schools regard the academic failure and inappropriate behavior of
African American male adolescents as axiomatic; however, there are
numerous examples of high-minority, high-poverty, and highachieving
schools (Education Trust, 2003a, 2003b). Districts that have reduced the
achievement gap share certain common elements: (a) clear goals related to

student performance, (b) challenging curricula that is aligned with standards, (c) supplementary instruction as needed, and (d) well-prepared teachers (Education Trust, 2003a, 2003b). The Education Trust has demonstrated more than 4,000 schools nationwide that have successfully closed the achievement gap. School counselors can use their repertoire of skills to help stem the growing tide of discipline referrals and suspensions for urban, African American male adolescents and help them achieve better educational outcomes. The recommendations cited in this article use as a point of departure the Education Trust's position that skill deficits can be overcome with supplemental instruction such as social skills training.

Urban African American adolescents have experienced a disturbing number of disciplinary infractions that jeopardize their academic achievement and prospects for the future (Bireda, 2002; Lee, 1996; Patton, 1998; Tucker, 1999). Their disproportionate representation among students who get referred for suspension and expulsion and who suffer from academic underachievement, subsequent school dropout, unemployment, and encounters with the penal system provides school counselors with a compelling reason to consider the symbiotic relationship between culture and discipline. Counselors who understand the central features of certain culturally derived behavior and thought patterns can help promote prosocial behaviors among urban African Americans by developing and implementing culturally congruent intervention strategies.

Norma L.Day-Vines is an associate professor with the College of William and Mary, Williamsburg, VA. Beth O. Day-Hairston is an assistant professor with Winston-Salem State University, NC. E-mail: nldayv@wm.edu

REFERENCES

Bireda, M. R. (2002). *Eliminating racial profiling in school discipline: Cultures in conflict.* Lanham, MD: Scarecrow Press.

Bradley, C. (2001). A counseling group for African-American males. *Professional School Counseling, 4,* 371–373.

Bryan, J., & Holcomb-McCoy. C. (2004). School counselors' perceptions of their involvement in school-family-community partnerships. *Professional School Counseling, 7,* 162–171.

Bryan, J., & Mitchell, N. (2004). *School-family-community partnerships: Strategies for school counselors working with Caribbean immigrant families.* Manuscript submitted for publication.

Butler, S. K. (2003). Helping urban African American high school students excel academically: The roles of school counselors. *High School Journal, 87,* 51–57.

Campbell, D. E. (2004). *Choosing democracy: A practical guide to multi-cultural education* (3rd ed.). Upper Saddle River, NJ: Pearson.

Cartledge, G., & Middleton, M. (1996). African Americans. In G. Cartledge (Ed.), *Cultural diversity and social skills instruction: Understanding ethnic and gender differences* (pp. 133–203). Champaign, IL: Research Press.

Celious, A., & Oyserman, D. (2001). Race from the inside: An emerging heterogeneous race model. *Journal of Social Issues, 57,* 149–165.

Corbin, S., & Pruitt, R. (1999). Who am I? The development of the African American male identity. In V. C. Polite & J. E. Davis (Eds.), *African American males in school and society: Practices and policies for effective education* (pp. 68–81). New York: Teachers College Press.

Davis, S., Jenkins, G., & Hunt, R. (2002). *The pact: Three young men make a promise and fulfill their dream.* New York: Riverhead.

Day-Vines, N. (2000). Ethics, power and privilege: Salient issues in the development of multicultural competencies for special education teachers serving African American children with disabilities. *Teacher Education and Special Education, 23,* 3–18.

Day-Vines, N. L., & Day-Hairston, B.O. (2004). *African American adolescents and the incidence of suicide: Strategies for prevention and intervention in urban school settings.* Manuscript submitted for publication.

Day-Vines, N., Patton, J., & Baytops, J. (2003). African American adolescents: The impact of race and middle class status on the counseling process. *Professional School Counseling, 7,* 40–51.

Education Trust. (1998). *Education Watch 1998: State and national data book, Vol. II.* Washington, DC: Author.

Education Trust. (2003a). *Achievement in America.* Retrieved July 14, 2004, from http://www2.edtrust.org/EdTrust/achievement+in+america.htm

Education Trust. (2003b). *African American achievement in America.* Retrieved July 14, 2004, from http://www2.edtrust.org/NR/rdonlyres/ 9AB4AC88-7301-43FF-81A3-EB94807B917F/0/AfAmer_Achievement.pdf

Ford, D.Y., Harris, J. J.,Tyson, C. A., & Trotman, M. F. (2002). Beyond deficit thinking. *Roeper Review, 24,* 52–58.

Gay, G. (2000). *Culturally responsive teaching: Theory, research,& practice.* New York: Teachers College Press.

Holcomb-McCoy, C. (1998). *School counselor preparation in urban settings.* Greensboro, NC: ERIC/CASS. (ERIC Document Reproduction Service No. ED418343)

Holcomb-McCoy, C., & Moore-Thomas, C. (2001). *Empowering African-American adolescent females.* Professional School Counseling, 5, 19–25.

Ingram, M. A. (n.d.). *Empathy through sociocultural poetry: A six step process.* Retrieved July 15, 2004, from http://www.thecounseling poet.com/research2.html

Justice Policy Institute. (2003, August 28). *Half of African American male dropouts and 1 in 10 white male dropouts have prison records.* Retrieved July 14, 2004, from http://www.justicepolicy.org/ article.php?id=242

Lee, C. C. (1996). *Saving the native son: Empowerment strategies for young Black males.* Greensboro, NC: ERIC Counseling and Student Services Clearinghouse.

Leighton, D. L. (1982). As I knew them: Navajo women in 1940. *American Indian Quarterly, 6*(1-2), 34–51.

Majors, R., & Billson, J. M. (1992). *Cool pose: The dilemmas of Black manhood in America.* New York: Touchstone.

National Center for Education Statistics. (2003). *Status dropout rate.* Retrieved July 14, 2004, from http://nces.ed.gov/ssbr/pages/ dropout.asp

Noguera, P. A. (2002,May 13). The trouble with Black boys: The role and influence of environmental and cultural factors on the academic per-formance of African American males (Part 2). *In Motion Magazine.* Retrieved July 15, 2004, from http://www.inmotionmagazine.com/ er/pntroub2.html

Ogbu, J.U. (2003). *Black American students in an affluent suburb: A study of academic disengagement.* Mahwah, NJ: Lawrence Erlbaum.

Patton, J. M. (1998).The disproportionate representation of African Americans in special education: Looking behind the curtain for understanding and solutions. *The Journal of Special Education, 32*(1), 25–31.

Patton, J. M., & Day-Vines, N. L. (2004). *A curriculum and pedagogy for cultural competence: Strategies to guide the training of special and general education teachers.* Richmond, VA: Virginia Department of Education.

Poussaint, A., & Alexander, A. (2000). *Lay my burden down: Suicide and the mental health crisis among African-Americans.* Boston: Beacon Press.

Suarez-Oroczco, C., & Suarez-Oroczco, M. (2002). *Transformations: Migration, family life, and achievement motivation among Latino adolescents.* Stanford, CA: Stanford University Press.

Tucker, C.M. (1999). *African American children: A self-empowerment approach to modifying behavior problems and preventing academic failure.* Boston: Allyn & Bacon.

Tyson, E. (2002). Hip hop therapy: An exploratory study of a rap music intervention with at-risk and delinquent youth. *Journal of Poetry Therapy, 15*, 131–144.

Vernon, A. (2004). *Counseling children and adolescents* (3rd ed.). Denver, CO: Love.

School Counselors Collaborating with African American Parents

By Carla Bradley, Phillip Johnson, Glenda Rawls
and Arlana Dodson-Sims

This article originally appeared in *Professional School Counseling*, Vol. 8, No. 5, 2005.

Parent participation has been strongly linked to student success. Yet, in urban schools, African American parents often are uninvolved. This article presents eight strategies that school counselors can use to better collaborate with African American parents.

The changing demographics of students in public schools have been a catalyst for reexamining the role of school counselors in the 21st century. Many writers have acknowledged that in order to effectively attend to the needs of students of color, school counselors need to be culturally competent and culturally responsive (e.g., Evans & Carter, 1997; Holcomb-McCoy & Myers, 1999; Paisley & McMahon, 2001). It is important to note, however, that the role of a school counselor is not just to work with students. School counselors also must be multiculturally competent to work with parents for the benefit of students' academic and developmental success.

Many studies have strongly linked parent participation to improved student achievement, accountability, and attendance (Samaras & Wilson, 1999; U.S. Department of Education, 1994, 1995). Yet, in urban schools, African American parents often are uninvolved (Gardner & Miranda, 2001; Troutman, 2001). Moreover, Abrams and Gibbs (2002), in their study of parent- school relationships, found that African American parents often are more alienated from public school institutions than are White American parents. Further, several studies have revealed that African American parents who question or challenge the authority of teachers and administrators or who do not mirror White middle-class norms often are made to feel unwelcome within the educational system (Harry, Rueda, & Kalyanpur, 1999; Samaras & Wilson, 1999).

Although "moments of inclusion" occur when African American parents are encouraged to participate in school activities such as parent/teacher conferences and athletic events, interaction with African American parents often does not occur outside of these traditional invitations. Gardner and Miranda (2001) have contended that this break in communication between schools and parents prevents the two stakeholders from understanding the requirements and expectations of the two environments (home and school) where the student must function.

Numerous scholars (Harry et al., 1999; House & Martin, 1998; Troutman, 2001) have posited that African American parent involvement also may be inhibited by the fact that many school personnel, who are mainly White American, middle-class women, receive limited or virtually no pre-service training with African American families. For example, the wide adoption of multicultural counseling as a critical component of school counselor preparation is fairly recent, and the effectiveness of its training efforts has yet to be evaluated (Holcomb-McCoy & Myers, 1999; Paisley & McMahon, 2001). Moreover, Bradley and Fiorini (1999), in their study of counseling programs accredited by the Council on the Accreditation of Counseling and Related Educational Programs, found that the majority of programs did not require multicultural training before practicum and only 18% of counseling programs required students to counsel clients from ethnic minority populations.

It is important to note that researchers (Abrams & Gibbs, 2002; Denby & Alford, 1996; Gardner & Miranda, 2001; Troutman, 2001) have found that African American parents value the educational success of their children. Because educators have found parental involvement to be a predictor of academic achievement, African American parents have become recognized "actors" in narrowing the achievement gap associated with African American children.

School counselors are ethically bound to make the academic environment more accessible to families and communities (American School Counselor Association, 2000). Yet, a review of articles published in *Professional School Counseling* revealed virtually no information on the interaction between school counselors and African American parents. Hence, the purpose of this article is to provide school counselors with nine strategies to better collaborate with African American families. These strategies are derived from techniques often used by culturally responsive teachers and from the collective counseling experiences of the authors of this article. It also is hoped that such strategies will identify and eliminate some of the institutionalized barriers that prevent these families from participating in schools.

NINE PRACTICAL STRATEGIES

1. Explore Your Own Attitudes About African American Families and Their Children

Well-intentioned school counselors may be under the impression that collaborating with African American parents from a "missionary" perspective is effective. According to Kunjufu (2002), educators who share a "missionary" perspective often believe that African Americans should be protected because they are culturally deprived. As a result, school counselors who embrace this notion may consciously or unconsciously have the attitude of either "White superiority" or pity for African Americans.

To circumvent this tendency, school counselors can read narratives by White American educators and counselors who share their own personal journeys toward cultural awareness and acceptance. For example, Weiner (1999), a White American, middle-class, female teacher who grew up in a predominately White American community, shared how she changed from perceiving African American children as "problem" youth to becoming a successful and responsive teacher in an inner-city school district. Moreover, D'Andrea (1999), a White American counselor educator, explained in his narrative on White racism that the process of reflecting on his own racist attitudes concerning African Americans was an important step in his understanding the impact of racism on the lives of African Americans.

School counselors can expand on what they learn from these narratives by becoming active participants in the African American community. Joining organizations such as the National Association for the Advancement of Colored People or attending African American religious institutions can provide a backdrop for deeper introspection and cultural and racial development among school counselors.

2. Obtain an Accurate and Well-Balanced Perspective of African American Family Life

African American families often are portrayed in the media as crisis-ridden with multiple problems. For example, Arnold (2002) has contended that the focus of counseling researchers has been on the minority of African American families who are female-headed, poor, and on welfare, and it depicts them as representing the majority of African American parents. This unbalanced, deficit-oriented approach obscures the broader picture of African Americans and creates "narrow, flat images" of African American family life (Arnold, 1994).

School counselors must be intentional in maintaining a comprehensive perspective of African American families. This may be accomplished by an expansion of knowledge through reading about various aspects of African American culture. For instance, books and articles by Giddings (1985) and Hill (1998) provide insight into the historical and current experiences of African Americans. Popular magazines such as *Ebony, Essence*, and *Black Enterprise*, which feature African Americans doing average and extraordinary things, also can assist school counselors in obtaining a realistic perspective of African American families.

3. Establish Rapport

School counselors should initiate contact with African American parents before problems arise. Additionally, communication with African American mothers and fathers should not be limited to the negative aspects of their children (Gardner & Miranda, 2001; Troutman, 2001). School counselors can utilize proactive strategies such as contacting parents at the beginning of the school year and asking them what types of educational goals they would like their children to achieve for the academic year. School counselors also could contact families during the middle of the school year via phone, letter, or e-mail to reaffirm the counselor's commitment in attending to the educational concerns of the parent. These strategies may eliminate the negative connotation that many African American parents have toward schools, especially if they perceive that school personnel only contact them with negative news (Troutman, 2001).

4. Make Flexible Meeting Times

Many African American family members work and find it difficult to attend meetings at school (Morris, 2002). Bernak and Cornely (2002) have suggested that school counselors advocate for institutionalized changes that include establishing early morning or evening meetings. According to Bernak and Cornely, this flexibility in the meeting times would allow families to become more involved in their children's education and would better include marginalized families. In addition, making such changes in the schedule of meeting times sends a strong message to parents that the school is willing to accommodate the time constraints experienced by many families.

5. Establish Community Relationships

Evans and Carter (1997) have stated that it is important that school counselors capitalize on the common interest that communities, families, and schools share in order to better serve students. One way of making such community collaborations is by tapping into community resources. For instance, a central part of the African American community is the church. Specifically, African American ministers have been recognized as major leaders in their communities and often are sought out by African American parents for assistance when their children are experiencing behavioral and academic problems. Adolescent African Americans in particular often rely on African American clergy for emotional support for achieving higher education and career goals (Lipford-Sanders, 2002).

Because the church plays such a significant role within the lives of African Americans, it would behoove school counselors to get to know the pastor and officials of the community church. This connection with the community also may increase a school counselor's ability to establish responsive relationships with African American young adults and their parents.

6. Perceive African American Students as "at Promise"

School counselors often are bombarded with negative images of African American children in general and African American young males in particular. Information disseminated via the media and/or educational literature frequently focuses on the African American male's problems with crime, drugs, and poor academic achievement. These negative messages could encourage school counselors to perceive African American males as "at risk" as opposed to "at promise." It is important to note that researchers (Denby & Alford, 1996; Hrabowski, Maton, & Greif, 1998) have found that African American parents who perceive school personnel to be disinterested or have low expectations for African American children are more likely to disengage with the educational system.

To this end, setting high expectations for academic achievement for African American youth and understanding African American culture and history can be the catalyst for school counselors establishing meaningful and responsive relationships with African American parents. Several writers (Abrams & Gibbs, 2002; Kunjufu, 2002; Weiner, 1999) have asserted, however, that formulating productive relationships with African American parents takes time. What may appear to be resistance on behalf of African American parents may in turn be their reluctance to convince yet another teacher that their child has potential.

7. Establish Parent Groups

School counselors also could formulate parent groups for African American families to discuss their children's education and their concerns regarding school personnel and resources (Bernak & Cornely, 2002). Through the sharing of experiences and ideas, African American parents can become empowered to collaborate with school officials in implementing change at the local, state, and national levels for African American children. In addition, by attending these meetings, school counselors could better understand the common issues and challenges that confront African American parents. To encourage attendance, special attention would need to be given to child care availability and alternative meeting times such as Saturday mornings or weekday evenings with dinner provided for the parents and their children (Gardner & Miranda, 2001).

8. Advocate on Behalf of African American Parents and Children

According to House and Martin (1998), the role of the school counselor also includes social advocacy. Therefore, school counselors should speak up when their colleagues and other school personnel have not considered the cultural aspects of working with African American families (Lipford-Sanders, 2002). For example, they could challenge the questionable placements of African American children in special education and/or the underrepresentation of African American children in gifted and talented courses (Harry et al., 1999). It is important to note that history has shown that advocacy efforts are effective. The desegregation of public schools, seating on public transportation, equitable housing, and college entrance were all changed because a diverse group of people advocated on behalf of African Americans.

9. Appreciate the Strengths of African American Families

A growing body of literature supports the importance of school counselors understanding and appreciating the unique strengths and contributions of African American mothers and fathers. Unlike White American parents, African American parents have the difficult role of orienting their children toward an environment that is restrictive and often hostile toward African Americans. This particular child-rearing practice also is known as racial socialization. Stevenson (1995) defines racial socialization as the "process of communicating messages and behaviors to children to bolster their sense of identity given the possibility and reality that their life experiences may include racially hostile encounters" (p. 51).

Researchers have documented that African American children whose parents provided positive protective, proactive, and corrective messages about the effects of race were better able to deter negative societal imagery (Sanders-Thompson, 1991), were better able to develop a healthy sense of self (Lipford-Sanders, 2002), and were better prepared academically than were African American children who had not received positive messages (Bowman & Howard, 1985).

CONCLUSION

The new vision for school counseling mandates that counselors remove systemic barriers that impede the academic success of poor and ethnic minority children (House & Martin, 1998). This requires school counselors to become proactive in changing the status of parent involvement in urban schools. Facilitating systemic change such as encouraging teachers and administrators to embrace and apply these nine strategies in their interactions with African American families is one way school counselors can maximize the potential for African American parent involvement. African American parents can play an effective role in schools and their presence can enhance the levels of success that school counselors can experience with African American students.

Carla Bradley is an associate professor, Phillip Johnson is an assistant professor, and Glenda Rawls is a doctoral student in the Department of Counselor Education & Counseling Psychology, Western Michigan University, Kalamazoo. E-mail: carla.bradley@wmich.edu. Arlana Dodson-Sims is a doctoral candidate at the University of North Carolina at Charlotte.

REFERENCES

Abrams, L. S., & Gibbs, J. T. (2002). Disrupting the logic of home-school relations parent involvement strategies and practices of inclusion and exclusion. *Urban Education, 37*, 384–407.

American School Counselor Association. (2000). *National standards for school counseling programs of the American School Counselor Association.* Retrieved December 12, 2003, from http://www.school-counselor.org/content.cfm

Arnold, M. S. (1994). Exploding the myths: African American families at promise. In S. Lubbeck & E. Swadener (Eds.), *Children and families at promise* (pp. 23–34). Albany, NY: State University of New York Press.

Arnold, M. (2002). African American families in the postmodern era. In J. Lipford-Sanders & C. Bradley (Eds.), *Counseling African American families* (pp. 3–16). Alexandria, VA: American Counseling Association.

Bernak, F., & Cornely, L. (2002). The SAFI model as a critical link between marginalized families and schools: A literature review and strategies for school counselors. *Journal of Counseling and Development, 80*, 322–331.

Bowman, P. J., & Howard, M. A. (1985). Race-related socialization, motivation, and academic achievement: A study of Black youths in three-generation families. *Journal of the American Academy of Child Psychiatry, 24*, 134–141.

Bradley, C., & Fiorini, J. (1999). Evaluation of counseling practicum: National study of programs accredited by CACREP. *Counselor Education and Supervision, 39*, 110–119.

D'Andrea, M. (1999). The evolution and transformation of a White racist: A personal narrative. *Democracy and Education, 2*, 7–12.

Denby, A., & Alford, K. (1996). Understanding African American disciplinary styles: Suggestions for effective social work intervention. *Journal of Multicultural Social Work, 4,* 81–98.

Evans, W., & Carter, M. J. (1997). Urban school-based family counseling: Role definition, practice applications, and training implications. *Journal of Counseling and Development, 75*(5), 366–374.

Gardner, R., & Miranda, A. H. (2001). Improving outcomes for urban African American students. *Journal of Negro Education, 70,* 255–263.

Giddings, P. (1985). When and where I enter. New York: Bantam.

Harry, B., Rueda, R., & Kalyanpur, M. (1999). Cultural reciprocity in sociocultural perspective: Adapting the normalization principle for family collaboration. *Exceptional Children, 66,* 123–133.

Hill, R. B. (1998). The strengths of African American families: Twenty five years later. Washington, DC: R & B Publishing.

Holcomb-McCoy, C. C., & Myers, J. E. (1999). Multicultural competence and counselor training: A national survey. *Journal of Counseling and Development, 77,* 294–302.

House, R. M., & Martin, P. (1998). Advocating for better futures for all students: A new vision for school counselors. *Education, 119,* 284–294.

Hrabowski, F. A., III, Maton, K. I., & Greif, G. L. (1998). *Beating the odds: Raising academically successful African American males.* New York: Oxford University Press.

Kunjufu, J. (2002). *Black students. Middle class teachers.* Chicago: African American Images.

Lipford-Sanders, J. (2002). Racial socialization. In J. Lipford-Sanders & C. Bradley (Eds.), *Counseling African American families* (pp. 41–57). Alexandria, VA: American Counseling Association.

Morris, J. (2002). A communally bonded school for African-American students, families, and a community. *Phi Delta Kappan, 84*(3), 230–234.

Paisley, P., & McMahon, G. (2001). School counseling for the 21st century: Challenges and opportunities. *Professional School Counseling, 5*(2), 106–115.

Samaras, A. P., & Wilson, J. C. (1999). Am I invited? Perspectives of family involvement with technology in inner-city schools. *Urban Education, 34,* 499–530.

Sanders-Thompson, V. L. (1991). Perceptions of race and race relations which affect African American identification. *Journal of Applied Social Psychology, 21*(18), 1502–1516.

Stevenson, H. C. (1995). Relationship of adolescent perceptions of racial socialization to racial identity. *Journal of Black Psychology, 21,* 49–70.

Troutman, M. F. (2001). Involving the African American parent: Recommendations to increase the decreasing level of parent involvement within African American families. *Journal of Negro Education, 70,* 275–285.

U.S. Department of Education. (1994). *Strong families, strong schools: Building community partnership for learning.* Washington, DC: Government Printing Office.

U.S. Department of Education. (1995). *America goes back to school: A place for families and the community: An initiative of the family involvement partnership for learning.* Washington, DC: Government Printing Office.

Weiner, L. (1999). *Urban teaching: The essentials.* New York: Teachers College Press.

Empowerment Groups for Academic Success: An Innovative Approach to Prevent High School Failure for At-Risk, Urban African American Girls

By Fred Bemak, Ed.D., Rita Chi-Ying Chung, Ph.D., and Linda A. Siroskey-Sabdo, M.A.

This article originally appeared in *Professional School Counseling*, Vol. 8, No. 5, 2005.

Twenty-first-century urban schools face unique challenges in being cultur-ally responsive and providing quality education to culturally diverse and low-income students. The academic achievement gap for low-income and ethnic youth poses the need for new and innovative interventions by edu-cational institutions. School counselors are in a unique position in schools to assume leadership roles in reducing academic disparity. This article dis-cusses the experience of urban youth identified as being at risk as well as some of the realities facing African American students in inner-city public education, and it describes the need for school counselors to emphasize a group counseling approach from a multicultural perspective. The article presents the Empowerment Groups for Academic Success approach that aims at preventing high school dropout and improving academic perform-ance for youth identified as being at risk.

Today's urban schools face significant challenges in being culturally responsive and providing quality education for culturally diverse urban youth (Bemak, Murphy, & Kaffenberger, 2004; Locke, 2003). The grow-ing academic achievement gap with lower success rates for inner-city impoverished youth has been clearly documented and is associated with fewer educational opportunities, a poor quality of education (College Board, 1999a, 1999b; Education Trust, 1998; House & Martin, 1998), high dropout rates as a result of cultural misunderstandings, negative stereotyping (Jackson, 1999), and fewer resources (Education Trust). Although youth problems stem from a wide range of both internal and external forces (Atkinson, Thompson, & Grant, 1993), oftentimes stu-dents having problems in school are preoccupied with concerns outside the school setting. This is evident when youth are faced with challenges from social problems, such as poverty, violence, and racism, and may result in disruptions in family and community life that can hinder the emotional, social, and academic growth and development of children and youth (Bauer, Sapp, & Johnson, 2000).

The aim of this article is to present an innovative group counseling approach called Empowerment Groups for Academic Success (EGAS), which was implemented in a Midwest inner-city high school that was experiencing high rates of expulsion and suspension, teenage pregnancies, absenteeism, poverty, and poor academic records. In an attempt to work with students who were identified by teachers, counselors, and administrators as being at the highest levels of risk for suspension, academic failure, and school dropout, we established an innovative group counseling intervention approach with the goal of resolving the difficult personal and interpersonal issues faced by these students. The group intervention would serve as a means of improving academic performance and attendance. It is important to note that this article is not an evaluation of the approach, but rather a description of a potentially effective intervention strategy to work with a very difficult population, an approach that may be replicated by other school counselors.

The group was composed of seven African American girls in 10th grade, all of whom were identified as being at the highest level of risk. The first author, as a principal investigator of one of the six national Transforming School Counseling Initiative DeWitt Wallace–Reader's Digest grants awarded through the Education Trust, developed the EGAS approach and worked closely with a school counselor to implement the group intervention in an urban school identified as having students at the highest level of risk for academic failure.

Before we present the EGAS approach, it is important to briefly present information that will assist the reader in understanding the difference between the EGAS approach and more traditional interventions and the relevance of EGAS in addressing the unique challenges of urban youth. Thus the article will begin with a brief overview of the unique problems facing inner-city youth regarding educational achievement and will include specific experiences of African American high school girls in public education, the role of the school counselor in inner-city schools, an examination of the research regarding group counseling as an effective intervention for youth, and a discussion about the importance of addressing multicultural issues in group counseling.

IMPACT OF UNIQUE CHALLENGES FACING INNER-CITY YOUTH ON EDUCATIONAL ACHIEVEMENT

Inner-city youth face numerous problems that are endemic to poor urban areas and that have the potential to interfere with their ability to learn and succeed in schools (Bemak, 2002; Bemak & Chung, 2003; Dryfoos, 1994, 1998; Jagers & Mock, 1993; Witherspoon, Speight, & Thomas,

1997). Findings have shown that inner-city youth experience elevated rates of delinquency, higher incidents of violent and aggressive behavior, greater degrees of psychological problems, heightened behavioral problems, and educational and occupational expectations that are discouraging rather than hopeful (Black & Krishnakumar, 1998). In fact, it has been found that inner-city high school students have higher rates of academic failure and greater school behavioral problems (Allen & Mitchell, 1998; Gallay & Flanagan, 2000; Kenny, Gallagher, Alvarez-Salvat, & Silsby, 2002; Sameroff & Seifer, 1995).

For example, the overall national dropout rates were 11% compared to 14% for children in poverty (Annie E. Casey Foundation, 2000). The condition of poverty correlated with increased risks for feelings of hopelessness and other associated problems (Bolland, 2003, Boyd-Franklin, 1995; Guerra, Huesmann, Tolan, Van Acker, & Eron, 1995), such as substance abuse, violent and aggressive behavior, and teenage pregnancy. Other studies have shown significantly higher dropout rates, with 3 times the number of dropouts in severely distressed, impoverished neighborhoods (Kasarda, 1993).

Another important factor in urban life is the presence of violence. Fitzpatrick and Boldizar (1993) found that almost 85% of low-income, inner-city African American youths had witnessed at least one violent act while 43.3% reported witnessing a murder, contributing to the higher rates of post-traumatic stress disorder. This is correlated with findings that children who witness domestic violence at home exhibit a variety of behavioral and emotional problems while children who witness community violence imitate the behavior and become more aggressive (Guerra, Huesmann, & Spindler, 2003; Osofsky, 1999). Bemak and Chung (1998) coined the term *psychological recoil effect*, based on findings from a national study of Amerasian youth who were resettled in the United States from Vietnam, where the actual observing of an act of violence contributed to higher levels of stress and trauma than actually being victimized. These findings can be generalized to other populations who witness violent acts, and it has particular relevance to high-poverty, high-crime areas.

Inner-city youth are aware of threats to personal safety, and hence they may be involved in gangs and drug and alcohol use to cope with living in dangerous neighborhoods and heightened feelings of hopelessness (Bolland, 2003; Dembo, Blount, Schmeidler, & Burgos, 1986). Studies have shown that adolescents who act out in the classroom, skip school, and experience academic failure and poor motivation are more likely to use alcohol, cigarettes, and marijuana (Bryant, Schulenberg, Bachman, O'Malley, & Johnston, 2000; Dryfoos, 1990; Voelkl & Frone, 2000).

Impoverished inner-city environments that contribute to adverse social conditions have been linked with narcotic addiction for many years and subsequently have an impact on educational performance and overall negative school climates (Chein, Gerard, Lee, & Rosenfeld, 1964; Gandossy, Williams, Cohen, & Harwood, 1980; Harries, 1990; Hawkins, Catalano, & Miller, 1992; Johnson, Williams, Dei, & Sanabria, 1990; Shaw & McKay, 1942).

EXPERIENCE OF AFRICAN AMERICAN HIGH SCHOOL GIRLS IN PUBLIC EDUCATION

It is not possible to consider the experience of African American girls in public education without examining a broader perspective that helps to understand the social, economic, political, historical, and ecological contexts. African American children continue to experience chronic school failure in disproportionately high numbers (Education Trust, 1998), arguably a continuation of historical discrepancies in equal educational opportunities that result in low expectations for future success and internalized self-perceptions that are reinforced by the educational system (Graham, Taylor, & Hudley, 1998). Research has shown that urban African American children may internalize feelings of powerlessness associated with racial identity and the depreciation of African American culture (Gibson, 1993; Justice, Lindsey, & Morrow, 1999).

Although a positive identification with one's own racial group provides a psychological buffer against such factors as racism, prejudice, and discrimination (Phinney, 1996), having exposure and internalizing negative attitudes about being African American can result in negative self-images and behaviors as well as delinquency (Belgrave et al., 1994; Kunjufu, 1986; Lyles, Yancey, Grace, & Carter, 1985). Counteracting this is the development of a positive and healthy racial identity that leads to a positive self-image and adoption of a value system that promotes personal and social well-being (Thomas, Townsend, & Belgrave, 2003).

A significant amount of the research on African American girls in public schools has targeted related social problems. Studies have found correlations between African American adolescent females and greater rates of teenage pregnancy, problems with substance abuse, violence and gang membership, and high infant mortality rates (Cousins & Mabrey, 1998). African American girls who observed high levels of violence and greater degrees of internalizing behaviors were found to be withdrawn, anxious, and depressed (Cooley-Quill, Boyd, Frantz, & Walsh, 2001). Possibly as a result of witnessing violence, African American adolescent girls reported physical fighting at the same rates as boys (Hudley, 2001) and greater degrees of internalized reactions, with higher rates of suicide attempts among African American girls as compared to their European American counterparts (Millstein, 1989). Despite the problems mentioned above that have an impact on academic performance and school completion, it must be kept in mind that there are numerous examples of students of color from urban areas attaining high standards of achievement (Sciarra, 2001).

SCHOOL COUNSELORS AND GROUP WORK: WHAT MAKES SENSE?

School counselors are in a unique position to effectively address issues facing inner-city youth. However, given the wide range of responsibilities that consume school counselors' time and energy, they may be involved to varying degrees with any number of tasks, including individual and group counseling, family consultations, student assessments, test interpretations, classroom guidance, teacher consultations, and linkages with outside agencies for referrals (Burnham & Jackson, 2000; Roland & Neitzschman, 1996). A significant portion of school counselors' work may be relegated to "clerk work," especially when they are perceived by school administrators as having less ability to contribute to the educational goals that are focused on academic achievement (Bemak, 2000; House & Hayes, 2002; Paisley & McMahon, 2001). Furthermore, budget constraints and school district priorities may reduce the number of available counselors and significantly define and limit their ability to effectively do their job. Therefore, it is not surprising that counselors have felt that they needed additional time to be effective and frequently complained about the paperwork and administrative responsibilities that have little to do with counseling (Dansby, 1996).

The American School Counselor Association recommends a counselor-to-student ratio of 1:300, while the National Education Association recommends an even lower ratio of 1:250 (Hobson, Fox, & Swickert, 2000; Montano & Bucher, 1999). Despite these recommendations, the ratios across the United States are frequently much higher, with disparities in different states, such as Minnesota (1:457), Michigan (1:709), Vermont (1:313), and California (1:1,182) (Hobson et al.; Montano & Bucher; Paisley & McMahon, 2001).

Given these realities of disproportionate ratios coupled with the assigned responsibilities of school counselors that go beyond the parameters of counseling, we would suggest that group counseling may be far more effective than individual counseling as a means of intervention that would reach the total student body in a school. This would require a major paradigm shift whereby group counseling becomes the intervention of choice rather than individual counseling. In turn, group counseling would become a "stand-alone" method of intervention (Bemak & Conyne, 2004) that does not necessitate supplemental individual counseling.

Redefining group counseling as the means of intervention would assist in meeting the demands of increased student loads and responsibilities assigned to school counselors. It is our belief, similar to other researchers, that school counselors can make a difference by assuming a new role and responsibilities to address the complex problems encountered by inner-city, impoverished youth (Bailey, Getch, & Chen-Hayes, 2003, Bemak, Chung, & Murphy, 2003; Bemak et al., 2004; House & Hayes, 2002; House & Martin, 1998). Our contention is that one part of the new role is to incorporate group counseling as a primary means of intervention. The following section further discusses this shift to group counseling as the intervention of choice.

GROUP COUNSELING AS THE INTERVENTION OF CHOICE IN SCHOOLS

Not only is group counseling an efficient means of coping with increased student loads and responsibilities for school counselors, but research has shown that group counseling is successful with children and in school settings (e.g., Becky & Farren, 1997; May & Housley, 1996; Phillips & Phillips, 1992; Prout & Prout, 1998). A review of the literature (McClanahan et al., 1998) found that group counseling in schools was more effective than individual interventions, fostering better developed social competencies within groups, bringing about new insights that were unavailable through individual work, and enhancing social skill development.

Children's school-based divorce groups were found to be the most practical and efficient intervention, reducing shame and providing important peer support (Yauman, 1991). Peer modeling, problem solving, and validation also were found to be important in groups (Shechtman, Bar-El, & Hadar, 1997; Yauman, 1991) and provided critical elements into the interpersonal process that did not exist in individual counseling. The efficacy of group counseling in schools has been argued by others (e.g., Proehl, 1995; Roland & Neitzschman, 1996) who contend that groups provide a framework that more efficiently manages time constraints and provides the greatest service delivery to the maximum number of students in the most efficient manner.

Subsequently, we would advocate that group counseling in public schools is a more effective intervention in addressing some of the serious social problems facing our youth, particularly at a time when peer relationships, social skills, and social interaction are not considered priorities in an era of high-stakes testing, test results, and academic productivity. In fact, group counseling meets earlier calls for schools to become training grounds for social development and moral development (Dewey, 1963) and remains an area of great concern in today's world.

GROUPS FOR YOUTH AT RISK

Group counseling has been shown to be effective in working with at-risk students (e.g., Becky & Farren, 1997; May & Housely, 1996; Phillips & Phillips, 1992; Praport, 1993; Rosen & Bezold, 1996; Zinck & Littrell, 2000). It has been linked to improvements in achievement scores and interpersonal relationships (Shechtman, 1993) and to enhanced learning, especially when the emphasis has been on self-awareness and responsible behavior (Campbell & Myrick, 1990). Group counseling also has been effective with at-risk children and youth at various developmental stages. For example, at the elementary level, groups aimed at increasing appropriate coping behaviors have been found to be beneficial (LaFountain, Garner, & Ellason, 1996), and students in groups showed enhanced self-perception and improvement in attitudes and behavior (Bretzing & Caterino, 1984; LaFountain & Garner, 1996; Myrick & Dixon, 1985; Nelson, Dykeman, Powell, & Petty, 1996).

At the preadolescence stage, a reduction in anxiety and an increase in self-esteem were found for female incest victims (De Luca, Hazen, & Cutler, 1993). For adolescents, peer groups have been found to be helpful (Henry & Kilmann, 1979) as well as reference groups for assessing personal, social, and academic achievements (Bemak & Greenberg, 1994; May & Housley, 1996). Enhancement of self-image and improved locus of control among adolescents from divorced families (Omizo & Omizo, 1988), and group therapy of sexually abused female adolescents, were found to be more effective than individual counseling (May & Housley, 1996). In a dating violence prevention group, participants acquired positive communication skills and self-efficacy (Rosen & Bezold, 1996). Praport (1993) demonstrated that group counseling was able to improve school attrition, while Bauer et al. (2000) found significant improvement in group members' self-esteem and academic self-concept.

THE NEED FOR MULTICULTURAL GROUP COUNSELING

It is imperative that school counselors be culturally competent and culturally responsive (Lee, 2001), especially in light of the history of psychological and educational theories and practices being derived from a Eurocentric perspective that is not representative of the worldviews of many students (D'Andrea & Daniels, 2001; Lee). The same holds true for the multicultural group counselor. Bemak and Chung (2004) point toward the unequivocal need for school counselors to be effective working with multicultural groups and present extensive recommendations for training multicultural group counselors.

It is essential that groups in schools be attentive to cultural differences that go beyond traditional European-American models. To facilitate effective groups, it is important that school counselors consider levels of racial consciousness and racial identity (see Cross, 1971; Helms, 1990) that impact the functioning and dynamics of the group (Johnson, Torres, Coleman, & Smith, 1995). This involves the school counselor knowing and understanding his or her own racial and ethnic identity and cultural worldview, and its impact on the racial identities and cultural worldviews of group members.

Studies have shown that students from culturally diverse backgrounds have benefited from culturally responsive groups. For example, students' self-perception increased for African American, European American, and Portuguese children (Walker, 1991), while Mexican American adolescents exhibited improvement in educational problems, quality of family life, and mental health (Baca & Koss-Chioino, 1997). Shechtman (1993) found significant student improvement in achievement scores and interpersonal relationships from short-term group counseling for Israeli children, while increased self-esteem and internal locus of control orientation were found for Native American adolescents who participated in group counseling (Kim, Omizo, & D'Andrea, 1998).

EMPOWERMENT GROUPS FOR ACADEMIC SUCCESS: A DESCRIPTION OF AN INNOVATIVE GROUP COUNSELING APPROACH

The EGAS approach takes into account the influence of social, psychological, and environmental factors on academic performance for inner-city youth, as well as the need for a changed role for school counselors and a culturally sensitive basis for developing effective interventions. This section includes a description of the group participants and leaders, a discussion of the selection of group participants, the rationale for the EGAS approach, and finally a description of the group sessions and their impact on group members.

Group Participants and Leaders

The target population for the group was girls identified by teachers and administrators as students at the highest levels of risk for school failure. At-risk criteria consisted of demonstrated poor school attendance, disruptive behavior, significantly low grades, and associated problems at home. These students were invited to a prescreening meeting. The format and goals of the group (support and help dealing with personal and social problems and improved school performance) were explained and interviewees were given a choice regarding participating in the group. Seven African American adolescent girls were interviewed during the prescreening process and all decided to join the group. The group leaders consisted of two European American facilitators, with the university professor being the lead facilitator and the school counselor co-facilitating. Two female, Asian master's degree intern students (Taiwanese and Korean) co-led the group during their respective internships during the winter and spring semesters.

Prescreening Interviews and Participant Selection

In choosing group members, it was important to ensure that the selection pertained to those who would benefit most from the format and style of the group (Ritchie & Huss, 2000). During prescreening, the needs, expectations, and commitment of the prospective group members were identified (Couch, 1995). A survey was sent to school staff requesting referrals of students who had very poor attendance, significant problems with study skills, and difficulties at home that appeared to cause marked disruptions in school behavior and academic performance. The school counselor and the university professor interviewed each of the students, attempting to find those students demonstrating the most significant problems related to these three areas. During the interviews they also challenged students' conceptions of personal failure and hopelessness, which have been identified as important in the screening process (Couch). Issues related to group goals, client's right to privacy, and informed consent were discussed. At the end of the prescreening interview, the leaders invited the students to participate in the group. All agreed and secured parental consent forms.

Rationale for EGAS Approach

Previous failed school interventions with the seven girls included detention, suspension, repeated disciplinary warnings, attempts at counseling targeted at behavior, linking with families, and behavior modification programs. Given the history of failed interventions, this group of individuals required an innovative and different approach. The EGAS approach to group counseling was unique and different in its emphasis on empowerment through group process, moving away from psycho-educational and traditional structured groups filled with exercises and activities planned by the facilitator. This allowed members a new way to openly explore and discuss issues that created disruption in their lives whereby group process was utilized as the basis for group intervention. The group interactions illuminated the members' interpersonal dynamics and created an environment in which they, as members, determined the content and design of the group.

One difficulty for school counselors who use the EGAS approach is the fear and concern that there is less control and focus, particularly with groups of students who have a history of disruptive behavior. EGAS is based on a core belief that facilitators should not "control" groups so that true empowerment results in members having an actual say in how a group is run. This is most effectively accomplished through an unstructured process group with clearly defined goals. By using the EGAS approach, group members developed ownership and had choices about discussing personal and social problems that were directly related to poor school behavior and performance and low attendance rates. The group's decision to discuss personal and social problems was, in our opinion, directly related to their poor school behavior and performance and low attendance rates. This provided a unique and different perspective in the group without replicating the many failed prior interventions that had discounted the profound personal, social, family, and community-based problems that negatively impacted each of the seven group members.

Subsequently, each week the group participants decided the agenda topic for group discussion. This was extremely different for the girls in the group who, given their poor school performance, were accustomed to being told what to do by authority figures. Reversing this pattern and having the group participants establish the discussion topics quickly changed the group dynamics and fostered a sense of self-control and group ownership. This was the first step in empowerment, whereby the group members engaged in a partnership and actual ownership of the group process and content rather than responding to authority that rested solely with the facilitators. This is in line with a shift in which participants increasingly guide their own decisions and process (Bemak, 1998).

Topics of discussion chosen by participants included family and peer relationships, the death of friends and loved ones, pregnancy and single parenting, experiences with first sexual encounters, smoking, confrontations and poor relationships with teachers, and general school and academic concerns. The group met once a week for 45 minutes, with the time rotating in order to alternate missed classes. Teachers and school administration were highly supportive of the group intervention, knowing that the goal of the group was to enhance academic performance for seven failing students.

Group Sessions

Early group meetings. The group began in October and was defined to all participants as an opportunity to work on personal problems and improve school performance. Early sessions focused on the group members agreeing on group norms and procedures. The girls were concerned about possible contravention of group norms and after a lengthy discussion determined how they would handle any future violations. Important in these early discussions was getting a "feel" for each other and the facilitators, particularly with all the group members being African American, the two facilitators being white and one being a male, and an international graduate student intern from Asia participating.

The issue of racial and ethnic differences within the group was openly discussed and explored, forging open dialogue that created trust and open communication. Initial conversations centered on relationships with extended family, discussions about relatives "borrowing" clothing, reactions to having to baby-sit for siblings, and the demands to do chores at home. As stories about these issues were discussed, a growing awareness about relationships in the group and with others began to take shape. Along with these insights, closeness began to develop with peers and with the group facilitators.

The holidays. As the group bonded during the weekly meetings, group members began to discuss the holidays. Interestingly, Thanksgiving and the Christmas holidays brought up memories of death and loss for all the members. For 4 weeks prior to Thanksgiving, the girls reminisced about friends and relatives who had died or were dying. They grieved, sharing their sadness and tears, and expressed their loneliness and lack of support in dealing with their losses. Years of loss and sadness poured out during the group sessions, and discussions centered on never before having a safe place to discuss these buried feelings. The group talked about feeling similar to a family and the closeness of the experience. In fact, a unanimous request to the group facilitators was made to see if we (the group) could spend Thanksgiving and Christmas together rather than at the students' homes. Deep and meaningful discussions ensued about home, relationships, and safety within and outside the group. The group celebrated the Christmas holidays just before the school break, having a party with food and drink. Although the conversation during the party once again centered on loss and death, it was done very differently than 2 months before, with an atmosphere of holiday celebration and joy in being and sharing together. This was a transformation and turning point for the group.

Post-holidays. The theme of loss and grief continued in the group following the holidays. One of the girls had lost her grandmother in December while another group member acutely felt the loss of a close family member earlier in the school year during the holidays. The group members continued to experience what they called a "special closeness" and began referring to the group as "the family." As they shared about the difficulties in their own biological families, their own intimacy and openness with each other grew, confronting a talkative group member about "talking too much," challenging each other more openly about behaviors toward one another without becoming defensive or angry, and experiencing greater self-disclosure within the group.

Later group meetings. A crucial difference between the EGAS approach and other groups is the responsibility placed upon the group members to establish their own agenda that centers on the goals of the group. Thus the facilitators deliberately did not introduce a discussion about grades, attendance, and school performance but rather decided to maintain a general awareness of the group goals – for example, improved school performance – and supported the group members in determining the content of the group based on this goal. The hypothesis of the first author based on past experience was that these issues would be addressed through the discussions about other problems and eventually would be introduced directly by group members themselves.

In early February, the group brought up the subject of school perform-ance. The girls shared that although their schoolwork had improved and their attendance rates were better, they were still struggling with "diffi-cult" teachers. They discussed grades and responsibility, exploring who and what was responsible for their school failures. Was it teachers, unrea-sonable assignments, or personal attitudes and behaviors? The girls dis-cussed the disrespect and prejudice they occasionally experienced from teachers, and they talked about ways to better deal with these situations. The discussion led to deep reflection about how they should in turn treat others, arriving at a strong consensual agreement not to mistreat anyone in ways they felt mistreated by some teachers.

A struggle with feeling mistreated by teachers and their own values and behaviors regarding the treatment of others was symbolized by a conflict over a bucket of candy in the group on Valentine's Day. The girls began to grab at the candy, trying to get their favorite kinds. The facilitators prompt-ed a discussion about how to divide the candy, generating a mixture of responses. A heated discussion followed with some of the girls arguing that those who weren't behaving properly should be "whooped" (beaten); oth-ers felt that names should be written on the board (one member actually stood and wrote names of those who were "misbehaving"); while another member declared that she was the "mother" of the group (she was the only member who had a child) and therefore everyone should listen to her. Expressing strong feelings while respecting and listening to each other's reactions eventually led to an agreement about how to amicably divide the candy. As the girls reflected on how they handled this difficult problem, they agreed and reaffirmed that the group was indeed a family!

The family theme deepened during the next session when the first counseling graduate student intern was finishing her placement. The group members wrote messages to the intern on the board expressing their sadness that she was leaving and mourning over the breakup of the "family." Group members agreed that it was too difficult to talk about saying goodbye to a "family member," and the loss of the intern was not only a painful event, but it reminded them of other losses. Even so, they found themselves talking to the intern about her leaving in an honest and open manner, reflecting on how different it was to talk about their pain in the group.

Intimacy within the group continued in the following session with one member discussing the abuse she suffered after an argument with her aunt. Two other members shared stories of abuse by family members for the first time. Feelings of abuse were associated with other neglectful situations, and they discussed emotional abandonment by parents or guardians who paid more attention to significant others. The group discussed the pain and hurt they felt at being second in their parent's or guardian's life, sharing their deep-rooted discomfort. One member actually wrote lyrics to a song during the group to express her feelings.

A few weeks later a new intern joined the group and was warmly accepted. She was also an international student from Asia, evoking memories of the first intern. Group members gently tested her out, asking questions to see if she would "fit." They quickly agreed to accept her into the group and labeled her a "sister." The topic of discussion shifted to smoking and health, and members expressed concern and care for those in the group who smoked. For the next few sessions the girls explored experiences about how two of them began to smoke at ages 6 and 8, respectively; desires to quit; and associations between smoking and other behaviors such as sex, substance abuse, and poor school performance.

Spring break and the beginning of the end. Following spring break, discussions centered on the students' boredom during the school vacation. Nothing "special" had happened and group members shared about staying at home doing chores, watching television, and babysitting family members. In fact, for the first time, they all found themselves glad to be back at school with their friends and the group. Finding group support for the tedium of being at home, they again revisited issues about difficulties in school. The hopelessness they felt about passing or succeeding in school was gone, bringing new feelings of hope and frustration as they entered the last months of school. They discussed having some control over their response to the teacher who called one of them "ignorant" and another teacher's rudeness.

In early May the first hints about the group ending were acknowledged. Along with an awareness of the group ending was a restlessness and an occasional lack of focus in the group. One member announced that she was pregnant, which produced significant discussion on what she would do, her future relationship with her boyfriend, and the practicalities of supporting herself and the baby. In mid-May the group facilitators reintroduced the subject of the group ending. The group was resistant to talking about this, changed the subject, became silent, wrote personal notes, played, and uncomfortably teased each other. Their behavior was reminiscent of early group meetings. One member even talked about not returning to the group, provoking tension with other members.

By the next session, group members had reflected on the group ending. A process of self-evaluation evolved, whereby the girls reflected on themselves, each other, and the group as a whole. Poignantly they linked personal changes with their future, sharing about where they were going and associated fears. The group took part in a powerful and deeply felt discussion, recalling their pasts, where they had grown up, positive relationships they had had as small children, and the deep sadness they had from missing that time and place. Interestingly, discussion shifted from deep feelings about the past to thoughts about the future that included marriage, babies, summer activities, and the coming of age for driver's licenses. Special activities were discussed including a presentation to a graduate group counseling class at the university about their experiences being in a group, coupled with a visit to an on-campus art museum and a special dinner celebration at a restaurant to end the group. The girls were excited and scared about the trip to the university, but they looked forward to the presentation and the restaurant celebration.

Final group meetings. The visit to the university made a profound impression on the group members. They were nervous and scared, and for many it was their first trip to the university, even though it was less than 5 miles from their homes. They expressed concern that the graduate students would see them as ignorant and immature and that their clothing would be inappropriate. Once the panel discussion began, the members became increasingly at ease and confident talking about their group experience. They answered the questions of the graduate students with self-assuredness and as an intimate and close-knit group. After the panel discussion, several group members commented about how the graduate students were "real people just like them" and "not some highly intelligent, stuck-up people." This had a deep impact on the group members who realized that college students were "normal" and that with hard work they also could attend university.

After the panel discussion, the group visited an art museum on campus. This was everyone's first trip to the museum, and they were awed by the vast differences in what people call art. They laughed and joked as they found some of the modern art "ridiculous" and others "beautiful and culturally relevant." The entire day was a journey into another world 5 miles away and a glimpse and realization that graduate students and a university life were attainable with hard work and effort.

A final luncheon celebration was at an Italian restaurant chosen by the group. For all but one of the group members, this was their first time in an "expensive" restaurant. They were highly inquisitive about items on the menu and surprised by the cost and greatly concerned that the male professor was going "to spend too much money" on them. They decided that for the final moment together they would rather be someplace more comfortable, so instead of having dessert at the restaurant the group went to a local ice cream parlor. Through tears and ice cream the group members hugged each other as they said their final farewells.

DISCUSSION

The EGAS approach facilitated profound discussions and deep reflection about the group experience and the group members' lives and its impact on their academic achievement. Contextually it is important to note the lack of effective interventions prior to this group for any of the girls who participated in the project. Teachers, school administrators, and the girls themselves all agreed that they were destined for failure as students and school dropout within the next year or two. The group was a means to intervene in a pattern of failure that we have named the "Cycle of Disengagement" and to explore difficult and painful issues within a group of peers.

Examples of the level of safety and importance of the group for these young women were illustrated in letters written by two group members and statements in post-group follow-up interviews. One letter was written after one of the girls was "jumped" (attacked) by a group of girls in school. The victim of the attack believed that one of the group members was part of the gang that attacked her, leading to a serious potential fissure in the group. The accused wrote the following letter to the facilitators:

> I know you probably wondering why her and I aren't talking. Well no, actually is because, maybe about Children services, the fight and her getting jumped. I really don't know. Could you put me and her to the side today or any other day to get us straightened out. Love Always …

The letter introduced an issue to the group for resolution that in the past would have generated anger, violence, and heightened personal and social problems. In fact, as the issue was discussed in group, there was a consensus that without the safety of the group this problem would have escalated into serious, full-blown school conflict.

In a second letter when the girls were asked to evaluate the group experience, another girl spoke about the importance and richness of the group experience. She wrote the following:

> This group has helped all of us. It has really helped in many different ways. It helped me to learn how to share and express my feelings and thoughts. It has helped to take some of the stress off of me because I got a lot off my chest. After a while the group has become a little family to me, and you [the female counselor] have become a second mother to me. You showed me love and support and you treated me like one of your own. You also showed me to make good choices for myself and my child and how when I make a mistake to learn from it and move on. Thank you for everything. Love Always ...

Other girls commented about the group's impact during a post-group taped interview 6 months after the group ended. One stated,

> The most important thing that I took from the group was when they [the group] were telling us about going to school and being on time. Because now I go to school and I am on time. ... I studied more and got more into it [schoolwork].

She also commented about the impact of the group on her personal life: "Me and my mom get along better now. Better than we did then." Another girl commented, "The group is helping me today by reminding me to be more open. ... It got me thinking more about my life." A third member reflected on her changes: "I go to school more compared to last year ... at the beginning my grades didn't change, but now they are up more." She added, "The most important thing I learned was how to communicate. ... It was uplifting and it helped me a lot. I improved in a whole bunch of things. I think we should have it this year."

We would attribute the self-reported impact of the EGAS approach to using a unique methodology that facilitates an open-ended process group aimed at true empowerment. This approach is very different when compared to more traditional structured group interventions in which established agendas and topics are determined by group facilitators. Using the EGAS approach, the young women determined the group content that was meaningful to them while maintaining the underlying goal of academic achievement. As one group member shared 6 months later when she was commenting on what she remembered about the group, "I remember us all crying together." Although a group crying together is not something one would typically link with academic improvement, it was what this student remembered most. In the EGAS approach we believe that the group experience and process will assist members to heal, and this is developmentally and culturally relevant in relationship to school performance. To disregard the intensity of the experience of inner-city youth without attention to the daily trials and tribulations that one faces because of poverty, discrimination, and social oppression is to neglect the deep-seated healing that is critical for the success of youth at risk for school failure.

Thus the aim of EGAS is to empower members so that they can discuss topics of concern by setting their own agenda rather than to impose a structured, theme-focused group on attendance or grades. This approach permitted the seven young women to share deep sadness and to help each other heal, all of which we believe are very closely associated with school failure. EGAS is rooted in the belief that beginning a group with discussions about school and schoolwork would repeat the Cycle of Disengagement, a pattern that is prevalent for many urban youth at risk of school failure.

Interestingly, group members pointed out how the group actually reconstructed a family with the male counselor/professor being identified as a father figure, the female school counselor being regarded as a mother figure, the interns seen as aunts, and peer members viewed as siblings. During the course of the group, members actually started referring to the group as a family, and they regularly discussed the idea of the facilitators being a surrogate father and mother. The healthy reenactment of the family (Yalom, 1995) is an important aspect of healing in groups and it provided a safe foundation for the members to discuss and resolve difficult emotional experiences.

A follow-up survey with group members 1 year later found positive long-range effects. The following is a general summary of those findings:

- The girls expressed a greater ability to share their individual feelings and to more effectively resolve interpersonal problems.
- There was continued support among the group members, with a general consensus that they could share difficult emotional issues with other members of the group in ways that were not possible to share with their own family members.
- The girls were unanimous in their prolonged experience of universality, knowing that they were not alone with their feelings and experiences.

- Self-reports (privacy records and inaccessibility to school records made a review of records impossible) included more attention to schoolwork, better attendance rates, and improved attitudes as a result of the group experience.
- All of the group members aspired to a future college degree as compared to when they entered the group and no one had college aspirations.
- Everyone wanted the group to continue. They missed the support and family nature of the group, and they were remorseful when talking about the absence of "laughing, arguing, fussing, and cussing together."

It is important to note that unexpected events happened that prohibited more formal data collection and analysis to determine school improvement for the seven group members.

SUMMARY

The EGAS approach is a unique and different way to address the depth and level of the personal, social, community, economic, and environmental problems of inner-city students identified as being at high levels of risk for school failure. Traditional intervention methods have not adequately addressed achievement gaps and school failure, with disproportionately large numbers of inner-city students continuing to be at risk of failing or dropping out of school. The EGAS approach was developed based on the belief that structured group interventions that narrowly target only one of many problem areas for students at high levels of risk, and group approaches that do not allow group members to assume responsibility and ownership for the group, fall short of dealing with the complexity and long-standing problems that many urban youth face.

The EGAS approach with the seven young women described in this article seemed to make an impact on improved attendance, more vigorous study habits, aspirations for the future, fewer disciplinary referrals, and enhanced grade performance. The approach is described in this article in hopes that other school counselors may be able to replicate EGAS and intervene in the Cycle of Disengagement that negatively impacts so many urban youth's lives.

The power of EGAS was instrumental in the personal, social, and academic changes exhibited by the students during the group. Furthermore, given the high ratios of students to school counselors in our schools, we believe that group work has the greatest benefit for meeting the needs of all students identified as being at risk and must be the intervention of choice for the professional school counselor, rather than individual counseling. The open structure in the EGAS approach allowed students, for the first time, to experience a true sense of empowerment and control over their lives and destinies. Many of the issues that the members discussed were spoken about for the first time, fostered by the environment of the group where they experienced a sense of safety and cohesion.

Through the exploration of interpersonal relations, discrimination, self-worth, anger, sadness, loss, behaviors, family relations, hopes, sexuality, and their future, for the first time group members examined the relevance and importance of school and the relationship of education to their future. As a result, marked improvements were evident in the group accompanied by self-reports about improved academic performance. Thus we would recommend an EGAS approach that is founded on a belief in self-exploration and empowerment through process and the necessity of having culturally sensitive interventions that are open to the exploration of differences. With the EGAS approach, there is an exploration through groups of associated issues and problems of students at high risk of failing, and an engendering of real empowerment, which we believe are keys to improving the school performance for students with untapped potential. Further studies of the EGAS approach with inner-city, high-risk youth are recommended.

Fred Bemak, Ed.D., is a professor and program coordinator and Rita Chi-Ying Chung, Ph.D., is an associate professor, Counseling and Development Program, Graduate School of Education, George Mason University, Fairfax, VA. E-mail: fbemak@gmu.edu. Linda A. Siroskey-Sabdo, M.A., is a school counselor in Columbus, OH. The authors would like to acknowledge the DeWitt Wallace–Reader's Digest Fund grant and the Education Trust, which supported this project with an aim toward equity and social justice through parity in academic achievement for low-income and ethnic minority students through the Transforming School Counseling Initiative.

REFERENCES

Allen, L., & Mitchell, C. (1998). Racial and ethnic differences in patterns of problematic and adaptive development: An epidemiological review. In V. C. McLloyd & L. Steinberg (Eds.), *Studying minority adolescents* (pp. 29–54). Mahwah, NJ: Lawrence Erlbaum.

Annie E. Casey Foundation. (2000). *Kids count data book: State profiles of child well-being.* Baltimore: Author.

Atkinson, D. R., Thompson, C. E., & Grant, S. K. (1993). A three-dimensional model for counseling racial/ethnic minorities. *The Counseling Psychologist, 21*, 257–277.

Baca, L. M., & Koss-Chioino, J. D. (1997). Development of a culturally responsive group counseling model for Mexican American adolescents. *Journal of Multicultural Counseling and Development, 25*, 130–141.

Bailey, D. F., Getch, Y. G., & Chen-Hayes, S. (2003). Professional school counselors as social and academic advocates. In B. T. Erford (Ed.), *Transforming the School Counseling Profession* (pp. 411–434). Upper Saddle River, NJ: Merrill Prentice Hall.

Bauer, S. R., Sapp, M., & Johnson, D. (2000). Group counseling strategies for rural at-risk high school students. *The High School Journal, 83*, 41–50.

Becky, D., & Farren, P. M. (1997). Teaching students how to understand and avoid abusive relationships. *The School Counselor, 44*, 303–307.

Belgrave, F., Cherry, V., Cunningham, D., Walwyn, S., Letlaka-Rennert, K., & Phillips, F. (1994). The influence of Africentric values, self-esteem, and Black identity on drug attitudes among African American fifth graders: A preliminary study. *Journal of Black Psychology, 20*, 143–156.

Bemak, F. (1998). Interdisciplinary collaboration for social change: Redefining the counseling profession. In C. C. Lee (Ed.), *Counselors and social action: New directions* (pp. 279–292). Greensboro, NC: ERIC/CASS.

Bemak, F. (2000). Transforming the role of the counselor to provide leadership in educational reform through collaboration. *Professional School Counseling, 3*, 323–331.

Bemak, F. (2002). Paradigms for future counseling programs. In C. D. Johnson & S. K. Johnson (Eds.), *Building stronger school counseling programs: Bringing futuristic approaches into the present* (pp. 37–49). Greensboro, NC: ERIC Counseling and Student Services Clearinghouse.

Bemak, F., & Chung, R. C.-Y. (1998). Vietnamese Amerasians: Predictors of distress and self-destructive behavior. *Journal of Counseling and Development, 76*, 452–458.

Bemak, F., & Chung, R. C.-Y. (2003). Multicultural counseling with immigrant students in schools. In P. B. Pedersen & J. C. Carey (Eds.), *Multicultural counseling in schools* (2nd ed., pp. 84–104). Boston: Allyn and Bacon.

Bemak, F., & Chung, R. C.-Y. (2004). Teaching multicultural group counseling: Perspectives for a new era. *The Journal for Specialists in Group Work, 29,* 31–41.

Bemak, F., Chung, R. C.-Y., & Murphy, C. (2003). A new perspective on counseling at-risk youth. In B. T. Erford (Ed.), *Transforming the school counseling profession* (pp. 285–296). Upper Saddle River, NJ: Merrill Prentice Hall.

Bemak, F., & Conyne, R. (2004). Ecological group work. In R. K. Conyne & E. P. Cook (Eds.), *Ecological counseling: An innovative approach to conceptualizing person-environment interaction* (pp. 195–217). Alexandria, VA: American Counseling Association.

Bemak, F., & Greenberg, B. (1994). A study of Southeast Asian refugee adolescents: Implications for counseling and psychotherapy. *Journal of Multicultural Counseling and Development, 22,* 115–124.

Bemak, F., Murphy, C., & Kaffenberger, C. (2004). Community-focused consultation. In C. Sink (Ed.), *Contemporary school counseling: Theory, research, and practice* (pp. 327–357). Boston: Houghton-Mifflin.

Black, M., & Krishnakumar, A. (1998). Children in low-income urban settings: Interventions to promote mental health and well-being. *American Psychologist, 53,* 635–646.

Bolland, J. M. (2003). Hopelessness and risk behavior among adolescents living in high-poverty inner-city neighborhoods. *Journal of Adolescence, 26,* 145–158.

Boyd-Franklin, N. (1995). Therapy with African-American inner-city families. In R. Mikesell & D. Lusterman (Eds.), *Integrating family therapy: Handbook of family psychology and systems theory* (pp. 357–371). Washington, DC: American Psychological Association.

Bretzing, B. H., & Caterino, L. C. (1984). Group counseling with elementary students. *School Psychology Review, 13,* 515–518.

Bryant, A. L., Schulenberg, J., Bachman, J. G., O'Malley, P. M., & Johnston, L. D. (2000). Understanding the links among school misbehavior, academic achievement, and cigarette use during adolescence: A national panel study of adolescents. *Prevention Science, 1,* 71–87.

Burnham, J. J., & Jackson, C. M. (2000). School counselor roles: Discrepancies between actual practice and existing models. *Professional School Counseling, 4,* 41–49.

Campbell, C. A., & Myrick, R. D. (1990). Motivational group counseling for low-performing students. *The Journal for Specialists in Group Work, 15,* 43–50.

Chein, I., Gerard, D. L., Lee, R. S., & Rosenfeld, E. (1964). *The road to narcotics, delinquency, and social policy.* New York: Basic Books.

College Board. (1999a). *Reaching the top: A report of the national task force on minority high achievement.* New York: Author.

College Board. (1999b). *Priming the pump: Strategies for increasing the achievement of underrepresented minority graduates.* New York: Author.

Cooley-Quill, M., Boyd, R. C., Frantz, E., & Walsh, J. (2001). Emotional and behavioral impact of exposure to community violence in inner-city adolescents. *Journal of Clinical Child Psychology, 30,* 199–206.

Couch, R. D. (1995). Four steps for conducting a pregroup screening interview. *The Journal for Specialists in Group Work, 20,* 18–25.

Cousins, L. H., & Mabrey, T. (1998). Re-gendering social work practice and education: The case for African-American girls. *Journal of Human Behavior in the Social Environment, 1,* 91–104.

Cross, W. E. (1971). The Negro-to-Black conversion experience: Toward a psychology of Black liberation. *Black World, 20,* 13–27.

D'Andrea, M. D., & Daniels, J. (2001). Facing the changing demographic structure of our society. In D. C. Locke, J. E. Myers, & E. L. Herr (Eds.), *The handbook of counseling* (pp. 529–540). Thousand Oaks, CA: Sage.

Dansby, V. S. (1996). Group work within the school system: Survey of implementation and role issues. *Journal for Specialists in Group Work, 21,* 232–242.

De Luca, R. V., Hazen, A., & Cutler, J. (1993). Evaluation of a group counseling program for preadolescent female victims of incest. *Elementary School Guidance & Counseling, 28,* 104–114.

Dembo, R., Blount, W. R., Schmeidler, J., & Burgos, W. (1986). Perceived environmental drug use risk and the correlates of early drug use or nonuse among inner-city youths: The motivated actor. *International Journal of Addiction, 21,* 977–1000.

Dewey, J. (1963). *Experience and education.* New York: Collier.

Dryfoos, J. G. (1990). *Adolescents at risk: Prevalence and prevention.* New York: Oxford University Press.

Dryfoos, J. G. (1994). *Full-service schools: A revolution in health and social services for children, youth, and families.* San Francisco: Jossey-Bass.

Dryfoos, J. G. (1998). *Safe passage: Making it through adolescence in a risky society.* New York: Oxford University Press.

Education Trust. (1998). *The Education Trust state and national data book* (Vol. II). Washington, DC: Author.

Fitzpatrick, K. M., & Boldizar, J. P. (1993). The prevalence and consequences of exposure to violence among African-American youth. *Journal of the American Academy of Child & Adolescent Psychiatry, 32*, 424–430.

Gallay, L. S., & Flanagan, C. A. (2000). The well-being of children in a changing economy: Time for a new social contract in America. In R. D. Taylor & M. C. Wang (Eds.), *Resilience across contexts: Work, family, culture, and community* (pp. 3–33). Mahwah, NJ: Lawrence Erlbaum.

Gandossy, R. P., Williams, J. R., Cohen, J., & Harwood, H. J. (1980). *Drugs and crime: A survey and analysis of the literature.* Washington, DC: U.S. Department of Justice. (NCJ 159074).

Gibson, C. M. (1993). Empowerment theory and practice with adolescents of color in the children welfare system. Families in Society: *Journal of Contemporary Human Services, 74*, 387–396.

Graham, S., Taylor, A. Z., & Hudley, C. (1998). Exploring achievement values among ethnic minority adolescents. *Journal of Educational Psychology, 90*, 606–620.

Guerra, N. G., Huesmann, L. R., & Spindler, A. (2003). Community violence exposure, social cognition, and aggression among urban elementary school children. *Child Development, 74*, 1561–1576.

Guerra, N. G., Huesmann, L. R., Tolan, P. H., Van Acker, R., & Eron, L. D. (1995). Stressful events and individual beliefs as correlates of economic disadvantage and aggression among urban children. *Journal of Consulting and Clinical Psychology, 63*, 518–528.

Harries, K. D. (1990). *Serious violence: Patterns of homicide and assault in America.* Springfield, IL: Charles C. Thomas.

Hawkins, J. D., Catalano, R. F., & Miller, J. (1992). Risk and protective factors for alcohol and other drug problems in adolescence and early adulthood: Implications for substance abuse prevention. *Psychological Bulletin, 112*, 64–105.

Helms, J. E. (1990). *Black and White racial identity: Theory, research, and practice.* Westport, CT: Greenwood.

Henry, S. E., & Kilmann, P. R. (1979). Student counseling groups in senior high school settings: An evaluation of outcome. *Journal of School Psychology, 17*, 27–46.

Hobson, S. M., Fox, R. W., & Swickert, M. L. (2000). *School counselor shortages: A statewide collaborative effort in counselor education.* Ypsilanti, MI: Eastern Michigan University. (ERIC Documentation Reproduction Service No. ED454484)

House, R. M., & Hayes, R. (2002). School counselors: Becoming key players in school reform. *Professional School Counseling, 5,* 249–256.

House, R. M., & Martin, P. J. (1998). Advocating for better futures for all students: A new vision of school counselors. *Education, 119,* 284–291.

Hudley, C. (2001). The role of culture in prevention research. *Prevention and Treatment, 4,* Article 5. Retrieved November 9, 2003, from http://journals.apa.org/prevention/volume4/pre0040005c.html

Jackson, R. L., II. (1999). *The negotiation of cultural identity: Perceptions of European Americans and African Americans.* Westport, CT: Praeger.

Jagers, R., & Mock, L. (1993). Culture and social outcomes among inner-city African-American children: An Afrographic exploration. *Journal of Black Psychology, 19,* 391–405.

Johnson, B. D., Williams, T., Dei, K. A., & Sanabria, H. (1990). Drug abuse in the inner city: Impact on hard-drug users and the community. In M. Tonry & J. Q. Wilson (Eds.), *Drugs and crime: Crime and justice, Vol. 13* (pp. 9–67). Chicago: University of Chicago Press.

Johnson, H. J., Torres, J. S., Coleman, V. D., & Smith, M. C. (1995). Issues and strategies in leading culturally diverse counseling groups. *The Journal for Specialists in Group Work, 20,* 143–150.

Justice, E. M., Lindsey, L. L., & Morrow, S. F. (1999). The relation of self-perceptions to achievement among African American preschoolers. *Journal of Black Psychology, 25,* 48–60.

Kasarda, J. D. (1993). Inner-city concentrated poverty and neighborhood distress: 1970–1990. *Housing Policy Debate, 4,* 253–302.

Kenny, M. E., Gallagher, L. A., Alvarez-Salvat, R., & Silsby, J. (2002). Sources of support and psychological distress among academically successful inner-city youth. *Adolescence, 37,* 161–182.

Kim, B. S. K., Omizo, M. M., & D'Andrea, M. J. (1998). The effects of culturally consonant group counseling on the self-esteem and internal locus of control orientation among Native American adolescents. *The Journal for Specialists in Group Work, 23,* 145–163.

Kunjufu, J. (1986). *Developing positive-self images and discipline in Black children.* Chicago: African American Images.

LaFountain, R. M., & Garner, N. E. (1996). Solution-focused counseling groups: The results are in. *The Journal for Specialists in Group Work, 21,* 128–143.

LaFountain, R. M., Garner, N. E., & Ellason, G. T. (1996). Solution-focused counseling groups: A key for school counselors. *The School Counselor, 43,* 256–267.

Lee, C. C. (2001). Culturally responsive school counselors and programs: Addressing the needs of all students. *Professional School Counseling, 4*, 257–261.

Locke, D. C. (2003). Improving the multicultural competence of educators. In P. B. Pedersen & J. C. Carey (Eds.), *Multicultural counseling in schools: A practical handbook* (2nd ed., pp. 171–189). Boston: Allyn and Bacon.

Lyles, M., Yancey, A., Grace, C., & Carter, J. (1985). Racial identity and self-esteem: Problems peculiar to biracial children. *Journal of the American Academy of Child Psychiatry, 24*, 150–153.

May, M., & Housley, W. (1996). The effects of group counseling on the self-esteem of sexually abused female adolescents. *Guidance and Counseling, 11*, 38–42.

McClanahan, K. K., McLaughlin, R. J., Loos, V. E., Holcomb, J. D., Gibbins, A. D., & Smith, Q. W. (1998). Training school counselors in substance abuse risk education techniques for use with children and adolescents. *Journal of Drug Education, 28*, 39–51.

Millstein, S. G. (1989). Adolescent health: Challenges for behavioral scientists. *American Psychologist, 44*, 837–842.

Montano, J., & Bucher, M. J. (1999). *Counselor assessment: Report to the legislature* (Rev. ed.). St. Paul, MN: Minnesota State Department of Children, Families, and Learning. (ERIC Document Reproduction Service No. ED449459)

Myrick, R. D., & Dixon, R. W. (1985). Changing student attitudes and behavior through group counseling. *The School Counselor, 32*, 325–330.

Nelson, J. R., Dykeman, C., Powell, S., & Petty, D. (1996). The effects of a group counseling intervention on students with behavioral adjustment problems. *Elementary School Guidance & Counseling, 31*, 21–33.

Omizo, M. M., & Omizo, S. A. (1988). The effects of participation in group counseling sessions on self-esteem and locus of control among adolescents from divorced families. *The School Counselor, 36*, 54–60.

Osofsky, J. D. (1999). The impact of violence on children. *Future of Children, 9*, 33–49.

Paisley, P. O., & McMahon, G. (2001). School counseling for the 21st century: Challenges and opportunities. *Professional School Counseling, 5*, 106–116.

Phillips, T. H., & Phillips, P. (1992). Structured groups for high school students: A case study of one district's program. *The School Counselor, 39*, 390–393.

Phinney, J. S. (1996). Understanding ethnic diversity: The role of ethnic identity. *American Behavioral Scientist, 40*, 143–152.

Praport, H. (1993). Reducing high school attrition: Group counseling can help. *The School Counselor, 40*, 309–311.

Proehl, R. A. (1995). Groups in career development: An added advantage. *Journal of Career Development, 21*, 249–261.

Prout, S. M., & Prout, T. (1998). A meta-analysis of school-based studies of counseling and psychotherapy: An update. *Journal of School Psychology, 36*, 121–136.

Ritchie, M. H., & Huss, S. N. (2000). Recruitment and screening of minors for group counseling. *The Journal for Specialists in Group Work, 25*, 146–156.

Roland, C. B., & Neitzschman, L. (1996). Groups in schools: A model for training middle school teachers. *The Journal for Specialists in Group Work, 21*, 18–25.

Rosen, K. H., & Bezold, A. (1996). Dating violence prevention: A didactic support group for young women. *Journal of Counseling & Development, 74*, 521–525.

Sameroff, A. J., & Seifer, R. (1995). Accumulation of environmental risk and child mental health. In H. E. Fitzgerald, B. M. Lester, & B. Zuckerman (Eds.), *Children of poverty: Research, health, and policy issues* (pp. 233–253). New York: Garland Publishing.

Sciarra, D. T. (2001). School counseling in a multicultural society. In J. G. Ponterotto, J. M. Casas, L. A. Suzuki, & C. M. Alexander (Eds.), *Handbook of multicultural counseling* (2nd ed., pp. 701–728). Thousand Oaks, CA: Sage Publications.

Shaw, C., & McKay, H. (1942). *Juvenile delinquency and urban areas.* Chicago: University of Chicago Press.

Shechtman, Z. (1993). School adjustment and small-group therapy: An Israeli study. *Journal of Counseling & Development, 72*, 77–81.

Shechtman, Z., Bar-El, O., & Hadar, E. (1997). Therapeutic factors and psychoeducational groups for adolescents: A comparison. *The Journal for Specialists in Group Work, 22*, 203–213.

Thomas, D. E., Townsend, T. G., & Belgrave, F. Z. (2003). The influence of cultural and racial identification on the psychosocial adjustment of inner-city African-American children in school. *American Journal of Community Psychology, 32*, 217–224.

Voelkl, K. E., & Frone, M. R. (2000). Predictors of substance use at school among high school students. *Journal of Educational Psychology, 92*, 583–592.

Walker, E. M. (1991). *Changing self-esteem: The impact of self-esteem changes on at-risk students' achievement.* Unpublished manuscript.

Witherspoon, K., Speight, S., & Thomas, A. (1997). Racial identity attitudes, school achievement, and academic self-efficacy among African American high school students. *Journal of Black Psychology, 23,* 344–357.

Yalom, I. D. (1995). *Theory and practice of group psychotherapy* (4th ed.). New York: Basic Books.

Yauman, B. E. (1991). School-based group counseling for children of divorce: A review of the literature. *Elementary School Guidance & Counseling, 26,* 130–138.

Zinck, K., & Littrell, J. M. (2000). Action research shows group counseling effective with at-risk adolescent girls. *Professional School Counseling, 4,* 50–59.

A Counseling Group for African-American Adolescent Males

By Carla Bradley, Ph.D.

This article originally appeared in *Professional School Counseling*, Vol. 4, No. 5, 2001.

An understanding of the unique experiences of and addressing the counseling needs of African-American male adolescents have become professional imperatives as school counselors encounter increasing numbers of African-American adolescents (Bradley & Sanders, 1999; Lee, 1987). Adolescence is a critical time for African-American males. In addition to dealing with the cognitive, physical, emotional, and social issues characteristic of adolescence, African-American males must work through racism and unique educational challenges (Hrabowski, Maton, & Greif, 1998; Lee, 1987; Majors & Billson, 1992;).

Several writers have asserted that the educational achievement and progress of many African-American adolescent males are substantially less than desired (Lee, 1991; Taylor, 1995; White & Parham, 1990). For example, a vast majority of referrals for African-American male youth are for poor academic achievement and behavioral problems, particularly hyperactivity and excessive aggression (Gibbs & Huang, 1998). Moreover, African-American male children are suspended three times more often and for longer periods of time than their European-American counterparts (Bradley & Sanders, 1999; Majors & Billson, 1992).

Several scholars (Lee, 1987; Majors & Billson, 1992; White & Parham, 1990) have acknowledged a disparity in evaluating and addressing the behavior of African-American adolescent males as compared to European-American adolescent males. They attributed this phenomenon to how the media has created vastly different images of the two groups. For example, Dowdy (1998) contended that leading newspapers have described European-American adolescent males who have committed crimes as "innocent looking choir boys" while depicting their African-American counterparts as "dangerous elements being unleashed into the community" (p. B2). Consequently, African-American males who gather at malls or other public settings are often approached by law enforcement officers who perceive their behaviors as menacing and suspicious (Hardy, 1996). Some scholars have posited that the internalization of such negative messages by African-American male adolescents can be linked to higher levels of anxiety, lower levels of self-esteem, and poor school performance

(Gibbs & Huang, 1998; Majors & Billson, 1992). Hence, the purpose of this article is to describe a group counseling experience for adolescent African-American males that was designed to clarify issues around race and the adolescent's ability to successfully negotiate environmental and educational challenges. In addition, a case study of an African-American adolescent male involved in this group experience is presented.

THE GROUP COUNSELING EXPERIENCE

The group counseling experience – consisting of six, one and one-half hour sessions – was intended for African-American 13- and 14-year-old males. The framework and content of the group were adapted from work completed by Lee (1987), who focused on the group counseling needs of adolescent African-American males.

Participants were selected to ensure a balanced mix of social, academic, and religious backgrounds. Teachers and administrators were encouraged to make referrals for the group. In addition, counselors solicited the help of clergy and other community leaders who were "in touch" with the needs and interests of African-American students.

It is recommended that the counselor facilitating the group understand the basic principles of multicultural counseling and be keenly aware of the unique experiences of African-American adolescent males. The following is an outline of the topics covered for each session of the group.

1. Introduction. To establish group rules and present the goals and activities of the group.
2. Understanding Prejudice and Racism. To examine the origins of racism and implications for African-American men in general and African-American adolescent males in particular.
3. Challenges within the Educational System. To discuss the experiences of African-American adolescent males within the educational system.
4. Survival Skills I. To explore and develop strategies needed to successfully negotiate challenging situations. Special emphasis was placed on interactions between African-American male youth and educational and environmental systems.
5. Survival Skills II. To practice newly acquired negotiation techniques.
6. Closure. To bring closure to the group by honoring the contributions of each group member.

LANGSTON: A CASE STUDY

The following case study illustrates a young man's journey through the 6-week counseling group. Langston is representative of African-American adolescent males who have participated in this counseling group. Langston was a 14-year-old, 8th grade African-American student who was referred to the group by the school principal. Both the principal and several of Langston's teachers characterized him as demonstrating low motivation and low morale. This was evident by his marginal academic performance and his body language as he slowly walked through the hallways.

Session 1

During the first group session, as the counselor discussed the goals and activities of the group, it appeared that the group was of little interest to Langston. As various members gave their input on group rules and consequences for rule violations, the counselor noticed that Langston was drawing a picture. The counselor also observed that while Langston was drawing, he was able to follow the discussion of the group.

Session 2

The counselor began the second session by discussing the etiology of racism in conjunction with African and African-American history. To encourage dialogue on these issues, the counselor showed a segment from the movie *Roots* (Haley & Wolper, 1977) in which Kunta Kinte, a slave, was being beaten by another Black slave at the order of their White slave owner. After the video, group members were asked to share their impressions. One student felt angry because "a Black man was forced to hurt another Black man." Langston, who slowly looked up from his drawing pad, asked, "Don't you have friends who sell drugs to Black folks?" The student acknowledged that he did, but told Langston that had nothing to do with what he just said. Langston replied, "Yes it does. Your friends are hurting Black people just like in the movie Roots. You and your friends are no better than White slave owners who beat and abused their slaves to make money." Langston's comments led other group members to question and discuss the etiology of "Black-on-Black" crime and internalized oppression.

To gain a more comprehensive perspective on the environmental experiences of the group participants, the counselor asked if students had ever been violated, humiliated, or discriminated against as a result of being African American. Several acknowledged this had occurred in their lives.

The counselor noticed that Langston had drawn a picture of a man dressed in black and a police car. The counselor asked Langston if he would share his drawing with the group. Langston explained that the man dressed in black was his father, who was stopped by the police after church and pushed to the ground. He indicated that he and his family were on their way to dinner when the police approached his father in the parking lot and demanded to see his driver's license. After his father asked, "Why?", the police pushed him up against the car and then to the ground. When the police reviewed his license and registration, they realized they had the wrong person and drove away.

Looking down at his drawing pad, Langston stated, "I have no rights or respect from the police." The counselor validated him by saying that he had a right to be angry and his father's civil liberties were violated by the police. This prompted other group members to share painful stories of their negative encounters with police and other authority figures, and to reflect on the status of African-American young men in this country.

Session 3

During the third session, several students including Langston voiced their concerns regarding authority figures within the educational system. One group member shared, "When I'm talking or daydreaming in class, the teacher yells at me, but when the White students do the same thing, she doesn't say anything." He went on to say that when he tried to bring this to her attention, she called him a "troublemaker" and sent him to the principal's office. Langston replied, "You shouldn't have said anything to her. She might have thought you were going to physically hurt her. That's what she told my parents when she caught me drawing in class, and I was trying to explain to her how drawing helps me to understand things." Most of the group members agreed that teachers and other school personnel perceived them as threatening.

The session closed with the counselor thanking group members for disclosing their reflections and personal experiences and their willingness to "keep going" after experiencing racial confrontation. The facilitator informed the group that the next two sessions would focus on successful African-American men who had encountered and navigated through similar challenging situations. In addition, the group would also explore skills that would be effective

Sessions 4 and 5

The next two sessions concentrated on strategies that African-American adolescent males could use to successfully negotiate educational and environmental challenges. To demonstrate effective verbal and nonverbal techniques, the counselor showed a segment from the movie Malcom X (Lee, 1992). The particular segment opened with Malcom X negotiating with White American police officers to have an African-American man, who was held and beaten by the police, receive medical treatment. The counselor then asked group members to identify three things that Malcom X had going for him to accomplish such a great triumph during the 1960s. Attributes such as discipline, respect, power, and faith in God were the most popular responses. Langston added, "Malcom X also had confidence. That's why the police granted his request." The group also identified other role models such as Nelson Mandela, Dr. Martin Luther King, Muhammad Ali, and the skills and attributes that facilitated the accomplishment of their goals. The counselor asked the students to assemble a list of survival skills and negotiation techniques used by these courageous men.

Role play exercises were conducted to assist group members with employing these skills within educational and environmental systems. Special emphasis was placed on navigating situations in which miscommunication or misinterpretation had occurred between group members and authority figures.

Session 6

The last session provided an opportunity for participants to reflect on their experience in the group. Each member expressed that the group had exposed him to new information and skills. Several of the students acknowledged that they also gained a sense of acceptance and validation as strong and responsible African-American young men. Finally, the counselor presented each group member with a gift that symbolized their unique qualities and contribution to the group.

Langston also displayed significant growth during the group process. During the last two sessions, he assumed more of a leadership role as he continued to question and challenge statements made by other students.

CONCLUSION

Although Langston continued to experience some academic difficulty following these group sessions, his teachers noticed a marked increase in his participation in class discussions. Langston also began to demonstrate a willingness to share and interpret his drawings with classmates.

As school counselors implement this type of group experience, they can become effective advocates for adolescent African-American males, enhancing their development. Such proactive interventions are essential in promoting and maintaining developmental counseling programs that meet the unique needs of ethnic minority students.

Carla Bradley, Ph.D., is an associate professor in the Counseling and Higher Education Department at Ohio University, Athens.

REFERENCES

Bradley, C., & Sanders, J. (1999). Counseling culturally diverse young clients. In A. Vernon (Ed.), *Counseling children and adolescents* (pp. 223–242) Denver, CO: Love.

Dowdy, Z. (1998, June 28). Killers as rascals? Depends on race. *Syracuse Herald American*, p. B2.

Gibbs, J. T., & Huang, L. (1998). *Children of color: Psychological interventions with culturally diverse youth*. San Francisco: Jossey-Bass.

Haley, A. (Producer), & Wolper, D. (Director). (1977). *Roots* [Film]. (Available from Warner Brothers, Inc., 4000 Warner Blvd., Burbank, CA 91522).

Hardy, K. V. (1996, May/June). Breathing room. *Networker*, 53–59.

Hrabowski, F. A., Maton, K. I., & Greif, G. L. (1998). *Beating the odds: Raising academically successful African American males*. New York: Oxford University Press

Lee, C. C. (1987). Black manhood training: Group counseling for male Blacks in grades 7–12. *Journal for Specialists in Group Work, 12*, 18–25.

Lee, C. C. (1991, December). Empowering young Black males. *Counseling and Personnel Services Digest*. ERIC Report No. EDO-CG-91-2.

Lee, S. (Director). (1992). *Malcom X* [Film]. (Available from Warner Home Video, Inc., 4000 Warner Blvd., Burbank, CA 91522)

Majors, R., & Billson, J. (1992). *Cool pose: The dilemmas of Black manhood in America*. New York: Simon & Schuster.

Taylor, R. (1995). *African American youth: Their social and economic status in the United States*. Westport, CT: Praeger.

White, J. L., & Parham, T. A. (1990). *The psychology of Blacks: An African-American perspective*. Englewood Cliffs, NJ: Prentice-Hall.

CHAPTER SIX

Practitioner Inquiry as the Promise for Multicultural School Counseling Practice and Educational Transformation

As we have learned throughout this book, in a time of rapidly increasing diversity, standardization and national accountability in schools, school counselors' roles are becoming steadily more multifaceted, complex and challenging. The dynamically evolving, comprehensive nature of contemporary school counselors' responsibilities necessitates that they continually engage in: (1) critical self-refection on their values and prejudices and how these map onto their professional attitudes, practices and relationships; (2) critical examination and critique of students' school and life experiences in relation to broader social, institutional and political issues of diversity and inequality; (3) substantive, meaningful and transformative professional development; and (4) constructive collaborations including outreach to colleagues, family members and community constituencies. The changing roles of school counselors also necessitates that they access and integrate cutting-edge theory, research and practice on issues of diversity and inequality into their practice. Engaging in these kinds of professional commitments and processes is necessary so school counselors can cultivate and continually refine a multicultural approach to their counseling practices.

However, becoming a multicultural practitioner does not simply require occasional self-reflection or exposure to outside experiences and resources; it requires that school counselors systematically look within, that they take an inquiry stance on their practice (Cochran-Smith & Lytle, 1993). Taking an inquiry stance on practice requires school counselors to develop and refine their understanding of the role of systematic reflection in counseling practice and to view practice-based inquiry as an ethic of their everyday work as well as a fundamental aspect of their vision of themselves as professionals. Taking an inquiry stance on practice means school counselors must be committed to their own process of self-reflection and the continual investigation into, and critique of, their practice. This stance on counseling practice translates into more person-centered counseling and a more systematic and proactive approach to empowering and advocating for youth and their families and communities.

There is considerable discussion about the powerful and important shifts that take place when practitioners engage in reflective practice (e.g., Cochran-Smith & Lytle, 1993; McIntyre, 1997; Nakkula & Ravitch, 1998; Sleeter, 1996). Because engaging in reflective practice has such a positive impact on the quality of counseling practices, school counselors must seek out sources and colleagues that motivate and inspire them to take an inquiry stance on practice in systematic ways throughout their careers. One opportunity for doing so is to engage in ongoing practitioner research in which school counselors pay close attention to the kinds of questions that emerge from their practice, reflect on and develop these questions and then design studies to investigate and respond to them. From a multicultural perspective, school counselors should continually ask questions that focus on issues of diversity and equity as these emerge within their daily practices. This kind of local, situated, equity-oriented inquiry is the promise for real change in practice, in schools and in the world more broadly. In terms of advancing their thinking and methods of practice around multicultural issues, engaging in practitioner research provides school counselors with necessary data with which they can base their understandings of the effectiveness and fit of specific strategies and approaches with diverse students, families and communities, as well as with other professionals within and around their schools.

ON THE NEED FOR LOCAL, SITE-BASED RESEARCH IN MULTICULTURAL SCHOOL COUNSELING

Practitioner research can be operationally defined as systematic, inquiry-based efforts directed toward creating and extending professional knowledge and associated understandings of professional practice. In practitioner research, questions emerge from practice and then studies are designed to collect practice-based data responding to those questions. Practitioner research is most often regarded as research undertaken by practitioners who seek to improve their own practice, and that of their colleagues, through the purposeful and critical examination of and reflection on aspects of their work; of their students' experiences; and of school functioning, policies and practices. Such examination is designed to increase awareness of the basis for professional actions, decisions and judgments, enabling practitioners to see their practices anew, to recognize and articulate the complexities of their work and the values that lie at the heart of professional practice. Practitioner research enables counselors to engage in inquiry directed toward creating and extending their professional knowledge, skills and strategies. It helps school counselors gain insight into what concerns or confuses them; what aspects of practice are most challenging and/or rewarding; about their roles as supporters, advocates and change agents; and about the parameters, possibilities and constraints of their work settings. Practitioner research offers possibilities for illuminating and improving practice and influencing policies in a data-driven, informed way that both informs and empowers school counselors as professionals. Finally, practitioner research elevates the status of school counselors; it professionalizes their positions in ways that empower and embolden them as individuals, as colleagues and as service providers (Ravitch, 2006).

As a former school counselor, teacher and counselor educator, and someone who has been teaching about issues of multicultural practice and practitioner research with an array of new and seasoned school and community mental health practitioners for more than a decade, I believe practitioner inquiry is the real hope for educational change and transformation in a time of increased standardization, top-down accountability and the decontextualized perspective on expectations for counselors, teachers, administrators and students that pervades educational policy at this historical moment. I believe local, site-based research focusing on issues of equity and reform is the promise for meaningful, evidence-based educational change.

Practitioner research allows for opportunities to work against the ways in which current educational policies disempower and constrain schools, and the practitioners and students within them, from engaging in the kinds of critical thinking, teaching, counseling and learning that we need both for the future of successful individuals and for the future of a nation of educated, informed and empowered citizens. The promise of practitioner-driven research is that the learning emerges from local, situated inquiry, the kind of inquiry that leads practitioners to engage in evidence-based

best practices and particularly the kinds of inquiry and research counselors can develop and engage in, in their own schools, their own practices, their own districts. And that is where the hope is, in the stories, in
the data and in the evidence that emerges from a more relational, contextualized kind of research. This is not the top down kind of research that is
being forced upon many of us but the kind that emerges from knowing
and caring about people in a setting, the kind that emerges when school
counselors take seriously the charge to care for, support and empower
their students. Clearly, the flavor-of-the-month approach to educational
change is not working. And it does not work because it does not do justice to counselors, teachers, students or administrators; it disempowers
everyone. And so we need practice-based research that can speak to what
is effective and meaningful in specific contexts and with specific populations in ways that are deeply contextualized and person-centered (Ravitch,
2006).

Sanday (1976) argues that educational practitioners must become
"introspective ethnographers" in their school settings in order to be able
to decipher the cultural meanings that they, their students and their colleagues bring to school. Research conducted by counselors in their own
settings is necessary so findings are grounded in the realities of contemporary schools and school counseling issues. There must be in-depth studies
of school counseling contexts that can articulate the complexity of students', counselors' and other school professionals' lived experiences.
Research in this area would greatly enhance the practices of multicultural
school counselors – and their colleagues – who are committed to counseling against the grain (Cochran-Smith, 1991).

COUNSELOR EDUCATION COURSES AND PROGRAMS AS CENTERS OF CRITICAL SELF-REFLECTION

One of the central goals of school counselor education courses and programs must be to encourage counselors to take an inquiry stance on their
practice and to teach them to engage in ongoing practitioner research as
an ethic of their work. Therefore, school counselor education classrooms
must become centers of reflective practice, places in which students learn
about the value of critical self-reflection and the importance of learning
how to systematically reflect on and evaluate their perspectives and their
practices. Within these programs and courses, students must be directly
taught about the value of societally contextualized, critical self-reflection
and the importance and value of taking an inquiry stance on their practice. To support these goals, students must be given concrete theoretical,
practical and research skills for learning how to become reflective practi-

tioners, both within their courses and for when their coursework is completed. This requires, among other things, that students be provided with a conceptual understanding that their personal and professional identities are intertwined and that both have been shaped by social norms and their particular socialization processes within an overarching social system fraught with racism and discrimination. Doing so requires facilitating in-depth conversations about the nature of counseling, about the relationship between schools and society and about the notion that counselors' decisions and practices reflect their own belief systems, perspectives and attitudes. It also requires cultivating an active sense of the value and import of inquiry and research for professional practice.

CONCLUDING THOUGHTS ON NEW BEGINNINGS

Lee (2001) reflects on the current state of school counseling with respect to issues of diversity and inequality, stating,

> "Appropriate educational processes require that schools move beyond the myth of a monolithic society to the reality of cultural diversity. Professional school counselors can be on the cutting edge of this movement. As the 21st century begins, it is becoming clear that a new American culture is emerging, a universal culture where diversity and pluralism are accepted hallmarks of the society. Young people, who represent diverse worldviews characteristic of this pluralism and are the future leaders of this new national order, are now maturing and developing their abilities and interests. They will need guidance in this developmental process from counseling professionals whose expertise includes sensitivity to human diversity and the skills to help develop talents within the context of cultural realities. When all of this is taken into consideration, professional school counselors and culturally responsive comprehensive guidance and counseling programs have the potential to be on the cutting edge of promoting access, equity and educational justice" (p. 261).

Given the enormity of the social, institutional and political issues that shape students' lives, schools and society more broadly, becoming a multicultural school counselor requires considerable thought, planning and focus; it must be founded in a desire to engage in practice that is equitable and empowering for all students with a particular focus on students who are traditionally marginalized and oppressed in schools. Developing and internalizing this perspective on school counseling practice is essential if, as Lee suggests, school counselors, counselor educators and counseling programs are to truly promote access, equity, and social and educational justice. Promoting positive change must be the primary task, though a daunting one, for school counselors who wish to follow the words of Mahatma Gandhi who has said, "You must be the change you wish to see in the world." It is time for this change. It is time for justice and equity for all students and for the building of a new society in which all experiences are valued and every voice is heard. School counselors, and those who educate them, can be the facilitators of this change and, ultimately, can plant the seeds of social transformation.

Bibliography

American School Counselor Association. (1999). *The professional school counselor and cross/multicultural counseling* (position statement). Alexandria, VA: Author.

Arredondo, P., Toporek, R., Brown, S., Jones, J., & Locke, D.C. (1996). *Operationalization of the multicultural counseling competencies.* Boston, MA: AMCD Professional Standards and Certification Committee.

Banks, J.A. (2003). *Teaching Strategies for Ethnic Studies.* Boston: Allyn & Bacon.

Baruth, L.G., & Manning, L.M. (2000). A Call for Multicultural Counseling in Middle Schools. *Clearing House, 73,* 243 – 246.

Beattie, M. (1997). Fostering Reflective Practice in Teacher Education: Inquiry as a Framework for the Construction of Professional Knowledge in Teaching (111 – 128). *Asia-Pacific Journal of Teacher Education, 25* (2). Retrieved December 4, 2002 from ProQuest Database: http://proquest.umi.com

Bryan, J. (2005) Fostering Educational Resilience and Achievement in Urban Schools through School-Family-Community Partnerships. *Professional School Counseling, 8* (3), 219–226.

Cochran-Smith, M., & Lytle, S.L. (1993). *Inside Outside: Teacher Research and Knowledge.* New York: Teachers College Press.

Cochran-Smith, M. (1991). Learning to Teach Against the Grain. *Harvard Educational Review, 61,* 279–310.

Coleman, H.L.K., & Baskin, T. (2003). Multiculturally Competent School Counseling. In D.B. Pope-Davis, H.L.K. Coleman, W. Ming Liu, & R.L. Arredondo (Eds.), *Handbook of Multicultural Competencies in Counseling and Psychology.* Thousand Oaks, CA: Sage.

College Board. (1999). *Reaching the Top: A Report of the National Task Force on Minority High Achievement* New York: Author.

Collins, P.H. (1989). *Toward a New Vision: Race, Class, and Gender as Categories of Analysis and Connection*. Memphis, TN: Research Clearinghouse and Curriculum Integration Project, Center for Research on Women.

Constantine, M.G., & Yeh, C. (2001). Multicultural Training, Self-Construals, & Multicultural Competence of School Counselors. *Professional School Counseling, 4*, 202 – 207.

Constantine, M.G., Arorash, T.J., Barakett, M.D., Blackmon, S.M., Donnelly, P.C., & Edles, P.A. (2001). School Counselors' Universal-Diverse Orientation and Aspects of their Multicultural Counseling Competence. *Professional School Counseling, 5* (1), 13 – 17.

Delpit, L. (1995). *Other People's Children: Cultural Conflict in the Classroom*. New York: New Press.

Erford, B.T. (Ed.). (2003) *Transforming the school counseling profession*. Upper Saddle River, NJ: Merrill Prentice Hall.

Erickson, F. (2004). Culture in Society and in Educational Practices. In J.A. Banks & C.A.M. Banks (Eds.), *Multicultural Education: Issues and Perspectives* (pp. 31 – 60). Hoboken, NJ: Jossey-Bass.

Gay, G. (1990). Multiethnic Education: Historical Developments and Future Prospects. *Phi Delta Kappan, 64*, 560 - 563.

Giroux, H.A. (1994). Insurgent Multiculturalism and the Promise of Pedagogy. In D.T. Goldberg (Ed.), *Multiculturalism: A Critical Reader* (pp. 325 - 343). Cambridge: Blackwell.

Goldberg, D.T. (Ed.). (1994). *Multiculturalism: A Critical Reader*. Cambridge, MA: Blackwell.

Gorski, P. (2000). *A Working Definition of Multicultural Education*. Virginia School of Education. http://curryedschool.virginia.edu/go/multicultural.

Grant, C.A. (1977). The Mediator of Culture: A Teacher Role Revisited. *Journal of Research and Development in Education, 11*, (1), 102 – 116.

Herring, R.D. (1997). *Multicultural Counseling in Schools: A Synergistic Approach*. Alexandria, VA: American Counseling Association.

Hidalgo, N.M. (1993). Multicultural Teacher Introspection. In T. Perry & J.W. Fraser (Eds.), *Freedom's Plow: Teaching in the Multicultural Classroom* (pp. 99 – 106). New York & London: Routledge.

Holcomb-McCoy, C. (2004). Assessing the Multicultural Competence of School Counselors: A Checklist. *Professional School Counseling, 7* (3), 178 – 187.

Hooks, B. (1994). *Teaching to Transgress: Education as the Practice of Freedom*. New York & London: Routledge.

Howard, G.R. (1999). *We Can't Teach What We Don't Know: White Teachers, Multiracial Schools.* New York: Teachers College Press.

Katz, J.H. (1985). The Sociopolitical Nature of Counseling. *The Counseling Psychologist, 13,* 615 – 623.

Ladson-Billings, G. (1995). Multicultural Teacher Education: Research, Practice, and Policy. In J.A. Banks & C.A.M. Banks (Eds.), *Handbook of Research on Multicultural Education* (pp. 747 – 759). New York: Macmillan.

Lee, C.C. (2001). Culturally Responsive School Counselors and Programs: Addressing the Needs of all Students. *Professional School Counseling, 4,* 257 – 261.

Levinson, B.A., & Holland, D.C. (1996). The Cultural Production of the Educated Person: An Introduction. In B.A. Levinson, D.E. Foley, & D.C. Holland (Eds.), *The Cultural Production of the Educated Person: Critical Ethnographies of Schooling and Local Practice.* New York: SUNY Press.

Locke, D.C. (1993). *Multicultural Counseling: ERIC Digest.* Ann Arbor, MI: ERIC Clearinghouse on Counseling and Personnel Services.

McCarthy, C. (1993). After the Canon: Knowledge and Ideological Representation in the Multicultural Discourse on Curriculum Reform. In C. McCarthy & W. Crichlow (Eds.), *Race, Identity, & Representation in Education* (pp. 289 - 305). New York & London: Routledge.

McIntyre, A. (1997). *Making Meaning of Whiteness: Exploring Racial Identity with White Teachers.* New York: SUNY Press.

McLaren, P. (1994). White Terror and Oppositional Agency: Towards a Critical Multiculturalism. In D.T. Goldberg (Ed.), *Multiculturalism: A Critical Reader* (pp. 45 - 74). Cambridge: Blackwell.

Nakkula, M.J., & Ravitch, S.M. (1998). *Matters of Interpretation: Reciprocal Transformation in Therapeutic and Developmental Relationships with Youth.* San Francisco: Jossey-Bass.

National Commission on Teaching and America's Future. (2003). *National Commission on Teaching and America's Future Report.* Washington, D.C.: Author.

Nieto, S. (2004). *Affirming Diversity: The Sociopolitical Context of Multicultural Education.* New York: Longman Press.

Nieto, S. (1999). *Critical Multicultural Education and Students' Perspectives. In S. May* (Ed.), Critical Multiculturalism: Rethinking Multicultural and Antiracist Education pp. 191 – 215. Philadelphia: Falmer Press.

Ogbu, J.U. (1987). *Variability in Minority School Performance. A Problem in Search of an Explanation.* Anthropology and Education Quarterly, 18 (4), 312 – 334.

Ogbu, J.U. (1995). Understanding Cultural Diversity and Learning. In J.A. Banks & C.A.M. Banks (Eds.), *Handbook of Research on Multicultural Education.* New York: Macmillan.

Pedersen, P. (1999). *Multiculturalism as a Fourth Force.* New York: Taylor & Francis.

Ponterotto, J.G. (1991). The Nature of Prejudice Revisited: Implications for Counseling Intervention. *Journal of Counseling and Development, 70,* 216 – 224.

Pope-Davis, D.B., Coleman, H.L.K., Ming Liu, W., & Toporek, R.L. (2003). *Handbook of Multicultural Competencies in Counseling and Psychology.* Thousand Oaks, CA: Sage.

Ravitch, S.M. (In Press). Interpretations in Practice: Multicultural Teacher Education. In S.M. Ravitch & M.J. Nakkula (Eds.), *Professional Development and Cultural Critique: Interdisciplinary Interpretations of Teaching, Learning, and Doing.*

Ravitch, S.M. Keynote speech to the Math and Science Partnership for Greater Philadelphia. Bryn Mawr College, Pennsylvania. March 25, 2006

Rogers, M.R., Ingraham, C.L., Bursztyn, A., Cajigas-Segredo, G.E., Hess, R, Nahari, S.G., & Lopez, E.C. (1999). Providing Psychological Services to Racially, Ethnically, Culturally, and Linguistically Diverse Individuals in Schools: Recommendations for Practice. *School Psychology International, 20* (3), 243 – 264.

Sanday, P.R. (1976). Cultural and Structural Pluralism in the U.S. In P.R. Sanday (Ed.), *Anthropology and the Public Interest.* New York: Academic Press.

Sciarra, D.T. (2001). School Counseling in a Multicultural Society. In J.G. Ponterotto, J.M. Casa, L.A. Suzuki, & C.M. Alexander (Eds.), *Handbook of Multicultural Counseling* (2nd ed.). Thousand Oaks, CA: Sage.

Sleeter, C.E. (1996). *Multicultural Education as Social Activism.* New York: SUNY Press.

Sue, D.W., & Sue, D. (2003). *Counseling the Culturally Diverse* (4th ed.). New York: John Wiley and Sons.

Tyson, L.E., & Pederson, P.B. (Eds.). (2000). *Critical Incidents in School Counseling* (2nd ed.). Alexandria, VA: American Counseling Association.

U.S. Bureau of the Census. (1996). *Population Projections of the U.S. by Age, Sex, Race, and Hispanic Origin: 1995 – 2030.* Washington, D.C.: U.S. Government Printing Office.

U.S. Bureau of the Census. (2000). *U.S. Census.* Washington, D.C.: U.S. Government Printing Office.

Acknowledgements

I am fortunate to have wonderful colleagues who offer continued support, insight and inspiration. Michael Nakkula, who guided me into the world of school counseling and university teaching, offering an unparalleled model of theory-research-practice integrations grounded in hermeneutics and phenomenology as well as a uniquely associative and collaborative way of conceptualizing school counseling practices. Your teaching, mentoring, support and friendship continue to influence my work and my life in immeasurable ways. Carol Gilligan, for continuing to have a tremendous impact on my thinking about issues of voice and resonance, the relational nature of psychology and inquiry, and the importance of engaged, contextualized, person-centered listening. Peter Kuriloff, your mentorship, modeling and collaboration in the areas of educational leadership, group dynamics and practitioner research are an important piece of my perspective on teaching, learning and professional development. Kathy Schultz, for your ongoing support, teaching and inspiration, you are a true role model and mentor. Frederick Erickson, for your profound influence on my thinking about research, schools, teaching and learning, counseling and issues of culture and diversity in education and life more generally.

I would like to thank my colleagues and friends at Arcadia University: Christina Ager, for your commitment to school-based tikkun olam and your deeply contextualized understanding of the myriad issues facing students, teachers, school counselors and their colleagues. Steve Gulkus, for your profound support, expansive vision and for being a model of collaborative research and professionalism. Graciela Slesaransky-Poe, for teaching me about the value, ethic and practices of full inclusion, collaboration and community empowerment through your passion, vision and commitment to these areas of research and practice. Peggy Hickman, for your understanding of the intersection of multicultural and special education issues and the ways in which these issues can be explored through qualitative research. Jeff and Norah Shultz, for your continued commitment to diversity, equity, pluralism and internationalization. Angela Gillem, for initiating our meaningful exchange of ideas about issues of diversity and equity across disciplinary borders. Peter Siskind, for your expansive vision of social and political history and its relationship to cutting-edge teaching and learning. Mary Dress and Ginny Blaisdell, for your sustaining humor and kindness, continued support and steadfast organization. Nicholas Bubel, for being an impressively focused, efficient and proactive research assistant; this book could not have happened without you. To my other colleagues at Arcadia who have mentored me, supported me and shared insights with me over the years, Steve Goldberg (of blessed memory), Bette Goldstone, Deborah Pomeroy, Ellen Skilton-Sylvester, Kim Dean, Lisa Holderman, Ana Maria Garcia, Leif Gustavson, Peter Appelbaum, Jane Duffy, Cindy Kennedy Reedy and all of the doctoral students in the university's doctoral program in special education.

To my husband, Andy Burstein, for your continued and unconditional love, support, friendship, your ongoing advice, your faith in me and for all of the daily sacrifices that you lovingly make to support me and my work. To my sons, Ari and Lev, for reminding me about the importance of just having fun.

To my parents, Arline and Carl Ravitch, for your generous and unending advice, love, nurturance and respect and for your abiding friendship and your unwavering faith in me. To my parents-in-law, Sheila and Larry Burstein, for your ongoing encouragement and understanding and your support – both emotional and tactical. To my siblings, Frank and Jamie Ravitch, Elizabeth and Auren Weinberg, Evan and Randi Burstein, Peter and Wendy Burstein, many thanks for your support, friendship and understanding.

Deep and abiding thanks go to my dear friends, Deborah Yaghoobzadeh, Laura Hoffman Meltzer, Wendy McGrath, Jen and Michael Finkelstein, Amy Leventhal, Alyssa Levy, Jaime Nisenbaum, Stefanie Gabel, Jen Groen, Deborah Caiola, Gabrielle Kaplan-Mayer, Deborah Waxman, Aaron Toffler, Shari Short, Karen Clark and Nathan Smith for your friendship, love and continued support.

I would like to thank Richard Wong, ASCA president, for inviting me to engage in this project and for giving me the freedom to develop and shape the book in ways that I hope do justice to the complicated issues of identity, social location and positionality in school counseling and society at large. I would like to both applaud and thank Kathleen Rakestraw for your fast and impeccable editing and your warm professionalism.

And finally, to my students at Arcadia University and the University of Pennsylvania, who continually challenge and inform my understanding of the issues that students, teachers, school counselors, administrators and educational leaders face every day in schools and other educational settings with respect to diversity and equity, I feel grateful to learn from your expertise and your experiences in the world.

– Sharon M. Ravitch, 2006